# Trade Unions in a Neoliberal World

## British Trade Unions under New Labour

*Trade Unions in a Neoliberal World* is the first book to provide readers with an authoritative and comprehensive assessment of the impact of New Labour governments on employment relations and trade unions. This innovative text locates changes in industrial politics since the 1990s in the development of globalization and the worldwide emergence of neoliberalism. The advent of Tony Blair's government in 1997 promised a new dawn for employment relations. In this rigorous but readable volume, a team of experienced and respected contributors explain in detail how the story has unfolded.

This book looks at all aspects of New Labour's policies in relation to employment relations and trade unionism. The first half of *Trade Unions in a Neoliberal World* presents an overview of industrial politics, the evolution of New Labour and an anatomy of contemporary trade unionism. It discusses relations between the Labour Party and the unions and the response of trade unionists to political and economic change. The second part contains chapters on legislation, partnership, organizing, training, strikes and perspectives on Europe.

Filling a gap in the current literature, this collection is an essential resource for academics and students of management and industrial relations, political science, contemporary history and sociology. It will appeal not only to academics but to managers, union activists and all those interested in employment relations and the state of Britain today.

**Gary Daniels** is a lecturer in Employment Relations at Keele University, UK. A former trade union activist, he is currently involved with the Union Ideas Network.

**John McIlroy** is Professor of Industrial Relations at Keele University, UK.

**Routledge Research in Employment Relations**
Series editors: Rick Delbridge and Edmund Heery
*Cardiff Business School, UK.*

Aspects of the employment relationship are central to numerous courses at both undergraduate and postgraduate level.

Drawing from insights from industrial relations, human resource management and industrial sociology, this series provides an alternative source of research-based materials and texts, reviewing key developments in employment research.

Books published in this series are works of high academic merit, drawn from a wide range of academic studies in the social sciences.

In a series of combative essays the contributors to *Trade Unions in a Neoliberal World* mount a sustained attack on the industrial relations and labour market policies of New Labour. Identifying New Labour with Neoliberalism, this impeccably researched book casts a baleful eye equally over the content of government policy and attempts within unions to accommodate it. It demonstrates that the radical wing of industrial relations scholarship is alive and kicking and provides an essential counterpoint to mainstream comment on British industrial relations.

Ed Heery
*Professor of Employment Relations*
*Cardiff Business School*

One of the central strategic tenets of New Labour's embrace of neoliberalism was to distance the party from its class base. This book soberly, intelligently and comprehensively assesses what the neoliberalization of social democracy has meant for trade unions in Britain. It thus breaks new ground and admirably fills a significant gap in the literature.

Leo Panitch
*Canada Research Chair in Comparative Political Economy,*
*Distinguished Research Professor of Political Science,*
*York University, Toronto*
*Co-editor,* The Socialist Register

Scholarly and committed, this immensely valuable text provides a wealth of meticulously researched material on contemporary trade unionism. It is essential reading for everybody interested in mobilising organized labour alongside other social movements in order to challenge neoliberalism.

Sheila Rowbotham
*Professor of Gender and Labour History, University of Manchester*

# Trade Unions in a Neoliberal World

## Edited by Gary Daniels and John McIlroy

Routledge
Taylor & Francis Group

LONDON AND NEW YORK

First published 2009 by Routledge
2 Park Square, Milton Park, Abingdon, Oxon OX14 4RN

Simultaneously published in the USA and Canada
by Routledge
270 Madison Ave, 3rd Floor, New York, NY 10016

*Routledge is an imprint of the Taylor & Francis Group, an informa
business*

Typeset in Times New Roman by
RefineCatch Limited, Bungay, Suffolk
Printed and bound in Great Britain by
MPG Biddles, King's Lynn, Norfolk

*British Library Cataloguing in Publication Data*
A catalogue record for this book is available from the British Library

*Library of Congress Cataloging-in-Publication Data*
Trade unions in a neoliberal world : British trade unions under New
Labour / edited by Gary Daniels and John McIlroy.
p. cm.
Includes bibliographical references and index.
1. Labor unions—Great Britain.   2. Labour Party (Great Britain)
3. Labor policy—Great Britain.   4. Industrial relations—Great
Britain.   I. Daniels, Gary.   II. McIlroy, John.
HD6664.T7218 2009
331.880941—dc22
2008021172

ISBN10: 0–415–42663–3 (hbk)
ISBN10: 0–203–88773–8 (ebk)

ISBN13: 978–0–415–42663–3 (hbk)
ISBN13: 978–0–203–88773–8 (ebk)

# Contents

# Figures

# Tables

# List of Contributors

**Richard Croucher** is Professor of Comparative Employment Relations at Middlesex University Business School

**Gary Daniels** lectures in employment relations and HRM at Keele University

**Dave Lyddon** lectures in industrial relations at Keele University

**John McIlroy** is Professor of Industrial Relations at Keele University

**Gary Morton** is a barrister who specializes in labour law

**Paul Smith** lectures in industrial relations at Keele University

**Graham Taylor** is a Reader in Sociology at the University of the West of England

**Martin Upchurch** is Professor of International Employment Relations at Middlesex University Business School

# Abbreviations

## Unions and Union Federations

| | |
|---|---|
| ACM | Association for College Management |
| AEEU | Amalgamated Engineering and Electrical Union |
| AEP | Association of Educational Psychologists |
| AEU | Amalgamated Engineering Union |
| AFA | Association of Flight Attendants |
| AFL-CIO | American Federation of Labor and Congress of Industrial Organizations |
| ALGUS | Alliance and Leicester Group Union of Staff |
| Amicus | Union formed in 2001 from AEEU and MSF |
| AMO | Association of Magisterial Officers |
| ANGU | The Abbey National Group Union |
| ASLEF | Associated Society of Locomotive Engineers and Firemen |
| ATL | Association of Teachers and Lecturers |
| AUT | Association of University Teachers |
| BACM-TEAM | British Association of Colliery Management – Technical, Energy and Administrative Management |
| BALPA | British Air Line Pilots Association |
| BDA | British Dietetic Association |
| BECTU | Broadcasting, Entertainment, Cinematograph and Theatre Union |
| BFAWU | Bakers, Food and Allied Workers Union |
| BIFU | Banking, Insurance and Finance Union |
| BMA | British Medical Association |
| BIOS | British and Irish Orthoptic Society |
| BSU | Britannia Staff Union |
| CATU | Ceramic and Allied Trades Union |
| CDNA | Community and District Nursing Association |
| CFDU | Campaign for a Fighting Democratic Union |
| CGNU | Norwich Union Staff Association |
| CIO | Congress of Industrial Organizations |
| COHSE | Confederation of Health Service Employees |

| | |
|---|---|
| Community | The Community Union |
| Connect | The union for professionals in communications |
| CPSA | Civil and Public Services Association |
| CSMTS | Card Setting Machine Tenters Society |
| CSP | Chartered Society of Physiotherapy |
| CWU | Communication Workers Union |
| CYWU | The Community and Youth Workers' Union |
| DGB | Deutscher Gewerkschaftsbund (German Confederation of Trade Unions) |
| EFTU | Engineering and Fastener Trade Union |
| EIS | Educational Institute of Scotland |
| Equity | The Actors' Union |
| ETU | Electrical Trades Union |
| ETUC | European Trades Union Congress |
| FBU | Fire Brigades Union |
| FDA | First Division Association |
| GMB | General Municipal and Boilermakers and Allied Trades *(Full name no longer used and de-registered with the Certification Officer)* |
| GPMU | Graphical, Paper and Media Union |
| GUDVSA | Guinness United Distiller and Vintners Staff Association |
| GULO | General Union of Loom Overlookers |
| HCSA | Hospital Consultants and Specialists Association |
| ISTC | Iron and Steel Trades Confederation |
| IUHS | Independent Union of Halifax Staff |
| KFAT | National Union of Knitwear, Footwear and Apparel Trades |
| MSF | Manufacturing, Science and Finance Union |
| MU | Musicians' Union |
| NACO | National Association of Co-operative Officials |
| NACODS | National Association of Colliery Overmen, Deputies and Shotfirers |
| NAEIAC | National Association of Educational Inspectors, Advisers and Consultants |
| NALGO | National and Local Government Officers Association |
| NAPO | The Trade Union and Professional Association for Family Court and Probation Staff |
| NAS/UWT | National Association of Schoolmasters / Union of Women Teachers |
| NATFHE | National Association of Teachers in Further and Higher Education |
| NGSU | Nationwide Group Staff Union |
| NUDAGO | National Union of Domestic Appliance and General Operatives |
| NUJ | National Union of Journalists |
| NULMW | National Union of Lock and Metal Workers |

| NUM | National Union of Mineworkers |
| NUMAST | National Union of Marine, Aviation and Shipping Transport Officers |
| NUPE | National Union of Public Employees |
| NUT | National Union of Teachers |
| PCS | Public and Commercial Services Union |
| PFA | Professional Footballers Association |
| POA | Prison Officers Association |
| Prospect | Professional Engineers Union |
| PTC | Public Services, Tax and Commerce Union |
| RCN | Royal College of Nursing |
| RMT | National Union of Rail, Maritime and Transport Workers |
| SCP | Society of Chiropodists and Podiatrists |
| SoR | Society of Radiographers |
| SEIU | Service Employees International Union |
| SWSWU | Sheffield Wool Shear Workers Union |
| TGWU | Transport and General Workers' Union |
| TSSA | Transport Salaried Staffs' Association |
| TUC | Trades Union Congress |
| UBAC | Represents staff in the Bradford and Bingley Group and Alltel Mortgage Solutions |
| UCATT | Union of Construction, Allied Trades and Technicians |
| UCU | University and College Union |
| Unifi | The Banking Union |
| Unison | The Largest Public Sector Union |
| Unite | Amalgamation of Amicus and TGWU |
| Unity | New name for CATU from 2006 |
| URTU | United Road Transport Union |
| USDAW | Union of Shop, Distributive and Allied Workers |
| UTW | Union of Textile Workers |
| WGGB | The Writers' Guild of Great Britain |
| WISA | The Union for Woolwich Staff |
| YISA | Yorkshire Independent Staff Association |

## Political Parties

| AWL | Alliance for Workers Liberty |
| BNP | British National Party |
| CP | Communist Party |
| CPB | Communist Party of Britain |
| PES | Party of European Socialists |
| SSP | Scottish Socialist Party |
| SLP | Socialist Labour Party |
| SP | Socialist Party |
| SWP | Socialist Workers Party |

## Other

| | |
|---|---|
| ACAS | Advisory, Conciliation and Arbitration Service |
| AES | Alternative Economic Strategy |
| ASHE | Annual Survey of Hours and Earnings |
| ASOS | Action Short of a Strike |
| CA | Court of Appeal |
| CAC | Central Arbitration Committee |
| CBI | Confederation of British Industry |
| CEEP | European Centre of Enterprises |
| CES | Commission for Employment and Skills |
| CIPD | Chartered Institute of Personnel and Development |
| CO | Certification Officer |
| CPAUIA | Commissioner for Protection Against Unlawful Industrial Action |
| CROTUM | Commissioner for the Rights of Trade Union Members |
| DCSF | Department of Children, Schools and Families |
| DIUS | Department of Innovation, Universities and Skills |
| DfEE | Department for Education and Employment |
| DfES | Department for Education and Skills |
| DTI | Department of Trade and Industry |
| DWP | Department of Work and Pensions |
| EA | Employment Act |
| EAT | Employment Appeal Tribunal |
| ECHR | European Court of Human Rights |
| ECJ | European Court of Justice |
| EDAP | Employee Development and Assistance Programme |
| EEF | Engineering Employers' Federation |
| EES | European Employment Strategy |
| EIRO | European Industrial Relations Observatory |
| ERA | Employment Relations Act |
| EMU | Economic and Monetary Union |
| ERM | Exchange Rate Mechanism |
| ETP | Employer Training Pilot |
| EU | European Union |
| EWC | European Works Council |
| GCHQ | Government Communications Headquarters |
| HL | House of Lords |
| HPWS | High Performance Work Systems |
| HRM | Human Resource Management |
| ILA | Individual Learning Account |
| ILO | International Labour Organization |
| IoD | Institute of Directors |
| IRLR | Industrial Relations Law Reports |
| LFS | Labour Force Survey |

| | |
|---|---|
| LLSC | Local Learning and Skills Council |
| LSC | Learning Skills Council |
| MSPs | Members of Scottish Parliament |
| NIPSA | Northern Ireland Public Service Alliance |
| NTO | National Training Organisation |
| NUTG | New Unionism Task Group |
| OECD | Organisation for Economic Co-operation and Development |
| ONS | Office of National Statistics |
| OPEC | Organization of the Petroleum Exporting Countries |
| QBD | Queen's Bench Division |
| QLFS | Quarterly Labour Force Survey |
| PHA | Protection from Harassment Act |
| SNB | Special Negotiating Body |
| SOCPA | Serious Organized Crime and Police Act |
| SSC | Sector Skills Council |
| SSDA | Sector Skills Development Agency |
| TEC | Training and Enterprise Council |
| TUA | Trade Union Act |
| TULC | Trade Union and Labour Party Liaison Committee |
| TULO | Trade Union and Labour Party Liaison Organisation |
| TULRA | Trade Union and Labour Relations Act |
| TULR(C)A | Trade Union and Labour Relations (Consolidation) Act |
| TURERA | Trade Union Reform and Employment Rights Act |
| UKEAT | United Kingdom Employment Appeal Tribunal |
| ULF | Union Learning Fund |
| ULR | Union Learning Representative |
| UMF | Union Modernisation Fund |
| UNICE | Union of Industrial and Employers' Confederations of Europe |
| WERS | Workplace Employment Relations Survey |
| WIRS | Workplace Industrial Relations Survey |
| WOW | Winning the Organized Workplace |

# Preface and Acknowledgements

This book stemmed from our teaching on the Contemporary Trade Union-ism course at Keele University which we relaunched in 2005 and have taught since then. We felt it important that students of HRM / Industrial Relations should receive a grounding in all aspects of contemporary trade unionism. The existing curriculum was strong on history and the detail of industrial relations. It sometimes failed to deal adequately with recent developments and the wider economic and political context in which trade unionists oper-ate. We were also aware that with the passing of time there was a need for a detailed analysis of the relationship of trade unions to the New Labour administrations of Tony Blair and Gordon Brown and a considered assess-ment of their fortunes since 1997. That is what this book is about.

Our debts are many. Among numerous students, our particular thanks go to Nicole Beckingham, Anna Carruthers, Kath Clarke, Steve Funnell, Andy Hodder, Adam Mason, Gary Morton and Matthew Price. Academics who have facilitated our work in various ways, some of which they may be unaware of, include: Frank Burchill, Sheila Cohen, Richard Croucher, Ralph Darlington, Paul Edwards, Ian Fitzgerald, Alhajie Saidy Khan, Richard Hyman, Ewart Keep, Kim Moody, Anna Pollert, Graham Taylor and Martin Upchurch. Ed Heery helped as editor of the series in which the book appears while special thanks go to John Kelly, not only for reading and commenting on the manuscript, but for his encouragement and advice over many years.

The book draws on a range of interviews, conversations and contacts with trade union officers, organizers and activists between 1999 and 2008, some of whom prefer to remain anonymous. We would like to thank them all, particu-larly the following: Brian Acton, TGWU Construction Organizer; Natalie Bell, GMB (Massive); Liz Blackshaw, Director of the TUC Organizing Academy; Steve Brown, Unison shop steward; Mark Burns, USDAW Organ-izing Academy Trainee; Julie Burgess, TGWU Organizer; Tony Burke, former GPMU Deputy General Secretary and Chair of New Unionism Task Group; Fran Cappa, TGWU Recruitment Support Worker; Sharon Cowell, TGWU Organizer; Liz Davies, former member of Labour Party NEC; Glen Dyson, USDAW Officer; Duncan Edwards, GMB Officer; Keith Elcoat, USDAW shop steward; Dave Evans, TGWU Organizer; Michael Fisher, PCS; Kate

Farrington, GMB (Massive); Helen Flanagan, PCS shop steward; John Fray, NUJ Deputy General Secretary; GMB; Pat Frost, USDAW Manchester Deputy Divisional Officer; Janice Godrich, PCS President; Rachel Hemingway, Unison shop steward; Michelle Kelly, USDAW shop steward; Allan Kerr, Unison Head of Organisation; Sharon Graham, TGWU; Anne Hickson, USDAW shop steward; Michelle Higgins, USDAW shop steward; Mark Holding, CONNECT Organizer; Colenzo Jarrett-Thorpe, Amicus (MSF) Officer; Jonathan Jewell, RCN; Gary Jones, GMB Lancashire Regional Secretary; Katey Jones, GMB (Massive); Chris Leach, NUJ; Dorothy Lovatt, CWU; Dave McCall, Regional Secretary TGWU; Paul McKenna, USDAW Organizing Academy Trainee; Dave Marsh, Amicus; Helen Masding, GMB (Massive); Sarah-Jane Miller, TSSA Organizer; John Murphy, TGWU Organizer; Paul Nowak, TUC Head of Organisation; Frances O'Grady, TUC Deputy General Secretary; Phil Pinder, TUC General Council, Youth Representative; Jon Rogers, Unison; Carl Roper, former Head of the TUC Organizing Academy; Maureen Rutter, USDAW shop steward; Steve, TGWU shop steward; Byron Taylor, TULO; Jennifer Torkington, USDAW shop steward; Jackie Wood, USDAW shop steward; Colin Woodward, PCS shop steward; Matt Wrack, FBU General Secretary. Needless to say, nobody is responsible for the conclusions reached in the book except the authors themselves.

# Introduction: Trade unions in a neoliberal world

*John McIlroy and Gary Daniels*

## I

*Trade Unions in a Neoliberal World* provides readers with a detailed assessment of the state of British trade unions over the last decade. That period has been dominated politically by New Labour, particularly its foundational leader, Tony Blair, and the spread of neoliberalism across the globe. The book embeds a history of British trade unionism since 1997 in a history of New Labour and neoliberalism. It analyses where New Labour came from; how it transformed the Labour Party and neoliberalized its policies; how it performed in government; and how it influenced the fortunes of trade unions. These years witnessed the consolidation of neoliberalism internationally. Politicians such as Blair in Britain and Bill Clinton in America refined the achievements of Margaret Thatcher and Ronald Reagan, China reinvented itself as a major capitalist power and the new global market extended its influence over millions of workers. The book sets the story of what happened in Britain after 1997 in a critical discussion of what neoliberalism is and how it developed. It discusses how neoliberalism became paramount in regulating the world economy, controlling political agendas across the globe and curbing the power of trade unions.

Our focus is on British trade unionism. *Trade Unions in a Neoliberal World* anchors discussion of contemporary issues in consideration of the role unions played during the long Keynesian boom of capitalism which commenced in 1945. It reviews the experience of trade unionists in the years after 1979 when Conservative governments applied the 'destructive-creative' policies of emerging neoliberalism to organized labour. It proceeds to examine changes in the membership, organization, strategy and politics of trade unionism since 1997. It looks at important developments in union organization, the role of leadership in the workplace, as well as on the national stage, and the part factionalism and internal politics play in the creation of union policy. There is detailed examination of union strategies for revitalization: partnership with employers and the urgent emphasis on organizing campaigns.

The current dilemmas of unions restlessly searching for resurgence in a new century in the aftermath of the defeats administered by Thatcherism are contexualized in the policies of New Labour governments. Particular attention is given to innovation in employment legislation and the labour market, to the political alliance between the Labour Party and the unions and important changes in the unions' attitude towards the European Union (EU). A range of other issues, from the role of the TUC to strikes and industrial conflict, figure in these pages. Unlike other volumes on trade unionism, *Trade Unions in a Neoliberal World* consistently relates its subject to its context: the current stage of capitalism and the dominant ideology which shapes economic, political and employment policies in Britain today.

The book is intended for students of employment relations / human resource management (HRM), political science, contemporary history and sociology. Many books on employment relations deal tangentially with the political forces which regulate and mould institutions and actors, with the political dimensions of trade unionism and with its recent history (cf. Kelly 1998). Texts which recognize the relevance of these issues (Edwards 2003; Blyton and Turnbull 2004; Williams and Adam-Smith 2006) perforce rehearse matters tersely. Research by political scientists has concentrated on the formal link between unions and the Labour Party, 'the contentious alliance', and on union leaders as actors on the national political stage (see, for example, Ludlam and Smith 2001, 2004). There is little about politics inside the unions or the competing political strategies of different groups of trade unionists (McIlroy 1998: 538–9).

This is nothing new. We have noted elsewhere the reticence of contemporary historians in integrating trade unionism and the role of union leaders and activists into their stories of Labour between 1945 and 1979. There is rather a tendency to treat unions as a reified adjunct of the party viewed largely through the eyes of politicians (McIlroy 2007: xxix–xxx). The recent spate of volumes chronicling the fortunes of New Labour under Tony Blair likewise have little to say about the circumstances and activities of trade unions (for example Seldon 2004; Seldon and Kavanagh 2005). We now have a library of texts dealing admirably with almost all aspects of New Labour in government. We are unaware of a single volume dedicated to the trajectory of trade unionism. Whatever their debilities, unions still represent seven million workers. They still play a noteworthy political role inside and outside the Labour Party. We hope *Trade Unions in a Neoliberal World* will help to fill this absence.

## II

'Neoliberalism', Andrew Gamble observes, 'is a term little used by neoliberals. They tend to prefer other labels' (Gamble 2006: 21). The same goes for many commentators and academics. Recent popular texts on New Labour scarcely mention the word – and then as an occasional epithet – let alone scrutinize what it means and whether the cap fits Blair, his successor Gordon

Brown and their policies (Riddell 2005; Seldon 2007ab). The majority of the scholarly estimations of the New Labour phenomenon work explicitly or implicitly on 'third way' criteria. Through strategic triangulation with the Conservatives and Old Labour, New Labour draws on the traditions of 1980s Conservativism and social democracy. It is not assimilated to either, indeed it is sometimes perceived as enigmatic. It is usually described as 'a party of the centre-left' purveying 'post-Thatcherite politics' (see, for example, Coates 2005; Driver and Martell 2006). The industrial relations literature is not greatly different. Labour lawyers have produced extremely insightful analyses of aspects of New Labour ideology and politics (Collins 2001; Fredman 2004; Ewing 2005) but they too eschew elaborated categorization.

There is an alternative approach exemplified by Colin Crouch, whose work crosses the boundaries of industrial relations and political science. Blair had just entered Downing Street in May 1997 when Crouch noted:

> And so the most spectacular crash of the world's most neoliberal government ushered in the neoliberal consensus. From now on both major contending parties in the British state accept the essential neoliberal tenets: markets should rule under the guidance of entrepreneurs with minimal intervention from governments; taxes and public spending and, in particular, the redistributive effect of direct taxation should be kept down; and trade unions should have as marginal a role as possible.
>
> (Crouch 1997: 352)

Despite its cogency, compelling argument and supportive detail, this has, somewhat surprisingly, remained a minority approach. True, the term neoliberalism may have deprecatory or pejorative connotations. It smacks of left critique. If power holders dislike this denomination, others may find it unhelpful. The developments which constitute neoliberalism have crept up on us. Few designated Mrs Thatcher a neoliberal in the 1980s. As she grappled, sometimes hesitantly, with the problems of turning ideology into practical politics, she was a monetarist, a partisan of the ideas of the New Right and, finally, the architect of Thatcherism. As global change quickened and the ideology and politics of the market burgeoned; as the economic crisis of the 1970s receded; as previously sheltered economies from Russia and China to India, Argentina, Brazil and Iran were drawn into the new global marketplace and inducted into the new rules of the game administered by international agencies; as Blair and Clinton embedded and built on the initiatives of their predecessors – it seemed time to take stock. By the late 1990s, analysts were better placed to integrate the diversity of developments and what had been, on the part of pioneering neoliberals, experimental, pragmatic innovation, albeit driven by ideology, within their underlying unity. It was appropriate to satisfy the intellectual and political urge for categorization.

Generalization has its hazards. It runs the risk of occluding difference and contradiction. Justice must be done to complexity and diversity. Theory must reflect, organize and inform empirical evidence, rather than compress it into neatly labelled boxes at the cost of distortion. That said, we believe that the concept of neoliberalism provides the best means of understanding the way capitalism operates and economics and politics are practised today in comparison with the recent past. The stagnation that gripped Keynesian capitalism in the 1970s and 1980s combined with emerging global forces and processes, enhanced economic integration, accelerated technological development and the communications revolution to provide neoliberals with their opportunity. Globalization evolved as the neoliberal project of establishing a global free market dominated by Anglo-American capitalism and its legitimizing discourse. Under American leadership and with its prospects bolstered by the restoration of capitalism across Asia and Eastern Europe, 'the end of history', as Francis Fukuyama put it, beckoned. Neoliberalism promised the opening of a new era where capitalism reigned triumphant and uncontested, and capitalists mastered the universe.

Neoliberalism represents the attempt to restructure global capitalism by moving towards a greater degree of market liberalization, deregulation, privatization, competitivity, productivity and profitability. It involves breaking down barriers to trade and competition, remoulding the state and reorganizing its functions to serve those purposes. It fosters individualism, 'economic man' and inequality, at the expense of collectivism, solidarity and egalitarianism. It aims at the extension of the market and the entrepreneurial ethic to all corners of the globe and the commodification of all aspects of contemporary life. Its purpose is the intensification of exploitation and a more relentless and ruthless search for profits. It is important to emphasize the nuances. Neoliberalism *attempts*, it *encourages*, it *tries*, to introduce a *degree of change*, it *strives* to *alter balances*. It endeavours to drive transformation in different political conjunctures with different histories through different forms of ideological, economic and political struggle. It does not always succeed. It remains a method of regulating capitalism and the extent to which it is capable of surviving a crisis of capitalism on the scale of the 1970s remains to be seen.

Neoliberalism does not, as a glance at America or Britain discloses, dispense with state regulation of the economy or the enterprise: it diminishes it and transforms its nature in comparison with the immediate past. It does not dissolve the welfare state: it tries to organize it so that, to a greater extent than hitherto, the welfare system serves the economy in global competition. It does not eliminate the public sector: it reduces it and attempts to assimilate it to the model of the market. The same applies to trade unionism. These are the dynamics of neoliberalism. It is nowhere fully realized in the political attainments of its disciples. There are, as with other creeds, fissures between ideology and practice, aspiration and outcome. Neoliberalism is far from uniform. Varieties of neoliberalism develop. Ideology mutates into distinctive political practices, combining different elements in the ideological repertoire. New Labour's soft neoliberalism is different from and similar to the Thatcherites' savage neoliberalism. The similarities and interconnections outweigh the differences, particularly when measured against the post-war past.

Those who challenge the utility of the characterization tend to target a monolith or indulge in caricature (cf. Peck and Theodore 2007). The assertion that the primordial liberal world dominated by imperial Britain in the nineteenth century can never be reproduced is easily conceded. It invalidates neither the term nor the analysis. Neoliberalism seeks to draw on and develop some of the ideas of classical laissez-faire; but it endeavours to apply them creatively to a different world. One critic continues:

> The characterization of developments in the global economy as 'neoliberalism' is misleading to say the least. For all the talk about free enterprise, freedom from state interference and the efficiency of 'the market', the fact is that today's economic giants find the state indispensable economically as well as politically.
>
> (Slaughter 2006: 36)

This is tilting at windmills. What is involved is not the withering away of the state. What is involved is its reconfiguration to better serve capitalism in its new phase. The obdurate fact that capital cannot do without the state is signalled by the key part the state has played in the process of constructing the neoliberal polity and economy and the role that state agencies undertake to sustain the market when it encounters difficulties. As it inevitably does.

# III

Problems remain in deepening our understanding of neoliberalism. Much of the growing literature is short on detailed empirical work. The grand sweep of David Harvey's (2005) analysis and the discursive explorations of Jamie Peck and Adam Tickell (Peck and Tickell 2002, Peck 2004) are invaluable. They require amplifying, extending and testing in relation to different states, different institutions and different varieties of neoliberalism. Empirical work would likewise benefit from greater engagement with theory. Address of trade unionism constitutes an important absence in the literature. Anything beyond passing reference remains rare. Yet trade unions were central to the emergence and unfolding of neoliberalism in theory and practice. They remain a potential constraint on its present. They could constitute part of a challenge to its future.

In the absence of detailed contextualized studies and with the continuing problems of comparable statistics, it is difficult to generalize about the impact of neoliberalism on trade unions across the world. Visser found that in the 1980s unions increased their membership in Australia, Canada, Denmark, Finland, Korea, Norway and Sweden. In Austria, Belgium, Germany, Japan and Switzerland, membership remained relatively stable. But it declined significantly in America, Britain, France, Holland and Ireland. Union density

– the percentage of the workforce who are union members – also fell. During the 1990s, measured by both aggregate membership and density, decline continued in Britain and America. But it also embraced Australia, New Zealand, Germany, Italy, Japan and Sweden. The position stabilized – but from a low ebb – in France and membership grew in Belgium, Canada, Ireland, Holland and Spain (Visser 2006; and see Blanchflower 2007).

The overall impression is that, with exceptions and variations, the reach of trade unionism was significantly curtailed in the last two decades of the twentieth century in comparison with the previous post-war decades. The period between 1997 and 2005 witnessed greater stabilization, but not resurgence, on what are again imperfect statistics, often of questionable comparability. There were slight declines in density in America, from 13.6 per cent to 12.5 per cent; in Britain, from 30.6 per cent to 29 per cent; and in New Zealand from 23.6 per cent to 22.1 per cent. Steeper falls in density were registered in Australia, from 30.3 per cent to 22.9 per cent; in Germany, from 27 per cent to 22.6 per cent; in Ireland, from 43.5 per cent to 35.3 per cent; in Italy, from 36.2 per cent to 33.7 per cent; and in Sweden, from 79.5 per cent to 74.1 per cent. In a small number of countries, such as Canada and Spain, the proportion of the workforce enrolled in unions increased. The general picture since the emergence of neoliberalism is one of union decline, significantly greater in the private sector and among the young, with increases in female density counteracted by falls in male density (ibid).

It remains difficult to correlate economic and political trends with union coverage. In the heartlands of neoliberalism the American unions lost two million members after 1980 – although this continued an already long decline in density. Membership and density showed even steeper falls in Britain and from a far stronger base. But decline was arrested and there was an element of consolidation after 1997. However, in the economy typically cited as the exemplar of market coordination, the German unions lost a third of their members after 1990. Again, there are complications as these calculations include the 'trade unions' of the former East Germany. The problem of using these sorts of figures as an indicator of union strength is suggested by the position in France. Density is less than a third of that in Britain. Yet over the last decade French workers' sustained and energetic approach to struggle stands in contrast to the relative quiescence in Britain.

Strike statistics are sometimes used as an index of workers' combativity and confidence. They need relating to a range of contextual factors and again there are problems of comparability given different methods of reporting industrial action in different countries. A decline in strikes may be interpreted as meaning that unions are powerful and do not need to resort to industrial action; or that they are fragile and lack the capacity to mobilize. The OECD statistics show an overall fall in the level of strikes across the world since the 1990s in comparison with past periods. Both Britain and America have low levels of industrial action. Between 1996 and 2005 the British strike rate was half that of the average for the core 14 EU states that made statistics available. The British rate was the same as Sweden's. The strike rate in France was more than double and in Spain more than eight times the rate in Britain. The problems of relating union activity to different economic and political regimes remains. America's strike rate is higher than Britain's while Germany's is negligible and strikes are rarer there than they are in Britain (Hale 2007).

In a review of the available evidence on union membership and strikes, employment, wages and working conditions across OECD countries, Glyn (2006: 104–28) notes downward pressure on wages, the fanning-out of differentials, the undermining of employment protection and welfare benefits and increases in hours worked, job insecurity and work intensity. He relates increases in exploitation, which he sees as particularly marked in the neoliberal economies, America, Britain, Australia and New Zealand, to the decline in union membership and industrial action and union strength. He concludes:

> Labour's position tended to be more eroded in the more free-market economies, like the USA and UK, than in European economies where social protection was already stronger . . . Those at the bottom of the pay distribution lost out in the liberal economies but not generally in Europe . . . The extraordinary gains at the very top of the income distribution, such a startling feature of the USA and UK, were not repeated in the European countries for which data is available. Coverage of union agreements generally held up even in those European countries where union membership fell, while coverage fell rapidly in most of the liberal economies and the impact of unions on pay and conditions was measurably lessened there.
>
> (Glyn 2006: 127)

But if things were worse in neoliberal economies, developments were increasingly interconnected: 'even in countries like Germany and Sweden, traditionally seen as bastions of union power, international competition may be making union solidarity more difficult to sustain' (ibid: 127).

Across the world unions have been weakened and, in some cases, labour movements have been substantially dissolved in their traditional form, by changes in the political sphere and the response to neoliberalism of social democratic parties to which unions were historically linked. From the 1980s such parties moved to the right. They often distanced themselves from their union allies in pursuit of new bases of support for market policies and the view that union leaders were no longer indispensable as mediators with the working-class electorate and deliverers of crucial votes. By the 1990s it was clear that social democracy was in the throes of 'de-social-democratization' (Moschonas 2002: 314). Labels such as 'modernization', 'the modernizing centre-left' and 'the third way' failed to disguise a gradual and uneven convergence of social democracy with neoliberalism and the diminution or breaking of 'the organic links' that bound social democratic parties to trade unions. There were differences in trajectories. In Spain in the late 1980s the governing Socialist Workers Party provoked conflict with its union base. In Germany by the mid-1990s serious tensions arose between the German Social Democrats, dubbed by their leader Gerhard Schröder 'the new centre', and the DGB unions. A similar process occurred in France with the Socialist Party of Lionel Jospin, although it remained, at least rhetorically, closer to the orthodoxies of the past. Similar developments occurred in different formations from the Polish Solidarity, initially based on trade unionists, to the Italian Communist Party, the strongest in Western Europe, and the South African Communist Party, entrenched in the leadership of the African National Congress, linked to the main union confederation.

The turn to neoliberalism did not always pave the path to electoral success. In 2005, the German Social Democrats were forced into a grand coalition with the Christian Democrats, Liberals and Greens; in the 2007 election, the French socialists presented a Blair-style programme and were defeated by the firmer 'Anglo-Saxon neoliberalism' of Nicolas Sarkozy while the historically strong Communist Party continued its apparently irreversible decline; a year later in Italy not a single representative of a party calling itself socialist, social democratic or communist was returned to Parliament. This process has weakened the political representation of workers and trade unionists. It has created dissension in parties and unions and in some cases spawned new parties espousing, to a greater degree, the cause of organized labour.

From the Alliance Party in New Zealand to Rifondazione Comunista in Italy and even in the attempt by a group of unions led by Tony Mazzocchi of the Oil and Chemical Workers to launch a Labor Party in America, rather than continue to finance the neoliberalizing Democrats, success has varied from the limited to the negligible. The most successful alternative has been Die Linke, the Left Party in Germany, based on a fusion of a group of Social Democrats and trade union leaders, headed by former Minister Oskar Lafontaine, and the former ruling party in East Germany, led by Gregor Gysi. The new formation won 54 seats in the Bundestag on the basis of defending coordination and 'the social state'. It has put pressure on the Social Democrats from the left. It still faces the difficulties encountered by new alternative parties from Brazil to Italy as to whether neoliberalism is best challenged from within, by entering government to civilize its administration, or by confrontation with it through mobilization from without.

Burgess (2004) offers a conceptual framework for examining the outcomes of crisis in alliances between parties and unions provoked by the party's turn in government to the politics of the market. Differences in the structures of party, unions and the alliance itself and relations of power and autonomy within and between organizations help us understand the divergent responses of disaffected union leaders, whether they cooperate with or oppose innovation and whether they seek to terminate, modify or maintain existing links. The balance of power between governments in which the party is involved, the party itself and the unions is central. A variety of issues – union membership and density; the degree of centralization or decentralization subsisting in the unions; the legal system regulating union behaviour; the structure of the party and its relationship to the government in terms of dependence or autonomy; and the electoral system itself – all require consideration.

The nature and depth of hardship suffered by union members and the availability of suitable alternative parties as a vehicle for opposition to government and articulation of union interests are also relevant to union leaders balancing between politicians and their members. The dilemma of union leaders struggling to reconcile their attachments to government and party with fidelity to their members is resolved calculatively by consideration of these factors. In the end: 'Their choice reflects who has the power to punish them most severely' (Burgess 2004: 8).

Although Burgess's research was based on studies of Mexico, Spain and Venezuela in the late 1980s and 1990s it confirmed a trend towards a loosening of links apparent in a number of other countries and has more general application.

In Britain, for example, the severe and sustained decline in union power prompted by Conservative policies after 1979, managerial withdrawal of support for unions and structural changes in industry and class composition influenced maintenance, rather than reduction, of support for the Labour Party as it turned to market policies. In the context of continuing union weakness and financial attrition, the Conservatives' employment legislation prompted a trend towards centralization of decision-making in the unions. This was facilitated and reinforced by the waning of workplace organization which cushioned national leaders from challenges from below. However, transformations in the labour market and changes in the electoral market convinced party potentates that they no longer needed union leaders, as previous Labour governments had, as brokers, to deliver incomes policy and wage restraint or their members' votes. The electorate was now addressed directly rather than through union mediation. Sections of working-class support could be taken for granted while unions were part of the problem, not the solution, when it came to winning over the crucial middle ground and wavering Conservative supporters.

The centralization of party decision-making in the hands of the leadership and the diminution of the institutional voice of trade unionists and constituency activists, who, in the recent past, had inclined to the left, largely closed down the possibility of the party as a competing power centre which unions could exploit. The domination of the leadership and subsequently the government over the party went hand in hand with the atomization and marginalization of the traditional party left organized around *Tribune* and the Campaign Group. Finally, Britain's 'first past the post' electoral system increased the costs to union leaders of supporting an alternative to New Labour. The absence of proportional representation handicaps new parties entering the electoral arena. While the formal structures of the alliance have been maintained in attenuated form, in substance, and in policy terms, both unions and party have remained politically subordinate to New Labour governments.

Burgess's framework helps to analyse change in a variety of situations but historical and cultural factors require emphasis. This is particularly so in the case of Britain. Neoliberalism has produced breaches with the past in many aspects of trade unionism and industrial relations. In terms of the union–party link, the constricting weight of tradition endures. In resolving the loyalty dilemma between party and union the behaviour of union leaders is not calculative in any simplistic or short-term sense. It occurs in the context of long-established convention and jurisprudence, the fixed division between the political and industrial, the deference of union leaders to the party and the customary precedence accorded party leaders (Minkin 1991). The increase in the specific weight of unions which are not affiliated to Labour does not seem to have encouraged a propensity to look to alternative political parties. What initiatives there have been, such as the Socialist Labour Party (SLP), led by the mineworkers' leader Arthur Scargill, soon subsided into insignificance. Crucially it reflected no substantial break from the Labour Party or mobilized any significant group of union leaders outside the declining NUM and the small railworkers' unions.

After a decade of New Labour, with an economic downturn developing, the weakness of trade unionism and its leaders' awareness, perhaps even amplification, of that weakness, underpinned by their wariness about strikes, extensive protest and mobilization, appears to preclude initiatives that might change the balance of power in favour of unions. There is a reluctance to take risks. Moreover, sharp-edged political analysis of the unions' predicament remains at a premium. For example, TUC general secretary, Brendan Barber, observed a contradiction between what he saw as New Labour's constructive attitude to unions in the field of skills formation, where the government pays the unions to deliver workplace learning, and its unhelpful position over employment legislation, where it adamantly maintains the Conservatives' restrictive laws, to the detriment of trade unionism (TUC 2006: 1). Analysis of New Labour's neoliberalism suggests symmetry not dissonance between the two. Combined with a tough macroeconomic policy, restrictions on public sector pay and resistance to industrial action, the legislation plays a significant role in keeping unions weak. Their fragility provides the state with opportunities to channel union activities and union functions away from militancy and joint regulation and towards moderation and servicing the labour market (Ewing 2005; McIlroy 2008).

Expressing further concern at government decisions, Barber explained:

> Ministers had made wrong judgements . . . The government needed to recover its political nerve . . . on a whole range of issues the call has been wrong . . . the government has been paying too much attention to the siren voices of those campaigning for the super-rich and the corporate

elite . . . They should not be intimidated by self-interested lobbies. They should have greater political confidence to set out their programme . . . The government should reflect the values of 'ordinary people' and the centre ground.

(*Observer*, 20 April 2008)

The problem, surely, is not one of lack of confidence or nerve. New Labour governments have set out their programmes with immense political confidence. But they remain neoliberal programmes, antagonistic to strong trade unionism. New Labour governments have rarely lost their political nerve: on the whole they have kept it; they have stuck to their guns. The view that they have been intimidated by the corporate elite or been taken in by the super-rich is very wide of the mark.

From the start New Labour based itself on the interests of the corporate elite as a matter of political and economic strategy. Blair and Brown saw capital as the instrument for economic and political success. They did so with conscious calculation: they put the interests of capital before the interests of labour. The idea that they can be persuaded through argument to return to 'the centre ground' demonstrates both a continuing inability to understand the nature of New Labour and the diminution of union ambition since the 1990s.

If you do not understand what New Labour is and what it stands for you are in some difficulty in seeking to change its trajectory, let alone chart an alternative course. Much of the argument and evidence in *Trade Unions in a Neoliberal World* should be of interest to trade unionists as well as to students and academics. Eliciting concessions from the state and reversing state policy so that it is more favourable to trade unions means building opposition and engendering resistance to New Labour, not placating it. A *sine qua non* for leadership in that endeavour is grasping its neoliberal ideology and policies.

## IV

*Trade Unions in a Neoliberal World* is in two parts. The first section, 'Trade Unions under New Labour', contains five chapters. Taken together they provide a detailed overview of industrial politics since 1997, their impact on trade unions and the response of trade unionists to political and economic change. Much analysis of trade unionism remains resolutely and debilitatingly locked into the present, minimizing understanding of how yesterday influences where we are today (McIlroy and Campbell 1999). In chapter 1, John McIlroy prefaces consideration of the development of New Labour and its employment policies with examination of the Golden Age of capitalism and trade unionism from the Second World War until the 1970s and its breakdown. He explores some of the explanations for the development of the neoliberalism that replaced it, how it emerged and what it means. The Conservative governments are seen as representing a breakthrough for neoliberalism, transforming the economic and political landscape and devastating trade unionism. They also represented significant limitations in terms of securing a new and enduring settlement. The chapter traces the fortunes of the unions in the 1980s and 1990s. It concludes with the birth of New Labour as a positive productionist alternative to Thatcherism.

McIlroy's second chapter constitutes an extended address of New Labour's policies in government. It assesses their economic success in the context of deregulation, privatization, commodification and greater social inequality. It then looks in some detail at New Labour's philosophy of trade unions as drivers of flexibility and competitivity in the enterprise and in the labour market which has left a lasting mark on developments since 1997. McIlroy returns to the discussion of neoliberalism in chapter 1 and probes arguments that New Labour represents continuity with social democracy or, alternatively, a new 'third way', halfway between social democracy and Thatcherism. The author finds these arguments unconvincing: New Labour is a variant within neoliberalism.

For trade unionists the last years of the twentieth century did represent, at least in some ways, 'the end of history' (Hyman 1995: 47–8). They witnessed the dissolution of the time-honoured traditions of voluntarism, collective laissez-faire and the attenuation of workplace organization, economistic militancy and social and political legitimacy. Since the change of government in 1997, trade union leaders and activists, not to say a substantial section of industrial relations academics, have devoted themselves to the issue of union renewal or revitalization. A persistent question has been whether, and if so how, unions can regain, or move significantly towards regaining, the place in the world they held during the post-war era. Can they make appreciable progress in extending their membership and coverage of the labour force, rebuilding workplace organization and achieving substantial political influence? Can they increase the voice of trade unionists in the economy and the enterprise, in Parliament and in society? Consequently, and crucially, can they better influence outcomes and improve the terms, conditions and lives of their members?

In chapters 3 and 4, McIlroy and Gary Daniels consider the evidence. Chapter 3 evaluates strategies for revitalization. Unions have oscillated between, and attempted to combine, a partnership model, based on winning support from employers by demonstrating the efficacy of unions in serving business ends, and the more adversarial model based on mobilizing the inherent antagonism at the heart of the employment relationship. The authors analyse trends in membership and density since 1997 and delineate changes in collective bargaining and industrial action. The evidence suggests that unions have stopped the rot so far as significant falls in membership are concerned: decline in density has continued. A balanced judgement would conclude that an element of consolidation, but not revitalization, is in train. However, immense efforts will be necessary to maintain progress since 1997. Chapter 4 scrutinizes the changing shape of trade unionism. It discusses the major unions, their membership and job territories in the context of recent mergers. It reviews the state of union organization at the national level and in the workplace, as well as the measures taken to secure appropriate representation of women and minority ethnic workers. It explores members' attitudes towards employment relations and allied issues. An extended section examines political organization and factionalism inside the unions as well as recent developments in the TUC.

In spring 2008, proposals for the reform of political funding, which could give New Labour greater control over the political funds of affiliated unions, sparked yet another in the perennial chain of spats between the party leadership and affiliated unions. The GMB raised the question of disaffiliation (*Guardian*, 18 April 2008). Over the decade since 1997 the alliance between the Labour Party and the unions has remained a matter of intense controversy. There have been changes in its conventions and ethos which confirm the subordinate position of the unions, illustrated in union leaders' acceptance of the self-denying ordinance of no votes on resolutions at conference in 2007 and, before that, the disaffiliation of two small unions who despaired of successfully pursuing their purposes inside New Labour. There has been no fundamental revision of the structures of the link itself. However, it is arguable that significant mutual relations are incrementally, gradually but remorselessly winding down or wearing out. In chapter 5, McIlroy explains the intricacies of the link and recent innovations before providing an extended review of the ups and downs in the contentious alliance since 1997. He argues that the situation is structured by sustained union weakness and by union leaders' perceptions of relative powerlessness. This is combined with their prioritizing of access to government for which the only realistic alternative contenders are the Conservatives. This means that the possibility of change emanating from the union side of the marriage remains unlikely. On present trends further change will be prompted by what is indubitably the senior partner.

In the second part of the book, a number of academics discuss in greater detail important aspects of issues central to the trajectory of trade unionism during the New Labour years. The Gate Gourmet dispute in 2005 highlighted the continuing difficulties employment legislation entails for unions and sparked renewed resistance by union leaders (see Ewing 2006). The Conservative laws, maintained although reformed by New Labour, remain a barrier to the re-emergence of powerful independent trade unionism in Britain. In chapter 6, Paul Smith and Gary Morton review the current state of play. They situate New Labour legislation, centred on the employment acts of 1999, 2002 and 2004 and the minimum wage measures, in the absences which bespeak the government's embrace of neoliberalism. They argue that the values behind the legislation as well as its detail reflect a minimalism which is part of a project to recreate trade unionism in a cooperative partnership mode. This is emphasized by the government's parsimonious attitude to EU directives. For the authors, New Labour legislates within the neoliberal paradigm. Its hostility to assertive, effective trade unionism should not be underestimated.

Martin Upchurch and Gary Daniels devote more attention to the partnership and organizing approaches reviewed in the first part of the text. In chapter 7, Upchurch notes the limited growth of partnership, at least if measured by partnership agreements and formal arrangements. He locates its development since the 1990s in New Labour's attempts to stimulate high-performance working and human capital development in order to increase productivity in the interests of competitivity. 'The third way', he notes, attempted to legitimize partnership while the imperatives of handling the continued flow of EU directives have kept partnership on the political agenda. Upchurch engages critically with the factors driving the partnership agenda and reviews both the academic literature and recent developments in the unions. Partnership, he concludes, is ultimately the application of management prerogative by other means. Trade unionists need partnership with other union members and other employees decidedly more than partnership with the employers.

Daniels draws up a balance sheet of the organizing project launched by the TUC in 1996. In chapter 8 he contributes a wide-ranging survey of the initiatives ignited by the TUC and developed in a variety of unions. He analyses the strengths and weaknesses of the organizing model and debates about it among academics. The evidence he deploys from diverse unions from Amicus and the TWGU to BECTU, Community and USDAW, suggests that there are few grounds for complacency. There is evidence of organizing success and the efficacy of new approaches. There are differences in recruitment and retention rates in different unions but the decline in aggregate membership stubbornly endures. A range of internal as well as external constraints curb progress. Nonetheless the TUC approach, imaginatively applied, as distinct from more radical versions of the organizing model, at least in a situation of relative rank-and-file quiescence, is the best instrument for revitalization presently available to union activists.

The growth of workplace learning during the New Labour years has been extolled by politicians, union leaders, activists and academics as a major success story for the unions. In chapter 9, McIlroy and Richard Croucher present a more critical take on recent developments. They set current initiatives against the background of trade union attempts to make vocational training and skills formation a matter of joint regulation as part of the TUC's stakeholder / HRM / partnership agenda which blossomed in the 1990s. On the admittedly limited evidence available, workplace learning has contributed slightly to this objective. It is typically organized separately from vocational training and collective bargaining as a fringe benefit / HRM perquisite, governed by management prerogative. The unions' new function in administering systems of state support for capital is financially lucrative and wins plaudits from the government. It raises fundamental questions about the role and independence of trade unions. If workplace learning contributes to union revitalization – and hard evidence that it is doing so is limited – a subaltern form of revitalization is likely to be the result.

In chapter 10, Dave Lyddon demonstrates that proclamations of the death of the strike are premature. New Labour has maintained the hostility to any form of industrial action cultivated by its Conservative predecessors. This was exhibited graphically in the 2002–3 firefighters' strike and the reintroduction of Conservative legislation to deal with the prison officers. It is routinely affirmed in government condemnations of strikes and strikers, most recently in the 2008 stoppages by teachers, other public sector workers and oil refinery employees (*Guardian*, 25, 26 April 2008). On all indices industrial action has declined to unprecedented levels. It is largely confined to transport and communications and public services. It has become more restricted in scope and time, more calculative and more tactical. The habit has not been eradicated.

Last, but not least, Graham Taylor explores the perspectives of New Labour and the unions on the EU and their development since the 1990s. Taylor argues in chapter 11 that evolving from social democracy to neoliberalism the New Labour project has combined a positive stress on market extension and integration with a distinctive approach to 'Social Europe' based on 'the so-called "Third Way"'. He notes the nuances and adumbrates differences within both party and unions which have surfaced on several occasions, most recently over the promised referendum on the EU constitution. He details the implementation of EU directives for employment relations and trade unionism. The government has demonstrated enthusiasm for the single market. Its opposition to the extension of the social dimension in Europe and in Britain is aptly illustrated in its restrictive attitude to EU legislation in Brussels and in London. In contrast, unions have placed the solidaristic and social partnership aspects of the EU at the heart of strategies for revitalization. This guarantees that differences will remain and may even deepen.

As Sinha (2005: 167) observes: 'neoliberalism threatens labour unions . . . labour politics seeks to reconstitute a regulatory and redistributive state, the opposite of the neoliberal ideal'. He is on weaker ground in relation to Britain when he goes on: 'older union formations have adapted to new conditions and have generated new forms of politics and independent unions have taken shape around "liberalisation" and privatization' (ibid: 168). Since 1997 it is the social movements and fringe parties that have made the running in challenging neoliberalism. British unions' contribution to wider struggles against neoliberalism and to new forms of politics has been slight. It is arguable that the engagement of unions as representative organizations of considerable social weight is necessary to progress. This, in turn, requires greater awareness of what is at stake if union leaders continue to pursue partnership with a neoliberal state and neoliberal employers, rather than mobilizing union members against neoliberalism. Union activists need to know what they are up against. They should also explore what might take the place of neoliberalism. It is imperative to construct new maps to different destinations. Seneca said centuries ago: 'If one does not know to which port one is sailing, no wind is favourable.' We hope that this book will further understanding of the political problems trade unionists must confront if they are to seriously pursue revitalization and the re-emergence of unions as significant economic and social actors.

## Bibliography

Blanchflower, D. (2007) 'International patterns of union membership', *British Journal of Industrial Relations*, 45:1, 1–28.

Blyton, P. and Turnbull, P. (2004) *The Dynamics of Employee Relations*, 3rd edition, Basingstoke: Palgrave Macmillan.

Burgess, K. (2004) *Parties and Unions in the New Global Economy*, Pittsburgh: University of Pittsburgh Press.

Coates, D. (2005) *Prolonged Labour: The Slow Birth of New Labour Britain*, Basingstoke: Palgrave.

Collins, H. (2001) 'Regulating the employment relationship for competitiveness', *Industrial Law Journal*, 30:1, 17–47.

Crouch, C. (1997) 'The terms of the neoliberal consensus', *Political Quarterly*, 68:4, 352–60.

Driver, S. and Martell, L. (2006) *New Labour*, 2nd edition, Cambridge: Polity Press.

Edwards, P. (ed.) (2003) *Industrial Relations: Theory and Practice in Britain*, 2nd edition, Oxford: Blackwell.

Ewing, K. (2005) 'The function of trade unions', *Industrial Law Journal*, 34:1, 1–22.

Ewing, K. (ed.) (2006) *The Right to Strike: From the 1906 Trade Disputes Act to a Trade Union Freedom Bill*, Liverpool: Institute of Employment Rights.

Fredman, S. (2004) 'The ideology of new labour law', in C. Barnard, S. Deakin and G. Morris (eds) *The Future of Labour Law*, Oxford: Hart Publishing.

Gamble, A. (2006) 'Two faces of neoliberalism', in R. Robison (ed.) *The Neoliberal Revolution: Forging the Market State*, Basingstoke: Palgrave.

Glyn, A. (2006) *Capitalism Unleashed: Finance, Globalization and Welfare*, Oxford: Oxford University Press.

Hale, D. (2007) 'International comparisons of labour disputes in 2005', *Economic and Labour Market Review*, 1:4, 23–31.

Harvey, D. (2005) *A Brief History of Neoliberalism*, Oxford: Oxford University Press.

Hyman, R. (1995) 'The historical evolution of British industrial relations', in P. Edwards (ed.) *Industrial Relations: Theory and Practice in Britain*, Oxford: Blackwell.

Kelly, J. (1998) *Rethinking Industrial Relations: Mobilization, Collectivism and Long Waves*, London: Routledge.

Ludlam, S. and Smith, M. (eds) (2001) *New Labour in Government*, Basingstoke: Palgrave.

—— (2004) *Governing as New Labour: Policy and Politics Under Blair*, Basingstoke: Palgrave.

McIlroy, J. (1998) 'The enduring alliance? Trade unions and the making of New Labour, 1994–1997', *British Journal of Industrial Relations*, 36:4, 537–64.

—— (2007) 'Reflections on British trade unions and industrial politics', in J. McIlroy, N. Fishman and A. Campbell (eds) *The High Tide of British Trade Unionism: Trade Unions and Industrial Politics 1964–79*, 2nd edition, London: Merlin Press.

—— (2008) 'Ten years of New Labour: workplace learning, social partnership and union revitalization in Britain', *British Journal of Industrial Relations*, 46:2, 283–313.

McIlroy, J. and Campbell, A. (1999) 'Still setting the pace? labour history, industrial relations and the history of post-war trade unionism', *Labour History Review*, 64:2, 179–99.

Minkin, L. (1991) *The Contentious Alliance: Trade Unions and the Labour Party*, Edinburgh: Edinburgh University Press.

Moschonas, G. (2002) *In the Name of Social Democracy, the Great Transformation: 1945 to the Present*, London: Verso.

Peck, J. (2004) 'Geography and public policy: constructions of neoliberalism', *Progress in Human Geography*, 28:3, 392–405.

Peck, J. and Theodore, N. (2007) 'Variegated capitalism', *Progress in Human Geography*, 31:6, 731–72.

Peck, J. and Tickell, A. (2002) 'Neoliberalizing space', *Antipode*, 34:3, 380–402.

Riddell, P. (2005) *The Unfulfilled Prime Minister: Tony Blair's Quest for a Legacy*, London: Politicos.

Seldon, A. (2004) *Blair*, London: The Free Press.

Seldon, A. (ed.) (2007a) *Blair's Britain 1997–2007*, Cambridge: Cambridge University Press.

Seldon, A. (2007b) *Blair Unbound*, London: Simon and Schuster.

Seldon, A. and Kavanagh, D. (2005) *The Blair Effect 2001–5*, Cambridge: Cambridge University Press.

Sinha, S. (2005) 'Neoliberalism and civil society: project and possibilities', in A. Saad-Filho and D. Johnston (eds) *Neoliberalism: A Critical Reader*, London: Pluto Press.

Slaughter, C. (2006) *Not Without a Storm: Towards a Communist Manifesto for the Age of Globalisation*, London: Index Books.

TUC (2006) *General Council Report*, London: TUC.

Visser, J. (2006) 'Union membership statistics in 24 countries', *Monthly Labor Review*, January, 38–44.

Williams, S. and Adam-Smith, D. (2006) *Contemporary Employment Relations: A Critical Introduction*, Oxford: Oxford University Press.

# Part I

# Trade unions under New Labour

# 1 A brief history of British trade unions and neoliberalism: From the earliest days to the birth of New Labour

*John McIlroy*

The history of British trade unionism demonstrates that its fortunes are bound up with a variety of interacting factors. Union strength, levels of membership, ability to mobilize and bargaining power, reflects the positions the state takes on employment relations; the attitude of employers and managers; the operation of the economic cycle, particularly the level of employment and the rate of inflation; the composition of the labour force and the structure of employment – historically some groups of workers have demonstrated greater propensity to organize than others, while size of enterprise and concentration of labour have proved relevant. Union strength is also a function of human agency, the quality of leadership at all levels, from head office to workplace, which enables unions to maximize the beneficial aspects of their environment and minimize its unfavourable features (Undy *et al.* 1981; Bain and Price 1983; Kelly 1998: 24–65).

The significance of the state and the strategies it adopts towards economic change, labour market issues and collectivism increased during the twentieth century. Its role has reflected the politics of its personnel but also wider political developments, trends in the world economy and embedded national traditions (Crouch 1993). The importance of the state in constructing industrial relations systems has been recently rehabilitated (Howell 2005). In the past the British state was restrained and sensitive to the independent development and autonomous cultures of capital and labour. Until relatively recently it was conventional to emphasize the continuity, distinctiveness and resilience of the tradition of voluntarism, collective bargaining and limited state intervention embodied in the system of collective laissez-faire (Hyman 2003: 37–8). The endurance and adaptability of the core of voluntarism when British capitalism adopted a regime of Keynesian economic regulation after 1945, despite arguable areas of incompatibility and unquestionable tensions with collective laissez-faire, pays testimony to the truth of this perspective.

Analysing European trade unionism as oscillating between ideal type polarities of market, class and society, Richard Hyman sees British unions as historically marked by the first two corners of the triangle. Prioritizing 'free' collective bargaining, industrial autonomy, insulation from legal regulation of collective employment relations, they represented class interests to the state, while accepting in practice the logical inevitability of capitalism. Despite their affiliation to the Labour Party, they treated politics and employment relations as distinctive, circumscribed spheres. There were pervasive tensions between class and market, 'free' collective bargaining and political reform, corporate responsibility and sectional assertiveness: 'occupying the terrain between class and market, British trade unions have traditionally displayed a militant, but sectional and defensive, economism' (Hyman 2001: 68).

The frictions between collective laissez-faire and union autonomy built up throughout the era of Keynesian demand management. Voluntarism was challenged and eroded by limited, largely unsuccessful attempts at quasi-corporatism centred on national understandings between the state, employers and unions about the reform and regulation of collective bargaining which developed from the 1960s and intensified in the following decade (Fox 1985: 373–414). The contours, core and culture of the old system remained. The appearance of neoliberalism in the late 1970s, its development in the 1980s and its consolidation after 1997 transformed British industrial relations. Global economic trends and free-market ideologies of capitalist revitalization triumphed over history and national particularities. A new politics of rupture propelled the dismantling of collective laissez-faire and the termination of union autonomy. Joint regulation of the workplace has been eroded, management prerogative has been enhanced and unions have been decisively weakened. The neoliberal counter-revolution has been planned and orchestrated by a state which in the past sustained trade unionism. Today, trade unionists face new challenges and they face them in an intractable environment.

To understand their predicament and the possibilities of transcending it we need to contextualize New Labour governments and assess their nature. We need to explore their ideology, politics and attitude to trade unionism in order to locate New Labour in the development of neoliberalism since the 1970s. There are different views on the extent to which the politics of Tony Blair and Gordon Brown represent a distinctive 'third way' or renewal of social democracy or whether they are the sons of Margaret Thatcher (Jenkins 2006) whose political DNA constitutes a variant of neoliberalism. What is clear is that both neoliberalism and New Labour are children of the crisis of Keynesian welfarism and the post-war settlement. This chapter starts by looking at the post-war compromise and the role trade unions played in it before examining the reasons why it disintegrated. It discusses the literature on neoliberalism and the ways in which scholars have understood its emergence. It explores the different phases of neoliberalism and its profound antagonism to trade unionism. It traces the way in which neoliberalism passed from marginal economic and political theories of the relationship between markets and the state, adumbrated in the obscure confines of the Mont Pelerin Society by the Austrian political philosopher Friedrich von Hayek and the American economist Milton Friedman, to an experimental and subsequently dominant politics. This chapter explains how in

Britain neoliberalism replaced Keynesianism as a means of revitalizing and re-regulating capitalism. It documents the development of Thatcherism as the pioneering iconoclastic neoliberalism that broke with both Keynesianism and collective laissez-faire in industrial relations and significantly undermined British trade unionism. It concludes by examining how the forward march of neoliberalism culminated in the 1990s with its annexation of the British Labour Party in the age of Tony Blair and Gordon Brown.

## Keynesianism and the Golden Age of trade unions

The crisis of Keynesianism characterized by the slowdown in capitalist accumulation, problems of profitability and state expenditure and embedded inflation, provided the opportunity for neoliberalism. But in the post-war period Keynesianism appeared an unsurpassed method of making capitalism work and integrating trade unions in its functioning. The years after 1945 constituted what Eric Hobsbawm (1994: 257–86) called 'The Golden Age' and witnessed the apogee of British trade unionism. The pioneering Labour governments of 1945–51 pledged themselves to full employment, an extended welfare state, a limited degree of public ownership, planning and fiscal redress of inequality. From 1951–64 their Conservative successors adapted to a circumscribed social democratic consensus. They accepted 'the mixed economy', state supervision of the market and government intervention and spending on welfare and defence to manage demand. The leading states were influenced by the failures of capitalism in the interwar years, the emergence of Fascism and Stalinism and the positive experience of collectivism, state planning and collaboration with labour during the war. Underpinned by technological development, American leadership and the strength of the US economy, the Bretton Woods Agreement, which fixed exchange rates, and institutions such as the International Monetary Fund, the state manipulated taxation and public spending to increase or reduce demand as necessary and ensure full employment. The result was sustained economic growth and the relative extension of prosperity to sections of the working class (ibid.; Armstrong *et al.* 1984: 309–50; Marglin and Schor 1990).

There was, however, failure to counteract the endemic short-termism of British capital, its privileging of shareholders and their profits, as well as the debilitating split between finance capital and industrial capital which produced under-investment in industry. Despite ad hoc initiatives centred on incomes policies, there was little attempt to coordinate the labour market or to enhance the coordinating capacity of union leaders (Crouch 2003). Rather, the 1950s and early 1960s represented the high point of collective laissez-faire which remained, in some ways, antagonistic to the ruling ethos of state intervention. Workers, and their purchasing power, were vital to the post-war settlement as consumers and organized workers were important as its facilitators and guardians, although women workers were largely consigned to the home and the new order was based on the male 'bread-winner' (Crompton

2006: 59). Unions became the fifth estate; their leaders were privileged and consulted by the state. They were recognized as rectifying the inequality of power inherent in the employment relationship and stimulating capital to introduce more efficient organization of work, adopt new technology and generate superior rates of productivity. Higher wages helped maintain demand. Collective bargaining was the preferred method of job regulation and it guaranteed the unions' role. They remained significantly free of either legal restriction or support. Immunity from common law, granted to union organization and industrial action by the 1906 Trade Disputes Act, endured. The disabilities introduced by the 1927 Trade Disputes and Trade Unions Act and wartime legislation were repealed in 1946 and 1951 respectively. Judicial hostility was muted (Flanders and Clegg 1954; Flanders 1960; Wedderburn 1965).

For union leaders, mediating between the state and their members, Keynesianism represented the best means of organizing capitalism that capitalists had as yet invented. For trade unionists, it was benign. Three-quarters of the labour force were covered by collective agreements (Milner 1995). Union membership expanded from 7.8 million in 1945 to 10.3 million twenty years later. However, the growth in the labour force and in service and white-collar occupations combined with the decline of traditionally organized sectors to ensure that density, which had increased from 38 per cent to 44 per cent, remained static thereafter (see table 1.1).

*Table 1.1* Aggregate trade union membership and density in the UK, 1945–67

| Year | Union Membership (000's) | Union Density (%) |
|------|--------------------------|-------------------|
| 1945 | 7,875 | 38.6 |
| 1948 | 9,363 | 45.2 |
| 1949 | 9,318 | 44.8 |
| 1950 | 9,289 | 44.1 |
| 1951 | 9,530 | 45.0 |
| 1952 | 9,588 | 45.1 |
| 1953 | 9,527 | 44.6 |
| 1954 | 9,566 | 44.2 |
| 1955 | 9,741 | 44.5 |
| 1956 | 9,778 | 44.1 |
| 1957 | 9,829 | 44.0 |
| 1958 | 9,639 | 43.2 |
| 1959 | 9,623 | 44.0 |
| 1960 | 9,835 | 44.2 |
| 1961 | 9,916 | 44.0 |
| 1962 | 10,014 | 43.8 |
| 1963 | 10,067 | 43.7 |
| 1964 | 10,218 | 44.1 |
| 1965 | 10,325 | 44.2 |
| 1966 | 10,259 | 43.6 |
| 1967 | 10,194 | 43.7 |

*Source:* Bain and Price (1983)

Broad sweep treatment minimizes diversity and underplays the persistence of instability and conflict. Stylized analyses of trade unionism predicating 'professional trade unionism', with full-time officers servicing quiescent members, giving way to 'participatory trade unionism' in the 1960s and 1970s, based on assertive lay activists (Heery and Kelly 1994) capture important aspects of the picture; but they require balancing by historical approaches (Campbell, Fishman and McIlroy 2007; McIlroy, Fishman and Campbell 2007). Inflationary tendencies, balance of payments problems, inequality and poverty were always present; and so from the 1940s were attempts at incomes policy and debates about legal intervention. Progress and prosperity was always uneven (Cronin 1984: 146–72). As America boomed, as Germany and Japan revived and were re-integrated into the world market, Britain's economic difficulties became harder to tackle (Price 1986: 208–34). Full employment combined with generational change bred security, reflected in the increasing confidence of trade unionists and the extension of shop steward organization and workplace bargaining over a widening range of issues. Unions became identified in public and political opinion as engines of inflation and obstacles to productivity; the accelerating strike rate crystallized concerns. The response, the incomes policies of the late 1960s and early 1970s, exacerbated matters (Panitch 1976).

Advertised as emergency measures, uneven in their impact, wage controls and the publicity about their failures combined with increasing encroachment of tax on wage packets, prompted by growing public expenditure, to ratchet up militancy and strikes and put pressure on productivity and profits (Glyn and Sutcliffe 1972; Gough 1979; Hyman 1989). Attempts at coordination were rendered more tenuous as collective bargaining moved down into the workplace from national and industry level. The distance between union leaders' support for national decisions at Labour Party conference or the TUC and union members' desire to compensate for tax and inflation with increased wages was extended by the burgeoning of shop floor organization. Decentralization inhibited national bargaining between unions, employers and the state; it undermined the impact of those bargains that were made (Cronin 1984: 173–92; Taylor 1993: 222–64). The twin tendencies of British trade unionism towards centralized tripartite pacts at the top and towards decentralized, sectional workplace bargaining at the bottom were increasingly incompatible.

The Royal Commission on Industrial Relations which reported in 1968 sought to act on this problem. It tried to restore order to collective laissez-faire, facilitate incomes policy and improve productivity. It attempted to persuade managers to negotiate extended agreements at plant and company level. They would regulate pay and conditions, mesh with industry-wide bargaining, integrate stewards in union and company structures and enable state supervision of voluntary reform through a Commission on Industrial Relations. The Donovan Report was overshadowed by legislative initiatives from impatient governments to control trade unions. Both Labour's *In Place of Strife*, 1969, and the Conservatives' Industrial Relations Act, 1971, proved unsuccessful and counterproductive in stimulating awareness of the power they possessed among trade unionists and reinforcing union resistance to change (Crouch 1977; Davies and Freedland 1993: 255–350).

From the early 1960s, with the establishment of the National Economic Development Council and subsequently the National Plan and National Prices and Incomes Board of the Wilson governments, the state had sought to foster a calibrated element of coordination. This cautious, incremental process was accelerated from 1974 by the Wilson and Callaghan administrations. The context was the collapse of Bretton Woods; the ending of fixed exchange rates; the 'shock' to the western economies administered by the OPEC oil embargo of 1973; the unprecedented combination of economic growth with inflation; growing unemployment; falling levels of profitability; and the difficulties of the US economy in the aftermath of the Vietnam war. These factors combined to provoke the crisis of Keynesianism (Glyn and Harrison 1980: 5–33; Marglin and Schor 1990). The first reaction of the British state was to harness the organizations which it now perceived as part of the problem to facilitate its solution. It attempted to use a balance of class forces unfavourable to capital to restore the fortunes of capitalism. It tried to strengthen the role and the reach of trade unions to save the social democratic state.

The ensuing process of shallow 'bargained corporatism' and juridification saw new rights for unions and enhanced access to the state exchanged for control of wages as part of the 'Social Contract'. Union leaders were involved in formulating the details of incomes policy and in deepening state intervention focused on the National Enterprise Board and 'planning agreements'. The Trade Union and Labour Relations Acts, 1974 and 1976, the Employment Protection Act, 1975, and the Health and Safety at Work Act, 1974, as well as anti-discrimination legislation, extended the rights of unions and their members. The unsuccessful proposals of the Bullock Commission on Industrial Democracy (1977) were intended to put the final touches to the edifice of neo-corporatism by complementing integrative rights for shop stewards with the appointment of worker directors (Coates 1980). But as the economic situation failed to improve, unions were confronted with government moves to combine monetarist remedies with quasi-corporatism (Glyn and Harrison 1980: 111–34). Cuts in public expenditure, the welfare state and the social wage, as well as rising unemployment, followed voluntary reduction of real income by trade unionists through wage restraint in 1976–7. Continuing pressure on wages provoked a new wave of militancy in 1978–9, the 'Winter of Discontent' and the demise of the Callaghan government.

In one sense, unions benefited from the experiment with corporatism. As table 1.2 demonstrates, membership increased dramatically in the decade from *In Place of Strife* to the Winter of Discontent. There were 10.2 million trade unionists in 1968 and 13.4 million in 1979. Density increased from

*Table 1.2* Aggregate trade union membership and density in the UK 1968–79

| Year | Union Membership (000's) | Union Density (%) |
|------|--------------------------|-------------------|
| 1968 | 10,200 | 44.0 |
| 1969 | 10,479 | 45.3 |
| 1970 | 11,187 | 48.5 |
| 1971 | 11,135 | 48.7 |
| 1972 | 11,359 | 49.5 |
| 1973 | 11,456 | 49.3 |
| 1974 | 11,764 | 50.4 |
| 1975 | 12,026 | 51.0 |
| 1976 | 12,386 | 51.9 |
| 1977 | 12,846 | 53.4 |
| 1978 | 13,112 | 54.2 |
| 1979 | 13,447 | 55.4 |

*Source:* Bain and Price (1983)

44 per cent to over 55 per cent, the highest level before or since. Time would prove this growth fragile and ephemeral. Arguably increased union influence exacerbated the problems of coordination it was intended to transcend without providing renewed conditions for 'constitutional insurgency' (Hyman 2001: 90). Unions were secondary actors in the drama: they cannot be blamed for its dénouement. Their identification with inflation, economic inefficiency and disorder would play a role in the next act as one component of change stimulated by seismic shifts in the world economy and new ruling ideologies.

## The birth of neoliberalism

Keynesianism crashed and a new regime for regulating capitalism began to emerge. At first it constituted an ideology, an intellectual critique which asserted the supremacy of the free market and the freedom of the individual in maximizing profitability, economic growth, optimal allocation of goods and the fairest distribution of income and wealth. The state intervention of the Keynesian era, it claimed, fuelled inflation and depressed profits. Solving the crisis required rejection of demand management, alleviation of burdens on business and transfer of costs from the state and capital to individuals and markets. To restore sound money and business confidence the state must control the money supply; restrict borrowing; slash public expenditure; reduce the welfare state to a safety net; and return the public sector to private capital. Taxes on business and the tax burden generally stifled entrepreneurialism and investment. They should be diminished while regressive indirect taxation should replace redistributive, direct taxation. The state should stimulate a return to human nature, individualism and entrepreneurialism rather than collectivism and dependency culture (McIlroy 1995: 76–7). Unions featured, in neoliberal ideology, as impediments to the market and the exercise of managerial prerogative to answer market demands. In Britain they had exploited the monopoly position state sustenance and full employment provided, to utilize the closed shop and the strike weapon to increase wages to artificial levels and generate inflation. Unions distorted efficient deployment of labour through job controls which crippled innovation, productivity, investment and competitivity (Coates 2000: 77–86).

Neoliberalism turned from ideology to practical politics in tandem with fundamental changes in the world economy later grouped together under the label 'globalization'. The specific relationship between global change in the 1970s and 1980s and the evolution of neoliberalism requires further investigation. The best view seems to be that trends towards globalization facilitated, although they did not cause, the political dominance of neoliberalism (Colás 2005: 75). There were shifts in production away from standard mass consumption products towards diversification of goods and services; increased competition, greater need for innovation, accelerated technology transfer and rapid product change; recomposition of the traditional working class; and greater commercialization of all aspects of life (Crouch and Streeck 1997). Growth in the scale and integration of activity by transnational corporations was fundamental. The end of financial controls and fixed exchange rates together with developments in information technology eased the movement of capital and production around the globe. The General Agreement on Tariffs prioritized free trade. The world was increasingly perceived as a single market in which the balance of power between states and global capital was transformed in favour of the latter (Dasgupta and Kiely 2006).

In extreme versions of globalization the state has been turned into little more than an instrument of global capitalism (Hardt and Negri 2000). The reality is that multinationals still operate from their home economy and look to 'their' nation state for support. Capital is not unproblematically footloose, labour is not simply reactive and locally embedded, and the state has not been rendered powerless (Dunn 2004). In more conventional and convincing accounts an overriding function of the state was to vie with competing states to provide an optimal environment for investment, minimal controls over business and a secure supply of skilled, compliant, productive and relatively inexpensive labour. Deregulation of national economies, privatization of state assets and liberalization of trade were key factors in providing a springboard for globalization (Castells 2000: 135–7).

The extent of globalization in comparison with past periods of liberalism has been contested (Hirst and Thompson 1996; Weiss 1998). Its origins, nature and implications have been widely debated (Held *et al.* 1999; Hardt and Negri 2000; Stiglitz 2002). What seems clear is that changes in the world economy and the restructuring of American capitalism which commenced after the oil crisis of the 1970s quickened after the collapse of the Soviet Union in 1989 (Crouch 2003: 212). This epochal change opened up new markets and freed the market model from challenge by Stalinism and its mutations. It intensified interest in neoliberalism and, in the context of its earlier adoption in Britain and America, stimulated its extension. These developments were accelerated by the crusading neoliberal states as well as the international bodies they sponsored, not only the Group of Seven economies but the Organization of Economic Cooperation and Development, the World Bank and the World Trade Organization (Callinicos 2001: 23).

Despite neoliberal ideology and discourse, actually-existing neoliberalisms have been achieved by state action. As the history of capitalism teaches, markets, global or otherwise, do not replace states. States make markets (Polanyi 2001: 58). Neoliberalism is the state-authored reorganization of capitalism aimed at extending the influence of the market and increasing the rate of profit; globalization became dominated by neoliberalism and it has evolved as neoliberalism's international dimension (Saad-Filho and Johnston 2005: 2–3). In contrast to its anti-statist rhetoric, states constituted neoliberal regimes, not least by removing working-class resistance. And states continue to play a significant role not only in providing legal frameworks for economic transactions and essential services, from defence to education and healthcare, but in economic management and coordination, in correcting and subsidizing market failure, in regulating privatized enterprise, and through fiscal and monetary policy. The term 'neoliberalism' can be misleading in relation to actually-existing neoliberalisms: they represent a remoulding of post-war regimes, make a variety of accommodations with the Keynesian and social democratic past and retain elements of it. Ideal types are just that. The world of 1860 has not been restored in Britain or China.

There is a great deal of controversy about neoliberalism. It is sometimes characterized as representing the hegemony of finance capital and an attempt to restore the economic fortunes and contested world domination of the USA (Chesnais 1997; Chesnais and Sauviat 2003). Others see it as an aberrant way of running capitalism (George 1999). In the best-known account, Harvey (2005) conceives neoliberalism as a new turn to primitive accumulation and extension of the market through globalization and plunder of state assets. Duménil and Lévy emphasize the interests of finance capitalism and the agency of key politicians, such as Margaret Thatcher in Britain and Ronald Reagan in the USA, in paving the way for neoliberal progress in alliance with owners of capital and business leaders (2004: 210–13). The 'Washington Consensus' was important. But other analysts stress the role of factions within the capitalist class and the influence of free market thinkers in discrediting Keynesianism and popularizing neo-liberalism (Van der Pijl 1998; Sklair 2001). The increasing importance of finance capital in the 'advanced' economies, its potential for profits and employment, its growing control of shareholdings, its stimulus to consumer credit and speculation, and its contribution to short-term stability but periodic crises, is well-evidenced (Glyn 2006: 50–76).

Actually-existing neoliberalisms have fallen short of neoliberal ideology.

They have demonstrated significant variation stretching from Bill Clinton's 'new economy' to the Anglo-American subaltern versions in Australia and New Zealand and Tiananmen Square neoliberalism in China (Harvey 2005: 120–51). If we eschew monolithic frameworks and remain sensitive to local difference and historical shifts within the paradigm, neoliberalism serves as a useful way of understanding and conceptualizing developments within capitalism since the 1970s and contrasting it with the post-war period (Larner 2000). Whatever the differences over causation and growth, Harvey's argument that neoliberalism represents a class project, a reassertion of class power, is persuasive and its profound antagonism to working-class collectivism and organized labour remains unquestionable (2005: 16, 53, 59). Neoliberalism emerged to counter capitalist crisis and revitalize capitalists. It sought to undermine the largely veto-based strength that trade unions had amassed under Keynesianism and their consequent resistance to domestication or curtailment of that strength (Panitch and Gindin 2004: 81). A central imperative of the new regime was 'to reduce the power of labour' (Saad-Filho and Johnston 2005: 3) and introduce 'a new discipline of labour and management to the benefit of lenders and shareholders' (Duménil and Lévy 2005: 10). Neoliberalism aspired 'to restore the [capitalist] class's revenues and power which had diminished since the Great Depression and World War II. Far from being inevitable this was a political action' (Duménil and Lévy 2004: 2).

Neoliberalism's engagement with trade unionism has changed as neoliberalism has developed. Peck and Tickell (2002) discern three phases. Proto-neoliberalism, a minority strand in economic and political thought from the 1930s which evolved as a critique of Keynesianism, influenced the 'roll-back neoliberalism' of the 1980s, pioneered by Thatcher and Reagan. This, in turn, prompted 'roll-out neoliberalism' as the unrelenting destructive onslaught and confrontational tactics and rhetoric of the founders mutated into a hegemonic institutionalized form of regulation in the 1990s. We might add in the case of Britain a preludial phase in which between 1976 and 1979 the social democratic government of James Callaghan laid some of the ground for the subsequent Conservative experiment (Artis and Cobham 1991). History may, despite the end of history proclaimed by neoliberals, usher in further phases. Neoliberalism may be challenged. It may unravel when confronted by new developments in capitalism, which historically has never stood still, as well as by its own contradictions.

The award of the Nobel Prize for economics to Friedrich von Hayek in 1974 and Milton Friedman in 1976 (Hobsbawm 1994: 408) announced the end of the marginality of neoliberal ideas. Friedman and other Chicago University economists, such as Gary Becker, who held that inflation, not unemployment, was the greatest evil and that fiscal responsibility and strict control of the money supply would curb inflation (Friedman 1962), had already influenced the policies of the Pinochet regime in Chile. Together with Hayek's stress on the centrality of 'economic man' the indispensability of laissez-faire and the injurious economic effects of trade unionism, their views attracted interest from a growing minority of economists and political thinkers in Britain (Cockett 1995). Monetarist ideas achieved an audience among Conservative and Labour politicians and civil servants. From 1976 they impacted on the policy of the Labour government which, in an attempt to placate the IMF, introduced monetary targets, cuts in state expenditure and attempted to reduce the budget deficit (McIlroy 1995: 188–93). Callaghan's advisers recalled that his administration had adopted, 'in primitive form', ideas which would be taken further by the Conservatives (Donoghue 1987: 96).

Mrs Thatcher studied Hayek (Young 1989: 207). Together with Sir Keith Joseph she established the Centre for Policy Studies and listened to right-wing gurus, notably Sir Alfred Sherman and economists such as Alan Walters (Cockett 1995). The liberation of the Conservative Party from paternalism and social democracy was facilitated by its 'corporatist' experiment in government under Edward Heath between 1970 and 1974 when it failed to discipline the unions, the passionate, if suppressed, attachment of sections of its supporters to anti-collectivism and individualism, as well as its hierarchical structure. Conquering the state took longer (Dorey 2001) and it was only consolidated after the Conservatives' 1983 election victory. The political application of neoliberal ideas was lubricated by the strategic thinking about the confrontations demanded for radical change, and about precisely how to devastate trade unionism, that the Conservatives undertook in opposition (Hoskyns 2000). It was eased by the insulation that Britain's 'first past-the-post-winner-takes-all' electoral system and potential Prime Ministerial domination of Parliament provides. It was bolstered by Thatcher's special relationship with America and Reagan (Morgan 1999: 454). The success of early neoliberalism was gradual, cautious and contingent on circumstances. It entailed pragmatic selection and adaptation of aspects of neoliberal ideology, the cultivation of a crusading mindset and flexibility combined with immense political will. It followed a burgeoning vision of possibility rather than a prepared blueprint.

Transformative change required statecraft to negotiate significant barriers, crucially the unions. From the start its purpose was to undermine trade unionism. For Hayek (1984: 52) British unions constituted 'the biggest obstacle to raising the living standards of the working class . . . The chief cause of the unnecessarily big differences between the best and worst-paid workers'. The unions were 'the prime source of unemployment . . . the main reason for the decline of the British economy. . . . Inflation and the problem of excessive [union] power have become inescapable' (ibid.). Hayek was not a practising politician and elected politicians were only ideologues if ideology enabled power. But there were politicians who were listening to this sort of thing. By the end of the troubled 1970s, Thatcher's lieutenant, Sir Keith Joseph, had come to believe, along with numerous other politicians, that 'solving the union problem is the key to Britain's recovery' (Joseph 1979).

## How neoliberalism broke Britain's trade unions

The Thatcherites were the crack assault troops of insurgent neoliberalism. In the heyday of its offensive, counter-revolutionary phase they rolled back regulation, recaptured wide tracts of the state sector for private capital, reinjected marketization into the remnants of state-owned enterprise and rooted out 'restrictive practices' and dependency culture. Transformation of the labour market was set in train by the removal of the commitment to full employment and the adoption of a primitive monetarism. In the context of world recession, this saw the number of jobless double between 1979 and 1981 and the unemployment count remain at 10 per cent of the labour force until the late 1980s. Tight labour markets lay at the root of union strength and trade unionists' confidence; the return of large-scale unemployment and the insecurity it brought sapped it. Deregulation and the opening of British industry to international competition; the decline in manufacturing and basic industries; the growth of service occupations; the increasing proportion of white-collar to manual jobs and the increase of atypical employment; the shrinking of the public sector; the shakeup redundancies engendered; and the decline of the size of the enterprise; in the context of a hostile state they all militated against trade unionism (McIlroy 1995: 71–3, 85–8). Privatization and contracting out jobs to private enterprise encouraged flexible labour markets. It restored service provision to competition and employees to market discipline, work intensification and downward pressure on wages. It weakened unions in public sector bargaining. At the same time privatization eased the state's financial problems, depoliticized workers' struggles and seeded business culture in employment and society (Fine 1999).

The institutions of an evanescent corporatism which had legitimized the unions' political and social functions from the NEDC to the Manpower Services Commission were gradually abolished. Union representation on the remaining tripartite institutions was reduced. Access to government decreased and what there was became ineffectual. The unions' positive influence on state policy after 1979 was negligible to non-existent (McIlroy 1995: 199–208). It is sometimes observed that collective laissez-faire's rejection of collective legal rights and dependence on union muscle rendered it vulnerable (Fredman 2004: 19). But everything, including the collective legal rights that did exist, was vulnerable to this new, calculatingly aggressive state.

Collective laissez-faire was finally extirpated by a series of legislative incursions: between 1980 and 1993 they transformed labour law. There were eight major statutes in that period as well as a mass of ancillary measures. The new Leviathan debilitated individual protections from dismissal to maternity rights in order to generate insecurity and to maximize flexibility. As the European Union's (EU) social dimension, which promised to extend such rights, came on stream, the British state legislated for directives it had opposed in Brussels; but it did so in attenuated form; witness the regulations on working time in 1993 and European Works Councils in 1996. It opted out of the Maastricht Social Chapter (Hall 1994). The reach of collective bargaining was diminished by a raft of initiatives: these ranged from the abolition of the union recognition procedure, the machinery for the extension of recognized terms and conditions to organized workers, the Fair Wages Resolutions and Wages Councils to the curtailment of shop steward rights and the excision of the obligation placed on ACAS to encourage collective bargaining (Brown *et al.* 1997).

The closed shop was progressively outlawed. The immunities which had protected unions since 1906 against liability when undertaking industrial action were branded 'a licence to coerce' and restrictively reformulated. The definition of a trade dispute was rewritten so as to open strikers taking secondary action or participating in disputes which went beyond basic terms and conditions of employment to legal liability. Picketing was limited to the pickets' workplace. The repeal of the *Taff Vale* clause in the 1906 legislation rendered unions liable to damages in such cases. Additionally they forfeited immunity where they failed to conduct secret ballots according to tightly-prescribed scripts before strikes or where they subsequently failed to repudiate industrial action without a secret ballot. Trade unionists who refused to join properly-balloted constitutional action were protected against disciplinary action by their union.

Compulsory secret ballots also applied to unions' internal arrangements. They covered not only elections of senior officials but union decisions to maintain a political fund, which impacted indirectly on relations with the Labour Party and political campaigning in general. To advise and finance action by complainants who wished to enforce these restrictions new state functionaries, a Commissioner for the Rights of Trade Union Members (CROTUM) and a Commissioner for Protection Against Unlawful Industrial Action (CPAUIA), were appointed. The Conservatives' step-by-step approach, developed while they were in opposition, navigated the barriers which had brought the 1971 Industrial Relations Act to grief. Each measure was carefully considered. Innovation was partial, piecemeal, targeted and tested before further problems were announced and further reform was scheduled (Auerbach 1990; McIlroy 1991; Undy *et al.* 1996; McIlroy 1999).

The legislative attack advanced from a project to repair the Keynesian diminution of employer bargaining power, confine trade union action to the enterprise and free up labour markets, towards an audacious neoliberal regulation of unions unparalleled in twentieth-century Britain or comparable economies. It was increasingly, if incompletely, based on Hayek's conceptions of collectivism as inherently pernicious (Wedderburn 1991). The administrations of John Major, Thatcher's successor, were 'relatively quiescent in policy terms' (Davies and Freedland 2007: 7). Nevertheless they continued what was now a far more ambitious project with the 1993 Trade Union Reform and Employment Rights Act. The 1996 Green Paper, *Industrial Action and Trade Unions* (DTI 1996), affirmed that the Conservatives' conception of regulating unions to deregulate the market was distinctive within neoliberal politics. It remained suggestive of the virulence of neoliberalism's repertoire and the crusading determination of it proponents.

Resistance was widespread. It was highlighted in symbolic pitched battles (Hyman 2001: 105–6). The successful victimization of Derek Robinson, the Communist convenor at British Leyland's Longbridge plant, revealed the weaknesses of shop steward organization which had intensified since 1974; it introduced the South African, Michael Edwardes, as the face of international 'macho management'. The defeat of the three-month steel strike of 1980 was far from fated, yet fundamental to progress. As the head of the Downing Street Policy Unit observed: 'If the steel strike had ended in humiliation for the government, it is quite possible that Thatcher would not now be a household name, nor would union reform, privatization or any other radical policies have been adopted' (Hoskyns 2000: 147).

The year-long miners' strike of 1984–5 was crucial: at key junctures it could well have ended in deadlock or even a major reverse for the government. If the 'Volcker Shock' in America, the decision to permit interest rates to rise until inflation was arrested, signalled the determination of the leading capitalist power to restructure the USA on neoliberal lines, victory over the miners set the seal on neoliberalism's breakthrough in Britain (Goodman 1985). Coercive intransigence, mobilization of working-class divisions and lack of solidarity in the unions ensured Conservative success. Rupert Murdoch's victory over the print unions in 1984–5, which followed Eddy Shah's earlier triumph over the NGA, struck a blow against the centuries-long traditions of craft control, affirmed the newfound confidence of that section of capital and encouraged the others. In each case the state directed the struggle or stridently supported management. These disputes were followed by further significant reverses for the seafarers and the dockers (McIlroy 1991: 143–51, 170–9). Cumulative defeats traumatized class consciousness and weakened workers' will to resist. These setbacks transformed the balance of class forces. They proved pivotal to the hegemony of neoliberalism in Britain and beyond.

Thatcher's first term provided the best terrain for resistance. But union leaders were disorientated by the struggles of the late 1970s, the difference and determination of the government, the speed of their exclusion from the corridors of power and the weakness of the Labour Party after the split of 1981. They were, we overgeneralize, bureaucratic, conservative and economistic. They were built for constitutionalism and collaboration, not for confrontation with governments which relished conflict. In the recent past the impetus for active opposition had come from workplace activists: they were confronting a surge in unemployment unprecedented since 1921. It dissipated confidence and brought the intrinsic weaknesses and 'factory consciousness' of shop steward organization to the surface. The conditions which had permitted a successful response to the more limited offensives of the 1970s were history.

Trade unionism aspires to unify but reflects fragmentation. Mobilization of workers' potential power requires convincing and coordination; it necessitates conjuring conviction and cohesion from sectional interests; or alternatively a balance of forces in which strategically-placed groups can generate sufficient power autonomously to bring employers to heel. The new state-constructed battlefield was rigged against both. Union leaders legitimized sectionalism: they exhibited minimal inclination to try to organize serious solidarity action to support either the steelworkers or the miners, the latter themselves racked by internal division; hitherto strategic groups like the printers were undermined by the availability of alternative technology and, in response to the neoliberal state, a new management determination. Union power in the postwar years was state-dependent. Stripped of the power the Keynesian state had endowed them with, confronted with an increasingly hostile context and a coercive anti-union state, the unions were forced into retreat. The TUC general secretary Len Murray signalled submission. He sponsored the 'new realism'. It reflected a scaling-down of expectations and a willingness to return to the down-to-earth trade unionism of the 1950s when unions had worked with Conservative governments. It was repulsed by Mrs Thatcher (McIlroy 1995: 210–12; McIlroy 2007: xxiii–xvi).

Where the state led, employers followed. In 1979 key sections of British capital accepted trade unionism. Disorientated by corporatism but drawing the line at the Bullock proposals, employers had responded positively to the invitation to reconstruct industrial relations at enterprise level issued by Donovan and reinforced by the employment legislation of the late 1970s. This cut with the grain of Conservative thinking. Decentralization of bargaining to relate pay to individual, workplace and company performance was buttressed by the new economic pressures. Industry-wide bargaining was dismantled and employer organizations gave way to enterprise autonomy in regulating employment (Brown and Walsh 1991; Millward *et al.* 2000: 204). Faced with the availability of new legal weapons and a new balance of forces on the one hand, and intensifying competitive pressures on the other, employers, particularly managers in new workplaces or employers confronted with new, harder product markets (Gospel 2005), 'generally acted to contain and reduce the autonomy of stewards and the influence of workplace unionism' (Terry 1995: 221). There was no overnight transformation, no dramatic ideological conversion to neoliberalism. Faced with the elements of a new state-induced framework, managers turned away from collective bargaining and collective laissez-faire in piecemeal fashion. They gradually rejected pluralism and derecognized or simply disregarded unions as membership fell away (Sisson 1993). Reviewing change on the cusp of the new century, the government's Workplace Industrial Relations Survey concluded:

The Conservative government that came to power in 1979 confronted a system of collective employment relations that was dominant . . . That system of collective relations, based on the shared values of the legitimacy of representation by independent trade unions and of joint regulation, crumbled in the intervening eighteen years to such an extent that it no longer represents a dominant model . . . This change is almost wholly in the direction in which public policy was directed. The Conservatives aimed to 'curb the power of the unions' – and overall union influence, on most of the measures available to us, has diminished.

(Millward *et al.* 2000: 234)

The state's role was primary and initiatory. But managers – and workers – responded: 'equally important was that the widespread assumption that voluntary joint regulation was the desirable basis for employment relationships was abandoned by swathes of managers and employees. If this change had not occurred, the crumbling of the institutional structure could not have happened on the scale that it did' (ibid.: 235). By the end of the Conservative years the contours of decline disclosed the extent of the counter-revolutionary transformation, although it should be stressed that the reduced public sector constituted an exception. There, union recognition remained in place, collective bargaining – albeit sometimes diluted via the pay review system by which specialist committees take evidence from both sides and make recommendations to the government – was maintained and union membership remained high (Winchester and Bach 1995; Carter and Fairbrother 1999).

Table 1.3 illustrates the unrelenting fall in overall union membership from 12.9 million in 1980 to 7.8 million in 1997. Density declined from 55.2 per cent in 1980 to 29.9 per cent in 1997. Union presence in the workplace held steady until 1984, despite erosion of membership; but it dropped

*Table 1.3* Aggregate trade union membership and density in the UK 1980–97

| Year | Union Membership (000s) | Union Density (%) |
|------|------------------------|-------------------|
| 1980 | 12,947 | 55.2 |
| 1981 | 12,106 | 52.6 |
| 1982 | 11,593 | 49.7 |
| 1983 | 11,236 | 47.6 |
| 1984 | 10,994 | 46.6 |
| 1985 | 10,821 | 45.0 |
| 1986 | 10,539 | 43.5 |
| 1987 | 10,475 | 43.4 |
| 1988 | 10,376 | 41.2 |
| 1989 | 10,132 | 38.6 |
| 1990 | 9,917 | 37.5 |
| 1991 | 9,512 | 37.0 |
| 1992 | 9,128 | 36.3 |
| 1993 | 8,804 | 34.9 |
| 1994 | 8,254 | 32.9 |
| 1995 | 8,068 | 32.0 |
| 1996 | 7,938 | 31.0 |
| 1997 | 7,801 | 29.9 |

*Source:* Certification Officer, *Annual Reports*; McIlroy 1995

from 73 per cent of workplaces in 1984 to 64 per cent in 1997 and 54 per cent in 1998 (Cully *et al.* 1999: 234). The proportion of workplaces with recognized unions plummeted from over 65 per cent to 53 per cent and then to 42 per cent over the same period. The coverage of collective bargaining fell from 70 per cent of all employees in 1984 to 54 per cent in 1990 and 41 per cent in 1998 (ibid.: 238–9, 241–2). The closed shop existed in only two per cent of workplaces (ibid.: 89). Contraction in collective bargaining contributed to wage inequality which accelerated in the 1980s (Machin 1996) and to increases in the share of income taken by the rich. The top one per cent saw their share of national income double to 10 per cent between 1980 and 1998 (Leys 2001: 46–8).

There was a marked decline in manifestations of industrial conflict. The average number of strikes and working days lost diminished from around 2,300 strikes and 11.6 million days lost in 1975–7; 1,300 strikes and 9.8 million days lost, including the miners' strike, 1980–5; 800 strikes and 3.5 million days lost 1986–90; and fewer than 250 strikes and 656,000 working days lost 1991–6. Blyton and Turnbull (2004: 336–40) distinguish three periods: 'coercive pacification', 1980–5, 'calculative bargaining', 1986–90, and 'economic pacification and legal self-restraint', 1991–6. These phases reflect the impact of state policies, the business cycle, changes in the structure of industry and the labour force, as well as union defeats and declining strength and growing caution, sometimes calculative and tactical.

## Early neoliberalism: limits and legacy

Thatcherism decisively debilitated trade unionism and broke up the established patterns of post-war industrial relations. In this sense, 'roll-back neoliberalism' was a success and much has been made of the engineering of consent in driving and consolidating success. Consent among ruling elites and key sections of politicians, civil servants, employers and managers was indispensable (Harvey 2005: 39–63), although the process seems to have been often gradual and a reaction to state success, certainly in the case of managers (Poole and Mansfield 1993). The assertion that the Conservative triumph of 1979 hinged on narration of union-inspired crisis and compelling tales of ungovernability, focused on the Winter of Discontent of 1978–9 (Hay 1996), is questionable (Hyman 2001; McIlroy 2007: xvi–xviii). The summation of Stuart Hall that by 1979 'the crisis has begun to be lived in *its* (Thatcherism's) terms' (quoted in Howell 2005: 144; and see Hall 1988) is exaggerated both as an estimation of consciousness and as a explanation for change.

Survey evidence contains its own problems: the picture it presents remains inconclusive but worthy of consideration. It is true that in January 1979 record numbers of respondents told opinion pollsters that unions were too powerful. Although they were evenly split on whether unions were 'a good thing' this, too, represented a major change in the public's perception of unions. Yet by August 1979, the indicators of public esteem had moved again, more favourably to unions: they were much the same as they had been in 1977. By August 1981, the proportion of voters who believed unions were too powerful was less than at any time since 1973 and fewer respondents approved of Thatcher's proposals for union reform than had commended Edward Heath's plans a decade earlier. A record third of trade unionists voted Conservative in 1979; but this was only marginally higher than the figure when Labour won in February 1974 and it declined in the 1983 general election (Taylor 1993: 370–3; McIlroy 2007: xviii, xxxiii).

In terms of evidence, rather than inference, the Conservatives won only 44 per cent of the vote in 1979, less than Heath's share in 1970; Labour's share, 37 per cent, was the same as it polled when removing Heath from office in February 1974. In the consolidating electoral victory of 1983, despite the popular Falklands war, the Conservative share of the vote dropped two points and in both 1987 and 1992 it was less than it was in 1979. In each case, the Conservative share was dwarfed by that of Labour, the Liberals and the Social Democrats, each of whom opposed its programme. In the 'winner takes all' system, small changes, such as the allegiance of the C2 category covering a wide range of 'skilled' workers, were decisive. But there was also an anti-Labour majority. One of Thatcherism's major successes was to disorientate its main competitor, while emerging neoliberalism won three elections according to the rules of the game, whatever we may think of them. By the early 1980s, most respondents to surveys carried out by social scientists still agreed that unions were too powerful but there was no great difference from responses to similar surveys in the early 1970s on that count. By 1987 things had changed dramatically: only 36 per cent, and by 1990, when Thatcher exited the political scene, only 30 per cent, felt unions were too powerful, while 42 per cent and 44 per cent in both those years claimed things were about right. By 1990, 70 per cent of respondents believed unions were a good thing compared with 17 per cent who disagreed (Taylor 1993: 370–3; McIlroy 1995: 285–90).

During the high tide of Thatcherism between 1983 and 1987, the *British Social Attitudes* survey recorded what it termed 'a shift to the left' (Jowell *et al.* 1987: 173). In 1984, 72 per cent of those surveyed considered that the gap between high and low incomes was too great; by 1987 this had increased to 77 per cent. In the same year 72 per cent of respondents believed that it was a government responsibility to reduce income differentials while 'readiness to pay increased taxes to provide valued welfare services had grown substantially, particularly between 1983 and 1985, from around a third of the population to nearly half' (ibid.: 3). There was no great enthusiasm for privatization. At the time of the miners' strike, 49 per cent of respondents believed that there should be less state ownership while 44 per cent felt that it should remain the same or be extended (Jowell and Airey 1984: 63). More than 80 per cent agreed that employers should share more of their profits with workers, 66 per cent supported the view that 'ordinary working people do not get their fair share of the nation's wealth' and 59 per cent accepted 'there is one law for the rich and one for the poor' (Jowell *et al.* 1987: 36).

The researchers concluded: 'The Thatcher policy revolution has simply *not* so far been accompanied by an equivalent revolution in public attitudes' (ibid.: 174). Actions speak louder than words. Such surveys are more rigorous than opinion polls but they capture complicated and shifting realities and the complex and fluid relationship of belief and action imperfectly. Overall, there is little compelling evidence, as distinct from *marxisant* rhetoric, for the view that the Conservatives' 'authoritarian populism' significantly influenced workers and elicited consent to neoliberalism (Jessop *et al.* 1988; McIlroy 1995: 285–90, 305–12).

In the unions, in local government, in numerous struggles, resoundingly in the successful campaign against the poll tax, and the cross-class support for the miners in the early 1990s, neoliberalism proved unpopular and was contested. The ability to form successive governments on a minority vote, control Parliament through domination of the cabinet, the disorientation of the Labour Party as it struck out to the left before recoiling towards neoliberalism, rather than providing the political leadership that might have mobilized, extended and deepened the oppositional attitudes outlined above, facilitated Thatcher and Major's control of the state. This not inconsiderable advantage permitted their philosophies of individualism and the market to be combined with moves to a strong state (Gamble 1988). A degree of coercion foreign to the post-war settlement secured acquiescence through sustained attrition and consequent acceptance of facts. Success bred success. Some, like the miners, fought back. Others, in education, particularly in the universities, did not. Defeat bred defeat. Changes in circumstances stimulated changes in consciousness. New structures, new systems, new demands, generational change, redundancy and early retirement changed facts and the way that ideas that motivated workers were articulated in practice and influenced their behaviour in the labour market.

The other side of acquiescence was enhanced material prosperity for enough sections of the population to maintain sufficient electoral success. Real take-home pay grew by 2.4 per cent between 1979 and 1997 compared with 0.7 per cent, 1974–9 and 0.2 per cent, 1972–4. Consumer expenditure increased by 2.7 per cent more than at any time since 1964. It was easy to correlate rising wages with the absence of incomes policy, although on a range of other indicators such as productivity and particularly on employment, the neoliberal record was inferior to that of Keynesianism (Wilkinson 2007: 828–29, 834). The stagnation of the 1970s was overcome at the cost of two recessions: there was no revolution in productivity, price stability or investment (Coates 2000: 91–4). There was success but it had its boundaries. The tax burden was not reduced; in fact it increased. But it shifted from direct to indirect taxation and increased inequality. Public expenditure was curbed, not slashed. Conservative governments spent slightly more as a proportion of national income than the Callaghan administration, although this was influenced by increased unemployment. They were able to cut back on housing and industry; education and health proved stubborn targets. The poll tax was pure neoliberalism: it engendered widespread and successful resistance. There appeared to be limits to how far neoliberalism could go and its ability to build popular consent as it went (Gamble 2006: 29–30).

Some political economists have also questioned the general verdict affirming neoliberalism's economic success. They have argued that by the 1990s global capitalism continued to experience an enduring impasse over profitability (Brenner 1998). Overall, the evidence suggested that restructuring helped to resolve crisis and stimulate an upturn (Panitch and Gindin 2005). But there were prices to be paid by some for what neoliberals called success. Inequalities widened dramatically, particularly between 1979 and 1990. The share of wages in national income declined from almost 70 per cent in the 1960s to 61 per cent in 1996. Among men, the ratio of the top 10 per cent of wage earners to the bottom 10 per cent increased from 2.38 per cent to 3.15 per cent. The share of income going to the top 10 per cent of households rose from 20.4 per cent in 1979 to 26 per cent in 1990. The share of the bottom 10 per cent fell from 4.2 per cent in 1979 to 2.9 per cent in 1990 (Arestis and Sawyer 2005: 206). Even the better-off workers paid for their own wage increases: higher earnings meant more intensive and extensive work (Edwards and Whitston 1991; Green 2000).

Gaining and maintaining active consent, still less commitment, constituted a problem for 'roll-back neoliberalism' in Britain. The fall of Mrs Thatcher in 1990, and the ensuing economic downturn, exemplified the fact that if she had cleared the ground and seeded a new system, she had not reaped the harvest. The achievements of neoliberalism had been hard-bought. They had been attained through disruption, conflict and not a little ruthlessness. Few forgot the two major recessions in the early 1980s and 1990s and the major stock market crash in 1987. The Conservatives had brought neither the promised social harmony nor economic transformation (Wilkinson 2007). Rampant individualism, the 'greed is good' philosophy and social exclusion of sections of the population and institutions like trade unions, provided tenuous grounds for a permanent settlement. John Major's government provided no solution to these difficulties (Seldon 1997). Neoliberalism seemed better at demolition than rebuilding.

Nowhere was this clearer than in employment relations. Unions had been significantly weakened. They had been excluded as potential partners buttressing state policy and as legitimate actors in civil society. Joint regulation had been abraded as a means of securing cooperation in the workplace. Nothing, certainly not any developed system of individual contractualism (Kelly and Kelly 1991; Colling 2003) had fully replaced the old system. There seemed to be a need for something more than macho management if Thatcher's heritage was to endure. One possible substitute seemed to be Human Resource Management (HRM). Starting from the belief that the quality and skills of social capital made a crucial difference in competitive advantage,

HRM stressed nurturing the human resource. A new breed of managers could close the gap between business strategy and people management, banish conflict from the workplace and commit employees to managerial goals and entrepreneurial culture. HRM prioritized training, flexibility, job insecurity combined with employment security and new forms of worker participation (Storey 1995).

The development of HRM was often linked to the 'Americanization' or 'Japanization' of British employment and the 'new economy' and the 'new industrial relations' driven by changes in markets and the structure of the enterprise, already developing but reinforced by Thatcherism. The 1970s had seen a turn towards internalization of labour markets, decentralization of management and refinement of management controls often in tandem with post-Donovan initiatives in industrial relations. First-phase neoliberalism with its drive to privatization, outsourcing and fragmentation reined this in. Conservative rule witnessed increased decentralization of management and casualization of labour. But models of flexible specialization, the flexible firm, with a core of secure strategic employees and a periphery of relatively unskilled workers, the learning company and so forth extrapolated from minority tendencies.

There was increasing internationalization and deindustrialization. But investment in people, autonomy for workers and the high-tech, high-knowledge, high-training enterprise remained relatively rare. Variations in company structure, management practice and the organization of work remained resilient. The low-wage, intensive labour route to productivity endured. Changes in the labour force, the growth of services and decline of manufacturing were real but restricted. Extensive publicity was accorded to new techniques such as 'just in time', 'total quality management' and 'continuous improvement'. Their reach and success was limited. Moreover, they were typically related to intensification of work and the exploitation rather than the development of the human resource (Elger 1990; Pollert 1991; Nolan and Walsh 1995).

The idea that pioneering neoliberalism had moved decisively to a new regime in employment characterized by strategic management, high-tech, high-skill, high-productivity, high-security networks of firms and a transformed flexible workforce is exaggerated (Edwards 2003: 514). By the early 1990s there was little evidence that HRM was replacing joint regulation outside a minority of situations, as distinct from constituting a new language which often obscured rather than informed management practice. Reality had more to do with the re-emergence of unilateral regulation and the reassertion of the management prerogative to cut costs and intensify the labour process, ill-disguised by labels such as 'strategic choice', 'lean production' and 'putting people at the top of the agenda' (Keenoy and Anthony 1992).

Beyond foreign-owned companies and greenfield sites there seemed to be few examples of textbook HRM (Sisson 1993). Outside the declining public sector, joint regulation was typically giving way to management prerogative and 'Bleak House' (Sisson and Marginson 1995) or 'Black Hole' (Guest 1995) industrial relations. Over growing tracts of employment there was neither nurturing nor regulating and only vestigial trade unionism. The state had deregulated employment. It had no compelling vision to replace collective laissez-faire and provided only weak support for HRM through supply-side measures such as training, which achieved minimal success (Davies and Freedland 1993: 599–615).

## Constructing constructive neoliberalism

Perry Anderson (2000: 11) stresses that conquering parties of the centre-left is indispensable to securing the long-term domination of neoliberalism. Governing in social democratic guise, neoliberalism fosters a new consensus. It demonstrates the survival in defeat of the ideas and endeavours of its initial protagonists. It provides the electorate with neoliberal competition and, as the market demands, a choice between parties purveying variants of neoliberalism. This hamstrings opposition and demoralizes the left by confirming that there is no alternative. Neoliberal governments with a social-democratic carapace may soften the strident political style of first-generation neoliberals, manage their failures, ameliorate the social dislocation engendered by greater inequality, divisions and social exclusion and exhibited in unemployment, crime and racism (see Walker and Walker 1997) in order to secure a greater degree of social order and popular consent. Building on the ground-clearing of the trailblazers they can complement and consolidate pioneering achievements employing a new 'hard-edged compassion', new initiatives which restore the state's legitimacy and its claims to balance different interests and new regulatory reform which lubricates the market (Peck and Tickell 2002: 384–5). As Burt Lancaster or Giuseppe di Lampedusa observed in *The Leopard*, if one is to defend a regime against the challenges of time, 'things must change so that they may remain the same'.

The core of neoliberalism, which in Britain and America had solved the crisis of the 1970s and produced economic renewal, endures. Succeeding the Conservatives, New Labour substantially endorsed and practised their attitude to the global market, fiscal policy, inflation, liberalization, deregulation, privatization, commodification and regressive taxation. It criticized their incompetence, intransigence, exclusion and corruption. New Labour combined acceptance of Thatcherite restructuring with 'subsidiary concessions and softer rhetoric. The effect of this combination ... is to suppress the conflictual potential of the pioneering regimes of the radical right' (Anderson 2000: 11). Neoliberalisms are contingent on local context and history: they are inevitably hybrid in relation to their distinctive evolution within Republican, Democratic, Conservative, Communist or Labour Parties. The shift in Britain from Thatcher and Major to Blair and Brown has been characterized as 'a social democratic variant of neoliberalism' (Hall 2003: 14).

This implies adjustments to retain solidarity from Labour's traditional base, including the unions, and some attention to the party's traditional concern with social cohesion and social inclusion including the redemption of excluded institutions, such as the unions and sections of the welfare state which had learned lessons and could prove useful in building a new consensus.

Concessions have been made, although in some cases they have diminished. From the start they were significantly prompted by settling accounts with the past and anxieties about the competitivity of British capital. In similar fashion, New Labour's conceptions of social inclusion have centred on the labour market, on encouraging flexibility, engendering employability, reducing the burden of welfare and taxation and extending entrepreneurial culture, rather than on engineering equality. New Labour programmes remain distinctive in comparison to the policies of previous social democratic governments in Britain. They are cut from the same neoliberal cloth woven by the Conservatives. There are discontinuities as well as continuities, but they are generally subordinate. New Labour neoliberalism is different – it is no less neoliberal.

Like its progenitor it has its limitations and some theorists confuse rhetoric with reality and aspiration with achievement. Boltanski and Chiapello (2007) accept much of the discourse of HRM as good coin. Taking it at face value they conflate the prescriptions of the business school and the language of managers with the quotidian realities of the workplace, asserting that the ethos and techniques of HRM have contributed to the sophisticated softer side of the neoliberal transformation of capitalism. Bureaucratic, autocratic management has given way to decentralized, people-friendly approaches. Autonomy and creativity have been appropriated by capital and reassembled to justify flexibility, multi-tasking, team-working and customer care. The evidence discussed earlier, as well as more recent estimations (Legge 2005), would not seem to support their views in terms of either the adoption of HRM or its power to facilitate neoliberalism.

Harvey (2005: 168–70) also appears to believe that neoliberalism does what it says and gets what it wants. He mistakes the promise of flexible labour markets and casualization – citing Thatcher's abolition of the relatively unique security of tenure in universities – for delivery. Temporary employment accounted for 7 per cent of all jobs at the turn of the century and while 25 per cent of jobs were part-time, most were secure (Nolan and Slater 2003: 61–6). As Edwards (2003: 514) concludes, although HRM has not become hegemonic and the turn to training and development is scarcely path-breaking, although the extensive emergence of the high-involvement workplace and qualitative changes in flexibility and productivity have not occurred, 'This is not to argue that nothing has changed'. But we should not confuse New Labour's ambition and ideology with what is actually happening in the workplace. Change is piecemeal and circumscribed, not systemic.

As the New Labour mutation emerged from its social democratic chrysalis and glided apparently effortlessly towards power as a more sophisticated instrument of neoliberalism than the Conservative Party, an astute political scientist remarked: 'its primary aims had, by 1997, become the control of inflation and the promotion of macro-economic stability. The Keynesian consensus of the post-war period would appear to have been replaced by the neoliberal consensus of the post-Thatcher period' (Hay 1999: 127). Sequential if uneven and contested adaptation to Thatcherism commenced after the devastating general election defeat of 1983. Labour increasingly disdained political leadership and education and rejected responsibility to its traditional working-class base. It sought to explore what it conceived as the electoral market through private polls and focus groups to discover what voters, particularly uncommitted voters and wavering Conservatives, wanted. Rather than trying to develop their views, the party sought to adapt policy to their preferences and sell the party as a profitable product (Gould 1998). Gradually, cumulatively, 'the fused objective of winning an electoral majority and governing efficiently led party leaders to make a political choice to adopt neoliberal policies as against alternatives and seek to reposition the party's representational role to elicit support from capital and former Conservative voters' (McIlroy 1998: 539).

Conditioned by further electoral defeat and the new economic and political terrain, policy convergence burgeoned after 1987. The Policy Review of the late 1980s conducted under the leadership of Neil Kinnock was a major step. It distanced the party from the unions; confirmed the move to individual rights for employees rather than trade unionists; strengthened New Labour's developing conception of unions as allies of employers in industry; and acknowledged there would be no return to collective laissez-faire or restoration of the statutory immunities. In Labour's ruling circles unions were increasingly perceived as obstacles to electoral success and impediments to a future Labour government (McIlroy 1998: 542). It was the 1992 rather than the 1997 election manifesto that first announced 'there will be no return to the trade union legislation of the 1970s. Ballots before strikes and for union elections will stay. There will be no mass or flying pickets' (Labour Party 1992: 13). New Labour was not simply the work of the late 1990s. Neil Kinnock's endeavours require greater recognition. More muted change proceeded under Kinnock's successor, John Smith. It accelerated and became more explicit and openly celebrated after Tony Blair's accession to the leadership in 1994 (Shaw 1994; Heffernan 2001).

Yet the potential for a more left-wing approach endured. By the mid-1990s, unions stood high in public esteem although, of course, they were different organizations and had lost influence and members, in comparison with the 1960s and 1970s. By 1992, only 21 per cent of workers thought unions were too powerful compared with 75 per cent who felt that they were not powerful enough or opined that things were just right. More than 60 per cent claimed unions were 'a good thing' while 26 per cent disagreed. There was no dramatic shift by the end of the decade (Taylor 1993: 370–3; Bryson 2007: 193). In 1998–9, 81 per cent of respondents to the *British Social Attitudes* surveys believed the gap between high and low incomes was too large and only 4 per cent thought it was about right. Almost 60 per cent thought that inequality persisted 'because it benefitted the rich and powerful' and only 17 per cent endorsed the view that 'large differences in incomes are necessary for Britain's prosperity'. It was observed:

> One of the recurring findings of the British Social Attitudes survey since the late 1980s has been the clear majority in favour of *increased* public spending on health, education and social benefits even if this means higher taxes. A correspondingly tiny proportion of the population opts for lower taxes and lower spending on these items . . . Attitudes now are much the same as they have been throughout the 1990s.
>
> (Hills and Lelkes 1999: 3)

Here surely lay the potential, if developed, if amplified by a party with Labour's traditions, for a challenge to Thatcherism which reflected and politically orchestrated these beliefs. Instead the Labour leadership chose to emulate the Conservatives. In doing so it removed an important obstacle to the domination of neoliberalism.

In one sense the times were propitious. Historians have seen in John Major's administrations from 1990 to 1997 'a long and unrelenting phase of crisis and decay' (Morgan 1999: 513). 'Black Wednesday', 1992, and Britain's withdrawal from the European Exchange Rate Mechanism followed the worst economic downturn since the last Conservative recession a decade earlier. Major's government was immersed in infighting over the EU and immured in sleaze. There was growing disillusion with what had followed the first two Thatcher governments and anxieties about the price paid for her achievements. Voters were looking for something new (Seldon 1997).

## The making of New Labour

Blair's successful initiatives to rebrand the party and remove Clause IV of its constitution were of immense ideological and symbolic significance in striking out towards neoliberalism. The change in nomenclature signalled that Labour was making a decisive break with a hundred years of history. The replacement of Clause IV – 'to secure for the producers by hand and brain the full fruits of their industry' – with a statement referring to the centrality of 'the enterprise of the market and the rigours of competition' spoke for itself. It coded the future. It left, or it should have left, the eternally optimistic organizations of producers in little doubt where they stood.

Blair's charismatic leadership and popularity was a significant factor in transformation (Ingle 2000: 132). Untrammelled by roots in the labour movement, identification with trade unionism or organic connections with democratic socialism or social democracy, he was governed by the drive to gain and keep power. His fundamental attitude to trade unions and their leaders was measured by his estimation of the extent to which they were an asset or a liability electorally, and he took the negative view. He made it crystal clear:

> These people [union leaders] are criminally stupid. They simply do not care if we win or lose ... They complain that we want to distance ourselves and then give us all the evidence why we should distance ourselves ... I'm finished with these people. Absolutely finished with them.
>
> (Campbell and Stott 2007: 56, 71–2)

He accepted that the writ of the markets constrained radical change: the Thatcher counter-revolution was essentially beneficial; the landscapes of power constructed by the Conservatives, and their beneficiaries, were untouchable. What was at issue was not the substance of neoliberalism, although there were differences over the role of the state and trade unions in relation to labour markets. What was at issue was technical competence, the Conservatives' confrontational, negative, unimaginative methods, crude political style and declining support. The issue in contention was: which party was best fitted to develop and consolidate neoliberalism, make it work and generate popular enthusiasm for it? Placing himself and an elite of supporters and professional advisers (Webb and Fisher 2003) who dealt in spin and marketed politicians as images, above party and above class, Blair continued to remould Labour and erode its institutional links with the working class. The reduction of the union vote at party conference to an overall 50 per cent was finalized in 1996 while the practice of unions sponsoring MPs was terminated. In early 1997 the national executive accepted proposals downgrading the role of conference and the executive in formulating policy in favour of new largely consultative policy forums which strengthened the role of the leadership in policy formation and made the party a more fitting receptacle for neoliberal politics (Russell 2005).

Blair was determined that the unions would not enjoy a special relationship with New Labour governments. His predilections, typified by his courtship of global media magnate Rupert Murdoch, were pro-business. This was not a matter of insincere manoeuvres in the interests of electability. His conviction that New Labour needed to gain and maintain support from capital conditioned his philosophy (Riddell 2005: 29–30). In consequence capital must not be burdened with undue regulation or onerous taxation: 'One of the requirements of our tax structure is to attract enterprise into the UK from overseas' (Blair 1996: 90). An unprecedented Business Manifesto provided employers with detailed reassurance: EU directives that threatened competitivity would be opposed. Employers would have direct access to ministers and action on long-standing commitments to the unions would be subject to discussion with the CBI (Edmonds 2006: 101–5). Imbrication between New Labour and business was reinforced by the increasing flow of funds to the party from entrepreneurs who knew instinctively there was no such thing as a free lunch (Osler 2002).

It was underpinned by Blair's belief that globalization constituted an overarching circumscription on what the state could do: 'The determining context of economic policy is the new global market. That imposes huge limitations of a practical nature – quite apart from reasons of principle – on macroeconomic policy' (Blair quoted in *Financial Times*, 22 May 1995). In consequence 'the control of inflation through a tough macroeconomic policy is even more important than the Tories have said' (Blair quoted in *Financial Times*, 23 May 1995). Therefore: 'the days of reflex tax and spend politics are over. . . . People do not want nor will they get a Labour government that will add to the burden of taxes' (Blair quoted in Panitch and Leys 1997: 251).

Unlike Blair, Gordon Brown, the other main architect of New Labour, had experienced a Damascene conversion from critic of Thatcherism (Brown 1989) to neoliberal proselytizer. He announced that 'business is in my blood', claiming that his mother had been a company director, something she subsequently denied (Peston 2005: 124–5). Like Blair, he accepted the inevitability of continuity with the Conservatives: 'In a global and integrated capital market there is little that any national government can achieve by manipulating interest or exchange rates . . . Stability and credibility are all' (Brown quoted, ibid.). For the Shadow Chancellor, globalization called all the shots: 'what were national decisions are now international and global and that is irreversible . . . the war on inflation is a Labour war. Brown's law is that the government will only borrow to invest, public debt will remain stable and the cost effectiveness of public spending must be proved . . . nobody should doubt my own resolve for stability and financial prudence' (Stevenson 2006: 21, 68).

New Labour pledges in the 1997 general election justified the verdict that they had broken from their party's past to embrace the Conservative past: 'the trajectory of change for Labour has been overwhelmingly in one direction, that of the dilution, weakening and selective abandonment of prior commitments' (Hay 1999: 140). New Labour had accepted the substance of the Conservatives' monetary and fiscal policy, the priority of state action on inflation, rather than unemployment, and the spending limits and restrictions on public sector pay set by Major's government for 1997–9. Its manifesto encapsulated neoliberal philosophy when it stated: 'to encourage work and effort we are pledged not to raise the basic and top rates of income tax throughout the next Parliament' (Labour Party 1997: 11).

This approach foreclosed on direct and fundamental redress of inequality. Labour had already resiled on promises to restore privatized industries to the public sector and watered down its 1995 assurance of renationalization of the railways. It had accepted the rationale, if not the detail, of Conservative commodification of the NHS. It had retreated on promises to restore the link between pensions and earnings. It differed from the Conservatives in some of the means to be used to achieve consensual objectives. Its emphasis on education and training, lifelong learning and 'the knowledge economy' and supply-side instruments to stimulate growth was distinctive. So were the specifics and the social justice setting of proposals to introduce 'new deal' and 'welfare to work' schemes. As with its employment of globalization as a disciplinary agent, excluding certain policies, requiring others, New Labour spoke a more persuasive, mellifluous, political language than the Conservatives (Riddell 2005: 24–5; Heffernan 2001). Underneath the packaging it agreed with them on the centrality of markets. The fundamental thrust of its policies, influenced by the soft-soap neoliberalism of Bill Clinton in the USA, was towards encouraging market efficiency first and social justice second (Marquand 1998: 19).

The 1997 manifesto repeated the now familiar message on change, on trade unions and on Labour's unacceptable past: 'there will be no return to flying pickets, secondary action, strikes with no ballots or the trade union laws of the 1970s . . . we will leave intact the main changes of the 1980s legislation' (Labour Party 1997: 3, 15). Key pledges promised a new procedure for union recognition and a national minimum wage. Their detail remained unsettled. The future Prime Minister summarized the position: 'the changes we propose would leave British law the most restrictive on trade unions in the Western world' (quoted in Panitch and Leys 1997: 254). New Labour's commitments to the unions distinguished it from the Conservatives who promised a further instalment of legislative restriction of trade unionism (DTI 1996). Nonetheless there was a union recognition procedure and a national minimum wage in the USA. The unions' new rights in Britain would be subject to discussion with employer organizations, endow debilitated unions and operate in a neoliberal environment. Just as the Conservatives in 1951 had accepted the key aspects of the post-war settlement, so, almost half a century on, New Labour had accepted the substance, if not the jot and tittle, of the neoliberal counter-revolution.

There had been largely rhetorical toying with an alternative. This took as exemplar the robust regulatory and institutional frameworks of more coordinated economies such as Germany as distinct from the liberal market model of the USA. Michael Albert's *Capitalism Against Capitalism* (1993) and particularly Will Hutton's *The State We're In* (1995) exercised a brief influence in New Labour circles with their vision of stakeholder capitalism. They accepted the need for governments to support capital and innovation. But they pointed out that countries such as Germany and Japan had successfully combined efficiency with greater equality. They highlighted the role that might be played by financial institutions, in generating long-term investment and long-term strategy in industry; by the state, in stimulating re-skilling and developing human capital; and by strong unions in fostering trust, cooperation and optimal utilization of human resources. This approach found resonance in Blair's Singapore speech in January 1996.

But progress entailed conflict with 'entrenched capitalist interests in the shape of the City and its allies in the Treasury and company boardrooms'

(Norris 1999: 30). Cutting with the grain of globalization, going with and stimulating the pace of change, they were not prepared to sacrifice short-termism and challenge the freedom rapid movement of capital in and out of markets gave financiers and entrepreneurs. Blair believed that, if crossed, the latter would quickly bring a New Labour administration to grief. Moreover, 'stakeholding was scuppered by suggestions that formally including stake-holders such as workers and consumers on company boards might interfere with managements' right to manage and directors' to direct, thus raising fears among the new business supporters of New Labour' (Gould 1998: 255; Riddell 2005: 35). As an item New Labour and stakeholding 'lasted little longer than a holiday romance' (ibid.). Dumping stakeholding was key to the making of New Labour.

As Leys (2001: 30–1, 44–6) suggests, the political struggle required to move towards creating coordination from uncoordinated systems of capital and labour in Britain in the face of hostile global trends would have been far-reaching (for an optimistic view see Garrett 1998). Harvey (2005: 62–3) is right to emphasize that events since 1979 seriously restricted New Labour's room for manoeuvre. His assertion that Blair had no alternative but to continue along the neoliberal path against his better instincts is less convincing. Blair enthusiastically, rather than reluctantly, embraced capitalist constraint and neoliberalism. Transformation was not on the agenda. More substantial change was (Hay 1999: 182–208). It is unlikely that renationalization of the railways, a halt to privatization, a superior recognition procedure, a better minimum wage, legislative support for basic structures for partnership in the workplace, the enactment of rights which subsisted in many of Britain's efficient competitors, or more significant constitutional reform would have bred disaster. The point is that by 1997 Blair's *preference* was for continuing, creatively and constructively, along the path of neoliberalism. He welcomed globalization and what he saw as the impossibilities and possibilities which flowed from it. He was persuaded that the American way and Clinton's and the New Democrats' accommodation to Reagan's reforms was the right way. Above all he was convinced that what was good for big business was good for Britain (Thompson 2006: 267–75).

Avoiding burdens on business and facilitating labour market flexibility took precedence over rights for workers, whether proposed in Westminster or in Brussels. New Labour's policy on the EU and social legislation had by 1997 moved decisively in a Thatcherite direction (Fella 2002). Trade unionists who advocated the European model might, with benefit, have noted New Labour's objective of 'a new Europe – more dynamic, competitive and open and learning a great deal from the entrepreneurial and flexible labour market of the American economy' (Stevenson 2006: 27). Not only had the die been cast in favour of 'Anglo-American' capitalism, New Labour wanted to turn 'Rhine' capitalism into 'Anglo-American' capitalism.

That represented a further and, as time would show, fundamental reverse for union leaders. They increasingly favoured the former and depicted the EU social dimension as a vehicle for its realization. A major actor, who carried the mainstream of union leaders with him, was John Monks, who succeeded Norman Willis as general secretary of the TUC in 1993. Monks was more fertile in ideas than any of his predecessors since George Woodcock in the 1960s. He was a proponent of the European model and an exponent of business unionism which emphasized the common interests of capital and labour at the expense of their structural conflicts. He believed that union activists could play a central part in the extension of HRM, untapping the knowledge and refashioning the skills of the workforce and channelling them constructively to the competitive advantage of the firm. His essential argument was that industrial relations and trade unions were no longer adversarial. In return for acceptance by management, unions could commit their members to the production of world-class commodities to meet the challenge of global competitivity. 'The unions', the TUC claimed, 'have a strategy for the management of change to meet the competitive conditions of the late 1990s. The focus must be on the production of competitive high quality products and services'. Unionized workplaces and HRM, Congress House insisted, produced more investment and more investment in human capital than their non-union comparators (Taylor 1994: 111–14).

The coinage to cover this enthusiasm for HRM was 'partnership'. A number of union leaders – John Edmonds of the GMB, Garfield Davies of USDAW and Bill Jordan of the AEEU – supported the Involvement and Partnership Association which pushed agreements and institutions centred on acceptance of unions, consultation, employee involvement, 'sharing in the success of the enterprise' and working towards the 'common goals of management and trade unions'. Edmonds and Alan Tuffin of the UCW produced a manifesto, *A New Agenda* in this vein (Edmonds and Tuffin 1992). There was measured support for HRM which stressed its potential for delivering job enrichment, better training, enhanced employee involvement and the exchange of flexibility for job security. But union leaders tended to downplay its disadvantages, work intensification, redundancy and the marginalization of workplace union organization (TUC 1994). As Monks explained:

> We do not fear the agenda of the human resource development manager. We prefer a people-orientated system . . . I believe that unions can have their own distinctive agenda with the human resource development company . . . in the areas of ensuring that training is linkable to external qualifications or ensuring that women at work receive special attention, reducing working time, of pointing up single status issues.
>
> (Monks 1993: 233)

This partial picture of HRM was complemented by an uncritical stance on global competition and its protagonists: 'we are encouraging a new language for activists with new terms – partnership; quality products and quality services; becoming competitive and staying there' (ibid.). There were strong New

Labour intonations in Monks' desire to turn union representatives into human resource managers and mobilize union members for a competitivity crusade: 'security and partnership underpin the priorities of the best British employers and I am proud of the pathfinding and progressive agreements which many unions have made to ensure that world class competition is mounted from this country' (TUC 1993: 365). The turn to the enterprise was part of a movement away from a never quite suppressed nostalgia for corporatist relations with the state which had centred on bargains over incomes policy:

> The ability of a relatively small number of national union officials to deliver pay restraint has been changed because the structure of bargaining has been changed. Leaving aside the public sector, the labour market is much more decentralised. So I don't think the old tradeoffs are relevant.
>
> (Monks 1995: 4)

But notions of workplace cooperation were only part of the wider conception of social partnership which informed the TUC's turn to Europe in the 1990s. The aspiration was formal collaboration with government as well as with employers. Models were the EU social dialogue based on the Protocol on Social Policy and the initiatives in creating framework agreements between the ETUC and the employer organizations, UNICE and CEEP, as well as the arrangements sponsored by the state for cooperation in Germany, Scandinavia and Spain. The TUC hoped social partnership would be generalized and reach Britain through EU legislation and a Labour government. The Conservatives' opt-out from the Social Chapter of the 1991 Maastricht Treaty blocked the extension of further progressive legislation to Britain. In this as in all other spheres, TUC willingness to work with the Conservatives failed to disguise its yearning for a Labour government and wishful thinking as to its possible trajectory. Monks reflected (1992: 217) that 'only in Britain is there this apparently ideological hostility to the very concept of social partnership'. But as time would demonstrate he underestimated New Labour's lack of enthusiasm not only for social partnership but for any partnership in the workplace which required meaningful state support. Monks made little secret of his preference for Rhine capitalism and the role trade unions played in it, even as New Labour's navigators steered away from stakeholding and social partnership. Unions, he believed, had been rendered fit for partnership purposes. They had been transformed into agencies for facilitating employer goals: 'The days when unions provided an adversarial opposition are past in industry' (Monks 1997).

Another strand in the New Unionism which Monks announced as part of the relaunch of the TUC as a campaigning organization in 1994 was the stress on unions as providers of services. Heery (1996: 187) described this as 'a managerial servicing relationship in which unions seek to research members' needs and design and promote attractive servicing packages in response. The relationship rests on the assumption that members are largely instrumental in their orientation to unions and behave as reactive customers'. Some unions and more commentators enthusiastically propagated the view championed by MSF leader Roger Lyons that members should be cast as individual consumers and that the AA constituted a model for union organization (Bassett and Cave 1993). There was renewed interest in organizing campaigns in the aftermath of the failure of TUC-coordinated experiments from the 1980s (Mason and Bain 1991). By 1996, interest in a more strategic planned approach developed as the TUC, influenced by the AFL-CIO in America, sought to implant a new campaigning organizing culture in British unions (TUC 1996: 61; Heery 1998). Despite the transatlantic connections this did not indicate any disillusionment with the European model. Organizing was necessary, particularly in the case of 'the bad employer', to build the forces which could deliver social partnership (TUC 1997: 63).

This encountered minimal opposition: there was little attempt to recharge the tradition of 'economistic militancy' or revive radical economic strategies. Years of intensifying debilitation had taken a cumulative toll on the union left. Unison, the TGWU, GMB, AEEU, MSF and USDAW went along with 'modernization', with varying degrees of enthusiasm. What opposition there was came from the smaller unions: the FBU, RMT, the bakers and the miners. The demand for 'the repeal of all the anti-union laws' remained a battleground at TUC congresses throughout the 1990s; but its supporters were increasingly ineffectual. Weakness was interwoven with expediency: if moderation, modernization and collaboration were what it took to get rid of the Conservatives, so be it. The case for a more militant stance on the part of trade unionists was eloquently argued (Kelly 1996). The conjuncture meant that the forces to develop it were not available (McIlroy 2000).

Unfortunately, modernization also encountered slight success. New approaches failed to break the spiral of decline. Union membership and density continued its apparently inexorable trend downwards (see table 1.3). The attempts by union leaders to arrange marriages between employers and their members typically met with hostility or indifference. This was not simply a function of their incongruity – 'Trade unions as agencies for the enhancement of shareholder value?' (Hyman 2001: 111). Large majorities of managers recorded their preference for consulting directly with employees rather than negotiating collectively with unions; far fewer than in the past recommended membership of unions to their workforce (Howell 2005: 140–1). The emphasis of the CBI, let alone the Institute of Directors, was now very firmly on individualism not collectivism (Gilbert 1993). As union leaders had moved from challenging management, towards partnership with it, management had moved away from trade unionism per se, let alone partnership with it. The costs for employers of disregarding, or less frequently derecognizing unions, were minimal in comparison with the past. On the same basis, less representative unions had less to offer companies in terms of 'partnership'.

HRM remained a minority phenomenon which sometimes acted to restrict union influence (Storey 1995: 246–50). Partnership agreements were often unfavourable to trade unionism and involved concessions and no-strike clauses in exchange for union, rarely employee, security. A fair judgement was that 'proponents of social partnership have seriously underestimated employer hostility to collective bargaining' (Kelly 1996: 90). The flirtation with servicing members proved short-lived as the experience of unions coincided with the findings of academic surveys. The TGWU, for example, concluded that workers joined and remained in unions not primarily, or even significantly, for financial or legal services or training opportunities. They joined unions for protection against the employer. Emphasis on the former in recruitment strategies could detract from the attractions of the latter (Taylor 1994: 144; Waddington and Whitston 1995: 191). A further implication was rarely drawn: workers wanted unions to challenge their employers, not assist their employers to manage them.

Problems in recruiting, organizing and establishing strong relationships with employers could be ameliorated by an effective recognition procedure. A national minimum wage could act as a focus for organizing. Politics and the question of government had never been more important (Towers 1997: 250–5). New Labour's neoliberalism was preferable to the Conservative variety. It could, through reversal of the Maastricht opt-out, begin to remove blockages to progress through the EU. The alternative, as then TUC President Nigel De Gruchy pointed out, was '[Conservative Minister] Ian Lang's Green Paper on further suffocating reform of trade unions' (TUC 1997: 62).

From the time of the Labour Party Policy Review, whatever the divisions and squabbles, TUC officials 'were often privately supportive of the Parliamentary leadership, playing a brokerage role between the political and industrial leaderships in an effort to produce change on sensitive issues' (Minkin 1991: 457). It was not change that they welcomed. But they swallowed it and 'by 1992 the unions had clearly accepted a new subordinate role. They had given over to the party leadership the cherished private domain of employment legislation' (McIlroy 1995: 301–2). Union leaders accepted that the future did not lie in the resurrection of either corporatism or collective laissez-faire but in partnership and a new legal framework with limited individual rights and severely circumscribed collective rights (Monks 1992: 218). Under the Blair leadership they actively reduced their demands on Labour, disregarding demands for a minimum wage of £4.15 an hour and pushing a figure of £3.60 an hour (TUC 1995). TUC leaders did their best to iron out differences and advise New Labour's ruling circles: 'Dinner with John Monks . . . He reckoned my problems were 1. Mandelson 2. Unions . . . 3. Shadow Cabinet . . . He said if you can keep them in line, you've cracked it' (Campbell and Stott 2007: 24).

As a Labour government drew within reach union leaders actively supported or acquiesced in the transformation of the party which they believed would ensure it. Given their voting power, reform could not have proceeded without their agreement. In the ballot for leader Blair polled 52 per cent of the union vote compared with 28 per cent for John Prescott and 19 per cent for Margaret Beckett, both, in the wider scheme of things, token candidates. On Clause IV, the union share of the vote was split 55 per cent to 45 per cent, with unions such as the AEEU, GMB and USDAW voting for its deletion and Unison leading the opponents. New Labour emerged as the second party of neoliberalism and big business. The unions accepted disempowerment. The decision to reduce the unions' vote at conference was opposed by only three small affiliates (McIlroy 1998: 551–3).

## Conclusion

By 1997 neoliberalism had made successful incursions into the British labour movement. It had captured the Labour Party but not the unions. It would be more correct to state that it had converted the dominant sections of the party leadership. Some of that leadership and probably most activists still held to social democratic or democratic socialist credos. But the overriding dynamic of the party, one which it had only occasionally neglected, and then never for long, was electoralism. The key to the success of Blair and his supporters was the fact that in that context they won the argument about policy. They convinced the majority of party and union activists that after 18 years of Conservative governments and the historic defeat of the labour movement that those governments had accomplished, the only way to turn things round electorally was to adopt much of the Conservatives' political premises. The unions were crucial to Blair's success. Their defeat and ensuing weakness as well the debilitation of the union left and its traditional links with a now-waning party left, removed an important obstacle to programmatic and organizational change. Electoralism and the fact that even in a small way New Labour would make a difference governed the concerns of the mainstream majority of union leaders. Consequently, if reluctantly, they supported the installation of neoliberalism in their party.

In the USA, neoliberalism had moved from its original base in the Republican Party to colonize Bill Clinton's traditionally more progressive and populist Democratic Party. Its supplanting of social democracy in the British Labour Party took things a significant step further. Unlike the Democrats, this was a party based on the working class in which organized labour had carved an extended and entrenched institutional and political role over almost a century. It was a party which only yesterday had been heavily marked by socialist ideas which were to neoliberalism like holy water to the devil. The long creation of the Labour Party from the 1890s to 1918 had represented a major achievement for class politics. It involved a decisive move away from liberalism and accommodation to liberalism, whatever its continuing influence, and a decisive move towards independent political representation and the socialist ideas embodied in its constitution, particularly

Clause IV. It was a landmark in the making of the twentieth-century working class (Hobsbawm 1998: 76–99).

Blair regretted all of this. He lamented the party's involvement with versions of socialism. He questioned the justification for its formation because of the breach with liberalism it entailed. Blair was a neoliberal in a very precise sense. He wanted to repair what he saw as the damage wrought to the politics of liberalism by reclaiming the party for an updated contemporary liberalism. For Blair, the birth of the Labour Party was 'a great mistake . . . that fatal deviation' (Beer 2001: 18). Socialism, democratic socialism, even social democracy, had been 'a blind alley'. With the birth of New Labour, redemption was not only possible, it was at hand. What Lenin had characterized as a contradictory formation, a bourgeois workers' party would become, in the hands of Blair and Brown, a straightforward bourgeois neoliberal party, its affairs complicated only by the institutional role of trade unions.

Where did this leave the unions with their potentially powerful position inside the party and the party's continued dependence on union finance and resources (see McIlroy, chapter 5, this volume)? They had gone along with New Labour although they did not share its neoliberalism. Their attachment to coordinated market models and collectivist politics might resurface once the party was in government. Most of the experience of the 1990s, however, suggested that the problem was containable formally, through a reduction in union representation in the party; or informally, through carefully crafted management to ensure that the union leaders and their block votes continued to serve the purposes of New Labour. With subtle application of statecraft they might be prevailed upon to play a subordinate role similar to that their Lib-Lab ancestors had played in the heyday of Liberalism, contributing financially, articulating union demands, but leaving the creation and execution of policy to the new liberal leaders of New Labour.

## Bibliography

Albert, M. (1993) *Capitalism Against Capitalism*, London: Whurr Books.

Anderson, P. (2000) 'Renewals', *New Left Review*, II:I, 5–24.

Arestis, P. and Sawyer, M. (2005) 'The neoliberal experience of the United Kingdom', in A. Saad-Filho and D. Johnston (eds) *Neoliberalism: A Critical Reader*, London: Pluto Press.

Armstrong, P., Glyn, A. and Harrison, J. (1984) *Capitalism Since World War II: The Making and Breaking of the Long Boom*, London: Fontana.

Artis, M. and Cobham, D. (eds) (1991) *Labour's Economic Policies 1974–1979*, Manchester: Manchester University Press.

Auerbach, S. (1990) *Legislating for Conflict*, Oxford: Clarendon Press.

Bain, G. and Price, R. (1983) 'Union growth: dimensions, determinants and destiny', in G. Bain (ed.) *Industrial Relations in Britain*, Oxford: Blackwell.

Bassett, P. and Cave, A. (1993) *All for One: The Future of the Unions*, London: Fabian Society.

Beer, S. (2001) 'New Labour: old Liberalism', in S. White (ed.) *New Labour: The Progressive Future?* Basingstoke: Palgrave.

Blair, T. (1996) *New Britain: My Vision of a Young Country*, London: Fourth Estate.

Blyton, P. and Turnbull, P. (2004) *The Dynamics of Employee Relations*, 3rd edition, Basingstoke: Palgrave Macmillan.

Boltanski, L. and Chiapello, E. (2007) *The New Spirit of Capitalism*, London: Verso.

Brenner, R. (1998) 'The economics of global turbulence', *New Left Review*, 229: 1–265.

Brown, G. (1989) *Where There is Greed: Margaret Thatcher and the Betrayal of Britain's Future*, London: Mainstream.

Brown, W. and Walsh, J. (1991) 'Pay determination in Britain in the 1980s: the anatomy of decentralisation', *Oxford Review of Economic Policy*, 7:1, 44–59.

Brown, W., Deakin, S. and Ryan, P. (1997) 'The effects of British industrial relations legislation 1979–97', *National Institute Economic Review*, 161:1, 69–83.

Bryson, A. (2007) 'New Labour, new unions?', in A. Park, J. Curtice, K. Thomson, M. Phillips and M. Johnson (eds) *British Social Attitudes: The 23rd Report*, London: Sage.

Callinicos, A. (2001) *Against the Third Way: An Anti-Capitalist Critique*, Cambridge: Polity Press.

Campbell, A., Fishman, N. and McIlroy, J. (eds) (2007) *The Post-War Compromise: British Trade Unions and Industrial Politics 1945–64*, 2nd edition, London: Merlin Press.

Campbell, A and Stott, R. (2007) *The Blair Years: Extracts from the Alistair Campbell Diaries*, London: Hutchinson.

Carter, B. and Fairbrother, P. (1999) 'The transformation of British public sector industrial relations: from model employer to marketized relations', *Historical Studies in Industrial Relations*, 7, 119–46.

Castells, M. (2000) *The Rise of the Network Society*, Oxford: Blackwell.

Certification Officer (1997–2007), *Reports of the Certification Officer*. London: Certification Office.

Chesnais, F. (1997) *La Mondialisation du Capital*, Paris: Syros.

Chesnais, F. and Sauviat, C. (2003) 'The financing of innovation-related investment in the contemporary global finance-dominated accumulation regime', in J.E. Cassiolato, H.M.M. Lastres and M.L. Maciel (eds) *Systems of Innovation and Development: Evidence from Brazil*, Cheltenham: Edward Elgar.

Coates, D. (1980) *Labour in Power? A Study of the Labour Government 1974–1979*, London: Longman.

—— (2000) *Models of Capitalism: Growth and Stagnation in the Modern Era*, Cambridge: Polity Press.

Colás, A. (2005) 'Neoliberalism, globalization and international relations', in A. Saad-Filho and D. Johnston (eds) *Neoliberalism: A Critical Reader*, London: Pluto Press.

Cockett, D. (1995) *Thinking the Unthinkable: Think-Tanks and the Economic Counter-Revolution 1931–1983*, London: Fontana.

Colling, T. (2003) 'Managing without unions: the sources and limitations of individualism', in P. Edwards (ed.) *Industrial Relations: Theory and Practice*, 2nd edition, Oxford: Blackwell.

Crompton, R. (2006) *Employment and the Family: The Reconfiguration of Work and Family Life in Contemporary Societies*, Cambridge: Cambridge University Press.

Cronin, J. (1984) *Labour and Society in Britain, 1918–1979*, London: Batsford.

Crouch, C. (1977) *Class Conflict and the Industrial Relations Crisis*, London: Heinemann.

—— (1993) *Industrial Relations and European State Traditions*, Oxford: Clarendon Press.

—— (2003) 'The state, economic management and incomes policy', in P. Edwards (ed.) *Industrial Relations: Theory and Practice*, 2nd edition, Oxford: Blackwell.

Crouch, C. and Streeck, W. (eds) (1997) *The Political Economy of Modern Capitalism*, London: Sage.

Cully, M., Woodland, S., O'Reilly, A. and Dix, G. (1999) *Britain at Work As Depicted by the 1998 Workplace Employee Relations Survey*, London: Routledge.

Dasgupta, S. and Kiely, R. (2006) *Globalization and After*, London: Sage.

Davies, P. L. and Freedland, M. (1993) *Labour Legislation and Public Policy: A Contemporary History*, Oxford: Clarendon Press.

Davies, P. and Freedland, M. (2007) *Towards a Flexible Labour Market: Labour Legislation and Regulation since the 1990s*, Oxford: Oxford University Press.

Department of Trade and Industry (DTI) (1996) *Industrial Action and Trade Unions*, London: DTI.

Donoghue, B. (1987) *Prime Minister: The Conduct of Policy under Harold Wilson and James Callaghan*, London, Jonathan Cape.

Dorey, P. (2001) *Wage Politics in Britain: The Rise and Fall of Incomes Policies since 1945*, Portland: Sussex Academic Press.

Duménil, G. and Lévy, D. (2004) *Capital Resurgent: Roots of the Neoliberal Revolution*, Cambridge, MA: Harvard University Press.

—— (2005) 'The neoliberal (counter) revolution' in A. Saad-Fillio and D. Johnston (eds) *Neoliberalism: A Critical Reader*, London: Pluto Press.

Dunn, B. (2004) *Global Restructuring and the Power of Labour*, Basingstoke: Palgrave.

Edmonds, J. (2006) 'Positioning Labour closer to the employers: the importance of the Labour Party's 1997 Business Manifesto', *Historical Studies in Industrial Relations*, 22, 85–107.

Edmonds, J. and Tuffin, A. (1992) *The New Agenda: Bargaining for Prosperity in the 1990s*, London: GMB/UCW.

Edwards, P. (2003) 'Concluding comments', in P. Edwards (ed.) *Industrial Relations: Theory and Practice in Britain*, 2nd edition, Oxford: Blackwell.

Edwards, P. and Whitston, C. (1991) 'Workers are working harder: effort and shop-floor relations in the 1980s', *British Journal of Industrial Relations*, 29:5, 592–601.

Elger, T. (1990) 'Technological innovation and work reorganisation in British manufacturing in the 1980s: continuity, intensification or transformation?', *Work, Employment and Society*, 4:5, 67–102.

Fella, S. (2002) *New Labour and the European Union: Political Strategy, Policy Transition and the Amsterdam Treaty Negotiation*, Aldershot: Ashgate.

Fine, B. (1999) 'Privatization: theory and lessons for the United Kingdom and South Africa', in A. Vlachou (ed.) *Contemporary Economic Theory: Radical Critiques of Neoliberalism*, Basingstoke: Macmillan.

Flanders, A. (1960) *Trade Unions*, 3rd edition, London: Hutchinson.

Flanders, A. and Clegg, H. (eds) (1954) *The System of Industrial Relations in Great Britain*, Oxford: Blackwell.

Fox, A. (1985) *History and Heritage: The Social Origins of the British Industrial Relations System*, London: Allen and Unwin.

Fredman, S. (2004) 'The ideology of new labour law', in C. Barnard, S. Deakin and G. Morris (eds) *The Future of Labour Law*, Oxford: Hart Publishing.

Friedman, M. (1962) *Capitalism and Freedom*, Chicago: University of Chicago Press.

Gamble, A. (1988) *The Free Economy and the Strong State: The Politics of Thatcherism*, Basingstoke: Macmillan.

—— (2006) 'Two faces of neo-liberalism', in R. Robison (ed.) *The Neoliberal Revolution: Forging the Market State*, Basingstoke: Palgrave.

Garrett, G. (1998) *Partisan Politics in the Global Economy*, Cambridge: Cambridge University Press.

George, S. (1999) *The Lugano Report: On Preserving Capitalism in the Twenty-First Century*, London: Pluto Press.

Gilbert, R. (1993) 'Workplace industrial relations 25 years after Donovan: an employer view', *British Journal of Industrial Relations*, 31:2, 235–53.

Glyn, A. (2006) *Capitalism Unleashed: Finance, Globalization and Welfare*, Oxford: Oxford University Press.

Glyn, A. and Harrison, J. (1980) *The British Economic Disaster*, London: Pluto Press.

Glyn, A. and Sutcliffe, B. (1972) *British Capitalism, Workers and the Profits Squeeze*, Harmondsworth: Penguin.

Goodman, G. (1985) *The Miners' Strike*, London: Pluto Press.

Gough, I. (1979) *The Political Economy of the Welfare State*, Basingstoke: Macmillan.

Gospel, H. (2005) 'Markets, firms and unions: a historical-institutionalist perspective on the future of unions in Britain', in S. Fernie and D. Metcalf (eds) *Trade Unions: Resurgence or Demise?* London: Routledge.

Gould, P. (1998) *The Unfinished Revolution: How the Modernisers Saved the Labour Party*, London: Abacus.

Green, F. (2000) 'It's been a hard day's night: the concentration and intensification of work in late twentieth-century Britain', *British Journal of Industrial Relations*, 39:1, 53–80.

Guest, D. (1995) 'Human resource management, trade unions and industrial relations', in J. Storey (ed.), *Human Resource Management: A Critical Text*, London: Routledge.

Hall, M. (1994) 'Industrial relations and the social dimension of European integration before and after Maastricht', in R. Hyman and A. Ferner (eds) *New Frontiers in European Industrial Relations*, Oxford: Blackwell.

Hall, S. (1988) *The Hard Road to Renewal: Thatcherism and the Crisis of the Left*, London: Verso.

—— (2003) 'New Labour's double-shuffle', *Soundings*, 24, 10–24.

Hardt, M. and Negri, A. (2000) *Empire*, Cambridge, Mass: Harvard University Press.

Harvey, D. (2005) *A Brief History of Neoliberalism*, Oxford: Oxford University Press.

Hay, C. (1996) 'Narrating crisis: the discursive construction of the "winter of discontent"', *Sociology*, 30: 2, 253–77.

—— (1999) *The Political Economy of New Labour: Labouring Under False Pretences*, Manchester: Manchester University Press.

Hayek, F. (1984) *1980s Unemployment and the Unions*, 2nd edition, London: Institute of Economic Affairs.

Heery, E. (1996) 'The new new unionism', in I. Beardwell (ed.) *Contemporary Industrial Relations: A Critical Analysis*, Oxford: Oxford University Press.

—— (1998) 'The relaunch of the Trades Union Congress', *British Journal of Industrial Relations*, 36:3, 339–60.

Heery, E. and Kelly, J. (1994) 'Professional, participative and managerial unionism: interpretation of change in trade unions', *Work, Employment and Society*. 8:1, 1–22.

Heffernan, R. (2001) *New Labour and Thatcherism: Political Change in Britain*. Basingstoke: Palgrave.

Held, D., McGrew, A., Goldblatt, D. and Perraton, J. (1999) *Global Transformations: Politics, Economics and Culture*, Cambridge: Polity Press.

Hills, J. and Lelkes, U. (1999) 'Social security, selective universalism and patchwork redistribution', in R. Jowell, J. Curtice, A. Park, K. Thomson, C. Bromley and N. Stratford (eds) *British Social Attitudes: The 16th Report*, Aldershot: Ashgate.

Hirst, P. and Thompson, G. (1996) *Globalization in Question: The International Economy and the Possibilities of Governance*, Cambridge: Polity Press.

Hobsbawm, E. (1994) *Age of Extremes: The Short Twentieth Century 1914–1991*, London: Michael Joseph.

—— (1998) 'The making of the working class, 1870–1914', first published 1984, in *Uncommon People: Resistance, Rebellion and Jazz*, London: Weidenfeld and Nicolson.

Hoskyns, J. (2000) *Just in Time: Inside the Thatcher Revolution*, London: Aurum Press.

Howell, C. (2005) *Trade Unions and the State: The Construction of Industrial Relations Institutions in Britain, 1890–2000*, Princeton, NJ: Princeton University Press.

Hutton, W. (1995) *The State We're In*, London: Cape.

Hyman, R. (1989) *Strikes*, 4th edition, Basingstoke, Macmillan.

—— (2001) *Understanding European Trade Unionism: Between Market, Class and Society*, London: Sage.

—— (2003) 'The historical evolution of British industrial relations', in P. Edwards (ed.) *Industrial Relations: Theory and Practice in Britain*, 2nd edition, Oxford: Blackwell.

Ingle, S. (2000) *The British Party System*, London: Continuum.

Jenkins, S. (2006) *Thatcher and Sons: A Revolution in Three Acts*, London: Allen Lane.

Jessop, B., Bonnett, K., Bromley, S., and Ling, T. (1988) *Thatcherism: A Tale of Two Nations*, Cambridge: Polity Press.

Joseph, Sir K. (1979) *Solving the Trade Union Problem is the Key to Britain's Recovery*, London: Centre for Policy Studies.

Jowell, R. and Airey, C. (eds) (1984) *British Social Attitudes: The 1984 Report*, Aldershot: Gower Publishing.

Jowell, R., Witherspoon, S. and Brook, L. (eds) (1987) *British Social Attitudes: The 1987 Report*, Aldershot: Gower Publishing.

Keenoy, T. and Anthony, P. (1992) 'HRM: metaphor, meaning and morality', in P. Blyton and P. Turnbull (eds) *Reassessing Human Resource Management*, London: Sage.

Kelly, J. (1996) 'Union militancy and social partnership', in P. Ackers, C. Smith and P. Smith (eds) *The New Workplace and Trade Unionism: Critical Perspectives on Work and Organization*, London: Routledge.

—— (1998) *Rethinking Industrial Relations: Mobilization, Collectivism and Long Waves*, London: Routledge.

Kelly, J. and Kelly, C. (1991) ' "Them and us": social psychology and the "new industrial relations" ', *British Journal of Industrial Relations*, 29: 1, 25–48.

Labour Party (1992) *It's Time to Get Britain Working Again. Election Manifesto*, London: Labour Party.

—— (1997) *New Labour: Because Britain Deserves Better. Election Manifesto*, London: Labour Party.

Larner, W. (2000) 'Theorising neoliberalism: policy, ideology, governmentality', *Studies in Political Economy* 63, 5–26.

Legge, K. (2005) *Human Resource Management: Rhetoric and Reality*, 2nd edition, Basingstoke: Palgrave Macmillan.

Leys, C. (2001) *Market-Driven Politics: Neoliberal Democracy and the Public Interest*, London: Verso.

Machin, S. (1996) 'Wage inequality in the UK', *Oxford Review of Economic Policy*, 21:1, 49–62.

Marglin, S. and Schor, J. (eds) (1990) *The Golden Age of Capitalism: Lessons for the 1990s*, Oxford: Oxford University Press.

Marquand, D. (1998) 'The "Blair paradox"', *Prospect*, May.

Mason, B. and Bain, P. (1991) 'Trade union recruitment strategies', *Industrial Relations Journal*, 22:1, 33–45.

McIlroy, J. (1991) *The Permanent Revolution? Conservative Law and the Trade Unions*, Nottingham: Spokesman.

—— (1995) *Trade Unions in Britain Today*, 2nd edition, Manchester: Manchester University Press.

—— (1998) 'The enduring alliance? Trade unions and the making of New Labour, 1994–97', *British Journal of Industrial Relations*, 36:4, 537–64.

—— (1999) 'Unfinished business – the reform of strike legislation in Britain', *Employee Relations*, 26:4, 377–91.

—— (2000) 'New Labour, new unions, new left', *Capital and Class*, 71, 11–45.

—— (2007) 'Reflections on British trade unions and industrial politics', in J. McIlroy, N. Fishman and A. Campbell (eds) *The High Tide of British Trade Unionism: Trade Unions and Industrial Politics 1964–79*, 2nd edition, London: Merlin Press.

McIlroy, J., Fishman, N. and Campbell, A. (eds) (2007) *The High Tide of British Trade Unionism: Trade Unions and Industrial Politics 1964–79*, 2nd edition, London: Merlin Press.

Milner, S. (1995) 'The coverage of collective pay-setting institutions in Britain, 1895–1990', *British Journal of Industrial Relations*, 33:1, 69–92.

Minkin, L. (1991) *The Contentious Alliance: Trade Unions and the Labour Party*, Edinburgh: Edinburgh University Press.

Millward, N., Bryson, A. and Forth, J. (2000) *All Change at Work? British Employment Relations 1980–1998 As Portrayed by the Workplace Industrial Relations Survey Series*, London: Routledge.

Monks, J. (1992) 'Gains and losses after twenty years of legal intervention', in W. McCarthy (ed.) *Legal Intervention in Industrial Relations: Gains and Losses*, Oxford: Blackwell.

—— (1993) 'A trade union view of WIRS 3', *British Journal of Industrial Relations*, 31:2, 227–33.

—— (1995) 'No shopping list', *New Statesman*, 8 September.

—— (1997) 'Interview', *Financial Times*, 10 September.

Morgan, K.O. (1999) *The People's Peace: British History since 1945*, 2nd edition, Oxford: Oxford University Press.

Nolan, P. and Slater, G. (2003) 'The labour market: history, structure and prospects', in P. Edwards (ed.) *Industrial Relations: Theory and Practice in Britain*, 2nd edition, Oxford: Blackwell.

Nolan, P and Walsh, J. (1995) 'The structure of the economy and labour market', in P. Edwards (ed.) *Industrial Relations: Theory and Practice in Britain*, Oxford: Blackwell.

Norris, P. (1999) 'New Labour and the rejection of stakeholder capitalism', in G.R. Taylor (ed.) *The Impact of New Labour*, Basingstoke: Macmillan.

Osler, D. (2002) *Labour Party PLC*, London: Mainstream.

Panitch, L. (1976) *Social Democracy and Industrial Militancy: The Labour Party, the Trade Unions and Incomes Policy 1945–1974*, Cambridge: Cambridge University Press.

Panitch, L. and Gindin, S. (2004) 'Finance and American empire', in L. Panitch and C. Leys (eds) *The Empire Reloaded, Socialist Register 2005*, London: Merlin Press.

—— (2005) 'Superintending global capital', *New Left Review*, II: xxxv, 101–23.

Panitch, L. and Leys, C. (1997) *The End of Parliamentary Socialism: From New Left to New Labour*, London: Verso.

Peck, J. and Tickell, A. (2002) 'Neoliberalizing space', *Antipode*, 34:3, 380–402.

Peston, R. (2005) *Brown's Britain*, London: Short Books.

Polanyi, K. (2001) *The Great Transformation: The Political and Economic Origins of our Times*, Boston: Beacon Press, first published 1944.

Pollert, A. (ed.) (1991) *Farewell to Flexibility*, Oxford: Blackwell.

Poole, M. and Mansfield, R. (1993) 'Patterns of continuity and change in managerial attitudes and behaviour in industrial relations 1980–90', *British Journal of Industrial Relations*, 31:1, 11–35.

Price, R. (1986) *Labour in British Society: An Interpretative History*, London: Routledge.

Riddell, P. (2005) *The Unfulfilled Prime Minister: Tony Blair's Quest for a Legacy*, London: Politico's.

Russell, M. (2005) *Building New Labour: The Politics of Party Organization*, Basingstoke: Palgrave.

Saad-Filho, A. and Johnston, D. (2005) 'Introduction', in A. Saad-Filho and D. Johnston (eds) *Neoliberalism: A Critical Reader*, London: Pluto Press.

Seldon, A. (1997) *Major: A Political Life*, London: Weidenfeld & Nicholson.

Shaw, E. (1994) *The Labour Party since 1979: Crisis and Transformation*, London: Routledge.

Sisson, K. (1993) 'In search of HRM', *British Journal of Industrial Relations*, 31: 1, 201–10.

Sisson, K. and Marginson, P. (1995) 'Management systems, structure and strategy', in in P. Edwards (ed.) *Industrial Relations: Theory and Practice in Britain*, Oxford: Blackwell.

Sklair, L. (2001) *The Transnational Capitalist Class*, Oxford: Blackwell.

Stevenson, W. (ed.) (2006) *Gordon Brown: Speeches, 1997–2006*, London: Bloomsbury.

Stiglitz, J. (2002) *Globalization and its Discontents*, New York: Norton.

Storey, J. (1995) 'Human Resource Management: still marching on or marching out?', in J. Storey (ed.) *Human Resource Management: A Critical Reader*, London: Routledge.

Taylor, R. (1993) *The Trade Union Question in British Politics: Government and Unions since 1945*, Oxford: Blackwell.

—— (1994) *The Future of the Trade Unions*, London: Andre Deutsch.

Terry, M. (1995) 'Trade unions: shop stewards and the workplace' in P. Edwards (ed.) *Industrial Relations: Theory and Practice in Britain*, Oxford: Blackwell.

Thompson, N. (2006) *Political Economy and the Labour Party: The Economics of Democratic Socialism*, 2nd edition, London: Routledge.

Towers, B. (1997) *The Representation Gap: Change and Reform in the British and American Workplace*, Oxford: Oxford University Press.

TUC (1993) *General Council Report*, London: TUC.

—— (1994) *Human Resource Management: A Trade Union Response*, London: TUC.

—— (1996) *General Council Report*, London: TUC.

—— (1997) *General Council Report*, London: TUC.

Undy, R., Ellis, V., McCarthy, W. and Halmos, A. (1981) *Change in Trade Unions: The Development of UK Unions since 1960*, London: Hutchinson.

Undy, R., Fosh, P., Morris, H., Smith, P., and Martin, R. (1996) *Managing the Unions: The Impact of Legislation on Trade Unions' Behaviour*, Oxford: Clarendon Press.

Van der Pijl, K. (1998) *Transnational Classes and International Relations*, London: Routledge.

Waddington, J. and Whitston, C. (1995) 'Trade unions: growth, structure and policy', in P. Edwards (ed.) *Industrial Relations: Theory and Practice in Britain*, Oxford: Blackwell.

Walker, A. and Walker, C. (eds) (1997) *Britain Divided: The Growth of Poverty and Social Exclusion in the 1980s and 1990s*, London: Child Poverty Action Group.

Webb, P. and Fisher, J. (2003) 'Professionalism and the Millbank tendency: the political sociology of New Labour's employees', *Politics*, 23:1, 10–20.

Wedderburn, K.W. (1965) *The Worker and the Law*, Harmondsworth: Penguin.

Wedderburn, Lord (1991) 'Freedom of association and philosophies of labour law', in Lord Wedderburn, *Employment Rights in Britain and Europe: Selected Papers in Labour Law*, London: Lawrence and Wishart.

Weiss, L. (1998) *The Myth of the Powerless State*, Cambridge, MA: Harvard University Press.

Wilkinson, F. (2007) 'Neo-liberalism and New Labour policy: economic performance, historical comparisons and future prospects', *Cambridge Journal of Economics*, 31:6, 817–43.

Winchester, D. and Bach, S. (1995) 'The state: the public sector' in P. Edwards (ed.) *Industrial Relations: Theory and Practice in Britain*, Oxford: Blackwell.

Young, H. (1989) *One of Us*, Basingstoke: Macmillan.

# 2 A brief history of British trade unions and neoliberalism in the age of New Labour

*John McIlroy*

Political history amply affirms that policies forged in opposition and elaborated in the heat of an election campaign may fail to withstand the tests of government and changing and challenging political and economic circumstance. Old Labour governments had been almost routinely excoriated for betraying their electoral promises, changing tack or turning tail when confronted with unforeseen but perhaps foreseeable pressures. This time, New Labour argued, things would be different: 'they had got their betrayal in first.' The new leadership contrived what it perceived as a pressure-proof programme: it was not only calculated to impress the electorate with its realism and competence, it would seamlessly translate into the practice of a government, which like that of an admired predecessor was not for turning. New Labour inherited a strong economy. It possessed a large majority and confronted a divided and demoralized Conservative opposition (Kavanagh 2007: 3–4). Nonetheless there was no shortage of academics hazarding that New Labour essentially represented a necessary exercise in rebranding, calculated to win a majority. They believed the social democratic soul of the Labour Party would reassert itself to reveal a reforming government rooted in party tradition and a clean break with Thatcherism (Kenney and Smith 1997; McAnulla 1999).

They could not have been more mistaken. Tony Blair, Gordon Brown and their supporters were men and women with a mission. They proved unstoppable in their determination to remedy the defects of pioneering neoliberalism, take what they considered to be its fundamentally healthy dynamics further and lead the opponents of the Conservatives into a new neoliberal consensus. In office New Labour was, for the most part, true to the approaches it had developed in the 1990s on the basis that social democracy was no longer feasible: 'The emasculation of social democracy followed inevitably from Blair's acceptance of the constraint of globalisation' (Bogdanor 2007: 182). In government New Labour remained faithful to what it saw as the best of the Conservative counter-revolution.

This chapter is in three parts. The first section examines the record of New Labour governments and assesses the framework of economic and social policy and the possibilities it provided for revitalization of the unions. It draws out similarities and contrasts with the politics of New Labour's Conservative predecessors and estimates its successes and failures. This is followed by exploration of how the unions fitted into New Labour philosophy. Blair was personally unsympathetic to trade unionism; indeed he perceived union leaders as well as the Labour left and much of the party mainstream who had been sympathetic to unions in the past as appeasers of what he saw as illegitimate power and the architects of the problems which had plagued the Labour Party since the 1960s. He observed of Harold Wilson and his attempts to restrict union influence in industry:

> Had he been allowed to implement *In Place of Strife*, the recent history of our country would have been hugely different. But he wasn't and there are many of his colleagues and his enemies alike who must take most of the blame for that.
>
> (Rentoul 1997: 464)

Weakened unions and the continuing availability of the Conservatives' employment laws suited Blair. The unions were no longer needed to police wage restraint. He sensed they would or could not play any significant positive role in modernized corporatist initiatives or national economic assessments which might compromise the role of government. The unions were not necessary to New Labour's success but they would be given a new brief as subaltern allies of business. If they accepted this, well and good. If not, and Blair was sceptical, little was lost. The final part of this chapter returns to the issue of the nature of New Labour which we raised in chapter 1. After discussing the view that New Labour represents a renewal of social democracy or a distinctive third way, it reaffirms that the party of Blair and Brown is best conceived as a distinctive variant of neoliberalism.

## Neoliberalism phase two: Neolib-labs in government

Reagan and Thatcher began to put capitalism back on its feet again (Panitch and Gindin 2005; for a different view see Brenner 2002). Neoliberalism provided a solution to the crisis of the 1970s but it came at a price. Thatcherism was running out of steam; after the exit from the EMU in 1992 its economic competence was increasingly questioned. Consolidation of its achievements demanded greater economic stability and more sophisticated politics. It required a softening of confrontation, enhanced economic competence, political methods which could mobilize more sustained and stable support and fashion some repair to the social fabric that Conservative contestation with the vested interests of Keynesianism had wrought. That was the direction the New Labour governments took. The notion that pre-election rhetoric represented opportunism and would yield to a renewal of social democracy was instantaneously dispelled. In the immediate aftermath of victory Blair declared: 'We were elected as New Labour and we will govern as New Labour' (Blair 1997). And he did.

A carefully contrived macroeconomic framework was fundamental to policy: it was intended to control inflation, restrain unemployment and banish the 'stop-go' of the Conservative years. Its allegedly novel inflation targets had been introduced by the Conservatives in 1992: New Labour's approach represented modification and continuity (Angeriz and Arestis 2007: 863). Responsibility for meeting the Conservative-set inflation target of 2.5 per cent was transferred from the government to the Monetary Policy Committee of the Bank of England. In future the Committee would fix interest rates which were perceived as the crucial monetary tool for securing price stability.

The move was seen as stabilizing New Labour's credibility with the markets. It resonated with neoliberalism, not only in its institutional entrenchment of low inflation as the central objective of policy, but in its depoliticization of decision-making and its assertion that political decisions were fundamentally matters of technical expertise which involved proficiency in reading and reassuring the markets. Having adopted the Conservatives' spending limits, New Labour announced that two fundamental principles of fiscal responsibility would govern future policy: over the economic cycle it would borrow only to finance public investment, not public consumption, while net debt as a preparation of Gross Domestic Product would be maintained at 'a prudent and stable level' (Balls and O'Donnell 2002; Keegan 2003). In distinction to previous Labour governments which had disparaged it as a force for conservativism, New Labour handed the Treasury a pivotal and wide-ranging brief. It exercised novel control over design and execution of policy and the allocation of resources through the system of Comprehensive Spending Reviews (Lee 2007: 72).

The Private Finance Initiative (PFI) – a private company finances the building of schools, hospitals or prisons and leases them back to the public sector, sometimes over a 25–30 year period – was important to fiscal policy. It replaced expenditure financed by debt with future interest payments. It kept borrowing for capital expenditure off the accounts while saddling future generations of taxpayers with the burden of repayment. Critics argued that PFI provided schools and hospitals inferior to public sector-financed projects and at greater cost. Moreover, workers experienced pay and conditions unsatisfactory in comparison with their public sector counterparts (Pollock and Price 2004; Craig and Brooks 2006).

The Chancellor, Gordon Brown, attempted to strike a balanced stance between provision by the market and provision by the state. He did so in a fashion which suggested the primacy of the former in his thinking: 'We need markets but we should normally tackle market failure not by abolishing markets but by strengthening markets . . . there are some areas where markets are not appropriate and where market failure can only be dealt with through public action' (Stevenson 2006: 124–5). In practice, examples of the latter seemed few and far between. New Labour preserved the Conservatives' extensive privatizations. Despite the absence of obvious candidates for further action, it struck out on a series of small-scale sell-offs, of the national air traffic control system, the Commonwealth Development Corporation and the Royal Mint. 'The Inland Revenue sold its entire estate to a property developer . . . The Treasury sold and then leased back its own headquarters in Parliament Square' (Jenkins 2006: 259–60). Even in a transparent case of market failure such as Railtrack, Blair baulked at state ownership, creating instead Network Rail, a limited company with no shareholders. In the case of Northern Rock in 2008 there was pleading with private enterprise and protracted agonizing before nationalization was announced, reluctantly and temporarily.

Reform of the public sector meant commercialization and commodification. Brown believed that '[public] utility reform must promote a market economy (and not just a privatised economy)' (Stevenson 2006: 133). The Post Office was a prime target for injection of deregulation and competition once attempts at privatization stalled. Across the public sector, the Treasury tied allocation of resources to policy through Public Service Agreements which offered 'money for modernization' and linked financial input to measurable efficiency targets, changes in management techniques and working practices (Lee 2007: 112–14). The public sector was expected to become more like the private sector, more entrepreneurial and the civil service was required to become dedicated to innovation and delivery (Monbiot 2000). It was pruned and reorganized after reviews by leading private sector managers and bevies of consultants in order to reflect the organization and culture of business – and its needs (Riddell 2005: 56–62). The introduction of consultants and New Public Management approaches was rife across the public sector (Finlayson 2003: 111–12).

In the National Health Service, the Conservatives' internal market was remoulded, not abolished. Outsourcing and Compulsory Competitive Tendering were refined, not abandoned. The government's mantra of 'choice', 'personalised public services' and 'earned autonomy' gave birth to Foundation Hospitals. Launched in 2004, they were allowed to own and manage their own assets, raise funds from private services and set their own terms and conditions of employment (Ham 2005). In education, the Conservatives' City Technology Colleges were recast as City Academies backed by private capital, the voluntary sector or religious groups. Governors were appointed by the sponsors with enhanced freedom over admissions, management, curriculum and staffing.

Education was increasingly subordinate to the labour market and economic ends. In breach of a manifesto commitment, New Labour walked where the Conservatives feared to tread by introducing top-up fees for university students. A pervasive theme as elsewhere was injection of private finance through 'private–public partnerships'. Building Schools for the Future, a partnership between government and private enterprise, worked in similar fashion to PFI; one of the major examination boards is now owned by Pearson, which owns the *Financial Times*; and Ofsted has given contracts to five companies to carry out inspections. By 2005, 500 PFI projects had been completed and the NHS had borrowed £6 billion with a further £11 billion to come for these schemes. The projection was that the majority of health investment would in future come from the private sector (Jenkins 2006: 272).

Control of inflation would, the government was convinced, contribute to the stability essential to attract long-term investment, stimulate productivity and maintain full employment. New Labour's second instrument was a labour market policy more active and rigorous than that of the Conservatives. Nonetheless, it remained within the neoliberal conception of the market-bound role of the state. The state would lubricate the market, not substitute for it. Unemployment, Brown accepted, could be involuntary and structural. In some cases it could result from demoralization, or from mismatches between the skills and wage expectations of the jobless, as well as the failure of welfare benefits to create an inducement to work. The state could facilitate market mechanisms through sponsoring training for reskilling and offering incentives to work by turning welfare benefits into wage subsidies, topping up pay, as well as introducing tax credits to help the low paid and a minimum wage. Enhanced competition in the labour market would reinforce downward pressure on wages. It would enable more expansionary demand management and stimulate the flow of jobs and taxes without inflationary consequences (Daguerre 2004; Glyn and Wood 2001: 204–6).

The neoclassical endogenous growth model adopted by Brown led him to target what he singled out as key factors in growth such as innovation, competitivity and investment (Balls *et al.* 2004). The Chancellor conceived knowledge, education, skills and research and development as at the heart of global competitivity (Kitson and Wilkinson 2007: 807–9). Supply-side neoliberalism would not only improve employability. By endowing individuals with skills and lifelong learning opportunities to continuously improve them, it could diminish social exclusion and poverty and contribute to equality of opportunity (Reich 1991; Dean 2004). The neoliberal state ruled out moves to engineer equality. Any significant and general redistribution of wealth and income through the taxation system was economically dysfunctional. But it *was* permissible for the neoliberal state to generate redistribution of opportunities – although only one endowment, education and training, and then emphatically centred on skills and work, appeared to figure in the equation. New Labour's restricted social vision of education and equality focused on economics, entrepreneurialism and the labour market. Brown demanded 'a society where all have the opportunity to realise their potential – to acquire skills, to work their way up, become self-employed or start a business and to rise as far as their talents and potential could take them . . . The modern way to personal prosperity is higher earnings through higher skills' (Stevenson 2006: 32–5).

This philosophy produced a series of measures starting with the New Deal programmes for long-term unemployed between 18 and 25 years of age. Accepting that 'work is the best form of welfare', the government offered young people a choice between subsidized employment or further training. But it combined incentives with coercion: simply continuing to draw benefits was not an option. Similar schemes were subsequently initiated for single parents, older workers and the disabled. There was even discussion about a 'new deal for depression' (Paz Fuchs 2008). Tax credits introduced in Blair's first term were reorganized in 2002 based on a Child Tax Credit and a Working Tax Credit. The National Minimum Wage Act 1999 sought to further enhance social inclusion, demonstrated the limits of state subsidy and emphasized the responsibilities of employers (Davies and Freedland 2007: 163–98). For critics, innovation represented a strategy of keeping taxes down and avoiding any general class-based redistribution while manipulating the tax system, rewarding some groups at the expense of others.

The decision to cut the main rate of income tax to 20p in the pound was accompanied by a decision to pay for it by axing the 10p starting rate. This hit the low paid. It left 5.3 million households earning less than £18,000 a year £200 a year worse off. They were referred to the complicated tax credit system for compensation but this only helped households with children. Distinguishing itself from first-phase neoliberalism by its stress on the supply side and on skills, New Labour rejected any return to the 'corporatist' training system that had existed before 1979 with compulsory levies on employers incentivizing human resource development driven by a web of tripartite training boards. Instead it relied on exhortation, example and institutional stimulation through an array of skill institutions intended to coax and cajole employers into action (McIlroy 2008).

Social inclusion through the market involved authoritarian remoralization of the excluded on the basis of entrepreneurial values. New Labour talked tough on crime, civil liberties, asylum and immigration. It attempted to outdo the Conservatives on nationalism, the nuclear family, policing and defence: 'the frequency with which Blair sent Britain's armed forces into battle became one of the defining features of his premiership' (Freedman 2007: 616). Responsible citizens were productive employees and acquisitive consumers, prepared to borrow to finance expenditure beyond their current means and keep the economy booming. All citizens and employees had to learn responsibility and how to manage themselves. State-orchestrated social anxieties from obesity and binge-drinking to the hazards of childbirth and the potentially recidivist genes of the children of criminals played their part in managing subjectivity 'to induce self-animation and self-government, so that citizens can optimize choices, efficiency and competitiveness in turbulent market conditions' (Ong 2006: 6). But New Labour appeared oblivious to the impact its own policies had on social problems. And 'neither a lender nor a borrower be' did not figure in the New Labour lexicon.

The welfare state was prodded by New Labour away from support and dependency towards facilitation and self-help. The vision was of a world where individuals would themselves provide 'for all their social needs – health, education, environment, travel, housing, parenting, security in unemployment and pensions in old age. Those who can . . . must. The rest – the residuum – must be targeted, means-tested and kept to a minimum of provision, lest the burden threaten "wealth-creation" ' (Hall 2003: 5). Despite all the efforts of the Social Exclusion Unit, many of the methods adopted such as the Anti-Social Behaviour Orders achieved little and risked deepening exclusion (Levitas 2005: 213).

What had been termed 'industrial policy' by social democratic governments became an attempt by New Labour to remove market rigidities and arrest tendencies to monopoly, albeit by weak means. Two pervasive themes were increasing competition and attracting foreign direct investment to Britain. The Competition Act 1998 and the Enterprise Act 2002 tried to control cartelization and restrictive agreements. It introduced a competition test for managers beyond 'the public interest' criteria supervised by a modernized Office of Fair Trading and the Competition Commission. The Department of Trade and Industry privileged global enterprise because New Labour believed that it was more competitive and not only created jobs but brought valued new technology, skills and innovative management practices to enterprise in Britain. Government organizations such as UK Trade and Investment sold neoliberal Britain to global investors:

> Wage costs are highly competitive . . . social costs on wage bills that are amongst the lowest in Western Europe . . . Businesses in the UK have long benefitted from one of the lowest corporate tax rates, making it one of the most competitive and attractive business locations . . . The UK has a highly flexible labour market which enables foreign investors to use a great deal of flexibility in their employment and management of staff . . . In the UK employees are used to working hard for their employers. In 2001 the average hours usually worked per week by full-time employees were 45.1 hours for males and 40.7 hours for females. The EU average was 40.9 hours and 38.8 hours for males and females respectively . . . UK law does not oblige employers to provide a written employment contract.
> (Arestis and Sawyer 2005: 203–4)

New Labour certainly delivered on a business-friendly Britain. After three years in office, the Chancellor was announcing 'the lowest small business corporation taxes in the industrialized world . . . the lowest ever corporation tax rate for business and the lowest ever capital gains tax for long-term investors' (*The Times*, 22 March 2000). A year later he reported:

> The Capital Gains Tax rate we inherited was 40p for investments held for one year. We cut it in Budget 2000 to 35p. I now propose a cut to just 20p. For investments held for two years, I propose to cut the rate from 30p to 10p . . . the Inland Revenue estimates that three quarters of taxpayers with business assets will pay only a 10p rate . . . For large companies we have already cut Corporation Tax from 33p to 30p, the lowest rate of

Corporation Tax in our history . . . All reflecting our goal to make and keep the UK as the best place for international business.

(Stevenson 2006: 31)

The Conservative counter-revolution on taxation was preserved. A stream of measures favoured business, although employers' National Insurance Contributions were increased while income tax, symbolically reduced in Brown's first budget, remained low in comparison with other countries: the top income tax rate in Sweden was 57 per cent, in France 56 per cent, in Germany 47 per cent and in Britain 40 per cent. The fiscal burden lay with regressive indirect taxation on consumption (Jackson and Segal 2004; Emmerson *et al.* 2005). Within this framework there was a certain amount of targeted 'redistribution by stealth' by means of allowing tax allowances to fall behind earnings, changes in pension taxation and the tax credit schemes (Dean 2004).

But the TUC estimated that tax avoidance by the rich cost the taxpayer £13 billion a year, a figure sufficient to increase old age pensions by 20 per cent (TUC 2008a). And faced with business pressure New Labour retreated from plans to reform capital gains tax and diluted plans to tax non-domiciled high earners, measures which would have contributed to meeting its child poverty targets (Elliott 2008). Earlier it had rejected changes in pension taxation when confronted with an elite group of multinational chairmen who enjoyed direct access to Downing Street (*Guardian*, 12 February 2008). Addressing the need for more spending on public services in 2008, the head of the civil service, Gus O'Donnell, remarked: 'Because of the competitive nature of globalisation, it is going to be hard to put tax rates up. The increasing demand for spending more means that we are going to have to do more with less' (quoted in *Guardian*, 8 February 2008).

Globalization was persistently invoked to explain and justify New Labour policy. It was advertised not simply as an unavoidable reality. It was potentially a beneficial development and its discipline must be imposed by New Labour not only on Britain but on all economies by means of British leadership in the Anglo-American-led global financial institutions. Brown believed that Britain was made for globalization; but others who failed to answer its imperatives must suffer:

The punishment for those who perform badly is now more instantaneous and more severe than in the past . . . the most important response when a country finds itself in difficulty is a strong commitment to implement the necessary policy reforms in conjunction with the IMF and the World Bank . . . it is essential that the international financial institutions attach tough conditions . . . covering both policy and the control of policy . . . Regional cooperation can play a part, but it is in no one's interest if this undermines the importance of the international financial institutions, of the IMF and the World Bank.

(Stevenson 2006: 21–2)

This reflected New Labour's belief that 'regional cooperation', like global economics, must develop on British lines. As presaged in opposition, its stance on the EU moved in a neoliberal direction as if reflecting the 'structural' interests of Anglo-American capitalism in rescuing Europe from the social market and the crippling illusion that globalization could be resisted (Hix 2000). Blair's bargain with the CBI was that in return for acceptance of New Labour's reversal of the opt-out from the Social Chapter the government would obstruct new EU legislation strengthening workers' rights (Taylor 2001: 261–3). In office the Prime Minister cut with the grain of the changing attitudes of member states to the social dimension, influenced by enlargement of membership. He manoeuvred with the right-wing Italian and Spanish governments to delay and gut directives on social policy. He argued that the social market was anachronistic. He urged, in continuity with Thatcher and Major, liberalization, deregulation and reform of the Common Agricultural Policy (Fella 2006: 389). In Europe, Britain was perceived as:

> having adopted a US-style economic model, achieving higher growth at the expense of increased poverty . . . As a result, British exhortations of the need for economic reform have been interpreted as a threat to Western Europe's much treasured institutions of social cohesion and solidarity.
>
> (Hopkin and Wincott 2006: 51)

This view was reinforced by New Labour foreign policy and its role as a junior partner in the pursuit of neoliberalism by other means in Iraq in conflict with France and Germany (Williams 2005). Blair's war dissolved or dented illusions in New Labour's 'ethical foreign policy'; it focused and amplified domestic discontents (Coates and Krieger 2004; Kampfner 2004). The doctrine of 'humanitarian intervention' in other countries (Freedman 2007) was maintained under Gordon Brown and five counterterrorism bills were introduced between 2000 and 2007.

Electorally, New Labour's record surpassed that of all its social democratic predecessors. Returned for an unprecedented third term, its majority of 179 seats in the 1997 election fell only slightly to 167 in 2001, but then significantly to 66 seats in 2005. Disillusion, particularly among traditional Labour voters, set in during its second term. At around 36 per cent, its share of the vote in the 2005 election was six points down on 2001 and eight points down on 1997. Despite the sustained inadequacies of the Conservative opposition, 'Never before had any party won an overall majority on such a low share of the overall vote . . . No previous Labour government had suffered so heavy a haemorrhage of support during its term of office' (Curtice *et al.* 2005: 235).

Measured by surveys, the attitudes of the public appeared somewhat to the left of New Labour, certainly on issues such as inequality. Collectivist attitudes to the welfare state which had increased under Thatcher remained resilient while support for increased taxes to finance increased spending remained high into the New Labour years (Sefton 2003: 24). More than 80 per cent of respondents in 2002 believed that the gap between rich and poor was too large and should be closed through changes in taxation: 'income inequality is no more acceptable now than it was in the early 1980s' (Bromley 2003: 90). However, there was greater fit between government policy and public attitudes over promotion of work, the benefits system and privatization of housing and pensions (Sefton 2003: 24). New Labour appears to have had some success, particularly in moving Labour supporters towards harder attitudes to welfare and equality. Some researchers tentatively conclude: 'It seems that Mr Blair has achieved what Mrs Thatcher failed to do; to move public opinion somewhat closer to the views espoused by the former Prime Minister' (Curtice and Fisher 2003: 249). Here, at least, soft neoliberalism may have made some progress towards creating the neoliberal consensus which eluded its Conservative precursor.

On the economic front New Labour enjoyed almost a decade of financial stability, what Gordon Brown referred to as the longest period of sustained growth since records began. As table 2.1 illustrates, the growth rate increased during New Labour's first term, peaking at 4.3 per cent in 2000 before dropping to 2.6 per cent in 2002. It subsequently recovered before dropping again to 1.86 per cent in 2005. Average growth was 2.8 per cent but this compared with an average of 3.1 per cent from 1992 to 1997. The longest period of sustained growth on record started under the Conservatives and continued for five years before New Labour took office. The record on inflation is also impressive. It never went above 3.5 per cent until 2008 and it averaged

*Table 2.1*  UK macroeconomic data 1992–2007

|      | Growth Rate (%) | Inflation Rate (CPI) (%) | Unemployment (Claimant Count) (%) | Unemployment (ILO) (%) |
|------|------|------|------|------|
| 1992 | 0.2  | 4.7  | 9.2  | 9.7  |
| 1993 | 2.3  | 3.0  | 9.7  | 10.3 |
| 1994 | 4.3  | 2.3  | 8.8  | 9.6  |
| 1995 | 2.9  | 2.9  | 7.6  | 8.6  |
| 1996 | 2.8  | 3.0  | 6.9  | 8.2  |
| 1997 | 3.1  | 2.8  | 5.3  | 7.1  |
| 1998 | 3.4  | 2.6  | 4.5  | 6.1  |
| 1999 | 3.0  | 2.3  | 4.1  | 6.0  |
| 2000 | 3.8  | 2.1  | 3.6  | 5.5  |
| 2001 | 2.4  | 2.1  | 3.1  | 4.8  |
| 2002 | 2.1  | 2.2  | 3.1  | 5.1  |
| 2003 | 2.8  | 2.8  | 3.0  | 4.8  |
| 2004 | 3.3  | 2.2  | 2.7  | 4.6  |
| 2005 | 1.8  | 2.3  | 2.7  | 5.0  |
| 2006 | 2.9  | 2.9  | 2.9  | n/a  |
| 2007 | n/a  | 3.2  | 2.8  | n/a  |

*Sources:* Statbase (ONS) and LaborSta (ILO)

2.58 per cent between 1997 and 2005. But as table 2.1 also demonstrates, the record of the Conservatives after the recession of the early 1990s was good, while the figures depress the rate of inflation measured by the Retail Price Index (RPI). The Consumer Price Index (CPI) which the government uses excludes the cost of mortgage interest payments, the major item of expenditure for most households, and council tax (Lee 2007: 82–3).[1]

Figure 2.1 shows inflation rates between 1992 and 2007 as measured by the CPI. Figure 2.1 illustrates the difference between inflation as measured by the CPI and as measured by the RPI. The latter gives us a better, if still incomplete idea, of the real rate of price increases. Table 2.2 sets out RPI inflation and increases in earnings. It demonstrates that on this basis, workers have not done too badly: for most of the period median earnings ran ahead of RPI inflation. Although this equation excludes taxation effects, it might have made membership of a union appear less attractive to some employees and curbed discontent and militancy (Bain and Price 1983).

Unemployment fell continuously through the New Labour years; a factor which might be seen as helping trade unions. But it also fell sequentially from 1992 to 1997 (table 2.1). While still declining it was higher on the more rigorous ILO measures than on New Labour's figures (Sawyer 2007: 886). High employment levels depressed public expenditure and inflated tax revenues. But prudence on public spending gave way to significant increases in health, education and transport during New Labour's second term, funded by economic growth rather than tax increases or borrowing, although spending fell thereafter.

The same trend was seen with public sector net debt: initial prudence was succeeded by higher spending. Net debt stood at 37 per cent of GDP in 2007,

*Figure 2.1* Inflation (RPI and CPI) January 1992 to January 2008.

*Source:* Statbase (ONS)

*Table 2.2* UK earnings and inflation 1999–2007

|  | Inflation Rate (RPI) (%) | Median Earnings (£) | Annual % Change (Median) | Mean Earnings (£) | Annual % Change (Mean) |
|---|---|---|---|---|---|
| 1999 | 1.5 | 14,888 |  | 17,702 |  |
| 2000 | 3.0 | 15,800 | 6.1 | 18,939 | 7.0 |
| 2001 | 1.8 | 16,438 | 4.0 | 19,822 | 4.7 |
| 2002 | 1.7 | 16,964 | 3.2 | 20,610 | 4.0 |
| 2003 | 2.9 | 17,508 | 3.2 | 21,327 | 3.5 |
| 2004 | 3.0 | 18,172 | 3.8 | 22,263 | 4.4 |
| 2005 | 2.8 | 18,949 | 4.3 | 23,389 | 5.1 |
| 2006 | 3.2 | 19,521 | 3.0 | 24,292 | 3.9 |
| 2007 | 4.3 | 19,943 | 2.9 | 24,908 | 3.2 |

*Sources:* Annual Survey of Hours and Earnings, Statbase (ONS)

*Table 2.3* Trends in UK public expenditure 1989–2006[a]

|  | Public Sector Current Expenditure | Public Sector Net Investment | Public Sector Gross Investment | Total Managed Expenditure |
|---|---|---|---|---|
| 1989/90 | 36.0 | 1.3 | 4.0 | 39.7 |
| 1990/91 | 36.4 | 1.4 | 3.9 | 40.0 |
| 1991/92 | 38.7 | 1.8 | 3.9 | 42.6 |
| 1992/93 | 40.5 | 1.9 | 3.9 | 44.5 |
| 1993/94 | 40.4 | 1.4 | 3.4 | 43.8 |
| 1994/95 | 39.4 | 1.4 | 3.3 | 43.3 |
| 1995/96 | 39.4 | 1.4 | 3.2 | 42.6 |
| 1996/97 | 38.5 | 0.7 | 2.3 | 40.8 |
| 1997/98 | 37.0 | 0.6 | 2.1 | 39.2 |
| 1998/99 | 36.0 | 0.7 | 2.1 | 38.1 |
| 1999/2000 | 35.3 | 0.5 | 1.9 | 37.1 |
| 2000/01 | 35.8 | 0.4 | 1.7 | 37.5 |
| 2001/02 | 36.3 | 1.1 | 2.4 | 38.7 |
| 2002/03 | 37.0 | 1.2 | 2.5 | 39.5 |
| 2003/04 | 37.8 | 1.4 | 2.6 | 40.4 |
| 2004/05 | 38.4 | 1.7 | 3.0 | 41.5 |
| 2005/06 | 39.1 | 1.8 | 3.1 | 42.2 |

*Source:* Sawyer (2007)

*Note:*
a  Figures expressed as percentage of Gross Domestic Product (GDP)

compared with 30.7 per cent of GDP in 2002 (ONS 2007a). Despite the tight restraints in which New Labour held public sector pay throughout the period, money earnings increased by 4.2 per cent between 1997 and 2004 and real take-home pay increased by 2 per cent. This compared with figures of 7.8 per cent and 2.4 per cent respectively between 1979 and 1997 (Wilkinson 2007: 834).

New Labour's conduct of the economy attracted widespread commendation, particularly from international bodies: 'macroeconomic performance over the last decade has been a paragon of stability'; moreover, success was attributed to competent management (OECD 2005: 24). More critical economists have stressed that the favourable circumstances operating from the early 1990s have exercised a benign influence. The expansion of the British economy has coincided with rapid global growth. Having established its credibility with the markets by sacrificing any hint of a radical agenda or deviation from neoliberal orthodoxy, New Labour liberated itself from the shock of balance of payments crises which had dogged Old Labour governments. The trade balance has steadily deteriorated since 1997. Yet there has been none of the traditional retribution from international finance. In that context growth has been sustained by increases in consumption, driven by easy credit, house price inflation and historically high levels of debt. Consumption has outstripped production and has been sustained by import growth, fuelled by the lower import prices globalization has delivered, and by recurring balance of payments deficits (Kitson and Wilkinson 2007: 811–12).

As Glyn documents, finance capital is at the heart of New Labour's boom, its strength and its weakness:

> The importance of financial activities has grown spectacularly . . . Consumer credit has boomed, allowing consumption to acquire temporary independence from the constraint of current incomes . . . shareholdings have become more concentrated in the hands of financial institutions, which pile on remorseless pressure for the maximization of share prices . . . The most significant winners have been chief executives and successful speculators on the domestic and international financial markets. The losers were workers whose jobs, working conditions and pensions were put at risk and investors not in the know.
>
> (Glyn 2006: 76)

Rising at twice the rate of productivity growth, consumer spending, and the debt incurred to maintain it, constituted an unstable foundation for New Labour's achievements. British neoliberalism continued to close the productivity gap with its leading competitors; but the gap remained. Productivity per worker in 2005 was 9 per cent below the G7 average and 25 per cent behind the USA, although New Labour did better than the Conservatives: in 1997 the figures were 15 per cent and 28 per cent respectively (ONS 2007b). OECD reports found that Britain ranked sixth among G7 countries on 'innovation performance' although it ranked first among G7 and OECD countries in liberal product market regulation (OECD 2005). Despite the extent and force of New Labour rhetoric about 'the knowledge society' and 'lifelong learning', class inequalities in education remained significantly entrenched (Piatt 2003). The gap in skills with leading competitors endured (Leitch 2006).

Deindustrialization, the decline in manufacturing and the growth of services has speeded up since 1997. It has been more marked under New Labour than under the Conservatives and it has affected Britain more than other comparable countries. It has contributed to the regional divide in jobs and prosperity (Coutts *et al.* 2007). Increased flexibility has undermined job quality and contributed to an insecure and overworked labour force. There is no evidence of a decrease in the intensification of work which developed in the 1990s. Stress levels have increased, job satisfaction and work–life balance have not improved (Crompton 2006; Green 2006). The inequality of the Conservative years has endured under Neolib-Labism. There is some evidence that wage inequality has been slightly reduced from a ratio of 7.28:1 between high and low earners in 1999 to a ratio of 6.93:1 in 2007. This is attributable to small but significant pay increases for the lowest-paid public sector workers. Inequality continued to increase in the private sector (New Earnings Survey / Annual Survey of Hours and Earnings 1999–2007).

The Gini index is a reasonable measure of income inequality: it is 100 when one person receives all the income and 0 when everyone has the same and there is perfect equality. Under New Labour the Gini – around 25 in the 1960s and 1970s – increased from 30 in 1997 to 34 in 2005. New Labour Britain is one of the most unequal countries in Europe. France's Gini is 28 and so is Germany's. Sweden's is 23, Denmark's 24 and Spain's 32. The average for the core EU-15 is 30 and for the extended EU-25 it is 31, although in the USA, New Labour's model, it is 45 (Eurostat 2008; United Nations Development Programme 2008).

Globalization affects all these countries. But political action seems to make a difference to equality. There is a choice and New Labour chooses inequality. The compiler of the *Richlist* reported that the wealth of top people had quadrupled since 1997: 'The 11 years of Labour have been absolutely fantastic for the super-rich . . . Having a friendly Labour government has almost been better than having a Tory one; it has neutered politicians on the left' (*Sunday Times*, 27 April 2008). The 'greed is good' of the 1980s mutated into Peter Mandelson 'feeling comfortable' with the increasing wealth of the rich and the softer explanation of New Labour's Business and Enterprise Secretary John Hutton, 'aspiration and ambition are actual human emotions'. New Labour, he protested, should 'celebrate huge salaries' (*Guardian*, 10 March 2008). Tony Blair certainly did, amassing more than £7 million in the year after he left office. Answering the neoliberal class war cry '*Enrichissez-vous!*', between 2006 and 2008 no fewer than 28 former New Labour ministers accepted lucrative private sector appointments (*Sunday Times*, 4 February 2008). One commentator observed: 'Hutton means this to be a tide-turner, the point where Labour kicks off the last irksome remnants of egalitarian nonsense' (Toynbee 2008).

He was pushing at an open door: under New Labour the rich got richer, (Lansley 2006; Peston 2008). Thatcherism produced a rise in inequality greater than in any western country. It left the richest 1 per cent of the population owning 17 per cent of Britain's wealth. By 2006 the figure has increased to around 22 per cent of total wealth (Lee 2007: 214). In 1979, the richest 10 per cent received 20 per cent of national income, by 1997 the figure was 28 per cent, and by 2002 it was 29 per cent. The share of the poorest 10 per cent declined from 4 per cent in 1979 to 2 per cent in 1997 and remained the same in 2002 (Levitas 2005: 231).

No significant inroads have been made into gender inequality at work. Recent research confirmed that from the age of 18 until retirement women earn less than men. In their twenties the gap is around 3 per cent. In their thirties women earn 11 per cent less than men and in their forties the gap increases to 23 per cent. A motherhood penalty still applies (TUC 2008b). Health inequality has worsened under New Labour, despite a government target to reduce it by 10 per cent by 2010. The infant mortality rate for manual workers was 19 per cent higher than for the total population in 2003, compared with 13 per cent in 1997 (Department of Health 2008). The anti-poverty strategy has had some success. But the initial target of reducing child poverty by a quarter was not met and the achievement of revised targets by 2010 appears unlikely. Poverty fell among pensioners but not among working-age adults. Moreover, 'despite the fall in poverty, three quarters of the extra income created over the last decade has gone to richer households . . . higher earnings have grown proportionately faster than average' (Palmer *et al.* 2006: 10).

Tax credits, it is argued, provide a subsidy to employers and help sustain a low pay culture (New Policy Institute 2004). At £5.73 per hour for adult workers in 2008, the minimum wage had increased 60 per cent on 1999 and was seen by many as a success. Trade unionists continued to criticize it on the grounds of the inadequacy of the rates, its interactions with subsidies to employers, the government's final say over Low Pay Committee recommenda-tions and its failure, unlike wage councils, to encourage joint regulation (Simpson 2004; Blackburn 2007: 196–200). A study of New Labour's welfare-to-work initiatives concluded: 'overall more working parents face reduced incentives to progress in the labour market through Labour's tax and benefit changes than face improved incentives to progress' (Brewer and Shepherd 2004: viii; and see McKnight 2005). A strategy based on targeted initiatives, which attempts to tackle poverty while simultaneously rejecting any general moves towards redistribution of wealth and income and greater equality, instead utilizing relatively discrete methods such as training in skills to gener-ate equality of opportunity, is unlikely to create a fairer society measured by the tenets of social democracy, let alone democratic socialism. 'Lifting the floor' but leaving the ladder of inequality intact is unlikely to create meaning-ful equality of opportunity. Eschewal of more ambitious goals weakens the possibility of achieving more limited goals: 'to tackle social exclusion without making serious inroads into inequality is to fight the battle with both hands tied behind our backs' (Levitas 2005: 234).

What progress New Labour has made is bounded by neoliberalism and the constraints it places on goals and methods. What progress there has been has occurred in favourable conditions. It has been achieved by a mixture of good management and good luck. New Labour has not as yet been tested as the Conservatives were tested by economic recession. As some economists have noted: 'History is replete with examples of periods of relative absence of inflationary pressure followed by major economic and financial crises' (Angeriz and Arestis 2007: 871). By 2008, recession was emerging in America and more difficult conditions were appearing in Britain. Fuelled by increases in the price of oil and petrol, food and utility bills, inflation was increasing at 2.2 per cent on the CPI but 4.1 per cent on the RPI; house prices were falling and mortgage costs increasing; the current account deficit was higher than at any time since 1955; low growth, accelerating inflation and unemployment were forecast by the Bank of England; and the government's ratings in the polls were lower than at any time since the 1980s. Together with the U-turn over the 10p tax rate, a defeat imposed by its own MPs, these difficulties were widely seen as marking the beginning of the end. By 2008 New Labour was in deep trouble facing recession and its most serious challenge since its inception.

## Neoliberalizing Britain's trade unions

Just before the 1997 general election, Millbank insiders described New Labour's take on trade unions:

> First, that they are in continuing decline; second, that they have nowhere else to go but Labour; third, that they must not be brought into the central policy-making centres once Labour is in government. They may take a role in elaborating training schemes and in setting a minimum wage. Beyond that nothing has even been mooted.
>
> (Lloyd 1996)

This was a reasonable summation of the thinking of party leaders. Strong trade unions on the pre-Thatcher model could constrain state policies based on market economics and the control of inflation. They were arguably incompatible with New Labour's macroeconomic policy; they could compromise entrepreneurial culture, puncture business confidence and endanger New Labour's political longevity. Stakeholding, and with it National Concordats with capital and labour and pacts over wages, taxes, competitiveness, productivity and industrial peace, had been rejected as weapons of economic management by the new neoliberalism. There was little doubt as to the attitude Tony Blair and his advisors took to trade unionism: 'Rodney Bickerstaffe, general secretary of Unison, came around for a general whinge. He said TB had to realise he would need the unions at a later stage. I reported back to TB who said they can just fuck off' (Campbell and Stott 2007: 58).

To the party leadership's way of thinking, unions were an unpleasant impediment to progress. Unfortunately they were still part of New Labour and still an aspect of political realities. They still had almost eight million members. For all the internal party reforms they remained constitutionally embedded in New Labour's structures while, as the general election confirmed, the party continued to be dependent on the unions for finance and resources. Longstanding, unavoidable commitments had been written into the manifesto. The question of what to do with the unions in a modified neoliberal paradigm required careful consideration.

New Labour's strengths lay in the weaknesses of the unions. In response to decisive defeat, unprecedented since the 1920s, the sinews of mobilization, reflected in the dwindling strike rate, had withered. The left was in decline. The 1997 generation of union leaders opposed any vision which called into question attachment to the party and deference to its leaders. They certainly believed they had nowhere else to go. In comparison with 1974 or 1979 their expectations had been trimmed. They had turned to moderation and partnership. They were only arriving at a realization that the moment of radical thinking, of stakeholding, of the EU, had passed; and that New Labour's first loyalty lay not with organized labour but with business. They were beginning to grasp that their future influence over government policy would be marginal (McIlroy 2000a: 20–5; McIlroy 2000b).

The decline which had facilitated the imposition of a neoliberal settlement was manifest. Overall union membership had fallen to 7.9 million; unions covered little more than a third of the workforce (see McIlroy and Daniels, chapter 3, this volume, table 3.3). Only 42 per cent of workplaces had recognized unions and in 1 in 7 of these workplaces no workers were covered by collective bargaining. Collective bargaining governed the terms and conditions of 67 per cent of workers in comparison with some 90 per cent in 1984. The previous decade had witnessed 'a progressive disintegration' of institutional industrial relations, 'facilitated by the weakening of both sides' commitment to both the structures and values of joint regulation' (Millward *et al.* 2000: 97, 160, 227). Little is irreversible. In a situation where the CBI opposed change of any significance and where the trend among managers ran ever more strongly in favour of direct dealings with employees, even where unions were recognized (Cully *et al.* 1999: 16–17), a government which prioritized capital and control of inflation had to proceed cautiously – even on prior commitments. As Undy (1999: 33) commented: 'Broadly the existing balance of bargaining power which favoured the employer was seen as appropriate.'

Maintaining it meant adopting the fundamentals of the Conservatives' anti-union legislation. The substance of Thatcherism's regulation of unions, the ballots for internal union elections and before industrial action, the restricted definition of a trade dispute, the curtailment of the statutory immunities and the restrictions on solidarity action and picketing were retained, in violation of international conventions (Ewing and Hendy 2002). Only 'excessive' regulation as manifested by the CROTUM and CPAUIA and the prohibition of union membership at GCHQ was removed. New Labour, Fredman noted, followed the Conservatives along a regulatory path sometimes conceived as inconsistent with neoliberalism. It 'refused to do anything but tinker with the worst excesses of neoliberal strike laws' (Fredman 2004: 32). The consequences of New Labour's macroeconomic framework created an environment far from conducive to union revitalization. It was stiffened by government restrictions on public sector pay increases, which were perceived as crowding out public spending and stimulating increased taxation, a firm line in opposing industrial action and willingness to use the law against trade unionists. Enhanced product market competition and increases in labour costs as a proportion of total costs ensured private sector employees were willing to resist union demands (Charlwood 2004: 380–4).

With these essential safeguards – and incentives to unions to change further – the government could proceed to a more inclusive policy aimed at steering unions away from adversarialism. Mrs Thatcher wanted to push unions out to the margins. To foster social cohesion and avoid conflict Tony Blair wanted to bring them back in. In contrast with its predecessors, New Labour saw no problem in restoring the legitimacy of organizations which were very different from their forebears of 1979. Union leaders were again appointed to public bodies from the Low Pay Commission to the Royal Commission on House of Lords reform, as well a wide range of quangos and taskforces. In contrast with the past, appointments were made on an individual, non-representative basis (McIlroy 2000b; Ewing 2005: 16–17). There was no difficulty in permitting union leaders renewed access to the state. They were soon meeting regularly with ministers and officials, not only at the DTI but at the DfEE, the Home Office and the Transport Department (TUC 2005: 3; TUC 2006: 2). If legitimacy and access were restored, their limits were carefully calculated. The new goodwill to organized labour was largely procedural; its impact on policy formation was negligible (McIlroy 2000b).

Blair and Brown's response to the union problem differed from that of Thatcher and Major. Rather than attempt to progressively brush them from the landscape, New Labour sought to remould them in its own, distinctive neoliberal image. Unions would be rehabilitated so long as they restructured their ideology, politics and activity. They would be reborn as labour market lubricators, as agents of supply-side neoliberalism doing the work of New Labour and the market inside the enterprise. They would foster employee identification with management and prosecute the goals of the business. They would contribute to harmonious employment relations as a vehicle to increase competitivity, help to attract investment and institutionalize lifelong learning and 'the knowledge economy' (Collins 2001). Historically unions have been advocates and, to some degree, instruments of greater equality (Blackburn 1967). By generating training opportunities and stimulating upskilling they could facilitate greater equality of opportunity within an enduringly unequal society that the decline of their political role and joint regulation gave them little chance to change. To these ends, the New Labour state 'sought to repress certain functions of trade unionism and to direct trade union purpose in a number of new directions' (Ewing 2005: 1).

The limited re-regulation embodied in inherited manifesto commitments would settle accounts with the party's social democratic past and constitute 'the last act of Old Labour' (Undy 1999: 33). Carefully calculated and circumspectly calibrated, convincingly explained and agreed with the employer organizations, these concessions could be made to serve New Labour purposes. They would come at a price. What transpired in the Employment Relations Act (ERA) 1999 and the minimum wage legislation represented light regulation, minimal burdens on business and, overall, a wider role for restricted legislation in setting very minimal standards at the expense of collective bargaining. The recognition procedure undeniably constrained management prerogative. But it excluded around 30 per cent of the labour force in the fastest growing sectors of the economy; required a high hurdle of consent, a majority of workers amounting to 40 per cent of the bargaining unit; and combined a wide range of safeguards for management with a number of obstacles for trade unionists. The statutory procedure terminated in what was an attenuated form of joint regulation covering pay, hours and holidays but not pensions or training. It was conditioned by New Labour's credo: 'employers must and will be free to organise their business in the way they choose' (DTI 1998a: para 4.18). This was scarcely a token of belief in powerful trade unionism or strong collective bargaining.

The procedure was justified not by the desirability of joint regulation as a necessary response to the power of employers but by the government assertion that 'collective representation can help achieve important business objectives' (ibid.: 4.3). Likewise, the limited changes in the qualification period for unfair dismissal rights were promoted as stimulating flexibility and labour mobility – workers had less to lose – rather than as enhancing employee security (ibid.: 3.9). Similarly, the government's measures to advance work–life balance stressed the need to strengthen the labour market rather than civilize lives (ibid.: 5.5). In the case of the minimum wage – if 'set sensibly, implemented sensibly' (Blair 1998: 3) – generating labour market efficiency could be reconciled with an element of decency, although the 'sensible' level was well below TUC expectations (Arrowsmith *et al.* 2003).

The message was that unions were legitimate economic, social and political actors and workers would receive minimal legal protection from the full rigours of the market. But equally fundamentally, public policy now demanded that unions should represent their members within a framework of support for management goals, for flexible systems of working, for increased competitivity. If it could – and the EU presented some problems here – New Labour would sponsor protection for workers which simultaneously oiled the wheels of productivity and competitivity. The purpose of unions was to sustain not challenge management. Legislation with a deleterious impact on capital – and this possibility would be scrupulously scrutinized by the DTI – was no longer on the agenda. This ensured that legislative and institutional backing for unions remained restrained and rudimentary.

New Labour philosophy should be distinguished from the ideas of stake-holding and from European models where strong unions stimulated entre-preneurs into the benign circle of high quality, high performance, high skills, high productivity (Freeman and Medoff 1984; Nolan 1992; Deakin and Wilkinson 1994). New Labour used these terms. In practice it disdained the robust and extensive regulation and rights which might produce the strong unions which could deliver these goals and close the road to competition through low skills and low wages. That particular project was too radical and too risky. The government's suspicion of joint regulation, and its negative attitude to reinforcing it, was suggested by the weak scaffolding of the recog-nition procedure; by the failure to re-enact the duty of ACAS to encourage collective bargaining; by refusal to restore the extension of bargaining machinery which the Conservatives had abolished; and by the rejection of any connection between the national minimum wage and joint regulation. Ewing reflected of collective bargaining: 'As a regulatory process it now has no public policy support' (Ewing 2005: 14).

Blair insisted that he 'was not in the business of overburdensome regula-tion'. All that was involved was placing 'a very minimum infrastructure of decency and fairness around people in the workplace'. Legal support for unions and workers would navigate 'a way between the absence of minimum standards of protection at the workplace and a return to the laws of the past' (Blair 1998: 3). In practice, fairness was downgraded from an end in itself to a means to efficiency (Fredman 2004: 21). Fairness and decency are conditional and contingent: where they are perceived by business interests to conflict with efficiency then it is the latter which prevails (Dickens and Hall 2006: 351–2). Moreover, New Labour's minimal package embodied in the legislation of the late 1990s (see Smith and Morton, chapter 6, this volume) aspired 'to draw a line under the issues of industrial relations law'. It was intended as substantially a final settlement. And Blair stressed the limits of retreat from the Conservative past. The new settlement endorsed, although it refined and strengthened, the neoliberal regime: 'Even after the changes we propose, Britain will have the most lightly regulated labour market of any leading economy in the world' (Blair 1998: 3). But, we should remind ourselves, the most regulated trade unions.

Blair meant what he said. The Employment Acts 2002 and 2004 both consisted of small-scale piecemeal measures. Arguments for more substantial change were off-message. Their proponents, it was made clear, were not ser-ious: they were endangering the prospects of more restricted change. There was no question of a New Labour government entertaining any integrated programme of legislative innovation as distinct from discrete refinements to existing law and the fine-tuning of the 1990s settlement. Even limited change was subject to 'regulatory impact assessment' by civil servants who estimated the likely impact of each measure on competitivity (McIlroy 2008: 296). The worldly-wise took some of these complex calculations about value added to the enterprise with a pinch of salt, as window-dressing to justify a priori political decisions. The development of labour law became dependent on the degree to which it could satisfy neoliberal aspirations which clashed with civil rights for workers and international conventions.

New Labour's policy for industrial relations was, from the outset, a component of neoliberal labour market policy. It constituted an integral, although not primary, part of the strategy for improving competitiveness focused on strong markets, modern companies and 'an enterprising nation' (DTI 1998a: 3.1).[2] The policy discourse was suffused with individualism and, like Thatcherism, privileged the contract of employment over the collective agreement. The primary labour market nexus subsisted between the entrepreneur and the individual employee: 'Individuals seek and obtain jobs and agree employment contracts with their employer . . . Employers and employees value individual achievement and individual ambition' (ibid.: 4.1). Trade unionism had its place. But that place was secondary or, at best, on a par with unmediated employer-employee relations. Social democracy had acknowledged the inherent structural disparity of power between employer and employee and the need for a general collective antidote. New Labour accepted the exceptional possibility of market failure: 'But individual contracts of employment are not always agreements between equal partners . . . Collective representation of individuals at work can be the best method of ensuring that employees are treated fairly' (ibid.: 4.2).

The validity of trade unionism was contingent. It depended on its utility to business: 'collective representation can help achieve important business objectives . . . Representatives who are respected by other employees can help employers explain the company's circumstances and the need for change' (ibid.: 4.3). In New Labour's policy discourse the role of unions in representing individuals is accepted; their role in regulating management and eroding its prerogatives through collective bargaining scarcely figures (cf. Ewing 2005: 13–15). The aspirations of union members and their attainment are conflated with the needs of the enterprise. Their inescapable potential for generating conflict with managerial goals is passed over: 'The neoliberal assumption that profitability represents the public interest', and one might add, the employee and union interest, 'is unchallenged' (Fredman 2004: 20). In New Labour's thinking, 'trade unionism is acceptable only when it contributes to the success of the enterprise and helps to deliver work reorganisation, flexibility, commitment and quality' (McIlroy 2000a: 20). Put more graphically: 'Unions are expected to be a useful tool of management' (Novitz 2002: 493).

The device New Labour adapted for developing neoliberal trade unionism as an adjunct to management and an instrument of flexibility and upskilling was partnership. It was different in crucial aspects from partnership as conceived by the TUC. The conceptions of earlier advocates of partnership were refashioned and diluted. As pursued by union leaders since the early 1990s it had attracted little interest from the Conservatives; it was picked up by their successors. New Labour's approach was rooted in the view that:

The keys to securing efficiency and fairness are employability and flexibility. Employability means ensuring that people are well-prepared, trained and supported, both initially, as they enter the labour market, and throughout their working lives. Flexibility means being able to adapt quickly to changing demand, technology and competition.

(DTI 1998a: 2.13)

New Labour's partnership agenda focused on HRM and supply-side neoliberalism; its primary actors were employers and individuals. Partnership could bond them together in pursuit of employability and flexibility. But partnership could in some cases transcend the fundamental contractual nexus:

In modern businesses relationships at work are flexible and tailored to the size and culture of the company or organisation. Sometimes, they are provided by a partnership between employers and trade unions which complements the direct relationship between employer and employee . . . each business should choose the form of relationship that suits it best . . . many employers and employees will continue to choose direct relationships without the involvement of third parties.

(ibid.: 2.5, 2.6, 1.9)

Many companies recognized unions and this was justified because:

Trade unions can make the task of forging effective partnerships easier for employers and employees. In recent years they have changed to reflect change in business. Many trade unions now focus much more strongly on working with management to develop a flexible, skilled and motivated workforce . . . Trade unions can be a force for fair treatment, and a means of driving towards innovation and partnerships.

(ibid.: 4.7)

Unions were an option; they were far from indispensable. Not only did partnership not *require* unions – in sharp contrast with the TUC view: 'you can't have partnership without unions' (Novitz 2002: 492) – but any union involvement in partnership required renunciation of conflict with employers, an unavoidable aspect of their *raison d'être*. Partnership – New Labour style – posited a utopian employment relationship, which was unitary or, at best, pluralist in a dilute form: it predicated a relationship in which unions accepted that business goals were paramount and overriding. The Prime Minister referred to 'a programme to replace the notion of conflict between employers and employees with the promotion of partnership' (Blair 1998: 3). The state demanded that employees 'accept their responsibilities to cooperate with employers' (DTI 1998a: 2.15).

Non-conflictual partnership remained, despite a modicum of state support, a matter for voluntary agreement. Some commentators discerned in the fragility of Blair's legislative rights an invitation to partnership: it certainly provided the setting for the 1999 initiatives while the 2002 legislation was promoted as a contribution to partnership (Parl. Debs H.L. vol. 375 col. 384, 27 November 2001). Others have discerned a lack of fit between state advocacy of partnership and New Labour legislation (Davies and Freedland 2007: 160–1). The freedom of employers to adopt or reject partnership was emphasized. Indeed, there was anxiety about legislation, EU-derived or otherwise, which might impose consultative forums on the enterprise (Collins 2001: 41–2). Finally, the locus of partnership was the workplace and enterprise: the 'social' was residual in New Labour pronouncements. But the government advocated HRM in the workplace (for a critical review see Nolan and O'Donnell 2003) forcefully if vaguely.

> Modern companies draw their success from the existence and development of partnership at work. Those who have learnt to cherish and foster the creativity of their whole workforce have found a resource of innovation and inventiveness that drives their companies forward as well as enriching their lives.
>
> (Blair 1998: 3)

Beyond such exhortations to cooperate and work together, partnership went undefined and without institutional support at work. Some classified it with New Labour's numerous other counterfeit coinages 'which amounted to little more than motherhood-apple-pie clichés' (Riddell 2005: 33). What the government offered was hardly, as New Labour seemed to believe, 'a blueprint for a lasting model' (DTI 1998a: 1.11). Whether ideological smokescreen or political weapon, partnership was of a part with Blair's other neologisms: 'Social-ism is not about class, or trade unions, or capitalism versus socialism. It is about a belief in working together to get things done' (Riddell 2005: 33). In New Labour's hands the concept was:

> Diffuse and open-ended . . . The language of partnership stresses cooperation, consultation and consensus and contains virtually no mention of disagreement, conflict or dispute. In so doing it comes at times close to an implicit negation of the existence or reality of conflict within the modern enterprise. This is not the case with the approaches espoused by the TUC and the IPA which clearly have a pluralist rhetoric.
>
> (Terry and Smith 2003: 18)

The language of partnership was predominantly aspirational, not descriptive. It offered employers a problematic means of harnessing workers to productivity imperatives and trade unionists a questionable means of redistributing profits, as distinct from neoliberalism's perennial promise that some of the added value that cooperation allegedly produced would 'trickle down'. The world had changed. In 1978–9 unions had rejected the Bullock proposals offering worker directors on the grounds that they compromised their independence. Now they were being required to take far less and give far more. New Labour partnership sought to resolve the historic contradictions of British trade unionism, the combination of collaboration with capital and defensive economistic militancy by asking trade unionists to renounce the latter as archaic.

The contribution partnership could make to the supply side and employability was particularly important for New Labour, given longstanding market failure and employer inaction over skills and training (DfEE 1998) as well as the recent lack of success of Conservative initiatives in this area (McIlroy 2000c). Commentators emphasised the historical significance of this projected transformation in the role of the unions:

> Government no longer needs trade union support to control wage inflation, or at least does not need it in the way it was needed in the past. The need now is for initiatives on the supply side to improve productivity, to train and educate the labour force and to remove barriers to labour market participation.
>
> (Ewing 2005: 18)

The evacuation of social democratic philosophy was affirmed by neoliberal refusal to legislate for an area particularly amenable to tripartism, as Old Labour had in the 1960s. Rather, government support for unions as agents for delivering state policy and acting as a stimulus to activate employers was characterized as resurrecting the public administration function that unions had exercised in the early years of the twentieth century – when they had administered national insurance legislation – at the expense of their diminishing, but hitherto central, regulatory function (Ewing 2005: 17–20).

In steering the unions away from regulating the labour market towards lubricating it through improving the supply of labour, the government was not prepared to use the law directly. Having granted concessions to the unions it expected concessions in return: the bargain was recognition and other rights in exchange for unions embracing partnership in the workplace. It remained ready to offer additional incentives. It was willing to legislate indirectly to provide financial support to influence union activity. The state's role was to 'spread the message', commission research on partnership initiatives and disseminate best practice to facilitate management choice rather than to impose institutional frameworks. However, it was prepared to provide funds 'to contribute to the training of managers and employee representatives in order to assist and develop partnerships at work' (DTI 1998a: 2.7). In the context of state support for management prerogative and the government's lack of enthusiasm for collective bargaining it was claimed that such funding tended to reinforce acceptance of the need 'to change the dominant interaction between management and trade union from one based around representation to one characterized as consultation' (Terry and Smith 2003: 9).

The Partnership at Work Fund dispensed some £12 million on a wide and diffuse range of partnership projects which stretched beyond initiatives to strengthen management and union cooperation into 'working together' over IT, bullying and harassment and work–life balance (ibid.).

It was succeeded by the Union Modernisation Fund (UMF). This distributed some £10 million to finance projects 'to help speed unions' adaptation to changing labour market conditions' in order to 'contribute to a *transformational* change in the organisational efficiency or effectiveness of a trade union or union' and 'to provide a *demonstration effect* to the broader trade union movement, enabling unions to realize more fully their potential to improve the world of work for workers and employers alike' (Stuart *et al.* 2006: 10). Priority themes were headed by: 'improving the understanding of modern business practice by full time officers and lay representatives to better enable unions to work constructively with employers as partners to improve business performance' (ibid.). The objective of state largesse was confirmed by the list of projects which would *not* be funded: 'Ineligible activity includes direct recruitment in respect of particular employers, activity that supports a union's ability to engage in collective bargaining and trade disputes and expenditure on political objectives' (ibid.: 11). The purpose was not to strengthen autonomous unions but to mould unions as helpmates of management, as deliverers of HRM and as lubricators of the labour market. The joint-interest and employer-hegemony ideology attached to the venture was sealed by the caveat that the first two exclusions could be overcome if employers gave their consent to the project.

A later initiative was intended to strengthen equality at work with £5 million of UMF finance dedicated to supporting union-sponsored equality projects and extending a system of union equality representatives. The objective was laudable: but once again unions were being given cash incentives to turn away from adversarialism and keep employers up to their mark on what were characterized and accepted by the unions as matters of joint interest (*Labour Research*, March 2008). Once again the workplace representative function was being reshaped: away from the conflictual bargaining shop steward and towards the consensual, partnership union learning representative (ULR) or equality representative. New Labour wanted to foster in limited forms the tendencies towards collaboration and partnership which had burgeoned within the unions in the 1990s: it was prepared to spend considerable amounts of taxpayers' money to make further change attractive.

The Union Learning Fund (ULF), established in 1998, sustained the unions' supply-side role in resourcing skills development (DfEE 1998). The ULF was part of 'a wide-ranging suite of policy initiatives aimed at improving UK competitiveness through increased skills and making the supply of education and training more responsive to demand from employers and individuals' (York Consulting 2006). The TUC, which strongly supported all these initiatives, orchestrated bids from unions for funding in conjunction with the DfEE. It helped to develop the system of ULRs whose effort to stimulate workplace learning were scrutinized and measured by the DTI. Most of the training resourced by unions involved basic skills, IT and literacy and some £100 million was passed from the state to the ULF to the unions to reinforce union efforts in this area (McIlroy 2008).

There was no guarantee that state funding would achieve its declared aim of transforming trade unions. Whether state strategy was more of an insurance policy to keep unions sweet, busy and out of trouble or whether great hopes were placed in its labour market impact by New Labour, remains a matter for speculation. The extent to which these initiatives would redirect the efforts and change the behaviour of trade unionists, beyond stimulating dependency on state revenues, was likewise a moot point. The TUC certainly appeared to have internalized state objectives to 'increase business/ serve competitiveness, enhance the employability of the workforce, build a partnership approach with employers and add value to the union card' (www.unionlearn.org.uk). Whether, and to what degree, this would impact in the workplace was more problematic.

What was clear was that New Labour differed from the Conservatives in its attitude towards trade unionism. But it was a difference within neoliberalism. The pioneers were determined to debilitate if not destroy collectivism in the interests of individualism and the market. Their more creative second-phase successors wanted to mould the already changing, relatively plastic fabric and ethos of trade unionism. New Labour tried to expedite existing directions within trade unionism, already stimulated by neoliberalism, and attach union leaders and activists more firmly to the purposes of the neoliberal state. It attempted to enrol them in the New Labour crusade to galvanize capital and revitalize labour markets. In doing this it sought to capitalize on the nature of unions as intermediate organizations, which are arguably closer to their members than managers are and which not only give voice to those members but influence their aspirations and attitudes. New Labour sought to take advantage of the unions' fragility and their search for a new role as well as to exploit their independence from management to expand the niche for unions stimulating and assisting management to refashion labour, spreading entrepreneurial opportunity through skills acquisition and improving the supply of labour to answer employer demand.

It was worth a try: 'The trade union is not a predetermined institution i.e. it takes on a definite historical form to the extent that the strength and will of the workers who are its members impress a policy and propose an aim that define it' (Gramsci 1977: 265). External agencies, particularly, as we have seen, the state and employers, have always exerted a powerful influence on the nature of trade unionism. A conjuncture in which the relative leverage that workplace activists could apply over strategy and policy had been dissipated by Thatcherism offered enhanced autonomy and freer play to the bureaucratic tendencies of union leadership and its attraction to the state (Muller-Jentsch 1985). Sustained loss of members and financial pressures (Willman 2005) were reinforcing factors. Destructive neoliberalism had failed to extirpate trade unionism. It remained to be seen whether constructive neoliberalism could transform it into a willing labour market ancillary of employers and the state.

## Conclusion

As the politics of New Labour developed, many commentators eschewed attempts to characterize it in relation to social democracy and neoliberalism. They contented themselves with empirical analysis or the view that it combined a bit of both in a 'post-Thatcherite politics' (see Budge 1999; Krieger 2007: 428). Others argued, strongly and at length, that New Labour represented continuity with the Labour Party's past. The party's methods had changed over time. Its values had stayed constant and they remained dominant in the party of Blair and Brown (Fielding 2003). More specifically some located New Labour's lineage in the party's longstanding traditions of modernization, best exemplified by the revisionist current of Hugh Gaitskell and Tony Crosland in the 1950s (Coates 1996 and see Driver and Martell 2006: 53–4). Blair's politics were new but not radically new: there was no caesura with the past.

After a decade of New Labour in government such judgements are hard to sustain. Even cursory address of the policies of the Clement Attlee administrations illustrates the gulf which yawns between democratic socialism and New Labour. The social democratic revisionists of the 1950s were singularly lacking in Blair and Brown's enthusiasm for markets, deregulation and privatization. Gaitskell opposed Clause IV – unlike Blair he was unsuccessful and accepted defeat. He did not oppose strategic public ownership and accepted nationalization as an instrument in managing 'the mixed economy'. The revisionists' commitment to Keynesianism, state intervention in markets and their understanding that enhanced equality of opportunity demanded greater equality, politically directed through state redistribution of wealth and income from rich to poor through taxation, stands in sharp contrast to New Labour dogma. So does their stance on the unions. The core values approach makes for evasive elasticity: equality, fairness, community are open to a diverse, sometimes competing, range of interpretations across the political landscape. Means are important. The perennial values argument is as unconvincing when it is used by historians or political scientists as it is when it is employed by New Labour politicians. As one critic of this approach has urged: 'To claim that a planned economy and a market economy are merely different means to the same end, even making due allowance for the changed circumstances that paralleled Labour's shift from supporting one to supporting the other, is surely an abuse of language' (Toye 2004: 95).

A different line of argument insisted that New Labour embodied a novel 'third way', steering its own course between social democracy's stifling reliance on the state and neoliberalism's socially corrosive dependence on the market (for critical discussion see White 2001). The third way, at least in the eyes of its proponents, transcended left and right and constituted 'an alternative political philosophy' (Giddens 2000: 32–3). Passing over the fact that social democracy was itself a third way between democratic socialism and liberalism (Salvati 2001), this approach offered 'a facilitative state' standing somewhere between the residual state of neoliberalism and the overbearing state of traditional social democracy. It stressed that egalitarianism, community and responsibility were at the heart of the third way and at the centre of New Labour's policy.

The state undoubtedly retained a significant mediating role under New Labour. But third way theorists inadequately acknowledged that the neoliberal Conservatives had themselves no intention of forging a nightwatchman state as distinct from a diminished state. Any convincing characterization of actually existing neoliberalism, as distinct from blackboard models of neoliberalism, recognizes, as neoliberals themselves do, that state expenditure, state intervention and state subsidy to capital and labour remain, with their nature and extent contingent on local factors and the balance of class forces (Harvey 2005: 50).

The manner of New Labour's employment of the state to facilitate the supply of labour to the market particularly distinguishes it from the Conservatives. But the Conservatives had been there before New Labour, albeit in a less coherent and forceful fashion. The Conservatives attempted to stimulate the supply side through the Training and Enterprise Councils (Keep and Rainbird 1995: 523–6). They introduced welfare-to-work with the Restart programme, the Social Security Act 1989 and the Jobseekers Allowance. As with other areas of policy there was continuity, although New Labour took things further and handled matters differently (Dolowitz 1997). These differences cannot obscure the fact that far from being a third way of any real significance, the facilitative state is a market-restricted state. It is closer to Thatcher's state than it is to Harold Macmillan's state. It operates within a defining framework of neoliberal economics closer to the economics of John Major than to the economics of Harold Wilson. Even the distinctive use of unions as supply-side agents is an attempt to manage them in order to improve the workings of the market, not regulate it.

New Labour's commitment to equality of opportunity is different from social democracy's commitment to greater – not complete – equality of outcome. Attainment of New Labour's commitment is crippled by the exclusion of the use of redistributive taxation to achieve it. This prohibition is premised by neoliberalism on the ground that the wealth and income of the rich entrepreneurs who master the market and create prosperity must remain set by the market (c.f. Stewart 2007: 433–4). Inequality has not diminished under New Labour and this constitutes a clear example of the intimate relation between ends and means. If you are serious about providing greater equality of opportunity you cannot transform entrenched differences through the use of one productive endowment, education and training. Inequality of opportunities in education reflects pre-existing and entrenched economic disparities which have to be tackled at source. The attack on poverty has met with only limited success. New Labour has failed to reach its own targets and its policies have left poverty and inequality resilient (Fredman 2004: 14–16). All this is better described as a variant of the *genus* neoliberalism than an authentic third way of any significance. Finally, if we look beyond phrasemongering and consider what New Labour has done, as an index of what it means by community and responsibility, we can discern substantial continuity with neoliberalism's 'free economy-strong-state' and the authoritarian populism of Mrs Thatcher (Callinicos 2001: 55–67).

Writing during the early years of New Labour, industrial relations scholars were hesitant about the validity of third way characterizations of employment policy. Howell (2004: 19) was prepared to acknowledge it 'as a policy adaptation specific to centre-left governments in weakly co-ordinated market economies'. Undy (1999: 333) felt that on the basis of Blair's early employment initiatives 'New Labour's "Third Way" industrial relations may be much closer to neoliberalism than the substance of the legislation would suggest'. Crouch (2001: 104–5) agreed. History quickly concurred. As New Labour's second term progressed, political scientists observed that 'the third way rather disappeared' (Driver and Martell 2006: 53). Labour lawyers judged: 'Third way terminology has outlived its purpose' (Fredman 2004: 39). Economists considered the third way to be opportunist and evanescent: 'It was frequently dismissed as vapid and vacuous and the term soon disappeared from the policy discourse' (Kitson and Wilkinson 2007: 805).

If we want to get a handle on what New Labour is about, neoliberalism is the best place to start. So long as we accept that it is not monolithic; reflects local history and context; makes compromises; changes and develops; possesses contradictions; and yields different outcomes (Peck and Theodore 2007: 757). If we recognize that all characterizations partake of elements of the arbitrary – Keynesianism is a good example – draw out and specify difference and variation and remain alert to reductionism (Gamble 2001: 134), then the most useful way of understanding recent developments in Britain and situating them against the past seems to be through the lens of neoliberalism.

Conversely it is unhelpful to measure practical politics against ideal types or caricatures in a way which would render Thatcherism itself precariously neoliberal. It is equally unhelpful to identify neoliberalism uniquely with the policies of the Conservative governments. We are confronting a neoliberal consensus. As with any consensus, as with Labour and Conservatives in the boom years of the Keynesian welfare consensus, this implies a spectrum along which different parties will purvey different and competing policies (Crouch 1997: 352). It is also unhelpful to isolate and dehistoricize New Labour's policies on employment relations, which is why we have spent some time contextualizing them. The New Labour project entailed the development of neoliberal trade unions. The following chapters will examine how successful it has been.

## Notes

1 The CPI, the official measure of inflation, thus excludes the major item of expenditure in most households. This artificial calculation is then used to justify public sector wage increases lower than 'inflation'. Even the RPI distorts the impact of price rises on many households. For example, it currently includes computers and electrical goods which have been falling in price, while housing costs, food, energy and transport, on which lower paid workers spend a disproportionate amount of their income, have been increasing.

2 *Fairness at Work* was remarkable as a clear and enduring statement of the government's philosophy and policy. It was complemented by the White Paper *Our Competitive Future* (DTI 1998b), an equally vivid declaration of New Labour's vision of reregulating employment relations to embed competitiveness (cf. Davies and Freedland 2007: 44–5).

## Bibliography

Angeriz, A. and Arestis, P. (2007) 'Monetary policy in the UK', *Cambridge Journal of Economics*, 31: 6, 863–84.

Arestis, P. and Sawyer, M. (2005) 'The neoliberal experience of the United Kingdom', in A. Saad-Filho and D. Johnston (eds) *Neoliberalism: A Critical Reader*, London: Pluto Press.

Arrowsmith, J., Gillman, M., Edwards, P. and Ram, M. (2003) 'The impact of the national minimum wage in small firms', *British Journal of Industrial Relations*, 41:3, 435–56.

Bain, G. and Price, R. (1983) 'Union growth: dimensions, determinants and destiny', in G. Bain (ed.) *Industrial Relations in Britain*, Oxford: Blackwell.

Balls, E. and O'Donnell, G. (2002) *Reforming Britain's Economic and Financial Policy: Towards Greater Economic Stability*, Basingstoke: Palgrave.

Balls, E., Grice, J. and O'Donnell, G. (eds) (2004) *Microeconomic Reform in Britain: Delivering Opportunities For All*, Basingstoke: Palgrave.

Blackburn, R. (1967) 'The unequal society', in R. Blackburn and A. Cockburn (eds) *The Incompatibles: Trade Union Militancy and the Consensus*, Harmondsworth: Penguin.

Blackburn, S. (2007) *A Fair Day's Wage for a Fair Day's Work? Sweated Labour and the Origins of Minimum Wage Legislation in Britain*, Aldershot: Ashgate.

Blair, T. (1997) quoted, *The Times*, 3 May.

—— (1998) 'Foreword', *Fairness at Work*, London: DTI.

Bogdanor, V. (2007) 'Social democracy', in A. Seldon (ed.) *Blair's Britain*, Cambridge: Cambridge University Press.

Brenner, R. (2002) *The Boom and the Bubble*, London: Verso.

Brewer, M. and Shepherd, A. (2004) *Has Labour Made Work Pay?* York: Joseph Rowntree Foundation.

Bromley, C. (2003) 'Has Britain become immune to inequality?', in A. Park, J. Curtice, K. Thomson, L. Jarvis and C. Bromley (eds) *British Social Attitudes: The 20th Report*, London: Sage.

Budge, I. (1999) 'Party policy and ideology: reversing the 1950s?', in G. Evans and P. Norris (eds) *Critical Elections: British Parties and Voters in Long-Term Perspective*, London: Sage.

Callinicos, A. (2001) *Against the Third Way: An Anti-Capitalist Critique*, Cambridge: Polity Press.

Campbell, A and Stott, R. (2007) *The Blair Years: Extracts from the Alistair Campbell Diaries*, London: Hutchinson.

Charlwood, A. (2004) 'Annual review article 2003: the new generation of trade union leaders and prospects for union revitalization', *British Journal of Industrial Relations*, 42:2, 379–97.

Coates, D. (1996) 'Labour governments: old constraints and new parameters', *New Left Review*, 219, 62–77.

Coates, D. and Krieger, J. (2004) *Blair's War*, Cambridge: Polity Press.

Collins, H. (2001) 'Regulating the employment relationship for competitiveness', *Industrial Law Journal*, 30:1, 17–47.

Coutts, K., Glyn, A. and Rowthorn, R. (2007) 'Structural change under New Labour', *Cambridge Journal of Economics*, 31:6 845–61.

Craig, D. and Brooks, R. (2006) *Plundering the Public Sector*, London: Constable.

Crompton, R. (2006) *Employment and the Family: The Reconfiguration of Work and Family Life in Contemporary Societies*, Cambridge: Cambridge University Press.

Crouch, C. (1997) 'The terms of the neoliberal consensus', *Political Quarterly*, 68:4, 352–60.

—— (2001) 'A Third Way in industrial relations?', in S. White (ed.) *New Labour: The Progressive Future*, Basingstoke: Palgrave.

Cully, M., Woodland, S., O'Reilly, A. and Dix, G. (1999) *Britain at Work: As Depicted by the 1998 Workplace Employee Relations Survey*, London: Routledge.

Curtice, J. and Fisher, S. (2003) 'The power to persuade? a tale of two Prime Ministers', in A. Park, J. Curtice, K. Thompson, L. Jarvis and C. Bromley (eds) *British Social Attitudes: The 20th Report*, London: Sage.

Curtice, J., Fisher, S. and Steed, M. (2005) 'The results analysed', in D. Kavanagh and D. Butler *The British General Election of 2005*, Basingstoke: Palgrave.

Daguerre, A. (2004) 'Importing workfare: policy transfer of social and labour market policies from the USA to Britain under New Labour', *Social Policy and Administration*, 8:1, 41–56.

Davies, P. and Freedland, M. (2007) *Towards a Flexible Labour Market: Labour Legislation and Regulation since the 1990s*, Oxford: Oxford University Press.

Deakin, S. and Wilkinson, F. (1994) 'Rights v efficiency? The economic case for transnational labour standards', *Industrial Law Journal*, 23:3, 289–310.

Dean, H. (2004) 'The implications of third way social policy for inequality, social cohesion and citizenship', in J. Lewis and R. Surender (eds) *Welfare State Change: Towards a Third Way*, Oxford: Oxford University Press.

Department for Education and Employment (DfEE) (1998) *The Learning Age: A Renaissance for a New Britain*, London: HMSO.

Department of Health (2008) *Tackling Health Inequalities: 2007 Status Report on the Programme for Action*, London: DH Publications.

Department of Trade and Industry (DTI) (1998a) *Fairness at Work*, London: DTI.

—— (1998b) *Our Competitive Future: Building The Knowledge Economy*, London: DTI.

Dickens, L. and Hall, M. (1995) 'The state: labour law and industrial relations', in P. Edwards (ed.) *Industrial Relations: Theory and Practice in Britain*. Oxford: Blackwell.

—— (2006) 'Fairness – up to a point. Assessing the impact of New Labour's employment legislation', *Human Resource Management Journal*, 16:4, 338–56.

Dolowitz, D. (1997) 'Reflecting on the UK welfare system', *Review of Policy Issues*, 3:1, 3–15.

Driver, S. and Martell, L. (2006) *New Labour*, 2nd edition, Cambridge: Polity Press.

Elliott, L. (2008) 'Poor children pay for non-doms tax break', *Guardian*, 3 March.

Emmerson, C., Frayne, C. and Tetlow, G. (2005) *Taxation*, London: Institute for Fiscal Studies.

Eurostat (2008) <http://epp.eurostat.ec.europa.eu> (accessed 3 July 2008).

Ewing, K. (2005) 'The function of trade unions', *Industrial Relations Journal*, 34:1, 1–22.

Ewing, K. and Hendy, J. (eds) (2002) *A Charter of Workers' Rights*, London: Institute of Employment Rights.

Fella, S. (2006) 'Robin Cook, Tony Blair and New Labour's competing vision of Europe', *Political Quarterly*, 77:3, 388–401.

Fielding, S. (2003) *The Labour Party: Continuity and Change in the Making of New Labour*, Basingstoke: Palgrave.

Finlayson, A. (2003) *Making Sense of New Labour*, London: Lawrence and Wishart.

Fredman, S. (2004) 'The ideology of new labour law', in C. Barnard, S. Deakin and G. Morris (eds) *The Future of Labour Law*, Oxford: Hart Publishing.

Freedman, L. (2007) 'Defence', in A. Seldon (ed.) *Blair's Britain 1997–2007*, Cambridge: Cambridge University Press.

Freeman, R. and Medoff, H. (1984) *What Do Unions Do?* New York: Basic Books.

Gamble, A. (2001) 'Neoliberalism', *Capital and Class*, 75, 127–34.

Giddens, A. (2000) *The Third Way and Its Critics*, Cambridge: Polity Press.

Glyn, A. (2006) *Capitalism Unleashed: Finance, Globalization and Welfare*, Oxford: Oxford University Press.

Glyn, A. and Wood, S. (2001) 'New Labour's economic policy', in A. Glyn (ed.) *Social Democracy in Neoliberal Times: The Left and Economic Policy since 1980*, Oxford: Oxford University Press.

Gramsci, A. (1977) *Selections from Political Writings 1910–20*, London: Lawrence and Wishart.

Green, F. (2006) *Demanding Work: The Paradox of Job Equality in the Affluent Society*, Princeton: Princeton University Press.

Hall, S. (2003) 'New Labour's double-shuffle', *Soundings*, 24, 10–24.

Ham, A. (2005) *Health Policy in Britain*, 5th edition, Basingstoke: Palgrave.

Harvey, D. (2005) *A Brief History of Neoliberalism*, Oxford: Oxford University Press.

Hix, S. (2000) 'Britain, the EU and the euro' in P. Dunleavy, A. Gamble, J. Holliday and G. Peele (eds) *Developments in British Politics 6*, Basingstoke: Palgrave.

Hopkin, J. and Wincott, D. (2006) 'New Labour economic reform and the European social model', *British Journal of Politics and International Relations*, 8:1, 50–68.

Howell, C. (2004) 'Is there a third way for industrial relations?', *British Journal of Industrial Relations*, 42:1, 1–22.

Jackson, B. and Segal, P. (2004) *Why Equality Matters*, London: Catalyst.

Jenkins, S. (2006) *Thatcher and Sons: A Revolution in Three Acts*, London: Allen Lane.

Kampfner, J. (2004) *Blair's Wars*, London: Free Press.

Kavanagh, D. (2007) 'The Blair premiership', in A. Seldon (ed.) *Blair's Britain, 1997–2007*, Cambridge: Cambridge University Press.

Keegan, W. (2003) *The Prudence of Mr Gordon Brown*, London: John Wiley.

Keep, E. and Rainbird, H. (1995) 'Training', in P. Edwards (ed.) *Industrial Relations: Theory and Practice in Britain*, Oxford: Blackwell.

Kenney, M. and Smith, M. (1997) '(Mis)understanding Blair', *Political Quarterly*, 68:3, 220–30.

Kitson, M. and Wilkinson, F. (2007) 'The economics of New Labour: policy and performance', *Cambridge Journal of Economics*, 31:6, 805–16.

Krieger, J. (2007) 'The political economy of New Labour: the failure of a success story', *New Political Economy*, 12:3, 421–32.

Lansley, S. (2006) *Rich Britain: The Rise and Rise of the Super-Wealthy*, London: Politico's.

Lee, S. (2007) *Best for Britain? The Politics and Legacy of Gordon Brown*, Oxford: Oneworld.

Leitch, Lord (2006) *Prosperity for All in the Global Economy – World Class Skills, Final Report*, London: HMSO.

Levitas, R. (2005) *The Inclusive Society: Social Exclusion and New Labour*, 2nd edition, Basingstoke: Palgrave.

Lloyd, J. (1996) 'With one bound', *New Statesman*, 9 August.

McAnulla, S. (1999) 'The post-Thatcher era', in D. Marsh, J. Buller, C. Hay, J. Johnston, P. Kerr, S. McAnulla and M. Watson (eds) *Post-War British Politics in Perspective*, Cambridge: Polity Press.

McIlroy, J. (2000a) 'New Labour, new unions, new left', *Capital and Class*, 71, 11–45.

—— (2000b) 'The new politics of pressure: the Trades Union Congress and New Labour in government', *Industrial Relations Journal*, 31:1, 2–16.

—— (2000c) 'Lifelong learning: trade unions in search of a role' in J. Field and M. Leicester (eds) *Lifelong Learning: Education Across the Lifespan*, London: Routledge.

—— (2008) 'Ten years of New Labour: workplace learning, social partnership and union revitalization in Britain', *British Journal of Industrial Relations*, 46:2, 283–313.

McKnight, A. (2005) 'Employment: tackling poverty through work for those who can', in J. Hills and K. Stewart (eds) *A More Equal Society? New Labour, Poverty, Inequality and Exclusion*, Bristol: Policy Press.

Millward, N., Bryson, A. and Forth, J. (2000) *All Change at Work? British Employment Relations 1980–1998 As Portrayed by the Workplace Industrial Relations Survey Series*, London: Routledge.

Monbiot, G. (2000) *Captive State: The Corporate Takeover of Britain*, London: Macmillan.

Muller-Jentsch, W. (1985) 'Trade unions as intermediary organizations', *Economic and Industrial Democracy*, 6:1, 3–33.

New Earnings Survey / Annual Survey of Hours and Earnings (NES/ASHE) (1997–2007) *Annual Reports*, London: ONS.

New Policy Institute (2004) *Why Worry Any More About Low Pay?* London: NPI.

Nolan, P. (1992) 'Trade unions and productivity: issues, evidence and prospects', *Employee Relations*, 14:6, 3–19.

Nolan, P. and O'Donnell, K. (2003) 'Industrial relations, HRM and performance', in P. Edwards (ed.) *Industrial Relations: Theory and Practice in Britain*, 2nd edition, Oxford: Blackwell.

Novitz, T. (2002) 'A revised role for trade unions as designed by New Labour: the representation pyramid and "partnership"', *Journal of Law and Society*, 29:3, 487–509.

Office of National Statistics (ONS) (2007a) *Public Sector Finances: April 2007*, London: ONS.

—— (2007b) *Social Trends, 37*, London: ONS.

Ong, A. (2006) *Neoliberalism as Exception: Mutations in Citizenship and Sovereignty*, Durham, NC: Duke University Press.

Organization for Economic Cooperation and Development (OECD) (2005) *Economic Survey of the United Kingdom*, Paris: OECD.

Palmer, G., Macinnes, T. and Kenway, P. (2006) *Monitoring Poverty and Social Exclusion 2006*, York: Joseph Rowntree Foundation.

Panitch, L. and Gindin, S. (2005) 'Superintending global capitalism', *New Left Review*, II: xxxv, 101–23.

Parl. Debs (2001) House of Lords, vol. 375, col. 384, 27 November.

Paz Fuchs, A. (2008) *Welfare to Work: Conditional Rights in Social Policy*, Oxford: Oxford University Press.

Peck, J. and Theodore, N. (2007) 'Variegated capitalism', *Progress in Human Geography*, 31:6, 731–72.

Peston, R. (2008) *Who Runs Britain? How the Super-Rich Are Changing Our Lives*, London: Hodder and Stoughton.

Piatt, W. (2003) 'Social mobility', *New Economy*, 10:4, 187–8.

Pollock, A. and Price, D. (2004) *Public Risk for Private Gain: The Public Audit Implications of Risk Transfer and Private Finance*, London: Unison.

Reich, R. (1991) *The Way of Nations*, New York: Alfred Knopf.

Rentoul, J. (1997) *Tony Blair*, London: Warner Books.

Riddell, P. (2005) *The Unfulfilled Prime Minister: Tony Blair's Quest for a Legacy*, London: Politico's.

Salvati, M. (2001) 'Prolegomena to the third way debate', in S. White (ed.) *New Labour: The Progressive Future?* Basingstoke: Palgrave.

Sawyer, M. (2007) 'Fiscal policy under New Labour', *Cambridge Journal of Economics*, 31:6, 885–99.

Sefton, T. (2003) 'What we want from the welfare state', in A. Park, J. Curtice, K. Thomson, L. Jarvis and C. Bromley (eds) *British Social Attitudes: The 20th Report*, London: Sage.

Simpson, B. (2004) 'The national minimum wage five years on: reflections on some general issues', *Industrial Law Journal*, 33:1, 22–41.

Stevenson, W. (ed.) (2006) *Gordon Brown: Speeches, 1997–2006*, London: Bloomsbury.

Stewart, K. (2007) 'Equality and social justice', in A. Seldon (ed.) *Blair's Britain 1997–2007*, Cambridge: Cambridge University Press.

Stuart, M., Charlwood, A., Martinez Lucio, M. and Wallis, E. (2006) *Union Modernisation Fund: Interim Evaluation of the First Round*, London: DTI.

Taylor, R. (2001) 'Employment relations policy', in A. Seldon (ed.) *The Blair Effect: The Blair Government 1997–2001*, London: Little, Brown.

Terry, M. and Smith, J. (2003) *Evaluation of the Partnership at Work Fund*, London: DTI.

Toye, R. (2004) '"The smallest party in history?" New Labour in historical perspective', *Labour History Review*, 69:1, 83–103.

Toynbee, P. (2008) 'This minister for fat cats is stuck in a Blairite time warp', *Guardian*, 11 March.

TUC (2005) *General Council Report*, London: TUC.

—— (2006) *General Council Report*, London: TUC.

—— (2008a) *The Missing Billions*, London: TUC.

—— (2008b) *Closing the Gender Pay Gap: An Update Report for TUC Women's Conference 2008*, London: TUC.

Undy, R. (1999) 'Annual review article: New Labour's "industrial relations settlement": the third way?', *British Journal of Industrial Relations*, 37:1, 315–36.

United Nations Development Programme (2008) <http://www.undp.org> (accessed 3 July 2008).

White, S. (2001) *New Labour: The Progressive Future?* Basingstoke: Palgrave.

Wilkinson, F. (2007) 'Neoliberalism and New Labour policy: economic performance, historical comparisons and future prospects', *Cambridge Journal of Economics*, 31:6, 817–43.

Williams, P. (2005) *British Foreign Policy under New Labour 1997–2005*, Basingstoke: Palgrave.

Willman, P. (2005) 'Circling the wagons: endogeneity in union decline', in S. Fernie and D. Metcalf (eds) *Trade Unions: Resurgence or Demise?* London: Routledge.

York Consulting (2006) *Evaluation of the Union Learning Fund, 2001–2005*, Nottingham: DfES.

# 3 An anatomy of British trade unionism since 1997

## Strategies for revitalization

*John McIlroy and Gary Daniels*

By 1997 British trade unionists had endured 17 years of sustained, historically unprecedented decline. The major damage in terms of membership loss was inflicted during the recessions of the early 1980s and 1990s: the unfavourable trend continued throughout the Conservative era. The last major reverse for the unions had occurred six decades earlier, in the dozen years between 1921 and 1933; but thereafter recovery commenced. In the early 1990s decline was accelerating ten years after it began; and unlike in the 1920s there were no years of growth (Bain and Price 1983; McIlroy 1995: 385–8).

Aggregate union membership slumped from 12.6 million in 1979 to less than eight million in 1996 and the proportion of trade unionists in the labour force dropped from more than 50 per cent to around 30 per cent. The TUC boasted more than 12 million affiliated members in 1979; less than 7 million in 1997 (Waddington 2000). Trade unionism was shrinking – even where unions were recognized. It was becoming a predominantly public sector phenomenon and its reach was increasingly skewed towards older, educated, professional workers. Collective bargaining coverage declined from 70 per cent of all employees in the mid-1980s to 54 per cent in 1990 and to 40 per cent by 1998. By 1998, 82 per cent of public sector employees were covered by collective bargaining but only 46 per cent in the traditional union heartlands of private manufacturing and 21 per cent in private services (Millward *et al.* 2000: 197). Only a little over 40 per cent of workplaces with 25 or more employees had recognized unions while in a quarter of workplaces in which unions were recognized there was no union representative (Cully *et al.* 1999: 96). The influence of workplace representatives over pay and conditions had diminished. There was a fall in the wage differential trade unionists had enjoyed over non-unionists in the past and in bargaining strength in the workplace (Stewart 1995). Management attitudes towards unions had hardened. Management control over the labour process from recruitment to pace of work had been restored (Gallie *et al.* 1998: 107) while managers increasingly bypassed recognized unions and preferred to deal directly with employees (Cully *et al.* 1999: 88).

More optimistic accounts attributed continuing 'significant influence over workplace industrial relations' to unions (Bryson 1999: 87). Sober assessment of the evidence favoured the view that, although there were exceptions, the overall picture displayed generalized debilitation in the workplace in comparison with the recent past. Even where unions continued to function as before they were often 'hollow shells', sidelined over key issues or serving enterprise purposes, their strength drained by restructured, insecure labour markets and constrained by the hostile legal environment (Hyman 1997). Unions faced economic attrition, political exclusion and loss of social legitimacy (McIlroy 1995: 385–400). In the workplace 'their organisations ha[d] been weakened and marginalised' (Terry 1995: 217). By 1997, militancy was in what was often seen as terminal retreat: the number of strikes and days lost through strikes reached their lowest point in the twentieth century (McIlroy 2000a: 14). The decline of the unions was unarguable. It was the product of the turn of the British state towards neoliberal economics and politics. It was driven by a complex of factors, by the maturing anti-collectivist state; hostile employment legislation; hardening attitudes among employers; unfavourable changes in the structure of employment and the composition of the labour force; as well as the belated, confused responses of the unions themselves (Metcalf 1991).

The election of New Labour was seen as heralding restoration of the fortunes of trade unions and presaging union revitalization. This was expressed in broad commonsensical terms:

> 'revitalisation' would entail halting and then reversing the decline in membership, heightened political influence, greater union effectiveness within the workplace, and a growing recognition on the part of workers and employers that unions were an important stakeholder in the economy and were here to stay.
>
> (Bryson 2007: 184)

This chapter explores some of the ways unions have tried to reverse decline in the employment field and considers how successful they have been since 1997. The first section scrutinizes the overarching strategy of partnership – organizing which the unions have placed at the heart of efforts at revitalization – and assesses its strengths and weaknesses. The second part of the chapter surveys the state of trade unionism after a decade of New Labour and discusses change and continuity since 1997.

## Trade union strategy

Since 1997 union strategy has contained two interrelated strands. Politically, the TUC has sought to pursue union revitalization through creative re-engagement with the state (see McIlroy, chapter 5, this volume). Industrially, it has attempted to reconnect with employers and facilitate union revitalization by rebuilding membership and organization. In the latter sphere two components were linked together under the rubric 'New Unionism' – intended to complement and benefit from 'New Labour' – partnership and organizing. A former TUC official recalled that '"organizing" and "partnership" were presented by the TUC leadership as two sides of the same coin' (Coats 2005: 22–3). This was politically adroit: those who advocated revitalization via accommodative 'modernized' trade unionism could flash the partnership side of the coin; those who embraced traditional adversarialism as the solution could flip it. TUC staff could emphasize statements demanding they 'promote organizing as the top priority' (TUC 1998a: 55). Alternatively they could cite general secretary John Monks' insistence on partnership and mobilizing the employer: 'It's about improving performance, enhancing competitiveness. That's the New Unionism, but it's also what smart managers want to do' (Monks 1999).

Tensions between the conflictual and cooperative aspects of New Unionism were negotiated by somewhat arbitrary distinctions between 'bad employers', who needed the shock of aggression to shake them up and change their attitudes, and 'good employers', who simply needed enlightening about their own self-interest through the force of argument (TUC 1999a: 60). Tony Blair explained to TUC delegates at the start of his first term that organizing unions *were* partnership unions:

> It was an essential part of the trade union role to seek to expose the bad employer. However, most workers did not believe that their employer was a bad employer . . . most people were proud of the organizations that employed them . . . Tomorrow's unions would be organizing unions, committed to the agenda of skills, equal opportunities and partnership. He urged both unions and employers to apply the partnership approach more widely.
>
> (ibid.)

But what Blair termed 'the partnership approach' was different in key aspects from the TUC's conception of partnership (see McIlroy, chapter 2, this volume). This constituted a fundamental difficulty although one the government and, to a large extent, the unions were prepared to diplomatically gloss over. New Labour and the TUC spoke the same language; but they were talking about different things. A second problem was that, unlike Blair, critics characterized organizing and partnership as distinct and sometimes contradictory approaches to revitalization (Kelly 2004; Taylor and Bain 2003). Acknowledging tensions, others have posed a sequential relationship: adversarial organizing may precede and pave the way for collaboration and partnership (Heery 2002). We look at each strand of the strategy in turn.

*Partnership*

The TUC's goal was expressed as 'social partnership', its inspiration a stylized European model based on the European Union's (EU) social dialogue, national economic assessments, social pacts, worker participation in the enterprise and works councils. Its purpose was reassertion of the unions' social and political legitimacy and revival of a more muted consensual tripartism (McIlroy 1995: 313–48). The canvas was broad and the economy was central: 'national social partnership discussions should be held on how the social partners could work together to achieve the government's medium-term economic objectives. This would require discussions on investment, productivity, fair rewards for public sector workers, and also how to reconcile growth, high unemployment and low inflation' (TUC 1998a: 73; TUC 1998b). Discussion would open the door to developing networks of dual or tripartite bodies on pay, productivity and training at regional and national level. This approach was based on the benign conception that unions provided a stimulus to increased competitivity and flexibility, goading management into efficiency. Channelling employee voice, mobilizing creativity and commitment, unions 'shocked' employers into proficiency in building the high-productivity, high-remuneration enterprise (Deakin and Wilkinson 1994; Nolan and O'Donnell 2003: 491–2).

In the context of attention to EU directives intended to transplant works councils to Britain (see for example, TUC 1998a: 92–5), social partnership at national level was perceived as part of a seamless web: 'partnership in the workplace' constituted one component. Located in the belief that partnership 'can both improve business performance in the private sector and greater efficiency in the public sector', the purpose was to position unions as 'organizations that can work with employers and government to solve some of the country's most difficult problems' (TUC 1998a: 74). In distinction to conceptions of partnership as something that could develop with or without unions, the TUC insisted that trade unionism was indispensable to 'genuine partnership' in the workplace. 'Genuine partnership' entailed shared commitment to the success of the enterprise but reciprocal recognition of the role of unions within it. Union commitment to job flexibility was exchanged for employer commitment to employment security. 'Real partnership' required enrichment of the quality of working life and a qualitative extension of training; willingness of employers to involve unions in future strategy; and joint understanding that partnership can deliver mutual gains and improvements for all parties (TUC 1999a: 59–60).

Union leaders were enthusiastic:

A new social phenomenon is sweeping throughout (*sic*) our society. Partnership is its name and cooperation is its game. Everyone is at it . . . the model of social partnership, so common and natural in continental

Europe is now being promoted by the Government and attracting the interest of employers.

(TUC 1999b: 58)

The TUC pressed the idea of a national framework of social partnership on the Prime Minister and Chancellor of the Exchequer (TUC 1998a: 73). It drew little response. There were early examples of social partnership bodies, loosely defined – the Low Pay Commission and the Skills Alliance. They were ad hoc and isolated. New Labour's neoliberal economic policy and vision of the limited utility of unions to the state (McIlroy, chapters 1 and 2, this volume) excluded any corporatist ethos and tripartite institutions on the model of the National Economic Development Council or the Manpower Services Commission as well as devolution of significant powers to capital and labour (McIlroy 2000b). State rejection of social partnership was intimately related to employer antagonism towards it. Addressing a TUC conference, Adair Turner, Director-General of the CBI, 'expressed real scepticism about social partnership at either national or European level. He was opposed to any widening of the social dialogue or major new social policy initiatives in the EU based on agreements between social partners' (TUC 1999a: 60).

So was New Labour. The government rejected successive appeals from the TUC to implement the 1997 party conference resolutions

which pledged the Party to helping and supporting the social partners at national, cross-sectoral and sectoral level, by providing the necessary political lead, technical support and legal back-up to promote the social partnership / social process.

(TUC 1999b: 25)

Whether in the conditions of the twenty-first century a 'competitive corporatist' strategy, centred on social partnership, pacts between unions and employers and formal 'national productivity coalitions' would have improved the condition of trade unionism we cannot know. Acknowledging that such an approach might involve exchanging wage restraint and cutting taxes for enhanced union legitimacy and membership, some saw it as preferable to 'unilateral neoliberalism' (Rhodes 1998: 52). The reality was that, even in the EU, moves to the single market and single currency went hand-in-hand with tighter fiscal policy, privatization and shifts towards neoliberalism. The extent to which the EU could act as a solidaristic shield for embattled national trade unionisms was diminishing (Huffschmid 2005). Moreover, New Labour was simultaneously critical and reluctant about EU directives which might have extended partnership in the workplace *and* hostile towards any significant support for EU-style dialogue between capital and labour which in other countries acted as a substitute for the legal regulation New Labour feared. Things never got much further than the Low Pay Commission or the ad hoc bipartite negotiations over the statutory recognition procedure.

The TUC kept up the struggle for social partnership. But it tended to emphasize a more amorphous partnership approach which, nevertheless, remained more coherent than government conceptions.

The content of that approach was increasingly the more specific and restricted 'partnership at work'. Employer support for workplace trade unionism in a period of decline could secure recognition and resources, from deduction of subscriptions at source (check off) to paid time off and facilities for union representatives. Social partnership has often been the product of union strength or threat. The contemporary impetus to workplace partnership stemmed from union weakness. The partnership transaction exchanges organizational maintenance and restricted influence for a role in motivating and managing members to meet employer objectives in the hope of future union recovery (Ackers and Payne 1998; Tailby and Winchester 2000). It depends on a degree of management commitment to human resource strategies which designate unions as vehicles for mobilizing human capital in the interests of the enterprise. Most agreements are management-driven (Oxenbridge and Brown 2004; Kelly 2004).

The response from organized labour's projected partner was again largely elusive or negative. The CBI accepted partnership at work subject to the devastating qualification that unions were unnecessary to it: '[Adair Turner] endorsed the view, which the General Council explicitly reject, that partnership can be established in the absence of recognised independent trade unions' (TUC 1999a: 60). Glossing over such fundamental difficulties, Blair was prepared to verbally endorse the TUC approach to workplace partnership (ibid.). But practical support from the government was restricted. It remained at arm's length and largely comprised the Partnership at Work Fund, the Union Learning Fund (ULF) and later the Union Modernisation Fund (UMF) to promote specific initiatives, combined with exhortations to cooperation. The root of the problem was that the government supported 'partnership' in the vague sense of cooperative employment relations and employers and employees 'working together'. Beyond the statutory recognition procedure and diluted EU directives they were not prepared to proceed to foster more formalized union-based versions of partnerships (see McIlroy, chapter 2, this volume).

Nothing daunted, energetically pursuing state funds to compensate for more direct and vigorous state support, offset depleted membership and assuage financial pressures, the TUC pressed ahead. Training in partnership was introduced into its educational programmes (TUC 1999a: 62). The TUC Partnership Institute was launched in 2001 with an advisory board of general secretaries, academics, the head of the Performance Directorate at the Cabinet Office and senior managers from Tesco and Terra Firma Capital Partners. Its canvas was workplace industrial relations not national politics; the enterprise not the economy. It aimed 'to create a sea change in British workplaces by establishing partnership as the modern and successful approach to industrial relations' (TUC 2002a).

The Institute was subsequently credited by the TUC with 'remarkable successes' and with attracting 'the wholehearted support of the Government . . . its success was recognised by the Prime Minister' (TUC 2002b: 4). It offered consultancy, training and research to management and unions to create better-quality jobs, greater investment in skills and enhanced flexibility and it secured DTI funding for major projects (TUC 2004a: 68). After 2002 and John Monks' retirement as general secretary the 'partnership at work' section, which had replaced the earlier 'building social partnership' section in the general council's annual report, vanished without trace. The Institute was hived off in 2005. The term 'partnership' does not appear in the index to the 2006 or 2007 general council reports.

Social partnership shrank into workplace partnership. That in turn has dwindled into partnership agreements dependent on bargaining. Both the critics and the critically supportive have concluded that there is a wide variation between partnership agreements ranging from the token to the meaningful; that the number of such agreements meeting TUC criteria are small; that there is no great management enthusiasm for meaningful partnership agreements; and that there is little evidence that such agreements either stimulate union growth or promote employment security. They may provide a mechanism for staving off derecognition of unions; but they may also domesticate the workforce, incorporate workplace representatives and divide unions. Well-publicized success stories such as Tesco or Blue Circle constitute the exception rather than the rule (Danford *et al.* 2003, and see Kelly 2004; Terry 2004; Upchurch, chapter 7, this volume).

Nonetheless, such agreements continue to be signed. Unions continue to seek state finance for 'partnership projects': The Partnership at Work fund was established in 1999 and phased out five years later, having disbursed £12.5 million on employer and union projects (http://www.berr.gov.uk/employment/trade-union-rights/partnership). The public sector and privatized utilities figured strongly in successful bids but there was a spread across industry while situations where formal partnerships were already developing were strongly represented. Unions played a noteworthy role in disseminating information about the fund, particularly Unison, MSF and perhaps surprisingly the RMT (Terry and Smith 2003: 32–3). The project was not without its difficulties:

> There was a problem for many union members and their representatives in supporting partnership approaches and practice. The evidence suggested that whilst senior union officers were able to build strong constructive relationships with senior executives and senior HR managers based on trust, officers at local levels experienced many difficulties in committing both their members and themselves to mechanisms which lead to a loss of independence. The evidence suggested that many rank-and-file members of trade unions remained uncertain and sceptical of activities which involved their members 'getting into bed'

with management, as some saw it, and thus unable to independently represent their interests.

(Terry and Smith 2003: 96–7)

Partnership was often shallow. Developed by managerial and union elites, its resonance with the rank-and-file was more limited and fundamental questions were raised about its impact on the functions of unions. It was pertinent to New Labour's insistence that partnership should replace conflict, that researchers concluded that moves towards partnership 'were no guarantee of conflict free patterns of industrial relations' (ibid.: 12). At least one bid for cash from the Partnership at Work Fund was delayed by a strike (ibid.: 95).

The Partnership Fund was replaced by the UMF (http://www.berr.gov.uk/employment/trade-union-rights/modernisation/page16097.html). In 2005–6 there were 49 applications to the UMF, of which 32 were approved after scrutiny by a committee of civil servants, four senior union officials, a senior company director and two academics – corporatism still lingers in this area. Unions had to provide matching funding for modernization projects. Almost three-quarters of unions with more than 100,000 members have applied to the UMF including Amicus-TGWU, the GMB, USDAW, CWU, RMT and the TUC itself. Applications centred on 'diversity issues or understanding modern business practices and working with employers as partners appeared to have been most successful' (Stuart *et al.* 2006: 7). In the absence of any rigorous evaluation of its impact it remains difficult to assess its effect on union goals, philosophy and practice. That it engages unions in the process of bidding for state subsidy to reform unions as state ancillaries in improving labour market policy and thus legitimizes that purpose and integrates it in union activity is not without significance. But there may be a gap between government intentions to neoliberalize unions and less clear-cut outcomes.

The ULF, now administered by the TUC, with an annual budget of over £10 million, is currently more important in developing what the government sees as the unions' 'partnership role' in lubricating and substituting for employers' failure to invest in human resource development. The new system of union learning representatives (ULRs) is perceived as an important increment not only to human resource management but to union activism in the workplace. Hard evidence of significant success is difficult to come by. But if ULRs are augmenting trade unionism, as well as stimulating training, it is arguable that the trade unionism they are augmenting essentially plays a subordinate role in informal productivity coalitions as a change-agent generating state-sponsored supply-side reforms. In employment relations there is always an opportunity cost. Substituting for management prerogatives in delivering workplace learning may divert unions from challenging management prerogative in other areas (see McIlroy and Croucher, chapter 9, this volume).

Partnership is not dead (see Upchurch, chapter 7, this volume). As a major strand in a national strategy for revitalization which predicated collaborative industrial politics from Whitehall to the workplace in order to galvanize competitivity while restoring union fortunes in the process, it has proved unsuccessful. Social partnership has been marginalized because it has been deemed imprudent in the context of New Labour's neoliberalism. In practice it is vestigial. At the start of the New Labour era surveys of IPA members, who might have been seen as advocates and pioneers, recorded that 62 per cent of respondents were making low or moderate progress towards partnership and only 28 per cent high progress. Around 4 per cent disagreed with the view that unions should have a strong role in partnership (Guest and Peccei 1998). Later surveys question qualitative progress and conclude that partnership agreements 'seem unlikely to figure as a major component of any revitalization of the union movement' (Kelly 2004: 290). For hard-headed, economic reasons, managers are antipathetic to trade unionism; thus they are resistant to partnership which involves unions (Bryson *et al.* 2004; Gospel 2005). The main hope of transforming a pragmatic patchwork of agreements into something more significant and strategic relies on EU directives prompting works council legislation and here scepticism is in order (Terry 2004). New Labour's unwillingness to provide institutional underpinning for partnership at work was embodied in its 2004 Information and Consultation Regulations. Instead of fostering European-style works councils, the government opted for weaker 'procedures' which uncouple union and employee representation (Ewing and Truter 2003; Davies and Kilpatrick 2004).

Associated with the imaginative and forceful advocacy of John Monks, partnership has, with good reason, been downgraded in revitalization strategy. Former TUC staff invoke the initial lack of state support and the consequent emergence of union leaders critical of the limited reality of partnership (Coats 2005: 22–3). TUC officials have responded to changes in the unions. Organizing has gradually taken precedence (ibid.; interviews with activists 2007).

### *Organizing*

The second aspect of TUC strategy required unions to

> ... promote organizing as the top priority and build an organizing culture ... boost investment of resources – people and money – into organizing and strengthen lay organisation ... strengthen their existing bases and break into new jobs and industries and win recognition rights ... sharpen unions' appeal to 'new' workers, including women, youth and those at the rough end of the labour market.
>
> (TUC 1997: 39)

What was new was that the TUC's New Unionism Task Group (fused in 2003 with the Representation at Work Task Group) was handed the brief of intervening to stimulate root-and-branch reconstruction of affiliates' recruitment methods (O'Grady and Nowak 2004: 153). The new approach drew comprehensively on lessons from the Australian Council of Trade Unions' 'Organizing Works' programme and the American AFL-CIO's Organizing Institute. It was based on the belief supported by recent research that workers joined unions to secure protection against employers, not to secure personalized financial or legal benefits (Waddington and Whitston 1997; Waddington and Kerr 2000). Further, the Task Group accepted that if decline was to be reversed, traditional recruitment of members and their integration into debilitated organizations with full-time officials or weak workplace representatives servicing members was insufficient. Qualitative recruitment and retention and meaningful union resurgence necessitated the building or rebuilding of self-sustaining workplace organization, the creation of new activists and the development of a responsive, participating membership (Heery *et al.* 2000).

In this perspective, the development of new structures in the workplace necessitates the transformation of unions at all levels. In a situation of financial stringency, with expenditure exceeding subscription income in many unions, the demand for greater investment in organizing often requires transfer of resources and restructuring of the role of union officers from servicing existing members to organizing and inspiring new ones. This, in its turn, necessitates cultural change; it demands building organizing into all union activities, whether the official's role is remoulded or whether organizing becomes a dedicated function. In the longer term, organizing, at least on an optimistic view, should generate its own resources by bringing in new members and training new representatives. In the short term scarcity requires reallocation of resources. Finally, unions have to cultivate the optimal mix between devoting resources towards making inroads into 'union-free' and 'union-weak' employment territories and 'infill' operations in established areas. Unions have to develop a portfolio of organizing ventures. They have to transcend market-share trade unionism and the temptation of organizing where it is easiest on the one hand; and campaigning exclusively where they possess a diminished presence on the other (TUC 1998a: 54–6).

American influence from the AFL-CIO and committed academics (Bronfenbrenner *et al.* 1998) motivated a more strategic approach. The stress was on developing change through developing cadres. Created in 1997, the TUC Organizing Academy recruited young people – half were women and more than half under 30 – from a range of unions, although some possessed little union experience, to lead campaigns. By 2004 almost 200 organizers had completed a year-long programme (TUC 2004a: 8). The Academy acted as a creator of change and a conduit and amplifier for a new adversarial organizing ethos and new aggressive campaigning ideas (see Daniels, chapter 8, this volume).

An organizing unit in Congress House considerably enhanced the professionalization of campaigns. It stressed targeting strategically important workplaces. It emphasized the necessity for researching companies and developing campaign plans which included targets, benchmarks and performance measures. There was a need to use the media, educate activists and develop representative organizing committees. One-to-one contact with potential members on the argument 'like-recruits-like' was indispensable, as was anticipation of employer responses (TUC 2005a, 2007a). Equipped with awareness of the company and its culture the organizers' task was to detect and develop discontent, amplify feelings of injustice, attribute problems to management and mobilize workers in full knowledge of the potential for employer counter-mobilization (Kelly and Badigannavar 2004).

The TUC can educate and proselytize: in the end affiliated unions have to organize. By 2005 a degree of progress appeared to have been made:

> Organizing is key, organizing built on the simple truth that unless you build strong self-confident, self-sustaining workplace organisation, you do not win . . . We have started by seeking to organize the workplaces where we have 800,000 members, through our 100 per cent campaign, making sure every worker is in the union . . . Next we need to organize unorganized workplaces always applying those organizing principles of helping workers to help themselves (TGWU) . . . Dozens of lay representatives have now spent six months each on secondment to the union – in fact 54 in the last three years – undergoing extensive training . . . we have a range of agreements with employers to second lay representatives, agreements to stand them down from their usual duties, to resource key organizing initiatives, all in addition to the work and resources we dedicate through our full-time people (USDAW) . . . we have increased the number of our branch organizers from 150 to 470 . . . We have trained all our lay organizers, developed with the TUC a strategic training for lead lay organizers, issued regular organizing newsletters, we have more full-time organizers, to find, train and support lay activists – all full-time organizers trained by the TUC Organizing Academy. We built organizing into our trade union education. We have held organizing conferences in every part of our regions and on a national basis as well. We have produced more campaigning literature; we have increased the number of activists in our union to around 8,000 (PCS).
>
> (TUC 2005b: 47–8)

Enumeration of such self-ascribed achievements has to be contextualized. The 2004 Workplace Employment Relations Survey observed in relation to union investment in organizing: 'In view of these efforts it is noteworthy that the vast majority of non-members (83 per cent) had never been asked to join a union or staff association at their workplace' (Kersley *et al.* 2006: 115–16). That sentence takes some pondering and considerable digesting in the light of the emphasis on organizing since 1997. So does the comment of TGWU organizing chief Jack Dromey, made nine years after the drive towards an organizing culture rooted in the workplace was launched: '[if] you do not win in the workplace you do not grow. Our hard-pressed officers are run ragged servicing a fragmented and declining membership' (TUC 2005b: 46).

Recent research highlights the continuing relevance of a variety of barriers to successful organizing within unions. They range from lack of resources for organizing staff to lack of support from union leaders, full-time officers and workplace activists (Heery and Simms 2008). Activists expressed the view that partnership sat uneasily with organizing and represented a distraction from it. Others affirmed that serious investment in organizing is lacking; if this *is* possible, even though finance is tight, organizing can still provide a host of problems from the dissatisfaction of existing members to the discontents of over-worked officers (interviews with activists, 2007). The problem is not simply one of enlightening, educating and changing. Existing members require representation. Servicing members is an inevitable aspect of trade unionism. Union resources are under pressure. Some members are under-represented and others do not take kindly to paying officers' salaries in return for injunctions to help themselves. Some do not benefit directly from collective bargaining. Problems are real, sometimes deep-seated and arguably intractable (Willman 2005).

Despite the narrative of achievement, recent reports from the TGWU suggest that serious reorientation and organization on the basis outlined above only commenced in 2003 after the union had extricated itself from unsuccessful engagement with partnership (Graham 2006). Other unions have concluded that the costs of a full-scale organizing strategy outweigh its advantages (BECTU 2003). Today, as at the start of the New Labour era, 'commitment to organizing still jostles uncomfortably with all the other demands on union efforts and resources' (TUC 1999b: 7). There can be no doubt, however, that, as one TUC official put it, 'the movement is moving in the right direction, although there is no room for complacency . . . if the TUC would not have launched its initiative, its affiliates would not have invested in organizing to anything like what they have done over the last ten years' (interviews with activists, 2007). That much remains to be done is recognized by the policy of increasing TUC and union resources devoted to organizing to 5 per cent and eventually 10 per cent of income (TUC 2007b: 19).

It has been argued that with the decline of workplace organization and the resources it generated, 'unions are paying for a higher percentage of total organizing activity than in the past' (Willman and Bryson 2006: 10). At some stage investment has to yield 'profits' in terms of more members, more workplace activists, and more subscriptions, if unions are to begin to achieve a financial turnaround. Significant investment in organizing which fails to yield substantial tangible results is likely to be short-term. Further fundamental questions centre on agency and environment. The TUC and the leadership of individual unions can and should play a role in organizing strategies. Yet history suggests that an essential precondition is, to a degree, autonomous and organic resurgence in the workplace in response to conditions in the enterprise. Such a movement from below may be developed, strengthened and channelled: it is questionable whether it can be created. Commentators note the problem of 'managed activism' inherent in organizing models (Heery 2002). But at the moment, leaving aside specific areas such as the railways and Royal Mail (see Lyddon, chapter 10, this volume), a militant rank-and-file of any weight requiring management by union officers shows little sign of taking the stage. Yet ultimately, whatever necessary strategy, sustenance and stimulation comes from above, it is grassroots workers who will be the decisive agents of change.

A healthy aspect of organizing is the primary postulate that organizers can make a difference, contribute to galvanizing non-members and facilitate workplace activism. But organizing can never be uncoupled from the attitudes of non-members to joining unions. When asked in one survey whether unions make a difference to what it is like at work, less than half of union members, only a third of employees who had never been trade unionists and little more than 25 per cent of former members said 'yes' (Cully *et al.* 1999: 212; and see Bryson 2007). Millward and his colleagues reported a decline in the attachment of workers to trade unionism (Millward *et al.* 2000: 92 and see Pencavel 2003). Charlwood (2002) and Kelly (1998: 48–9) locate perceptions of unions as deliverers of workplace change as the key to positive attitudes to joining. The central question for potential recruits is: how effective are unions likely to be? An inevitable problem is that we don't know the answer until we and others join and organize. There may be some distance between abstract responses to survey questions and real-life decisions which have real-life consequences. Given the current balance of power in many – but by no means all – workplaces, there may be a tendency on the part of prospective members to make negative assessments. It is transparent and central to strategy that in many situations employee reluctance to join unions remains an important barrier to successful organizing. Moreover, there is evidence that employee discontent, the grist of mobilization, peaked in the 1990s and has subsequently declined (Kelly 2005b: 73).

The role of employers as agents in the partnership strategy may minimize these difficulties. But advocates of partnership are casting managers as major actors in union revitalization when the great bulk of evidence suggests that managers possess little appetite for either union recognition or joint regulation. Surveying the last 25 years, researchers have concluded: 'something has made union organisation, particularly union-only voice, much less attractive to employers over this period' (Bryson *et al.* 2004: 138). Partnership shares with organizing the pivotal problem that a significant majority of managers are, at best, indifferent or, at worst, hostile to unions; it does not avoid it (Gall 2004; Heery and Simms 2008). And some perceive a lack of fit between partnership and organizing with the former's weaknesses contaminating the latter, arresting its progress and thus handicapping revitalization (McIlroy 2000a). There are significant tensions between the two approaches (Heery 2002). The ethos of independence, adversarialism, movement and empowerment that surrounds organizing contradicts, to some degree at least, the imperatives of collaboration, managing members and delivering flexibility and productivity to employers inherent in partnership. Organizing poses mobilization and grassroots democracy; partnership poses incorporation, the positioning of the union closer to management and potential withering of the sinews of adversarial mobilization. Both, organizing and partnership, may, in favourable circumstances, develop their own dynamic.

Arguments that if sequenced they may prove compatible – successful organizing paves the way for successful partnership – may be hard to realize in practice. If – and it is a big 'if' – organizing has delivered on its promise of mobilization and employee empowerment then a transition to partnership may be awkward to manage; just as failed partnership may be difficult to redeem by organizing, if the union is compromised as an independent agency and its membership disillusioned. Historically, British trade unionism developed differentially, and pragmatically, with distinctive admixtures of moderation and militancy, cooperation and conflict, adversarialism and 'partnership', emerging in different contexts. To yoke the two together in a coordinated national strategy for revitalization is a different matter and a greater challenge.

Fundamentally, as reflected in its downgrading by the TUC, major unions have concluded that as a national narrative for regeneration, partnership fails to compel. The TGWU has decided that partnership 'is built on incorrect assumptions and only successful if used to undermine effective union organisation' (Graham 2006: 3). Partnership is still pursued by other unions. And question marks remain as to the success of whatever strategic ensemble is employed in the current environment unions confront. If the macro-context since 1997, at least in terms of the business cycle, inflation and employment levels, has had benign aspects, constraints still exist and they include the state and its orientation towards powerful trade unionism (see McIlroy, chapters 2 and 5, this volume). The role of the state in legitimizing and legislating for trade unionism since 1997 still leaves much to be desired – at least if we want strong unions. The problem is encapsulated in the limitations of the recognition procedure in the 1999 Employment Relations Act (see Smith and Morton, chapter 6, this volume).

David Metcalf provides a compelling snapshot of the immense difficulties unions have confronted over the last decade. They have had to devote resources to representing 5–6 million members whose pay is set by collective bargaining, while attempting inroads into the 3 million workers covered by collective bargaining who are not members. Simultaneously they have had to try to recruit around 3 million workers in non-union industries where unions have some base. And they have had to endeavour to enrol non-members among the 14 million workers in sectors where trade unionism is rare (Metcalf 2001, 2005). Mantras about empowerment and self-organization are no substitute for fruitful strategy. Turning things around in significant fashion is the test of revitalization. We turn next to examine how successful unions have been in doing this.

## Trade unionism under New Labour

The vitality of British trade unionism has typically been judged by reference to a range of factors. These have included aggregate union membership; union density – the proportion of the labour force who are union members; recognition of unions by employers; collective bargaining coverage; the movement of wages; strike statistics; and the state of union organization, particularly in the workplace. There is disagreement about the degree to which some of these factors capture the condition of trade unionism and particularly the ever-elusive issue of union power. Overall, they provide some understanding of its comparative strength at a particular time (Kelly 1998: 9–18). This section examines each in turn.

### *Membership and density 1997–2006*

As table 3.1 demonstrates, both the aggregate membership and the membership of TUC affiliated unions continued to decline under New Labour. Overall membership now stands at 7.6 million and TUC membership at 6.4 million. Unions can take encouragement from the fact that total membership increased in the three years, 1998 to 2000, albeit by small, and in the case of the growth in 2000, tiny percentage increases. That this was not simply a once-and-for-all effect associated with New Labour's early pro-union reforms is suggested by the increase in membership recorded in 2006 – the largest since 1979. In contrast, changes in TUC membership are associated with an impending statutory recognition procedure effect in the early years and the sole increase of any significance, in 1999, was related to a new affiliation, although minor progress occurred in 2005 and 2006.[1]

The arrest of the downward escalation of membership which continued throughout the Conservative years is of importance both practically and in

*Table 3.1*  UK trade union membership 1997–2006

|      | *Overall Membership* | *% Change* | *TUC Membership* | *% Change* |
|------|------------|---------|------------|---------|
| 1997 | 7,801,315  |         | 6,756,544  |         |
| 1998 | 7,851,904  | 0.65    | 6,638,986  | −1.74   |
| 1999 | 7,897,519  | 0.58    | 6,749,481  | 1.66    |
| 2000 | 7,898,293  | 0.01    | 6,745,907  | −0.05   |
| 2001 | 7,781,077  | −1.48   | 6,722,118  | −0.35   |
| 2002 | 7,752,381  | −0.37   | 6,685,353  | −0.55   |
| 2003 | 7,735,983  | −0.21   | 6,672,815  | −0.19   |
| 2004 | 7,559,062  | −2.29   | 6,423,694  | −3.73   |
| 2005 | 7,473,000  | −1.14   | 6,452,267  | 0.44    |
| 2006 | 7,602,842  | 1.74    | 6,463,159  | 0.17    |

*Source:* Certification Officer, *Annual Reports* (1997–2007) and TUC, *Report of Congress* (1997–2006)

terms of symbolism and morale. The best complexion that can be put on table 3.1 is that while decline has been stemmed, it has not been reversed. There is no real evidence here that revitalization is in train. To put things in a broader context, unions had 13.4 million members in 1979 and 9.8 million members 50 years ago.

Union density – a harder measure of growth and decline – gives us a firmer indication of union presence, reach and voice. The results of three different methods of estimating density, calculating union membership against employees, all those in employment and all those economically active, are reported in table 3.2 and table 3.3. In each case density has declined sequentially under New Labour with only an upward blip on the first measure in 2005 (see table 3.2) It has dropped from 31 per cent to 28.4 per cent, from 27.9 per cent to 25.8 per cent and from 27.5 per cent to 24.8 per cent on the different measures. On these estimations things have deteriorated under New Labour. If we use Bain and Price's figures, which calculate density as a percentage of the labour force, including those registered unemployed, as a reference point, the 2006 density figure of 24.8 per cent compares with 55.4 per cent in 1979, 45.2 per cent in 1948 and 30.5 per cent in 1938. Density is approaching its lowest level since the 22.6 per cent of 1933 – the product of the interwar depression and the defeat of the 1926 general strike (Bain and Price 1983: 4–6).

Density varies substantially by sector and industry. Table 3.4 confirms that the public sector constitutes the heartland of trade unionism and holds up both aggregate membership and density figures. Even here density has dropped from 61.3 per cent in 1997 to 58.8 per cent in 2006. Decline has again been continuous, with upward blips in 2000 and 2001. The public sector has seen job increases but it remains under pressure from privatization and deregulation. The figures for the private sector, the engine room of the British

*Table 3.2* Aggregate trade union density UK 1997–2006

| Year | Employees (%)[a] | In employment (%)[b] |
|------|------------------|----------------------|
| 1997 | 31.0 | 27.9 |
| 1998 | 30.1 | 27.2 |
| 1999 | 29.8 | 27.2 |
| 2000 | 29.7 | 27.2 |
| 2001 | 29.3 | 26.8 |
| 2002 | 29.2 | 26.6 |
| 2003 | 29.3 | 26.6 |
| 2004 | 28.8 | 26.0 |
| 2005 | 29.0 | 26.2 |
| 2006 | 28.4 | 25.8 |

*Source:* Grainger and Crowther (2007)

*Notes:*
a Wage and salary earners but excludes members of the armed forces.
b All employees and self-employed but excludes members of the armed forces, unpaid family workers and those on college-based schemes.

*Table 3.3* UK trade union density 1997–2006 (all economically active)

|  | *Economically Active (includes unemployed)[a]* | *Employment[a]* | *Unemployed[a]* | *Trade Union Membership[b]* | *Density[c] (%)* |
|---|---|---|---|---|---|
| 1997 | n/a | n/a | n/a | 7,801,315 | n/a |
| 1998 | 28,509,000 | 26,721,000 | 1,788,000 | 7,851,904 | 27.54 |
| 1999 | 28,833,000 | 27,090,000 | 1,743,000 | 7,897,519 | 27.39 |
| 2000 | 29,061,000 | 27,461,000 | 1,599,000 | 7,898,293 | 27.18 |
| 2001 | 29,167,000 | 27,694,000 | 1,472,000 | 7,781,077 | 26.68 |
| 2002 | 29,420,000 | 27,905,000 | 1,515,000 | 7,752,381 | 26.35 |
| 2003 | 29,655,000 | 28,192,000 | 1,464,000 | 7,735,983 | 26.09 |
| 2004 | 29,844,000 | 28,412,000 | 1,433,000 | 7,559,062 | 25.33 |
| 2005 | 30,126,000 | 28,693,000 | 1,433,000 | 7,473,000 | 24.81 |
| 2006 | 30,613,000 | 28,930,000 | 1,683,000 | 7,602,842 | 24.84 |

*Notes:*

a *Labour Market Trends*, December 2006

b Certification Officer, *Annual Reports* 1997–2007 (CO)

c Based on a simple calculation of the proportion of trade union members (CO) who are economically active, including the unemployed. We have used CO figures because unemployed trade union members are counted (unlike with the Labour Force Survey (LFS)) which provides a more accurate measurement.

*Table 3.4* UK trade union density by sector 1997–2006

|  | *Public (%)* | *Private (%)* |
|---|---|---|
| 1997 | 61.3 | 20.2 |
| 1998 | 61.0 | 19.5 |
| 1999 | 59.9 | 19.3 |
| 2000 | 60.2 | 18.8 |
| 2001 | 59.3 | 18.6 |
| 2002 | 59.7 | 18.2 |
| 2003 | 59.1 | 18.2 |
| 2004 | 58.8 | 17.2 |
| 2005 | 58.6 | 17.2 |
| 2006 | 58.8 | 16.6 |

*Source:* Grainger and Crowther (2007)

economy, are particularly worrying for trade unionists. Less than 17 per cent of the private sector labour force are union members and, again, the drop from 20.2 per cent since 1998 brutally underlines the absence of advance under New Labour.

Gloom is sustained when we look at density by industry. The relative strength of the public sector is again affirmed. Density in education has increased, but only slightly. It has declined in public administration and health and social services: the figures here remain high, 57.3 per cent and 43.4 per cent respectively. But these are sheltered areas where trade unionism *should* be growing, where it should be possible to develop in-fill organizing from a relatively protected base (table 3.5). The problems which continue to constrain trade unionism in the all-important private sector stand out. In hotels and restaurants, where unions have mounted series of organizing initiatives, density has dropped from 7.2 per cent to 5.6 per cent. It remains relatively high, although reduced, in transport and in declining industries such as manufacturing and mining which were traditional strongholds of trade unionism. Wholesale and retail, where unions have also been actively organizing, registered increased density in 2006 in comparison with 1997, although there has been a small drop in coverage since 2002. Privatized industries, such as electricity, gas and water, have long traditions of trade

*Table 3.5* UK Trade union density by industry 1997–2006 (%)[a]

| | 1997 | 1998 | 1999 | 2000 | 2001 | 2002 | 2003 | 2004 | 2005 | 2006 |
|---|---|---|---|---|---|---|---|---|---|---|
| Agriculture, forestry and fishing | 9.0 | 12.3 | 9.0 | 10.5 | 8.8 | 8.9 | 9.3 | * | 8.5 | 9.0 |
| Mining and quarrying | 32.1 | 29.9 | 36.2 | 31.8 | 25.3 | 23.6 | 28.0 | 27.3 | 21.2 | 23.5 |
| Manufacturing | 30.4 | 29.9 | 28.5 | 27.7 | 27.2 | 26.7 | 26.2 | 24.6 | 24.8 | 22.2 |
| Electricity, gas and water | 62.7 | 57.7 | 52.4 | 53.9 | 53.4 | 50.5 | 47.4 | 46.9 | 47.9 | 49.3 |
| Construction | 21.8 | 20.6 | 21.1 | 20.1 | 19.2 | 17.5 | 18.9 | 16.7 | 15.7 | 15.8 |
| Wholesale, retail and motor | 10.8 | 10.9 | 11.7 | 11.4 | 11.7 | 11.3 | 11.7 | 11.5 | 11.0 | 11.1 |
| Hotels and restaurants | 7.2 | 6.7 | 6.2 | 5.4 | 5.4 | 5.9 | 5.4 | 5.0 | 4.2 | 5.6 |
| Transport, storage & communication | 45.7 | 42.5 | 42.2 | 42.5 | 42.2 | 41.5 | 42.3 | 41.3 | 42.2 | 41.2 |
| Financial intermediation | 33.7 | 31.1 | 30.2 | 29.9 | 27.0 | 27.2 | 25.9 | 26.6 | 24.4 | 24.3 |
| Real estate and business services | 11.7 | 11.3 | 11.4 | 10.3 | 10.6 | 10.6 | 11.0 | 10.5 | 10.1 | 10.0 |
| Public administration and defence | 62.8 | 60.7 | 60.7 | 59.4 | 59.3 | 59.5 | 56.9 | 56.2 | 57.1 | 57.3 |
| Education | 54.8 | 53.8 | 54.1 | 54.0 | 53.2 | 54.7 | 54.8 | 54.9 | 56.0 | 55.1 |
| Health & social | 47.2 | 46.1 | 45.0 | 46.3 | 44.7 | 44.9 | 44.4 | 43.8 | 44.2 | 43.4 |
| Other services | 21.1 | 21.1 | 22.1 | 21.8 | 21.2 | 20.9 | 22.2 | 18.0 | 18.6 | 20.3 |

*Source:* Grainger and Crowther (2007)

*Notes:*
* sample size too small for a reliable estimate.
a All employees but excludes members of the armed forces.

unionism; but density has dwindled dangerously since 1997. Rather than moving forward on this important front under New Labour, trade unionism has retreated further. On any sober account, if private sector services continue to grow and former union fortresses like manufacturing continue to shed jobs, then unions face slow but unremitting decline, balkanization and fragmentation on the model of the USA. The necessary qualification is that the future does not always follow the patterns of the past. Nevertheless, it has done so since 1979 and it has done so broadly since 1997.

Density differs by occupation as well as by sector and industry. Overall membership is increasingly skewed towards 'managers and senior officials' and 'professional occupations', although it has once more increased faster in the public sector where density remains high for these groups – around 70 per cent in 2005. The aggregate figure is again deflated by inferior performance in the private sector where once again there is a drop on the 1997 figure (Grainger and Crowther 2007). Over half of all trade unionists are now concentrated in the 'managerial', 'professional' and 'associate professional and technical' categories. At the other end of the spectrum only around 20 per cent of the least skilled workers are union members. These are often vulnerable workers. On present trends, trade unionism has the potential to move towards a new 'labour aristocracy' of professional workers with higher pay, status and security, embracing at the bottom end of the pile only a minority of the 'unskilled', highly exploited workers who need it most.

Trade unionism could also become the gerontocratic preserve of older workers. Only one-tenth of workers aged 16 to 24 were union members in 2006. Again this is related to the employment situation: young workers in the public sector are more likely to be members than their private sector counterparts. Moreover, workers unionize as they grow older: density in 2006 was 23.5 per cent in the 25–34 age group, 33.9 per cent in the 35–49 age group and 34.8 per cent for workers over 50 (Grainger and Crowther 2007: 16).

Tendencies towards elite workers and gerontocracy have been accompanied by an overdue propensity towards feminization. Arguments that women were less likely to unionize than men gained credence from the fact that in the past female density lagged behind male density. However, this was related to the concentration of women in lower-density areas of employment with small establishments, small workgroups and high turnover. The gender gap gradually decreased with changing employment patterns and it has been reversed since 1997.

Using different methods we can calculate that female density increased from 29.1 per cent or 27.4 per cent in 1997, to 29.7 or 28.1 per cent in 2006. Male density, in contrast, decreased from 32.8 per cent or 28.3 per cent in 1997, to 27.2 per cent or 23.7 per cent in 2006 (table 3.6). While this is important, the significant factor is decreasing male density and the resilience of overall density in the public sector, where women constitute 60 per cent of employees, compared with 40 per cent in the private sector.

Despite their concentration in low-paid unskilled jobs, minority ethnic

*Table 3.6* UK trade union density by sex 1997–2006

|      | Employees[a] | | In Employment[b] | |
|------|-------|-----|-------|-----|
|      | Women | Men | Women | Men |
| 1997 | 29.1 | 32.8 | 27.4 | 28.3 |
| 1998 | 28.7 | 31.4 | 27.0 | 27.3 |
| 1999 | 28.5 | 31.1 | 27.1 | 27.3 |
| 2000 | 29.1 | 30.4 | 27.7 | 26.7 |
| 2001 | 28.4 | 30.1 | 27.0 | 26.6 |
| 2002 | 29.0 | 29.4 | 27.6 | 25.8 |
| 2003 | 29.3 | 29.4 | 27.8 | 25.5 |
| 2004 | 29.1 | 28.5 | 27.6 | 24.7 |
| 2005 | 29.9 | 28.2 | 28.1 | 24.6 |
| 2006 | 29.7 | 27.2 | 28.1 | 23.7 |

*Source:* Grainger and Crowther (2007)

*Notes:*
a  Wage and salary earners but excludes members of the armed forces.
b  All employees and self-employed but excludes members of the armed forces, unpaid family workers and those on college-based schemes.

*Table 3.7* UK trade union density by ethnicity 2003–6

|      | 2003 | 2004 | 2005 | 2006 |
|------|------|------|------|------|
| White | 29.6 | 29.0 | 29.2 | 28.7 |
| Mixed | 20.8 | 25.4 | 25.6 | 23.6 |
| Asian or Asian British | 25.5 | 23.5 | 25.7 | 24.3 |
| Black or Black British | 30.1 | 32.5 | 30.1 | 33.1 |
| Chinese | 19.3 | 20.9 | 21.1 | 18.0 |

*Sources:* Palmer, Grainger and Fitzner (2004); Grainger and Holt (2005); Grainger (2006); Grainger and Crowther (2007)

workers were historically just as likely to be union members as their white counterparts. Table 3.7 demonstrates that the pattern has continued. The 'black or black British' category increased its density from 30.1 per cent in 2003, to 33.1 per cent in 2006; the 'Asian or Asian British' category fell slightly from 25.5 per cent to 24.3 per cent; while density of white workers decreased from 29.6 per cent to 28.7 per cent. Given the growth of a diverse ethnically-mixed workforce and the increasing role of migrant labour, these figures offer a modicum of hope for holding the line against a further numerical decline of trade unionism (TUC 2004b).

*Recognition, collective bargaining and strikes*

The incidence of union recognition declined sequentially and substantially from 1979 to 1997 (Millward *et al.* 2000: 95–108). Using similar methodology, researchers have concluded that the proportion of establishments with recognized unions fell from 33 per cent in 1998 to 27 per cent of workplaces, employing 48 per cent of all employees by 2004. Decline is largely confined to the private sector, where the proportion of establishments recognizing unions fell during the same period from 20 per cent to 15 per cent, and, although this is far from comforting, it is also concentrated in new workplaces. Around 80 per cent of public sector workplaces still recognize unions (Kersley *et al.* 2006: 120). By 2006 unions had secured recognition through resort to the new statutory procedure in the ERA 1999 in 162 cases although this fails to take account of employers who agreed recognition in order to avoid legal entanglements (CAC 2007). Whatever the overall impact of ERA, decline has progressed at a substantial rate: the trajectory of the Conservative years has continued.

On one calculation, as New Labour's legislation loomed, the number of recognition agreements signed increased from 109, covering 24,500 workers in 1997 to 365, covering 130,446 workers in 1999. In 2000, the year the ERA came into effect, the figure accelerated to 525 agreements, covering 157,000 workers and the following year to 685 agreements, covering 122,033 workers. However, by 2005, the figures had fallen to pre-ERA levels: there were only 131 agreements involving 27,400 workers (Gall 2007). Under New Labour there was a positive recognition effect. However, it was small and transient and it is not reflected in increases of significance in either membership or density. In terms of union security, the uprooting of the closed shop in the 1980s and 1990s has not been reversed; but 76 per cent of unionized workplaces with 25 or more employees still deduct union dues at source (Millward *et al.* 2000; Willman and Bryson 2006: 8).

The erosion of collective bargaining and joint regulation of pay and conditions developed from the mid-1980s. The advent of New Labour provided little respite: the restructuring of industrial relations and the re-emergence of unilateral regulation and management prerogative was not reversed. The government's Workplace Employment Relations Survey (WERS) data showed the coverage of collective bargaining falling from 70 per cent in 1984 to 40 per cent in 1998 (Millward *et al.* 2000) The 2004 WERS concluded:

> By far the most common form of pay determination in 2004 was unilateral pay-setting by management . . . the percentage of workplaces engaged in any collective bargaining over pay fell from 30 per cent in 1998 to 22 per cent in 2004 . . . The decline was largely confined to the private sector where bargaining incidence fell from 17 per cent to 11 per cent.
>
> (Kersley *et al.* 2006: 181–2)

The serious diminution of collective bargaining over pay during the last two decades has been complemented by a move from negotiation to consultation over non-pay issues. However, the resilience of collective bargaining over public sector pay, as well as the limited arm's-length negotiation, represented by the pay review bodies, should be underlined. In 2004

> collective bargaining was the dominant form of pay setting – it was present in around four-fifths (83 per cent) of public sector workplaces and covered 82 per cent of public sector workers. In contrast, only 14 per cent of private sector workplaces used collective bargaining.
>
> (ibid.: 179–81)

Figures from the Labour Force Survey tell a similar story of sustained but slow decline. The percentage of employees across industry whose pay was affected directly or indirectly by collective bargaining dropped from 34.5 per cent, or around 8.2 million workers, in 1996 to 33.5, or under 7 million workers, in 2006. There were, however, increases in 1999, 2000 and 2005 and these aggregate figures cloak the substantial public–private split (table 3.8).

Pay itself has been relatively buoyant under New Labour. Annual percentage changes in median earnings outpaced percentage increases in the RPI between 2000 and 2005, although the gains were small for many workers after taxes. During that period, median earnings grew at 4 per cent annually before falling behind inflation in 2007 (see McIlroy, chapter 2, this volume, table 2.2). In the public sector median earnings increased at 4.3 per cent while in the private sector they increased at 3.9 per cent, although the public sector lagged behind until limits on public expenditure were relaxed in 2003. There were, again, differences between the public and private sector in relation to differentials. In the public sector differentials between the top and bottom narrowed. Given union strength here in comparison with the private sector, unions like the PCS continued their traditional function as 'a sword of justice'.

*Table 3.8* UK collective bargaining coverage 1997–2006

|      | *Employee's pay affected by collective agreement (%)* |
| --- | --- |
| 1997 | 33.3 |
| 1998 | 32.3 |
| 1999 | 36.2 |
| 2000 | 36.3 |
| 2001 | 35.7 |
| 2002 | 35.7 |
| 2003 | 35.9 |
| 2004 | 34.9 |
| 2005 | 35.3 |
| 2006 | 33.5 |

*Source:* Grainger and Crowther (2007)

Across sectors, the growth in differentials which developed during the Conservative years has not been significantly arrested under New Labour. In 1999 the gap between the bottom 10 per cent of earners and the top 10 per cent stood at £26,718. By 2007 it had increased to £36,710. Once more there were differences between the public and private sectors with the gap between the top and bottom percentiles greater in private enterprise. There has been a slight decline in wage inequality in the public sector from a ratio of 7.28:1 in 1999 to 6.93:1 in 2007, attributable to small but significant pay increases for lower-paid workers. In the private sector, however, the earnings gap has increased (New Earnings Survey / Annual Survey of Hours and Earnings 1999–2007).

A historic attraction of union membership and a historic achievement of collective bargaining was the gap in wages between union members and non-members. Recent research suggests that the union mark-up fell from 14.2 per cent in 1993 to 6.3 per cent in 2000 and that this fall affected all groups (Metcalf 2005: 91–2). A wage premium for members may still apply in specific occupations and certain sectors. The conclusion of many labour economists is that generally it no longer pays to join a union (Machin 2001: 13). Unions still act as a force for equality, compressing wage differentials between men and women, black and white, manual and non-manual workers: '. . . unions still wield the sword of justice in the workplace. Unions narrow the distribution of pay, promote equal opportunity and family-friendly policies, lower the rate of industrial injuries and handle grievances' (Metcalf 2005: 102). But they do so to a lesser extent than they did at key periods in the past.

Strikes are conceived by many commentators as an index of the confidence and combativity of workers; in some quarters they are considered to signify union decline or revitalization. Allowing for the variability induced by circumstance and contingency, the fall in the number of stoppages, the number of workers involved and the number of striker days, which set in during the late 1980s and became established in the 1990s, has continued under New Labour (see table 3.9). The leap on all three indicators in 2002 was largely due to the FBU strikes in that year while the 905,000 working days lost in 2004 was the highest since 1996. There was an increase in striker-days and workers involved in 2006: in terms of fluctuations in the recent past this represented a small upturn in a sustained pattern of decline. In comparison with the 1960s, 1970s and 1980s, indeed with the entire twentieth century, strikes remain at a historic low with a decline deeper than elsewhere in Western Europe.

Since 2000 there has been no great difference in the number of strikes occurring in the public and private sector – although the former has had the edge. Strikes have been concentrated in public services, the Royal Mail and the railways. Moreover, there has been a turn away from the straightforward strike to targeted, selective and discontinuous action. The legal framework continues to be restrictive with ballots often simultaneously impeding but legitimizing action and being tacitly utilized to test membership opinion, demonstrate discontent and exercise pressure on employers. The sustained

*Table 3.9* Strikes in the UK 1997–2006

|  | Working days lost (000's) | Stoppages in progress | Workers involved (000's) |
|---|---|---|---|
| 1997 | 235 | 216 | 130 |
| 1998 | 282 | 166 | 93 |
| 1999 | 242 | 205 | 141 |
| 2000 | 499 | 212 | 183 |
| 2001 | 525 | 194 | 180 |
| 2002 | 1,323 | 146 | 943 |
| 2003 | 499 | 133 | 151 |
| 2004 | 905 | 130 | 293 |
| 2005 | 157 | 116 | 93 |
| 2006 | 755 | 158 | 713 |

*Source:* Hale (2007)

low level of strike activity can be related to the enhanced power and resources – including legal resources – of employers and the antipathy and determination, every bit as intense as that of its Conservative predecessors, of New Labour to resist industrial action. In that context, the indisputable decline of the strike appears plausibly rooted in more cautious and calculative use of the strike weapon rather than any sea change in attitudes to collective action. An element of rank-and-file resilience is reflected in the fact that a substantial percentage of strikes remain unofficial (see Lyddon, chapter 10, this volume).

## Conclusion

The gains that trade unionism registered in the Golden Age of Keynesianism were reversed between 1979 and 1997. The decline of the unions went hand in hand with privatization; diminution of employment protection; intensification of work; greater insecurity for workers; increased levels of unemployment; pressure on wages; and increases in wage differentials which particularly affected the less skilled, most vulnerable workers (see McIlroy, chapters 1 and 2, this volume). This was part of a worldwide offensive by neoliberalism, although its impact was greater in the pioneering neoliberal regimes of Anglo-American capitalism than in many EU economies (Glyn 2006: 126–7). In this chapter we have looked at the strategies unions have adopted in an attempt to end the retreat and reverse decline and how they have tried to set in train a process of union revitalization.

History does not repeat itself but in the past a ten-year period has often provided a reasonable timescale for change to occur – witness the upturn of union fortunes between 1906 and 1914 and from 1968 to 1979 – although we also have to consider the longer periods of relative sluggishness, 1945–66, and significant decline, 1979–97 (see Bain and Price 1983). On that basis we can conclude that partnership has failed to provide a compelling answer to the unions' strategic impasse, while organizing has also failed to deliver on its promises. Union membership has stabilized but density continues to fall. The predicament of private sector trade unionism is of particular concern. Revitalization is not underway. It can be argued that unions have enjoyed some success: they have halted the retreat. But it can also be claimed that with all-embracing, bottomless state hostility replaced by at least some elements of state support, unions have proven incapable of seizing the opportunities the situation has presented them with to mount a revival of any substance (Kersley *et al.* 2006).

Underpinning this unsatisfactory position is a neoliberal state and a neoliberal political environment which unions appear unable to significantly influence (see McIlroy, chapter 5, this volume). This is complemented by an employment environment which does not significantly facilitate union growth. It is characterized by employer disinterest or hostility and an economic context where inflation has been successfully controlled and real earnings have proved buoyant. Only 20 per cent of managers favour union membership for their employees (Kersley *et al.* 2006: 112–13). Employee attitudes, in the context of what is happening at work and in the economy, remain vital. With real earnings increasing slightly over the last decade, although work pressures have remained intense, employee discontent has been restricted: there has been no apparent accumulation of dissatisfaction from below which might presage a future upsurge. While decline in union power presently inclines workers to doubt whether unions can deal successfully with employers, rising inflation, continuing pressure on public sector wages, long hours, intensification of work and the host of problems afflicting the New Labour state and neoliberalism may change things. However, a review of recent survey evidence suggests that:

> There has been no improvement in unionized workers' perceptions of union effectiveness since 1998, two-fifths of those eligible to join their workplace union do not and there is no sign that this is changing . . . only one-sixth of unorganized workers actually believe a union would make their workplace a better place to work.
>
> (Bryson 2007: 22)

The relationship between agency and structure is dialectical: trade unionists can improve things by working to maximize the potential opportunities that the current unfavourable environment still offers. They can attempt to ameliorate their position by working to minimize the dangers and solve the problems the contemporary context throws up. They cannot voluntaristically will that context away. Possibilities are not determined by the current position; but they are limited by it. An important step forward in combating external constraints would be a more successful grappling with the internal difficulties union organizers face (see Heery and Simms 2008). In searching for solutions, skilled imaginative leadership is essential. Servicing existing members is, to a degree, if not to a fixed degree, inevitable. Diversion of resources to organizing from other important functions comes at a price and an opportunity cost. And so on. On that sober note we turn to look at changes in union organization and internal politics since 1997.

## Note

1 The Certification Officer reports total union membership. In 2005–6 the total number of members paying dues was 11.1 per cent less than the figures for total membership. In 2004–5 it was 10.7 per cent less (*Annual Report of the Certification Officer*, 2006–7, p.23). Moreover, the returns submitted by unions to the Certification Officer and the TUC, may, for a variety of reasons, inflate membership. For a useful discussion see Charlwood and Metcalf, 2005, pp. 238–9.

## Bibliography

Ackers, P. and Payne, J. (1998) 'British trade unions and social partnership: rhetoric, reality and strategy', *International Journal of Human Resource Management*, 9:3, 529–50.

Bain, G.S. and Price, R. (1983) 'Union growth: dimensions, determinants and destiny', in G.S. Bain (ed.) *Industrial Relations in Britain*, Oxford: Blackwell.

BECTU (2003) *Conference Report*, London: BECTU.

Bronfenbrenner, K., Friedman, S., Hurd, R., Oswald, R., Seeber, R. (eds) (1998) *Organizing to Win: New Research on Union Strategies*, Ithaca, NY: ILR Press.

Bryson, A. (1999) 'Are unions good for industrial relations?', in R. Jowell, J. Curtice, A. Park and K. Thomson (eds) *British Social Attitudes: The 16th Report*, Aldershot: Gower.

——(2007) 'New Labour, new unions?', in A. Park, J. Curtice, K. Thomson, M. Phillips and M. Johnson (eds) *British Social Attitudes: The 23rd Report*, London: Sage.

Bryson, A., Gomez, R. and Willman, P. (2004) 'The end of the affair? the decline in employers' propensity to unionize', in J. Kelly and P. Willman (eds) *Union Organisation and Activity*, London: Routledge.

Central Arbitration Committee (CAC) (2007) *Annual Report 2005–2006*, London: CAC.

Charlwood, A. (2002) 'Why do non-union employees want to unionize? evidence from Britain', *British Journal of Industrial Relations*, 40:3, 463–91.

Charlwood, A. and Metcalf, D. (2005) 'Appendix: trade union numbers, membership and density', in S. Fernie and D. Metcalf (eds) *Trade Unions: Resurgence or Demise?* London: Routledge.

Coats, D. (2005) *Raising Lazarus: The Future of Organized Labour*, London: Fabian Society.

Cully, M., Woodland, S., O'Reilly, A. and Dix, G. (1999) *Britain at Work*, London: Routledge.

Danford, A., Richardson, M. and Upchurch, M. (2003), *New Unions, New Workplaces: A Study of Union Resistance in Restructured Workplace*, London: Routledge.

Davies, P. and Kilpatrick, C. (2004) 'UK worker representatives after single channel', *Industrial Law Journal*, 33:2, 121–51.

Deakin, S. and Wilkinson, F. (1994) 'Rights v efficiency? the economic case for transnational labour standards', *Industrial Law Journal*, 23:3, 289–310.

Ewing, K. and Truter, G. (2003) *Implementing the Information and Consultation Directive in the UK: Lessons from Germany*, London: Institute of Employment Rights.

Freeman, R. and Medoff, J. (1984) *What Do Unions Do?* New York: Basic Books.

Gall, G. (2004) 'British employer resistance to trade union recognition', *Human Resource Management Journal*, 14:2, 36–53.

—— (2007) 'Trade union recognition in Britain: an emerging crisis for trade unionism', *Economic and Industrial Democracy*, 28:1, 78–109.

Gallie, D., White, M., Cheng, Y. and Tomlinson, M. (1998) *Restructuring the Employment Relationship*, Oxford: Oxford University Press.

Glyn, A. (2006) *Capitalism Unleashed: Finance, Globalization and Welfare*, Oxford: Oxford University Press.

Gospel, H. (2005) 'Markets, firms and unions: a historical-institutionalist perspective on the future of unions in Britain', in S. Fernie and D. Metcalf (eds) *Trade Unions: Resurgence or Demise?* London: Routledge.

Graham, S. (2006) *Organizing Out of Decline – The Rebuilding of the UK and Ireland Shop Stewards Movement*, London: TGWU.

Grainger, H. (2006) *Trade Union Membership 2005*, London: Office of National Statistics.

Grainger, H. and Crowther, M. (2007) *Trade Union Membership 2006*, London: Office of National Statistics.

Grainger, H. and Holt, H. (2005) *Trade Union Membership 2004*, London: Office of National Statistics.

Guest, D. and Peccei, R. (1998) *The Partnership Company*, London: IPA.

Hale, D. (2007) 'Labour disputes in 2006', *Economic and Labour Market Review*, 1:6, 25–36, London: Office of National Statistics.

Heery, E. (2002) 'Partnership versus organizing: alternative futures for British trade unionism', *Industrial Relations Journal*, 33:1, 20–35.

Heery, E. and Simms, M. (2008) 'Constraints on union organizing in the United Kingdom', *Industrial Relations Journal*, 39:1, 24–42.

Heery, E., Simms, M., Delbridge, R., Salmon, J. and Simpson, D. (2000) 'Union organizing in Britain: a survey of policy and practice', *International Journal of Human Resource Management*, 11:5, 986–1007.

Huffschmid, J. (2005) *Economic Policy for a Social Europe: A Critique of Neoliberalism and Proposals for Alternatives*, Basingstoke: Palgrave.

Hyman, R. (1997) 'The future of employee representation', *British Journal of Industrial Relations*, 35:3, 309–36.

Kelly, J. (1998) *Rethinking Industrial Relations: Mobilization, Collectivism and Long Waves*, London, Routledge.

—— (2004) 'Social partnership agreements in Britain: labor cooperation and compliance', *Industrial Relations*, 43:1, 257–92.

—— (2005a) 'Social partnership agreements in Britain' in M. Stuart and M. Martinez Lucio (eds) *Partnership and Modernization in Employment Relations*, London: Routledge.

—— (2005b) 'Social movement theory and union revitalization in Britain', in S. Fernie and D. Metcalf (eds) *Trade Unions: Resurgence or Demise?* London: Routledge.

Kelly, J. and Badigannavar, V. (2004) 'Union organizing campaigns', in J. Kelly and P. Willman (eds) *Union Organization and Activity*, London: Routledge.

Kersley, B., Alpin, C., Forth, J., Bryson, A. Bewley, H., Dix, G. and Oxenbridge, S. (2006) *Inside the Workplace: Findings from the 2004 Workplace Employment Relations Survey*, London: Routledge.

Machin, S. (2001) *Does it Still Pay to Be in or Join a Union?* London: Centre for Economic Performance, London School of Economics.

McIlroy, J. (1995) *Trade Unionism in Britain Today*, 2nd edition, Manchester: Manchester University Press.

—— (2000a) 'New Labour, new unions, new left', *Capital and Class*, 71, 11–45.

—— (2000b) 'The new politics of pressure: the Trades Union Congress and New Labour in government', *Industrial Relations Journal*, 31:1, 2–16.

Metcalf, D. (1991) 'British unions: dissolution or resurgence?', *Oxford Review of Economic Policy*, 7:1, 18–32.

—— (2001) 'British unions: dissolution or resurgence revisited', in R. Dickens, J. Wadsworth and P. Gregg (eds) *The State of Working Britain*, London: Centre for Economic Performance, LSE.

—— (2005) 'Trade unions: resurgence or perdition? An economic analysis', in S. Fernie and D. Metcalf (eds) *Trade Unions: Resurgence or Demise?* London: Routledge.

Millward, N., Bryson, A. and Forth, J. (2000) *All Change at Work? British Employment Relations 1980–1998*, London: Routledge.

Monks, J. (1999) Speech to Partners for Progress conference, London, 21 May 1999.

New Earnings Survey / Annual Survey of Hours and Earnings (NES/ASHE) (1997–2007) *Annual Reports*, London: ONS.

Nolan, P. and O'Donnell, K. (2003) 'Industrial relations, HRM and performance', in P. Edwards (ed.) *Industrial Relations: Theory and Practice*, 2nd edition, Oxford: Blackwell.

O'Grady, F. and Nowak, P. (2004) 'Beyond new unionism', in J. Kelly and P. Willman (eds) *Union Organisation and Activity*, London: Routledge.

Oxenbridge, S. and Brown, W. (2004) 'A poisoned chalice? Trade union representatives in partnership and co-operative employer-union relationships', in G. Healy, E. Heery, P. Taylor and W. Brown (eds) *The Future of Worker Representation*, Basingstoke: Palgrave.

Palmer, T., Grainger, H. and Fitzner, G. (2004) *Trade Union Membership 2003*, Office of National Statistics: London.

Pencavel, J. (2003) 'The surprising retreat of union Britain' in D. Card, R. Blundell and R.B. Freeman, (eds) *Seeking a Premier Economy: The Economic Effects of British Economic Reforms, 1980–2000*, Chicago: University of Chicago Press.

Rhodes, M. (1998) 'Defending the social contract', in D. Hine and H. Kassim (eds) *Beyond the Market*, London: Routledge.

Stewart, M. (1995) 'Union wage differentials in an era of declining unionization', *Oxford Bulletin of Economics and Statistics*, 7:2, 143–66.

Stuart, M., Charlwood, A., Martinez Lucio, M. and Wallis, E. (2006) *Union Modernization Fund: Interim Evaluation of the First Round*, London: DTI.

Tailby, S. and Winchester, D. (2000) 'Management and trade unions: towards social partnership?', in S. Bach and K. Sisson (eds) *Personnel Management*, Oxford: Blackwell.

Taylor, P. and Bain, P. (2003) 'Call center organizing in adversity: From Excell to

Vertex', in G. Gall, (ed.) *Union Organizing: Campaigning for Union Recognition*. London: Routledge.

Terry, M. (1995) 'Trade unions: shop stewards and the workplace', in P. Edwards (ed.), *Industrial Relations: Theory and Practice in Britain*, Oxford: Blackwell.

—— (2004) ' "Partnership": a serious strategy for the UK trade unions?', in A. Verma and T. Kochan (eds) *Unions in the 21st Century: An International Perspective*, Basingstoke: Palgrave.

Terry, M. and Smith, J. (2003) *Evaluation of the Partnership at Work Fund*, London: DTI.

TUC (1997) *General Council Report*, London: TUC.

—— (1998a) *General Council Report*, London: TUC.

—— (1998b) *Economic Policy and Social Partnership*, London: TUC.

—— (1999a) *General Council Report*, London: TUC.

—— (1999b) *Report of Congress*, London: TUC.

—— (2002a) *Partnership Works*, London: TUC.

—— (2002b) *General Council Report*, London: TUC.

—— (2004a) *General Council Report*, London: TUC.

—— (2004b) *Migrant Agency Workers*, London: TUC.

—— (2005a) *Planning for Organizing: A Guide for Unions*, London: TUC.

—— (2005b) *Report of Congress*, London: TUC.

—— (2007a) *Guide to Organizing*. London: TUC.

—— (2007b) *General Council Report*. London: TUC.

Waddington, J. (2000) 'United Kingdom: recovery from the neo-liberal assault', in J. Waddington and R. Hoffman (eds) *Trade Unions in Europe: Facing Challenges and Searching for Solutions*, Brussels: European Trade Union Institute.

Waddington, J. and Kerr, A. (2000) 'Towards an organizing model in Unison? a trade union membership strategy in transition', in M. Terry (ed.) *Redefining Public Sector Unionism: Unison and the Future of Trade Unions*, London: Routledge.

Waddington, J. and Whitston, C. (1997) 'Why do people join unions in a period of membership decline?' *British Journal of Industrial Relations* 35:4, 515–46.

Willman, P. (2005) 'Circling the wagons: endogeneity in union decline', in S. Fernie and D. Metcalf (eds) *Trade Unions: Resurgence or Demise?* London: Routledge.

Willman, P. and Bryson, A. (2006) *Accounting for Collective Action: Resource Acquisition and Mobilization in British Unions*, London: Centre for Economic Performance, London School of Economics.

# 4 An anatomy of British trade unionism since 1997

## Organization, structure and factionalism

*John McIlroy and Gary Daniels*

Consideration of the position and prospects of trade unions in contemporary Britain needs to address not only their size, inclusiveness and strategy but their external and internal structures, the shape of unions, how they are organized internally, the degree of membership influence and how they are led. Union structures reflect past struggles as well as contemporary challenges; indeed the former may impede adjustment to the latter (Turner 1962: 14; Hyman 1975: 62–3). Structure interacts with consciousness. One or several big unions does not necessarily reflect or reinforce unity between their members. But the way unions organize – for example, small scattered unions, fragmented by adhesion on political or religious grounds to competing centres, as distinct from larger bodies, articulated with employment structures and affiliated to a single centre – may influence trade unionists' capacity for collective action. So may the centralization or dispersion of power within individual unions, the nature of internal democracy, members' ability to participate in decisions and the intensity of their identification with their union. The problems which impede unions' ability to act, however, are often less administrative than political and ideological (ibid.: 56–62).

Labour history teaches us that national leaders can, and often do, play a key role in union strategy, action and politics. This understanding has been echoed in recent years in positive assessments of the so-called 'awkward squad' of contemporary union leaders as significant agents of change (Murray 2003). Yet national leaders are subject not only to pressures from members but pressures from their structural position and their role as bargainers with employers, politicians and state functionaries and as managers and custodians of often sizeable organizations and their resources, efficiency and survival. Mediating between their members on the one hand and employers and the state on the other, they may be susceptible to bureaucratization. They may seek to foster accommodative and subordinate relations with external agencies or endorse compromises unacceptable to union members (for different views on this, see Hyman 1971, 1979; Kelly and Heery 1994). But national leaders are far from autonomous or insulated from their members. Leadership at other levels of the union exerted through workplace organization but also through factions and caucuses may seek to repair what is perceived as a representation gap or democratic deficit.

Muller-Jentsch (1985) has elaborated the significance of workplace activism and organization in developing union resources and values: it can constitute a constraint and sometimes an alternative to the union hierarchy, dispersing power through the organization. Conversely the weakness of workplace leaders amplifies the role of national leaders. As Kelly (1998: 32–6, 49–51) has argued, leadership at all levels is intrinsic to the maintenance and development of union organization and membership mobilization and the forms they take (and see Darlington 2006). Leaders, nationally, regionally and particularly in the workplace, imbue a sense of grievance and identity and organize and legitimate workers' activity. But conflict may develop between them over policy and strategy. Factional struggles between different groups of leaders and members representing distinctive occupational, geographical, structural or political concerns are likewise intrinsic to the definition of member interests and how grievance is articulated and organized.

This chapter looks at recent changes in trade unions in the light of these issues. It begins by documenting the current shape of trade unionism in Britain marked, as it is, by amalgamations, concentration of members and increasing size of unions. It proceeds to examine recent trends in organization at the workplace and nationally before scrutinizing changes in leadership and detailing what we know about today's union leaders and members' attitudes to their unions. There is then a discussion of developments in the neglected but important area of internal factionalism. Recent changes in the role of the TUC are explored and the chapter concludes with a brief summation of the current position.

## Union organization: The changing shape of trade unionism

The continuing decline of trade unionism has fostered the continuing merger of unions and consequent concentration of membership. Here again the tendencies of the Conservative years have been sustained. There were 177 unions in 2006, compared with 245 in 1997 and 453 in 1979. There has been a similar decline in the number of TUC affiliated unions (table 4.1). There are still 88 unions with less than 1,000 members but unions with membership over 100,000 constitute 84 per cent of total membership. Eighteen unions went out of existence in 2005–6: five were dissolved through merger, the remainder were wound up. The increasing weight of public sector trade unionism is also noteworthy: seven of the biggest ten unions organize predominantly in the public sector (Certification Officer 2006, 2007).

The major unions and their membership are set out in table 4.2. Unite was formed in 2007 as an amalgamation of Amicus and the TGWU. Amicus, then Britain's second biggest union, was itself established as recently as 2002 in a merger between MSF, whose core membership was technical, craft and supervisory and managerial workers, and the AEEU, an amalgamation of

*Table 4.1* Number of unions in the UK and number of TUC affiliated unions 1997–2006

|      | All | TUC affiliated unions |
|------|-----|------------------------|
| 1997 | 233 | 75 |
| 1998 | 224 | 74 |
| 1999 | 221 | 77 |
| 2000 | *   | 76 |
| 2001 | 206 | 73 |
| 2002 | 199 | 70 |
| 2003 | 197 | 69 |
| 2004 | 195 | 70 |
| 2005 | 185 | 66 |
| 2006 | 177 | 63 |

*Sources:* Certification Officer, *Annual Reports* (1997–2007) and TUC, *Report of Congress*, 2006.

*Note:*
*In 1999 The Certification Officer changed the census date from Dec 31 to March 31. There is no exact figure in this adjustment year.

engineers and electricians established during the 1990s. Organizing primarily in the private sector, Amicus attracted the GPMU, a recent merger of print and media unions, and Unifi, an amalgamation of unions in finance. Amicus recruited across sectors from manufacturing, aerospace and education to local authorities, foundries and finance and across occupations, from bank assistants to skilled technical workers and senior managers. Its partner in Unite, the TGWU, had, likewise, a strong private sector base, although it also organized in the public sector, local government and the health service. It was badly hit by the decline of manufacturing and traditional industries such as the docks. Sustained falls in the membership of both Amicus and the TGWU were an important factor in the merger.

Displaced by Unite as Britain's biggest union, Unison is the product of a 1993 amalgamation between three public sector unions, COHSE, NUPE and NALGO. It recruits across local government, the NHS and education as well as in the voluntary sector and privatized utilities such as electricity, gas and water. Unison embraces a variety of occupations from professionals and managers to manual workers. The GMB refused to join Unite, preferring to maintain its own identity. Historically, the main competitor of the TGWU as a general union, the GMB organizes across the public and private sectors and recruits in a wide range of occupations. The biggest non-TUC affiliate is the RCN. It projects a strong professional image, contrasting itself favourably with Unison, which also enrols nurses. But the need to extend its base in the health service has led it to recruit less-skilled health care assistants.

*Table 4.2* Largest 15 trade unions in the UK 2006

| Union | | | Membership |
|---|---|---|---|
| Unite | Amicus | 1,200,000 | 1,977,325 |
| | Transport and General Workers Union | 777,325 | |
| Unison | | | 1,317,000 |
| GMB | | | 575,105 |
| Royal College of Nursing | | | 391,347 |
| Union of Shop Distributive and Allied Workers | | | 340,653 |
| Public and Commercial Services Union | | | 312,725 |
| National Union of Teachers | | | 254,862 |
| National Association of Schoolmasters / Union of Women Teachers | | | 248,479 |
| Communication Workers Union | | | 244,461 |
| British Medical Association | | | 137,361 |
| Union of Construction Allied Trades and Technicians | | | 121,109 |
| University and College Union | | | 116,310 |
| Association of Teachers and Lecturers | | | 113,408 |
| Prospect | | | 102,161 |
| National Union of Rail, Maritime and Transport Workers | | | 73,347 |

*Sources:* TUC, *Report of Congress*, 2006 and Certification Officer, *Annual Report*, 2006–7

Schoolteachers are represented by a number of competing organizations, notably the NUT, NAS/UWT and ATL. In the past the NAS/UWT was rooted in secondary schools. It presented itself as the 'career-teachers' union'. This was sometimes seen as a euphemism for 'the mens' union', given the NUT's large female primary school teacher membership. The NAS/UWT still contrasts its 'realism' with the NUT's 'militancy'. The ATL, a recent affiliate to the TUC, initially recruited in grammar schools and independent schools; it now organizes across the school sector and in further education colleges. Although it projects a professional image, it has opened its doors to classroom assistants. The UCU is a 2006 amalgamation of NATFHE, which organized lecturers in further education and the former polytechnics, and the AUT, which represented lecturers in the 'old' universities.

The shopworkers' union, USDAW, enrols members from packers to managers in wholesale, retail and related factories and warehouses. Basing itself on organizing supermarkets, notably Tesco, USDAW has resisted the lure of amalgamation. In contrast, the PCS is the product of a 1998 merger of the CPSA and the Public Service and Commerce Union, itself the fruit of a 1996 marriage between the Civil and Public Services Union and the

Inland Revenue Staff Federation. Membership includes a wide range of civil servants, from cleaners, computer operators, messengers, kitchen staff and security guards, to employees in managerial and professional grades. The PCS also recruits in privatized agencies and IT companies.

The CWU was established in 1995 via a merger of the Union of Communication Workers, representing a variety of Post Office workers, and the National Communications Union, made up of engineers in the Post Office and subsequently in BT and Girobank. The CWU also organizes in Cable and Wireless, cable TV and related companies. The BMA is often regarded as a professional association of doctors: in reality it is perhaps Britain's most effective trade union.

A 1971 merger of the craft unions in construction created UCATT. Over the last decade it has resisted overtures from the TGWU, which organizes building labourers. Prospect represents engineers and scientific, professional and managerial staff in a variety of industries from electricity supply and engineering to agriculture and defence. It resulted from a 2001 merger between two unions made up of senior engineers and managers. Likewise, Community was created via the 2004 merger of two steel and textile unions – the ISTC and KFAT. The RMT, which aspires to organize all railway workers and seafarers, is the product of a 1990 merger of the NUR and NUS, although it is constrained by the presence of other unions, such as ASLEF, which consists of train drivers, the TSSA, which represents clerical and allied staff on the railways, and the TGWU, which also enrols seafarers. Other organizations with more than 50,000 members include the Educational Institute of Scotland, which recruits teachers north of the border, and the Fire Brigades Union.

Table 4.3 suggests that the aggregate decline in union membership (see table 3.1, chapter 3) hides a more complicated picture at the level of individual unions. Calculations are difficult and imperfect but at one end of the scale the BMA, NUT and PCS increased their membership significantly, between 17 and 30 per cent, between 1997 and 2006 and the RCN also enjoyed substantial expansion. At the other end of the scale, the GMB, Amicus and the CWU suffered appreciable decline. Returns for individual years add to the complexity of the picture. Declining over the decade, Amicus increased its membership by 26 per cent in the two years to 2006. In the same period, the TGWU, which also declined substantially over the New Labour decade, increased its membership by 5 per cent. The NUT grew by 9.5 per cent, 2004–6, while its competitor, the NAS/UWT contracted by 11.6 per cent, although it had expanded by some 7.5 per cent between 2003 and 2005 (Certification Officer 2003–7).

It is impossible to draw firm conclusions. But these figures do suggest the need to look more closely at the environment in which different unions operate and the potential importance of leadership and strategy as well as situational factors as an influence on growth and decline. Unions such as Amicus and the GMB operate in a hostile and concentrated private sector context. They are characterized by dispersed membership and have far-flung

*Table 4.3* Membership of major trade unions 1997 and 2006

| | 2006 | | 1997 | | Change +/– | |
|---|---|---|---|---|---|---|
| | CO | TUC | CO | | No's | % |
| Unison | 1,317,000 | 1,317,000 | | 1,300,451 | 16,549 | 1.27 |
| Unite    Amicus | 1,179,655 | 1,200,000 | | 1,497,509[a] | −317,854 | −21.23 |
| Transport and General Workers Union | 777,325 | 777,325 | | 881,357 | −104,032 | −11.8 |
| Unite (Total) | 1,956,980 | 1,977,325 | | 2,378,866[a] | −421,886 | −17.7 |
| GMB | 575,105 | 575,105 | | 709,708 | −134,603 | −19.0 |
| Royal College of Nursing | 391,347 | | | 312,141 | 79,206 | 25.38 |
| National Union of Teachers | 361,987 | 254,862 | | 276,819 | 85,168 | 30.77 |
| Union of Shop Distributive and Allied Workers | 340,653 | 340,653 | | 293,470 | 47,183 | 16.08 |
| Public and Commercial Services Union | 312,725 | 312,725 | PTC 154,245 CPSA 111,657 Total 265,902 | | 46,823 | 17.6 |
| National Association of Schoolmasters / Union of Women Teachers | 289,930 | 248,479 | | 245,932 | 43,998 | 17.9 |
| Communication Workers Union | 244,461 | 244,461 | | 273,814 | −29,353 | −10.72 |
| Association of Teachers and Lecturers | 203,241 | 113,408 | | 153,343 | 49,898 | 32.54 |
| British Medical Association | 137,361 | | | 104,344 | 33,017 | 31.6 |
| Union of Construction Allied Trades and Technicians | 121,109 | 121,109 | | 113,555 | 7,554 | 6.7 |
| University and College Union | 106,713[b] | 116,310 | AUT 32,551[c] NATFHE 55,918[c] Total 88,469[c] | | 18,244 | 20.6 |
| Prospect | 102,161 | 102,161 | IPMS 64,493[c] EMA 29,562[d] Total 94,055[d] | | 8,106 | 8.6 |
| Rail, Maritime and Transport Union | 73,347[c] | 73,347 | | 56,337[c] | 17,010 | 23.19 |
| Community | 31,978[c] | 67,450 | KFAT 38,075[c] ISTC 32,299[c] Total 70,374[c] | | −38,396 | −54.6 |
| Fire Brigades Union | 45,556[c] | 46,811 | | 51,426[c] | −5,870 | −11.4 |
| National Union of Journalists | n/a | 30,210 | | 19,384[d] | n/a | n/a |

| | | | | |
|---|---|---|---|---|
| Transport and Salaried Staff Association | 30,989[c] | 29,493 | 31,123[c] | −134 | −0.4 |
| Connect | n/a | 19,856 | n/a | n/a | n/a |
| Associated Society of Locomotive Steam Enginemen and Firemen | 18,141[c] | 3,190 | 14,255[c] | 3,886 | 27.26 |

*Sources:* Certification Officer, *Annual Reports*, 1997–2007 and TUC, *Report of Congress*, 1998

*Notes:*
a Amicus in 1998 = AEEU 720,926; MSF 416,000; GPMU 204,882; Unifi = 42,729; BIFU 112,972
b The sum total of political fund membership and non-membership of the AUT and NATFHE.
c The CO only reports membership figures for unions with 100,000 members or more. However, the membership figures from smaller unions can be extracted from the Political Fund table (contributors and exemptions). It should also be noted that the sum of these two figures might not represent an individual union's total membership because, for example, honorary, retired and unemployed members are neither required to pay the political levy nor seek exception from it. But these are the nearest 'official' figures available.
d These unions did not have a political fund and therefore, we have used the figures reported in TUC, *Report of Congress*,1998.

engagements in comparison with the more compact BMA and RCN, both of which have operated in relatively benign public sector territory. The potential of leadership and strategy is posed by the NUT and NAS/UWT: they have enjoyed very different fortunes at different times since 1997, while organizing on the same relatively favourable terrain.

On the other hand, the PCS has performed well in the face of privatization and cuts. But it still faces challenges. It has a small membership in the privatized sector. Density in some areas is less than 10 per cent, workplace organization is vestigial and the organizing it advocates expensive. USDAW, too, has grown in a traditionally hostile landscape of intensely competitive employers, a dispersed part-time workforce and high turnover. Its membership is concentrated in larger enterprises and the partnership it advocates to secure recruitment may come at the expense of membership voice and mobilization. The fact that the PCS has adopted an adversarial stance and USDAW has pursued and implemented partnership may point not simply to the importance of strategy but to the centrality of its effective implementation by leaders at all levels and its fit with the union's environment. The pattern of growth and decline in individual unions presents at least a chink of light for Britain's embattled labour movement.

Table 4.4 lists all transfers of engagement – where a small union is swallowed up in a larger organization – and amalgamations – where two or more unions of more comparable size merge – since 1997. It confirms that merger activity has continued at a high level under New Labour (for background, see Waddington 1995). The absorption of smaller unions by larger organizations has significantly reduced the overall number of unions (table 4.1). It is gradually bringing to an end the historic mosaic of small, local, craft and employer-based unions which burgeoned as recently as the 1970s. Ancient textile unions

*Table 4.4* Amalgamations and transfers 1997–2007

| Year | Activity | From | To |
| --- | --- | --- | --- |
| 1997 | Transfer of Engagements | United Association of Power Loom Overlookers | General Union of Loom Overlookers |
| | | Amalgamated Power Loom Overlookers | General Union of Loom Overlookers |
| | | Health Care Chaplains | MSF |
| | | National and Provincial Building Society Staff Association | BIFU |
| | | Association of University and College Lecturers | AUT |
| | | Government Communications Staff Federation | Public Services, Tax and Commerce Union (PTC) |
| | | National Association of Licensed House Managers | TGWU |
| 1998 | Amalgamations | CPSA-PTC | PCS |
| | Transfer of Engagements | Amalgamated Association of Beamers Twisters and Drawers (Hand and Machine) | KFAT |
| | | Clerical Medical Staff Association | Independent Union of Halifax |
| | | Communications Managers Association | MSF |
| | | Gas Managers Association | GMB |
| 1999 to March 2000 | Amalgamations | BIFU, Unifi and NatWest Staff Association | Unifi |
| | Transfer of Engagements | Cabin Crew 89 | AEEU |
| | | Royal Sun Alliance Staff | NatWest Staff Association |
| | | Nielson Staff Association | MSF |
| | | Lufthansa Staff Association | MSF |
| | | Corporation of London Staff Association | MSF |
| | | Britannic Supervisory Union | MSF |
| | | National Union of Insurance Workers | MSF |
| | | National League of the Blind | ISTC |

| April 2000 to March 2001 | Transfer of Engagements | Society of Chief Officers of Probation | Managerial and Professional Officers Union |
|---|---|---|---|
| | | Scottish Prison Officers Association | Prison Officers Association |
| | | Northern Carpet Trades Union Hambro Staff Association | TGWU Nationwide Group Staff Union |
| | | Power Loom Carpet Weavers and Textile Workers' Union | ISTC |
| | | British Aerospace Senior Staff Association | AEEU |
| | | Lloyds Register (UK) Staff Association | MSF |
| | | AXIS The AXA Sun Life Staff Association | Unifi |
| | | Managerial and Professional Officers Union | GMB |
| | | Associated Metalworkers Union | AEEU |
| April 2001 to March 2002 | Amalgamations | Institution of Professional Managers and Specialists (IPMS) and Engineers and Managers Association (EMA) | Prospect |
| | | Amalgamated Engineering and Electrical Union (AEEU) and Manufacturing, Science and Finance Union (MSF) | Amicus |
| | Transfer of Engagements | Leicester Housing Association Staff Association | MSF |
| April 2002 to March 2003 | Transfer of Engagements | WISA – the Union for Woolwich Staff | Unifi |
| | | Union of Textile Workers | Amicus |
| | | Girobank Senior Managers Association | Alliance and Leicester Group Union of Staff |
| | | CGNU Staff Association | Amicus |
| April 2003 to March 2004 | Transfer of Engagements | Midlands Area Association of Colliery Officials | NACODS |
| | | National Association of Colliery Overmen, Deputies and Shotfirers (Yorkshire Area) | NACODS |
| | | Scottish Further and Higher Education Association | Educational Institute of Scotland |

(*Continued Overleaf*)

*Table 4.4* Continued

| Year | Activity | From | To |
|------|----------|------|-----|
| April 2004 to March 2005 | Amalgamations | ISTC and KFAT | Community |
| | Transfer of Engagements | Anchor Group Staff Association | Amicus |
| | | Diplomatic Services Association | FDA |
| | | Unifi | Amicus |
| | | GPMU | Amicus |
| | | National Union of Lock and Metal Workers | TGWU |
| | | Staffordshire Building Society Staff Association | Portman Staff Association |
| | | Association of Magisterial Officers | PCS |
| April 2006 to March 2007 | Amalgamations | AUT and NATFHE | UCU |
| | Transfer of Engagements | National Union of Domestic Appliances and General Operatives | Community |
| | | General Union of Loom Overlookers | GMB |
| | | Audit Commission Staff Association | Prospect |
| | | Community and Youth Workers Union | TGWU |
| April 2007 | Amalgamations | Amicus and TGWU | Unite |
| | Transfer of Engagements | Alliance and Leicester Group Union of Staff | CWU |

*Source:* Certification Officer, *Annual Reports* (1997–2007)

and modern finance sector staff associations are quietly disappearing. Most significant are the mergers between larger bodies such as the AEEU and MSF, NATFHE and the AUT and Amicus and the TGWU. The basic impetus, as in the Conservative years, has not been rationalization of representation according to occupation and employment, but financial retrenchment, attempts to achieve economies of scale and curb competition, and a degree of political compatibility between leaders. However, merger activity has not delivered a reduction of per capita costs and contributed to a reduction of financial pressures on unions (Willman and Bryson 2006: 10). The creation of the PCS

and the GPMU, for example, certainly achieved an element of rationalization. But the latter then merged with Amicus while, to take other instances,
there have been no decisive moves to amalgamate the competing school-
teachers' unions or ASLEF, the RMT and TSSA on the railways.

Since 1997, mergers have combined with the extinction of smaller organizations – as Unite emerged in 2007, the TUC's smallest affiliate with ten
members, the Sheffield Wool Shear Workers, finally expired – to transform
the shape of British trade unionism. But mergers have typically lashed
together diverse memberships across sectoral and occupational boundaries to
form conglomerates. The tendency to concentration marked by the creation
of Unison in 1993 has been taken further with the establishment of Unite,
whose leaders have stated that they see the initiative as presaging further
mergers. The RMT has already expressed interest. In response, Unison has
approached the GMB. Such initiatives would involve augmentation of conglomerates as against industrial unions. Current tendencies have important
implications for the destiny of the TUC and the Labour Party but also for the
future of membership representation and union democracy.

If the development of trade unionism as a concentrated and public sector
phenomenon requires emphasis, so does its changing gender composition
(see McIlroy and Daniels, chapter 3, this volume, table 3.6). Again, as table 4.5
illustrates, there is diversity and divergence between individual unions. In
the NUT, 76 per cent of members are women and in Unison, the figure is
74 per cent. In largely private sector unions, like the GMB, the proportion
is smaller but women still represent 42 per cent of members as against a
58 per cent male membership. All-male organizations, such as UCATT, where
more than 98 per cent of members are men, persist. But the New Labour
years have witnessed the continuation of the long-term feminization of
British trade unionism.

In the 1990s this phenomenon and the increasing diversity of the labour
force stimulated reform of union structures to attract under-represented
groups into membership and activism. The TUC now has annual conferences
for women, minority ethnic workers, gay, lesbian, bisexual and transsexual
(LGBT) members and disabled workers as well as a young members' conference. Each can submit one resolution to Congress, although the TUC has
resisted reserved seats for under-represented groups on the general council.
This process was pioneered by Unison, which reserves seats on its executive
for women and also provides for nomination by 'self-organized groups'. In
2007 nine unions had reserved seats on their executive for women and eleven
had reserved seats for minority ethnic members. Over 60 per cent of unions
with more than 12,000 members had a national committee for minority
ethnic workers while over 50 per cent had such a body for women and
LGBT members. A third of unions convened a national conference for women
and 42 per cent held such a conference for black members (TUC 2007a).

The current position in relation to female representation can be seen from
table 4.6. Arguments continue as to whether positive action stimulates

*Table 4.5* Male / female membership of major UK unions 2006

|  |  | *Male* | *%* | *Female* | *%* |
|---|---|---|---|---|---|
| | Amicus | 933,014 | 77.75 | 266,986 | 22.25 |
| Unite | Transport and General Workers Union | 614,455 | 79.05 | 162,870 | 20.95 |
| | Total (Unite) | 1,547,469 | 78.26 | 429,856 | 21.74 |
| Unison: The Public Service Union | | 340,923 | 26.06 | 967,077 | 73.94 |
| GMB | | 337,731 | 58.32 | 241,374 | 41.68 |
| Royal College of Nursing | | Not available | | | |
| National Union of Teachers | | 61,116 | 23.98 | 193,746 | 76.02 |
| Union of Shop Distributive and Allied Workers | | 143,168 | 42.03 | 197,485 | 57.97 |
| Public and Commercial Services Union | | 124,241 | 39.73 | 188,484 | 60.27 |
| National Association of Schoolmasters / Union of Women Teachers | | 77,026 | 31.00 | 171,453 | 69.00 |
| Communication Workers Union | | 195,329 | 79.90 | 49,123 | 20.10 |
| Association of Teachers and Lecturers | | 29,767 | 26.25 | 83,641 | 73.75 |
| British Medical Association | | Not available | | | |
| Union of Construction Allied Trades and Technicians | | 119,554 | 98.72 | 1,555 | 1.28 |
| Prospect | | 80,781 | 79.07 | 21,380 | 20.93 |
| University and College Union | | 61,032 | 53.48 | 53,085 | 46.52 |
| Transport and Salaried Staff Association | | 21,091 | 71.51 | 8,402 | 28.49 |
| Rail and Maritime Transport Union | | 65,629 | 89.48 | 7,718 | 10.52 |
| National Union of Journalists | | 17,824 | 59.00 | 12,386 | 41.00 |
| Fire Brigades Union | | Not available | | | |
| Community | | 55,505 | 82.29 | 11,945 | 17.71 |
| Connect | | 15,686 | 80.09 | 3,900 | 19.91 |
| Associated Society of Locomotive Steam Enginemen and Firemen | | 2,998 | 93.98 | 192 | 6.02 |

*Source:* TUC, *Report of Congress*, 2006

activism, involvement and commitment or alternatively represents a politically correct token which improves matters for, at best, a small unrepresentative minority. In a union like the PCS, where there are two seats reserved for black members but none for other groups, opinion remains divided. The number of women general secretaries has increased and the combination of

*Table 4.6* Women in senior positions in largest TUC unions 2006

| | | No. of members | Members (%) | NEC (%) 2008 | TUC delegation (%) 2007 | FT National Officers (%) 2008 | FT Regional Officers (%) 2008 |
|---|---|---|---|---|---|---|---|
| | | *Women as percentage of:* | | | | | |
| Unite | Amicus[a] | 266,986 | 22.25 | 20.0 | See Unite | 21.0 | 23.0 |
| | Transport and General Workers Union | 162,870 | 20.95 | 32.5 | See Unite | 26.0 | 17.0 |
| | Total (Unite) | 429,856 | 21.74 | – | 31.0 | – | – |
| Unison: The Public Service Union | | 967,077 | 73.94 | 65.0 | 59.0 | 43.0 | 43.0 |
| GMB | | 241,374 | 41.68 | 41.0 | 49.0 | 30.0 | n/a |
| National Union of Teachers | | 193,746 | 76.02 | 41.0 | 49.0 | 29.0 | 50.0 |
| Union of Shop Distributive and Allied Workers | | 197,485 | 57.97 | 41.0 | 41.0 | 71.0 | 27.0 |
| Public and Commercial Services Union | | 188,484 | 60.27 | 34.0 | 61.0 | 30.0 | 27.0 |
| National Association of Schoolmasters / Union of Women Teachers | | 171,453 | 69.00 | 23.0 | 45.0 | 63.0 | 42.0 |
| Communication Workers Union | | 49,123 | 20.10 | 19.0 | 29.0 | 22.0 | 8.0 |
| Union of Construction Allied Trades and Technicians | | 1,555 | 1.28 | 0.0 | 0.0 | 0.0 | 0.0 |

*Source:* TUC, *Report of Congress*, 2006; *Labour Research*, March 2008

*Notes:*
a  Only includes figures for AEEU/MSF sections. GPMU and Unifi figures are not available.

Bill Morris, the first black general secretary of a British union and the first black general secretary to enter the House of Lords and Margaret Prosser, later Lady Prosser, led the TGWU in the New Labour years. It remains unclear whether this has improved the position of oppressed females and black members more generally.

## Workplace organization and national leadership

Organization in the workplace and a system of direct, accountable representation which protected union members and in some cases facilitated bargaining over pay and conditions was, if its prevalence and power were sometimes exaggerated, a distinctive and enduring feature of British trade unionism. In strong form it was a minority phenomenon. Nonetheless, in the 40 years to 1985, workplace organization constituted a significant channel for employee voice and strengthened union democracy. It mobilized resources: activism from members, services and paid time off from employers. It sometimes exhibited a degree of independence from formal union structure and it could act as a significant supplement and counterweight to the activities of full-time officials and official union machinery. The weakening of workplace organization was one of the achievements of the Conservative administrations after 1979.

There has been no revitalization of workplace trade unionism since 1997. By 2004 union representatives were present in 13 per cent of workplaces, compared with 17 per cent of workplaces in 1998. Even where unions were recognized, only 45 per cent of workplaces had an on-site representative from at least one union. This represented a decline from 55 per cent in 1998 (Kersley *et al.* 2006: 123–5). There are differences between the public sector, where representation is more resilient, and the private sector where representatives are far fewer and concentrated in large workplaces. If decline has been slower than in the 1980s and 1990s it remains a reality (Charlwood and Terry 2007). Tentative estimates suggest that the number of representatives of recognized unions employing 25 or more workers dropped from 156,700 in 1998 to 137,000 in 2004 (DTI 2007: 19). These figures are approximate. They include representatives carrying out specialist functions notably in relation to health and safety and union-resourced learning.

Union learning representatives (ULRs) have developed since 1999 and the TUC claimed that by 2006 there were 14,000 ULRs. Equality representatives – a still more recent development – have received encouragement and financial support from the state via the Women at Work Commission and the Union Modernisation Fund (UMF), which has provided £5 million for 'capacity building'. The function of ULRs is to advise members and employers on the skill needs of the enterprise and employees and arrange relevant training. They possess statutory backing to carry out this function but few negotiate over these issues (McIlroy 2008). Equality representatives take up workplace practices related to equality and diversity and work with management to seek solutions (*Labour Research*, March 2008). These new functions do not involve collective bargaining and joint regulation. They represent the state's attempt to reshape workplace trade unionism and channel its functions away from adversarialism and towards working with management. If such developments provide opportunities for trade union activists, their formal purpose and the restricted nature of the roles they offer cannot be minimized or downplayed.

The majority of union representatives work full-time and are over 40 years of age: their average age is 46. They were formed as members and activists during the period of management ascendancy since the 1980s (cf. Terry 2003: 261). While 56 per cent are male and 44 per cent female – a narrowing of the gender gap – 96 per cent are white (DTI 2007: 20). In the minority of work-places where there are representatives, vestiges remain of the powerful struc-tures of the 1960s and 1970s. Around 13 per cent of union representatives are full-time and 43 per cent spend five hours or more a week on union duties, with 89 per cent being paid while on union duties and the majority claiming that they received adequate facilities. Moreover, 48 per cent of senior union representatives reported that they negotiated over pay, 37 per cent over hours, and 32 per cent over holidays (Kersley *et al.* 2006: 145–55).

Despite minority resilience and developments such as the growth of ULRs, there is little reason to doubt the substance of Mike Terry's verdict that a change of great significance occurred during the Conservative years and that the endurance of transformative decline requires acknowledgement. Under New Labour, workplace organizations remain decisively debilitated and overall they no longer negotiate to any significant extent. Joint regulation as the cornerstone of industrial relations and the token of trade unionism's ability to provide, with all its inadequacies, a democratic voice for members in decision-making at work and restrict management prerogative has – at least for the moment – been laid aside in general terms and has, often, turned into consultation where managers are so inclined (Terry 2004: 205). The trad-ition of rank and file organization which generated crucial resources in terms of activism, voice and democracy for British trade unionism has been qualitatively diminished across extensive tracts of employment. The view that, despite decline, 'unions continued to have a significant influence over management and workplace outcomes in 1998' (Millward *et al.* 2000: 183) can only be justified today in relation to specific, limited situations in the public sector and parts of the private sector such as the railways. It does not work as a general description of workplace relations at the end of the millen-nium or in the early years of the new century (cf. ibid.: 234–6; Hyman 1997).

Given their traditionally small and commonly inadequate corps of full-time officers and comparatively low subscriptions (Kelly and Heery 1994), unions have depended on membership activism, and its ability to generate employer subsidy in terms of collecting dues (check-off) and providing paid time off and facilities in the workplace, to sustain and extend representation of mem-bers. There are ways of examining activism other than scrutinizing the state of workplace organization. One study assessed self-defined union activism 1991–2003 using a nationally representative panel data-set. Between 4.5 and 6.3 per cent of employees considered themselves activists. But activism peaked on this measure in the mid-1990s and fell to a low point in 2003 (Charlwood *et al.* 2006). Moreover, the attenuation of workplace activism and organization is continuing at a time when unions need activism most.

Unions are under financial pressure. Since the 1990s subscriptions have increased faster than average earnings but per capita growth in expenditure exceeds increases in earnings and prices despite the concentration of trade unionism. It has been argued that union statistics on income, expenditure and reserves which often show unions in the red nonetheless underestimate resource depletion. In terms of conventional financial measures, 'the union movement which is seeking to revitalize itself in the early part of the 21st century following substantial membership loss in the late 20th century is financially weaker than it has been for the last 50 years' (Willman and Bryson 2006: 3). In the awareness that state funding (see McIlroy, chapter 2, and McIlroy and Daniels, chapter 3, this volume) is no substitute for self-generated resources and autonomous grassroots vitality, some unions have begun to attempt to grapple with the problem. The TGWU has mounted an initiative to rebuild representative structures in the workplace (Graham 2006). The RMT has gone further and sponsored a National Shop Stewards Network (www.shopstewards.net).

Many accounts of contemporary trade unionism tell us more about workplace activists than about ordinary members, their attachment to their organizations, their perceptions of trade unionism and their political attitudes. Recent research has been limited and surveys suggest a mixed picture. In one study, more than 60 per cent of employees believed that unions do a good job, although that leaves a sizeable minority who did not. There has been little change in such responses since the 1980s. However, only 51 per cent of employees in 1998 and 57 per cent in 2005 who worked in unionized workplaces thought 'unions made a difference' to the workplace, while 42 per cent of respondents in 1998 and 36 per cent in 2005 felt unions made no difference. Attitudes to unions have thus become more positive under New Labour but again there are sizeable critical minorities. And what should worry trade unionists is the proportion of employees who believe that unions do not make a difference. Some 59 per cent of employees in unionized workplaces agreed that unions took notice of members' problems and complaints – which leaves a very unhealthy 40 per cent who did not – while the proportion who agreed 'strongly' fell from 13 per cent in 1998 to 9 per cent in 2005 (Bryson 2007).

A degree of dissatisfaction with the present position might be suggested by the fact that 36 per cent of employees, well over a third, felt unions possessed too little power. But this compared with 47 per cent in 1998, while 51 per cent of current respondents believed unions had 'about the right amount of power', compared with 45 per cent in 1998. The view that there are significant levels of discontent, like the belief that non-unionists think unions will improve the position at their workplace, is not affirmed by answers to survey questions related to the climate of employment relations: how employees view their interaction with managers. In 1998, 25 per cent of employees in union workplaces felt the climate was not good, while over 70 per cent declared it 'very good' or 'quite good'. In 2005, 77 per cent of respondents in union workplaces were positive about the employment relations climate and only 22 per cent were unenthusiastic. In non-union workplaces, 83 per cent of employees were positive about employment relations in 1998 and 85 per cent in 2005. On this, albeit imperfect and partial, evidence, things have improved under New Labour. Large majorities are satisfied with things as they are in employment relations and their sense of grievance is relatively subdued (Bryson 2007). This is not good news for union revitalization or its advocates: in terms of recruitment and organizing, unions can take little encouragement from this research. However, attitudes exist in context. A changing economic and political situation may, as in the past, provide the basis for a change in the way trade unionists look at the world and act on the world.

The *British Social Attitudes* survey yields little evidence of political radical-ism among union members. Although they are more likely to be left-wing than the general population, their radicalism is declining. Between 1998 and 2004, 42 per cent of union members agreed with the view that government should redistribute income from the better off to the less well off. This com-pared with 37 per cent of non-unionists. But it represented a drop from 54 per cent between 1991 and 1996. While 67 per cent of trade unionists believed that 'ordinary working people do not get their fair share of the nation's wealth', compared with 59 per cent of non-unionists, this had declined from 73 per cent in the Conservative years. And while 30 per cent of trade unionists agreed strongly that 'there is one law for the rich and one law for the poor', this represented a drop of eight points on the response between 1991 and 1996. There were similar changes in attitudes to increased taxation and welfare benefits. Trade unionists are still more likely to identify with Labour than other respondents: but there was a decline from 54 per cent of union respondents identifying with the party, 1991–6, to 51 per cent identify-ing with it, 1997–2004 (Curtice and Mair 2005).

Whether these changes are related to developments in the workplace and the decline of union workplace organization is conjectural. But that decline has undoubtedly facilitated shifts in power from shop floor to union office, from shop stewards and members to full-time officers, and raised issues of union democracy (Cohen 2006). There are question marks about the extent to which decline can be reversed from the top, from head offices, in the absence of significant change emanating from the bottom, from the work-place – and there are few signs of that. In the present context there is a danger that mergers driven by bureaucratic and financial considerations may further centralize decision-making, curtail rank-and-file influence, diminish grass-roots voice and circumscribe activism.

Unions have traditionally responded to such concerns about democracy and activism by providing for trade and sectional representation at regional and national level. Historically these mechanisms were complemented in some unions by direct election of officials at district and regional levels and the election of active, informed delegates to national and regional executives and conferences who could play a role in controlling bureaucracy and 'the machine'. However, the trend in recent years has been towards appointment rather than election of full-time officials, sometimes from outside the union.

This has complemented tendencies towards central control of policy which intensified in the 1980s and 1990s and were driven by a range of factors from legislation on industrial action and balloting, to an understandable desire to conserve resources at a time of retrenchment (Willman *et al.* 1993). Senior officials have always played a management role (Dunlop 1990) and there has been a recent tendency towards performance management in unions with appraisals, development reviews and, in some cases, detailed targets (Dempsey 2004).

Some of these problems can be seen in the Unite merger. The executive of the new union has 80 members drawn from a wide range of sectors and occupations and meets bimonthly. The two joint general secretaries wield executive power between meetings and if they declare an issue vital for policy, the executive can only reverse their decision on a 75 per cent vote. Full-time officials at regional and district level, subject to election in the Amicus rule-book, will be appointed in Unite – a practice which historically cemented the power of the leading officials in the TGWU. In the new conglomerate, twice the size of each of its components, some activists fear that power will be concentrated at the top in a way which affirms the worst, rather than the best, traditions of the merging unions (www.btinternet.com/~davidbeau mont/msf).

In this context the orientations, perspectives and abilities of national leaders may be vital in developing, in conjunction with activists, strategies which can empower members and stem decline. The New Labour years have been widely seen as producing a new generation of leaders more assertive industrially and more left-wing politically than their predecessors. The leaders of the main unions in 1997 are listed in table 4.7. The vast majority became officials, usually at district or regional level, in the late 1960s and 1970s and embraced activism a little earlier. This was a period of relative union strength, militancy and sophisticated workplace organization. It has been suggested that such generational experience may exercise enduring influence on the values and orientations of officials; it may incline them more towards adversarialism and radicalism to a greater extent than their counterparts who became active in periods of union weakness and retreat (Kelly and Heery 1994: 198–207). However, this hypothesis may underplay both initial variation in values between officers and the impact on them of changing circumstances and structure as they pass from district to national level (McIlroy 1997: 115–20).

For the cohort in table 4.7, what may have been more important by 1997 was their negative experience of the 1980s and 1990s and their relief at the election of Tony Blair, rather than their experience of the 1960s and 1970s. Far from opposing New Labour's turn to neoliberalism, some were prepared to support the explicit rejection of that era of union strength which lay at the heart of Blair's 'no return to the 1970s' line (McIlroy, Campbell and Fishman 2007: 1–2). Historical change is also important. Five of the fifteen leaders listed in the table had degrees: this would have been unlikely in earlier

Table 4.7 Leaders of major unions 1997

| Union | General Secretary | Full-time officer | Born | Education | Political Position | Remuneration (financial package) | |
|---|---|---|---|---|---|---|---|
| | | | | | | Salary | Benefits |
| TGWU | Bill Morris | D 1972; N 1979; DGS 1986; GS 1992–2003; K 2003; L2006 | 1938 | Left school 15 | Centre | 56,812 | 14,216 |
| Unison | Rodney Bickerstaffe | D 1966; N 1974; GS 1981–2001 | 1945 | College of technology | Centre | 49,456 | 11,461 |
| GMB | John Edmonds | R 1967; D 1968; N 1972; GS 1986–2003 | 1944 | University | Centre | 57,000 | 14,000 |
| AEEU | Ken Jackson | D 1992; N 1996; GS 1996–2003; K 1999 | 1937 | Left school 15 | Right | 45,300 | 10,451 |
| MSF | Roger Lyons | D 1966; N 1970; AGS 1987; GS 1997–2004 | 1942 | University | Centre-right | 62,465 | 10,997 |
| RCN | Christine Hancock | GS 1989–2001 | 1943 | n/a | Centre-right | 78,650 | 17,264 |
| USDAW | Bill Connor | D 1971; N 1978; DGS 1987; GS 1997–2004; K 2003 | 1941 | Left school 15 | Centre-right | 56,328 | 11,288 |
| NUT | Doug McAvoy | DGS 1975; GS 1989 | 1939 | Left school 15 | Right | 70,003 | 6,106 |
| CWU | Derek Hodgson | D 1980s; N 1990s; GS, 1997–2001 | 1940 | Left school 15 | Centre-right | 58,260 | n/a |
| NASUWT | Nigel De Gruchy | DGS 1978–89; GS 1990–2002 | 1943 | University | Centre-right | 61,385 | 15,152 |
| GPMU | Tony Dubbins | D 1971; DGS 1976; GS 1983–2004; N 1974; DGS 1982 GS 1988; GS 1992–2004 | 1944 | Left School 15 | Centre | 55,167 | 14,373 |

(Continued Overleaf)

Table 4.7 Continued

| Union | General Secretary | Full-time officer | Born | Education | Political Position | Remuneration (financial package) | |
|---|---|---|---|---|---|---|---|
| | | | | | | Salary | Benefits |
| ATL | Peter Smith | AGS 1974; DGS 1988; GS 1992 | 1940 | Left school 15 | Centre-right | 77,122 | 14,853 |
| UCATT | George Brumwell | D 1971; N 1984; GS 1991 | 1939 | Left school 15 | Left | 29,038 | 5,155 |
| BIFU | Ed Sweeney | R 1976; N 1986; DGS 1991; GS 1996 | 1955 | University | Centre-right | 43,480 | 8,794 |
| CPSA | Barry Reamsbottom | D 1976; E 1979; GS 1992–1998 | 1949 | Left School 17 | Right | 47,969 | n/a |

Sources: Who's Who; individual unions.

Notes:
Please note that the average salaries used in the text are taken from the New Earnings Survey 1997 which was replaced by the Annual Survey of Hours and Earnings (ASHE) in 2004.
Abbreviations: D = District or equivalent officer; E = Education Officer; N = National Officer; R = Research Officer; AGS = Assistant Secretary / General Secretary; DGS = Deputy General Secretary; GS = General Secretary; K = Knight; L = Lord

generations. Leaders such as Bickerstaffe and Edmonds, in comparison with, say, Brumwell or Dubbins or many leaders of past eras, had little direct experience of their members' work. While the majority had followed the traditional route from district office to national leadership, some had been directly elected or appointed, sometimes from outside the union, to national leadership. At one end of the spectrum, Brumwell had supported the Communist Party (CP); at the other end, Jackson came from the hard-right ETU tradition. Reamsbottom was, in trade union terms, an ideological right-winger and McAvoy a crusading but maverick 'moderate'.

Whatever their personal predilections, the majority had experienced the years of union reverses in leading positions. They could be considered, by 1997, centre or centre-right, at least in relation to the trade union politics of the 1970s and 1980s. With an average age of 55 they were not young, but in comparison with their members, they were well rewarded and financially secure. Their average salary was £55,987 and their average benefits £11,855. This compared with an average for all salaries in 1997 of £13,982 and the highest figure, for 'specialist managers', of £28,808 (New Earnings Survey 1997; see table 4.7).

With varying degrees of criticism these leaders were supportive of New Labour's first term. By 2007 the position had changed (see McIlroy, chapter 5, this volume). The leaders of the main unions, after a decade of New Labour, are listed in table 4.8. Again the table demonstrates variety and complexity. Six of the 2007 cohort had attended university. One had been a university lecturer, one had a PhD and one had been chief executive of a NHS trust. They contrasted with more traditional representatives: Simpson had been a CP member in the 1960s and 1970s and Woodley had been a shop steward in the car industry. The difference with their predecessors is that the majority of the 2007 group became full-time officers in the late 1980s and 1990s, a period of union defeat. This again raises questions about generational theories because there has been a relative turn to the left, not to the right, in trade union terms since 1997. But it would be wrong to exaggerate this in practical terms. The 2007 cohort had an average age of 54 and an average salary of £87,726 plus benefits of £24,759. This contrasts with a median for all employees of £19,496 and a figure of £34,887 for 'corporate managers' in 2006 (Annual Survey of Hours and Earnings, 2006).

The election of a succession of new leaders in 2002–3 – in some cases in opposition to right-wing incumbents such as Jackson in Amicus and Reamsbottom in the PCS, figures viewed as fringe members of the New Labour establishment – was perceived as affirming a new, harder attitude to the government and demonstrating greater support for industrial militancy among union members who voted for them (Murray 2003). As we have seen there is little evidence suggestive of the development of significant discontent at grassroots level, although dissatisfaction in the workplace may have escaped social science surveys. Alternatively, the old common sense of union representation may have been at work: members elect representatives because

Table 4.8 Leaders of major unions 2007

| Union | General Secretary | Full-time officer | Born | Education | Political Position | Remuneration (financial package) | |
|---|---|---|---|---|---|---|---|
| | | | | | | Salary | Benefits |
| Unite | Derek Simpson | D 1981; GS 2002 | 1944 | Left school 15 OU degree | Left | 86,927 | 66,410 |
| | Tony Woodley | D 1989; N 1991; DGS 2002; GS 2003 | 1948 | Left school 15 | Left | 80,043 | 10,221 |
| Unison | Dave Prentis | DGS 1993; GS 2001 | 1948 | University | Centre | 87,659 | 29,967 |
| GMB | Paul Kenny | D 1979; GS 2006 | | Left school 15 | Centre-left | 78,000 | 21,000 |
| RCN | Peter Carter | Executive of NHS Trust; GS 2007 | 1949 | University | Centre | 123,588 | 19,838 |
| USDAW | John Hannett | D 1985; N 1990; DGS 1997; GS 2004 | 1953 | Left school 16 | Centre-right | 76,061 | 19,828 |
| NUT | Steve Sinnott | Teacher EC member; DGS 1994; GS 2004 | 1951 | University | Left | 84,042 | 20,844 |
| NASUWT | Chris Keats | Teacher; AGS 1998; DGS 2001; GS 2004 | 1953 | University | Centre | 87,847 | 23,776 |
| PCS | Mark Serwotka | GS 2002 | 1963 | Left school 16 | Left | 83,115* | 29,427 |
| CWU | Billy Hayes | N 1992; GS 2001 | 1953 | Left school 15 | Left | 77,188 | 22,813 |
| ATL | Mary Bousted | University lecturer; GS 2003 | 1959 | University | Centre | 96,735 | 21,309 |
| UCATT | Alan Ritchie | D 1983; N 1991; GS 2004 | 1951 | Left school 15 | Left | 59,382 | 10,714 |
| Prospect | Paul Noon | N 1981; AGS 1989; GS 1999 | 1952 | Left school 18 | Centre | 85,560 | 25,654 |
| UCU | Sally Hunt | N 1991; AGS 1995; GS 2002 | 1964 | University | Centre | 129,345** | 26,477** |
| RMT | Bob Crow | AGS 1997; GS 2002 | 1961 | Left school 16 | Left | 80,394 | 23,100 |

Sources: Who's Who; individual unions

Notes:
Abbreviations: D = District or equivalent officer; E= Education Officer; N = National Officer; R = Research Officer; AGS = Assistant Secretary / General Secretary; DGS = Deputy General Secretary; GS = General Secretary; K = Knight; L = Lord
*Mark Serwotka donates everything above the average wage of a PCS member to the union strike fund.
**Payment made for a period of more than 12 months.

they believe that they will represent them vigorously, not because they endorse their politics. Moreover, members vote, as they did in the past, in relatively small numbers. The designation 'awkward squad' captured one aspect of the attitude of some of the new leaders, at least from a New Labour viewpoint. There was more criticism, more objection and more argument: they were less clubbable and pliable and harder for politicians to manage. But with a few exceptions they proved better at talking than acting and were, when tested by the neoliberal state, ultimately willing to fall in line. The term 'awkward squad' imposed too great a degree of homogeneity; it abstracted personalities and their history from structure and environment (Charlwood 2004).

Several of the group had received political training in left-wing organizations. Serwotka and Wrack had been members of Trotskyist groups, Simpson and Crow had been in the CP and the latter, together with Rix, had been prominent in Arthur Scargill's Socialist Labour Party (SLP). But while Crow and Serwotka worked amicably with like-minded executives, Rix was defeated in 2003 by a right-wing candidate. Another member of 'the squad', Gilchrist, was defeated in 2005 by the more militant Wrack, who then presided over a divided executive. Serwotka operated in a PCS which was not affiliated to Labour, and neither Crow nor Wrack had any objections to their unions' disaffiliation from the party. In contrast Simpson, Woodley and Hayes firmly opposed disaffiliation and campaigned, albeit decreasingly, on a 'reclaim the Labour Party' basis. In Amicus, Simpson harassed a left wing which appeared to think very much like Serwotka, Crow and Wrack. In the latter three cases, and in the case of Hayes and the CWU, leaders were voicing the views of activists in relatively compact unions whose employment situation disposed them to criticism of the government and action against it. The awkward squad reflected a move to the left but the group was neither composite nor cohesive (see table 4.9).

The emergence of the squad was awkward for the government. The group was more difficult than its predecessors. Taken together it posed no fundamental political threat, still less a coherent political alternative to neoliberalism. In terms of industrial policy and membership militancy, Serwotka, Crow and Wrack held different, more critical views than Simpson and Woodley. Fundamentally, this trend to the left among union leaders and many activists was not accompanied by any significant trend to militancy among rank-and-file members.

## Factionalism and internal politics

Since 1997 British trade unionism has been marked by factionalism and infighting. Amicus, now part of Unite, was the product of the 2002 merger of two heavily factionalized unions, the AEEU and MSF. The AEEU was among the firmest supporters of New Labour and a powerful protagonist of partnership, single-union agreements and 'no-strike deals' – sometimes to the

*Table 4.9* The Awkward Squad

| Member | Born | Union | Elected GS | Background |
|--------|------|-------|------------|-----------|
| Tony Woodley | 1948 | TGWU | 2003 | Works convenor, Vauxhall Motors. Full-time official 1989. Deputy General Secretary 2002. Labour Party member. |
| Derek Simpson | 1944 | Amicus | 2002 | Engineering shop steward. District Official supported by Broad Left. Communist Party member. Joined Labour Party in 1994. |
| Mark Serwotka | 1963 | PCS | 2002 | Rank-and-file office member of Socialist Caucus before election. Former supporter of *Socialist Organizer*, Alliance for Workers Liberty. Endorsed Respect candidates in 2005 general election. |
| Billy Hayes | 1955 | CWU | 2001 | Executive member and national officer before election. Member of the Labour Party. |
| Bob Crow | 1961 | RMT | 2002 | Local rep, national officer, assistant general secretary before election. Former member of the Communist Party, Communist Party of Britain and Socialist Labour Party. No longer a member of any party. |
| Andy Gilchrist | 1960 | FBU | 2000 | Full-time officer. Labour Party member. |
| Matt Wrack | 1963 | FBU | 2005 | Rank and file activist before election. Supporter of *Militant* and Socialist Party. |
| Mick Rix | 1963 | ASLEF | 1998–2003 | Local activist in union and Labour Party. Former member of Socialist Labour Party. |
| Paul Mackney | 1950 | NATFHE | 1997–2007 | Full-time officer. Former member of International Socialists. |
| Jeremy Dear | 1966 | NUJ | 2002 | University. National Organizer. Unaffiliated left. |
| | | Average age when elected: 44 | | |

*Sources: Who's Who*; individual unions

detriment of competing unions. Its leadership around Ken Jackson had reconstructed the union in the centralized image of the electricians' union, from which they largely came, extinguishing much of the democracy of the old engineering union. They were supported by a right-wing caucus, AEEU United: it based itself on full-time officials and controlled the national executive. Increasing disillusion with New Labour, the impending retirement of Jackson and better organization prompted the revival of a group around the left-wing paper, *Engineering Gazette*. More open than some union broad lefts, it was marked by the rank-and-file traditions of the old AEU. The *Gazette* called for greater internal democracy, election of officials and a programme to revive manufacturing industry. Despite having to resign from his union post in order to stand and a gruellingly difficult election campaign, the *Gazette* candidate, Derek Simpson, defeated Jackson in the 2002 contest for general secretary.[1]

The MSF executive was similarly dominated by the right and aligned with New Labour. The main grouping 'MSF for Labour' backed general secretary, Roger Lyons, in his 1997 election victory over an official from Northern Ireland, Joe Bowers. Its aftermath saw intense infighting as Lyons, supported by the executive, sought to sideline Bowers and his supporters and discipline other opponents such as leading members of the London regional council. A torrent of allegations concerning inflated expense claims, financial mismanagement and unfair dismissal of staff by the general secretary surfaced in the press and were contested in employment tribunals. With his domination of the executive threatened by the merger and the rise of the left in the AEEU and amid appeals and cross-appeals to the Certification Officer, Lyons stepped down, leaving Simpson as general secretary of Amicus.

The elections for the executive of the new union saw a shift to the left. The *Amicus Unity Gazette*, a fusion of the AEEU group and the MSF Broad Left, won 23 out of 48 seats. Tensions emerged between the leadership and those who saw the *Gazette*'s job as deferring to it and activists who took a more critical stance. In late 2004, four Socialist Workers Party members were barred from *Gazette* meetings for voting against the leadership's repudiation of the Multiplex strike. There were fierce arguments about including election of full-time officials in the new rulebook and implementing the new rules. The 'ATU group' of full-time officers, including some supporters of the previous regime, emerged pledging support to Simpson. By 2006 his lieutenants dominated the *Gazette* and three officials prominent in his election campaign, but now critical of his leadership, had been dismissed. The deputy general secretary informed a *Gazette* meeting that he had been nominated by Simpson as his successor and sole general secretary of Unite. The order of the day was to get Amicus officials into position so that the TGWU did not take control of the merged organization.

By the turn of the century there was dissatisfaction in the TGWU with the increasingly conservative role played by Bill Morris and Margaret Prosser as general secretary and deputy general secretary. They were seen on the left as too soft on New Labour. The major faction in the union, the Broad Left, had backed the election of both: it had always been primarily a top-down election organizer, primed and prompted by full-time officers. With the decline of workplace trade unionism, it reflected struggles inside the machine rather than bringing workplace struggles into the higher echelons of the union. Moreover, by the late 1990s, there were significant differences between the two main forces in the Broad Left. The London left possessed an old-style orientation to building bridges with the centre-right and influencing the general secretary. The other main group, whose traditional base was in the North-West, shared much of this approach; but it advocated a more aggressive style and greater emphasis on organizing. By 2002 there was a cold split and rough parity on the executive. The situation was transformed when Tony Woodley, national automotive officer and a long-standing member of the second group, defeated Peter Booth, a national organizer, supported by the London left, in the contest for deputy general secretary.

Using this success as a launching pad to develop further realignment round the slogan of 'unity', Woodley secured support from the Communist Party of Britain (CPB) as well as the centre. He defeated Barry Camfield, the London regional organizer – long identified with the old Broad Left and the CPB – Jack Dromey, traditionally identified with New Labour, and the Scottish candidate Jimmy Elsby, in the race to succeed Morris. A new Unity coalition was sealed when Dromey, who was given an important role in the new organizing strategy associated with Woodley, subsequently defeated Camfield to become Woodley's deputy. This led to the retirement of figures such as Camfield and a gradual reassembly of the Broad Left. Traditional problems were reiterated in its failure to secure the TGWU's backing for John McDonnell MP – whom the Broad Left publicly supported – as Labour Party deputy leader in 2006 in the face of reluctance from Woodley and the new leadership.

Differences in Unison are more transparently political: here the opposition is driven by the hard left. It is marked by division and, like the TGWU, characterized by changing partnerships. In the late 1990s the left was split between the Campaign for a Fighting Democratic Union (CFDU) led by the Socialist Party (SP), the Socialist Workers Party (SWP), which operated independently, and the small Unison Labour Left. The advent of New Labour, and leadership loyalty towards it, led to bans on branches supporting campaigns unacceptable to the executive, a 60–40 per cent conference decision to prohibit provision of finance and resources by branches to the CFDU and disciplinary measures against left-wing activists. This provoked regroupment. The SWP joined the new Unison United Left (UUL). But the SP subsequently decamped on the grounds that the new organization refused to take a sufficiently strong positive position on Unison disaffiliating from the Labour Party.

New Labour's policies on pay, pensions and privatization have ensured that there is continuing questioning of Unison's funding of the party and its leadership's management of the Unison Labour Link – the affiliated fund

– and the General Political Fund. The left has maintained a minority position on the executive in the face of administrative measures from the leadership and is able to poll around a quarter of the vote in elections for general secretary. It has not been successful in uniting its potential supporters in a project of constructing alliances beyond its limited natural constituency in order to harness wider membership discontent with New Labour or in defining itself as a credible alternative to the existing leadership. In 2000, the well-known and experienced CFDU candidate, Roger Bannister, won over a third of the votes when standing against Dave Prentis. In 2005, representing the SP, Bannister took around 15 per cent of the vote, while the UUL candidate, Labour Party activist, Jon Rogers, won around 10 per cent.

The GMB is a union with little history of political factionalism. The retirement of the able John Edmonds as general secretary against a background of financial difficultly provoked rivalries, although their political content was subdued. In the 2003 election for Edmonds' successor, Kevin Curran, the Northern regional secretary, and Paul Kenny, London regional secretary, were both backed by ad hoc organization which appeared to owe more to local differences than to politics. Curran, the successful candidate, was suspended by the executive after a series of allegations and the appointment of an inquiry into the bankrolling of his campaign and its use of union staff. He resigned in 2003 and was eventually succeeded by Kenny, who was perceived as slightly to the left of his predecessor.

Factionalism has usually been mild in USDAW. Under the leadership of Bill Connor the union was seen as 'the bedrock of New Labour' and energetically pushed partnership with employers. Since 1997, the left has been a marginal force. In the run-up to the election for Connor's successor as general secretary, there were unsuccessful attempts to get the Broad Left to support the deputy general secretary, John Hannett, another New Labour loyalist. In the end, the Broad Left candidate, Maureen Madden, received 27.3 per cent of the vote, which reasonably reflected the balance of forces in a union where partnership is still seen as a viable option.

The NUT's two hard left factions, the Socialist Teachers Alliance and the CFDU, had long harassed the authoritarian general secretary Doug McAvoy and his centre and right-wing supporters. On his retirement in 2004 success eluded them. Under the single transferable vote system the SP candidate and John Bangs, McAvoy's favoured successor, were both eliminated. In the run-off the deputy general secretary, Steve Sinnott, generally seen as soft left, defeated Ian Murch, backed by the CFDU and STA, by 27,287 votes to 22,340 votes. Sinnott adopted a more open and inclusive stance than his predecessor and secured a greater degree of unity. He supported the executive's opposition to the 'social partnership' with the government, accepted by the other leading unions. He criticized the National Workload Agreement and the Rewards and Incentives Group involving the employers, government and other leading teaching unions.[2]

Prolonged argument about the resolution to the 2006 industrial action over pay and the hotly contested tussle for general secretary between the centre-leaning Sally Hunt and the left candidate, Roger Kline, paved the way for the creation of a new open UCU Left. Influenced by the SWP, this grouping emphasized the importance of politics to union struggle and took up the trajectory of New Labour, the Middle East and the War in Iraq as well as traditional university issues. The situation remained unstable: Hunt won the election but the left gained a strong presence on the executive.

In contrast to the traditionally non-political culture of both the UCU's components, NATFHE and the AUT, the predecessors of the PCS, particularly the CPSA, were marked by organized political competition. Barry Reamsbottom, CPSA general secretary at the time of the merger, led the hard right National Moderate group. It dominated the executive and was confronted by Left Unity – an alliance in which the SP was the most influential component. The right-wing faction in the PTC, Members First, was distinctly milder than its CPSA counterpart while the opposition Unity group was basically a broad left on the old CP model. After the merger the two right-wing groups failed to coalesce while the Unity group lost ground. The right still held a majority on the new executive but with the retirement of the joint general secretary, John Sheldon, ex-PTC, a wrangle commenced as to whether Reamsbottom should continue as sole general secretary until his retirement or whether there should be an election. In the event, Members First, increasingly critical of the Moderates, worked with the left to ensure that conference demanded an election in 2001.

Believing Reamsbottom would stand, Left Unity supported the Members First candidate, the assistant general secretary and New Labour supporter, Hugh Lanning. They reversed their position when Reamsbottom failed to secure sufficient nominations and Lanning was challenged by an 'independent socialist', Mark Serwotka. The latter was a benefits office worker who had never served as a full-time officer and a supporter of the small Socialist Caucus within Left Unity. Serwotka's victory led to attempts by the Moderates to render the election null and void through an executive vote securing Reamsbottom another two years in office and through resort to the courts. Matters culminated in legal confirmation of the election result and a new general secretary. The trend towards the left provoked by the impact on members of New Labour's policies on pay, conditions and job cuts was reinforced by revulsion at the Moderates' methods; it was driven by superior and more inclusive organization of the left. It has been maintained by the restoration of annual elections and conferences, mothballed by the Moderates, and reflected in the election of successive left-wing executives and Serwotka's return, unopposed, as general secretary.

Together with the president, Janice Goodrich, an SP member, he leads an executive dominated by the Democracy Alliance – essentially Left Unity, the SP, SWP, Scottish Socialist Party (SSP), the Communist Party of Britain (CPB) and independent socialists – working in harness with the PCS Democrats, a strand of the old Members First Labour Party supporters. Left Unity, in which the SP possesses the strongest presence, is the most sophisticated faction in the unions. It has engineered an alliance with those to its right. It holds a national conference which elects a national committee, debates motions both domestic and international, and agrees nominations for all elected positions. Currently the three opposition groups, the Moderates, '4 the Members' – a split from the latter – and the small Socialist Caucus, which now stands on an Independent Left slate in elections, remain peripheral. Nonetheless, problems remain over how to combat job losses and campaign for national terms and conditions and pay-bargaining. The PCS's difficulties were encapsulated in divisions over the executive's acceptance of the 2005 pension deal. This secured the pension entitlements of existing employees but conceded that new entrants would have to work to 65, not as now to 60, to receive a full pension.

Members of the CWU also face an insecure environment with threats of privatization, liberalization of services, job losses and pay curbs. In 1998, the Broad Left candidate, postal worker Billy Hayes, attracted 17,000 votes against centre-right incumbent, Derek Hodgson. In 2001, Hayes' sustained opposition to the New Labour agenda saw him defeat the assistant general secretary, John Keggie, who was backed by the establishment and some sections of the left in telecommunications. An SWP member, associated with the rank-and-file paper, *Postworker*, Jane Loftus, was subsequently elected president. Hayes' political credentials are strong but together with executive members, he has been criticized from the left for an insufficiently firm stance on industrial action, particularly during the 2007 national pay dispute.

Together with the PCS, the RMT is the most left-wing and, together with the CWU, the most strike-prone of Britain's unions. Again, radicalization stems from the environment in which members work. It is fuelled by increasing antagonism to New Labour's refusal to reverse privatization of rail, its privatization of the London Tube and outsourcing of jobs, reinforced by employers' use of employment legislation on ballots to undermine industrial action. In the late 1990s, Arthur Scargill's SLP had a powerful presence on the executive and among leading officers, and the left candidate, Greg Tucker, performed creditably against the general secretary, Jimmy Knapp. The executive prescribed the increasingly successful CFDU. But Knapp's death in harness in 2001 and the overwhelming victory of the CFDU supporter and assistant general secretary, Bob Crow, signalled the ascendancy of the left. Phil Boston became president and leading activists, such as Alex Gordon, dominated the executive. In contrast to the earlier CFDU, there is, today, no organized broad left but rather a plethora of rank-and-file platforms, groupings and bulletins such as *Across the Tracks, The Red Line* and *Tube Worker*. In the context of left control of the apparatus these operate with remarkable unity and cohesion, focusing both on elections and member mobilization.

If the right in the RMT is vestigial, the situation is different in the train drivers' union, ASLEF. Here, the left chalked up a major success with the 1998 election of Mick Rix as general secretary, replacing the more right-wing

Lew Adams. Success was fleeting in a union with a conservative membership, often inclined to the right, which had not backed the RMT campaigns against privatization. Some of Rix's proposals, such as a return to national bargaining, control over overtime and extension of the equality agenda proved unpopular; so did his high profile in wider union politics. Against this, hard bargaining increased drivers' pay during his tenure. Nonetheless, the right regrouped and in 2003 Rix was replaced by Shaun Brady.

The new general secretary expressed concern at the state of ASLEF finances and commissioned an accountant's report which confirmed that there were problems. The executive in turn commissioned a report from a QC which recorded a degree of mismanagement but ruled out more serious allegations. Conflicts between the general secretary and head office staff, threats of dismissal, fisticuffs between leading officers and TUC intervention, terminated in the dismissal of Brady by the executive, protracted litigation and fresh elections, won by the centre candidate, Keith Norman.

The conduct of the FBU pay dispute of 2002–3 produced discontent among members and fractured the support of the general secretary, Andy Gilchrist, elected in 2000 as the left candidate in succession to the old CPer Ken Cameron. A number of oppositional groupings such as 'Red Watch' criticized Gilchrist's handling of the dispute. Out of it came Grassroots FBU, established in 2004 to build an activist network which would develop support for radical policies and challenge for electoral positions based on a critique of the existing leadership. Grassroots was swiftly investigated and proscribed by the executive – a move which presaged success for its supporters. Matt Wrack, an official in the militant London region, was elected deputy general secretary in February 2005. A year later Wrack defeated Gilchrist in the contest for general secretary. The union continues to regroup with a leadership divided between two competing left tendencies.

Factionalism is arguably as strong as it ever was, although in most cases it is closer to the model of the electoral machine than the grassroots caucus. It rarely attracts attention unless it erupts in open warfare and it is usually deemed of dubious legitimacy. Union leaderships have themselves often emerged from factional activity and in some cases are sustained by it. They almost invariably consider such activity on the part of their opponents as illegitimate and even unconstitutional. They sometimes place obstacles in its path and, from time to time, prohibit or restrict oppositional groups and discipline their activists. Nonetheless, organized internal conflict is an inevitable aspect of trade unionism and has been considered functional and positive in safeguarding democracy and making it work (Lipset *et al.* 1956; Martin 1968; Undy and Martin 1984). It remains the preserve of a small number of activists and mobilizes only a fraction of union members: Left Unity has around 700 members, the United Left in Unison around 500. Union democracy itself is a minority pursuit. In the last election for Unison's general secretary only 16.6 per cent of members voted. Even where there is greater interest and media publicity, as in the recent UCU election, turnout was a mere 14 per cent. There are exceptions: at a time of intense interest in union policy, 38,000 of the FBU's 53,000 members voted in the Gilchrist/ Wrack contest.

The antipathy to New Labour among union activists has to be located in this context and, like factionalism, the intensity of antagonism has varied according to the territory that individual unions cultivate, the problems their members encounter and the viability of political and industrial alternatives to cooperating with New Labour. The advance of the left has occurred to different degrees in different situations. It has proceeded against a background of union decline. Crucially, policy forged internally must be delivered externally, in a world of major constraints; they include the neoliberalism of the state, the economic and industrial relations context, the quality of union leadership internal contention provides and the depth of membership support for consequent policy. The right wing has been defeated: in unions like Unite and the PCS it has been routed. Yet the substantive achievements of the left and the degree to which it has dented neoliberalism have been slight. Its retreat at the 2007 Labour Party conference over the issue of voting on motions (see McIlroy, chapter 5, this volume) symbolized its failure to deliver on its rhetoric. In a situation where the myriad of problems which impede industrial mobilization were absent the episode again raised doubts about the nerve, will and strategic acumen of left-wing leaders in combat with neoliberalism. It prompted the question of how left the union left really is when push comes to shove, when policy must be practised.

## The changing TUC

The TUC maintained its representative nature as the national union centre during the Blair governments. It still represents 6.4 million trade unionists. However, this compares with 12 million in 1979 and 8.1 million in 1990. Since 1997, the decline in affiliated membership has been arrested but not reversed. The TUC no longer speaks for the majority of British workers, although it remains the voice of the vast majority of trade unionists (see McIlroy and Daniels, chapter 3, table 3.1). The number of its affiliates has continued to fall. The adhesion of small bodies does little to enhance overall membership and affiliation of bodies such as the British Dietetic Association and the Guinness Staff Association is countered by merger activity. The ATL has been the single sizeable new affiliate while the RCN has remained unwilling to join.

The 1993 Conservative legislation which gave individuals the right to join a union of their choice organizing in their occupation compromised the TUC disputes committee's role in regulating inter-union disputes under the 1939 Bridlington Agreement. The TUC still maintains a more limited conciliatory and adjudicatory role. There are only a small number of such cases annually – 25 in 2001, 11 in 2005: 'it is clear that the trend towards fewer inter-union disputes is continuing' (TUC 2005: 151). Such disputes still raise problems: in

1998 the road haulage union, URTU, disaffiliated after a TUC judgement, although it returned to the fold in 2003 (TUC 2004: 150).

The TUC continues to provide valuable services for affiliates in terms of publicity, research and education. These services develop activists, make them more efficient and contribute to union strategy. The resumption of state funding for education courses, axed by the Conservatives, has been particularly important. Congress House acts as both a think tank for new ideas and as an indispensable forum for debate about union futures. In this sphere it has adopted a more professional approach, increasingly commissioning research and reports from consultants and academics. It has continued to provide support for members in a range of disputes over public sector pay and pensions. It has involved itself in conflicts in the fire service, Royal Mail, the universities and Gate Gourmet. It continues to act as a spokesperson for affiliates in both national and, indispensably, international arenas.

The attenuation of its political role in coordinating its affiliates' dealings with the state in the 1980s and 1990s stimulated the relaunch of the TUC in 1994. It now places far greater emphasis on what it can do as a campaigning body (Heery 1998; McIlroy 2000). A more dynamic outward-looking structure has turned on leadership from Task Groups headed by experienced general council members. The list of campaigns over the last decade, over issues such as disability, racism and the BNP, working time, pensions, equal pay and Iraqi trade unions has been extensive and impressive. The Campaigns Unit has forged links with a variety of organizations from Help the Aged to Stonewall. The TUC's political role has been reasserted through quarterly meetings with the Chancellor and Secretary of State for Trade and Industry and regular contact at all levels with other relevant departments. The successes such campaigning has chalked up remain limited.

The TUC also maintains links with the Trade Union Group of MPs at Westminster and Brussels and with the spokespersons of the Conservative, Liberal Democrat and Plaid Cymru and the Scottish National Party. It has pushed for a stronger EU social model and developed its involvement in Europe – despite differences among affiliates – through the General Council Europe Monitoring Group, the ETUC and the European Economic and Social Committee (TUC 2006: 98–102). Nonetheless, outcomes have not matched persistent and often imaginative efforts (see for example Taylor, chapter 11, this volume).

Finance has been a recurring difficulty in the context of the problems facing affiliates and the inelasticity of affiliation fees. This partly motivated unsuccessful proposals for biennial Congresses: they were rejected on the grounds that this move would diminish the TUC's visibility and curtail its accountability (TUC 2005: 150). However, the TUC has extended its financial relationship with the state and cash problems have moderated with the influx of state funds for workplace learning and the handover of the ULF to Congress House. This increases the TUC's potential dependency on the state. It decreases its dependence on affiliates; indeed the fact that Congress House annually dispenses £12.5 million to affiliated unions may lubricate relationships with them and stiffen the rationale for affiliation. The burgeoning of state funding also suggests a potentially significant change in the TUC's portfolio of activities in a situation where its political role is vigorously pursued but is, like much of its activity, far from successful (see McIlroy, chapter 5, this volume). A further factor is the growth of 'super unions' and associated tensions between the TUC and major affiliates.

John Monks, general secretary 1993–2003, and his successor Brendan Barber (they might have been dubbed, at least in New Labour circles, as the 'sensible squad') were university graduates who followed the traditional pattern of becoming general secretary after a career inside Congress House rather than in the unions. Monks was an able leader whose dedication to partnership and initially to New Labour provoked criticism. He did his utmost to maintain a constructive stance towards the government and liaised closely with sympathetic ministers such as Ian McCartney, although their loyalty to New Labour overrode their empathy with union leaders. Monks was active in opposing moves to the left in TUC policy, over the anti-union laws and privatization. He was unsympathetic to changes within the unions, in the CWU, PCS and RMT, which were seen as endangering relations with New Labour. There was evidence that at least one TUC employee had helped New Labour supporters to campaign against the left in union elections during 2001 (Foot 2002; Kimber 2002). Such initiatives were unsuccessful and the TUC was confronted by the election of the 'awkward squad' and switches in policy in the big unions. Barber, elected unopposed, was another moderate, initially seen as equally pledged to partnership. However, facilitated by staff changes, such as the exit of David Coats – a partnership enthusiast – the emergence of younger figures such as the new deputy general secretary, Frances O'Grady, his own efforts during the Gate Gourmet dispute, which were appreciated by the TGWU, and the decline in the 'awkwardness' of some union leaders, Barber mended fences and presided over the decreased visibility of partnership (interviews with activists, 2007).

Nonetheless the leaders of 'the big four unions' were, as the Warwick Agreement illustrated, willing at times to go it alone and approach government through the Labour Party link rather than through the TUC. Problems were also posed by the Unite amalgamation, declarations by its leaders that they hoped to attract more unions into their fold and the assertions of activists that Unite could become an alternative to the TUC. It was observed: 'Given the General Secretary and Executive of this new union will be subject to direct election by the membership, the merger represents a step forward . . . a powerful progressive and accountable alternative to the TUC apparatus' (www.workersliberty.org/node/7533). The concern of smaller unions that they are not adequately represented on TUC bodies or listened to sufficiently seriously (TUC 2000: 142) is likely to be bolstered by such developments.

The general council – currently 55 members, general secretaries and other senior union representatives – is elected at Congress in sections determined by the membership of affiliates, with additional representation based on gender, ethnicity and sexual orientation. A smaller executive is elected on the basis of recommendations from the general secretary and president. Recent suggestions that all unions should be represented on the general council, that election of the executive should be revised and that the three TUC equality conferences should be entitled to submit two resolutions rather than one to Congress and have their own seats on the general council, have been unsuccessful. However, all general secretaries can now attend council meetings as observers while the executive slate will be made more transparent and open to amendment. With changes in representation consequent on the Unite merger – TUC rules did not provide for a union with more than 1.5 million members – Unite now has twelve seats and Unison eight, the next biggest union, the GMB, three and CWU, NAS/UWT, NUT, PCS and USDAW two each, and other affiliates which qualify, one seat (TUC 2007b: iv–v).

Tendencies to super-unions and the development of the TUC as a funding agency for affiliates pose important issues. In relation to the former, fragmentation is not on the agenda. A split similar to that which occurred in the AFL-CIO in America during 2005 would constitute a step backwards. Unlike Unite or Unison, the TUC represents the interests of the entirety of organized (and even unorganized) labour. Whatever the problems, this gives it a unique strategic and political role. The latter development requires continuing scrutiny. In the past, unions have found it in their interests to act as delivery agents for the state. In the context of decline it is important to ensure that this is not to the detriment of their central role in regulating the workplace and influencing government.

## Conclusion

Assessing the unprepossessing position that unions confronted in 1998, the TUC general council pronounced: 'The scale and urgency of the task ahead is awesome' (TUC 1998: 54). Little has changed. Decline has been stemmed; there has been no revitalization of significance. Perhaps progress demands further shifts in the environment and the business cycle, a dose of inflation and consequent pressure on real earnings. As in the past, change may develop through a build-up of discontent from below which generates resistance in the workplace. Even in those circumstances, transformation would seem to require a more pro-union attitude from the state, although the only realistic alternative to New Labour's benign neutrality is currently Conservative hostility.

A quarter of a century ago, as the first incursions of the neoliberal offensive were digested, Bain and Price considered the degree to which trade unionism had become embedded in the managerial process a potential safeguard against catastrophic decline (Bain and Price 1983: 33). The attitude of management to trade unionism and joint regulation remains crucial. But management has changed its ways. The virtuous circle by which recognition of unions powered recognition of unions, with the exercise fostered by a collectivist social-democratic state, has been replaced by a vicious circle. Lubricated by a market-orientated neoliberal state, decline in employer propensity to work with unions has ratcheted up further decline. It has done this to such a degree that vigorous state intervention, rather than New Labour's mild legislation, would be necessary to begin to significantly reverse it. From the early 1980s a hostile state, a neoliberal economy, enhanced competition and a transformed balance of forces emerged gradually and incrementally; slowly but surely management adapted to neoliberalism and lost the union habit. So, whatever their abstract aspirations, did many workers in the private sector. It is questionable whether the latest placebo, works councils, are any more likely than the last palliative, the ERA 1999, to prompt fundamental change.

Union leaders have tried a variety of approaches to the central question of how to build power and influence so that they become more attractive to employees. They have not succeeded in engineering significant advances and they have not mounted a serious political challenge to neoliberalism. More emphatic attention to organizing may yield greater dividends for union revitalization. But, as we have seen, money is tight and it remains the sinews of war. Organizing and union leaders who endorse it have not lived up to their rhetoric (Heery and Simms 2008). Partnership has foundered against the rocks of a neoliberal state reluctant to intervene in employment relations, the opposition or indifference of management and the absence of any great degree of dissatisfaction among employees with things as they are (Kersley *et al.* 2006; Bryson 2007).

These are factors that unions which remain relatively weak may find difficult to transcend. Responsible accommodative trade unionism combined with episodic and volatile opposition to government has not turned the trick with New Labour. The endeavours and overtures of many mainstream union leaders have been registered but rejected. More militant leaders on the model of 'the awkward squad' have taken the stage. Arguably they have done too little to encourage resistance from below. On the whole they have been constrained by the situation and have been prepared to countenance only a moderate degree of calculated militancy with mixed success. Perhaps we have got to get used to a trade unionism of roughly current proportions and accept that in an economic downturn immense efforts will be needed to achieve consolidation rather than revitalization. What stands out from our review of the unions' industrial fortunes is the intense relevance of the state and political change. We move on in the next chapter to discuss progress in this sphere.

## Notes

1 This section is based on information from a number of activists, many of whom prefer to remain anonymous (see Preface and Acknowledgements), and from a variety of websites such as amicus.cc, amicusunitygazette.org.uk, labournet.net,

leftunity.org.uk, pcssocialistcaucus.org.uk, socialist-teacher.org, shopstewards.net, jonrogers1963.blogspot.com, cwurankandfile.wordpress.com, civilunrest.org.uk and fightingunions.org.uk.
2 Steve Sinnott died in April 2008 at the relatively young age of 56.

## Bibliography

Bain, G.S. and Price, R. (1983) 'Union growth: dimensions, determinants and destiny', in G.S. Bain (ed.) *Industrial Relations in Britain*, Oxford: Blackwell.

Bryson, A. (2007) 'New Labour, new unions?', in A. Park, J. Curtice, K. Thomson, M. Phillips and M. Johnson (eds) *British Social Attitudes: The 23rd Report*, London: Sage.

Certification Officer (1997–2007), *Reports of the Certification Officer*. London: Certification Office.

Charlwood, A. (2004) 'Annual review article: the new generation of trade union leaders and prospects for union revitalization', *British Journal of Industrial Relations*, 42:2, 379–97.

Charlwood, A., Greenwood, I. and Wallis, E. (2006) 'The dynamics of trade union activism in Great Britain, 1991–2003', paper presented to the 24th Annual International Labour Process Conference, 10–12 April, London.

Charlwood, A. and Terry, M. (2007) '21st century models of employee representation: structures, processes and outcomes', *Industrial Relations Journal*, 38:4, 320–37.

Cohen, S. (2006) *Ramparts of Resistance: Why Workers Lost their Power and How to Get it Back*, London: Pluto Press.

Curtice, J. and Mair, A. (2005) 'Are trade unionists left-wing any more?', in A. Park, J. Curtice, K. Thomson, C. Bromley, M. Phillips and M. Johnson (eds) *British Social Attitudes: The 22nd Report*, London: Sage.

Darlington, R. (2006) 'The agitator theory of strikes re-evaluated', *Labor History*, 47:4, 485–509.

Dempsey, M. (2004) *Managing Trade Unions: A Case Study Examination of Managerial Activities in Four UK Trade Unions Formed by Merger*, unpublished PhD, Cranfield University.

Department of Trade and Industry (DTI) (2007) *Workplace Representatives: A Review of Their Facilities and Facility Time*, London: DTI.

Dunlop, J. (1990) *The Management of Labor Unions*, Lexington, MA: Lexington Books.

Foot, P. (2002) 'TUC's own official part of plots against left leaders', *Socialist Worker*, 19 January.

Graham, S. (2006) *Organizing Out of Decline – The Rebuilding of the UK and Ireland Shop Stewards Movement*, London: TGWU.

Heery, E. (1998) 'The relaunch of the Trades Union Congress', *British Journal of Industrial Relations*, 36:3, 339–60.

Heery, E. and Simms, M. (2008) 'Constraints on union organizing in the United Kingdom', *Industrial Relations Journal*, 39:1, 24–42.

Hyman, R. (1971) *Marxism and the Sociology of Trade Unionism*, London: Pluto Press.

—— (1975) *Industrial Relations: A Marxist Introduction*, London: Macmillan.

—— (1979) *The Political Economy of Industrial Relations*, London: Macmillan.

—— (1997) 'The future of employee representation', *British Journal of Industrial Relations*, 35:3, 309–36.

Kelly, J. (1998) *Rethinking Industrial Relations: Mobilization, Collectivism and Long Waves*, London: Routledge.

Kelly, J. and Heery, E. (1994) *Working for the Union: British Trade Union Officers*, Cambridge: Cambridge University Press.

Kersley, B., Alpin, C., Forth, J., Bryson, A., Bewley, H., Dix, G. and Oxenbridge, S. (2006) *Inside the Workplace: Findings from the 2004 Workplace Employment Relations Survey*, London: Routledge.

Kimber, C. (2002) 'Interference in other election', *Socialist Worker*, 19 January.

Lipset, S.M., Trow, M. and Coleman, J.S. (1956) *Union Democracy: The Internal Politics of the International Typographical Union*, New York: Doubleday.

McIlroy, J. (1997) 'Still under siege: British trade unions at the turn of the century', *Historical Studies in Industrial Relations*, 3, 93–122.

—— (2000) 'The new politics of pressure: the Trades Union Congress and New Labour in government', *Industrial Relations Journal*, 31:1, 2–16.

—— (2008) 'Ten years of New Labour: workplace learning, social partnership and union revitalization in Britain', *British Journal of Industrial Relations*, 46:2, 283–313.

McIlroy, J., Campbell, A. and Fishman, N. (2007) 'Approaching post-war trade unionism', in J. McIlroy, N. Fishman and A. Campbell (eds) *British Trade Unions and Industrial Politics: The High Tide of Trade Unionism, 1964–79*, 2nd edition, London: Merlin Press.

Martin, R. (1968) 'Union democracy: an explanatory framework', *Sociology*, 2:2, 82–124.

Millward, N., Bryson, A. and Forth, J. (2000) *All Change at Work? British Employment Relations 1980–1998*, London: Routledge.

Muller-Jentsch, W. (1985) 'Trade unions as intermediary organizations', *Economic and Industrial Democracy*, 6:1, 3–33.

Murray, A. (2003) *A New Labour Nightmare: The Return of the Awkward Squad.* London: Verso.

New Earnings Survey / Annual Survey of Hours and Earnings (NES/ASHE) (1997–2007) *Annual Reports*, London: ONS.

Terry, M. (2003) 'Employee representation: shop stewards and the new legal framework', in P. Edwards (ed.), *Industrial Relations: Theory and Practice in Britain*, 2nd edition, Oxford: Blackwell.

—— (2004) '"Partnership": a serious strategy for the UK trade unions?', in A. Verma and T. Kochan (eds) *Unions in the 21st Century: An International Perspective*, 2nd edition, Basingstoke: Palgrave.

TUC (1998) *General Council Report*, London: TUC.

—— (2000) *General Council Report*, London: TUC.

—— (2004) *General Council Report*, London: TUC.

—— (2005) *General Council Report*, London: TUC.

—— (2006) *General Council Report*, London: TUC.

—— (2007a) *TUC Equality Audit 2007: A Statistical Report on Trade Union Action on Equality*, London: TUC.

—— (2007b) *General Council Report*, London: TUC.

Turner, H. (1962) *Trade Union Growth, Structure and Policy*, London: Allen and Unwin.

Undy, R. and Martin, R. (1984) *Ballots and Trade Union Democracy*, Oxford: Blackwell.

Waddington, J. (1995) *The Politics of Bargaining: The Merger Process and British Trade Union Structural Development, 1892–1987*, London: Mansell.

Willman, P. and Bryson, A. (2006) *Accounting for Collective Action: Resource Acquisition and Mobilization in British Unions*, London: Centre for Economic Performance, London School of Economics.

Willman, P., Morris, T. and Aston, B. (1993) *Union Business: Trade Union Organization and Financial Reform in the Thatcher Years*, Cambridge: Cambridge University Press.

# 5   Under stress but still enduring

The contentious alliance in the age of Tony Blair and Gordon Brown

*John McIlroy*

Heckles, jeers, silence and a walkout greeted Tony Blair's last speech to the TUC in September 2006. Commentators reflected on what a world of difference nine years can make. In 1997 Blair had been treated to a rapturous welcome and tumultuous standing ovation as Congress acclaimed the end of 18 years of Conservative rule. 'The rhetoric of opposition', TUC general secretary John Monks remarked, 'is no longer appropriate' (TUC 1997: 4). Within a few short years many union leaders spoke little else. As Blair prepared to quit Downing Street, relations between a Labour government and the unions were at their lowest ebb since the Winter of Discontent of 1978–9.

Fast forward a year. It is now summer/autumn 2007. The leaders of the unions affiliated to New Labour are expressing pride in nominating Blair's neoliberal co-thinker, Gordon Brown, as his successor to the exclusion of pro-union candidates; without exception they are declaring that the link between party and unions is indissoluble; they are affirming their unselfish loyalty to the new leader by accepting a qualitatively diminished role in the party conference – one of their last remaining arenas of real influence in the party (Woodley 2007). Such oscillations emphasize that what Lewis Minkin termed 'the contentious alliance' has always been characterized by ups and downs, flare-ups and make-ups and the occasional crisis. But it has endured and unions have typically, although not always, accepted a subordinate role in it.

It is the question of the survival of the alliance which dominates the literature tracking the trajectory of union–party relations since 1997. That literature is marked by a tendency to base assessment on the short term. It sometimes moves too easily from discussion of conjunctural conflicts within the alliance to predictions of its transformation. New Labour was scarcely settled in government before it was observed: 'The disdain with which Tony Blair appears to view trade unions has reactivated the question of whether the Labour Party and the unions will formally disengage to become two separate and independent entities' (Dorey 1999: 203). Before New Labour's first term had run its course it was concluded:

> Whether in the front-page divorce settlement, pressed by modernisers, or a longer process of mutual disengagement, the 100-year-old labour

alliance, in its historic constitutionally united form, is unlikely to last long into its second century.

(Ludlam 2001: 129)

Historicism is often at work. As Minkin observed, since the 1960s 'the tendency has been to forecast the continuation of whatever particular problematic trend happened to be at the forefront at the time' (Minkin 1991: 633). Yet two years after the demise of the alliance had been forecast, it was claimed that significant developments in downgrading the unions' role in the party, still less a divorce, were unlikely in the near future (Ludlam and Taylor 2003: 747).[1] Political science, like industrial relations, lacks a historical sweep. A glance at the 1960s and 1970s, with their conflicts between union and party leaders over incomes policy and employment legislation (Thorpe 2007) and 'the constitutional revolt, 1979–82' (Minkin 1991: 192–207) confirms the frequent turbulence of relations. But the past also demonstrates the resilience of the alliance and the strength of tradition. Its participants are neither prisoners of history nor always guided by precedent: in novel contexts, new actors can make fresh choices. History – and the history of the labour movement – suggests potential for change as well as continuity (Quinn 2004). But there are historical and contemporary constraints on change. A decade of New Labour in government provides a more adequate evidential base for reflection and judgement on these questions.

This chapter outlines the institutional and financial arrangements which underpin the alliance. It proceeds to critical examination of the changing relations between party and unions since 1997 and their impact on the link. It concludes with an assessment of the current situation and likely future trends.

## How the link works

In 2006 sixteen trade unions, all of them affiliated to the TUC and with a total membership of 4,744,380, affiliated 2,639,284 members to the Labour Party. Unions that have successfully balloted members to establish a political fund resource that fund by means of a political levy. Members may opt out of paying the levy, which is usually deducted from the ordinary union subscription. Opt-out rates vary widely according to tradition, publicity and changing member attitudes. They are small in the TGWU and GMB, far higher in Amicus and Unison. Affiliation to Labour constitutes a further step: the PCS, for example, has a political fund but the union is not affiliated to the Labour Party. Affiliation is related to the number of members paying the political levy but this is not applied rigorously. Unions typically 'over-affiliate' or 'under-affiliate'. For example, in 2006, the TGWU, now part of Unite, affiliated 400,000 members, although 720,274 members paid the levy; BECTU affiliated just over a quarter of its 26,550 levy payers while USDAW affiliated all of its 323,652 levy payers.

These decisions reflect to varying degrees the current political situation, the electoral cycle, the political and financial state of the party, the state of the unions and the overall judgment that union opinion-formers make on these matters. Decisions on affiliation are relevant to New Labour's financial position, the voting power of unions within the party and the ability of trade unionists to influence party decisions. Each union affiliates nationally by paying an annual fee of around £3 per member compared with a £36 fee paid by individual members. In addition, regional offices of unions can affiliate to the regional party by paying up to £12.50 per 100 members; and union branches can affiliate to constituency parties at a rate of 6p per member. As well as paying affiliation fees, unions donate substantial sums to the party, particularly during election periods.

Tables 5.1 and 5.2 compare the position in 2006 when 16 unions (including Amicus and the TGWU, now merged as Unite) affiliated 2,639,284 members to the Labour Party, with the situation in 1997 when 23 unions affiliated 3,286,133 members. The drop in the number of unions largely reflects mergers, although two unions, FBU and RMT, disaffiliated from the party in 2004 and the tiny textile union GULO abandoned its political fund. The drop in members affiliated represents these last two factors, as well as political and financial decisions to affiliate on less than the number of members paying the levy and decline in the membership of some affiliates. In 1997, 63.6 per cent of the membership of affiliated unions were affiliated to Labour; by 2006, the proportion had dropped to 55.6 per cent. In 2006, a little over a third (35.2 per cent) of *all* union members were affiliated to the Labour Party compared with more than two-fifths (42 per cent) in 1997. The biggest unions, Unite, Unison, GMB and USDAW are affiliated. But other large unions, the RCN, PCS, NAS/UWT and NUT are not.

That two-thirds of British trade unionists are not affiliated to the party is a cause for concern for supporters of the link, at least if measured by past conceptions of the alliance as comprehensively uniting the two wings of the labour movement. Nonetheless, the officialdom of unaffiliated unions sometimes look towards Labour rather than the Conservatives or Liberal Democrats. The division between conglomerate unions such as Unite, organizing 'traditional' trade unionists from a strong private sector base, and public sector professional unions recruiting in sectors that are now bastions of union membership is also notable; particularly in the context of unions, such as the PCS, which have recently established political funds but have not affiliated to the Labour Party.

The mechanism of the alliance is set out diagrammatically in figure 5.1. However, the link works differently in individual unions. Unison is unique in that members have a triple choice: they can choose not to pay the levy or to pay it to one of two funds, the Unison-Labour Link (ULL), which is affiliated to Labour, and the General Political Fund (GPF), which is not. In 2005–6, 476,216 members contributed to ULL and 770,404 members contributed to the GPF, suggesting minority support for New Labour (Unison 2006a). The GPF has a structure which is restricted in terms of specific democracy.

*Table 5.1* Trade unions affiliated to the Labour Party 1997

| Union | Members 1997 | Political fund payers 1997[a] | Political fund payers as % of members | Members affiliated to the Labour Party[b] | Members affiliated to the Labour Party as % of union members | Members affiliated to the Labour Party as % of political fund members |
|---|---|---|---|---|---|---|
| AEEU | 720,296 | 429,421 | 59.62 | 400,000 | 55.5 | 93.2 |
| ASLEF | 14,255[c] | 13,940 | 97.79 | 15,260 | 107.0 | 109.5 |
| BFAWU | 28,743[c] | 28,731 | 99.96 | 20,100 | 70.0 | 70.0 |
| BECTU | 28,650[c] | 28,555 | 99.67 | 12,000 | 41.9 | 42.0 |
| CATU | 20,478[c] | 20,259 | 98.93 | 22,335 | 109.0 | 110.3 |
| CWU | 273,814 | 231,748 | 84.64 | 224,888 | 82.1 | 97.0 |
| FBU | 51,426[c] | 41,374 | 80.45 | 20,000 | 38.9 | 48.3 |
| GULO | 331[c] | 225 | 67.98 | 200 | 60.4 | 88.9 |
| GMB | 709,708 | 662,446 | 93.34 | 700,000 | 98.6 | 106.0 |
| GPMU | 204,822 | 72,771 | 35.53 | 70,000 | 34.2 | 96.2 |
| ISTC | 32,299[c] | 26,832 | 83.07 | 48,000 | 148.6 | 179.0 |
| MSF | 416,000 | 167,294 | 40.21 | 135,100 | 32.5 | 80.8 |
| MU | 28,577[c] | 27,657 | 96.78 | 10,500 | 36.7 | 38.0 |
| NACODS | 783[c] | 781 | 99.74 | 1,000 | 127.7 | 128.0 |
| NUDAGO | 2,250[c] | 2,247 | 99.87 | 590 | 26.2 | 26.3 |
| NUKFAT | 38,075[c] | 37,484 | 98.45 | 41,000 | 107.7 | 109.38 |
| NUM | 5,935[c] | 5,543 | 93.40 | 5,001 | 84.3 | 90.2 |
| RMT | 56,337[c] | 55,655 | 98.79 | 50,000 | 88.8 | 90.0 |
| TGWU | 881,357 | 809,373 | 91.83 | 500,000 | 56.7 | 61.8 |
| TSSA | 31,123[c] | 27,211 | 87.43 | 30,000 | 96.4 | 110.3 |
| UCATT | 113,555 | 81,644 | 71.90 | 20,000 | 17.6 | 24.5 |
| Unison | 1,300,451 | 1,184,333 | 91.07 | 700,000 | 53.8 | 59.1 |
| USDAW | 293,470 | 271,984 | 92.68 | 260,159 | 88.6 | 95.7 |
| TOTAL | 5,252,735 | 4,227,508 | 80.48 | 3,286,133 | 62.6 | 77.7 |

*Sources:* Certification Officer, *Annual Report*, 1998 and Trade Union & Labour Party Liaison Organisation (TULO)

*Notes:*

a Certification Officer, *Annual Report* 1998

b Trade Union & Labour Party Liaison Organisation (TULO)

c The CO only reports membership figures for unions with 100,000 members or more. However, the membership figures from smaller unions can be extracted from the Political Fund table (contributors and exemptions). The sum of these two figures might not represent an individual union's total membership because, for example, honorary, retired and unemployed members are neither required to pay the political levy nor seek exception from it. But these are the nearest 'official' figures available.

| Union | Members 2006 | Political fund payers 2006 | Political fund payers as % of members | Members affiliated to the Labour Party | Members affiliated to the Labour Party as % of union members | Members affiliated to the Labour Party as % of political fund members | Union members affiliated to the Labour Party compared with 1997 +/- |
|---|---|---|---|---|---|---|---|
| Unite Amicus[1] | 1,179,655 | 591,004 | 50.10 | 630,100 | 53.4 | 106.6 | 25,000 |
| TGWU | 777,325 | 720,274 | 92.66 | 400,000 | 51.7 | 55.5 | -100,000 |
| Total | 1,956,980 | 1,311,278 | 67.01 | 1,030,100 | 52.6 | 78.6 | -75,000 |
| ASLEF | 18,141 | 17,829 | 98.28 | 15,500 | 85.4 | 87.2 | -240 |
| BFAWU | 26,843 | 25,801 | 96.12 | 5,100 | 19.0 | 19.8 | -15,000 |
| BECTU | 27,354 | 26,550 | 97.06 | 7,310 | 26.7 | 27.5 | -4,690 |
| Community[2] | 34,528 | 29,965 | 86.78 | 55,246 | 160.0 | 184.4 | -34,344 |
| CWU | 244,461 | 201,678 | 82.50 | 210,000 | 86.0 | 104.1 | -14,888 |
| GMB | 575,105 | 546,635 | 95.05 | 400,000 | 69.6 | 73.2 | -300,000 |
| MU | 31,148 | 28,072 | 90.12 | 10,500 | 33.8 | 37.4 | 0 |
| NACODS | 833 | 450 | 54.02 | 410 | 49.2 | 91.1 | -590 |
| NUM | 10,793 | 1,675 | 15.52 | 1,813 | 16.8 | 108.2 | -3,188 |
| TSSA | 31,356 | 28,970 | 92.39 | 27,653 | 88.2 | 94.4 | -2,347 |
| UCATT | 121,109 | 85,301 | 70.43 | 51,000 | 42.1 | 59.8 | 31,000 |
| Unity[3] | 8,076 | 7,604 | 94.16 | 1,000 | 12.4 | 13.2 | -21,335 |
| Unison | 1,317,000 | 476,216[4] | 36.16 | 500,000 | 38.0 | 105.0 | -200,000 |
| USDAW | 340,653 | 323,652 | 95.01 | 323,652 | 95.0 | 100.0 | 63,493 |
| TOTAL | 4,744,380 | 3,111,676 | 65.59 | 2,639,284 | 55.6 | 84.8 | -646,849 |

*Sources:* Certification Officer, *Annual Report*, 2006–7; Electoral Commission website; individual trade union returns to the Certification Officer 2006; *TULO Directory*, 2007.

*Notes:*
1 Amicus comprises AEEU, MSF and GPMU. Another major union that became part of Amicus was Unifi but this union did not affiliate to the Labour Party.
2 Community comprises ISTC, KFAT and NUDAGO.
3 Unity is the new name for CATU (Ceramic and Allied Trades Union)
4 Unison has two political funds (GPF and APF) which 1,022,812 million members pay into. In 2006 this was split between 476,216 payers into the APF and 770,404 into the GPF.

**Union Member**

Union member pays subscription fee

**Collective Union Membership**

Every ten years, a ballot is held to determine whether to have a political fund

Union votes to have a political fund

Union votes not to have a political fund

Subscription fee normally reduced by level of contribution to political fund

**Union Member**

UNISON members tick a box to determine which political fund to contribute to.

This amount is **not** the same for all unions & **not** necessarily £3.

Union member contributes to a political fund

Union member decided **not to** contribute and has proactively *opted out* of paying the political fund

**Union Executive**

Union votes & representation at Conference and NEC calculated according to number affiliated.

Votes in Electoral College are sent to each individual affiliated member.

This may not be exactly the same as the number who contributed to the political fund.

Contribution goes in to political fund.

Union calculates how much affiliation to Labour Party will cost based on membership.

Balance of political fund.

**Union Political Activity**

TU branches can affiliate to Constituency Labour Parties for £6 per 100 members

Union pays affiliation fees to Labour Party.

May be used for campaigning as a third party

Used for other political activities.

May be used to make donations to Labour Party.

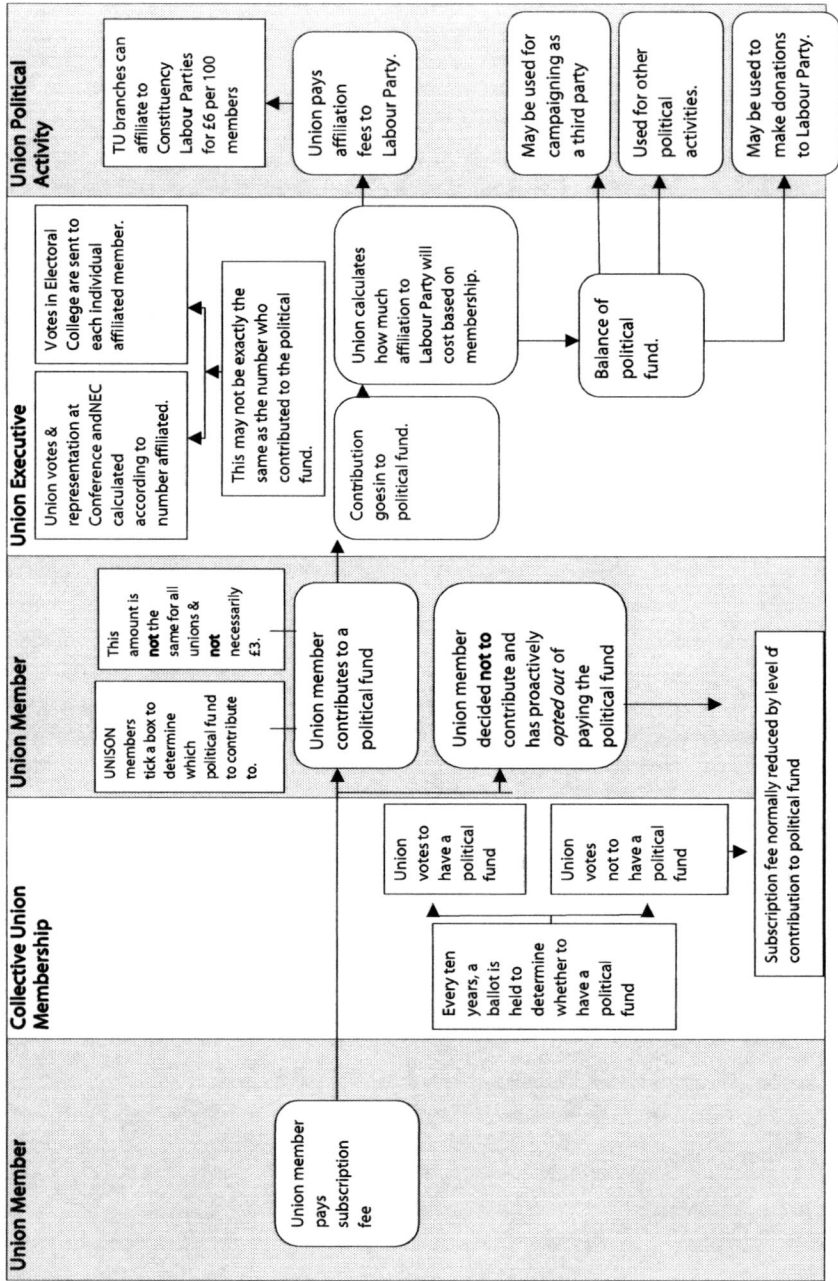

*Figure 5.1* Unions affiliated to the Labour Party and political funds.

Source: Phillips (2007)

Decisions as to the use and operation of the fund lie in the hands of elected members of Unison's national executive, not elected members of the GPF. Contributions to political parties from the GPF are constitutionally prohibited. The fund is used for general political campaigning in accordance with union policy. There is an element of devolution and branches seek approval from the regional committees for expenditure (Unison 2006b).

In contrast, the committee of ULL consists of a mixture of members elected from the national executive and ULL activists elected from the regions in a members' ballot. ULL funds can only be used to support the Labour Party, not for wider political campaigns. Unusually, Unison's national policy-making bodies cannot instruct the union on policy positions to be taken in relation to the Labour Party: this is the prerogative of the ULL. The fact that officials of ULL beyond the branch are required to be members of the Labour Party, rather than simply levy-payers who want their money to go to Labour, has also provoked argument. There is choice but it is circumscribed. This is managed democracy: in contrast with the wishes of many Unison members it accords priority and protection to the link with New Labour at the expense of plural political alignments (Jones 2000; Sawyer 2000; Unison 2006c; interviews with activists, 2007).

In affiliated unions without the competing traditions of the three unions that formed Unison – NALGO was never affiliated to Labour; COHSE and NUPE were – there is only one political fund. Its governance is typically assimilated to the union's constitutional structure with ultimate power vested in conference and day-to-day supervision exercised by a political subcommittee of the executive. Broadly, that was the situation in the TGWU, although in the GMB the regions have played a greater role in decisions over expenditure. In Amicus there was a more complex structure which will develop as the merger with the TGWU in Unite is implemented.

Affiliation provides the basis for representation of trade unionists within what has traditionally been a federal party pledged to a mix of representative and activist democracy. Representative structures have changed over time and New Labour's transformative neoliberal policies had organizational implications. The visible involvement of unions in party policy-making and the party's financial dependence on organized labour were perceived by Tony Blair as significant constraints on developing neoliberalism, implanting it in the party and implementing it in government. The unions' role in the party was perceived as a vote-loser in 'middle England' and a barrier to winning key sections of the electorate back from the Conservatives. Blair was intent on restructuring to create a modernized 'rational-efficient' party in which policy-making is centralized in the hands of a charismatic leader and a quasi-autonomous parliamentary elite surrounded by professional advisers tapping directly into public opinion. In line with neoliberalism's antipathy to democracy, inner-party democracy and parliamentary democracy are downgraded to privilege flexible policy-initiation with the party's 'professional class' free to play the fickle electoral market. The role of trade unionists and constituency activists is steered towards legitimizing leadership policy through plebiscitary democracy and turning out the vote. Ideally they are passive in making policy and active in mustering support for it (McIlroy 1998; Moschonas 2002: 123–34).

Building on changes introduced earlier, a series of reforms between 1994 and 1998 took the party further in this direction. Theoretically annual conference remained the sovereign body. In the past the leadership had claimed the right to decide the priority and timing of implementing conference decisions. New Labour determined that it would not be bound at all by conference resolutions. The union vote at conference was reduced from more than 80 per cent at the start of the 1990s to 49 per cent (the small affiliated societies made up the 50 per cent often quoted). The National Executive (NEC) was remoulded. Unions maintained their prerogative of electing 12 out of 32 representatives, but forfeited their preponderant role in electing five women representatives and the party treasurer. In 2006 activists from Amicus, Community, the CWU, GMB, TGWU, TSSA, UCATT and Unison sat on the NEC (TULO 2007). Fundamentally it was deprived of any policy-making role (Quinn 2004: 50–63).

In practice policy-making began and ended with the party leadership: top-down policy creation and implementation was mediated only by consultative structures that substantially bypassed conference and the NEC. A joint policy committee chaired by the leader with equal numbers from the government and NEC and three members elected by the National Policy Forum (NPF) dominated the process. Proposals were developed in similarly constituted Policy Commissions. They progressed to the NPF. This body was made up of representatives from all sections of the party with the unions electing 30 out of 183 members – around 17 per cent (Russell 2005: 133–68). In 2006 activists from Amicus, ASLEF, BFAWU, Community, GMB, MU, TGWU, TSSA, UCATT and Unison were members of the NPF (TULO, 2007). The documents coming out of the NPF were discussed at conference although amendments of substance were difficult to achieve. They were fed back into the policy machinery and at the end of the two-year cycle were voted on at conference.

In addition, conference could debate four motions dealing with contemporary issues not substantially addressed in the policy documents, as well as emergency motions. The unions still possessed a third of the votes in the selection of the party leader, deputy leader and leaders of devolved assemblies. But selection of parliamentary candidates was subject to central vetting and ratification and 'one member one vote' at constituency level (Russell 2005: 81–93).

The Trade Union and Labour Party Liaison Committee (TULC) provides an additional forum for informal consultation and discussion. It comprises the general secretaries of all affiliated unions; the party leader; key party officials; the chair of the NEC; and the party treasurer and representatives of the Trade Union Groups of MPs and MEPs. These groups are open to all members of the respective parliaments who belong to affiliated unions or whose constituencies are supported by them. They embrace almost the entire party at Westminster, with some MPs belonging to more than one group. For example, the Amicus Group has 114 MPs, the GMB 108, the TGWU 76 and Unison 70 (TULO 2007).

TULC is backed by the Trade Union Liaison Organisation (TULO). Its staff are paid by the unions. Its purpose is to strengthen the link, generate finance from unions and mobilize union resources in the party interest, particularly during elections. The majority of party income comes, as it did typically in the past, in donations and some 65 per cent of donation income comes from the unions (Phillips 2007: 9; Electoral Commission 2007). Despite New Labour's drive to escape union influence, it has not transcended its historic financial dependence on the unions. This continues (see table 5.3). Substitutes such as the development of a mass individual membership, with members cast in the mould of donors and executors of established policy rather than traditional socialist activists, proved a fiasco. Membership more than halved from 400,000 in 1997 to around 180,000 in 2007. We are left with the leadership-sponsored Labour Supporters Network. Persistent attempts to

*Table 5.3* Donations to the Labour Party 2001–6

| Union | Donations (£) |
|---|---|
| Amicus[1] | 14,555,819.69 |
| ASLEF | 345,775.00 |
| BFAWU | 46,346.00 |
| BECTU | 129,970.00 |
| Community[2] | 1,117,368.09 |
| Connect | 84,160.00 |
| CWU | 5,049,778.12 |
| FBU | 199,458.00 |
| GMB | 8,371,090.98 |
| Musicians' Union | 199,599.00 |
| NACODS | n/a |
| NUM | 107,922.02 |
| RCN | 11,750.00 |
| RMT | 277,608.66 |
| TGWU | 7,497,246.58 |
| TSSA | 506,586.02 |
| UCATT | 920,152.00 |
| Unison | 10,613,012.17 |
| Unity[3] | 594,303.00 |
| USDAW | 5,906,119.90 |
| TOTAL | 56,534,065.23 |

*Source:* Electoral Commission (2007)

*Notes:*
1 Amicus includes MSF, AEEU and GPMU.
2 Community includes KFAT and ISTC.
3 Unity is the new name for CATU (Ceramic and Allied Trades Union).

attract millionaire donors provided no stable alternative source of finance. But they fuelled a series of Conservative-style scandals from the debacle involving Bernie Ecclestone in 1998 to the cash-for-honours affair of 2006–7 (McIlroy 2007) and the secret subventions from David Abrahams which provoked a further police investigation and the resignation of Labour's general secretary, David Watt, in 2007 (for arguments about the funding of political parties generally see Ewing 2007 and Phillips 2007).

Five points are important to contextualize discussion of union–party relations. First, union leaders acquiesced in and, in some cases, fostered the remoulding of the party (McIlroy 1998). They did this with some illusions but ultimately because they preferred their chances with New Labour's variant of neoliberalism than with the Conservative version. Second, Blair's reform of the party remained incomplete. Affiliated unions do not always act collectively in the party although they have increasingly done so. To some degree they represent different memberships, reflect different interests and articulate different policies: 49 per cent of the conference vote has rarely been cast one way. But, in the context of recent, successful attempts to coordinate strategy, unions still possess potential to influence what the party – if, more questionably, the government – decides (Kelly 2005: 78).

Third, arguments about democracy are involved. These range from the 'disenfranchisement' of thousands of members who want their union to contribute to parties other than Labour and the publicity, or lack of it, routinely given to the right to opt out of paying the political levy, to the fact that the three biggest unions wield more than 90 per cent of the total union vote at conference. They include perennial controversies about balancing that block vote against the votes of individual members and ensuring that it is used in accordance with the aspirations of the union's members or levy payers, not just their interests as perceived by union leaders.[2]

Fourth, New Labour's attempt to escape dependence on union funding and the consequent scandals, has ensured that the funding of political parties remained a controversial issue (Ewing 2007). Fifth, as we have seen, some commentators have suggested that developments since 1997 could provoke the end of the alliance. Yet Minkin's emphasis was on the rooted nature of the attachment and this was confirmed by events between 1991 and 1997 (McIlroy 1998). A less dramatic, but perhaps more pertinent inquiry, might be whether, as New Labour's policies unfolded in government, union leaders would sustain the traditional restraint they had exercised inside the party (Minkin 1991: 26–48) or act more vigorously and more instrumentally.

### New morning, New Labour, new unions

Tony Blair had set out his stall in opposition. His closest confidante, Alistair Campbell, recalled the new leader's speech to the 1995 TGWU conference:

TB wrote a very strong section himself, the strongest I'd yet seen, saying we would listen to the unions, but making clear there would be no special relationship and certainly no favours . . . He was raging on the train. 'What really gets me is the way they beg me to go to their conference, otherwise nobody will take them seriously, then they go out of their way to embarrass me. It's pathetic, it's just not serious.' Even TB would struggle to hide the contempt today.

(Campbell and Stott 2007: 72)

Trade union leaders still greeted the first Blair government with keen but realistic expectations. Unlike some on the left (see McIlroy 2000a) they were far from starry-eyed although important policy orientations, notably the completeness of New Labour's retreat from 'Rhine capitalism' as a model in favour of the American market approach, remained unclear. They were conscious that in the context of weakened unions, balkanized labour markets and attenuated collective bargaining, New Labour opposed any return to the quasi-corporatism of the 1970s. Blair's statement to the 1996 TUC was one of many:

I want to be quite blunt with you about the modern relationship between today's Labour Party and the trade unions. There was a time when a large trade union would pass a policy and then it was assumed Labour would follow suit. Demands were made, Labour responded and negotiated. These days are over. Gone.

(quoted in McIlroy 1998: 542)

Union leaders were aware that in their priority areas, particularly the repeal and reform of the Conservatives' employment laws, there would be no return to the past and much hard bargaining.

You have heard me say this many times: I will say it again. There is not going to be a repeal of all Tory trade union laws. It is not what the members want; it is not what the country wants. Ballots before strikes are here to stay. No mass or flying pickets. All these are ghosts of time past . . . It is not for reasons of politics; actually it is for reasons of principle.

(ibid.)

Allowing for the caricature it was evident where Blair stood. But Labour prime ministers had, in the unions' calculations, stood there before and been rendered amenable to union persuasion. At least some union leaders overestimated New Labour's sympathy for the EU social model and social partnership and underestimated its blossoming Eurosceptic streak and overriding orientation to business and the market (interviews with activists, 2007). There was, it transpired, a place for unions in government strategy but it was a secondary place. It was located within a neoliberal economic policy framework unfriendly to significant union recovery. The decision to observe

Conservative spending limits, prioritize control of inflation and transfer power to set interest rates to an independent Bank of England committee were intrinsic to the emphasis on neoliberal financial rectitude. This embraced strict limits on direct taxation, restrictions on public spending and public sector wage increases, and an intense antipathy to strikes, little different from the hostility of New Labour's Conservative predecessors (Charlwood 2004). New Labour's preference for capital promised the unions only a subordinate ad hoc role as subaltern agents in workplace productivity coalitions where they seemed to fit the bill; rather than the institutionalized national role as social partners they desired (Hyman 2001: 110–11).

Comparison with the immediate past remained a potent yardstick and the TUC quickly re-established easy access to ministers and civil servants. However, this was a government which orientated primarily to business (Edmonds 2006). Business people were closer to Blair as ministers and advisors than trade union leaders. Employers enjoyed quality access and greatly outnumbered trade unionists in appointments to government bodies. Moreover, if union exclusion was reversed its fruits were limited. The nearest the unions got to social partnership was the Low Pay Commission, the 'Social Dialogue' with the CBI over the union recognition procedure and the beginnings of a new framework for vocational training (McIlroy 2000b). Nonetheless, the spectacular growth of a funding stream, directed towards unions, with the Union Learning Fund and the Partnership at Work Fund established during the first term stood favourable comparison with the parsimony of the Conservative years (see McIlroy and Croucher, chapter 9, this volume).

The unfolding of Labour's programme demonstrated the nature of the new settlement. At the 1998 Congress, the moderate TUC general secretary, John Monks, was already reflecting:

> The government is intent on maintaining the broad coalition which saw it elected . . . That means maintaining the support of employers as well as employees . . . There is a tendency with New Labour to demonstrate the newness at the expense of the traditional links with labour, with workers and with unions . . . The White Paper [on employment legislation] clearly falls short of what Congress hoped for . . . The [minimum wage] rates agreed by the Low Pay Commission fall short of what we believe the economy can afford as well as what the low paid deserve . . . Our failure to join the majority of the European Union in the first wave of the economic and monetary union could potentially do us a great deal of harm . . . Then there are plenty of other concerns about the government . . .
>
> (TUC 1998: 4–5)

New Labour's manifesto had affirmed 'retention of the key elements of trade union legislation of the 1980s – on ballots, picketing and industrial action'

(Labour Party 1997: 14). Blair's introduction to the White Paper, *Fairness at Work*, affirmed that after reform, Britain would still possess 'the most lightly regulated labour market of any leading economy in the world' (DTI 1998). Moreover the most substantial innovations, the national minimum wage and the recognition procedure in the Employment Relations Act (1999), had been developed as policy before the advent of New Labour. That implementation of his predecessors' policy was far from sacrosanct was demonstrated by Blair's rejection of their pledges to activate individual rights such as unfair dismissal from 'day one' of employment. The level at which new entitlements were set and their coverage intensified concern.

At £3.60 an hour the minimum wage was 20 per cent below the TUC benchmark. The small firms loophole in the ERA excluded six million work-ers from the union recognition procedure; the requirement that 40 per cent of the bargaining unit vote for recognition constituted a practical obstacle as well as being questionable in terms of democracy. The detail of New Labour's pro-union legislation bore the imprint of discussions with employ-ers and rarely transcended employer imperatives (Howell 2005: 178, 180) while the core of anti-union legislation remained on the statute book (see Smith and Morton, chapter 6, this volume). Further, the unions' vision of Europe as a conveyor belt for social partnership and a cornucopia of helpful legislation was soon unravelling. The renunciation of Britain's opt-outs from the Maastricht social chapter opened the way to a stream of EU directives. In more sophisticated fashion New Labour replicated the methodology of its Conservative predecessors: these directives were restrictively considered, amended and delayed in Brussels and phased in, in mutilated form, at Westminster. Already, and symbolically, by 2000 the TUC was taking the government to task for its failure to implement the parental leave directive (TUC 2000: 4 and see Taylor, chapter 11, this volume).

Union leaders looked on the bright side: during the first term they had enjoyed 'victories as well as setbacks'. They accepted that a second term was the priority. They hoped for progress after the next election 'as the govern-ment matures'. They put the 'guerrilla warfare' that they had endured, over ERA and Blair's insistence on employer consent to legislative reform and demonstrable negligible negative impact on business goals, down to political insecurity and preoccupation with public relations, rather than the neoliberal politics from which that insistence derived. Understanding and acceptance rather than criticism and consequent antagonism would, or so TUC opinion formers believed, pave the path to progress. New Labour's commitment to the Conservative legislation, privatization and the injection of private capital and market mimicry into the public sector remained worrying. Nonetheless the TUC general council acted vigorously in this period to minimize conflict (TUC 1999: 4–6; McIlroy 2000b).

In New Labour's first term, criticism and opposition were typically chan-nelled through the TUC and direct talks with ministers. In the Labour Party itself union leaders were supportive of government policy. This was perceived as demonstrating loyalty and utility and lubricating future concessions. On the NEC, what criticism there was came, not from the union representatives – they perceived their primary responsibility as sustaining the government – but from left-wing constituency representatives. When the centre-left Grassroots Alliance promoted a slate of candidates critical of New Labour's political direction they encountered trade unionists manoeuvring with ministers to dampen opposition. When representatives of the CWU, GMB or RMT criticized the government they attracted cursory support from other unions. The view from the NEC left was:

> None of the other trade union representatives uttered so much as a whisper of protest at privatisation, cuts to public sector workers, the low level of the minimum wage or the government's pension policy. Yet nearly all of them represented unions opposed to privatisation and in favour of an index-linked minimum wage and restoration of the link between pensions and earnings.
>
> (Davies 2001: 88–9, 174–5)

They were playing their traditional role of deferring to the parliamentary leadership (Minkin 1991: 37, 406, 622–4). In 1998 the AEEU liaised with party headquarters to finance an unsuccessful campaign for an alternative loyalist slate in the constituency section of the NEC (Shaw 2004: 65). A number of unions were involved in abetting the prime minister's preferences in leadership elections. In 1998 Blair backed Alun Michael against Rhodri Morgan as leader of the Welsh party, ensuring that the panel was reopened to permit Michael's late application. Morgan secured a majority of the votes of individual members of the electoral college, but he was defeated by union votes in the affiliates section. After alleged backroom deals, the AEEU, GMB and TGWU failed to ballot their members before casting their votes for Michael. In Unison, the only union that did ballot its members, two-thirds of those voting favoured Morgan (Flynn 1999). Some change of mood was signalled in the selection process for the London Mayoral contest in 2000 where Blair's candidate Frank Dobson narrowly defeated Ken Livingstone. While the latter gained 72 per cent of the vote in the affiliates section, the role of the AEEU, which again refused to ballot its members before casting its block vote for Dobson, was a significant factor in Livingstone's defeat (Alderman 2000).

In the NPF union initiatives were muted. Opposition was minimal, even over the maintenance of Conservatism embodied in Public Private Partnerships (PPP) and the Public Finance Initiative (PFI).[3] At conference the unions made no significant attempt to challenge the government. But the rerun of their traditional role in bolstering party leaders against critics would prove short-lived. Things were changing. Even in Unison, where New Labour loyalists Maggie Jones and Lord Tom Sawyer were prominent, as well as in other unions whose representatives on the NEC and NPF had been generally supportive of the government, pressure was beginning to build (Davies 2001: 83–191, 181).

But the only substantial conflict came over pensions. Union leaders were dissatisfied by government assurances, unfulfilled in the NPF, over the restoration of the link between pensions and earnings. At the 2000 conference the GMB and Unison submitted contemporary motions on this issue which saw the leadership's first defeat since 1994. More than 80 per cent of union votes were cast against the government although New Labour carried the constituencies by 64:36 per cent. The Chancellor of the Exchequer, Gordon Brown, insisted that the resolutions would not influence policy. It was 'not for a few composite motions to decide the policy of this government and the country' (*Guardian*, 28 September 2000). Unison's outgoing leader, Rodney Bickerstaffe, was suitably apologetic: 'We weren't instructing the Chancellor to do anything . . . All we wanted to do was show that we believed in something' (Jones 2002: 36).

Blair treated union general secretaries as conveniences or inconveniences: 'TB spoke to Edmonds [of the GMB] to try to get him to move his members on the Scottish executive and thankfully he did so. We won 18–12 . . . [TB] was furious at the GMB . . . said he intended to give Edmonds a real hammering' (Campbell and Stott 2007: 51, 559). If they reciprocated with a public deference which reflected the balance of the relationship, greater tensions were developing. The RMT, ASLEF and TSSA were exercised by projected privatization of the tube and failure to renationalize the railways. The RMT's 1998 conference demanded that the union's MPs take a stand on these issues or forfeit financial support for their constituencies. A motion calling on the union to end all financial support for New Labour was only narrowly defeated. The funding issue was also taken up in the FBU. At Congress, the TUC general council struggled to contain opposition demanding an end to PPP and PFI (McIlroy 2000b).

New Labour's first term was a time of relative stability for the alliance. Union leaders proved helpful in a number of ways, for example, with their strong condemnation of the fuel protests by drivers in 2000: 'TB spoke to Bill Morris and John Monks and the unions are being terrific' (Campbell and Stott 2007: 471). The 2001 general election witnessed a union campaign which proved the value of TULO: it had a significant impact in mobilizing finance and resources and orchestrating canvassing in key seats (Ludlam and Taylor 2003: 735–6). The years from 1997 had demonstrated a large degree of surface compatibility. But there was an underlying misunderstanding. The government perceived its pro-union measures as substantially a final settlement. Many union leaders saw them, or wanted to see them, as a first instalment: they believed that a more confident government would acknowledge the utility of union support and provide trade unionists with further substantial concessions. Moreover, some union leaders appear to have underestimated New Labour's attachment to privatization (Edmonds 2001; interviews with activists, 2007).

**High noon: the confrontation that never came**

Disillusionment can be gauged from pronouncements of moderate union leaders early in the second term. GMB leader John Edmonds tumbled to the government's implacable commitment to privatization (Edmonds 2001). Monks observed:

> Increased private sector involvement in public services, far from solving the problems of poor quality service delivery, actually compounds them. Railtrack has been the most high profile case, but there have been many other examples of private sector failure – in the health service, in transport and especially in local government. Secondly, despite the limited protection offered by the Transfer of Undertakings Protection of Employment Regulations (TUPE), private sector service providers tend to offer poor pay and conditions and a more aggressive management.
>
> (TUC 2001: 4)

PFI and Foundation Hospitals[4] were flashpoints (Waddington 2003: 345–6). Yet active opposition was slow to emerge. The unions probed the possibilities and discovered the limits of the NPF: they proved unable to shake the privatization drive. At the 2002 conference the unions went public: they carried a resolution which called for a review of PFI; not, however, for a moratorium or termination. Again, the government announced that it would ignore the decision (Shaw 2004: 58).

The Foundation Hospitals initiative had never been discussed at the NPF; it was developed unilaterally by the cabinet. Again union votes carried the day against the constituency delegates and the NEC. Again Blair was furious, accusing the unions of 'playing with fire' by using democratic machinery to hold him to account. Again the government announced it would not accept the conference decision (Russell 2005: 206). The matter was pursued by Unison's viscerally moderate new general secretary, Dave Prentis, who pointed out that the government had unilaterally initiated policies on faith schools and top-up fees in universities as well as Foundation Hospitals independently of the party. This prompted a review of the NPF process (Prentis 2003).

It had been surmised that in its second term New Labour might 'feel free to complete the modernizers' unfinished business with the unions . . . [and] persuade some friendly union leaders to help lead a voluntary move to change the party constitution' (Ludlam 2001: 128). By 2003, with disenchantment stiffened by Blair's war in Iraq, there were few friendly union leaders around and it was the unions, not the government, which moved to amend the constitution. Against the opposition of the leadership they pushed through a decision to double the number of contemporary motions that conference could debate. Nevertheless the limits to how much embarrassment union leaders were prepared to inflict on Blair and the limits of their policy vision were evident in their well-publicized, unprincipled refusal to support attempts to secure a debate on Iraq at conference, despite the TUC view that on Blair's war, 'as on a number of other issues, the government appeared out of touch with public opinion as well as trade union opinion' (TUC 2003: 2; Russell 2005: 207–8).

Yet some on the left remained unhappy at their union leaders' failure to use the NEC to pursue union policy. The future FBU general secretary, Matt Wrack, remarked:

> The union representatives on Labour's National Executive have been some of the most loyal Blairites going. What is the point of electing trade union delegates onto Labour's executive if they subsequently ignore the policies of their own union at every opportunity?
>
> (Wrack 2002: 11)

Nor was there any follow-through when the government, true to its word, ignored conference and pushed ahead with legislation on Foundation Hospitals and new PFI projects. The unions had to be content with concessions which helped mitigate the impact of these measures on their members: the government agreed that the terms and conditions of employees taken on as a result of privatization initiatives in local government should be no less favourable than those of local government employees (Waddington 2003: 345–6).

The FBU dispute of 2002–3 confirmed that New Labour meant what it said about public-sector pay limits and remained committed to the imperatives of neoliberal economics. Blair's stance suggested a resolve every bit as firm as Mrs Thatcher's in 'facing down' workers and 'toughing it out' to cow public-sector trade unionists (Seldon 2007: 131–2). The episode was exemplary in more ways than one: it demonstrated both the state's enduring antagonism to militant trade unionism and the persisting weaknesses of British trade unionism. The firefighters' strike fed into the mood of hostility.

Matters were not helped by Blair's characterization of the strikers as 'wreckers' and 'Scargillite'. Or by the party headquarters at Millbank's interventions in Amicus to sustain its right-wing general secretary Sir Ken Jackson against the left (Waddington 2003: 335, 339). The mood was reflected in elections for senior union positions. It was difficult for Blairites to win office. Among incoming general secretaries Billy Hayes of the CWU, Bob Crow of the RMT, Mick Rix of ASLEF and Andy Gilchrist of the FBU were vigorous critics of New Labour. In Amicus, Derek Simpson, the left candidate, replaced Jackson; in the TGWU, Tony Woodley, hardly a firebrand himself, took over from the more biddable Bill Morris; and in the PCS, the relatively unknown Mark Serwotka, a partisan of the hard left, was elected. There was, however, a good deal of exaggeration and hyping of the left credentials of 'the awkward squad'. USDAW continued to be a bastion of Blairism. ASLEF moved right. It was difficult to see Dave Prentis, Rodney Bickerstaffe's successor in Unison, Kevin Curran, the new GMB general secretary, or

Brendan Barber, Monks' successor at the TUC, as men of the left, still less militants. The rhetoric of others remained to be tested in practice (Charlwood 2004: 387–8).[5]

That change was in the air was suggested by a more politicized attitude to financing the party. In 2002–3 a range of unions – ASLEF, BECTU, CWU, FBU, GMB and RMT – responded to government policy by reducing donations. Blair's response was to launch a 'debate' on state funding of political parties which in the face of public disillusion with the political class never really got off the ground (Cain and Taylor 2002; Ewing 2002). Most of these cutbacks represented knee-jerk reactions or at best short-term tactics, rather than calculated strategy. However, the question raised by thousands of trade unionists as to why they should finance a party far from friendly to union policies whose government was, in some cases, attacking their conditions and their pay packets, from which contributions to New Labour were deducted, a party whose wealthy leaders branded strikers with legitimate grievances as 'wreckers', was answered more forcefully in the FBU and RMT.

The RMT had backed Livingstone, expelled by New Labour for standing against Dobson, in his subsequent London Mayoral triumph. At conferences in 2003 and 2004 its members decided that branches could apply for executive permission to affiliate to parties other than Labour. This was an attempt to democratize the political process in the union and cater for members alienated by New Labour's transport policy. When some branches affiliated to the Scottish Socialist Party (SSP), the RMT was expelled from the Labour Party in 2004 (interviews with activists, 2007). In the FBU, from the 1990s, one faction had favoured democratization. Its hand was strengthened by what was perceived to be New Labour's unfair handling of the pay dispute. In its aftermath, attitudes hardened. The leadership's position of targeting funds on campaigns in line with FBU policy while maintaining the link with Labour was a casualty of the strike: members voted for disaffiliation at the 2004 conference (Seifert and Sibley 2005: 217–86).

Both unions were relatively small with a discrete public-sector/former public-sector membership which harboured specific grievances against New Labour. Many RMT members shared FBU activists' frustrations. They had to live with the government's refusal to reverse privatization. They often saw the rail companies as profiteering and inefficient employers. More than any other union the RMT suffered the impact of anti-union legislation on strike ballots (McIlroy 1999; interviews with activists, 2007). Despite the break with New Labour, neither union exhibited enthusiasm for launching a new party apart from brief flirtations with the Campaign for a New Workers' Party, the SSP and the George Galloway / Socialist Workers Party (SWP) Respect. Politicization of funding was important. But disaffiliation remained a minority tendency. The BECTU conference instructed its executive to provide a report on alternatives to New Labour. Its recommendation of continued affiliation was confirmed in a membership ballot (Leopold 2006: 196). The sentiments of many leaders of the major unions were summarized by TGWU general secretary Tony Woodley:

> It is time to put Labour back into the party. Not walk away from it as a few on the fringes would argue but restore it to the values of working class men and women, the values of socialism. If the present leader doesn't listen . . . and that threatens a Labour victory at the next election then you change your leader . . . Obviously the answer is not to have the Tories back. That is why I don't support breakaways from Labour, there is just no sense in it.
>
> (quoted in Murray 2003: 181–2)

Similar views were expressed by Derek Simpson of Amicus. Like Woodley, Simpson was forthright in his criticism of the party leaders. Like the TGWU, Amicus never questioned the alliance: it forcefully defended it.

> The value of the link has been called into question from a number of different quarters. In the main these calls have come from two political extremes of the Labour Party: the ultra New Labour 'Islington Set' and the hard left of the trade union movement. The hard left attack the link because they overlook and don't want to acknowledge what Labour actually delivers . . . Perhaps a greater threat to the sustainability of the link comes from those on the ultra right of the Labour Party. Certain forces, more 'Nouveaux Labour' than New Labour, find the link an acute embarrassment to their middle class preferences.
>
> (Amicus 2004)

Unison, whose interests were bound up with the future of the public sector, also conceived of opposition as circumscribed by the need to keep the Tories out. Its leaders believed that constructive criticism within a framework of loyalty and cooperation could win New Labour hearts: 'On key issues government often takes most notice of people it normally considers to be supportive . . . walking away does not help our members' (*Unison Labour-Link News*, Autumn 2004).

There was a substantial deterioration in relations. If we give due weight to the removal of the FBU and RMT from the party, the link frayed at the edges. For the majority of affiliates, it was never under threat even if criticism of the government was strong. In spring 2004, Amicus, the GMB, TGWU and Unison supported a 'Working for a Radical Third Term' conference. In an important development the 'big four' began to put forward a common position at both the TUC and party conference (Ludlam and Taylor 2003: 739). But none of the big unions followed the BFAWU, CWU, FBU and RMT in affiliating to the Labour Representation Committee established in July 2004 to 'reclaim the Labour Party', although some of their branches did (*Guardian*, 22 July 2004).

Concern over privatization intensified through New Labour's second term. At the 2004 party conference 99.5 per cent of the union vote supported a TSSA resolution calling for renationalization of the railways. The platform was also defeated over council housing (Russell 2005: 207).The first national one-day strike of civil servants for a generation took place in November 2004. It underlined continuing problems in the public sector (TUC 2005: 107). Disquiet deepened over New Labour's continuing failure to provide more significant labour law reforms. In his farewell message John Monks had presented a balanced view:

> The government has made some important and positive changes to employment law over the past five years – rights to recognition and representation and the minimum wage to name a few ... We would have hoped for further progress and have been disappointed both by government actions and attitude ... The government does not appear to address the issues at stake but occupies the middle ground between our quest for justice and a positive role for people in their workplaces and employers' complaints about so-called 'red tape'.
>
> (TUC 2002: 4)

What trade unionists saw as valuable but insufficient changes in legislation were subject to prolonged consultation and exacting, sometimes questionable scrutiny by ministers, advisors and civil servants of their potential impact on employers and the economy. What finally came out of this process was viewed as demonstrably inadequate. On what many union activists perceived as 'the big issues', such as industrial action and ballots, there was little movement. The Employment Act 2002 contained improved provisions on maternity and parental leave and rights for union learning representatives. But the government also responded to the employers' 'burdens on business' agenda. It made realization of existing individual rights more difficult in practice by making it harder to bring a case before employment tribunals and by requiring that problematic procedures were followed before legal claims for unfair dismissal could be initiated. The government's review of the 1999 Act rejected all the TUC's key demands for improvements in the recognition procedure while the Employment Act 2004 contained minor reforms (see Smith and Morton, chapter 6, this volume). The position was similar with regard to EU legislation. There was increasing frustration about the way in which directives on working time, works councils and consultation and information were implemented in half-hearted fashion (see Taylor, chapter 11, this volume). There was satisfaction with the continuing flow of finance from government to unions through the Partnership Fund, the Union Modernisation Fund and the unions' new niche in workplace learning (see McIlroy and Croucher, chapter 9, this volume). But the effect of the legislation of the late 1990s was diminishing in the workplace and in its impact on membership trends (Gall 2004).

The much-vaunted Warwick agreement – policy pledges covering employment legislation, the public services, manufacturing and pensions – of autumn 2004 provided a compromise. It illustrated the potential and the limits of the relationship. Orchestrated by ministers and the big four unions at the NPF – rather than through direct talks involving the TUC or motions to party conference – the agreement was based on, but not simply a product of, the party machinery. New Labour desperately needed money and resources for the impending 2005 election (McIlroy 2007). The 'awkward squad' desperately needed legislative concessions. Both sides needed a New Labour government. Warwick papered over the cracks. This temporary *entente* represented a rerun of a now familiar script. The big issues – repeal of the Conservative laws, a halt to privatization, an end to PFI, and an improved recognition procedure – were not resolved. Warwick constituted an extensive package; some of its concessions were valuable; many were marginal; others were vague; and so, to put it mildly, was the timetable for implementation.

There were piecemeal pledges. Bank holidays would not be included in the four-week statutory paid leave guaranteed by EU directives. The TUPE requirements, that workers moving into new jobs should be employed on terms and conditions no less favourable than their public sector counterparts, would be extended from local government to the NHS and education. The protection of strikers against dismissal for the first eight weeks of the stoppage would be extended to twelve weeks. Other promises were more restricted. There would be no moratorium or independent review of PFI: instead the government would consult with 'stakeholders' about monitoring it. The Low Pay Commission would examine the minimum wage rates for 18- to 21-year-olds. There was an assurance that New Labour would support the EU directive on agency workers. Some commitments were firm: there would be a new Women at Work commission and a system of public services forums. Others were pious: the government pledged itself to 'dialogue' over pensions, committed itself to full employment and assured the unions it would work in partnership with them (*Labour Research*, January 2005).

During New Labour's second term, relations between party and unions remained tense. Ideological and political consensus diminished. In the party and more broadly, given the ineptitude of the Conservatives, the unions were sometimes seen as 'the opposition'. Criticism of the government united unions across the boundaries of membership and employment sectors. It reflected the changing political process within unions. Amicus and the TGWU, with large private-sector memberships, were as critical of New Labour as Unison, directly confronted by the government as paymaster and privateer, although private-sector unions such as USDAW remained loyal.

But we have to distinguish between troubled relations between the parties to the alliance and their impact on the maintenance of the alliance. Heery is right to emphasize a graph of declining and increasing union influence which followed the electoral cycle (Heery 2005: 6). It is important to emphasize that union influence on the government remained restricted throughout the cycle;

and the electoralism and desire to keep the party in government which burgeoned in 2001 and 2005 has always been intrinsic to what the alliance is about and a perennial pervasive consideration for union leaders. The dissatisfaction of the FBU and RMT with events should neither be glossed over nor exaggerated. They had no emulators. Cuts in funding did not lead to the end of funding; or a turn towards new political organizations. There was anger, bitterness and cynicism: a strong element of restraint remained. The belief that the alliance was under threat proved as insubstantial as scenarios promising a wave of industrial militancy or over-optimistic assessments of the radicalism of 'the awkward squad'.

## Third term tensions, trials and tribulations

The 2005 election witnessed another bravura performance from the unions: more than in any previous election they pulled out all the stops in providing finance (see table 5.3) and manpower. Apart from extremely generous funding, TULO mounted

> . . . a programme of direct mails to union members in key marginals; a postal vote recruitment exercise amongst union members; a website encouraging union members to get involved; and a national network of Key Seat Co-ordinators and drivers on the ground to harness the energies of union volunteers . . . the overall approach has marked a departure for how the affiliated trade unions organize to help the Party at election times.
>
> (TULO 2005: 1)

The government's determination to increase the public-service pensionable age from 60 to 65 threatened to overshadow the election. There had been a TUC 'national campaign day' to oppose the measure in February 2005 and the threat of a strike by public-service unions that March. The strike was avoided by government promises to negotiate. In October 2005 agreement was reached enabling civil servants, teachers and health workers in post to retire on full pension at 60: but the retirement age for new employees would be 65. The framework agreement reflected the balance of power. It gave the unions something; but it created a two-tier workforce and did not apply to local government. The dispute rumbled on through 2006 with a Unison day of action in March (TUC 2006: 47–51). Its effect on relations was highlighted when Unison 'withdrew active support' from the party in the May 2006 local elections. Unison emphasized that this was a pragmatic decision which would have no impact on the alliance. A minority claimed that the decision 'had weakened Unison's influence with New Labour'. Union leaders stressed in the aftermath of the elections the need for 'strengthening further our relations with the Labour Party' (*Unison Labour-Link News*, June 2006).

'The government's obsession with privatisation' continued to undermine relations (TUC 2006: 2). Unison maintained its campaign against attempts to marketize the health service. There was another national one-day strike by PCS members protesting against privatization and redundancies and the Chancellor's 2 per cent cap on public sector pay. The phasing in of the 2007 recommendations of the pay review bodies in order to keep increases below inflation stoked more resentment (*Guardian*, 23 September 2006; *The Times*, 2 March 2007).

Dissatisfaction on the legislative front was focused by the Gate Gourmet dispute in summer 2005. This episode highlighted the fact that workers such as British Airways (BA) TGWU members at Heathrow Airport were prohibited from taking action in solidarity with low-paid workers, also in the TGWU, who had been hived off by BA to the catering company Gate Gourmet (Hendy and Gall 2006). Woodley remarked: 'How can this be right in Britain today? We do need to redraft those laws. We do need to make solidarity a basic human right and we do need to campaign now' (TUC 2005: 45). Congress carried an extensive programme for legislative reform which was later boiled down to demands for specific rights to take solidarity action and changes in the law on balloting in the Trade Union Freedom Bill (TUFB) (Ewing and Jones 2006).

Legislating Warwick proved immensely harder than negotiating it had been. Its implementation remained a union priority (TUC 2005: 1–2). But testing proposals for their impact on the market continued, and so did the delays engendered by the now established ritual of prevarication, reviews and, perhaps, minor concessions (DTI 2006). Protection for strikers was extended and redundancy pay increased. A Women at Work Commission was created; maternity leave was further extended in the Work and Families Act. TUPE-style protection for pensions affected by company mergers was introduced together with a corporate manslaughter bill – without directors' liability – and training for pensions trustees. But with even a seemingly straightforward commitment such as the exclusion of bank holidays from employees' statutory leave entitlement it took 2½ years before the government announced that the measure would be phased in from October 2007. On making training a negotiating issue as part of the statutory recognition procedure, an issue debated for almost a decade, there was no progress (*Labour Research*, October 2006; Bewley 2006; *Tribune*, 19 January 2007).

For many trade unionists it was all too familiar: too little too late. Simpson remarked: 'We should now be moving towards Warwick Mark II, not quibbling over attempts to dilute and delay the initial agreements' (*Tribune*, 19 January 2007). Brendan Barber referred to 'the contrast between the positive and welcome engagement with government in some areas and the negative relationship in others' (TUC 2006: 1). He cited government support for workplace learning (see McIlroy and Croucher, chapter 9, this volume) as an example of the first, and the refusal of 'fairer employment legislation' as symptomatic of the second (ibid.). For New Labour, generous funding of unions to resource skills training was not a problem; significant legislative change was a different matter.

There was continuing consternation that 'ministers are more willing to take account of the business point of view than that of people at work. We see this in terms of both domestic legislation and on the major issues at European level – working time and the service directive for instance' (TUC 2006: 2). The government's attitude to legal rights was confirmed in March 2007. Despite a promise to implement the EU directive on agency workers, ministers talked out a private member's bill supported by unions and the TUC. The TUFB, sponsored by the unions and almost 180 MPs, did not survive the balloting process for these bills (*Guardian*, 3 March 2007).

As in 2001, Blair was hardly back in Downing Street before criticism revived. Prentis was scathing about the New Labour campaign: 'A complete absence of vision. All the things we believe in absent'. The government's passion for privatization, he termed 'a criminal abuse of taxpayers' money and it has got to stop' (Prentis 2005a). At the party conference the government was again defeated – where card votes were taken, defeated comprehensively – on the composites based on resolutions from 'the big four'. The TGWU-initiated motion on removing the prohibition on solidarity action was carried by 70 per cent to 30 per cent. The Amicus motion insisting that the government sign the temporary workers directive, end the opt-outs from the working time directive and oppose the directive opening public services to the market; the Unison motion criticizing privatization and calling for a review of the plans for primary care trusts and an end to competition in the health service; and the GMB motion on compulsory pensions for all wage earners were all successful (*Tribune*, 23 and 30 September 2005).

The response was pre-emptive and more public than in the past. Employment Minister Gerry Sutcliffe announced that there would be no reform of strike law: Gate Gourmet made no difference. The Education Secretary and former CWU leader, Alan Johnson, announced that there should be a reduction in the unions' share of the conference vote from 49 per cent to 15 per cent. Blair reflected: 'A situation where constituency delegates can get voted down by a block union vote doesn't do any good for our relationship or credibility' (*Observer*, 16 October 2005; *Tribune*, 14 October 2005; *Guardian*, 14 November 2005).

The 2004 conference had demanded a further review of party structure. But the situation for the government was increasingly difficult. By 2006 Blair was a lame duck prime minister, forced to agree to step down in 2007. The Conservatives were ahead in the polls while a reduced majority of 66 MPs made the parliamentary rebellions which had characterized Blair's second term more costly (Cowley 2005). Calls for constitutional change to restrict union involvement in the party continued to come: from former cabinet minister Stephen Byers, from Gordon Brown and from Lord Bill Morris (*Tribune*, 3 March 2006; *Morning Star*, 10 June 2006). The unions presented a straight bat. They argued that New Labour wanted to ditch its own rules when it lost the game. Unison claimed that the issue was not the necessity for constitutional change but rather the need to implement conference policy: 'What we need to discuss is what happens to motions which gain a majority at conference' (*Tribune*, 21 October 2005).

This latter was potentially the unions' Achilles heel. What was the point of public conflict each year at conference if the process achieved nothing of substance? Some commentators argued that the conference confrontation simply publicized the unions' political weakness (Charlwood 2004: 392). Prentis disagreed: 'Does it make any difference that we win the votes at Labour conference? Some people say not but, believe me, government ministers think it matters. They hate being overturned in public' (Prentis 2005b). There was still negligible follow-through by union leaders. The government simply ignored its defeats and moved ahead with *its* policy. The unions, with the partial exception of the TUFB and the agency workers bill, did little to influence MPs and achieved less. Blair was unfazed. He believed union leaders were aware their opposition represented little more than an empty ritual. In a world of globalization they realized that they had lost their political power 'irrespective of votes or arithmetic at party conference . . . Whatever is sometimes said publicly, that is accepted by union leaders. They know it' (*Tribune*, 10 March 2006).

They were waiting for Blair to go. The cash-for-honours scandal, which erupted in March 2006, further embarrassed the government. In raising the issue of party finance it raised the issue of union representation in the party based on affiliation fees. The affair illustrated the problems of a party leadership standing above the party. Neither the unions, the party treasurer (the TGWU's Jack Dromey) nor the NEC were consulted about Downing Street fundraising by 'loans' before the 2005 election. The incident publicized the party's financial crisis and underlined that the unions remained its financial anchor (McIlroy 2007). The response from union leaders was angry but restrained. They failed to profit from the disarray of Blair's third government. And they kept their ammunition dry when faced with the issue of his successor. As events moved towards a coronation of Gordon Brown rather than a political contest, and as candidates emerged for leadership and deputy leadership positions, the unions, with a third of the vote in elections, reacted cautiously.

Prentis responded that 'a challenge from the left, that Gordon Brown defeats, that is not in our union's interests' (*Tribune*, 23 June 2006). Unison's deputy general secretary back-pedalled on platform rhetoric suggesting that the next prime minister should be an opponent of the Iraq war. Critics of the union leadership called for a challenge to Brown on the grounds that he opposed Unison policies (*Tribune*, 21 July 2006). Asserting the exhaustion of neoliberalism and criticizing adherence to US foreign policy, Woodley urged on a new leader a halt to privatization, radical reform of labour law and the need to base government policy on conference policy. He did not name the candidate to undertake this programme even after a committed pro-union candidate, John McDonnell, declared an interest (Woodley 2006, 2007).

Simpson had apparently shed earlier illusions about Brown compared with

Blair: 'I don't think you can get a cigarette paper on policy between the two men' (*Guardian*, 9 March 2007). However, he showed little enthusiasm for McDonnell. Simpson insisted that it would be difficult for McDonnell to gain the support of the 45 MPs necessary to stand: 'If you don't have to fight and you don't think you can win, why expose weakness . . . I agree with most of the points raised by John McDonnell but I don't see the point of going out on the field for a glorious defeat' (*Morning Star*, 9 March 2007). Despite the strength of the Trade Union Group in parliament, union attempts to muster the signatures required were apparently ruled out on the grounds of the constitutional independence of MPs.

The prognosis seemed to be that opposition to Brown would count against the unions once Brown became prime minister. Yet Brown represented neo-liberalism, not an alternative to it. A smaller union such as the CWU passed conference motions insisting that it would only back candidates committed to the TUFB and public ownership of Royal Mail. The big battalions kept their counsel while supporting the outsider for deputy leader, former Blair aide, Jon Cruddas (*The Times*, 12 March 2007). As Simpson put it: 'There is no credible alternative to Gordon Brown . . . The best way to exert pressure for policy change is to support the leftwing deputy candidate Jon Cruddas so that he might put pressure on Mr. Brown' (ibid.). Cruddas was an advocate of the TUFB: but he also contended that the unions' share of the vote in the party should be a uniform third, thus supporting a cut in the union share of the conference vote (Cruddas and Harris 2006).

The game the unions played remained bargaining for small concessions rather than negotiating for significant reforms, still less arguing a political alternative to neoliberalism. In return for minimal change, they were willing to sponsor Brown, the architect of many of their discontents. The legitimacy and stability of trade unionism was underpinned by the 1999 legislation, by access to government and by the stream of funding that flowed with increased liberality to the unions through the TUC. But privatization and downward pressure on wages continued while legislative reform had slowed to a trickle. The nuances had been seen at the 2006 TUC. Blair lectured the unions: his stance remained unchanged since 1997. The RMT organized a walkout. Most delegates received the prime minister in silence. But Brendan Barber congratulated Blair (*Guardian*, 13 September 2006). Union leaders were unhappy: but what was the alternative?

The 2006 party conference followed what were now routine lines. A Unison motion rejected the selling-off of NHS Logistics to a German company, a move which provoked strike action. It called on the government to drop its latest plans to privatize the NHS and it was carried with considerable support. Motions from the TGWU and UCATT on tightening the corporate manslaughter bill, from Amicus on carrying out the Warwick Agreement and from the GMB condemning the government's failure to raise the pension wage were also successful. The possibility of conference policy being translated into government policy remained remote (*Tribune*, 22 September 2006).

But it was the union leaders themselves who refused to make their policies an issue in the succession contest. Despite support from another putative candidate, Michael Meacher, John McDonnell failed to secure sufficient nominations from MPs to spark a contest. The big unions, led by Unite and Unison, then nominated Brown: in June 2007 he became party leader and prime minister unopposed. In the contest for deputy leader the union vote was dispersed. Unite funded Cruddas, Unison backed the Blairite, Alan Johnson, who like Brown held out few hopes for more union-friendly policies. ASLEF, BFAWU, the GMB, NUM, TSSA and UCATT voted for another loyal member of Blair's cabinet, Peter Hain. Hain, they hazarded, 'stands for real partnership with working people and their unions and retention of the unions' conference rights' (*Guardian*, 13 June 2007). Within months Hain too was engulfed in a scandal about donations to his campaign. The CWU executive was censured by the union's conference for supporting Johnson (*Guardian*, 5 June 2007). The awkward squad, it seemed, had been finally laid to rest. The unions had, in the end, taken the field; but they went down to a 'glorious defeat' as Harriet Harman won the contest before becoming involved in a further funding scandal.

Any misapprehensions that Brown would be more helpful to them than Blair were speedily dissipated. Brown bonded, not as Labour Prime Ministers had in the past, with trade unionists, but, as New Labour had always done, with capital. His inclusive state encompassed a range of politics and expertise to the exclusion of labour. Brown announced his admiration for Mrs Thatcher; assigned two Conservatives and a Liberal Democrat MP to lead reviews of government policy; recruited a surgeon, a sea lord, a Scotland Yard commissioner and a QC to advise his administration; established a Business Council of Britain to liaise with his cabinet which included free marketer Alan Sugar and private equity boss Damon Buffini; and appointed non-party member, Digby Jones, former director-general of the CBI, to the new Department for Business. On leaving the CBI, Jones had remarked: 'I don't meet the unions. They are an irrelevance. They are backward-looking and not on today's agenda' (*Guardian*, 2 July 2007).

It was neoliberal business as usual. Even more than Blair, the new Prime Minister was the author of New Labour's core policies. In style he was different from Blair. But he demonstrated that politically he had no intention of being different from Brown! He promised repeal and replacement of the unfair dismissal procedures introduced in 2002, extension of parental rights to flexible working and tighter enforcement of the minimum wage. There were no concessions on the unions' outstanding legislative agenda, privatization or PFI. At the 2007 Congress, Brown reiterated his determination to stick with neoliberal economics and impose pay awards below inflation, provoking delegates to agree coordinated action over public-sector pay.

But in the context of speculation about an early general election the union leaders' history of public bluff and bleating preceding quiet acceptance of neoliberal initiatives continued. GMB general secretary Paul Kenny secured headlines with his claim that his union could consider disaffiliation in frustration at New Labour policies. Weeks later, with an election still mooted, the leaders of Unite articulated where their colleagues in the big unions really stood: 'Mr Simpson and his fellow leader Tony Woodley said it was "Mr Brown's call" and they would provide the cash if needed' (*The Times*, 13 August, 8 September 2007).

Brown appeared to have ushered in a new era of acquiescence even on issues over which union leaders had drawn a line in the sand. The contemporary motions at party conference and the votes against government policy they facilitated had been pronounced non-negotiable. Such motions remained a residual redoubt of party democracy, one union leaders were pledged to maintain and extend. For New Labour, conference votes were an embarrassing relic of the past they wished to remove. Brown turned the trick. The 2007 consultation document *Extending and Renewing Party Democracy* proposed there would only be 'deliberative debates' at conference. Votes, which the unions had stressed were indispensable to democracy, would no longer be permitted. Contemporary motions chosen for debate in a 'priorities ballot' would be despatched after discussion, but not votes, to the NPF. The NPF might, or might not, consider them in developing policy. The issues would not return to conference and final policy statements would be put to members in a one-member-one-vote national ballot. After the conventional oppositional noises the union leaders tamely submitted, declaring: 'We don't want a bloodbath at this conference . . . the first conference . . . we have to get a fourth Labour term.' The only concession was that the matter would be reviewed in two years time (*Labour Research*, October/November 2007).

Few of the lessons of the 1990s, when union leaders played their part in the making of New Labour, appeared to have been absorbed in the new century. Here was another milestone in the consensual reduction of union voice in the party. The union leaders' surrender of their members' rights to vote on issues which affected their lives, without any mandate from those members, represented a further significant increment in remaking the realities of the alliance. Before the dust had settled the issue of political funding again hit the headlines in the shape of the secret donations made by property millionaire David Abrahams, prima facie in breach of New Labour's own Political Parties Act 2000.

## The enduring alliance after ten years of New Labour

New Labour governments have placed strains on the alliance. They have not precipitated the rupture of the link or sizeable defections from the party. The power balance between government and union leaders remains tilted in favour of the former, particularly in the perception of the latter. No large-scale mobilization is on their agenda. They calculate that the costs of any breach would outweigh the gains. Change in the party linked to change in the unions would seem a necessary prelude to a new phase. The party has remained dominated by its leadership. There has been little attempt by trade unionists to mobilize MPs against the government. The left has declined with the unions. No alternative party has emerged to challenge neoliberalism. In a period of union weakness and economic growth and stability, union leaders have gained concessions and there has been no significant challenge from below. In terms of Burgess's (2004) analytical framework for assessing the changes in interrelations between parties moving towards neoliberalism and their union supporters, the leaders of the 16 unions affiliated to Labour perceive disaffiliation as more costly than the status quo. Their members cannot be ignored and thus 'they vacillate between cooperation and resistance' (ibid.: 7; and see McIlroy and Daniels, introduction to this volume).

The alliance endures although some of the factors that Lewis Minkin perceived as binding both sides have been eroded (Ludlam and Taylor 2003). Its physiognomy has been remoulded to the advantage of the party leaders and the detriment of unions. Key factors remain to sustain it. The unions are significantly less of a shield against opponents of the leadership than they have been at times in the past. There is increasing divergence, at least in theory, over political goals and projects. The unions' traditional role in conveying the state of working-class consciousness to the leadership is disregarded. But they remain an indispensable source of finance, electoral resources and of electoral mobilization. Millions of members mean that they still represent, albeit imperfectly, a slice of civil society. The political price of provoking the break-up of the alliance is less easily calculated than the cost to the party in terms of money and mobilization. From the union side, ten years of New Labour have witnessed a degree of achievement. How it is measured is more problematic. Access and the legitimacy it brings – a traditional pillar of the link – constitutes a relative success story. As Brendan Barber put it:

> Our contacts with government are now as regular and as detailed as at any time in our history. Over the past year a senior General Council team has met the Prime Minister on a number of occasions. There are regular quarterly meetings with the Chancellor of the Exchequer and with the Secretary of State for Trade and Industry. The Public Services Forum, the Trade Union Sustainable Development Advisory Committee and the TUC / FCO Advisory Committee are formally constituted and have provided vehicles for detailed discussions carrying forward contacts between government and the trade union movement . . .
>
> (TUC 2006: 1; and see Marsh 2002)

Substantive attainments have been less impressive: they have declined through the period. Conversely, the access and influence of employers have grown. A balanced view would conclude that what the unions gained by political action has contributed to retrenchment but not union revitalization. Specific reforms and the direction of economic policy have provided inadequate stimulation to union resurgence. How this is viewed by union actors, rather than academics, in the context of dominant neoliberalism and the marginalizing of the left, is key to any assessment. Measured against union achievements under the Labour governments of 1974 to 1979 success appears scant. Measured against the position under Conservative governments from 1979 to 1997, the assessment may be different. So may be the estimation of what has and what can be achieved under New Labour if calculated against the potential for regression that a future Conservative government holds.

Under the rhetoric it is the latter comparison which informs the judgement of most union leaders: 'All our experience tells us that whatever our differences with Labour, Conservative governments have been consistently hostile to trade unions' (Prentis 2006). This philosophy ensures that for the most part they are determined to maintain rather than rupture the alliance. A defective recognition procedure and an inadequate minimum wage are better than no recognition procedure and no minimum wage.[6]

Academics have raised the possibility of a move towards 'lobbying models'. In this conspectus the unions' constitutional role is diminished, or alternatively severed so that the unions attempt to exert influence as an external pressure group (Ludlam and Taylor 2003: 728–9). As they recognize, radical change is unlikely. On New Labour's side there is no great enthusiasm for dissolving the link. Why should there be? They have got the substance of what they want through persuasion and union money matters. For their part, given recognition of relative achievement and the fact that New Labour is a party of government or potential government, union leaders perceive no viable alternative. They have not been prepared to confront neoliberalism politically or consider what might replace it. Given the political alternatives on offer the latter is understandable.

The point is made by a glance at the Scottish Socialist Party (SSP), which lost its MSPs and split in two in 2006–7. It is affirmed by any realistic assessment of Respect, the alliance of George Galloway MP, the Socialist Workers Party and Muslim community activists with perhaps 2,000 members and a handful of council seats which split in two in 2007. It is underlined by the fortunes of the Campaign for a New Workers' Party or the fate of the 1990s breakaway, Arthur Scargill's Socialist Labour Party, which briefly attracted union officials. For most union leaders and for their members, it is an electorally successful party and, through that party, access to government which counts. Ending the link is not a realistic choice. There is, as far as union leaders are concerned, at least in the short and medium term, only one alternative to New Labour: the Conservative Party.

This central constraint, and in some cases strong individual loyalty to the party, conditions their attitude to New Labour. As their consent to the demise of voting on contemporary motions at the party conference demonstrates, that attitude is one of vocal protest typically succeeded by grudging assent to unpalatable realities. In a culture of complaint there is no plan B, no alternative strategy. In practice, the majority of British union leaders have adapted to neoliberalism. Their desire for a return to the securities of the 'Old

Labour' state, regulating, redistributing and nurturing collectivism, constitutes, if measured against their actions, an exercise in platform declamation and nostalgic yearning. The Labour Party, they assert, should be reclaimed. Far from doing anything to reclaim it, the events of 2007 affirmed their willingness to endorse the claims of the neoliberal party leaders and reinforce their own marginalization. They are prisoners and pensioners of neoliberalism, sometimes reluctant prisoners – over employment legislation – sometimes enthusiastic pensioners – over training and the funds that go with it. New Labour's subordination of the unions is an outstanding political triumph. The party's leaders have taken the unions with them a long way down the neoliberal road. They have demonstrated that the contentious alliance can endure while changing its constitution and its policies to their advantage.

More extensive state funding of the parties appears unlikely. Any revised legislation introduced by New Labour to restrict donations in the light of recent scandals is likely to protect collective union donations by treating them as aggregated *individual* donations. More radical scenarios which could impinge on the link appear dependent on a deepening of New Labour's growing political problems, further deterioration in the economic situation, a New Labour defeat at the polls and Conservative reform of political funding. If this cannot be ruled out, significant change still appears as unlikely as a wave of anger from below forcing the leadership of big unions to permit branches to affiliate to other political parties, thus courting disaffiliation. It is notable that neither the FBU nor RMT have affiliated to another party – the RMT has severed its short-lived links with the SSP – while the number of branches requesting permission to do so remains negligible. Through 2007 the FBU was considering its position: nothing, including re-affiliation, was ruled out (interviews with activists, 2007). These unions run campaigns and sustain active groups of MPs. It is difficult to discern that they are doing anything qualitatively different from unions that do this *and* use the additional lever of exercising pressure inside the Labour Party. Smaller unions, however, possess less purchase in the party than the large unions and both disaffiliated unions would argue that the funding–influence transaction did not work in their favour. In a world of transactional funding, where few donate without hope of reciprocal benefit, they did not get value for money, which arguably could be put to work more profitably elsewhere.

It is a strong argument and the prevailing situation remains unprepossessing for affiliates. Constitutional reforms have created a leadership-dominated party which marginalizes opposition (Shaw 2004). The removal of the FBU and RMT has divided the opposition. Yet *potential* for change favourable to trade unionists remains; the opportunity to mobilize is still there (Kelly 2005: 80). In theory, there is no compelling obstacle to unions using New Labour's dependence on their political funds to negotiate on a 'no say no pay' basis (McIlroy 2007). Or to combating the sharp decline in constituency organization and membership through affiliating union activists and constructing coalitions of protest on specific issues with a range of pressure groups (Frege, Heery and Turner 2004; Kelly 2005).

What is at issue is the will and ability to build power, of trade unionists: there have been few signs of power-building strategies. Union leaders have been aggressive at party conference, at Warwick and in the press. What is striking is the extent to which they have maintained traditional restraint in practice. Union leaders with a variety of sectoral and vocational member-ships and interests have increasingly opposed government policy. But the opposition is partial and restricted – improve employment legislation – often negative – end privatization. Union leaders have responded; they have rarely taken the initiative. No alternative set of policies on the lines of, say, the Alternative Economic Strategy of the 1970s has been presented. There is no orientation to extra-parliamentary mobilization. In the work-place and in Parliament, socialist ideas remain marginal. The left remains debilitated.

Other inhibiting factors in a context of union weakness are their leaders' traditional concern for observing the frontier between the industrial and pol-itical and respect for the party leaders' domination of the latter – despite New Labour's failure to honour tradition in industrial relations policy. Acknowledgement of the hegemony of party leaders remains, and with it anxiety about courting their political antagonism and the disapproval of popular opinion. Many of the traditional roles are still observed. There is above all fear of another period of Conservative rule and worry that internal conflict in the party could facilitate it. Under the rhetoric this motivates the continuation of Minkin's rule-governed restraint: it places limits on what union leaders are prepared to do to challenge the party leadership and develop a strategy to reclaim the party.

A coalition with radical MPs would be central to any such strategy: some MPs who benefit from union support do little to support union policies. The response of Derek Simpson is to reiterate parliamentary convention:

> Individual MPs, who happen to be in the union, are not under any obli-gation under rule to support our policies. We'd probably take the view that it would be wrong that an outside body should dictate what is determined in parliament.

> (*Morning Star*, 9 March 2004)

In March 2007, Woodley wrote to all TGWU MPs before the vote on renewal of the Trident nuclear missile system. He emphasized the TGWU's long-standing opposition to nuclear weapons. More than 90 Labour MPs rebelled against the government but the majority of TGWU MPs, like the majority of Unison MPs, whose union also opposes Trident, supported the government and Trident (interviews with activists, 2007). There is still little evidence that, as distinct from union delegates at conference, union representatives on the NEC act as a group – although they appoint a convenor – still less an oppositional group. Or that they perceive themselves as answerable for union policy to union members (*Tribune*, 23 September 2005).

There are no signs of unions using the TULC to confront the government over policy in the context of funding; or injecting TULO, which they finance, with union goals. The associated website is dedicated to anti-Toryism and to praise from ministers of what they have done for the unions. There are few comments from trade unionists on what has not been achieved (*Unions Together* 2007). There has been little appetite for building alliances within the party, despite the emergence of the Grassroots Alliance, Save the Labour Party and the Labour Representation Committee. The TUC has linked up with pensioner campaigns. Many unions are affiliated to the Stop the War Coalition: their leaders play little part in its direction or activity. Neither strikes nor demonstrations have suggested a capacity to influence the government's political course.

Union leaders are typically realists. It is arguable that in the past trade unionists have only been able to extract significant concessions from the state when there is a policy consensus favourable to trade unionism or where unions have the propensity to act to deliver key state policies. Unions must be growing or relatively strong. These conditions have not existed since 1979. There is little evidence that they are likely to pertain in the near future. Yet within this general judgement there is diversity, as the differences in the trajectories of the key public sector unions, PCS and Unison, suggests. They may be taken as examples of, on the one hand, an attempt to build a militant orientation to the state and, on the other hand, to make gains through accommodation with government. They may also be taken as illustrations of the argument that affiliation to Labour delivers little; or alternatively that support for Labour is beneficial (interviews with activists, 2007).

After ten years, the ambition of the majority of union leaders remains limited in terms of both what they think they can get from New Labour and what they will do to get it. Their aspirations have diminished.[7] Life is full of contradictions. Most union leaders seem content to continue bankrolling neoliberalism with their members' money while claiming that such donations help to win New Labour over to improving the work prospects of those members. If, as some have claimed, there are only inches between the Conservatives and New Labour, for the majority of union leaders inches remain vital. That belief ensures that changes of significance in the alliance cannot be read off from the latest row spun as crisis or even from developments in political economy or electoral trends. The resilience of the contentious alliance is not a law of history. It will require a longer, more troubled stretch of history and the impact of greater events to consummate its demise.

## Notes

1 Despite the fact, that in many eyes, relations between party and unions had deteriorated between 2001 and 2003 – see, for example, Charlwood (2004).

2  The issue of who should be involved in taking decisions about union political funds is a complex one. There are differences between trade unionists over whether this is a matter for all members, political levy payers or Labour Party members. There are also differences over the extent to which union policy-making in relation to Labour and execution of policy inside the party should be subject to the norms of union democracy. The role of union 'representatives' on the NEC – executing union policy or applying their own judgement – has been particularly controversial (interviews with activists, 2007).

3  PFI involved the government contracting out new capital projects such as building schools, hospitals or prisons, projects funded in the past by the Treasury, to private companies. The latter financed, designed, built and ran the facility with the government repaying them over some 25–30 years.

4  Foundation Hospitals are a halfway house to privatization. Successful hospital trusts are given greater independence from the Department of Health, permitted to manage their own assets, set their employees' wages and compete with other hospitals.

5  For a less critical view, see Murray (2003).

6  A future Conservative government might not radically change relations with the unions (cf. Howell, 2005: 190). At times, Conservative spokespersons have stressed the need for cooperation with the unions. At others, they have suggested the need for further employment legislation 'to curb union power' (see, for example, *The Times*, 29 April 2008). Union leaders are not prepared to risk it.

7  See, for example, Dubbins (2007) where the failure of the Agency Workers Bill, despite all the unions' efforts, is portrayed as a success, largely because of the number of MPs who attended the debate.

## Bibliography

Alderman, K. (2000) 'Stranger than fiction? The selection of the Conservative and Labour London Mayoral candidates', *Parliamentary Affairs*, 53:1, 737–52.

Amicus (2004) *The Political Fund*, London: Amicus.

Bewley, H. (2006) 'Raising the standard? The regulation of employment, and public sector employment policy', *British Journal of Industrial Relations*, 44:2, 351–72.

Burgess, K. (2004) *Parties and Unions in the New Global Economy*, Pittsburgh: University of Pittsburgh Press.

Cain, M. and Taylor, M. (2002) *Keeping it Clean: The Way Forward for State Funding of Political Parties*, London: Institute of Public Policy.

Campbell, A and Stott, R. (2007) *The Blair Years: Extracts from the Alistair Campbell Diaries*, London: Hutchinson.

Certification Officer (1998–2007) *Annual Report*, London: Certification Office.

Charlwood, A. (2004) 'Annual review article: the new generation of trade union leaders and prospects for union revitalisation', *British Journal of Industrial Relations*, 42:2, 379–97.

Cowley, P. (2005) *The Rebels: How Blair Mislaid His Majority*, London: Politico's.

Cruddas, J. and Harris, J. (2006) *Fit for Purpose? A Programme for Labour Party Renewal*, London: Compass.

Curtice, J. and Mair, A. (2005) 'Are trade-unionists left-wing any more?', in A. Park, J. Curtice, K. Thomson, C. Bromley, M. Phillips and M. Johnson (eds.) *British Social Attitudes: the 22nd Report*, London: Sage.

Davies, L. (2001) *Through the Looking Glass: A Dissenter Inside New Labour*, London: Verso.

Department of Trade and Industry (DTI) (1998) *Fairness at Work*, London: HMSO.
—— (2003) *Review of Employment Relations Act 1999*, London: DTI.
—— (2006) *Success at Work: Protecting Vulnerable Workers, Supporting Good Employers*, London: DTI.
Dorey, P. (1999) 'The Blairite betrayal: New Labour and the trade unions', in G. Taylor (ed.) *The Impact of New Labour*, Basingstoke: Macmillan.
Dubbins, T. (2007) Agency and Temporary Workers Bill – The Result <www.unionstogether.org.uk/articles/article19.html> (accessed 3 July 2008).
Edmonds, J. (2001) 'The unions and the party', *Socialist Campaign Group News*, September.
—— (2006) 'Positioning Labour closer to the employers: the importance of the Labour Party's 1997 Business Manifesto', *Historical Studies in Industrial Relations*, 22, 85–107.
Electoral Commission (2007) <http://registers.electoralcommission.org.uk/regulatory-issues/regpoliticalparties.cfm> (accessed 3 July 2008).
Ewing, K.D. (2002) *Trade Unions, the Labour Party and Political Funding*, London: Catalyst.
—— (2007) *The Cost of Democracy: Party Funding in Modern British Politics*, Oxford: Hart.
Ewing, K.D. and Jones, C. (2006) 'From the Trade Disputes Act to a Trade Union Freedom Bill', in K. Ewing (ed.) *The Right to Strike: From the Trade Disputes Act 1906 to a Trade Union Freedom Bill 2006*. Liverpool: Institute of Employment Rights.
Flynn, P. (1999) *Dragons Led By Ponies*, London: Politicos.
Frege, C., Heery, E. and Turner, L. (2004) 'Comparative coalition building and the revitalisation of the labour movement', in C. Frege and J. Kelly (eds) *Varieties of Unionism: Strategies for Union Revitalization in a Globalizing Economy*. Oxford: Oxford University Press.
Gall, G. (2004) 'Trade union recognition in Britain, 1995–2002: turning the corner?', *Industrial Relations Journal*, 35:3, 249–70.
Heery, E. (2005) 'Trade unionism under New Labour', *The Shirley Lerner Memorial Lecture*, Manchester: Manchester Industrial Relations Society.
Hendy, J. and Gall, G. (2006) 'British trade union rights today and the Trade Union Bill', in K.D. Ewing (ed.), *The Right to Strike: From the Trade Disputes Act 1906 to a Trade Union Freedom Bill 2006*. Liverpool: Institute of Employment Rights.
Howell, C. (2005) *Trade Unions and the State: The Construction of Industrial Relations Institutions in Britain 1890–2000*, Princeton, NJ: Princeton University Press.
Hyman, R. (2001) *Understanding European Trade Unionism: Between Market, Class and Society*. London: Sage.
Jones, M. (2000) 'Working with Labour: the impact of Unison's political settlement', in M. Terry (ed.) *Redefining Public Sector Trade Unionism: Unison and the Future of the Unions*. London: Routledge.
Jones, N. (2002) *The Control Freaks: How New Labour Gets Its Own Way*, 2nd edition, London: Politico's.
Kelly, J. (2005) 'Social movement theory and union revitalization in Britain', in S. Fernie and D. Metcalf (eds) *Trade Unions: Resurgence or Demise?* London: Routledge.
Labour Party (1997) *New Labour: Because Britain Deserves Better*, London: Labour Party.

Leopold, J. (2006) 'Trade unions and the third round of political fund review balloting', *Industrial Relations Journal*, 37:3, 190–208.

Ludlam, S. (2001) 'New Labour and the unions: the end of the contentious alliance?', in S. Ludlam and M. Smith (eds) *New Labour in Government*. Basingstoke: Palgrave.

—— (2004) 'New Labour, "vested interest" and the union link', in S. Ludlam and M. Smith (eds), *Governing as New Labour: Policy and Politics Under Blair*. Basingstoke: Palgrave.

Ludlam, S. and Taylor, A. (2003) 'The political representation of the labour interest in Britain', *British Journal of Industrial Relations*, 41:4, 727–49.

McIlroy, J. (1998) 'The enduring alliance? Trade unions and the making of New Labour 1994–97', *British Journal of Industrial Relations*, 36:4, 537–64.

—— (1999) 'Unfinished business: the reform of strike legislation in Britain', *Employee Relations*, 21:6, 521–39.

—— (2000a) 'New Labour, new unions, new left', *Capital and Class*, 71, 11–45.

—— (2000b) 'The new politics of pressure – the Trades Union Congress and New Labour in government', *Industrial Relations Journal*, 31:1, 2–17.

—— (2007) 'Defend the link – but make it work for union members! Cash for honours, New Labour and the trade unions', Union Ideas Network <http://uin.org.uk/content/view/199/71/> (accessed 3 July 2008).

Marsh, H. (2002) 'Changing pressure-group politics: the case of the TUC 1994–2000', *Politics*, 22:3, 143–51.

Minkin, L. (1991) *The Contentious Alliance: Trade Unions and the Labour Party*, Edinburgh: Edinburgh University Press.

Moschonas, G. (2002) *In the Name of Social Democracy, the Great Transformation: 1945 to the Present*, London: Verso.

Murray, A. (2003) *A New Labour Nightmare: The Return of the Awkward Squad*, London: Verso.

Phillips, Sir H. (2006) *The Review of the Funding of Political Parties: An Interim Assessment*, London: HMSO.

—— (2007) *Strengthening Democracy: Fair and Sustainable Funding of Political Parties*, London: HMSO.

Prentis, D. (2003) 'No hidden surprises, no late extras', *Fabian Review*, 115:3, 14–15.

—— (2005a) 'Step up the fight against privatisation', *Tribune*, 24 June.

—— (2005b) 'Unison: winning the arguments', *Unison Labour-Link News*, Autumn.

—— (2006) 'Dave Prentis says . . .', *Unison Labour-Link News*, Summer.

Quinn, T. (2004) *Modernising the Labour Party: Organisational Change Since 1983*, Basingstoke: Palgrave.

Russell, M. (2005) *Building New Labour: The Politics of Party Organisation*, Basingstoke: Palgrave.

Sawyer, T. (2000) 'Unison and New Labour: searching for new relationships', in M. Terry (ed.) *Redefining Public Sector Trade Unionism: Unison and the Future of Trade Unions*, London: Routledge.

Seifert, R. and Sibley, T. (2005) *United they Stood: The Story of the UK Firefighters Dispute 2002–2004*, London: Lawrence and Wishart.

Seldon, A. (2007) *Blair Unbound*, London: Simon and Schuster.

Shaw, E. (2003) 'What matters is what works: the third way and the case of the Private Finance Initiative', in W. Leggett, S. Hale and L. Martell (eds) *The Third Way and Beyond: Criticisms, Futures and Alternatives*. Manchester: Manchester University Press.

—— (2004) 'The control freaks? New Labour and the party', in S. Ludlam and M. Smith (eds) *Governing as New Labour: Policy and Politics Under Blair*, Basingstoke: Palgrave.

Stuart, M., Charlwood, A., Martinez Lucio, M. and Wallis, E. (2006) *Union Modernisation Fund: Interim Evaluation Of First Round*, London: DTI.

Terry, M. and Smith, J. (2003) *Evaluation of the Partnership at Work Fund*, London: DTI.

Thorpe, A (2007) 'The Labour Party and the Trade Unions' in J. McIlroy, N. Fishman and A. Campbell (eds), *British Trade Unions and Industrial Politics: The High Tide of Trade Unionism, 1964–1979*, London: Merlin (1st edition, 1999).

TUC (1997) *General Council Report*, London: TUC.

—— (1998) *General Council Report*, London: TUC.

—— (1999) *General Council Report*, London: TUC.

—— (2000) *General Council Report*, London: TUC.

—— (2001) *General Council Report*, London: TUC.

—— (2002) *General Council Report*, London: TUC.

—— (2003) *General Council Report*, London: TUC.

—— (2005) *Report of Congress*, London: TUC.

—— (2006) *General Council Report*, London: TUC.

TULO (2005) *General Election 2005: The TULO Strategy Delivered*, London: TULO.

—— (2007) *Directory*, London: TULO.

Unions Together (2007) *Unions Together 2007* <www.unionstogether.org.uk> (accessed 3 July 2008).

Unison (2006a) *Annual Return to the Certification Officer*, London: Unison.

—— (2006b) *General Political Fund. Decentralising Decision Making*, London: Unison.

—— (2006c) *Unison in Labour*, London: Unison.

Waddington, J. (2003) 'Annual review article: heightening tensions in relations between trade unions and the Labour government in 2002', *British Journal of Industrial Relations*, 41:2, 335–58.

Woodley, T. (2006) 'New policies can win back the core voters we have lost', *Guardian*, 6 September.

—— (2007) 'For a fourth term we will have to move beyond Blairism', *Guardian*, 5 March.

Wrack, M. (2002) *Whose Money is it Anyway? The Case For Democratising The Trade Union Political Funds*, London: Socialist Alliance.

# Part II
# Issues

# 6 Employment legislation

## New Labour's neoliberal legal project to subordinate trade unions

*Paul Smith and Gary Morton*

Since 1997 New Labour governments have implemented a major programme of employment law reform, comprising three major statutes – the Employment Relations Act (ERA) 1999, the Employment Act (EA) 2002, and the Employment Relations Act (ERA) 2004 – and over 80 statutory instruments. Important innovations such as the national minimum wage, statutory union recognition, a right to accompaniment in grievance and disciplinary procedures, and family-friendly policies have been enacted. These measures represent a significant rupture with the policy of preceding Conservative governments, 1979 to 1997. They originate in New Labour's ambition to improve labour-market efficiency and to create new individual employment rights; the latter in response to its social and political constituency and the European Union's (EU) agenda for the social market.

There are, however, important aspects of continuity – a steadfast hostility to any resurgence of trade unionism capable of mounting an effective challenge to employers' determination of the pay–effort bargain, and a light touch in employment protection. Both dimensions are underpinned by neoliberal assumptions and norms (see McIlroy, chapters 1 and 2, this volume). These are repackaged in a language of 'fairness', 'flexibility' and social partnership 'to replace the notion of conflict between employers and employees with the promotion of partnership' (DTI 1998: 3) and to promote competitiveness (ibid.: 13–14, paras 2.9–2.19; see also DTI 2002, 2003a).

New Labour's concept of trade unionism is imbued with unitary values: 'New Labour re-legitimized collectivism but on one central condition: that it be imbricated with management objectives' (McIlroy 1998: 543). In his first speech to the TUC as prime minister after the election victory of 1997 Blair was explicit.

> The crusade for competitiveness has to be a national crusade . . . fought in every business in the country . . . I want the trades unions and the trades union movement to be part of that fight. Let us build trades unions and businesses that are creative, not conservative, unions that show they can work with management . . . Let us build unions that people join not just out of fear of change or exploitation but because

they are committed to success, . . . that support workers and foster the true adaptability they need to be secure in that competitive and fast-changing world. Agree as much as possible with employers and let there be a genuine dialogue to try and resolve some of the practical problems in any such legislation . . . We are not going to go back to the days of industrial warfare, strikes without ballots, mass and flying pickets and secondary action . . . I will watch very carefully to see how the culture of modern trades unionism develops.

(Blair: 1997: 103)

In contrast to its Conservative predecessors (Smith and Morton 1993), New Labour seeks to contain and domesticate rather than exclude the workers' voice. The goal, however, is the same – a reduced scope for workers to challenge the terms of the pay–effort bargain. New Labour's enthusiastic adoption of Conservative legislation on industrial action, and on union government and administration, is intended to maintain trade unions' weakness and subordination. Innovative measures, such as the statutory union-recognition procedure and state funds for unions, promote cooperative trade unionism (Müller-Jentsch 1985: 19). Although the Conservative government's derogation from the European Union's Protocol on Social Policy (the social chapter) of the Treaty of Maastricht 1992 was ended in 1997, New Labour remains sceptical of the European model of a regulated labour market. It declared: 'Some aspects of the social models developed in Europe before the advent of global markets have arguably become incompatible with competitiveness' (DTI 1998: 10; see also Wedderburn 2001; Treasury 2002; Taylor, chapter 11, this volume). Thus it has continued the Conservatives' policy of delay and dilution of EU Directives.

## Industrial action and the law

From 1979, successive Conservative governments, influenced by a free-market ideology that developed and intensified over time, enacted an unfolding programme to reform trade union law 'step by step' in six major statutes (Smith and Morton 2001a; Wedderburn 1991). The technique used was successively to narrow trade unions' protection against civil wrongs – tort immunity – established by the Trade Disputes Act (TDA) 1906 and reaffirmed by the Trade Union and Labour Relations Act 1974, as amended in 1976 (Wedderburn 1986: 578–9). Today tort immunity is only retained in a dispute between workers and their employer that relates 'wholly or mainly' (s. 244(1) Trade Union and Labour Relations (Consolidation) Act (TULR(C)A 1992) to their pay, terms and conditions of employment in the United Kingdom. Disputes between workers and workers (over a closed shop or union jurisdiction), between workers and other employers (by taking solidarity action or in sector-wide disputes where an employer's workers are not in dispute), or between a union and an employer (over the closed shop or the extent of collective agreements and union recognition by other employers) are outside the immunity (s. 218 TULR(C)A 1992).

The courts' definition of an employer does not permit extension of industrial action to associated companies or incorporated subsidiaries of multi-divisional corporations or holding companies (Davies and Freedland 2004: 136–40; Wedderburn 1986: 96–103). This obscures the reality of managerial power within large corporations and their contractors. Neither will the courts entertain industrial action against an existing employer in a dispute over future terms and conditions.[1] The opening of union funds by the Employment Act (EA) 1982 (s. 22 TULR(C)A 1992) to claims for damages by employers, neutralizing the 1901 *Taff Vale* judgment, was for Wedderburn (1991: 223) the point at which the philosophy of Hayek, a pioneer of the neoliberal project, became embedded in the legislative programme. The EA 1990 (ss. 219–46 TULR(C)A 1992) made unions vicariously liable for industrial action in which *any* officer (lay or paid) participated. To escape liability a union had to renounce any unofficial action (with statutory rules as to the procedure to be followed). If it wished to support such action it was necessary to use the statutory balloting procedure (see below), but unions were debarred from doing so if any officer had at any stage supported the action. During this period it is open to an employer to selectively dismiss any workers engaged in strike action without having to face a claim of unfair dismissal.

The right to picket was narrowed by the EA 1980 (s. 220 TULR(C)A 1992): only workers who are a party to a trade dispute (and their union officers) can attend at or near their place of work. In an era of complex webs of ownership and contracting, large multi-divisional corporations controlling a range of subordinate business units, and shifts in the location of production, this is a major limitation. In combination with the restriction of tort immunity to disputes between workers and their contractual employer, the effect is to confine workers' collective power to units often irrelevant to the locus of decision-making, and to prevent picketing of strategic points in the 'real' employer's supply chain or production system rather than any nominal legal entity.[2] Strikers' difficulties are compounded by the Code on Picketing (DTI 1992), which recommended a limit of six pickets at any entrance; this quickly achieved the status of a rule for courts and the police.

The Protection from Harassment Act (PHA) 1997 and the Serious Organized Crime and Police Act (SOCPA) 2005 allow prosecutions against those whose behaviour on more than one occasion causes alarm or distress: harassment is defined by s. 125 of the SOCPA as seeking 'to persuade any person ... not to do something that he is entitled or required to do, or to do something that he is not under any obligation to do'. The PHA has been used against peaceful environmental protestors, and has been cited in employment law[3] (though not yet in a trade union or industrial action case), and the implications of SOCPA's definition of harassment for unions are obvious.

Legal intervention did not stop there. Conservative governments imposed ever more stringent procedural requirements with which unions must comply in order to retain tort immunity. The intended result is that the ability to take effective action is narrowed in practice. The rationale for regulation switched from articulating workers' consent to industrial action, measured by and conforming to statutory requirements, to delaying the action and giving employers extensive grounds with which to mount legal challenges based on procedural irregularities (Trade Union Reform and Employment Rights Act (TURERA) 1993) (Simpson 2005: 331–7). A union is required (ss. 226–35 TULR(C)A 1992) to employ a body approved by the Department of Trade and Industry to supervise a postal ballot of members called upon to take industrial action; use a specified ballot paper and form of questions; notify the employer of the ballot; and give details of the ballot paper and the workers to be balloted, the result, and seven days' notice of the industrial action and categories of worker who are to be called upon to take it. Employers, union members and citizens are entitled to go to court to seek an injunction against any union that has not fully complied with this complex procedure.

The 1993 Act's requirement for unions to specify the workers whom they intend to ballot over industrial action was interpreted to mean that, where an employer could not readily identify the relevant members, then a union must provide their names to the employer.[4] In many cases, this would occur where union membership was low or dispersed, and therefore easily open to employers' countermeasures. In response to TUC protests, Schedule 3 of the Labour government's Employment Relations Act (ERA) 1999 amended the TULR(C)A 1992 so as to preserve union members' anonymity, but required a union to give employers 'such information in the union's possession as would help the employer to make plans and bring information to the attention of those of his employees whom the union intends to induce or has induced to take part, or continue to take part, in industrial action.' This was soon followed by a legal challenge in *National Union of Rail, Maritime and Transport Workers v London Underground Ltd* [2001]. The Appeal Court ruled that a union's officials must provide the information called for in the statute, even when it did not possess it (Wedderburn 2001: 209–10).

After more protests by the TUC, the Labour government amended the legislation again in ss. 22 and 25 ERA 2004. The outcome is scarcely less onerous: it requires unions, when balloting members for industrial action, to provide employers with a list of members (by category and workplace) and the figures involved (total, number in each category, and the number in each workplace) who may take action. 'Workplace' has a complex definition. Such information 'must be as accurate as is reasonably practicable in the light of the information in the possession of the union at the time', and is declared to be in the possession of the union if held in a document, in electronic form 'or any other form', and 'in possession or under the control of an officer or employee of the union' (ss. 226A, 234A TULR(C)A 1992). These amendments 'underline the function of the law . . . in assisting employers to limit the impact of any industrial action' (Simpson 2005: 333). The new Code of Practice (DTI 2006) 'has added significantly to the body of "soft law" with which trade unions "should" comply in the form of advice on how they should provide the "lists and figures" now required in sections 226A and 234A notices' (ibid.: 336). The law today is 'intricate, often arcane and sometimes scarcely comprehensible . . . and frequently does render the space for legitimate industrial conflict largely illusory' (Simpson 2006: 191). This is the intention. Recently a shift in focus has seen employers seeking disclosure of ballot procedures and claims for damages for losses incurred as a result of industrial action, or threats to make claims if the industrial action is proceeded with.[5] This has proved an effective weapon.

New Labour's commitment to protect the liberty of individual workers to take lawful industrial action (DTI 1998: 26–7) emerged in a stunted form: employers' freedom to dismiss workers taking industrial action was regulated, not abolished, by the ERA 1999. Unfair dismissal protection was extended to employees dismissed for taking 'protected industrial action' (action within the boundary of union tort immunity) which fell within an eight-week period after the beginning of the action, or after eight weeks if the employer did not take 'such procedural steps as would have been reasonable for the purposes of resolving the dispute'. The period was extended normally to twelve weeks by s. 26 ERA 2004 (s. 238A TULR(C)A 1992).

There is no explicit statutory declaration that industrial action shall not be regarded as a breach of contract. Protection is further qualified: of particular importance is the reference to employer or union adhesion to agreed procedures and other stances taken in the course of negotiations (s. 238A(6) TULR(C)A 1992). The sanction is an application to an employment tribunal for unfair dismissal. The only case to come to a tribunal – the Friction Dynamics dispute – showed the weakness of the law (Hendy and Gall 2006: 253–4). There is no protection for those who take industrial action outside the immunities. The liberty of individuals to take industrial action remains precarious and in breach of international standards.

New Labour has striven to prevent the European Community Charter of the Fundamental Social Rights of Workers 1989 from being incorporated in any legally binding document. The UK denied any Community right to strike in the hearing before the European Court of Justice (ECJ) in *Viking Line v International Transport Workers' Federation*,[6] the only member-state to do so (Bercusson 2007: 300). The Advocate-General's opinion,[7] despite important reservations, stating that 'the rights to associate and to collective action are of a fundamental character within the Community legal order, as the Charter of Fundamental Rights of the European Union reaffirms' (para. 60), represented a setback for the UK. A remedy was soon at hand in the form of negotiations during 2007 for the new EU constitutional treaty, by which the UK secured a derogation from the Community Charter, with 'potentially very serious consequences for the protection of workers' and trade unions' rights in the UK, giving rise to a risk that EU law will apply differently in the UK to its application in other Member States' (Ford and Hendy 2007: 9). The decision of the ECJ affirmed the right to strike but hedged this with major qualifications.

This represented a significant victory for the British government and its allies (Wedderburn 2008: 8–12).

The Gate Gourmet dispute, in August 2005, revealed the strategic advantage of employers when confronted by industrial action (Hendy and Gall 2006: 248–50). The TGWU had no immunity for the industrial action taken by Gate Gourmet workers (s. 219 TULR(C)A 1992): the union had not complied with the statutory procedure – notification of the ballot (including the questions to be asked) and the workers concerned, the ballot and a count supervised by an external, approved agency, and notification of the result and the action to be taken (ss. 226, 226A, 231A, 234A). The TGWU was obliged to repudiate the action (s. 226).The High Court granted an injunction restraining picketing away from site B (500 metres from the company's premises), limiting to six the pickets at site A (opposite the company's premises), and preventing picketing at bus stops close to the plant.[8] The workers had no claim for unfair dismissal (ss. 237, 238). The TGWU was also obliged to repudiate solidarity action by BA workers because the action was against an employer that was not a party to the dispute (ss. 224, 244). Gate Gourmet's UK managing director, Eric Born, was a director of Versa Logistics, a subsidiary of Gate Gourmet which supplied temporary workers to Gate Gourmet. There could be no question of a legal dispute between Gate Gourmet workers and Versa Logistics, a separate employer. The TGWU was forced to walk away from the dispute: 'Of the 813 workers sacked, 272 were reinstated [on worse terms] and 411 given the equivalent of their [statutory] redundancy entitlement. For 130 there was neither employment nor compensation' (Hendy and Gall 2006: 249).

Gate Gourmet was a defining moment when New Labour's attitude to trade unions and industrial action was starkly revealed. No words of partnership or supply-side reforms could mask its distaste for industrial action; no condemnation of the employer's actions was forthcoming from ministers. New Labour is content with the law: capital is free to remould its relationship with labour; labour is often powerless to resist. Employers' confidence in disputes increases; a new tactic is the use of counter-pickets by managers and security guards (some hired for the occasion), unrestricted by any statutory restrictions or codes as to employment, place or number.

## Union recognition and workers' representation

The union-recognition provisions of the ERA 1999, implemented in June 2000 (as Schedule A1 of the TULR(C)A 1992), were seen by many as an opportunity to rebuild trade unions. But the Schedule contained 'a series of rigorous tests that [established] a highly circumscribed right to trade union representation' (Smith and Morton 2001b: 124) that have not lowered the costs of unionization in any significant way.

The definition of collective bargaining is restricted to 'negotiations relating to pay, hours and holidays' (para. 3(3)). The broader and conventional definition embracing the wider pay–effort bargain, in s. 178 TULR(C)A 1992, was expressly excluded and has been maintained.[9] Other matters may be agreed voluntarily. All of the major statutory underpinnings to collective bargaining were removed by Conservative governments; none have been restored by New Labour, including the promotion of collective bargaining in the Advisory, Conciliation and Arbitration Service's (ACAS) terms of reference (deleted by the TURERA 1993). This narrow view of, and limited support for, collective bargaining reflects New Labour's suspicion of workers' collective voice. Its view of 'partnership' does not involve any special role or status for trade unions: relationships are 'Sometimes . . . provided by a partnership between employers and trade unions which *complements* the direct relationship between employer and employee. On the other hand, some organizations achieve effective working relationships in other ways' (DTI 1998: 12, emphasis added).

With respect to statutory recognition the Schedule (para. 7) only applies to employers of at least 21 workers (those who work under a contract of employment or a contract to perform any work or services). This excludes 31 per cent of the workforce, 8.1 million workers (Simpson 2000: 196). This is particularly important given the absence of tort immunity for secondary industrial action, which inhibits unions from mobilizing support for workers employed in small companies in dispute, or enforcing recognition and collective agreements across sectors.

Employers have a major voice in determination of bargaining units, whose boundaries determine the viability of a union's claim to represent workers. The general duty of the Central Arbitration Committee (CAC) in deciding union recognition and derecognition applications is to 'have regard to the object of encouraging and promoting fair and efficient practices and arrangements in the workplace' (para. 171), but this duty must be consistent with other provisions, among them 'the need for the [bargaining] unit to be compatible with effective management' (para.19B(2)(9)). Sensitivity to employers' requirements is also evident in the absence of any three-year moratorium for an application by employers to change the contours of the bargaining unit (in contrast to union recognition applications; see below) and the 'business' criteria specified – a change in the employer's organization, structure or activities, or a substantial change within the original bargaining unit in the number of workers (Part III, para. 67(2)). Employers have sought to dilute union membership within wide bargaining units (countering the trend of recent years to devolve bargaining to subordinate business units), thus reducing the likelihood of unions winning a majority of votes and the support of 40 per cent of the workforce in a recognition ballot.

The existing structure of collective representation is protected. The CAC cannot accept an application from an independent union if there is a collective agreement in existence as a result of which a union is entitled to bargain on behalf of any workers (even one) in the bargaining unit (para. 35(1)). This extends to any independent union or employer-sponsored workers' association, whatever their representative status – a fatal obstacle to some applications for recognition (Davies and Kilpatrick 2004: 131).[10] Moreover, the agreement need not cover pay and conditions. For Simpson, 'The decision to leave voluntary recognition of a demonstrably unrepresentative independent union beyond challenge . . . must have been a conscious one' (Simpson 2007: 297).

A number of further tests restrict applications for recognition. An application from a number of unions is not admissible unless they show that they will cooperate with each other and demonstrate that they will enter into single-table bargaining arrangements if the employer wishes (para. 37(2)). If a recognition application is accepted but is unsuccessful, then there is a three-year moratorium before a new application can be submitted (para. 39(2)(a)).

A union may apply to the CAC to decide if the union has the support of a majority of workers constituting the bargaining unit (paras 11–12). But the application may only proceed if union members number at least 10 per cent of workers constituting the bargaining unit and if a majority of the workers would be likely, as assessed by the CAC, to favour union recognition (para. 36). If these criteria are met then the CAC will organize a ballot. Where a union has already recruited a majority of the relevant workforce, then the CAC must award recognition unless it believes that any of three qualifying conditions are fulfilled. These provide ample opportunity for challenge by employers,[11] although the CAC has exercised its discretion not to order ballots without appropriate evidence (Bogg 2006: 261–70).

Employers are required to cooperate with a recognition ballot, the union and the CAC-appointed ballot administrator (para. 26). The employer must provide the relevant union with access to the workforce during the period of the ballot. If it fails to do so the CAC may issue a declaration that a union be recognized (para. 27(2)), but proceedings for contempt of court have been avoided. The formal equality of access accorded to unions is restricted to the period of the ballot; there are no restrictions upon employers in the preceding period. Despite employers' opposition the ERA 2004 amended the statutory procedure to give unions improved access to a workforce. However, the new procedures embodied employers' wishes at almost every turn, disregarding unions' concerns.

After the CAC has accepted an application, a qualified and independent person, acting on behalf of a union and appointed by the CAC, may distribute material by post to workers (paras 19C–F, Sch. A1 TULR(C)A 1992). New duties have been imposed on employers informed of a ballot (para 19D(2), and sanctions and remedies against unfair practices by both employers *and* unions with respect to recognition and derecognition ballots (paras 27A–F, 119A–I, 166B). Both areas of legislation are complex (Bogg 2005: 75–81). The definition of unfair practices is 'inclusive enough to encapsulate many of the employer abuses identified by the TUC' (ibid.: 79), but protection is narrow and limited to the period of the ballot. A new Code of Practice provides guidance on access and unfair practice but its scope is restricted: 'the employer's typical methods of communicating with his workforce should be used as a benchmark for determining how the union should communicate with members of the same workforce during the access period' (DTI 2005: para. 28). The Code applies to both parties: of the four complaints received by the CAC in 2006–7, one was from an employer (CAC: 4, 13).

If, after either statutory or voluntary union recognition, the parties are unable to reach an agreement on a method for conducting collective bargaining, then either may request assistance from the CAC (paras 30, 58). Should it be unable to promote an agreement, then the CAC is required to specify a procedural agreement which is legally binding (paras 31, 63). If one or more of the parties fails to adhere to the agreed method of conducting collective bargaining reached under the procedure, then either may apply to the CAC, which is required to impose a legally binding agreement (para. 32). A model agreement is given in The Trade Union Recognition (Method of Collective Bargaining) Order 2000. If one party breaches a legally binding procedural agreement, the other may apply for an order for specific performance (paras 31(6), 63(5)). This will be limited to the holding of meetings as required by the agreement (Simpson 2000: 215–16). There is no access to arbitration as was the case under the Employment Protection Act 1975. Any failure by either party to observe an order for specific performance could constitute contempt of court (none has arisen to date).

The Schedule establishes procedures for derecognition (Parts IV and V). An unprecedented innovation, in defiance of international standards (Ewing 2000a), is the protection given to recognition agreements with employer-sponsored, non-independent workers' associations (Part VI: Derecognition where union not independent). The wider definition of collective bargaining in s. 178(1) TULR(C)A 1992 is excluded (para. 136) but no other is specified; it can be very narrow or consist only of consultation (para. 35(2)(b)). There is no three-year restriction, after a recognition agreement between an employer-sponsored workers' association and an employer, for an application for derecognition, but the application must be made by workers (para. 137) rather than by an independent union (which has no status in the application). Workers applying for derecognition have no right of access to the workforce, in contrast to the employer and its sponsored association (paras 147, 118). This compounds the subordination of workers indicated by the very existence of an employer-sponsored association.

The CAC will not admit an application for derecognition unless it considers that at least 10 per cent of the workforce favours an end to the bargaining arrangements and that this will be supported by a majority (para. 139). If the CAC calls a derecognition ballot, then the same onerous rules apply (a simple majority and at least 40 per cent of the workforce in the existing bargaining unit). If an employer-sponsored association obtains a certificate of independence then any application for derecognition is inadmissible. An independent union may apply for statutory recognition only if an application for derecognition of an employer-sponsored association has been successful and the employer has responded by recognizing the same body for substantially the same bargaining unit (paras 148, 35(4)).

The government's review of ERA declared that it was 'working well' (DTI 2003b: 23). A number of issues were put forward for consultation but any change to the statutory protection of employers' recognition of non-independent unions – a measure that contravenes International Labour Organisation conventions (ILO)[12] – and the inability of an independent union to challenge this or the bargaining unit was rejected. The evidence cited was that only two CAC applications had been received, both later withdrawn (ibid.: 54–5, paras 2.95–2.99). That this might result from the very subordination of workers that trade unionism seeks to challenge is something that the government cannot acknowledge. Derecognition of non-independent unions is a right that exists in theory rather than practice (Simpson 2007: 296). The government did not address the issue of employers' recognition of independent trade unions with no viable representative base.

The impact of the statutory recognition procedure has been minimal, and confined to its early years. Total union membership has fallen slightly, from 7,898,000 in 2000 to 7,603,000 in 2007 (see McIlroy and Daniels, chapter 3, this volume). Unions won recognition largely where they had retained or quickly built membership before employers learned to mitigate or use the procedure's provisions, including ballots (Moore *et al.* 2004). Two studies, using different methodologies (Gall 2004; Wood *et al.* 2003), indicated its limited effect. By March 2007, the CAC had received 566 applications in its seven years of existence, of which 333 were accepted: 74 resulted in union recognition without a ballot and in 143 cases a ballot was held; unions were successful in only 88 – a significant failure rate (CAC 2006: 23). Voluntary agreements outside the procedure increased (Moore *et al.* 2004: 79–83), before falling (TUC 2006). The 'shadow effect' soon dissipated.

The Labour government defended the UK state's legal position (i.e. it defended the stance of the Conservative government) in the *Wilson and Palmer* case at the European Court of Human Rights (ECHR). It lost decisively. The issue was whether denial of pay increases to employees who had refused to sign new contracts that removed pay from collective bargaining constituted anti-union discrimination. A succession of hearings in the UK concluded with the House of Lords' judgment in 1995, which rejected the applicants' case. The Conservative government had intervened with the so-called Ullswater amendment[13] (to what became the TURERA 1993), which prevented a legal challenge if the employer's purpose was to further a change in its relationship with employees (Ewing 2000b). The ECHR criticized both the 1993 Act and the Law Lords' judgment as a violation of Article 11 of the European Convention on Human Rights (Schedule 1 of the Human Rights Act 1998) as regards both the individual applicants and their trade unions.

New Labour responded in minimalist fashion (Bogg 2005: 72–5). Section 29 ERA 2004 (see ss. 145A–F TULR(C)A) gave workers the right not to be made offers to induce them not to be or to seek to become members of independent unions, to take part in their activities (at the appropriate time), or to use their services. The definition of the latter expressly excluded both union representation (ignoring the judgment of the ECHR)[14] and collective bargaining. Members of recognized and independent unions have the right not to be made offers which, as the employer's 'sole or main purpose', have the result that the workers' terms of employment 'will not (or will no longer) be determined by collective agreement negotiated by or on behalf of the union' (s. 145B). This is intended to permit employers to make offers to workers to derogate from collective agreements where the sole or main purpose is not to exclude a union's role in collective bargaining – 'a striking continuity with New Right perspectives' (ibid.: 74).

Despite its narrow scope, the ERA 2004 has added a new layer of protection. Thus ASDA was ordered by an Employment Tribunal to pay £2,500 compensation to 340 members of the GMB, a total of £850,000, because 'on the balance of probabilities . . . the removal of collective bargaining was the main purpose of the [cash] offer. . . . when we take other matters into account then we move to a position of having no doubt at all that it was the main purpose'.[15] The tribunal's findings were a major political victory for the GMB in its campaign to build union organization at ASDA.

## Union administration and government

Conservative governments imposed ever more detailed regulation of union government and administration in three statutes – the TUA 1984, EA 1988 and TURERA 1993 – based upon an individualist model of representation and a presumption of undemocratic practices within unions. The state laid claim to be the guarantor of union democracy and accountability (DTI 1991: 17–21): the object was to delegitimize unions as collective and democratic organizations. The legislation was important for its political symbolism, the additional burdens imposed upon unions, and for its impact upon industrial action.

Workers have a statutory right to join a relevant union of their choice (s. 174 TULR(C)A 1992). Unions have only residual power to discipline members (s. 65) and are forbidden to impose any sanctions on members who refuse to take industrial action.[16] Members have extensive, unprecedented access to unions' financial reports (s. 30); union officers who do not comply with statutory requirements face draconian sanctions (with no discretion left to the court) and the Certification Officer (CO) has wide, independent powers of investigation (ss 37A–E). All executive officers and members of the principal executive committee are subject to periodic election by individual-member postal ballot, supervised by an external agency approved by the DTI (ss. 46–61). Political fund ballots must be held every ten years (s. 73(3)) and members were required (s. 68 TULR(C)A 1992) to renew their authorization of the payment of union subscriptions by employers at source (the 'check-off'). This measure was repealed in 1998 by New Labour.

The Labour government also abolished (s. 28 ERA 1999) the offices of the Commissioner for the Rights of Trade Union Members (CROTUM) and the Commissioner for Protection Against Unlawful Industrial Action, which had been established by the Conservative government (EA 1988, EA 1990, TURERA 1993) to support union members' complaints against unions, and to provide members of the public with an avenue to challenge industrial action. Their powers were transferred to the CO, whose role was strengthened by Schedule 6 of the Employment Relations Act 1999. Whereas the CROTUM could only advise on and support complaints by union members, the CO now possesses a quasi-judicial function. Declarations and enforcement orders made by the CO in relation to a wide range of issues relating to union government and administration (breach of rule or statutory duty by a union), most of which were introduced by the Conservative government, have the status of court orders. Non-compliance may lead to contempt proceedings.

This legislation is indebted to Hayek (Wedderburn, 1991: 218–19). For Wedderburn, the ban on disciplining of union members who refuse to take industrial action (now ss. 64–5 TULR(C)A 1992) is quintessential Hayek: 'No principles of collective conduct which bind the individual can exist in a society of free men' (cited in Wedderburn 1991: 217). Embedded within the legislation is a conception of unions as voluntary organizations of individuals (hence the closed shop has no legal protection) who give limited consent to delegate aspects of their economic autonomy, and who should not subject other workers to coercion in the form of collective agreements and industrial action.

Such sentiments are routinely echoed by New Labour, without seemingly any knowledge as to their origin. Thus unions are conceived as 'extremely important organisations that regulate, or strongly influence, the employment relationship between many millions of people and their employers. That sets them apart from other voluntary organisations' (DTI 2003c: 68). In response to a legal dispute between the Amalgamated Society of Locomotive Engineers and Firemen (ASLEF) and a member over the latter's activity as a British National Party (BNP) member[17] (Ford and Hendy 2007: 3) the government amended the TULR(C)A 1992 (by ss. 33, 34 ERA 2004) so as to allow expulsion of members on the basis of their political activities. ASLEF appealed to the ECHR, where the UK state reaffirmed its view of unions as special organizations.[18] The Court ruled that s. 174 TULR(C)A infringed Article 11 of the European Convention on Human Rights, that is the right of ASLEF's members to freedom of association. This is interpreted widely (para. 38) (Ford and Hendy 2007: 7). As with the ECHR's decision in *Wilson and Palmer*, the Labour government's response minimized the scope of the court's judgment.

> The Court did not give any opinion as regards other limitations under UK law on the ability of trade unions to expel, exclude or otherwise discipline their members. Nor do the general principles set out in the

Court's judgment imply that there can be no justification under Article 11 for other limitations on the freedom of trade unions to determine their membership. The UK Government therefore firmly maintains its position that the other legal restrictions under UK law in this area are necessary in a democratic society and strike a fair balance between the interests of trade unions, their members and their prospective members.

(DTI 2007a: 12)

Time and again the legal provisions preventing unions exercising discipline over members have been condemned by authoritative international bodies (Ford and Hendy 2007: 12), only to be ignored by both Conservative and Labour governments.

## Representation of workers: information and consultation

New Labour's values are revealed in the regulations to implement the EU Information and Consultation of Employees Directive, whose passage had been delayed by the UK government (Beckett and Hencke 2004). Any conception of codetermination is alien to both the Directive and the Information and Consultation of Employees Regulations 2004, which establishes bodies that bear no relation to works councils as 'institutions of market-independent industrial citizenship . . . [that bring] non-competitive "social" interests to bear on managerial decision-making' (Streeck 1997: 330). As with statutory union recognition, information and consultation has been imposed on employers despite their opposition but in a manner acceptable to them.

The scope of the Regulations is narrow. They establish a right of employees (itself a restrictive criterion) in undertakings of more than 50 full-time employees (thereby excluding seven million employees) 'carrying out economic activity' – which may exclude much of central and local government (Ewing and Truter 2005: 628) – to receive information, subject to commercial confidentiality, and to be consulted. Pre-existing agreements are given a measure of protection. Employees' representatives are entitled only to a 'reasoned response' to their opinions. Procedures may also consist of direct communication with employees. For Davies and Kilpatrick (2004: 148) the TUC's acceptance of this is 'a measure of just how weak the negotiating position of unions is in the UK today'. The sanctions for non-compliance are weak (Ewing and Truter 2005: 634–6).

The Regulations have 'disconnected union-based structures from the representative structures of information and consultation' (Davies and Kilpatrick 2004: 141), giving statutory support to a second channel of communication from which trade unions are excluded, even where they are recognized or possess members (ibid.: 143–7, 149–50). This is unprecedented. It is in stark contrast to existing issue-specific statutory consultative procedures (ibid.: 141–7), for example over collective redundancies and transfers of undertakings, and allows employers to determine the boundaries of information and consultation procedures. This flows logically from New Labour's determination to restrict trade union recognition to predetermined paths acceptable to employers.

A three-stage process of implementation (April 2005 to April 2008) has required employers of undertakings with 50 or more employees to establish information and consultation procedures when a request is made in writing by 10 per cent of the employees (subject to a minimum of 15 and a maximum of 2,500). If one or more agreements already exist – which must be inclusive, in writing and 'approved by the employees' – and at least 10 per cent (but less than 40 per cent) of employees have supported the request, the employer must initiate negotiations or organize a ballot. The latter must be conducted in a fair manner, but it need not be postal or independently supervised (the contrast with ballots for industrial action, principal executive committees and executive officers could not be more tellingly drawn). To succeed, the request must be supported by at least 40 per cent of the undertaking's employees and a simple majority of those voting. The employer has wide discretion as to employee constituencies: these may embrace all employees or 'such constituencies as the employer may decide' if the employer 'considers that . . . separate ballots . . . would better reflect the interests of the employees as a whole' (Sch. 2, para. 2(a)). The employer is the judge of employees' interests: a unitary perspective with a vengeance!

Some consultative bodies will provide opportunities for workers' collective representation and organization on a company-wide basis, but given the nature of the regulations in many cases employers will dominate (Dickens and Hall 2006: 344), and the new bodies may weaken or displace union organization (Moore *et al.* 2004: 82) and provide the foundation for new staff associations – non-independent trade unions – to the detriment of statutory recognition applications by independent unions (Hall 2002: 14).[19] Managerial prerogative will not be reduced or constrained; if anything it will gain a new legitimacy.

## Employment protection

Since 1997 New Labour has introduced a range of employment protection measures in established areas such as unfair dismissal and discrimination, and extended it to encompass new ones such as the national minimum wage, working time, family leave, part-time workers and fixed-term employees. The goal is to raise standards of 'fairness' (DTI 1998) and 'to raise employment and develop a diverse pool of skilled labour' (Treasury 2002: 6) in order to improve labour-market efficiency. But such regulation must not impose labour-market rigidities or disproportionate costs on employers; the latter must be able to 'adjust total pay, including overtime and bonuses, as well as employment numbers quickly and flexibly in response to changes in market conditions' (Treasury 2002: 8). This explains New Labour's openness to pressure from the CBI, *and* their differences with it, as well as the government's inability to accept counter-arguments and evidence (Crouch 2001: 105), leading to 'a downward drift in aspirations and achievement' (McIlroy 1998: 7).

The reduction of the qualifying period for unfair dismissal to one year and the increase in compensation, which is index-linked (ERA 1999 s. 34), were both significant measures. However, the formula for the basic award remains low, based upon gross pay capped at £330 a week (and a total of £9,900) from 1 February 2008, which for male employees is half of its real value when first established in 1976. The median award for unfair dismissal in 2005–6 was £4,228 (Gibbons 2007: 21) – a weak sanction, apart from the difficulty some applicants have in obtaining payment.

The right not to be unfairly dismissed was diluted in three major ways by Part 3 of the Employment Act 2002, implemented from 1 October 2004 (amending the Employment Rights (ERA) Act 1996). First, new statutory standard and modified disciplinary procedures undercut the ACAS Code of Practice and the standards of reasonableness developed by the courts (Hepple and Morris 2002: 259). Any employer that does not follow the statutory procedures is open to a claim of unfair dismissal, with the remedy of four weeks' basic pay in compensation (S120(1A) ERA 1996) – hardly an impressive sanction; under specific circumstances the compensatory award may be increased by a maximum of 50 per cent (s.124A ERA 1996). Second, except in specified circumstances, claims to an employment tribunal are permitted only after the relevant statutory procedure has been completed. Third, *Polkey v A. E. Dayton Services* was partly reversed (s. 98A ERA 1996): that is, employers are no longer required to follow a procedure other than the statutory procedure at the *time* of dismissal. The case law has interpreted this widely (Sanders 2007).[20]

Tribunal claimants now face a very real fear of costs being awarded against them. The Employment Tribunals (Constitution and Rules of Procedure) Regulations 2001 raised the maximum award by an employment tribunal from £500 to £10,000, and the Employment Tribunal Regulations 2004 (under ss. 13A and 34 Employment Tribunals Act 1996) permit non-legal preparation costs to be awarded in specific circumstances.[21] There is evidence that some employers' legal representatives use this fear to cause applicants, especially those without representation, to withdraw claims (Citizens' Advice 2004).

Despite their deregulatory intent, the impact of these changes has not been to the liking of employers or the government. The unintended consequences, formalizing early recourse to the law, were too great. With remarkable alacrity a review was commissioned by the DTI in 2006, reported in just over three months (Gibbons 2007), and was quickly followed by a consultation document (DTI 2007b). The Employment Act 2007 repealed the statutory procedures and reinstated *Polkey*.

The National Minimum Wage Act 1998 (Deakin and Morris 2005: 285–92) applies to workers ordinarily working in the United Kingdom (rather than employees) who have ceased to be of compulsory school age, overriding any contractual agreement. The minimum hourly rate is determined by the Secretary of State, after consultation with the Low Pay Commission, and applies to most types of payment in a pay-reference period. It is regularly uprated although there is no automatic procedure for cost-of-living increases. From 1 October 2007 the national minimum rates are: for those above 22 years, £5.52; for those of 18–22 years, £4.60; and for those under 18, £3.40. The Act has improved the position of the very lowest-paid workers although its impact has been reduced by its level and difficulties in enforcement in some sectors (Dickens and Manning 2003).

There are many examples of the government's minimalist approach to transposing EU Directives. The initial attempt to restrict the Directive on Part-time Workers (97/81 EC) to employees (rather than workers) proved unsustainable. Nevertheless, the regulations as implemented (Part-time Workers (Prevention of Less Favourable Treatment) Regulations 2000) restrict the right of comparable pay and terms to a narrow band of full- and part-time workers within the same employer, thereby excluding agency workers. Only 400,000 part-time workers were affected.[22] McColgan (2000a: 267) concluded that the scope of the Regulations 'is so narrow and their protections so few' that embedded disadvantage will continue. The first tranche of family-friendly policies, although establishing new principles in the face of CBI opposition, were minimalist in design (McColgan 2000b: 142), and although subsequently extended by the Work and Families Act 2006 its provisions are hardly radical (Caracciolo di Torella 2007; James 2007).

Agency workers possess an ambiguous legal status (Wynn and Leighton 2006), outside much protective legislation, and are vulnerable to abuse. For Forde and Slater (2005: 250) such workers are 'one of the least protected groups . . . in the British labour market'; not so for the Treasury for which they are an essential part of a flexible labour market (Treasury 2002: 9). In its opposition to all calls to increase protection of agency workers, New Labour displayed 'the heights of negativity' (Davies and Freedland 2007: 88). This position has proved unsustainable and in May 2008 the government announced that it would no longer oppose the draft Agency Workers Directive. Typically, this is to be implemented in a manner that, though giving significant improvements to some workers, is acceptable to the CBI. The new rights will not apply to sick and maternity pay or pensions (the statutory minima will apply), and will only be triggered after twelve weeks' employment (rather than the six weeks proposed by the draft Directive). This will exclude 30 per cent of all agency workers (and more, if their employment is carefully planned to be within twelve weeks). Only 20 per cent would be excluded if this were a six-week exemption (Forde *et al.* 2000: 15). Although the scope of the gangmasters' legislation is narrow in that it only applies to food harvesting and processing (Davies and Freedland 2007: 78–80), it remains important for groups that fall within its jurisdiction (Lawrence 2007).

Perhaps the most vivid example of New Labour's attitude is the transposition of the Working Time Directives. The Working Time Regulations 1998 took every opportunity to minimize the impact of the maximum working week of 48 hours – exemption for all workers in specific sectors and occupations, and those on unmeasured working time; flexible time-periods for the calculation of hours; and derogation from the 48-hour week by collective or workforce agreements (the latter made by workers not represented by an independent and recognized trade union), and individual choice (Barnard 1999, 2000). The most recent study of the Regulations' impact noted the absence of collectively agreed derogations, the prevalence of individual derogation, and the pressure exerted on some workers to agree to this (Barnard *et al.* 2003: 231–52). It concluded that the 'Directive has yet to have a significant impact on employment relations in the UK' (ibid.: 251). The only exception is the statutory right to payment for holidays (even here compliance had to be enforced by legal action),[23] though its impact in small companies and casual employment may be doubted. The Labour government opposed the European Commission's proposals for safeguards that regulate but did not abolish individual derogation (Hobbs and Njoya 2005: 308–13), which were introduced in an attenuated form.

Without powerful unions the law's efficacy to regulate the employment relationship is limited (Kahn-Freund 1977: 8–10). Hence many of the new rights prove in practice to have a limited impact upon workers, both in terms of coverage and the degree of change. For Pollert (2005: 237) the 'vulnerability of the majority of unorganized workers does not register in . . . [New Labour's] thinking or its programme' (see also Colling 2006: 144). Another route was open, given that evidence shows that trade union presence reduces claims to employment tribunals (Colling 2004: 557) – to strengthen trade unions. But this would have had consequences unacceptable to employers and the government: both are content with unions' weakness.

## Conclusion: purpose and impact

The package of small measures announced in the 2007 Queen's Speech – changes to statutory unfair dismissal procedures, tighter enforcement of the minimum wage, facilitation of expulsion from unions on political party grounds – emphasized the essential continuity between the administrations of Blair and Brown (*Labour Research*, December 2007). New Labour's employment law policy is intended to restrict and regulate trade unions and industrial action: hence the maintenance of the overwhelming bulk of Conservative legislation. It is prepared to introduce new and improved individual and collective rights, but once the headlines are ignored, the practical effect is rarely more than minimal. This is achieved by their limited scope, specific derogations and weak sanctions.

A novel policy, not prefigured in New Labour's programme when in opposition and which has grown in importance over the course of its period in office, is state sponsorship of trade union activities – some new, acceptable to employers and the government – to support cooperative trade unionism (Smith and Morton 2006). State funds have been provided to promote partnerships at work (ERA 1999 s. 30), to train union-learning representatives (EA 2002 s. 43) and for union 'modernisation' (ERA 2004 s. 55), as well as for training shop stewards and international work. There is now a massive state subsidy to trade unionism (see McIlroy, chapter 2; and McIlroy and Croucher, chapter 9, this volume).

Although the policy of state finance emerged pragmatically, it stems from the deeply held view of New Labour as to the appropriate nature and activity of unions. The policy promotes activities that strengthen the dynamic of cooperative trade unionism at a time of unions' weakness, organizational flux and amalgamation. Unions' support reflects a search for financial and organizational subsidies and new roles at a time of a historic decline in financial reserves (Willman 2005: 50; 53–5), a shift away from union recognition by employers (ibid.: 58; Bryson *et al.* 2004: 139–41), and their reduction of subsidies for workplace representation (Willman 2005: 50). Within unions a constituency of representatives and full-time officers dependent financially and politically upon these roles and funds has been quickly created.

The impact of the law should not be underestimated: it is a powerful independent factor in the hostile environment that confronts unions. The narrowed tort immunity to take industrial action, and the complex statutory procedure, has significantly reduced unions' effectiveness, altering 'the calculus facing employers as they considered changing their industrial relations policies' (Howell 2005: 142, 146–7). New avenues to articulate collective voice – the recognition procedure and the information and consultation regulations – are characterized by their modesty, indeed weakness. Neither has lowered the cost of constructing collective organization – deliberately so.

There are other consequences, important over time. The limited effectiveness of unions reduces their attractiveness to workers, making recruitment more difficult. Within each workplace the threshold for the viability of collective organization is raised by the restriction of external pressure that unions can mobilize by secondary action. This in turn compounds unions' difficulties in organizing and servicing members and collective bargaining. The imposition of individual-member postal ballots for the election of principal executive committees and executive officers is not only expensive, but eliminated the role of intermediate bodies as electoral colleges, ending their function in mediating the interests of distinct constituencies. Organizational coherence has been impaired in some cases. The prohibition of workplace ballots for constitutional elections and industrial action prevented unions from asserting their collective identity and presence at work – a powerful tool of legitimation. Moreover, the low turnout in postal ballots in turn delegitimates outcomes and unions. Unions' inability to enforce members' legal rights by industrial action has compelled them to develop their legal services, again at a high financial cost, and with limited impact.

Ewing has pointed out the void at the centre of New Labour's programme of employment law reform – the absence of any commitment to trade union autonomy in conformity with ILO conventions 87 and 98 and other international standards. He notes that unions

> are being compelled by government to accept their changing role in the contemporary economy. . . . in the Warwick agreement the Labour Party is continuing to remould trade union function and to push it in directions that are consistent with the interests and programmes of the government. We are witnessing the emergence of a new supply side trade unionism, with the functions of trade unionism being determined in Whitehall rather than in the workplace.
>
> (Ewing 2005: 2)

He comments that unions' support for Labour 'mask(s) a series of bitter disappointments which for political reasons it is in no one's interests to dwell upon' (ibid.).

Although this disappointment is palpable to anyone casually acquainted with union members at any level, it has rarely been articulated within unions in a political assessment of New Labour. Too often particular policies and absences are seen as aberrations rather than the logical outcome of a consistent perspective. Hall has argued that New Labour *is* distinct from previous Conservative governments in that it is a '*hybrid* regime' (Hall 2003: 19), a '*social-democratic variant of neo-liberalism*' (ibid.: 22). This eludes McCartney (2005: 95): 'Some people say our approach is neoliberal and Thatcherite. I think that is very offensive.' It is the way in which Labour's reforms have been conceived and formulated that displays its commitment to neoliberalism. In its own way this is as closed a system of truth and hostility to autonomous and effective trade unionism as that of the Conservatives. It is inspired at one remove by Sir Keith Joseph, and, at two, by Hayek, even if New Labour's leaders dare not acknowledge this, or – now that such values, suitably remodelled, are their own – have forgotten their origins.

No one should underestimate the hostility of New Labour to effective trade unionism and any legal measures that might support it. One reading of the DTI consultation on workplace representatives (DTI 2007c) is the view that the rights accorded to union representatives are too generous and even unnecessary given the transformation of industrial relations (the decline of trade unions to a minority of the workforce), the number of non-union representatives, and the willingness of employers to offer facilities (ibid.: 51–5). Only by an acknowledgment of the values that lie within this project – the bitter fruit of neoliberalism – can effective opposition be mounted.

## List of cases

*Alexander v Bridgen Enterprises* [2006] IRLR 422, EAT.

*Allonby v Accrington and Rossendale College* [2004] IRLR 224, ECJ.

*ASLEF v Lee* (EAT/625/03, 24 February 2004, unreported).

*ASLEF v UK* [2007] IRLR 361, ECHR.

*Blackpool and the Fylde College v NATFHE* [1994] ICR 648, CA.

*First Global Locums Ltd v Cosias* [2005] IRLR 873, QBD.

*Gate Gourmet London Ltd v (1) TGWU (2) The Individuals Named in Schedule 1 to this Order (3) Persons Unknown* [2005] EWHC 1889, QBD.

*International Transport Workers Federation, Finnish Seamen's Union v Viking Line ABP, OÜ Viking Line Eesti* [2007] ECJ.

*National Union of Rail, Maritime and Transport Workers v London Underground Ltd* [2001] IRLR 228.

*Majrowski v Guy's Hospital and St Thomas's NHS Trust* [2006] IRLR 695, HL.

*Polkey v A. E. Dayton Services* [1988] ICR 142, HL.

*R (On the application of Gatwick Express) v CAC* [2003] EWHC 2035 Admin.

*R (NUJ) v CAC* [2005] ICR 493, QBD.

*R (NUJ) v CAC* [2006] IRLR 53, CA.

*R. v Secretary of State for Trade and Industry ex parte BECTU* [2001] IRLR 560, ECJ.

*Software 2000 Ltd v Andrews* [2007] IRLR 568, EAT.

*UNIFI v Bank of Nigeria* [2001] IRLR 712, CAC.

*Union Traffic v Transport and General Workers' Union* [1988] ICR 98, CA.

*Unison v UK* [2002] IRLR 497, ECHR.

*University College London Hospital NHS Trust v Unison* [1999] IRLR 31, CA.

*Viking Line Abp v International Transport Workers' Federation and another* [2006] IRLR 58, CA.

*Willerby Holiday Homes Ltd v UCATT* [2003] EWHC 2608, QBD.

*Wilson and NUJ, Palmer, Wyeth and RMT v United Kingdom* (2003) 35 EHRR 523, [2002] IRLR 568.

## Notes

1 An appeal to the European Court of Human Rights was not accepted: *Unison v UK* [2000]. See *University College London Hospital NHS Trust v Unison* [1999].

2 *Union Traffic v Transport and General Workers' Union* [1988].

3 *Majrowski v Guy's Hospital and St Thomas's NHS Trust* [2006].

4 *Blackpool and The Fylde College v NATFHE* [1994].

5 UCATT was compelled to pay £130,458 in damages plus costs for losses incurred in a two-week strike because it had given the employer erroneous information on the members to be balloted: *Willerby Holiday Homes v UCATT* [2003].

6 Case C-438/05, *International Transport Workers' Federation and the Finnish Seamen's Union v Viking Line and OÜ Viking Line Eesti*. And see now *International Transport Workers Federation, Finnish Seamen's Union v Viking Line ABP, OÜ Viking Line Eesti* [2007].

7 Opinion of the Advocate-General Poiares Maduro, 23 May 2007, Case C-438/05.

8 *Gate Gourmet London Ltd v (1) TGWU (2) The Individuals Named in Schedule 1 to this Order (3) Persons Unknown* [2005].

9 The CAC's decision that pay could include pensions was overturned by s. 20 ERA 2004 (para. 171A Sch. A1 TULR(C)A 1992).

10 *NUJ and Sports Division: MGN Ltd*, TUR1/307/2003; *R (NUJ) v CAC* [2005], upheld by the Court of Appeal in *R (NUJ) v CAC* [2006].
11 There are three conditions: a ballot should be held in the interest of good industrial relations; a significant number of union members within the bargaining unit inform the CAC that they do not wish the union to bargain on their behalf; or evidence leads the CAC to conclude that there are doubts as to whether a significant number of members within the unit wish the union to bargain on their behalf (para. 22).
12 The Certification Officer reported 'that a number of enquiries . . . about the formation of new trade unions have come from human resource departments' (2004: 123).
13 *Wilson and NUJ, Palmer, Wyeth and RMT v UK* [2002]. S. 148(3) Trade Union and Labour Relations (Consolidation) Act 1992.
14 'The union and its members must however be free, in one way or another, to seek to persuade the employer to listen to what it has to say on behalf of its members', *Wilson and Palmer v United Kingdom* [2002], para. 44.
15 B. Davies and Others and ASDA Stores Ltd, Employment Tribunal case number 2501510/05, para 43.
16 For the case of the subcontractor's employees who worked throughout the Liverpool dockers' strike, 1995–97, see N. M. Salinas and Others and TGWU, 2001 (Employment Tribunal case no. 2101223/00).
17 *ASLEF v Lee* [2004] EAT.
18 *Associated Society of Locomotive Engineers and Firemen (ASLEF) v The United Kingdom* [2007], Application no. 11002/05, reprinted in DTI (2007a), pp. 15–30, p. 23 at para. 34.
19 *TGWU and Jordan (Cereals) Ltd*, TUR1/258 [2003] established guidelines that an employer must follow for a staff association to be judged capable of concluding a collective agreement.
20 See *Software 2000 Ltd v Andrews* [2007].
21 The DTI proposed moves to a full-cost regime, as in the county courts (2001: 31, para. 5.11).
22 *Allonby v Accrington and Rossendale College* [2004]. Department of Trade and Industry press release, 3 May 2000.
23 *R. v Secretary of State for Trade and Industry ex parte BECTU* [2001].

## Bibliography

Barnard, C. (1999) 'The Working Time Regulations 1998', *Industrial Law Journal*, 28:1, 61–75.
—— (2000) 'The Working Time Regulations 1999', *Industrial Law Journal*, 29:2, 161–71.
Barnard, C., Deakin, S. and Hobbs, R. (2003) 'Opting out of the 48-hour week: employer necessity or individual choice? An empirical study of the operation of Article 18(1)(b) of the Working Time Directive in the UK', *Industrial Law Journal*, 32:4, 223–52.
Beckett, F. and Hencke, D. (2004) *The Blairs and their Court*, London: Arum Press.
Bercusson, B. (2007) 'The trade union movement and the European Union: Judgment Day'. *European Law Journal*, 13: 3, 279–308.
Blair, A. (1997) *Report of Congress 1997*, London: TUC.
Bogg, A.L. (2005) 'Employment Relations Act 2004: another false dawn for collectivism?', *Industrial Law Journal*, 34:1, 72–82.

—— (2006) 'Politics, community, democracy: appraising CAC decision-making in the first five years of Schedule A1', *Industrial Law Journal*, 35:3, 245–71.

Bryson, A., Gomez, R. and Willman, P. (2004) 'The end of the affair? The decline in employers' propensity to unionize', in J. Kelly and P. Willman (eds) *Union Organization and Activity*, London: Routledge.

CAC (Central Arbitration Committee) (2006) *Annual Report 2005–2006*, London: CAC.

—— (2007) *Annual Report 2006–2007*, London: CAC.

Caracciolo di Torella, E. (2007) 'New Labour, new dads: the impact of family friendly legislation on fathers', *Industrial Law Journal*, 36:3, 318–28.

Certification Officer (2006) *Annual Report*, London: Certification Office.

Citizens' Advice (2004) *Employment Tribunals. The Intimidatory Use of Costs Threats by Employers' Legal Representatives*, London: Citizens' Advice Bureaux.

Colling, T. (2004) 'No claim, no pain? The privatisation of dispute resolution in Britain', *Economic and Industrial Democracy*, 25:4, 555–79.

—— (2006) 'What space for unions on the floor of rights? Trade unions and the enforcement of statutory employment rights', *Industrial Law Journal*, 35:2, 140–60.

Crouch, C. (2001) 'A third way in industrial relations?', in S. White (ed.) *New Labour: The Progressive Future?* Basingstoke: Palgrave.

Davies, P. and Freedland, M. (2004) 'Changing perspectives upon the employment relationship in British labour law', in C. Barnard, S. Deakin and G.S. Morris (eds) *The Future of Labour Law*, Oxford: Hart.

Davies, P. and Kilpatrick, C. (2004) 'UK worker representation after single channel', *Industrial Law Journal*, 33: 2, 121–51.

Davies, P. and Freedland, M. (2007) *Towards a Flexible Labour Market: Labour Legislation and Regulation since the 1990s*, Oxford: Oxford University Press.

Deakin, S. and Morris, G. (2005) *Labour Law*, Oxford: Hart.

Department of Trade and Industry (DTI) (1992) *Code of Practice on Picketing*, London: DTI.

—— (1991) *Industrial Relations in the 1990s*, London: DTI.

—— (1998) *Fairness at Work*, London: DTI.

—— (2001) *Routes to Resolution*, London: DTI.

—— (2002) *High Performance Workplaces: The Role of Employee Involvement in a Modern Economy*, London: DTI.

—— (2003a) *High Performance Workplaces: Informing and Consulting Employees*, London: DTI.

—— (2003b) *Review of Employment Relations Act 1999*, London: DTI.

—— (2003c) *Review of the Employment Relations Act 1999:Government Response to the Public Consultation*, London: DTI.

—— (2005) *Code of Practice on Access and Unfair Practices during Recognition and Derecognition Ballots*, London: DTI.

—— (2006) *Code of Practice on Industrial Action Ballots and Notice to Employers*, London: DTI.

—— (2007a) *The Judgment of the European Court of Human rights in the ASLEF v UK Case: Implications for Trade Union Law*, London: DTI.

—— (2007b) *Success at Work: Resolving Disputes in the Workplace*, London: DTI.

—— (2007c) *Workplace Representatives: A Review of their Facilities and Facility Time*, London: DTI.

Dickens, L. and Hall, M. (1995) 'The state: labour law and industrial relations', in P. Edwards (ed.) *Industrial Relations: Theory and Practice in Britain*. Oxford: Blackwell.

—— (2006)' Fairness – up to a point: assessing the impact of New Labour's employment legislation, *Human Resource Management Journal*, 16: 4, 338–56.

Dickens, R. and Manning, A. (2003) 'Minimum wage, minimum impact', in R. Dickens, P. Gregg and J. Wadsworth (eds) *The Labour Market under New Labour*, Basingstoke: Palgrave Macmillan.

Ewing, K. (2000a) 'Trade union recognition and staff associations: a breach of international standards', *Industrial Law Journal*, 29:4, 267–73.

—— (2000b) 'Dancing with daffodils', *Federation News*, 50: 1–22.

—— (2005) 'The function of trade unions', *Industrial Law Journal*, 34:1, 1–22.

Ewing, K. and Truter, G. M. (2005) 'The Information and Consultation of Employees Regulations: voluntarism's bitter legacy', *Modern Law Review*, 68: 4, 626–41.

Ewing, K., Moore, S. and Wood, S. (2004) *Unfair Labour Practices: Trade Union Recognition and Employer Resistance*, London: Institute of Employment Rights.

Ford, M. and Hendy, J. (2007) *ASLEF v UK*, Liverpool: Institute of Employment Rights.

Forde, C. and Slater, G. (2005) 'Agency working in Britain: character, consequences and regulation', *British Journal of Industrial Relations*, 43:2, 249–71.

Forde, C, Slater, G. and Green, F. (2008) *Agency Working in the UK: What Do We Know? Centre for Employment Relations, Innovation and Change Policy Report 2*, Leeds: Leeds University.

Gall. G. (2004) 'British employer resistance to trade union recognition', *Human Resource Management Journal*, 14:2, 36–53.

Gibbons, M. (2007) *Better Dispute Resolution: A Review of Employment Dispute Resolution in Great Britain*, London: DTI.

Hall, M. (2002) *The Implementation of the EU Employee Consultation Directive*, London: TUC.

Hall, S. (2003) 'New Labour's double-shuffle', *Soundings*, 24:1, 10–24.

Hendy, J. and Gall, G. (2006) 'British trade union rights today and the Trade Union Freedom Bill', in K. Ewing (ed.) *The Right to Strike: From the Trade Disputes Act 1906 to a Trade Union Freedom Bill 2006*, Liverpool: Institute of Employment Rights.

Hepple, R. and Morris, S. (2002) 'The Employment Act 2002 and the crisis of individual employment rights', *Industrial Law Journal*, 31:3, 245–69.

Hobbs, R. and Njoya, W. (2005) 'Regulating the European labour market: prospects and limitations of a reflexive governance approach', *British Journal of Industrial Relations*, 43:2, 297–319.

Howell, C. (2005) *Trade Unions and the State: The Construction of Industrial Relations Institutions in Britain, 1890–2000*, Princeton: Princeton University Press.

James, G. (2007) 'The Work and Families Act 2006: legislation to improve choice and flexibility', *Industrial law Journal*, 35:3, 272–8.

Kahn-Freund, O. (1977) *Labour and the Law*, London: Stevens.

Kelly, J. (2004) 'Social partnership agreements in Britain: labor cooperation and compliance', *Industrial Relations*, 43:1, 267–92.

Lawrence, F. (2007) 'The miracle of cheap food depends upon illegality', *The Guardian*, 17 July 2007.

McCartney, I. (2005) *Report of Congress*, London: TUC.

McColgan, A. (2000a) 'Family friendly frolics? The Maternity and Paternity Leave etc Regulations 1999', *Industrial Law Journal*, 29:2, 125–43.

——— (2000b) 'Missing the point? The Part-time Workers (Prevention of Less Favourable Treatment) Regulations 2000 (SI 2000, No 1551)', *Industrial Law Journal*, 29:3, 260–7.

McIlroy, J. (1998) 'The enduring alliance? Trade unions and the making of New Labour, 1994–97', *British Journal of Industrial Relations*, 36:4, 537–64.

Moore, S., McKay, S. and Bewley, H. (2004) *The Content of New Voluntary Trade Union Recognition Agreements, 1998–2002: Vol. 1. An Analysis of New Agreements and Case Studies*, London: DTI.

Müller-Jentsch, W. (1985) 'Trade unions as intermediary organizations', *Economic and Industrial Democracy*, 6:1, 3–33.

Offe, C. and Wiesenthal, H. (1985) 'Two logics of collective action', in C. Offe, *Disorganized Capitalism*, Cambridge: Polity Press.

Pollert, A. (2005) 'The unorganized worker: the decline in collectivism and new hurdles to individual rights', *Industrial Law Journal*, 34:3, 217–38.

Sanders, A. (2007) 'Expanding the "no-difference" rule in the law of unfair dismissal', *Industrial Law Journal*, 36:3, 355–63.

Simpson, B. (2000) 'Trade union recognition and the law, a new approach – Parts I and II of schedule A1 to the TULR(C)A 1992', *Industrial Law Journal*, 29: 3, 193–222.

——— (2005) 'Strike ballots and the law: round six', *Industrial Law Journal*, 34:4, 331–7.

——— (2006) 'The 1906 Act: the second fifty years – from *Thomson v Deakin* in 1952 to *P v NASUWT* in 2003', in K. Ewing (ed.) *The Right to Strike: From the Trade Disputes Act 1906 to a Trade Union Freedom Bill 2006*, Liverpool: Institute of Employment Rights.

——— (2007) 'Judicial control of ACAS', *Industrial Law Journal*, 36:3, 287–314.

Smith, P. and Morton, G. (1993) 'Union exclusion and the decollectivization of industrial relations in contemporary Britain', *British Journal of Industrial Relations*, 31: 1, 97–114.

——— (2001a). 'The Conservative governments' reform of employment law, 1979–97: "Stepping Stones" and the "New Right" Agenda', *Historical Studies in Industrial Relations*, 12: 131–47.

——— (2001b) 'New Labour's reform of Britain's employment law: the devil is not only in the detail but in the values and policy too', *British Journal of Industrial Relations*, 39:1, 119–38.

——— (2006) 'Nine years of New Labour: neoliberalism and workers' rights', *British Journal of Industrial Relations*, 44:3, 401–20.

Streeck, W. (1997) 'Neither European nor works councils: a reply to Paul Knutsen', *Economic and Industrial Democracy*, 18:2, 325–37.

TUC (2004) 'Focus on recognition', *Trade Union Trends Survey*, London: TUC.

——— (2005) 'Focus on recognition', *Trade Union Trends Survey* 1, London: TUC.

——— (2006) 'Focus on recognition 2006', *Trade Union Trends Survey*, London: TUC.

Treasury (2002) *Full and Fulfilling Employment: Creating the Labour Market for the Future*, London: Treasury.

——— (2005) *Global Europe: Full-employment Europe*, London: Treasury.

Undy, R., Fosh, P., Morris, H., Smith, P. and Martin, R. (1996) *Managing the Unions: The Impact of Legislation on Trade Unions' Behaviour*, Oxford: Clarendon Press.

Wedderburn, Lord (1986) *The Worker and the Law*, 3rd edition, Harmondsworth: Penguin.

—— (1991) 'Freedom of association and philosophies of labour law', in Lord Wedderburn, *Employment Rights in Britain and Europe: Selected Papers in Labour Law*, London: Lawrence and Wishart.

—— (2001) 'Underground labour injunctions', *Industrial Law Journal*, 30:2, 206–14.

—— (2008) *Yes to a Referendum? A Labour View*, Liverpool: Institute of Employment Rights.

Willman, P. (2005) 'Circling the wagons: endogeneity in union decline', in S. Fernie and D. Metcalf (eds) *Trade Unions: Resurgence or Demise?* London: Routledge.

Wood, S., Moore, S. and Ewing, K. (2003) 'The impact of the trade union recognition procedure under the Employment Relations Act, 2000–2002', in H. Gospel and S. Wood (eds) *Representing Workers: Trade Union Recognition and Membership in Britain*. London: Routledge.

Wynn, M. and Leighton, P. (2006) 'Will the real employer please stand up? Agencies, client companies and the employment status of the temporary agency worker', *Industrial Law Journal*, 35:3, 301–20.

# 7 Partnership
## New Labour's Third Way?

*Martin Upchurch*

Partnership at work has been a central theme of the New Labour years. Defining what the phrase means in theory and practice has proved difficult and contentious. Despite this, debate over partnership has dominated the industrial relations literature combining case study analysis with broader commentary.[1] Formalized union–employer collaboration was already evident in the 1980s under the Conservative governments in the guise of the 'single union deal' version of business unionism. The 'new realist' turn many unions made in the 1980s was a defensive response to the onslaught launched by the Thatcher governments. However, inter-union disputes over single union sweetheart deals left a bad taste in the mouth of the TUC and its affiliates and this form of business unionism fell into disrepute (McIlroy 1995: 215–19). Despite these early difficulties partnership has become a prominent feature of New Labour's industrial strategy since its election in 1997, indicating some continuity with the previous experiment.

Yet the number of recorded partnership deals is small: the database of the independent pro-partnership IPA registers no more than 150,[2] while Bacon and Samuel (2007) note 219 formal agreements signed from 1990 onwards and Gall (2004) reports that between 1995 and 2002 only 18 per cent of union recognition deals under the new legislation involved partnership arrangements. What is significant is the seeming alliance that has developed between the government, employers and TUC over the desirability of partnership. It is the reasons and outcomes of this alliance that this chapter seeks to explore and understand.

Under the rhetoric, New Labour is cautious of any institutional implications. As Terry and Smith (2003) observe in their evaluation for the Department of Trade and Industry (DTI) Partnership at Work Fund:[3] 'The government's approach, as reflected in the materials disseminated by the DTI Partnership Fund, is altogether more open-ended and diffuse *than under the Conservatives*' (emphasis added). Avoiding any attempt at definition the department argues that 'there is no ideal example of partnership work'. Various government documents (DTI 1998, 2002, 2004) often omit the word 'social' when referring to partnership, implying a perceived need to distance themselves from the kind of institutional support that is given to a consensus-based industrial relations system to be found in the German or European 'Social Models' (Hyman 2005). Far from proffering an institutional framework of participatory bodies, the government does not consider trade unions as a necessary ingredient of partnership, preferring instead to utilize the term 'employee representatives' in a multi-channel model of worker representation. Partnership thus appears both with and without unions, and includes non-union forms of representation (Ackers *et al.* 2005; Upchurch *et al.* 2006).

In terms of legislation, partnership at work was declared by Prime Minister Tony Blair to be central to the flagship *Fairness at Work* document (DTI 1998) later enshrined in the Employment Relations Act 1999. The establishment of a Partnership Fund to encourage workplace initiatives reinforced the approach. New Labour's view of what partnership should achieve was revealingly outlined by the Prime Minister himself in his foreword to *Fairness at Work*. Blair is worth quoting to help us understand how partnership fits in to New Labour's industrial strategy:

> This White Paper is part of the Government's programme to replace the notion of conflict between employers and employees with the promotion of partnership . . . this White Paper goes far wider than the legal changes we propose. It is nothing less than to change the culture of relations in and at work – and to reflect a new relationship between work and family life . . . Already modern and successful companies draw their success from the existence and development of partnership at work. Those who have learnt to cherish and foster the creativity of their whole workforce have found a resource of innovation and inventiveness that drives their companies forward as well as enriching their lives.
>
> (DTI 1998)

The government wants to reinforce a consensus-based industrial regime at the expense of conflict. The relationship between employees, their unions and employers has always been located on a spectrum of cooperation and conflict, but this spectrum has traditionally been skewed towards an adversarial approach to distributive bargaining. New Labour's intervention is important as it reflects an attempt to construct a new ideological framework for British industrial relations based *solely* on consensus and enacted in practical terms through the process of partnership.

The response of the peak organizations of labour and capital to this model has been generally supportive. The British TUC established its own semi-independent Partnership Institute to act as a lobby group and consultancy to business, and promotes partnership as a potential strategy of union revival. Training and development schemes and the creation of a system of accredited Union Learning Representatives is a central pillar of this approach (see McIlroy and Croucher, chapter 9, this volume). The Confederation of British Industry (CBI 2003) was clearly anxious not to concede ground to trade union representation, preferring instead to emphasize the value of direct rather than indirect employee representation. However, despite its caution, the CBI endorsed the TUC's 1999 *Partners for Progress* document (TUC 1999). The professional body for human resource managers, the Chartered Institute of Personnel and Development (CIPD), has also supported the concept, with a caveat that partnership should be centred on employer–employee relations and not necessarily trade unions. If partnership at work was the New Labour mantra what precisely would be the implications for the world of work and the collective interest of labour? How likely is it that partnership would become embedded in Britain's industrial relations culture? Is partnership a route to trade union revival? To answer these questions this chapter first explores the sources of partnership in the UK, and then proceeds to review the evidence of partnership working in practice.

## The sources of partnership

We can identify several sources of partnership at work in the UK. The first is the desire of the UK Government to find a way out of Britain's continuing problem of lagging productivity by encouraging a capital accumulation regime centred on high-performance working and human capital development. The second source interplays with the first by the construction of an ideological framework contained within the discourse of the Third Way and its dismissal of the contemporary relevance of the politics of class struggle. The third source flows from the institutional imperative of continued membership of the EU and its legislative expansion of employee representative rights manifested in both the European Works Council and Information and Consultation Directives. What has emerged in the UK, as Guest and Peccei (2001) have outlined, is a hybrid model of partnership which borrows from the US model of mutual gains while adopting selected aspects of the European model of social partnership and its institutional framework. We proceed to look more closely at some of these issues.

### *Productivity and high performance*

The 1997 New Labour government inherited a production regime that had been described by Rubery (1994) as a 'low wage, low skill economy, unable to compete in or effectively adjust to the demands of new international competition'. The reasons for this deficiency were considered to be the specific societal conditions of shareholder-based short-termism that militated against a 'high road' approach. Despite the wide-scale restructuring of the UK's industrial base during the Conservative years the productivity gap between the UK and its major competitors remained. This gave grounds for New Labour to contend that a different approach was needed (see Porter and Ketels 2003). As Hay (2004), has observed, New Labour's approach transmuted into the 'dual objectives' of credibility in financial markets and competitiveness in the productive economy. This approach assumes that risks in the international product market can be minimized by adopting supply-side solutions (Thompson 1996; Green *et al.* 2001). The strategy involved both a drive to increase labour market flexibility (a continuation of the Thatcher project) and to upgrade human capital through education and skill training (the main area of change). Human capital is constructed through 'employability' and 'adaptability' under the aegis of former Chancellor Gordon Brown's post neoclassical endogenous growth theory. The model is consistently presented as progressive and necessary in a globalized economy (cf. McIlroy, chapter 2, and McIlroy and Croucher, chapter 9, this volume).

At the level of the workplace the model is framed within concepts associated with high-performance working, or High Performance Work Systems (HPWS), and its associated partnership framework. The essential proposition of the advocates of the HPWS is that previous efforts to intensify work by lean production, peer pressure, surveillance and control are inferior to systems which allow more worker discretion and autonomy. In the early 1990s there was growing concern that productivity growth in America was suffering from the aftershocks of a decade of de-layering of jobs. One potential by-product of increasing job insecurity was a decline in workplace trust deemed necessary within organizations to develop a spirit of creativity and innovation.

In effect, eulogies of the excellence of lean production (Womack *et al.* 1990) became usurped by a more labour-friendly approach (Kochan and Osterman 1994; Appelbaum *et al.* 2000). These authors claimed that a shift in management–employee relations was necessary if organizations were to overcome lack of trust and create the conditions for increased productivity. Kochan and Osterman's work explored an argument for the HPWS that places job security, management–worker trust, worker participation and up-skilling as central features. Their prescription claims a 'win-win' game for employees and employers whereby mutual gains are made by twinning job security with higher productivity. This shift towards collective employee involvement as a strategy for managing workplace performance has provided the opening for partnership agendas to grow. It helps explain a convergence between business managers, sections of the trade union leaderships and government policymakers towards a partnership agenda.

In terms of public policy the government reported the following in respect of productivity in its 2002 discussion paper:

> UK productivity remains lower than that of France and Germany, and substantially lower than that of the US – output per worker in the US is 38 per cent higher than in the UK, in France it is 18 per cent higher and in Germany 9 per cent higher . . . The productivity gap is due to a number of factors. One of these is the relative failure to invest in the skills and abilities of the workforce . . . the Government believes productivity can be boosted by firms and employees working together to build high

> performance workplaces. The characteristics of high performance work-places are high levels of adaptability, flexibility and involvement by both employees and employers . . . Information and consultation can be one of the ingredients of a modern, high performance workplace.
>
> (DTI 2002)

The discussion paper was prepared in the light of earlier responses to the government's Productivity Initiative from the Engineering Employers' Federation (EEF) and from a joint paper produced by the TUC and CBI. The EEF had commissioned its own study of the productivity gap in manufacturing between the USA and UK (EEF 2001). Called *Catching Up with Uncle Sam*, it extolled the virtues of skill enhancement as a tool 'to overcome barriers to investment, and the uptake of lean manufacturing'.[4] The TUC/CBI submission (TUC/CBI 2001) took up the same themes, stating that 'management leadership and employee involvement are complementary features of the high performance/high commitment model'. Further support came from a joint EEF/CIPD Report (2003) which identified workplace practices which could be identified with HPWS, which have implications for the organization of work as well as HR practice. They included many aspects associated with workplace flexibility and team-working including work improvement teams and job redesign, as well as 'employee autonomy and involvement in decision-making'.

The emphasis on high performance and employee involvement is not confined to the manufacturing sector. The government introduced its Best Value 'modernisation' programme in the public sector under the rubric of partnership (Geddes 2001; Whitfield 2001; Richardson *et al.* 2005). Indeed, since 2001 the majority of partnership agreements have been signed in the public sector (Bacon and Samuel 2007). In financial services the shift to an increasingly competitive environment has also created opportunities for employers to introduce work flexibility and high-performance agendas (Danford *et al.* 2003: 97–121). Neither is it the case that high-performance working is always the key employer motive for the introduction of partnership. Both Gall (2001) and Kelly (2005) note that there has been a sharp increase in partnership agreements utilized by employers in the banking industry as an attempt to counter-mobilize against the rise of union adversarialism.

The TUC's position on competitiveness is further outlined in its response to the DTI Discussion Paper in 2002 (this time divorcing itself from the CBI). It drew a link between high performance and collective worker representation. Citing evidence from academic studies and surveys, the TUC report stated:

> Engaging the expertise and knowledge of workers will help to ensure that bad judgements are avoided – and as a consequence, the legitimacy of the outcome is enhanced. It is important to recognise that while differences of interest between employers and workers are inevitable there are many

areas where interests are shared. This fundamental principle must be understood if change is to be managed successfully and if more organisations in the UK are to become high performance workplaces.

(TUC 2002)

The TUC embrace of partnership also has a strategic intent, reflecting its desire to once more be seen as a legitimate social and political actor. The TUC also sought to draw upon the labour-friendly institutional implications of the 'European Social Model' (see Taylor, chapter 11, this volume). Six principles of partnership were devised by the TUC as an expression of the nature of 'good' as opposed to 'bad' partnership practice (TUC 1999, 2002) (Figure 7.1).

There is an emphasis in the six principles on the necessity of independent trade unions to foster effective employee voice as well as reference to the 'mutual gains' inherent in the American Model. This was in contrast to the 1980s New Realist alternative strategy of the TUC which promoted collaborative concepts of business unionism and which Kelly (2005) has described as 'first generation' partnership. Proponents of the high-performance work system argue that trust can only be obtained alongside increased job security. This particular argument was taken on board by the TUC. In 2000 John Monks, then general secretary of the TUC, emphasized the point:

> To create a real spirit of partnership – we found it essential to have a commitment to employment security. We all know and accept that employment levels in any enterprise can fall as well as rise. But we cannot expect people to commit themselves wholeheartedly to an organisation without any reciprocal commitment. Genuine partnership requires a trade off between employee flexibility and security of employment. No employer could ever realistically guarantee that there would never be compulsory redundancies, but he or she could and should make

---

**TUC Principles of Partnership**

- A joint commitment to success of the enterprise.
- Unions and employers recognising each other's legitimate interests and resolving difference in an atmosphere of trust.
- A commitment to employment security.
- A focus on the quality of working life.
- Transparency and sharing information.
- Mutual gains for unions and employers, delivering concrete improvements to business performance, terms and conditions, and employee involvement.

---

*Figure 7.1* TUC Principles of Partnership.

it clear that this would be the last resort, and not the first response to a crisis.

(Monks 2000)

The emphasis on a supposed link between partnership and increased business performance is also evident in TUC literature, as well as that of the TUC-sponsored Partnership Institute. In 2002 the TUC surveyed evidence from 46 companies utilizing the Partnership Institute and claimed that 'partnership workplaces are one-third more likely to have financial performance that is a lot better than average; and are a quarter more likely to have labour productivity that is a lot better than average' (TUC 2002).

Crucially, the Partnership Institute sought to draw the link between high-commitment management practices, high performance and a strong recognized union. The emphasis on a 'strong' union creates space for the TUC to define a difference between 'good' partnerships and 'bad', without specifically defining what 'strong' trade unions means in practice. 'Good' partnership deals or agreements presumably not only achieve the six principles but are underpinned by union independence at the workplace, while 'bad' partnership deals fall short of the criteria and would presumably not be supported by the TUC.[5] With this distinction between good and bad in mind it should be noted that some employers may wish to introduce partnership arrangements not so much as a 'high road' route to competitiveness, but rather as a 'survival strategy' by which concessions can be gained from unions as an alternative to the threat of workplace closure (Heery 2002). Following Crouch (1992), such arrangements have been labelled by Kelly (2005) as 'employer dominant'. They stand in contrast to arrangements which might arise when the union is well established, when the enterprise is well placed in the product market and the labour market is tight. In these circumstances it would be expected that the bargaining power of the workforce expressed through the union is high and in consequence some degree of 'good partnership' might be achievable.

However, Gall's (2004) review of partnership arrangements in union recognition deals highlights that only a small proportion of self-styled partnership arrangements would fulfil the TUC's criteria for 'good partnership'. Despite this evidence, there remains an underlying assumption from the TUC that it is possible to achieve its six principles if the underlying conditions for 'good' partnership are in place. According to the TUC, such underlying conditions may be absent due to unfavourable profiles of corporate governance, reflecting the general critiques of 'short-termism' and shareholder benefit at the expense of 'stakeholders' outside of the boardroom.[6] Counter-arguments for a refined form of company pluralism have been set out by the TUC's Stakeholder Task Group, where TUC Policy Officer Janet Williamson argued for a company web of stakeholder interests, 'each of which is based on mutual dependence' (Williamson 1997). Good partnership practice would thus sit side-by-side with 'good' corporate governance.

What emerged was a triple alliance between New Labour, employers and the TUC on the value of high-performance work systems and employee involvement. This alliance was held together by a perceived need to boost productivity in the 'national interest'. Differences existed within the alliance on the role and emphasis that should be placed on employee representation, but there was nevertheless an implicit commitment by the employers' side to recognize the value of employee voice (at least in some form) as a potential vehicle for enhancing creativity and innovation within the workplace. It is in this context that we should understand the interest in partnership.

### Partnership and the Third Way

Experiments in union–employer collaboration have occurred before in British industrial relations. The Mond–Turner agreements of the late 1920s, for example, occurred in the aftermath of a major defeat for unions in the 1926 General Strike. The context was a relatively closed economy, and the purpose was to press home employers' bargaining advantage and neutralize the resurgence of class struggle. The short-lived flirtation by the state with industrial democracy in the 1970s was an attempt to placate union demands for more organizational power, while the period of the social contract, in contrast, acted to contain rank-and-file wage militancy in the face of continuing balance of payments crises. Similarly, as Ramsay (1977, 1996) observed, employer interest in techniques of employee involvement have ebbed and flowed, more often than not reaching their peak as employers seek to institutionalize and contain workers' increasing aspirations for workplace voice. How then can we assess the nature of partnership in the new millennium? What is the political economy of partnership and how might it differ from previous instances of worker–employer collaboration?

Martínez Lucio and Stuart (2005) have described partnership at work as 'new industrial relations in a risk society'. They equate the partnership discourse to the concepts of risk introduced by Beck (1992) and Giddens (1998) and suggest that partnership 'assumes a sharing of risk by capital and labour' in a 'marriage of convenience'. Such risk-sharing would provide the ideological impetus for 'mutual gains' in the workplace, whereby employees work collaboratively with employers to protect the organization from business failure. Contributions to the literature from Ackers and Payne (1998) and Coats (2004) regard partnership as an extension of pluralist principles within which trade unions can achieve new societal and workplace legitimacy. Ackers (2002) and Ackers and Wilkinson (2003) develop the argument and make a plea to locate social partnership in terms of a 'neo-pluralist' framework which they claim can provide a response to the threat of wider societal breakdown resulting from new forms of work and employment. Leaning on the sociology of Durkheim, they argue the need for new normatively based institutions that can protect the citizen in an era of societal change and risk. Ackers (2002: 15) fancifully suggests that new institutional mechanisms associated with partnership can enable employers to make a 'constructive contribution to community and society'. This analysis argues that trade unions are subject to the perils of global competition but can redefine their role as protectors within society against the subsequent *anomie*.

Trade unions, Coats (2004) claims, are a source of both bonding and bridging *social capital* – bonding capital in terms of developing intra-colleague solidarity, and bridging capital in terms of seeking common cause between employee and employer. 'All of this contributes to the "ontological security" that Giddens deems necessary for social cohesion – workers understand their place in the world and have a sufficient sense of continuity to withstand the vicissitudes of their working lives' (Coats 2004: 38). But there is an implicit assumption here that as 'workers understand their place in the world' the 'bonding' social capital employed by trade unions is *class neutral*. This downplays the possibility that social capital is a product of social relationships within society and as such is likely to reflect divisions. As Das (2006) observes, trade union social capital *can* lubricate the capitalist production regime, as in a partnership orientation, or *obstruct* it as in a class conflict orientation. To view social capital solely as a lubricator (in either its bonding or bridging version) reduces the analysis to the dismal science of economics without any appreciation of the social structures within which all types of capital are formed and utilized (Fine 2001).

In terms of social and business policy the Third Way produces additional initiatives (participatory democracy and corporate social responsibility) to cope with the excesses of global capitalism. Both initiatives are seen as enabling mechanisms by which the market can be constrained. It is this distinction which makes the Third Way different from the pure market imperative of neoliberalism. In other words, while it is suggested that 'there is no alternative' (TINA) to the forces of globalization, it may be possible to use forms of ethical voluntarism to maintain social democratic values. Giddens relays the theme by suggesting that

> the left is defined by its concern with the dangers of [the] market, whose excesses need constantly to be reined back by the state. Today, however, this idea has become archaic. The left has to get comfortable with markets, with the role of business in the creation of wealth, and the fact that private capital is essential for investment.
>
> (Giddens 1998: 34)

In adopting this philosophical approach New Labour cleared the ground for the abandonment of socialist critique of the market. Or, as the then Chancellor Gordon Brown told the CBI at their 1999 Conference, 'we must never again be seen as anti-success, anti-competition, anti-profit, anti-markets' (*Guardian*, 27 September 1999). If we are to believe Gordon Brown then any ideological difference with the market imperative must be buried. Once again the government would have us subjugated to the world of economics and subsumed within a milieu of what Weltman and Billig (2001) describe as 'anti-politics'. What remains is a form of 'ethical socialism' that gives priority to community over class: '. . . in which the S-word is retained but in its hyphenated form of social-ism' (Callinicos 2001: 46). It is within this ethical communitarianism that we can locate the development of the 'neo-pluralism' (or social-ism) found in the arguments of Ackers and others. New forms of participative and associative democracy are deemed necessary because of a decline of social solidarity allied with the risk society, which in turn has created a crisis of representative democracy (e.g. Cohen and Rogers 1995).

This crisis is a cause of economic inefficiency, in that the negation of 'voice' combined with rising income inequality means that real solutions to real problems are less likely to be found within civil society. In other words there is a link between the social institutions of capitalism and economic efficiency. In this Third Way vision old forms of representative democracy, associated with mass state provision of goods and services, are no longer appropriate to peoples' needs. The Third Way project becomes in essence Giddens' (2000) 'social investment state' whereby the role of the state mutates to one which discourages welfare dependency while at the same time providing incentives for personal advancement via education and training. Associative democracy, with horizontal networks of individuals acting as pressure within a renewed civil society, is presented as a more democratic framework designed to increase rates of social capital formation, participation and societal efficiency. Translated to the restructured workplace the process of *participation* is again postulated as key to economic and production efficiency, either as pluralist networks of stakeholders in the corporation (Hirst 1994, 1997; Kelly *et al.* 1997: Kelly and Parkinson 2001) or, as Archer (1996) suggests, in terms of economic democracy expressed through Works Councils.

Finally, Third Way commentators reject the irresponsible and unethical exercise of power by multinational corporations in the global market (e.g. Giddens 2000). Corporate power should be subject to voluntary restraint and moral imperative. Restraint is voluntary because anything statutory or regulatory might upset the market process. Alternatively, corporate power should be constrained by bringing the corporations into partnership with policy-makers within a new remit of corporate social responsibility referenced by such initiatives as social and environmental audits, and a willingness of the corporation to engage more openly in public affairs in a progressive rather than regressive fashion (Prabhakar 2003).

Pressure also comes from non-governmental organizations, and agencies such as the United Nations and the World Bank with its new emphasis on 'civil society' empowerment (World Bank 2005). The International Monetary Fund has also entered the fray by extolling the virtues of social capital formation as an essential means by which market transaction costs can be lowered (Fukuyama 1999). Efforts to reduce poverty and to ensure 'democracy' in developing countries are essentially good for business, creating political stability and new generations of consumers. There thus emerges a crossover between government and business agendas in this respect, and the concept of *partnership* between government and business emerges as a central plank of Third Way policy.[7]

Indeed, partnership is postulated in UK government discourse on a variety of fronts beyond the workplace – between government and business but also between the agencies of state, markets and society in general (Catney 2002). This emphasis is even conceived as a form of 'new governance', typifying the ethic of the European Social Model (e.g. Kristensen 2001), or as 'sustainable work systems' linked to a continuous regeneration of human resources (Docherty *et al.* 2002: 223). Indeed, the suggestion that global restructuring of work is the precursor of more collaborative industrial relations is reinforced by other authors when considering the impact of EU legislation. Brown (2000), for example, suggests global re-regulation is taking place, more inclusive of trade unions domestically and based on New Labour's commitment to developing partnership in practice. Brown constructs an institutional analysis by examining New Labour's domestic legislation, EU initiatives and developments in the 'social institutions' such as the Advisory, Conciliation and Arbitration Service (ACAS) and the Low Pay Commission. This is combined with a defensive change in UK trade unions towards 'a co-operative rather than a confrontational stance', which, according to Brown, meant that 'Social partnership appeared to be taking root' in the UK (figure 7.2).

## Critique

The argument presented so far is that partnership in the UK context had its precedents in the business unionism of the 1980s, but has been refined under New Labour to embrace worker voice as a means to close the UK's continuing productivity gap. The approach has been consolidated by the construction of Third Way ideology which seeks to negate class struggle and inject a consensus-based industrial relations framework in the 'national' interest. Inherent in this approach is a reliance on a voluntaristic development of ethical social-ism in which trade unions are valued not because they represent workers' interests in a class fashion but because they can use their social capital to enhance business efficiency in the new globalized market. Such an analysis raises questions about union strategy towards the government's agenda.

Academic comment on these debates has been voluminous, focusing either on the nature of partnership agreements, the processes involved in partnership, or the cultural characteristics of partnership attached to the employer–employee relationship. Academics are not immune from positioning themselves for or against the ideological implications of partnership and the 'objective' conclusions from case study research will no doubt have been influenced by the subjective. Broadly speaking, academic dialogue can be characterized as contestation between those who might be labelled 'advocates'

| Concept | Origin | Outcome Related to Partnership |
|---|---|---|
| *Associative democracy* | Crisis of representative democracy evidenced by<br>- fall in electoral turnout<br>- decline in participation in mainstream parliamentary parties<br>- volatility in election<br>- fragmentation of class identity<br>- shift from collectivism to individualism | New forms of representative participation evidenced by<br>- workplace participation<br>- networks<br>- stakeholder interest groups<br>- public/private partnerships |
| *Corporate Social Responsibility* | Concerns over excessive corporate power in a new era of globalization evidenced by<br>- environmental damage<br>- social problems<br>- rising income inequality<br>- economic exploitation | - Social and environmental audits.<br>- Business in the Community<br>- Public/private partnerships<br>- Ethical concern for workforce |
| *Stakeholderism* | Concerns over short-termism of Anglo-Saxon capitalism.<br>Concern over lack of employee voice and consequent inefficiencies. | Widening participation in corporate affairs and decision making by<br>- individual participation (New Labour version)<br>- development of organizational learning and skills<br>- employee financial participation |

*Figure 7.2* Third Way origins of partnership.

of partnership, and those who are 'critics', although some, such as Heery (2002), sit between the two camps. The advocates generally present the arguments for partnership as a necessary strategic reorientation for unions if they are to survive and thrive in an increasingly competitive environment (e.g. Haynes and Allen 2001; Samuel 2005). They are joined by those such as Ackers (2002) and Ackers and Wilkinson (2003) who have championed the 'new pluralist' vision of the role of trade unions. Both sets of authors represent a pessimistic view of the ability of trade unions to continue to progress through adversarialism, and in so doing can be accused of denying the continued validity of unions as agents of class struggle in the workplace.

The critics tend to focus on the deleterious outcomes for workers of partnership in the workplace. Such negative outcomes include a general intensification and extensification of work as employer flexibility agendas impact on the labour process (e.g. Taylor and Ramsay 1998; Martínez Lucio and Stuart 2002; Findlay and McKinlay 2003; Danford *et al.* 2005). Criticism is also framed in terms of an attack on New Labour's accommodation to neoliberal agendas through the 'side door' of the Third Way. McIlroy describes the limitations of partnership in the face of neoliberal market imperatives and contends that New Labour has embraced the neoliberalism of its Conservative predecessor. He posits that far from introducing 'new pluralism', 'It [partnership] embraced a unitary framework of industrial relations and the rhetoric of human resource management' (McIlroy 1998: 543). Such a theme is supported by Martínez Lucio and Stuart (2000), who suggest that partnership is simply an extension of 'tired' HRM, and is an attempt by employers to re-invigorate processes of employee involvement whereby worker commitment to organizational goals can be used to increase worker productivity. In summary, partnership cannot be viewed outside of the context of employer (and government) attempts to restructure industry and to increase worker productivity. As such, as Danford *et al.* (2005: 236) argue, partnership and high-performance working 'cannot mask irreconcilable conflicts of interest that are prime characteristics of capitalist workplace dynamics'.

Indeed, it is these irreconcilable conflicts that are the source of both intra- and inter-union differences over partnership. Much evidence from case study research would suggest that partnership has been highly divisive in the workplace. Of course, workers and their unions are often divided but what is notable in many cases of partnership is the *ideological* rather than sectional nature of division. Such is the case in Danford *et al.*'s (2005) study of the aerospace industry, whereby in two enterprises the manual and non-manual unions were on opposite sides when it came to willingness to establish partnership with the two respective employers, with the manual sections opposed to partnership in one case but in support in the other. Where partnership arrangements have been introduced they have also been found to create new divisions between senior union activists and the rank and file. The senior activists became either 'detached' from the membership (Marks *et al.* 1998; Danford *et al.* 2003) or 'displaced' (Geary and Roche 2003). Such detachment derives largely from the emphasis on consultation that is prominent within partnership arrangements and agreements. As Terry and Smith report in their evaluation of projects conducted under the DTI's Partnership Fund:

> In organisations where trade unions were recognized the partnership initiative often involved a change in the structures through which unions and management interacted. Such changes were almost universally associated with an intention, explicit or otherwise, to change the dominant interaction between management and trade unions from one based around *negotiation* into one characterised as *consultation*.
>
> Terry and Smith (2003: 9)

The processes involved in negotiation codify the outcomes of bargaining power into transparent written agreements. In contrast, the process of consultation de-codifies arrangements between the parties. Partnership replaces traditional written agreements with informal, unwritten and consensus-based 'agreements'. The lack of formal codification in partnership thus produces 'agreements' between the union leaderships and employers which are less transparent and accountable to the rank and file than those previously produced under traditional bargaining structures. In addition, more business-related information is released to senior union activists and full-time union officials by the employer in the consultation/partnership process, but this is often on a 'need to know' and confidential basis. Thus further division is created between 'information rich' senior workplace representatives and 'information poor' union members. The dangers of detachment may also occur where the union has sought to reach a partnership arrangement with the employer that trades employee compliance for union privilege in recruiting members. Such was the outcome in Heery *et al.*'s (2005) study of the Manpower staff agency, whereby 'an officer-dependent, passive form of trade unionism has been viewed as a constraint upon, and not a condition for, the development of a broader exchange with the company' (ibid.: 182).

Most importantly the process of partnership runs the risk of pacifying the rank and file (Blyton and Turnbull 1998: 106). This is because the consensual nature of the process, when combined with detachment of senior activists, can undermine activism and marginalize 'oppositionism'. Employers' agendas to utilize partnership processes as a vehicle for the management of change have also necessitated the 'cultivation' of union activists who are sympathetic to the general project. In his study of Legal and General and Amicus-MSF, Samuel highlights how opposition to partnership was overcome by union activists who 'were given extended reach into management decision-making'. These 'cultivated' activists proceeded to enable the workplace union 'to exert pressure as the "conscience" of the company' (Samuel 2005: 73). Lastly partnership can divide workers both at the time when new partnership projects are conceived and also as the outcomes of the agreements begin to unravel. Kelly (1999) refers to the opposition from stewards to partnership before it was introduced at Blue Circle, the 49 per cent vote against the introduction of partnership at Scottish Power, and its initial rejection at United Distillers. Beale (2005), in the case of the Inland Revenue, and Gall (2005), in the case of Royal Mail, also provide evidence of workers turning against partnership once the outcomes unravel and disappointment sets in.

We can track a developing divide within the unions at national level. This is exemplified by the election of the 'awkward squad' of union leaders and the renewal of a dividing line in industrial disputes crystallized in the fire-fighters' dispute and the consequent decision of the union to disaffiliate from the Labour Party (see McIlroy and Daniels, chapter 4, this volume). Central to the emergence of the new opposition within trade unions to New Labour have been the issues of continuing privatization, Public–Private Partnership, the Private Finance Initiative, Foundation Hospitals and, at the workplace, partnership practice itself (see McIlroy, chapters 2 and 5, this volume). Derek Simpson, since being elected as general secretary of Amicus (now Unite), has challenged the TUC concept of partnership as a precursor for reviewing all the partnership agreements signed by the union. He claimed that partnership, as presently constructed, is 'all smoke and mirrors' (quoted in Murray 2003: 125). The mood of change at the time was summarized in comments by the CWU general secretary Billy Hayes:

> I think the other important difference between us and the 1980s–1990s model is the issue of partnership. I'm not against working with the employer; it's what used to be called collective bargaining. We've worked with the Post Office management to get £2.5 billion from the government for investment in the industry. But I've found anything that is announced as 'partnership' is more like supplication than negotiation. Weakness invites aggression; that's the reality. Anyone who's ever been an activist knows that the first word you learn not to hear is 'No'. When I've been with people who follow the partnership agenda they say: 'The employers said we can't have it.' And they accept it. This sort of partnership agenda is dead.
>
> (Hayes 2000)

Indeed, the three largest unions within the TUC have now cautioned against partnership. The public service union Unison's submission to the TUC 2004 Review argued:

> We suspect Congress House has always had its own agenda based on the social partner imperative, but. . . . could point to the need to maintain a political equilibrium among affiliates. Now that the pendulum has swung to the left, is this being reflected adequately?[8]

And in similar vein, the TGWU suggested:

> There is a danger . . . in the TUC being seen as an intermediary . . . or in being concerned to keep in with the government – at the expense of the forthright presentation of working people's agendas.
>
> (*Guardian*, 10 March 2004)

Such ambivalence to the partnership agenda is rooted within ideological differences in the unions at national level between New Labour values of 'modernization' and Old Labour values of public service provision and industrial relations adversarialism. This disjuncture between government and union policy in the public sector has created a particular focus for the retention of partnership discourse by the TUC and public sector unions over the future of public service delivery in Britain. A 2003 TUC resolution referred to a 'spirit of partnership which needs to be adopted between government departments and agencies and the trade unions representing workers in these important and demanding public services'. However, the strains between unions and government are highlighted in the resolution's caveat: 'Congress urges those in government to enact their obligations under international law, and not seek to remove the ability of the trade unions to protect their members by the use of industrial action. The trade union movement demands of its "political arm", the Labour Party, that all partnership agreements are enacted with the full backing of international law, and that these are partnerships of equals and do not demand trade unions to be "silent partners"' (TUC 2003).

From a position of general support in the early years of New Labour many trade unionists have moved to a position of criticism (see McIlroy, chapter 5, this volume). This is not to say that there is outright opposition to partnership, but rather retreat to a position in which partnership is viewed merely as a possible tactical approach with employers reluctant to deal with unions on other terms. Amicus, for example, signed a major partnership agreement in the print industry when in 2005 it sought the services of Professor Frank Burchill through the DTI Strategic Partnership fund to review previous partnership arrangements. The agreement contains 12 key objectives such as increasing dialogue between employers, employees and their union, improving productivity, reducing excessive overtime working, assisting employees to adapt to change, and enabling effective recruitment and development of employees. It also contained new provisions on key issues, such as sick pay, the regulation of agency and temporary workers, information and consultation, and flexible working patterns (*Personnel Today*, 2005). The CWU also continues to sign partnership agreements with small employers on the fringe of the industry. General secretary Billy Hayes outlined the tactic: 'We actually have partnership agreements in some telecommunication firms, where we do not have full negotiating rights. We regard partnership agreements in these certain instances, as an interim measure on the way to more mature and respectful relationship between equals' (Hayes 2006).

Cautious opposition to partnership developed as more left-wing union leaders have emerged, and as the outcomes of previous partnership arrangements proved disappointing to the rank and file. The election of a 'broad left' leadership of the Public and Commercial Services Union (PCS) in 2003 is one example, whereby the previous long-held support for partnership in principle has been reversed (Beale 2005). However, there are deeper constraints to the development of partnership which would indicate grim prospects for the vision. Indeed, as Robert Taylor concludes in his review of the evidence for the government-funded Economic and Social Research Council (ESRC):

The critics of partnership at work in Britain have certainly grown more widespread and influential in recent years. Their attacks have begun to exercise a significant influence over the attitude of public policy-makers towards the concept. Partnership has never been without its opponents

who see it as an inappropriate means for developing new forms of industrial relations. Now it is finding it difficult to remain on any public policy
agenda at all.

(Taylor 2004: 6)

### Conclusion: the limits of partnership

The argument presented in this chapter is that the partnership paradigm has
been introduced into industrial relations as a response to declining business
competitiveness and lagging productivity. The route chosen by New Labour
to solve these problems has been to adopt the premises of high-performance
working and to use partnership as a vehicle for its introduction. Central to
this shift has been Third Way ideology which seeks to justify and facilitate the
negation of class conflict in the workplace and to replace traditional adversarial industrial relations with consensus and consultation. Worker voice is
valued as a way of tapping creativity and innovation, but the role of trade
unions is downplayed and multi-channel forms of representation, both direct
and indirect, are emphasized instead. There are specific constraints on the
chemistry of partnership which mean that the vision of the unions' view of
'good partnership' is difficult to achieve if not unattainable.

First, where 'good' partnership exists with 'strong' union presence workplace bargaining may mean that industrial relations practices are little
removed from those that pertained under past adversarial traditions. This
may be tested by studying outcomes from the distinction between 'labour
parity' and 'employer dominant' partnership whereby we might expect to find
more evidence of employee gains in the former as opposed to the latter.
However, when he examined matched sectoral pairs of partnership and non-
partnership agreements, Kelly (2005) found that for 'labour parity' types, the
gains for unions, while outstripping the non-partnership match, were as
much a product of union power obtained through increased membership and
better shop-floor organization as partnership practice itself. We might sus-
pect that in such cases there might be little difference between what might be
labelled 'good partnership' and the 'shrewd' collective bargaining identified
by Martínez Lucio and Stuart (2000: 21), with partnership expressed merely
as a pragmatic adjunct to the bargaining process, rather than an alternative
industrial relations framework. Such a distinction would also correspond
with the evidence of 'nurturing' partnership identified by Oxenbridge and
Brown (2002: 273), whereby informal partnership arrangements had been
developed on management initiative and where the management strategy was
to seek 'greater control over communication structures ... and to shift
worker loyalty away from the union, but [where] unions retained an active
role on employment regulation'.

Second, the evidence would suggest that the implantation of the core
values of both high-performance working and partnership has been only
sporadically applied in Britain. Both White *et al.* (2003) and Danford *et al.*

(2005), in surveys conducted for the ESRC's Future of Work Programme, found that HPWS can deleteriously affect employees' work–life balance and intensify work. The discretion over tasks that is so necessary for creative innovation is often contained solely within management grades, and does not reach down to lower-grade occupations. Danford *et al.* (2005: 8) further argue that many of the constraining and controlling aspects of lean production 'have been cannibalized most successfully in the current ideology of the high performance workplace'. Indeed, the difficulties of introducing effective HPWS are also recognized by practitioners. Porter and Ketels' (2003) government-commissioned report into UK competitiveness suggested that UK companies are less likely to adopt modern management techniques than their competitors. The role of line managers in implementing the process is crucial, and it is here that some resistance to relaxing control may take place.

Findings from the Workplace Employment Relations Survey (WERS) 2004 would seem to confirm the constraints, as the proportion of workplaces utilizing a combination of high-involvement practices has shown only a 'marginal increase' since the 1998 survey (Kersley *et al.* 2005). Most importantly there appeared a continued lack of trust between employers and employees (an essential ingredient of the HPWS), which appeared in only a 'minority' of workplaces. A 2006 CIPD Survey of 2000 employees confirms the WERS pessimism about the reluctance of British managers to engage seriously with their employees. The survey reported 30 per cent of employees responding that they rarely or never received feedback on performance; only 38 per cent of employees said directors and senior managers treated them with respect; and 42 per cent of employees did not feel they were kept well-informed about what was going on in their organization (CIPD 2006).

The reasons for management reluctance to engage creatively with employees may well lie in the continuing structural problems of UK industry. In particular, corporate turbulence due to continuing shareholder value short-termism makes it particularly difficult to establish job security and trust (Sisson 1995, Driffield 1999; Upchurch and Danford 2001). This point was well recognized by no less than the TUC's ex-general secretary John Monks (now general secretary of the ETUC) in his Aneurin Bevan memorial lecture given in November 2006. Monks, the erstwhile foremost advocate of partnership, stated:

> Partnership with who? There has been a disintegration of the social nexus between worker and employer – a culture containing broad rights and obligations. The new capitalism wants none of it . . . I did not fully appreciate what was happening on the other side of the table . . . it cannot be easy running a firm . . . when you are up for sale every day and night of the year.
>
> (Monks 2006)

Further, Monks argued that the short-term behaviour of 'overpaid corporate executives' was 'shameless . . . more and more they resemble Bourbons – and they should be aware of what eventually happened to the Bourbons' (ibid.). In re-assessing the 'UK Model' ten years on from an original paper published in 1994 Rubery *et al.* (2005) seem to confirm that there remains a lack of institutional support for the type of high-performance model so desired by the government. While progress might have been made in educational provision and training in order to boost human capital, Britain has not taken up the necessary aspects of the Rhine model of institutional support for the high-road route to business competitiveness. The long-term decline of manufacturing and its steady replacement with a service economy may also have affected capacity to reach the target model so that 'it may be argued that the opportunities to move onto a high value added manufacturing development path were already lost' (ibid.: 31). This does not mean to say, of course, that the search for productivity improvement in UK industry is likely to be fruitless, but rather that it is more likely to continue to come from more intensive and extensive exploitation of the existing workforce than from 'enlightened' policies of employee engagement. As such, adversarialism is alive and well in UK workplaces, enacted by the majority of UK managers if not always by the union side.

All this might suggest that the ideological framework of partnership gathered in the Third Way and supported by sympathetic academics may be in disarray. Many of the concerns associated with globalization addressed by Third Way theories, such as social inequality and increasing job precariousness, are concerns which are central to the everyday lives of working people and their trade unions. However, rather than a route to neo-pluralist nirvana this analysis would suggest that partnership at work, at least in the UK context, is simply an application of management prerogative by other means. It comes with a neo-unitarist rather than a neo-pluralist flavour sprinkled liberally with the ideological message of class de-alignment. But it is firmly located in employer efforts to intensify work and maintain the rigid discipline of capital accumulation. Hyman (2005: 263) has already observed that trade unions and their members need partnership, but with each other rather than with their employers. If unions are to survive and thrive such partnership between employees and their unions may also need to be a precursor to a renewed adversarialism.

## Notes

1 See Stuart and Martínez Lucio (2005) for a review.
2 <http://www.ipa-involve.com> (accessed 30 June 2008)
3 The DTI Partnership Fund ran from 1999 to 2004. It funded 249 workplace projects between unions and employers, over 20 strategic projects and committed £12.5 million to individual projects.
4 <http://www.eef.org.uk/UK/preview/policy/public/publication21112003.htm> (accessed 30 June 2008)
5 Author's interview with officers of the TUC Partnership Institute, 2002.

6 Debates on corporate governance have crystallized under New Labour within the guise of stakeholderism, theorized in the varieties of capitalism literature and politicized by writers such as Michel Albert and Will Hutton. What is intriguing is the capriciousness of many third way politicians and academics towards the stakeholder vision. The 'individual' version of stakeholderism concentrates in outlining the need to boost education and training so that everyone is provided with the opportunity to participate in the new global economy. As Soskice (1997) argued, this is essentially a new labour market contract between the government and individuals whereby the state will take on the responsibility of establishing a framework in which learning and mass higher education can take place. As for business, in this scenario, its role is restricted to harnessing the creative skills and competencies of individuals through participation and cooperative working (or partnership). The incoming New Labour government was committed to this watered-down version of stakeholding, heavy on individual learning but stripped of its governance aspects or any critique of power relations within the workplace. As Coates (2000) recorded, by the 1997 General Election even the term 'stakeholding' had been excluded from the Labour Party Manifesto. All that was left of the stakeholding discourse was references to 'partnership' as an alternative to conflict and encouragement of Employee Share Ownership schemes and cooperatives.

7 The UK delegation to the 2002 Earth Summit in South Africa was an interesting example of such an approach, in that the delegation was composed of both government representatives and corporate leaders.

8 Quoted in 'New trade unions in the making', *Red Pepper TUC Special*, London, 2002.

## Bibliography

Ackers, P. (2002) 'Reframing employment relations: the case for neo-pluralism' *Industrial Relations Journal*, 33:1, 2–19.

Ackers, P. and Payne, J. (1998) 'British trade unions and social partnership: rhetoric, reality and strategy', *International Journal of Human Resource Management*, 9:3, 529–50.

Ackers, P. and Wilkinson, A. (2003) 'Introduction: the British industrial relations tradition – formation, breakdown and salvage' in P. Ackers and A. Wilkinson (eds) *Understanding Work and Employment: industrial relations in transition*, Oxford: Oxford University Press.

Ackers, P., Marchington, M., Wilkinson, A. and Dundon, T. (2005) 'Partnership and voice, with or without trade unions: changing UK management approaches to organisational participation', in M. Stuart and M. Martínez Lucio (eds) *Partnership and Modernisation in Employment Relations*, London: Routledge.

Appelbaum, E., Bailey, T., Berg, P., and Kallenberg, A.L. (2000) *Manufacturing Advantage: Why High Performance Work Systems Pay Off*. Ithaca, NY: Cornell University Press.

Archer, R. (1996) 'Towards economic democracy in Britain' in P. Hirst and S. Khilnani (eds) *Reinventing Democracy*, Oxford: Blackwell.

Bacon, N. and Samuel, P. (2007) 'Partnership: agreement, adoption, form and survival in Britain'. Paper presented to the Eighth European Congress of the International Industrial Relations Association, Manchester, September.

Beale, D. (2005) 'The promotion and prospects of partnership at work at Inland Revenue: employer and union hand-in-hand' in M. Stuart and M. Martínez Lucio (eds) *Partnership and Modernisation in Employment Relations*, London: Routledge.

Beck, U. (1992) *Risk Society: Towards a New Modernity*, London: Sage.

Blair, T. (1998) Foreword to *Fairness at Work*, London: DTI.

Blyton, P. and Turnbull, P. (1998) *The Dynamics of Employee Relations*, 2nd edition. Basingstoke: Macmillan Business.

Brown, W. (2000) 'Putting partnership into practice in Britain', *British Journal of Industrial Relations*, 38:2, 299–316.

Callinicos, A. (2001) *Against the Third Way*, Cambridge: Polity Press.

Catney, P. (2002) 'New Labour and associative democracy' Paper given to the Political Studies Association Conference, Aberdeen, April.

Chartered Institute for Personnel and Development (CIPD) (2006) *How Engaged are British Employees?* Annual Survey Report 2006, London: CIPD.

Coates, D. (2000) 'New Labour's industrial and employment policy' in D. Coates and P. Lawler (eds) *New Labour in Power*, Manchester: Manchester University Press.

Coats, D. (2004) *Speaking Up! Voice, Industrial Democracy and Organisational Performance*, London: Work Foundation.

Cohen, J. and Rogers, J. (1995) 'Secondary associations and democratic governance' in J. Cohen and J. Rogers (eds) *Associations and Democracy*, London: Verso.

Confederation of British Industry (CBI) (2003) *High Performance Workplaces: The Role of Employee Involvement in a Modern Economy – CBI Response*, London: CBI.

Crouch, C. (1992) 'The fate of articulated industrial relations systems: a stock-taking after the neo-liberal decade', in M. Regini (ed.) *The Future of Labour Movements*, London: Sage.

Danford, A., Richardson, M. and Upchurch, M. (2003), *New Unions, New Workplaces: A Study of Union Resilience in the Restructured Workplace*, London: Routledge.

Danford, A., Richardson, M., Upchurch, M., Tailby, S. and Stewart, P. (2005) *Partnership and the High Performance Workplace: Work and Employment Relations in the Aerospace Industry*, London: Palgrave Macmillan/ESRC.

Das, R. (2006) 'Putting social capital in its place' *Capital and Class*, 90, 65–92.

Department of Trade and Industry (DTI) (1998) *Fairness at Work*, London: DTI.

—— (2002) *High Performance Workplaces – The Role of Employee Involvement in a Modern Economy*, London: DTI.

—— (2004) *Achieving Best Practice in Your Business. Maximising Potential: High Performance Workplaces*, London: DTI.

Docherty, P., Forslin, J. and Shani, A. B. (2002) 'Sustainable work systems: lessons and challenges', in P. Docherty, J. Forslin and A. B. Shani (eds) *Creating Sustainable Work Systems*, London: Routledge.

Driffield, N. (1999) 'Indirect employment effects of foreign direct investment into the UK', *Bulletin of Economic Research*, 51:3, 207–21.

Engineering Employers Federation (EEF) (2001) *Catching Up with Uncle Sam: The Final Report on US/UK Manufacturing Productivity* London: EEF.

Engineering Employers Federation / Chartered Institute for Personnel and Development (EEF/CIPD) (2003) *Maximising Employee Potential and Business Performance: The Role of High Performance Working*, London: CIPD.

Findlay, P. and McKinlay, A. (2003) 'Organizing in electronics: recruitment, recognition and retention – shadow shop stewards in Scotland's "Silicon Glen"', in G. Gall (ed.) *Union Organizing: Campaigning for Union Recognition*, London: Routledge.

Fine, B. (2001) *Social Capital vs. Social Theory*, London: Routledge.

Fukuyama, F. (1999) 'Social capital and civil society', prepared for delivery at the IMF Conference on Second Generation Reforms, <https://www.imf.org/external/pubs/ft/seminar/1999/reforms/fukuyama.htm> (accessed 30 June 2008).

Gall, G. (2001) 'From adversarialism to partnership? Trade unionism and industrial relations in the banking sector in the UK', *Employee Relations*, 23:4, 353–75.

—— (2004) 'Trade union recognition in Britain, 1995–2002: turning a corner?' *Industrial Relations Journal*, 35:3, 250–70.

—— (2005) 'Breaking with, and breaking, "partnership": the case of the postal workers and Royal Mail in Britain', in M. Stuart and M. Martínez Lucio (eds) *Partnership and Modernisation in Employment Relations*, London, Routledge, 154–70.

Geary, J.F. and Roche, W.K. (2003) 'Workplace partnership and the displaced activist thesis', *Industrial Relations Journal*, 34:1, 32–51.

Geddes, M. (2001), 'What about the workers? Best Value, employment and work in local public services', *Policy and Politics*, 29:4, 497–508.

Giddens, A. (1998) *The Third Way*, Cambridge: Polity.

—— (2000) *The Third Way and its Critics*, Cambridge: Polity.

Green, R., Steen, M. and Wilson, A. (2001) 'The third way in Europe: New Labour's employment and industrial relations strategy', in D. Foden, J. Hoffman and R Scott (eds) *Globalisation and the Social Contract*, Brussels: European Trade Union Institute.

Guest, D. and Peccei, R. (2001) 'Partnership at work; mutuality and the balance of advantage', *British Journal of Industrial Relations*, 39:2, 207–36.

Hay, C. (2004) 'Credibility, competitiveness and the business cycle in "third way" political economy: a critical evaluation of economic policy in Britain since 1997', *New Political Economy*, 9:1, 39–56.

Hayes, B. (2006) Billy Hayes Blog <http://www.billyhayes.co.uk/permalink.php?id=P640_0_1_0_C> (accessed 30 June 2008).

Haynes, P. and Allen, M. (2001) 'Partnership as union strategy: a preliminary evaluation', *Employee Relations*, 23:2, 166–87.

Heery, E. (2002) 'Partnership versus organizing: alternative futures for British trade unionism', *Industrial Relations Journal*, 33:1, 21–35.

Heery, E., Conley, H., Delbridge, R and Stewart, P. (2005) 'Seeking partnership for the contingent workforce', in M. Stuart and M. Martínez Lucio (eds) *Partnership and Modernisation in Employment Relations*, London: Routledge.

Hirst, P. (1994) *Associative Democracy: New Forms of Economic and Social Governance*. Cambridge: Polity Press.

—— (1997) *From Statism to Pluralism*, London: UCL Press.

Hyman, R. (2005) 'Whose (social) partnership?', in M. Stuart and M. Martínez Lucio (eds) *Partnership and Modernisation in Employment Relations*, London: Routledge.

Kelly, G., Kelly, D. and Gamble, A. (1997) 'Conclusion: stakeholder capitalism', in G. Kelly, D. Kelly and A. Gamble (eds) *Stakeholder Capitalism*, London: Macmillan.

Kelly, G. and Parkinson, J. (2001) 'The conceptual foundations of the company: a pluralist approach', in J. Parkinson, A. Gamble and G. Kelly (eds) *The Political Economy of the Company*, London: Hart.

Kelly, J. (1999) 'Social partnerships in Britain: good for profits, bad for jobs and unions', *Communist Review*, 30, 3–10.

—— (2005) 'Social partnership agreements in Britain', in M. Stuart and M. Martínez Lucio (eds) *Partnership and Modernisation in Employment Relations*, London: Routledge.

Kersley, B., Alpin, C., Forth, J., Bryson, A., Bewley, H., Dix, G. and Oxenbridge, S. (2005) *Inside the Workplace: First Findings From the 2004 Workplace Employment Relations Survey*, London: DTI.

Kochan, T. and Osterman, P. (1994) *The Mutual Gains Enterprise: Forging a Winning Partnership Among Labor, Management and Government*, Boston: Harvard University Press.

Kristensen, J.E. (2001) 'Corporate social responsibility and new social partnerships', in C. Kjægaard and S. Westphalen (eds) *From Collective Bargaining to Social Partnerships: New Roles of the Social Partners in Europe*, Copenhagen: The Copenhagen Centre.

McIlroy, J. (1995) *Trade Unions in Britain Today*, 2nd edition, Manchester: Manchester University Press.

—— (1998) 'The enduring alliance? Trade unions and the making of New Labour 1994–97' *British Journal of Industrial Relations*, 36:4, 537–64.

Marks, A., Findlay, T., Hine, J., McKinlay, A. and Thompson, P. (1998) 'The politics of partnership? Innovation in employment relations in the Scottish spirits industry', *British Journal of Industrial Relations*, 36:2, 209–26.

Martínez Lucio, M. and Stuart, M. (2000) 'Swimming against the tide: social partnership, mutual gains and the revival of "tired" HRM', Working Paper 00/03, The Centre for Industrial Relations and Human Resource Management, Leeds University.

—— (2002) 'Assessing the principles of partnership: workplace trade union representatives' attitudes and experience.' *Employee Relations*, 24:3, 305–20.

—— (2005) ' "Partnership" and new industrial relations in a risk society: an age of shotgun weddings and marriages of convenience', *Work, Employment and Society*, 19:4, 797–817.

Monks, J. (2000) *Address to the Institute of Directors Convention by TUC General Secretary John Monks*, Press Release, London: TUC, 19 April.

—— (2006) Interview in *Financial Times*, 20 November.

Murray, A. (2003) *A New Labour Nightmare: The Return of the Awkward Squad*, London: Verso.

Oxenbridge, S. and Brown, W. (2002) 'The two faces of partnership? An assessment of partnership and co-operative employer/trade union relationships', *Employee Relations*, 24:3, 262–76.

*Personnel Today* (2005) *Partnership Working* <http://www.personneltoday.com/Articles/2005/12/06/32899/partnership-working.html> (accessed 30 June 2008).

Porter, M. and Ketels, C. (2003) *UK Competitiveness: Moving to the Next Stage*, DTI Economics Paper No. 3, London: DTI.

Prabhakar, R. (2003) *Stakeholding and New Labour*, London: Palgrave Macmillan.

Ramsay, H. (1977) 'Cycles of control', *Sociology*, 11:3, 481–506.

—— (1996) 'Involvement, empowerment and commitment', in B. Towers (ed.) *The Handbook of Human Resource Management*, Oxford: Blackwell.

Richardson, M., Tailby, S., Danford, A., Stewart, P. and Upchurch, M. (2005) 'Best Value and workplace partnership in local government', *Personnel Review*, 34:6, 713–28.

Rubery, J. (1994) 'The British production regime: a societal-specific system?', *Economy and Society*, 23:3, 335–54.

Rubery, J., Grimshaw, D., Donnelly, R. and Urwin, P. (2005) *Revisiting the UK Model: From Basket Case to Success Story?* Manchester: Manchester University Business School.

Samuel, P. (2005) 'Partnership working and the cultivated activist', *Industrial Relations Journal*, 36:1, 59–76.

Sisson, K. (1995) 'Change and continuity in British industrial relations', in R. Locke, T. Kochan and M. Piore (eds) *Employment Relations in a Changing World Economy*, Cambridge, MA: MIT Press.

Soskice, D. (1997) 'Stakeholding yes; the German model no', in G. Kelly, D. Kelly and A. Gamble (eds) *Stakeholder Capitalism*, London: Macmillan.

Stuart, M. and Martínez Lucio, M. (2005) 'Introduction,' in M. Stuart and M. Martínez Lucio (eds) *Partnership and Modernisation in Employment Relations*, London: Routledge.

Taylor, P. and Ramsay, H. (1998) 'Unions, partnership and HRM: sleeping with the enemy?', *International Journal of Employment Studies*, 6:2, 115–43.

Taylor, R. (2004) *Partnership at Work: The Way to Corporate Renewal?* Swindon: Economic and Social Research Council (ESRC).

Terry, M. and Smith, J. (2003) *Evaluation of the Partnership at Work Fund*, London: DTI.

Thompson, N. (1996) 'Supply side socialism; the political economy of New Labour'. *New Left Review*, 216, 37–54.

TUC (1999) *Partners for Progress: New Unionism in the Workplace*, London: TUC.

—— (2002) *Partnership Works*, London: TUC.

—— (2003) *Congress Decisions* <http://www.tuc.org.uk/congress/tuc-7138-f0.cfm> (accessed 1 July 2008).

TUC/CBI (2001) *The UK Productivity Challenge*, London: TUC/CBI.

Upchurch, M. and Danford, A. (2001) 'Industrial restructuring, "globalisation", and the trade union response: a study of MSF in the south west of England', *New Technology, Work and Employment*, 16:2, 100–14.

Upchurch, M., Richardson, M., Tailby, S., Danford, A. and Stewart, P. (2006) 'Employee representation and partnership in the non-union sector: a paradox of intention?', *Human Resource Management Journal*, 16:4, 393–410.

Weltman, D., and Billig, M. (2001) 'The political psychology of contemporary anti-politics: a discursive approach to the end-of-ideology era', *Political Psychology*, 22, 367–82.

White, M., Hill, S., McGovern, P., Mills, C. and Smeaton, D. (2003) ' "High performance" management practices, working hours and work-life balance', *British Journal of Industrial Relations*, 41:2, 175–95.

Whitfield, D. (2001), *Public Services or Corporate Welfare: Rethinking the Nation State in the Global Economy*, London: Pluto Press.

Williamson, J. (1997), 'Your stake at work: the TUC's agenda', in G. Kelly, D. Kelly and A. Gamble (eds) *Stakeholder Capitalism*, London: Macmillan.

Womack, J.P., Jones, D.T. and Roos, D. (1990) *The Machine that Changed the World: The Triumph of Lean Production*, New York: Rawson Macmillan.

World Bank (2005) *Issues and Options for Improving Engagement between the World Bank and Civil Society Organisations*, Washington DC: World Bank.

# 8   In the field

## A decade of organizing

*Gary Daniels*

De Turberville encapsulates the flavour of organizing as 'a proactive bottom-up model of collective organization in which members constantly use innovative techniques to empower themselves' (de Turberville 2004: 777). The TUC's version, which draws on experience in Australia and the USA, embodies this vision; but overall it is perhaps better captured by the phrase 'managed activism' (Heery 2003; Simms 2007). For strategy, stimulation, pressure and coordination come largely from Congress House, the offices of affiliated unions and professional organizers: from above, not from below. There must be some discontent, grievance, desire for change, impetus within workplaces: its transformation into organizing involves a dialectic between workers and external leadership. But organizing campaigns are orchestrated by the union leadership rather than stemming organically from the workforce. 'Managed activism' involves the TUC and unions implanting a culture of organizing inside Britain's workplaces rather than nurturing an already emergent culture. Mobilization has a strong external and sometimes a weak internal dimension. The organizing agenda was driven, at least initially, not by a grassroots shop stewards movement but by a TUC Academy and by paid organizers trained by the TUC. However, it was anticipated that 'top-down' action would eventually produce bottom-up organizing (TUC 1997: 43–4).

In 1997 workplace unionism was weak (see McIlroy, chapter 2; McIlroy and Daniels, chapter 3, this volume). The TUC top-down model of 'empowerment' was seen as indispensable if unions were to consolidate their position in areas of existing presence, break into new jobs and industries, win recognition rights, and sharpen unions' appeal to 'new' workers, including women, youth and those at the rough end of the labour market (TUC 1997: 31). This required rejection of 'market share' approaches (Willman 1989) to union growth and necessitated using messages and methods attractive to workers in particular circumstances. For the TUC, organization was 'based not merely on recruitment per se but on processes of membership mobilisation through renewed workplace activism and rank and file participation' (Danford *et al.* 2002: 2). Organization involved seeding, not servicing, rooting self-sustaining collectivism in the workplace. This in turn required strengthening representative structures at work and emphasizing retention of members as well as recruitment. Organizing demanded increased investment by unions (TUC 1998: 55) and a switch from servicing members with officials doing things for them, to workers' self-organization and members learning to do things for themselves (Carter 2000).

Heery and his colleagues note the managing role of the TUC and unions but conclude: 'the organizing model represents an attempt to rediscover the "social movement" origins of labour, essentially by redefining the union as a mobilising structure which seeks to stimulate activism among its members and generate campaigns for workplace and wider justice' (Heery *et al.* 2000a: 996). In their view, union organizing is more than simply recruiting: it is about rebuilding participative unionism (Heery *et al.* 2000b: 38) through the identification and grooming of activists while involving workers and future members in the process of 'collective organisation' (Heery *et al.* 2003ab: 81). For academic interpreters the model rests on a set of assumptions. First, workers join unions for protection at work (Waddington and Whitston 1997). Second, a reversal of decline is only achievable through higher levels of membership participation and self-organization (Waddington and Kerr 2000: 234). Third, members discover a sense of ownership vis-à-vis their union and share decision-making with union officials (Heery *et al.* 2003b). Fourth, successful organizing comes from a militant stance (Badigannavar and Kelly 2005: 530). Finally, 'unionisation is most likely to be triggered by a sense of injustice, a breach of legal or collective agreement rights or of shared social values' (Badigannavar and Kelly 2005: 520; see also Kelly 1998).

The organizing model integrates recruitment, retention and organizing; it places the workplace at the centre of unionism and sees developing workplace organization as a continuous project. It is aggressive and adversarial; it can involve the wider community; it encourages membership participation; and it questions the model of trade union advance by providing services to individual members. This approach matches closely the TUC's stated objectives laid out in its New Unionism strategy and developed by the Organizing Academy. However, de Turberville makes important points: the radical language and conceptual plasticity of the TUC model makes it inclusive: it attracts support across the political spectrum and it attracts radicals. But 'managed activism' can mean that activism and radicalism are moulded to ensure replication of existing trade unionism rather than transformation of the status quo (de Turberville 2004: 778–80). The classic example which comes from America is that of the CIO in the 1930s where a conservative but organizationally dynamic leadership around John L. Lewis used radical methods and Communist organizers for their own purposes. But this does not conclude matters. For managed activism provides opportunities for radical trade unionism and may produce its own dynamic.

Organizing is only half the story and half the strategy. The TUC model is expressed more precisely as an organizing and partnership model (see McIlroy and Daniels, chapter 3, this volume). Dualism is driven by opportunism. State support for partnership, however vestigial, provides legitimacy and offers openings to employers. The TUC's distinction between 'good' and 'bad' employers (*Labour Research*, October 1997) provides the means for harmonizing partnership and organizing: different strokes for different folks. Academic commentators note the theoretical tensions between collaboration and adversarialism (Heery 2002). These tensions may be practical as well as theoretical. Aggressive organizing may place obstacles in the path of partnership while partnership may compromise a union's representative ability and weaken its independence. It may demand a quiescent rather than an active membership (Taylor and Bain 2003; Danford *et al.* 2005).

Academic critics of this approach have argued that partnership contaminates organizing and have urged a one-track strategy focused solely on organizing (Fairbrother 2000; McIlroy 2000; McIlroy and Daniels 2007; and see Upchurch, chapter 7, this volume). Other critics have gone further stressing the contradictions between centralized bureaucratic-led organizing with its potential for accommodation and a more autonomous participative bottom-up approach. Different approaches to organizing will produce different forms of trade unionism. While initiatives from workers themselves are present in contemporary organizing these authors are concerned that the maintenance in practice of a servicing model, whether lay or professionally based, and the failure to actively encourage self-activity and transfer resources into organizing, detracts from the radical vision of grassroots empowerment (Carter 2000, Carter 2006, Fairbrother and Stewart 2003).

In this chapter I first present an overview of the TUC adoption of the organizing model and allied projects before surveying organizing initiatives by its affiliates. While not intended to be exhaustive, this will give a flavour of the organizing agenda in Britain in the first ten years of New Labour and provide a background to the subsequent more critical discussion of some of the problems with union organizing which will draw on the past as well as international examples and assess the scope for the *real* organizing advocated by a minority of radical academics.

## Organizing: The TUC

The establishment of the New Unionism Task Group (NUTG) and creation of the Organizing Academy gave impetus to the TUC initiative. The purpose of the Academy is to train and motivate young salaried organizers to strengthen existing, and create new, membership bases and support and build workplace organization. Trainees are sponsored by affiliated unions with the possibility that on graduation they will be employed by their sponsors. While many trainees go on to work full-time for their sponsoring or other unions, some have not secured employment once their temporary contract expires (Waddington 2003: 240–1). In 1997 the Academy recruited the first cohort of 36 trainees. Launched as a one-year pilot, the Academy is now (2008) in the process of recruiting its eleventh intake. Over 220 trainees have passed through the Academy, sponsored by 27 TUC affiliated unions (see table 8.1).

*Table 8.1* TUC Organizing Academy

| Year | | Number of trainees |
|------|------|------|
| 1998 | | 35 |
| 1999 | | 27 |
| 2000 | | 36 |
| 2001 | Two intakes | 24 |
| | | 13 |
| 2002 | | 20 |
| 2003 | | 17 |
| 2004 | | 13 |
| 2005 | | 13 |
| 2006 | | 19 |
| 2007 | | 19 |
| Total | | 226 |

The 28 sponsoring unions were AEEU, Amicus, ASPECT, ATL, AUT, BALPA, CATU, CMA, Community, Connect, CWU, FDA, GPMU, IPMS, ISTC, KFAT, MPO, MSF, NATFHE, NUJ, PCS, Prospect, SoR, TGWU, TSSA, Unifi, Unison and USDAW.

*Sources:* Heery *et al.* (2003a); <http://www.tuc.org.uk/organisation>.

In addition to training new organizers, the Organizing Academy now trains existing union officials, and two TUC-affiliated unions, TGWU and USDAW, have set up their own internal academies.

Assessing success is difficult because there are no published data or recorded accounts of campaigns in which Academy trainees have been involved. The verdict of Heery and his colleagues after two years of the Academy was upbeat. However, only one of the 17 unions involved in the Academy between 1998 and 2000, USDAW, recorded an increase in membership (Heery *et al.* 2000c: 402). There are occasional accounts of Academy successes: for instance, in the TUC's *Organizing to Win* (TUC 2003b), a campaign at Hugh Baird College in Merseyside is recalled in which NATFHE-sponsored Academy trainee, Martyn Moss, worked with the local branch and, after six months, membership tripled and density increased to around 80 per cent. Subsequently the branch won 'negotiation rights on pay, hours and other conditions, a newly constituted consultative body and facilities with time-off for branch officers' (TUC 2003b: 7). Another Academy trainee at Unison, Phil Siddle, was drafted in to support Sandwell Unison branch, which covered three hospitals in the Black Country where membership had dropped below 1,000 with only five branch officers. After an organizing campaign that involved mapping and newsletter distribution as well as employing the TUC-developed Winning the Organized Workplace (WOW) – training for 12 new activists – and targeted recruitment at particular occupational groups, they recruited 200 new members and identified 25 new activists (TUC 2003b: 8–9).

WOW was intended to complement the drive into new areas by mopping up and in-fill operations. Recognizing that it is rare for even the best-organized workplaces to have 100 per cent density, noting research that there are over three million non-members employed in recognized establishments and conceding that approximately one-third of recognized workplaces have no union representative, the TUC launched WOW as a national skills training programme (TUC 1997: 3.7). Its aim was to equip union officials and lay representatives with the tools of best practice in organization and recruitment. WOW sessions would be relevant to particular workplaces where the students are employed and operate on a workshop basis.

The TUC's new role has also taken unions and Academy trainees out of the workplace and into the community. In 1998 Academy organizers attended the Glastonbury Festival and flooded the event with 'I want to join a union' leaflets. They combined this activity with a questionnaire intended to determine where the young people at the festival worked and their attitudes to unions (TUC 1998: 65). Whilst acknowledging that there is 'no substitute for workplace based organizing', the TUC argued that community activities such as this 'help warm up the climate and . . . provide a useful complementary route to unionisation' (ibid: 65). It also forms part of their strategy to get younger workers into the union movement (TUC 1999: 32–3). Similar initiatives included Students at Work – a collaborative project with the National Union of Students (NUS) – and Union City – a TUC initiative in the Midlands to bring various unions together in a geographical area to highlight issues such as 'unemployment, low skill levels and issues around enforcement of the minimum wage' (TUC 2002: 67).

Following recommendations in the *Reaching the Missing Millions* report (TUC 2001b) the TUC launched a website, workSMART, to provide 'advice, information and some limited services for people at work . . . a gateway to union membership' (TUC 2002: 72). A year later the TUC launched the 'Union Reps – Winning Respect at Work' campaign with an associated website which would use 'a system of electronic discussion boards [for] reps . . . to discuss their work with each other and with expert specialist guides' (TUC 2003a: 115). The UnionReps website has over 10,000 registered users and in 2007 the TUC launched UnionScope which aims to 'track down exactly where unions have recognition or membership . . . use the power of the web to help reps, members and union officers collaborate in mapping out our deals and members, in one place for the first time . . . [it] will be used to help recommend unions to prospective members, powering services such as the workSMART unionfinder, and the TUC's Know Your Rights Line' (TUC 2007).

In 2003 the NUTG merged with the Representation at Work Task Group to form the Organizing and Representation at Work Task Group. This aimed to 'integrate more effectively' the organizing work of the TUC with its campaigns for rights in the workplace (TUC 2004: 7). This step could be seen to help rectify the anomaly of well-prepared organizing campaigns counting for little because of the failure to have any post-recognition workplace strategy (cf. Simms 2006). This approach was strengthened two years later when the TUC launched 'Bargaining to Organize' (B2O), which aimed to use collective bargaining as a focus for organizing and recruitment and improve support for workplace representatives (TUC 2006: 7).

## Organizing: individual unions

In response to TUC activity, its affiliated unions have mounted a variety of organizing initiatives. They range from campaigns by Amicus to organize students and attempts by the GMB to use language training to organize Polish workers to global initiatives between the TGWU and American workers (Tattersall 2007). However, as table 8.2 demonstrates, in numbers alone at least, the outcome across unions is uneven and patchy.

The TGWU was one of the first to take action. It allocated funds for increased recruitment and organizing, and emphasized the need for a new culture in which the emphasis should shift to the 'most important resource – the active and committed lay member' (TGWU 1998). There was a considerable gap between this rhetoric and any discernible national TGWU organizing orientation. For a long period, only Region 6 in the north-west of England had an organizing section which employed organizers. Even here, there were problems and tensions. These organizers were on temporary contracts, paid substantially less than union officers and struggled for resources and general commitment from the union at large (interviews with organizers, 1999–2002). More recently the TGWU claimed to have adopted the principles of the organizing model and increased its activity in greenfield sites (TGWU 2005).

In 2003 the union launched a Strategy for Growth and concentrated national organizing campaigns in four sectors: the meat industry, logistics, aviation and building services, including cleaning. They now have 86 full-time organizers across the regions. After two years the TGWU were claiming success with 549 new shop stewards and more than 19,000 new members from the national campaigns. These successes were achieved at EasyJet, FlyBe, TNT, UPS, Two Sisters and, for cleaners, at Canary Wharf, the Houses of Parliament, Marshalls and Thomas Cook. The organizing successes also included bargaining wins such as an agreement to include flight allowances in holiday pay at EasyJet and a 10 per cent pay rise at UPS (TGWU 2007). In addition to its sector-specific organizing, the TGWU also launched a 100 per cent campaign which encouraged existing full-time officers to increase membership in workplaces where there is already a membership base.

Today the TGWU forms part of the new super union, Unite. In 2006 its partner union, Amicus, implemented an Organizing for Growth Strategy: this centres on officials providing leadership to workplace representatives. The

*Table 8.2* Union growth / decline (disaggregated) 1997–2006: selected unions

| | 2005–6 | 1997–98 | Growth / Decline |
|---|---|---|---|
| Amicus | 1,179,655 | 881,625 (AEEU); 416,000 (MSF); 203,229 (GPMU); 106,007 (Unifi)[a] 1,606,861 (TOTAL) | –427,206 |
| ATL | 203,241 | 168,027 | +35,214 |
| BMA | 137,361 | 106,864 | +30,497 |
| CATU / Unity | 7,239 | 20,478 | –13,239 |
| CWU | 244,461 | 287,732 | –43,271 |
| GMB | 575,105 | 712,000 | –136,895 |
| Community (ISTC) | 33,459 | 50,001 (ISTC) 32,164 (KFAT) | –48,706 |
| NASUWT | 289,930 | 250,783 | +39,147 |
| NUT | 361,987 | 286,503 | +75,484 |
| PCS | 312,725 | 245,350 | +67,375 |
| Prospect | 102,161 | n/a (EMA) 62,515 (IPMS) | n/a |
| RCN | 391,347 | 320,206 | +71,141 |
| TGWU | 777,325 | 881,625 | –104,300 |
| TSSA | 30,570 | 31,132 | –562 |
| UCATT | 121,109 | 111,804 | +9,305 |
| Unison | 1,317,000 | 1,272,330 | +44,670 |
| USDAW | 340,653 | 303,060 | +37,593 |

*Source:* Certification Officer, *Annual Reports* (1997–2007); individual union returns to the Certification Officer (2007); TUC (1998).

*Note:*
a This figure only includes the membership of BIFU. The membership numbers for BWSU, NWSU and WISA were unavailable. Therefore, Unifi membership figures (1997–8) cited in the table are an underestimation of real membership which makes the decline for Amicus between 1997 and 2006 even greater.

strategy necessitates every Amicus official identifying two key targets within their area of responsibility where there is potential to build higher membership levels and stronger workplace organization. All Amicus officials are required to attend training which has been jointly developed with the TUC Organizing Academy. Training is key to Amicus strategy. It is based on *Organizing Skills* courses – one-day training modules specific to a particular region, sector or workplace (Amicus 2006: 9). It remains to be seen how the organizing agenda will be pursued in the newly merged union and whether the TGWU's own organizing academy will survive restructuring. However, it should be noted that membership decline was an important driver of the Unite merger and the investment in organizing of neither of its components had managed to stem it (see McIlroy and Daniels, chapter 3, this volume).

In contrast USDAW has increased its membership. In 2003 it became the first TUC affiliate to establish its own Academy with 15 organizing officers. It subsequently enrolled 18 organizing officers in 2004, 23 in 2005 and 29 in 2006 (USDAW 2007). Organizing officers are recruited from USDAW's membership. The union arranges time off with employers and pays their wages. On completion of the six-month secondment, the reps return to their workplaces to further their organizing work. USDAW claims that its Academy organizers have recruited 25,000 new members and 2,000 new reps and activists (USDAW 2007). This is a union that has had historical difficulties organizing in sectors with a high turnover of workers. Union density in the retail sector is around 11 per cent. However, its partnership agreement with Tesco has created a membership density of over 50 per cent – greater than any other national bargaining unit in the private sector. For the most part USDAW has eschewed 'bottom-up' organizing for a 'top-down' approach. The union attempts to secure recognition from employers and then use its organizers as 'travelling recruitment officers' to generate membership from within (Heery *et al.* 2003b: 83). USDAW has recently introduced new software which functions as a database of its workplace representatives across the UK.

Only the TGWU and USDAW have set up specific organizing academies. Other unions have chosen to up-skill existing staff. For example, PCS, through its Organizing and Learning Services Department, is providing all staff with an organizing remit. In 2007 Unison overhauled its internal structures, developed organizing roles for all its staff and mounted intensive training programmes. Training is seen at the heart of developing organizing by the TUC and many affiliates have got the message.

> The move towards organizing has involved a fundamental cultural change. For it to succeed, we will need to engage our entire membership. TSSA's reps have a vital role to play in this process and TSSA continued to prioritise their training and development . . . The training offered to staff and safety reps is designed to build skills and knowledge . . . The theme of TSSA's summer school . . . was building an organizing union.
>
> (TSSA 2005: 8)

But training has not halted membership decline: 2005 proved to be another disappointing year for TSSA. The union's membership fell by a further 3.3 per cent; 4,638 members left TSSA, of whom only around 1,432 did so because they had left their jobs. Compared to 2004 there was a large decline (17 per cent) in the number of new members joining the union in 2005 (TSSA 2006). The union leadership reflected:

This disappointing performance was due, in part, to TSSA lacking its full complement of paid recruiters, organizers and other staff for a significant proportion of the year. Our staff make numerous visits to a multitude of workplaces, and our experience continues to demonstrate that face-to-face contact is still the best way to get people to join TSSA. However, it should also be noted that recruitment from lay reps and members remained stable when it would have been reasonable in the circumstances to expect it to increase during 2005.

(TSSA 2005: 4)

Nevertheless, their five-year campaign to organize the travel trade, which was launched in 2002, has notched up some successes. Wills (2003) examined the work of the Greenfield Site Team (GST) of the TSSA and followed their first organizing campaign at Seacat. She stresses the importance of significant resources to sustain an organizing campaign and nurture workplace organization. Paradoxically, Wills found greater willingness to join a union among the sea-going workers than the offshore call centre workers. Yet it was the latter, in Belfast and Liverpool, who finally won a recognition agreement with Seacat. Despite identifying issues of discontent and workers ready to become activists, the GST met formidable problems, including some degree of inter-union competition with the RMT, court injunctions and management importing of strike-breaking labour from Estonia, the Isle of Man, Belfast and Liverpool.

MSF moved into organizing early. But their experience demonstrated the problems. According to Carter, 'no other union in Britain ha[d] witnessed attempted change as dramatic as MSF in its adoption of . . . the organizing model' (Carter 2000: 119). However, there was widespread resistance from full-time officers and Carter believes that this frustrated the very real opportunities that existed for building organizing by mobilizing rank-and-file activists to rebuild workplace organization. The ISTC and the GPMU had 'shown particular commitment to organizing non-union sites' (Heery *et al.* 2003b: 80). The GPMU set up its own Recruitment, Retention and Re-Organisation Programme which combined organizing and recruiting new members with providing an effective service for existing members. The union was also the strongest supporter of the TUC Organizing Academy (Gennard *et al.* 2000: 44–5). The ISTC has been widely cited as adopting core practices of the organizing model (see, for instance, Heery *et al.* 2003a; Wills 2001; Findlay and McKinlay 2003ab). In one case, at Fullarton Computer Industries (FCI) in Ayrshire, worker disenchantment broke out when management withdrew a ten-minute break. This provided the catalyst for an ISTC organizing campaign. Although there had been a works council, this lost credibility with employees at FCI when management announced 'it was not a negotiating body but existed simply to relay information to the workforce' (Findlay and McKinlay 2003b: 56). Employee grievance and employer intransigence were important ingredients that fired this campaign but it was the readiness

of the union to lead a militant organizing campaign and challenge management that was most significant (Findlay and McKinlay 2003b: 57–8).

In 2002 MSF became part of Amicus. The GPMU followed in 2004. Amicus
itself is now part of Unite, which was formed in 2007. The ISTC merged with
KFAT to form Community (see McIlroy and Daniels, chapter 4, this volume). Before this merger activity the ISTC and the AEEU (the union that
merged with MSF to found Amicus) were the subjects of a study of organizing.
Researching Scotland's 'Silicon Glen', Findlay and McKinlay (2003a) consider the role of *shadow stewards* (unofficial workplace representatives in non-
recognized workplaces) in organizing campaigns. Using three case-studies at
IBM, Chunghwa Picture Tubes (CPT) and Fullerton Computer Industries
(FCI), Findlay and McKinlay map the fortunes of the AEEU and ISTC in
campaigns initiated and led by lay activists. In each instance the campaigns
faltered due to different degrees of 'basic inadequacies in union support
mechanisms' and, in the AEEU case, their accommodative approach. The
lesson drawn was the need to overcome the difficulties of the complex balance
between bottom-up adversarialism and top-down co-ordination (ibid.: 132).
It is this lack of coordination between the official structures of the union and
organization in the workplace that can be a significant contributor to recognition failure. Simms (2003) has emphasized the problems MSF encountered in
attempting to organize a diverse workforce in the not-for-profit sector. She
concluded that issue-campaigning alone does not suffice. Such an approach
had some merit in the charity's headquarters, where workers were more geo-
graphically and occupationally cohesive and there was greater opportunity
to exchange ideas and discuss workplace issues. It is much more problematic
when a union is attempting to organize atomized shop workers where
opportunities for workplace discourse are limited.

Current organizing activity by Community appears patchy. It has recently
initiated campaigns to organize workers in the 'Big 3' bookmakers (with
support from television betting pundit, John McCririck) and those working
'behind the scenes' in the football industry, but there is little information
about the success rate. All three bookmakers (Ladbrokes, Coral and William
Hill) have resisted union attempts to organize their staff with Ladbrokes
claiming that the existing Staff Council proves to be 'a very effective channel
of communication' (Community 2007). Community's website only mentions
two 'successful' organizing campaigns. The first was MultiServ (formerly
Brambles) at Corus in Port Talbot, which, over 18 months, almost doubled its
membership and regenerated the branch. The second is a small company – 60
staff, of which 40 are union members. It has recognized the union since the
1970s but recently signed a partnership agreement with Community – there is
no mention of an organizing campaign. Despite early enthusiasm from
Community evidenced by their prominent role (in the form of ISTC and
KFAT) in the TUC's Organizing Academy, organizing now appears partial
and limited with servicing being emphasised to potential members: 'Community has a better ratio of full-time officers to members than any other

union. We also have a member service centre ready to answer any questions, give advice and assist you at work' (Community 2008).

One of the major unions continuously involved in the TUC Organizing Academy has been the Public and Commercial Services Union (PCS). Its membership of 313,000 (60 per cent female) includes a wide range of occupations, from cleaners to middle managers, in departments and agencies in the civil service and in newly privatized agencies – the common employer of the civil service has been fragmented since 1994 into 229 bargaining units. With the TUC, the PCS has developed a strategic training programme, enabling all full-time organizers to be trained by the TUC Organizing Academy, as well as training all lay organizers. The PCS has built organizing into its union education programmes and holds regular organizing conferences in every region (TUC 2005: 47–8). In a difficult environment, where many members are threatened with severe job cuts through government plans to overhaul the civil service, the PCS, as part of its National Organizing Strategy, has recorded some success including recognition campaigns at the Electoral Commission, BAA Business Services Centre in Glasgow and the National Maritime Museum where the union was de-recognised in 1997. PCS also secured recognition for agency workers in Workington at the British Cattle Movement Service (PCS 2007: 3). Despite the impact of privatization and workforce reductions, it has increased its activists by about 8,000 and total membership by 27 per cent since 1997 (see table 8.2). In the face of major changes in its organizing and bargaining environment, PCS has become one of the few successful organizing unions.

The CWU has established its own national organizing department, which oversees recruitment and organizing, the conduct of ballots, and union structure below headquarters. At their 2006 conference it was decided to double the number of organizing trainees. Despite its high-profile and unsuccessful campaign at T-Mobile, the CWU continues to focus a lot of its organizing activity on the big mobile phone companies. One union that has had some success in this industry is Connect, which has recently secured recognition in part of Vodafone. Perhaps the most successful of the organizing campaigns which have been documented in detail is that of the CWU at Excell and then Vertex (Taylor and Bain 2003).

This initiative was not without problems and significant lessons continue to be ignored. The ingredients for success were apparent: deep-rooted discontent among workers ranging from monotony, performance targets, poor wages, long shifts, management bullying and an unpopular bonus scheme. Despite a strong sense of injustice, the CWU was unable to mobilize more than 30 per cent of workers as tensions mounted between workplace activists and national officials who had blocked various organizing activities for fear of upsetting ongoing partnership negotiations with Cable and Wireless – Excell's major client. After sixteen months of campaigning, Excell launched a counter-mobilization against the union, including the sacking of two key workplace activists for disclosure of poor working conditions to the media.

This attracted adverse publicity and Cable and Wireless transferred its operations to an alternative outsource supplier, Vertex. It took a further two years to win a recognition ballot (ibid.: 169). This did not stop recriminations about union officers from local activists who believed they could have won recognition within weeks of the transfer had it not been for the union's more accommodative strategy. The experiences at Excell and Vertex bring into question the 'TUC's perspective that the "organizing model" can co-exist with partnership without the emergence of profound contradictions' (ibid.: 171).

But the problems are not just at the organizing stage. Simms explored the transition from a successful CWU organizing campaign to post-recognition representation at CallCo – 'an autonomous business unit of the CallCare charity' – employing around 350 workers at two sites in Liverpool (Simms 2006: 170). In an unanticipated lengthy campaign initiated by a CWU-sponsored Organizing Academy trainee, union recognition was achieved after two years. Simms argues that unions lack a post-organizing strategy which serves to alienate a newly won membership, undermine activism and contribute to an early decline in workplace organization (ibid.: 180).

Following the Unison merger the union adopted aspects of both servicing and organizing models. For instance, it spent over £14 million on member benefits and services. However, in the light of survey data on union-leavers which indicated that union services were considerably less important than collective issues, Unison shifted its emphasis towards the 'organizing model' and an attempt to increase lay member participation through the 'be active!' initiative (Waddington and Kerr 2000: 249–52). Over recent years Unison has concentrated its organizing agenda on the training of its lay representatives.

The GMB created its own National Organizing team in 2006, headed by Martin Smith, but despite this, and in keeping with the traditions of the union, there is still a great deal of autonomy in the regions. On a national level, in 2006 the GMB successfully secured a recognition agreement with Securicor where it now organizes 15,500 workers. More widely it has formed a coalition with Solidarność, the widely known Polish trade union, to ensure Polish workers coming to the UK are familiar with their individual employment rights as well as, for instance, in the southern region, providing language training, job training and work placement (GMB Press Release, 12 January 2007).

Smaller unions, like the NUJ, have grown significantly as they orientated to organizing. The NUJ was one of the unions which suffered most from derecognition by employers through the 1980s and early 1990s. Consequently, it lost a great deal of members. Since 1997, utilizing New Labour's legislation and prosecuting issue-based organizing campaigns, the NUJ have turned the tide. However, even if, as the NUJ has done, these smaller unions increase their membership by 15 per cent, this is going to have little impact on the overall aggregate UK union membership.

### Problems in organizing

But not all TUC affiliated unions have embraced organizing. Following a study of three unions (Connect, GPMU and TSSA), BECTU decided the costs outweighed the benefits. For instance, TSSA employed 16 organizing officials and, in 2003, developed a 'business plan' to ensure that the costs of such investment in organizers would be met in increased membership dues by 2005. However, after two years of this initiative they were significantly behind target. Even though they stopped the decline in union membership and showed a small growth, this was at the cost of a significantly higher wage bill (BECTU 2003). Connect faced a similar financial predicament '. . . some people inside Connect would tell you it has been a success, but at this stage by our calculations the union is still subsidising it to a level of approximately £100,000 per annum' (ibid.: para. 214). BECTU further observed that:

> The GPMU initiative has been a failure, mostly because the branches were not signed up to the initiative and many of them resented the idea of head office sending them staff which they had to pay for. Also, there was no coherent policy on what these individuals would do.
>
> (BECTU 2003: para. 213)

The TUC's objective of promoting a culture of organizing within affiliated unions has proved immensely difficult. BECTU is not the only union to have rejected it. Resistance has been strong. Chiefly, this is because of union officer opposition to the relocation of resources from servicing to organizing (Carter 2000: 119; Heery *et al.* 2003b: 83). In some unions, organizers and officers 'do not speak to each other' (interviews with activists, 2008). Fletcher and Hurd noted similar resistance in the United States: union officials wedded to the servicing approach were unwilling to let go; a reluctance, on the part of union officials, to let members organize their own workplace; and steward dependence on union officials vis-à-vis advice (Fletcher and Hurd 1998: 42).

But internal impediments have not been the only problem: rhetoric from the top is not matched by practice on the ground. The TUC has repeatedly asserted its explicit commitment to break into new sectors and 'organize the unorganized': 'we need to get into new areas of the economy where we have no base – the media, telecoms and services' (interviews with activists, 2001). But there is little hard evidence of unions penetrating new workplaces. While accompanying trade unionists on organizing activities with both organizers within and outside of the Academy, it was clear to this author that 'favourable' relatively high-density organizing environments were preferred. In effect, organizing the (partly) organized. One regional union official explained:

> We haven't [taken on greenfield sites] because we have so much potential in existing companies where we have existing membership or agreements

and we have got massive potential even in the likes of Tesco where we have got 80,000 members so it's still another 60,000 to get.

(interviews with activists, 2002)

The rhetoric of the proponents of the organizing model, to the effect that organizing is more than recruitment, rings rather hollow. Insights from interviews and participant observation are backed by an assessment of recently-won recognition deals in which 'the overwhelming bulk of these new deals have been secured in areas of traditional strength – manufacturing, production and engineering, and to a lesser extent, parts of the former public sector' (O'Grady and Nowak 2004: 157). In effect, trade unions in the UK are 'circling the wagons' (Bronfenbrenner and Juravich 1998: 19).

Nevertheless, for TUC staff 'there are enough new "wins" in areas such as catering, new media and, more generally, the private sector as a whole, to suggest that unions can make inroads into areas of traditional weakness' (O'Grady and Nowak 2004: 157). But the evidence of significant organizing activity in these sectors remains thin. Breaking out of existing union terrain has proved difficult for most TUC-affiliated unions. Whether to consolidate where there is strength or to organize new workers is an age-old conundrum. But for many unions, although far from all, despite the novel rhetoric of the organizing model, today's approach appears little different to that taken by unions in the 1980s and 1990s (see, for example, Beaumont and Harris 1990: 274–86; Kelly and Heery 1994). The traditional and, in some cases, entrenched proclivity to concentrate recruitment in union heartlands and 'mop up' in existing workplaces where unions are recognized has proved hard to resist. This was evident even in the early days of the Academy when two-thirds of the first cohort of Organizing Academy trainees reported that they had had limited success in identifying 'new' recruitment targets (Cardiff Research Bulletin 1999: 6). In one sense, consolidation is a perfectly rational response in terms of resources when millions of potential members are at arm's length. Yet continuing to concentrate on a 'healthy' unionized environment is likely to enlarge the gulf between an organized core and the non-organized areas. This will erode union influence in the rapidly growing sectors of the economy and exacerbate future union membership difficulties.

Infill, per se, does not necessarily contradict the ethos of the organizing model. Strengthening existing union bases is an important part of today's renewal strategy: 'in-fill organizing can be "adversarial", based on identifying and exploiting grievances around traditional union issues, such as health and safety, workplace discipline and management style' (Heery *et al.* 2003b: 81). But infill campaigns take different forms. Most such activity takes the form of service-selling. This activity fails to mobilize the membership, revitalize workplace organization or pose any challenge to management prerogative.

Some employers are engaged in mounting counter-mobilizations with a range of union-busting tactics such as appointing armies of barristers to engage in litigation – often frivolous – to draw out a union-recognition process as long as possible: the threat of site closures or relocations; the fostering of division between employees; supervisor one-to-ones; staff forums and disciplinary action; and even dismissal against workplace union leaders on trumped-up charges (see, for example, Moore 2004: 16–21; Kelly and Badigannavar 2004). The experience of the CWU at T-Mobile (see O'Grady and Nowak 2004: 152), where union-busting consultants were employed to counter union campaigning, is also instructive. However, employer counter-mobilizations are par for the course and have always been something unions have had to face. Employer hostility, in and of itself, is not a reason for defeat. In fact, it is tactical errors by unions that often contribute to failure (Kelly and Badigannavar 2004).

More generally, strengthening the workplace branch is a key part of the strategy. According to one senior union official on the New Unionism Task Group there is the need for 'building up representatives' confidence and skills because an organizing union very much depends on the lay reps to do much of the work in the workplace' (interviews with activists, 2002). But organizers themselves are increasingly, in many unions, 'organized' top-down through systematic techniques such as performance management targets. This has encouraged some union organizers 'to focus more on returning back to the office with a briefcase full of membership forms than on encouraging reps and activists to take responsibility, and credit, for this work for themselves' (O'Grady and Nowak 2004: 155). The New Labour obsession with targets has infused the TUC's prescribed activism; all too often activism is directed, controlled and managed from the top.

Even senior officials have conceded the shortfalls in such an approach: 'as a top-down project, it has also been difficult to inculcate an organizing culture amongst the . . . workplace representatives with only a small minority prioritising recruitment and organizing' (O'Grady and Nowak 2004: 155). The centrality of the workplace activist in the organizing model does raise the pertinent question, if the TUC is, as it says, convinced that revitalization must come from below and that the basis of organizing is self-activity in the workplace, why has it fostered such a top-down approach? The workplace activist is crucial to union renewal: their efforts (without pay and often in their own time) are the single most important factor in reaching out to non-members, promoting member participation and mobilizing workers in the quest for collective demands and against employer attacks. Indeed, in any practical sense, most unions are financially dependent on the voluntary labour of workplace activists (Willman and Bryson 2006).

I asked today's TUC head of organization, Paul Nowak, for his thoughts about organizing over the last ten years and his summary evoked *A Tale of Two Cities*: 'It was the best of times, it was the worst of times, it was the age of wisdom, it was the age of foolishness, it was the epoch of belief, it was the epoch of incredulity. . . .' Overall Nowak believes that the union movement is moving in the right direction but problems remain. He insists that the TUC has made a difference. He compared today with before 1997: 'Then we were fighting off derecognition in all corners of the economy – today we are out there doing a lot more organizing and winning new deals.'

## Arguments, problems and contradictions

The TUC organizing model has thus encountered a range of difficulties in practice and its success is so far limited. It is still seen as central to union revitalization by trade unionists at every level and by academics. Advocacy sometimes rests on invocation of the past as inspiration, utilization of the experience of organizing in other countries and the assertion that the practice of organizing in Britain in recent years derives from models developed by academics, the implementation of which would make revitalization more likely. I will look at each in turn.

### 1. Long ago

De Turberville exaggerates when he includes in the underpinning of contemporary organizing 'a golden-age of organizing hypothesis that legitimizes the model as being historically effective' (de Turberville 2004: 778). Proponents of organizing do not 'rely' on the past (Carter 2006: 418). But activists do sometimes invoke it to legitimate and inspire what they are doing (Daniels 2006) and while American academics have found explanations of the past useful for understanding the present (Fiorito 2003), the relative failure of their British colleagues to undertake proper historical reconstruction, as distinct from occasional reference to trade union history, arguably debilitates our understanding of contemporary industrial relations (Lyddon 2003).

The past is important

> so long as we realise that what we are dealing in are the complexities and complications of history, not the simplistic narratives and cosmeticised protagonists of myth and iconography. So long as we are conscious of the differences as well as the similarities that exist between distinctive eras. So long as we perceive what we have in common and what distinguishes us from previous generations of trade unionists.
>
> (McIlroy and Daniels 2007)

The shop stewards movement of 1914–18, the campaigns in America of the Industrial Workers of the World and the organizing drives of the 1930s in both Britain and America are sometimes discussed as examples of what can be and what cannot be achieved (de Turberville 2004; McIlroy and Daniels 2007). The most recent persistent parallel I found being made by activists in the early days of the TUC's New Unionism was one from long ago. They drew comparisons between the contemporary situation and the upsurge of New Unionism at the end of the 1880s. Activists would refer to the matchworkers' strike at Bryant and May and the struggle for 'the docker's tanner' in 1888 (Daniels 2006).

What they took from their understanding of those events was a sense of potential, élan and mission. The past encouraged optimism and drove action in the present. It strengthened their confidence and affirmed for them that workers were not simply victims of economic and political events beyond their control. They could make a difference. They could make their own future. Specifically, they could organize the unorganized. There are few matchworkers or dockers today. Exploited young people – women, migrant workers, the unskilled – remain with us (Daniels 2006).

In today's world we must re-emphasize the role of agency (Heery and Simms 2008). But we must remember that the growth of New Unionism in the 1880s developed in particular circumstances and encountered counter-mobilization. Like the shop stewards movement during the First World War or the CIO organizing drive in America in the 1930s, we have to see the human factor and organizing strategy in specific contexts. We have to relate action and leadership, which are indispensable, to a web of interrelating factors from the policy of the state and the state of the economy to conditions of consciousness of the working class and the effectiveness of trade unionism (Bain and Price 1983; Undy *et al.* 1981). If we do so we see that although we can learn from the past that we can make gains in the present, these gains are constrained by factors which were not present during past eras of union success (Charlwood 2004).

Differences in context are important. So are differences in leadership and approach. The most significant impetus in key periods of growth based on organizing, rather than state policies as in the 1960s and 1970s (Towers 2003: 188), came from the bottom, not the top of the movement. The impetus came from the workplace, not from Congress House. The organizers were lay militants, often socialist activists, often opposed to the then existing forms of trade unionism and its current leadership, not salaried professionals trained by that leadership (McIlroy and Daniels 2007). Perhaps what the lessons of history hold for us today is not the absolutist conception that initiatives always have to come from below but the more nuanced lesson that if initiatives come from above they will not succeed unless they stimulate and hand over control to activists in the workplace. The past can help in developing the organizing model. It can also help in giving us a realistic idea of what is and what is not possible today.

## 2. And far away

The lessons of history can provide inspiration for union activists today. In terms of strategy, positive pointers from the past necessitate adaptation to a different world. The lessons from abroad employed by the TUC also require careful consideration and flexible adaptation. It is the American movement and the turn to organizing of the AFL-CIO in the mid-1990s which has exercised the greatest influence on the TUC approach since 1997. The writings of radical US academics have had at least as great an impact on the ideas of their British counterparts. Yet as interest burgeoned, sceptics observed:

> Can we see the future of British trade unions in America today? If so, it looks like a future of declining influence. Membership dropped from 22 million in 1975 to 16 million by 1990 with density today around 15 per cent . . . the USA would seem to provide lessons of what to avoid rather than emulate.
>
> (McIlroy 1995: 414–15)

Despite increased investment in organizing, heralded by John Sweeney as head of the AFL-CIO, there has been little increase in membership, density or power. Despite an impressive array of activities, including coalition-building and international campaigns, as well as organizing, partnership and political action, American unions have continued to decline on all dimensions of revitalization (Kelly and Frege 2004). American unions are not better off in terms of density than they were in 1952.

The growth of organizing, the influence of the AFL-CIO Organizing Institute and the specialist organizing departments in individual unions has to be set in this context. So has the influence of the organizing model developed by American academics which prioritizes aggressive, adversarial, creative campaigning using trained organizers to mobilize grassroots and stimulate self-organization (Bronfenbrenner and Juravich 1998). Much of the rhetoric and some of the substance has been absorbed into union activity. There has been an increase in the resources devoted to organizing in some unions (Hurd *et al.* 2003). But progress has been uneven. One commentator judges: 'the focus on organizing by the AFL-CIO in the last few years has clearly not uncapped a powerful wellspring of desire for unionization' (Heckscher 2001: 59). The radical view that recruiting at the grassroots just needs the right approach is questionable. A recent survey concluded that even unions which have led the 'transforming to organize movement' have failed to score consistently impressive organizing gains (Fiorito and Jarley 2003: 207–8).

Academics maintain on the basis of their studies of wins and losses that their approach holds the key to success (Bronfenbrenner 2003: 41). Evidence for this is cited from case studies (see for example the collections by Milkman 2000 and Milkman and Voss 2004). But the success of specific initiatives finds little reflection in the stubborn endurance of aggregate membership decline, despite increases in particular years. Despite everything, the USA has not seen union revitalization. As in Britain, success may rest on the fact that organizing staves off what would have been a more extensive decline. Nonetheless, aggregate statistics and systemic studies provide little evidence for the confident assertion that 'at the dawn of a new century the American labour movement shows signs of resurgence that make it as much a model of renewal as a prototype to decline' (Bronfenbrenner 2003: 32). Fiorito, who provides a sober and nuanced picture, suggests the need for greater coordination and centralization (Fiorito 2003: 209). It is more than a little ironic that shortly after he wrote, the AFL-CIO split: part of the reason was disputation over its organizing approach, lauded by the TUC. The main components of the 2005 split were the Teamsters and the Service Employees International Union (SEIU). The SEIU and particularly its leader, Andy Stern, have attracted support in Britain from the TUC and latterly the TGWU for the vigour and vision of their organizing strategy.

There can be little doubt about its success. Under Stern's leadership the SEIU has tripled its membership to 1.8 million. But its critics assert that in the new 'Change to Win' Coalition the organizing model adopted is qualitatively different from that elaborated by American and British radicals. It is argued that innovation involves:

> . . . a sternly top-down structure which would, as one critique puts it, 'bureaucratize to organize' . . . locals have lost all control over bargaining and answer to business agents appointed from above . . . As an example of 'organizing' rather than the 'service' model, it is not a promising portent.
>
> (Cohen 2006: 154–5)

If Stern's organizing zeal is unquestionable, it is firmly inserted into the politics of partnership. Stern insists that trade unionists must 'find ways to persuade business leaders to work in partnership with them' (Stern 2006: 37). He supports the free market, signs no-strike agreements against the wishes of his members and believes that 'the distrust [of employers] can be rightfully earned, but this class-struggle mentality was a vestige of an earlier, rough era of industrial unions' (ibid.: 70–1). A measured scepticism about what is happening in America still seems preferable to exaggerated views of what has been achieved as a basis for emulation in Britain.

### 3. Real organizing

For some academics, organizing has become a significant vehicle for a transformation of British trade unionism driven by antagonism between bureaucracy and accommodation on the one hand and a democratic participative independent rank and file on the other expounded in the 1990s (Fosh 1993; Fairbrother 2000; Cohen 2006). From this perspective the fragmentation of national pay bargaining, particularly in the public sector, under Conservative governments provided a significant potential stimulus towards active self-regulating workplace organization. It opened the possibility of a new militant unity and coordination across employment based on rank-and-file organization with the external union at best a secondary support (Fairbrother 1996). This approach to renewal was criticized from different vantage points: it was seen as fetishizing democracy; marginalizing politics and consciousness;

downplaying agency; and glossing over the harsh realities of contemporary industrial relations (McIlroy 1995; Gall 1998; Terry 2003).

In their analysis of organizing, proponents of this rank-and-file, transformative version of renewal continue to stress the primary initiating role of grassroots activism and the centrality of democratic participative workplace structure. *Real* organizing on this basis is the route to qualitative change in the very nature of trade unionism (Carter 2006). Despite their radicalism, the TUC's advocacy of union transformation seems to have been taken by at least some of these writers as good coin. But its realization in practice is obstructed by the inability of Congress House – presumably as part of the bureaucratic element of trade unionism they criticize – to intervene in the internal activities of affiliates and undermined by the attempt to combine organizing with partnership (Fairbrother and Stewart 2003: 167–75). In contrast, for these academics real organizing as elaborated by American scholars centres almost completely on 'support for democratization, training and militant action' from below. Those in Britain who adopt this vantage point go on to take other British academics to task for an insufficiently critical view of official initiatives and for reducing 'the radical vision' of real organizing into the TUC's 'managed activism'. By doing this, mainstream academics allegedly indulge in the 'distortion of the original idea' (Carter 2006: 218).

There may, genuinely and legitimately, be different conceptions of 'the original idea' and how best to realize it. Any organizing model has to be related to the specific conditions of British trade unions and the practice of the TUC and affiliated unions. 'Original ideas' have to reflect, and in some cases adapt, to reality. A prerequisite of any viable strategy of transformative organizing is acknowledgement of the difficulties it confronts in the face of the current weakness and conservative culture of British trade unionism at all levels. This is rooted in both the contemporary climate and in history.

Grassroots organization, rank-and-file ambition and the 'challenge from below' are at their lowest ebb since the early 1930s. Proponents of 'real organizing' claim that this verdict 'ignores evidence of initiatives in the direction of democratization and militancy from workers themselves' (Carter 2006: 418). Although no examples are given, they certainly do exist in continuing strikes and the efforts of factions and rank-and-file groups (see McIlroy and Daniels, chapter 4, and Lyddon, chapter 10, this volume). They are weak and often unsuccessful, isolated and circumscribed; and the only example of organizing per se, cited in a reply to critics, was, likewise, limited (Carter 2006: 421). Downplaying the conflict between bureaucratization and hierarchy and the rank and file which figured strongly in the earlier accounts of renewal (Cohen, 2006: 150–1), we are now told by advocates of rank-and-fileism that 'the role of national and local leaders in transforming unions is central. Members and leaders have a complex and frequently contradictory relationship' (Carter 2006: 422). Indeed they do. But evidence that the present leaders of British unions have a genuine interest in radical transformation as distinct from recruiting more activists and more members remains slight.

In contrast, mainstream commentators such as Waddington do not view the organizing model and the servicing model as mutually exclusive (Waddington 2003: 238–40). For the advocates of real organizing they are opposites. The role of organizers is to stimulate self-activity, not substitute for it. This recipe requires a seismic shift in all the traditions of British unions. Trade unionism has always entailed a combination of organizing and servicing, and in all probability always will. What is at stake is the mix and balance between the two. All that is on the current agenda is more organizing and less servicing. In contrast, 'the radical vision' would dissolve and reconstruct the existing social relations and the existing organization of British unions. That would in all likelihood require the dissolution and reconstruction of work, employment and society. If the TUC is an unlikely agent of such transformation it is difficult to see others accomplishing the project. 'The radical vision' is not so much revolutionary as utopian. The current task for radicals is the development of openings and possibilities in the TUC model, not its replacement by abstract blueprints.

## Conclusion

Claims that the organizing model has contributed to union renewal and revitalization in Britain (Heery *et al.* 2003a) are difficult to assess. Basic aggregate data on organizing campaigns across the UK is not available. Neither individual unions nor the TUC collate it: chiefly this is because of internal opposition to 'performance management' and 'targets'. Measuring and assessing union organizing strategy is difficult without data on campaign outcomes but 'no one wants performance management' (interviews with activists, 2008). But if we were to measure the turn to organizing on membership numbers alone then it has been an abject failure. With the exception of two relatively small increases between 1998 and 2000, aggregate union membership in Britain has continued to decline over the last ten years (see table 8.3).

*Table 8.3* Increases / decreases in aggregate union membership 1998–2006

| Year | Membership | Increase / Decrease |
|------|------------|---------------------|
| 1998 | 7,801,315  |                     |
| 1999 | 7,851,904  | +50,589             |
| 2000 | 7,897,519  | +45,615             |
| 2001 | 7,779,393  | −118,126            |
| 2002 | 7,750,990  | −28,403             |
| 2003 | 7,735,983  | −15,007             |
| 2004 | 7,559,062  | −176,921            |
| 2005 | 7,473,000  | −86,062             |
| 2006 | 7,602,842  | +129,842            |

*Source:* Certification Officer, *Annual Reports* (1997–2007)

But this is elastic inference. We cannot know how much union membership would have declined if British unions had not orientated (albeit in a limited way) to an organizing agenda. As John Monks stated: 'You never know the degree of your success since there's no way of knowing what would happen if you had done nothing' (cited in Mason and Bain 1991: 37).

By 2002 Organizing Academy graduates had 'targeted more than 1,200 employers, added nearly 40,000 new members and identified nearly 2,000 new activists. They ha[d] also established membership at 600 greenfield sites and helped secure or raise the question of recognition for more than 300 bargaining units' (Heery *et al.* 2003a: 9). In and of themselves, these figures are not overly impressive over five years. When they are broken down, they are even less remarkable: only half (659) of the workplaces targeted had previously no union presence, only a quarter of targeted workplaces had their membership rates increased to over 50 per cent, trainees were only responsible for the direct recruitment of 19,596 workers (that is 169 workers per organizer) and *actual* recognition deals numbered 84 (that is, on average, one deal every three weeks and less than one recognition victory (0.72) per Organizing Academy trainee). To date, there has been no further analysis of the TUC's Organizing Academy contribution to growth and subsequent TUC General Council Reports (2003, 2004, 2005, 2006 and 2007) make no mention of membership figures via their organizing initiatives.

Furthermore, the prospects for union growth look bleak. If we look at unions whose membership is greater than 100,000 or unions that have been involved with the Organizing Academy, a worrying picture emerges. Most unions have lost a considerable proportion of their membership since 1997. The exceptions are public sector unions, as well as UCATT and USDAW, operating in areas of employment growth (see table 8.2). Given that the organizing model's crucial aspect is the revitalization of workplace organization, a key indicator of UK success would be an upturn in the number of workplace representatives. But, according to the WERS 2004 survey, only 30 per cent of workplaces in the UK have a recognized trade union; 64 per cent of workplaces have no union members whatsoever; and less than a fifth (18 per cent) of workplaces have majority unionization – i.e. 50 per cent or more union membership (Kersley *et al.* 2005). Furthermore, numerical revival in individual workplaces in and of itself would not suffice. If workplace representatives are unable to secure greater influence over management decisions, it is likely that any membership growth would soon be reversed. For instance, at FCI, the ISTC recruited 65 per cent of the workforce within six months but management insistence on a single-plant agreement based on procedural-only issues and an initial pay rise offer of only 11p ensured this membership rate withered quickly (Findlay and McKinlay 2003b: 59–60).

It is clear that organizing has risen up the list of many union agendas over the last decade. But it is no panacea. In and of itself, it cannot reverse the severe decline that has occurred over the last three decades. The forces out there that operate against trade unions have changed, but they have not changed enough, since 1997. The New Labour governments have not made a significant difference. While they have put forward reforms such as the Employment Relations Act recognition procedure, the evidence is that New Labour's reforms have not qualitatively enhanced the possibilities of organizing.

The current context is a powerful source of constraint. The macro-economic framework of neoliberal economic policy (see McIlroy, chapters 1 and 2, this volume) and the government's resistance to further legislative reform of any substance restricts progress in organizing. An environment where employer opposition to trade unionism and the absence of large-scale discontent amongst employees, underpinned by the fact that wages have been rising at reasonable levels – although statistics show averages – in relation to low inflation, curbs employee propensity to organize (see McIlroy and Daniels, chapters 3 and 4, this volume). This does not mean that unions should adopt a fatalistic approach and renounce organizing: structural constraints are not fixed within different and across sectors. As the recent increases in inflation and the turmoil in financial markets suggest, economic stability and a benign climate for employees are far from inevitable or enduring.

Nonetheless, organizers perceive external constraints as restrictive of success, particularly 'employer opposition to trade unions'; 'lack of access to workplaces'; 'inadequate supporting legislation'; and 'poor union image' in relation to non-members whose values often do not chime with the need for organization (Heery and Simms 2008: 33–5). These problems are not insuperable. Pressures from the environment vary: some unions have done better in organizing and recruiting than others (see table 8.2). External problems may be diminished by increased political pressure and the leverage union financing of New Labour can provide – if exercised. We cannot consider the future of organizing without considering the future of trade union action in the political sphere and the development of greater political pressure and clout if the environment in which unions operate is to change.

Unions also need to develop their own organizations' practice and ideology if organizing is to possess a greater chance of achieving success. Heery and Simms demonstrate the very real internal constraints on organizing that exist in many ways. Significant problems range from the lack of resources and experience of organizers to absence of commitment or experience from workplace activists, and, further, to lack of support from full-time union staff and union leaders. As these authors argue, there are some grounds for optimism: at best some of these internal weaknesses are remediable (Heery and Simms 2008: 39). But there are grounds for pessimism in that after a decade of organizing some of these difficulties are fundamental. As the period since 1997 has demonstrated, changing the orientation of full-time officers, securing a real and practical rather than rhetorical and abstract degree of commitment to organizing from the union hierarchy and convincing potential and existing members of the necessity of collective organization are stubborn problems. They have, thus far, proved resistant to change.

There is space to change things and combat conservativism. History demonstrates that trade unionists have changed in the past and they can change today and tomorrow, although the task will not be an easy one. The fundamental challenge is this: if organizing does not succeed, then decline appears inevitable. There is no alternative to organizing, even if success has to be measured in terms of maintaining membership and density rather than the more ambitious goal of union revitalization. Influencing change in the environment of trade unionism entails trade unionists changing trade unions. This has always constituted the central challenge of the organizing model. In this important and fundamental sense, the future of British trade unions lies in the hands of their leaders and activists.

## Bibliography

Ackers, P. and Payne, J. (1998) 'British trade unions and social partnership: rhetoric, reality and strategy', *International Journal of Human Resource Management* 9:3, 529–49.

Amicus (2006) *Industrial Report 2006*, London: Amicus.

Badigannavar, V. and Kelly, J. (2005) 'Why are some union organizing campaigns more successful than others?', *British Journal of Industrial Relations*, 43:3, 515–35.

Bain, G. and Price, R. (1983) 'Union growth: dimensions, determinants and destiny' in G. Bain (ed.) *Industrial Relations in Britain*, Oxford: Blackwell.

Bassett, P. and Cave, A. (1993) *All for One: The Future of the Unions*, Fabian Pamphlet 559, London: Fabian Society.

Beaumont, P. and Harris, R. (1990) 'Union recruitment and organizing attempts in Britain in the 1980s', *Industrial Relations Journal*, 21:4, 274–86.

BECTU (2003) *NEC Report to Conference*, London: BECTU.

—— (2008) *NEC Report to Conference*, London: BECTU.

Bland, P. (1999) 'Trade union membership and recognition 1997–98: an analysis of data from the Certification Officer and the Labour Force Survey', *Labour Market Trends*, London: DTI.

Blyton, P. and Turnbull, P. (2004) *The Dynamics of Employee Relations*, 3rd edition, Basingstoke: Palgrave.

Bronfenbrenner, K. (2003) 'The American labour movement and the resurgence in union organizing', in P. Fairbrother and A. Yates (eds) *Trade Unions in Renewal: A Comparative Study*, London: Routledge.

Bronfenbrenner, K. and Juravich, T. (1998) 'It takes more than house calls: organizing to win with a comprehensive union-building strategy', in K. Bronfenbrenner, S. Friedman, R. Hurd, R. Oswald and R. Seeber (eds) *Organizing to Win: New Research on Union Strategies*, Ithaca, NY: ILR Press.

Bryson, A., Gomez, R. and Willman, P. (2004) 'The end of the affair? The decline in employers' propensity to unionize', in J. Kelly and P. Willman (eds) *Union Organization and Activity*, London: Routledge.

Cardiff Research Bulletin No. 4 (1999) *New Unionism Project*, Cardiff: Cardiff University.

Carter, B. (2000) 'Adoption of the organizing model in British trade unions: some evidence from manufacturing, science and finance (MSF)', *Work, Employment and Society*, 14:1, 117–36.

—— (2006) 'Trade union organizing and renewal: a response to de Turberville', *Work, Employment and Society* 20:2, 415–26.

Certification Officer (1997–2007) *Annual Report of the Certification Officer 1997–2007*, London: Certification Office.

Charlwood, A. (2004) 'The new generation of trade union leaders and prospects for union revitalization', *British Journal of Industrial Relations*, 42:2, 379–97.

Coats, D. (2005) *Raising Lazarus: The Future of Organized Labour*, London: Fabian Society.

Cohen, S. (2006) *Ramparts of Resistance: Why Workers Lost Their Power, and How to Get It Back*, London: Pluto.

Community (2007) Ladbrokes staff page < http://www.community-tu.org/information/101895/101479/lad/> (accessed 16 July 2008).

Community (2008) *Betting Shop Workers*, <http://www.community-tu.org/information/101478/bsc/> (accessed 16 July 2008).

Cully, M., O'Reilly, A., Millward, N., Forth, J., Woodland, S., Dix, G. and Bryson, A. (1998) *The 1998 Workplace Employee Relations Survey: First Findings*, London: DTI.

Cully, M., Woodland, S., O'Reilly, A. and Dix, G. (1999), *Britain at Work As Depicted by the 1998 Employee Relations Survey*, London: Routledge.

Danford, A., Richardson, M. and Upchurch, M. (2002) ' "New unionism", organizing and partnership: a comparative analysis of union renewal strategies in the public sector', *Capital and Class*, 76, 1–27.

Danford, A., Richardson, M., Upchurch, M., Tailby, S. and Stewart, P. (2005) *Partnership and the High Performance Workplace: Work and Employment Relations in the Aerospace Industry*, London: Palgrave Macmillan.

Daniels, G. (2006) 'Reflections on new unionism: past and present', *Historical Studies in Industrial Relations*, 21, 35–62.

De Turberville, S. (2004) 'Does the organizing model represent a credible union renewal strategy?', *Work Employment and Society* 18:4, 775–94.

Disney, R. (1990) 'Explanations of the decline in trade union density in Britain: an appraisal', *British Journal of Industrial Relations*, 28:2, 165–78.

Fairbrother, P. (1996) 'Workplace trade unionism in the state sector', in P. Ackers, C. Smith and P. Smith (eds) *The New Workplace and Trade Unionism*, London: Routledge.

Fairbrother, P. (2000) *Trade Unions at the Crossroads*, London: Mansell.

Fairbrother, P. and Stewart, P. (2003) 'The dilemmas of social partnership and union organization: questions for British trade unions', in P. Fairbrother and C. Yates (eds) *Trade Unions in Renewal: A Comparative Study*, London: Routledge.

Findlay, P. and McKinlay, A. (2003a) 'Organizing in electronics: recruitment, recognition and representation – shadow shop stewards in Scotland's "Silicon Glen" ', in G. Gall (ed.) *Union Organizing: Campaigning for Trade Union Recognition*, London: Routledge.

Findlay, P. and McKinlay, A. (2003b) 'Union organizing in Big Blue's backyard', *Industrial Relations Journal*, 34:1, 52–66.

Fiorito, J. (2003) 'Union organizing in the United States', in G. Gall (ed.) *Union Organizing: Campaigning for Trade Union Recognition*, London: Routledge.

Fiorito, J. and Jarley, P. (2003) 'Union organizing commitment: rhetoric and reality', *Proceedings of the Fifty-fifth Annual Meeting of the Industrial Relations Research Association*, Champaign, IL: IRRA.

Fletcher, B. and Hurd, R. (1998) 'Beyond the organizing model: the transformation process in local unions', in K. Bronfenbrenner, S. Friedman, R. Hurd, R. Oswald and R. Seeber (eds) *Organizing to Win: New Research on Union Strategies*, Ithaca, NY: ILR Press.

Fosh, P. (1993) 'Membership participation in workplace unionism: the possibility of union renewal', *British Journal of Industrial Relations*, 31:4, 577–92.

Freeman, R. and Pelletier, J. (1990) 'The impact of industrial relations legislation on British union density', *British Journal of Industrial Relations*, 28:2, 141–64.

Gall, G. (1998) 'The prospects for workplace trade unionism: evaluating Fairbrother's union renewal thesis', *Capital and Class*, 66, 149–57.

Gennard, J., Ramsay, H., Baldry, C., Snape, E. and Bain, P., (2000) *Globalisation of the Graphical Industry and the Future of Graphical Trade Unions*, Report, Centre for European Employment Research (CEER), University of Strathclyde.

Heckscher, C. (2001) 'Living with flexibility', in L. Turner, H. Katz and R. Hurd (eds) *Strategies for Renewal: Transforming the Labor Movement in the 1990s and Beyond*, Ithaca, NY: Cornell University Press.

Heery, E. (1998) 'The relaunch of the Trades Union Congress', *British Journal of Industrial Relations*, 36:3, 339–60.

—— (2002) 'Partnership versus organizing: alternative futures for British trade unionism' *Industrial Relations Journal*, 33:1, 20–35.

—— (2003) 'Trade unions and industrial relations', in P. Ackers and A. Wilkinson (eds) *Understanding Work and Employment: Industrial Relations in Transition*, Oxford: Oxford University Press.

Heery, E., Simms, M., Delbridge, R., Salmon, J. and Simpson, D. (2000a) 'Union organizing in Britain: a survey of policy and practice', *International Journal of Human Resource Management*, 11:5, 986–1007.

Heery, E., Simms, M., Simpson, D., Delbridge, R. and Salmon, J. (2000b) 'Organizing unionism comes to Britain', *Employee Relations*, 22:1, 38–57.

Heery, E., Simms, M., Delbridge, R., Salmon, J. and Simpson, D. (2000c) 'The TUC's Organizing Academy: an assessment', *Industrial Relations Journal*, 31: 5, 400–15.

Heery, E., Delbridge, R. and Simms, M. (2003a) *The Organizing Academy – Five Years On*, London: TUC.

Heery, E., Kelly, J. and Waddington, J. (2003b) 'Union revitalization in Britain', *European Journal of Industrial Relations*, 9:1, 79–98.

Heery, E. and Simms, M. (2008) 'Constraints on union organizing in the United Kingdom', *Industrial Relations Journal*, 39:1, 24–42.

Hurd, R. W., Milkman, R. and Turner, L. (2003) 'Reviving the American labour movement: institutions and mobilization', *European Journal of Industrial Relations*, 9:1, 99–117.

Hyman, R. (1989) *The Political Economy of Industrial Relations: Theory and Practice in a Cold Climate*, London: Macmillan.

Kelly, J. (1998) *Rethinking Industrial Relations; Mobilization, Collectivism and Long Waves*, London: Routledge.

Kelly, J. and Badigannavar, V. (2004) 'Union organizing campaigns', in J. Kelly and P. Willman (eds) *Union Organization and Activity*, London: Routledge.

Kelly, J. and Heery, E. (1994) *Working for the Union: British Trade Union Officers*, Cambridge: Cambridge University Press.

Kelly, J. and Frege, C. (2004) 'Union strategies in comparative context', in J. Kelly and C. Frege (eds) *Varieties of Unionism: Strategies of Union Revitalization in a Globalizing Economy*, Oxford: Oxford University Press.

Kersley, B., Alpin, C., Forth, J., Bryson, A., Bewley, H., Dix, G. and Oxenbridge, S. (2005) *Inside the Workplace: Findings from the 2004 Workplace Employment Relations Survey*, London: Routledge.

Lyddon, D. (2003) 'History and industrial relations', in P. Ackers and A. Wilkinson (eds) *Understanding Work and Employment: Industrial Relations in Transition*. Oxford: Oxford University Press.

McIlroy, J. (1995) *Trade Unions in Britain Today*, 2nd edition, Manchester: Manchester University Press.

—— (1998) 'The enduring alliance? Trade unions and the making of New Labour, 1994–97', *British Journal of Industrial Relations* 36:4, 537–64.

—— (2000) 'New Labour, new unions, new left', *Capital and Class*, 71, 11–43.

McIlroy, J. and Daniels, G. (2007) 'History matters: understanding the future, the present and the past of trade unionism', *Union Futures*, London: Labour Research Department.

Martínez Lucio, M. and Stuart, M. (2005) 'Suspicious minds? Partnership, trade union strategy and the politics of contemporary employment relations', in P. Stewart (ed.), *Employment, Trade Union Renewal and the Future of Work: The Experience of Work and Organisational Change*, Basingstoke: Palgrave Macmillan.

Mason, B. and Bain, P. (1991) 'Trade union recruitment strategies: facing the 1990s', *Industrial Relations Journal*, 22:1, 36–45.

Milkman, R. (2000) *Organizing Immigrants: The Challenge for Unions in Contemporary California*, Cornell: Cornell University Press.

Milkman, R. and Voss, K. (2004) *Rebuilding Labor: Organizing and Organizers in the New Union Movement*, Cornell: Cornell University Press.

Millward, N., Bryson, A. and Forth, J. (2000) *All Change at Work? British Employment Relations 1980–98. As Portrayed by the Workplace Industrial Relations Survey Series*, London: Routledge.

Moore, S. (2004) 'Employer and union mobilisation in the statutory recognition process', in J. Kelly and P. Willman (eds) *Union Organization and Activity*, London: Routledge.

O'Grady, F. and Nowak, P. (2004) 'Beyond new unionism', in J. Kelly and P. Willman (eds) *Union Organization and Activity*, London: Routledge.

PCS (2007) *Protecting our Future: Defending Jobs, Pay and Conditions*, London: PCS.

Simms, M. (2003) 'Union organizing in a not-for-profit organization', in G. Gall (ed.) *Union Organizing: Campaigning for Trade Union Recognition*, London: Routledge.

—— (2006) 'The transition from organizing to representation: a case study', in G. Gall (ed.) *Union Recognition: Organizing and Bargaining Outcomes*, London: Routledge.

—— (2007) 'Managed activism: two union organizing campaigns in the not-for-profit sector', *Industrial Relations Journal*, 38:2, 119–35.

Snape, E. (1994) 'Reversing the decline? The TGWU's Link Up Campaign', *Industrial Relations Journal* 25:3, 222–33.

Stern, A. (2006) *Getting America Back on Track: A Country that Works*, New York: Free Press.

Tattersall, A. (2007) 'Labor-community coalitions, global alliances, and the potential of SEIU's global partnerships', in K. Bronfenbrenner (ed.) *Global Unions:*

*Challenging Transnational Capital Through Cross-Border Campaigns*, Ithaca, NY: Cornell University Press.

Taylor, P. and Bain, P. (2003) 'Call centre organizing in adversity: from Excell to Vertex' in G. Gall (ed.) *Union Organizing: Campaigning for Trade Union Recognition*, London: Routledge.

Terry, M. (2003) 'Can "partnership" reverse the decline of British trade unions?', *Work, Employment and Society*, 17:3, 459–72.

TGWU (1998) *1998 Action Plan*, London: TGWU.

—— (2005) *T&G Logistics Strategy*, London: TGWU.

—— (2007) *Organizing: Strategy for Growth*, <http://www.tgwu.org.uk/Templates/Internal.asp?NodeID=92090> (accessed 6 July 2008).

Towers, B. (2003) 'Comparisons and prospects: industrial relations and trade unions in North America and Britain', in G. Gall (ed.) *Union Organizing: Campaigning for Trade Union Recognition*, London: Routledge.

TSSA (2005) *Annual Report*, London: TSSA.

—— (2006) *Annual Report*, London: TSSA.

TUC (1997) *General Council Report*, London: TUC.

—— (1998) *General Council Report*, London: TUC.

—— (1999) *General Council Report*, London: TUC.

—— (2001a) *General Council Report*, London: TUC.

—— (2001b) *Reaching the Missing Millions*, London: TUC.

—— (2002) *General Council Report*, London: TUC.

—— (2003a) *General Council Report*, London: TUC.

—— (2003b) *Organizing to Win*, London: TUC.

—— (2004) *General Council Report*, London: TUC.

—— (2005) *General Council Report*, London: TUC.

—— (2006) *General Council Report*, London: TUC.

—— (2007) *UnionScope* <http://www.tuc.org.uk/organisation/tuc-12903-f0.cfm> (accessed 1 July 2008).

Undy, R., Ellis, V., McCarthy, W. and Halmos, A. (1981) *Change in Trade Unions: The Development of UK Unions Since the 1960's*, London: Hutchinson.

USDAW (2007) *Building the Union*, <http://www.usdaw.org.uk/getactive/academy> (accessed 1 July 2008).

Waddington, J. (2003) 'Trade union organization', in P. Edwards (ed.) *Industrial Relations: Theory and Practice in Britain*, 2nd edition, Oxford: Blackwell.

Waddington, J. and Kerr, A. (2000) 'Towards an organizing model in Unison? A trade union membership strategy in transition', in M. Terry (ed.) *Redefining Public Sector Unionism: Unison and the Future of Trade Unions*, London: Routledge.

Waddington, J. and Whitston, C. (1997) 'Why do people join unions in a period of membership decline?' *British Journal of Industrial Relations* 35:4, 515–46.

Willman, P. (1989) 'The logic of market share trade unionism: is membership decline inevitable?', *Industrial Relations Journal*, 20:4, 260–71.

Willman, P. and Bryson, A. (2006) *Accounting for Collective Action: Resource Acquisition and Mobilisation in British Unions*, Discussion Paper No. 768, London: Centre for Economic Performance, London School of Economics.

Willman, P., Morris, T.J. and Aston, B. (1993) *Union Business: Trade Union Organisation and Financial Reform in the Thatcher Years*, Cambridge: Cambridge University Press.

Wills, J. (2001) 'Community unionism and trade union renewal in the UK: moving beyond the fragments at last?', *Transactions of the Institute of British Geographers*, 26:4, 465–83.

—— (2003) 'Organizing in transport and travel: learning lessons from TSSA's Seacat campaign', in G. Gall (ed.) *Union Organizing: Campaigning for Trade Union Recognition*, London: Routledge.

# 9 Skills and training

## A strategic role for trade unions or the limits of neoliberalism?

*John McIlroy and Richard Croucher*

When the Northern Rock crisis erupted in 2007 the British government intervened to prop up the failing business. The state provided loans and guarantees worth £100 billion of taxpayers' money to dig Northern Rock out of the hole its managers had got it into playing the financial markets. Britain's neoliberal administration temporarily nationalized the building society to restore it to health, pending a sell-off to private capital reluctant to invest in a failed business. They paid two consultants their market value of £90,000 and £75,000 a month respectively to do the job. Adam Applegarth, the company's chief executive, who was responsible for Northern Rock's failure in the market, received a pay-off of £760,000 while the market simultaneously judged that 2,000 Northern Rock employees should be made redundant. As the credit crunch bit, the Bank of England swopped rock-solid government bonds for billions of pounds of mortgage-backed securities that nobody else wanted in order to bail out the banks and restore confidence in the market.

In neoliberal theory, individuals take responsibility for their actions: they pay for their failures. Investors make or lose money by taking risks. Things are different in practice: banks which take reckless decisions are protected from the consequences by taxpayers' money. Risk is restricted. There are clearly limits to neoliberal governments' belief in the market. In a similar way, in the crisis over high interest–low security mortgages in the USA, thousands of poor Americans saw their homes repossessed by predatory lenders. Meanwhile the Federal Reserve threw money at the banks and lenders who had painfully discovered greed was not always good: the state purchased 'toxic' mortgage-backed securities from the banks in order to correct the market. In twenty-first-century Anglo-American capitalism, the poor get neoliberalism; the rich still get Keynesianism.[1]

If the nationalization of Northern Rock, with its distant echoes of social democracy, was portrayed by opposing politicians and the media as a source of embarrassment to a neoliberal administration, New Labour's proactive policy on skills and training which involves the state in financially feather-bedding employers – and trade unions – to train workers to meet the demands of the market, has attracted considerably less controversy. Beyond the confines of the rhetoric of competing political factions the fact that the state acts to buttress, subsidize, even regulate capital and guarantee markets is incongruous only to purist proponents of neoliberal ideology. It is part of the woof and warp of practical politics and the political maintenance of neoliberal regimes in Britain and America. Dilemmas about 'market fundamentalism' among neoliberals have tended to resolve themselves in policies of reorganizing and modernizing public expenditure and welfare states rather than dismantling them (Shaikh and Tonak 2000; Shaikh 2003). Marxists have got many things wrong. They remain right in stressing that national capital still needs its state to establish the political and institutional basis of markets and help provide a regular supply of healthy, compliant, suitably socialized and suitably skilled labour.

The social market strands of second phase, constructive neoliberalism tell us that if the market is to operate optimally, the state has to construct institutions which support and lubricate it. This legitimates *inter alia* welfare safety nets, limited forms of redistribution, environmental protection and investment in human capital (Gamble 2006: 21–2) – on condition that intervention serves market purposes and that entrepreneurial culture and self-help, opportunity but not dependency, solidarity or equality, predominate. 'Social neoliberalism', which redefines citizenship in terms of market participation and recasts state approaches to equality as extending access to the market rather than direct redistribution of wealth and income has characterized various neoliberal governments – including New Labour in Britain (Robison 2006: 5–6).

A new politics of economic inclusion, social mobility and productivist welfare has marked New Labour's policy on skills and training. It has pledged itself to 'the continuous development of the skills, knowledge and understanding that is essential to employability and fulfilment' (DfEE 1998a: 11). Personal fulfilment was part of its alleged purposes: it was, initially and increasingly, subordinate to the global economic imperatives of competitivity and flexibility: 'In our rapidly-changing world, having a highly skilled workforce isn't an optional extra: it's an economic necessity' (DIUS 2007: 4). Inclusion, mobility and the good life were presented as the consequences of the enhanced access to labour markets that greater equality of opportunity, redistribution through improvements in skills and training, would afford: 'developing the right culture for skills and employment isn't just about being able to compete in the global economy. It's also the most effective way of . . . increasing social mobility' (DIUS 2007: 4; see also DfES *et al.* 2003).

In New Labour's thinking the state could not and should not seek to engineer equality by employing social democratic methods. In the interests of social cohesion and economic efficiency it could and should provide a greater measure of equality of opportunity. What were ruled out were the traditional redistributivist methods, welfarism and taxation, which debilitated the market, burdened business and discouraged the entrepreneurial ethic. The way forward lay in the state developing labour rather than controlling capital and minimizing handicaps so that everyone got a fairer start in the market. But only by influencing 'the distribution of productive endowments so that market interactions lead to a greater initial equality of income, lessening the need for subsequent redistribution' (White 1997: 170–1).

Although it enunciated similar aims and appropriated its language of the 'high quality, high skills, high performance, high value' enterprise and economy, New Labour rejected stakeholding, coordination of markets, social partnership and strong trade unions, perceived by many analysts as the indispensable means to achieve those goals (see McIlroy, chapters 1 and 2, this volume). It refused to return to the mild corporatism which had regulated skills formation in Britain between the 1960s and the 1980s and favoured a system singularly distinctive from those operating in successful EU economies (Stuart and Wallis 2007). New Labour rejected robust regulation, attempts by the state to penetrate the workplace, the locus of much skill formation, and any significant cramping of management prerogative, which governs the development and utilization of skills. The state refused to confront capital, the dominant social force shaping skills and influencing economic performance (Coates 2000: 144). It opted instead for an arm's-length approach based on human capital theory and largely restricted to state stimulation and subsidization of inadequate entrepreneurial effort. This constitutes a voluntarist active-state variant of the free market model of skills development (Ashton 2004: 26–8).

The purpose of New Labour's protracted and complicated interventions has been to try to forecast employers' needs and, having predicted future trends, help satisfy them by working to generate the optimal supply of trained, flexible labour. The problem is essentially conceived as one of supply-side weakness. Employers are lacking in information on the need for better skills and the resources available to develop them. The model is one in which employers do not understand the need to up-skill or lack the wit, will or skill to do it. Low skills are at the heart of Britain's productivity gap with its key competitors. The instruments of correction that the state can apply must remain consonant with neoliberalism's *omerta* on robust regulation. New Labour has largely confined itself to exhortation, dissemination of best practice and financial incentives to encourage employer enlightenment; changes in the educational and training system designed to reform the supply side; and the intricate and continuous building of facilitative institutions, intended to identify and plan training and engage employer interest. But New Labour's ability to intervene is circumscribed by the intrinsic difficulties of this kind of predictive planning, the restricted powers it deems legitimate and the fragility of its chosen methods of intervention (Keep and Mayhew 1999; Keep 2006).

With nuances and a growing, if still unrealized, turn away from supply to engage with the problems of demand, this has constituted the gist of New Labour policy since 1997. To its underlying continuities with constructive elements of Conservative policies, which were largely devoted to the pioneering neoliberal project of clearing the corporatist landscape, we must add elements of discontinuity. The changes which inspire and characterize constructive neoliberalism can be observed both in New Labour's imaginative assimilation of skills policy to social policy and in its confident formulation of a new role for trade unions. In the skills script of the early twenty-first century, unions are destined to play the part of loyal, energetic and well-remunerated servitors of New Labour. Trade unionists are, as the then New Labour Minister, David Blunkett, put it, foot soldiers in the perennial but recharged project of creating high-skill, flexible, competitive labour markets as the gateway to economic regeneration and equality of opportunity (*Guardian*, 28 August 2000). Since 1997 the unions have come in out of the skills cold to which the Conservatives had consigned them.

With a vengeance. By 2007 the TUC was managing a Union Learning Fund (ULF) of some £15 million, provided by the state so that unions could resource government-supported projects. This had facilitated the establishment of Unionlearn, which grouped together TUC education and training initiatives with an annual income of £22 million. State finance had underpinned a growing network of union learning representatives (ULRs). Gordon Brown blessed Unionlearn at its launch. Bill Rammell, the Minister for Skills, and the government's skills adviser, Lord Leitch, addressed TUC meetings (TUC 2007a: 115). Union leaders perceived themselves to be major actors in the skills narrative. In their estimation, unions had developed a strategic role and exercised significant leverage on government: 'The General Council has also continued to influence policy on learning and skills' (ibid.: 114). Unlike other protagonists, trade unionists did the business where it mattered. Their involvement, the TUC asserted,

> has made a real impact in the workplace and has made an important difference to many people's lives. With government and business emphasising the crucial importance of learning and skills to our future prosperity it is the trade union movement that is delivering in a positive and practical way.
>
> (ibid.: 3)

New Labour's refusal of what many saw as the preconditions for using skills formation as a vehicle for union advance – legal support and institutionalized social partnership at the level of state, region and workplace, an absence conditioned by the limits of neoliberalism (Streeck 1989), did not daunt union leaders. They retained a belief that participation in state-authored skills and training agendas not only furthered the unions' financial health but advanced union organizing and union revitalization. The TUC repeatedly claimed: 'There continues to be evidence that the rapidly increasing number of union learning representatives is boosting union organizing' (TUC 2006a: 7). The formal functions of Unionlearn included 'promoting integrated learning and organizing strategies' (ibid.: 121).

In the next section of this chapter we look in more detail at how New Labour's policy on skills and training has evolved since 1997 and discuss the criticisms that have been made of its direction and limitations.[2] This is followed by exploration of the ways in which the TUC has responded to government policy. At one level it has criticized its thrust and advocated social partnership and joint regulation. At another level it has participated enthusiastically in the delivery of New Labour initiatives within a neoliberal framework conspicuously lacking in the fundamental requirements of union policy. The dilemmas of acting as an agent for neoliberalism when the state has persistently refused to circumscribe management prerogatives, endow unions with regulatory powers or substantially support collective bargaining over skills formation are addressed. They are related to wider arguments about New Labour's calculated rehabilitation of a reformed trade unionism and the conditions of that redemption. Finally we discuss the role the unions' participation in the state's skills agenda may play in strengthening the development of cooperative tendencies towards capital and the state and the suppression of the conflictual and adversarial tendencies integral to trade unionism. We consider to what extent involvement in New Labour initiatives has provided unions with a strategic role which facilitates union revitalization; or, alternatively, has demonstrated the limits of trade union practice in a neoliberal skills regime.

## New neoliberalism – old skills problem[3]

Insurgent neoliberalism terminated the mild and transient corporatist experiment that had been ushered in by the Industrial Training Act 1964. The Thatcher governments gradually dismantled the system of levies and subsidies administered by the Industry Training Boards; presided over the demise of the boards themselves; and delivered the *coup de grâce* to corporatism's figurehead and powerhouse, the Manpower Services Commission. At its zenith this approach had been constrained by the political and structural limitations of neo-corporatist concertation in Britain and tendencies in industrial relations and collective bargaining which hampered the emergence of social partnership on the European model (Crouch *et al.* 1999: 157–62). Even in its first destructive phase, neoliberalism maintained a mild interventionist role for the state, mediated through the system of Training and Enterprise Councils (TECs) and the development of National Vocational Qualifications (NVQs) (Grugulis 2003). The TECs, which lingered under New Labour, played a prominent part. They operated as limited companies, comprised of high-ranking exemplary entrepreneurs, and achieved some success in engaging employers, building local networks of business and training bodies and administering training programmes (King 1993; Wood 1998).

New Labour shared but extended the Conservatives' concern that better skills were essential to better productivity and improved economic performance and that the state had a role, albeit a restricted facilitative role, in their development. The nature of the problem was common ground. New Labour's diagnosis was formulated more compellingly in precise relation to globalization. Its message was more urgent and expressed more intensely: 'in the modern global economy, where capital, raw materials and technology are internationally mobile and tradeable worldwide, it is people – their education and skills – that are necessarily the most important determinant of economic growth' (Brown 1994a). As a consequence of New Labour's adoption of neoclassical endogenous growth theory (see McIlroy, chapter 2, this volume), investment by employers in training greater than the Conservatives had achieved was imperative. So was more extended involvement by the state than pioneering neoliberalism had been prepared to countenance. Nonetheless, New Labour was not, at least not on its own estimation, 'a party of out-dated ideology . . . what counts is what works' (Labour Party 1997: 3–4).

On that basis there could be no regression to the party's social democratic past. Before it came to power New Labour had broken with its long-standing commitment to return to the 1970s and legislate for a revamped levy system or tax-based approach. It had renounced any significant re-regulation of employer prerogative and any rights-based approach to encouraging individuals to invest in skills training (Labour Party 1996). Characteristically, the most powerful influence on innovation was the attitude of employers and the CBI's adherence to voluntarism (King and Wickham-Jones 1998). Replacement proposals centred on Individual Learning Accounts. They minimally addressed, indeed they bypassed, 'how to tackle the free market voluntarism which until recently had been at the core of the Party's diagnosis of the UK's skills shortage' (ibid.: 447). This formative decision established the limits of New Labour's pragmatism. Rejecting what the party had considered for thirty years 'worked best', it conditioned to a large degree the trajectory of future policy.

New Labour – *nouveau langue*. Or rather, the appropriation and adaptation of extant educational discourses which might lend charm and power to government strategy. The stolid-sounding 'Vocational Education and Training' was superseded by the more mellifluous and attractive 'lifelong learning', 'workplace learning' and 'the learning society'. Such terms evoked lives brimming with possibilities to develop the whole person and active, creative engagement in a new open-ended system of learning, which could embrace humanistic agendas, personal growth and self-fulfilment. They elevated the vocational skills often disdained in mainstream education. The programme was, and would remain, fundamentally economic, entrepreneurial and individualistic: 'learning is the key to individual employability and business competitivity' (DfEE 1998b). The individual was first and foremost a human resource, a hand and a brain, a component of social capital. Learning as a critical process, learning to think, was subordinate to learning as the acquisition of profitable skills; the inculcation of technique and socialization in entrepreneurial culture; and the adaptation of citizens as employees and consumers to the constraints of existing economic and social relations, employability, flexibility and competitivity. Really useful knowledge was knowledge that was really useful to British entrepreneurs in global competition (McIlroy 2000a: 300–1).

New Labour saw little problem in reconciling enhanced company performance and profitability with equality of opportunity and personal liberation. Better skills produced social justice. The road to individual emancipation ran through increasing the value of labour and improving the operation of the labour market rather than, as democratic socialists and social democrats had mistakenly conceived in antiquity, regulating the power of capital (Brown 1994b: 116). Skills became, at least in New Labour's market-restricted vision of the good society, the answer to almost everything.

> Improving skills will help individuals to improve their employability, progress in their careers, and secure better wages. It will help employers to secure increased productivity and profitability for their businesses. It will help us to reduce unemployment, tackle child poverty and improve social mobility. And it will help to reduce crime, improve health outcomes, and improve civic and community participation.
>
> (DIUS 2007)

Skills were the new socialism, or at least the old social democracy. They acted as a substitute for the inadequacies of New Labour social policy as measured by the commitment to overt planned redistribution of wealth, income and education of the party's past. Policy was less utopian and more prosaic. Concrete measures, as distinct from rhetorical effusions, were slow to emerge: much early effort was focused on the 'New Deal' and 'welfare to work' legislation which provided unemployed workers with learning options (Davies and Freedland 2007: 113–82). The Individual Learning Account (ILA) initiative introduced in England in 2000 produced 1.4 million accounts but was quickly terminated after allegations of fraud. Conservative innovations such as the Investors in People Award, certifying best practice in skill development, were maintained and new projects such as the University of Industry, later Learn Direct, were mounted. The Conservatives' employer-led, but state-financed, Industry Training Organisations became National Training Organisations (NTOs). Without a great deal of convincing explanation the TECs were replaced in 2001 by the Learning Skills Council (LSC) and the NTOs by the Skills for Business Network, which consisted of new Sector Skills Councils (SSCs) and the Sector Skills Development Agency (SSDA) (DfEE 1999a, 1999b).

The LSC was complemented by 47 Local Learning and Skills Councils (LLSCs) and given a budget of £5.5 billion with responsibility for funding all post-16 provision outside Higher Education. It set National Learning Targets and, together with the LLSCs and sectoral bodies, endeavoured to engage with employers to forecast and train the labour necessary to fulfil employer needs. The SSCs, established in 2002, attempted to assess and respond to sectoral requirements and design provision to match them through Skills Sector Agreements and Sector Qualification Strategies (Ashton 2006). Regional Development Agencies also provided training, while the Skills

Alliance, created in 2003 to supervise the operation of government strategy, consisted of government ministers with an involvement, and representatives of the CBI, the Small Business Council and the TUC (DfES *et al.* 2003; McIlroy 2008: 286–8).

The institutional web was complex. But the system remained voluntary and employers retained their freedom to engage or not to engage, to train or not to train. The difficulties of forecasting and planning for the needs of a myriad of distinctive enterprises across the economy lay somewhere between immense and impossible. The system depended on relatively weak institutions with 'fragile technologies' capable of eliciting only what data employers were willing or capable of offering. It operated on a diagnosis of a skills crisis expressed in terms of deficiencies in the supply of skills and a consequent conception that if the supply of skills grew, demand would increase to meet it. Nonetheless, by 2002, signs were surfacing which suggested that demand was beginning to emerge as the key issue (Keep 2002: 458).

Employer Training Pilots (ETPs) offered free or highly subsidized training for employees to attain basic skills or first full Level 2 qualifications (five good GCSEs or vocational equivalent). By 2006, 30,000 employers and 250,000 employees had participated. Despite criticism of 'dead weight' training standing in for employers' own effort (Abramovsky *et al.* 2005), the ETPs were extended into the National Employer Training Programme, 'Train to Gain'. This was criticized on similar grounds: it required no contribution from employers, and taxpayers' money paid for what employers should, and in many cases would, have done anyway (Wolf 2007: 24).

It was in this context that Lord Leitch's review of skills strategy, commissioned in 2004, reported in December 2006. Its verdict on the results of almost a decade of constructive neoliberalism was mixed. Leitch estimated that the average French worker produces 20 per cent more per hour, the average American worker 18 per cent more per hour and the average German worker 13 per cent more per hour, than their British counterparts. He concluded that the UK's relatively poor skills were responsible for 20 per cent of the gap. There were encouraging signs. The number of apprentices had increased from 76,000 in 1997 to 256,000 in 2005. The government had exceeded its target of 750,000 adults taking basic skills qualifications, while two-thirds of workers now possessed a Level 2 qualification and only around 15 per cent lacked any qualifications. Nonetheless, almost half of adults, around 17 million, had numeracy problems and a seventh, around 5 million, were not functionally literate. Leitch observed:

> While the UK's skills base has improved significantly over the last decade, [it] remains weak by international standards, holding back productivity growth and social justice . . . Our nation's skills are not world class and we run the risk that this will undermine the UK's long-term prosperity.
>
> (Leitch 2006: 13)

New Labour could take little satisfaction from Leitch's succinct evaluation of strategy since 1997: 'The Review's analysis shows that previous approaches to delivering skills have been too "supply driven", based on the government planning supply to meet ineffectively articulated employer demand. This approach has a poor track record' (ibid.: 12). In Leitch's estimation the methods embodied in the ETPs and Train to Gain were more effective in gauging demand and responding to it, than earlier attempts to plan supply. Moreover – and this was a damning indictment of New Labour's institution-building – 'employers are confused by the plethora of advisory, strategic and planning bodies they are asked to input to' (ibid.: 49). A more demand-led approach, building on Train to Gain and refashioning institutions to strengthen employer voice and engagement with employer demand, was imperative.

Leitch recommended that the much-vaunted LSC should no longer involve itself in detailed planning while a new overarching Commission for Employ-ment and Skills (CES) should replace the Skills Alliance, advise government and drive strategy. It would relicence and reform SSCs as vehicles of employer voice and apply the demand-led principles of Train to Gain across the system. The state should fund most basic skills training but for Level 3 intermediate skills, employers and individuals should contribute at least 50 per cent, and for higher skills at Level 4 most of the costs, 'as they will benefit most' (ibid.: 15). This would be complemented by the reintroduction of refurbished Learner Accounts. However, Leitch did not rule out an element of future selective regulation. The government should launch a new voluntary pledge by employers to train all employees up to Level 2. In 2010 the government should review progress: if it was insufficient, it should introduce a statutory entitlement to such training (ibid.: 4).

The government accepted Leitch's general argument and his suggested line of march. A new Department for Innovation, Universities and Skills (DIUS) was created in 2007 and the CES was scheduled to become operative in 2008. It was proposed that the LSC would be abolished, with its brief for young people being transferred to the local authorities and its remit for adults to a new Skills Funding Agency. The restructured SSCs would undertake a review of vocational qualifications privileging 'economically valuable skills'. Insti-tutional innovation was sustained: the CES would also charter a network of local employer-led Employment and Skills Boards. The extension of Train to Gain would involve an employer training fund of over £900 million by 2010, when total expenditure on employer-focused training would reach £1.3 bil-lion. New Skills Accounts, providing matched funding of up to £100 to help pay for approved courses, would further facilitate up-skilling. Moreover, the government endorsed Leitch's recommendation on the Skills Pledge and promised a review of progress by 2010. A mass of ancillary undertakings concluded in exposition of new targets. New Labour committed itself to becoming a world leader in skills by 2020, when it hoped that 95 per cent of adults would possess basic skills, 90 per cent Level 2 qualifications and more than 40 per cent of adults would be qualified at Level 4 (DIUS 2007; DCSF and DIUS 2008).

Some remained sceptical. They felt that despite movement, the government was still reading from substantially the same script that had failed to engage successfully with enduring difficulties, a text that had been subject to sustained criticism from analysts through the New Labour years. Commentators have argued that while the connection between skills and economic performance is plausible at a general level, the assertion that skills are the crucial factor in economic success is more questionable. Productivity depends not just on training, but on technology, work organization and management strategy (Shackleton 1995: 233–4). Questions have been raised about the nature of Britain's skills problem: what sort of skills does the economy need and to what degree does it require high skills? Lloyd and Payne (2002a, 2002b) interrogate the influential literature suggesting a paradigm shift to 'the knowledge economy' and a global trend towards higher level skills (for example, Castells 1996; Giddens 2000). They conclude that there is insufficient evidence to predicate such a shift. Despite tendencies in that direction, low-wage, low-skills, low-cost approaches remain viable in many companies and sectors of the economy. The High Performance Workplace remains rare in Britain and changes in the labour process and the labour force are often exaggerated (Nolan and Slater 2003). Surveys do not always sustain the state vision of the deleterious economic impact of skill shortages while our understanding of the relationship between demand for skills and training continues to be inadequate (Campbell *et al.* 2001; Keep and Rainbird 2003; LSC 2006).

This raises issues about New Labour policy premised on the basis that employers need an expanded supply of higher-skilled, better-qualified labour. The difficulty in moving to a more productive and competitive economy may lie rather with the low level of employer demand for a wider range of skills and the factors conditioning it (Keep and Mayhew 1999). New Labour's strategy may be too blunt, partly because of failure to acknowledge the entrenched short-termism and quick-profit orientations of many British companies and the mix in the economy between the high-wage, high-skills enterprise which practises or is susceptible to Human Resource Management; and low-wage, labour-intensive companies which are perhaps preponderant, certainly in some sectors, and which remain unamenable to exhortations about up-skilling and training. Current strategy may produce a mismatch between highly qualified workers and low-paid unskilled jobs and things can only be taken forward by more sophisticated intervention going beyond a focus on skills as a discrete phenomenon and relating them to the context in which they are developed and operate.

As Keep has observed: 'Rather than a training problem, what we may be faced with, at least in certain parts of the economy, is a problem with product market strategies, work organisation, job design and therefore demand for and usage of skill' (Keep 2002: 468). This takes us further into, on the one hand, the integration of skills into the wider organization of education and, on the other, into the structure and operation of the enterprise and its markets. It suggests that state intervention needs to take greater account of the nature of the economy and the structure of industry and reach into the production process more firmly than hitherto. It affirms that skills cannot stand alone in analysis, in policy or in the workplace. It raises the question of new employment strategies to promote innovation, research and development, and investment, even 'an alternative economic and social model in the UK' (Lloyd and Payne 2002b: 389). As Cutler (1992: 165) argues, a focus on skills tends to stereotype the problem, yet again, as a problem of labour. This characterization may detract from the central role of capital in economic strategy and skills formation and the need to regulate workplace and market to galvanize employers into action.

In the present context that seems unlikely. The continually changing galaxy of skills institutions has lacked coherence and power. Control of policy and strategy has remained firmly in the hands of the neoliberal state and success has proved elusive (Keep 2006). It is questionable whether the government's post-Leitch plans will qualitatively change matters. New Labour's conception of a demand-led approach seems, at least at this stage, limited: 'What all our reforms have in common is that they are trying to put the customer – in this case adult learners and employers – first. We call this our "demand-led" approach' (DIUS 2007: 7). Reflecting on Leitch's central recommendation that all adult skills funding should flow through demand-led routes, it tellingly and a little coyly 'endorses the direction of travel'. But it refuses to implement the proposal immediately for fear of 'destabilising existing networks of colleges and training providers' (ibid.: 18).

Train to Gain stands at the centre of the new thinking. But critical evaluations of the impact of this approach in the ETPs are disregarded (Abramovsky *et al.* 2005). Moreover, as one iconoclastic critic comments:

> The idea that government should fund employers' training directly is, if you stop to think about it, a very odd one. Such training is, after all, something that is meant to contribute directly to production and productivity. We do not usually go around giving direct subsidies for machinery or other investment: in fact, that is definitely frowned upon as disturbing competition, reducing efficiency and favouring established firms over new entrants.
>
> (Wolf 2007: 24)

Social neoliberalism combines brittle state control of skills development and training with generous state largesse towards employers. The consequences may be dysfunctional: 'if these are the fruits of market failure, it makes sense to ensure that the market keeps on failing' (Keep 2006: 53). New Labour has demonstrated flexibility, introducing changes of emphasis and rejigging of institutions within an evolving approach. Evolution is firmly bounded by inflexible principles: light, limited, targeted regulation is a weapon of last resort; Britain has little to learn from European models; confrontation with organized capital is to be avoided at all costs (Keep 2002: 473–4). Once again the barriers to radical change are ideological and political and based on the limits of neoliberalism.

### Skills training: A strategic role for unions?

Critical analysts of New Labour's policies on skills and training have noted that moves towards more radical, regulative, and potentially more effective models, would entail trade unions taking a significant role and adopting a strategic approach to skill formation embedded in the organization of work and markets (Lloyd and Payne 2002b: 370–1). What would a strategic trade union take on skills training look like? The work of the German sociologist Wolfgang Streeck provides the bones of a starting point. Streeck distances himself from a model of cooperation with management that is all too common and which in Britain is sometimes dignified by the term 'partnership'.

> Today, unions are again and again invited to 'cooperate' with management in restructuring, in rebuilding competitiveness, improving quality ... typically such cooperation is not meant to entail more than union leaders explaining to their members why it is necessary to comply with whatever management determines is required – for example, more training and retraining. The rewards held out for such cooperation are improved economic performance with an uncertain share of benefits accruing to union members, and perhaps management abstention from trying to break unions and run the workplace unilaterally.
>
> (Streeck 1992a: 253)

In contrast with this kind of 'partnership', which we might more aptly designate 'subaltern integration' into management goals, what we might denote as 'productivist strategy'

> requires forceful intervention in and regulation of management behaviour with unions potentially and eventually appropriating, through *collective political action*, a significant share of responsibility for productive performance. This is so, and indeed is 'necessary' in the sense that it is *competitively superior* to managerial unilateralism.
>
> (ibid.: 254, original emphasis)

If partnership over skills and training is to mean more than the subordination of unions to management, it demands joint regulation. Management prerogative is deficient because management is a source of incomplete, sometimes faulty, intelligence which requires enriching with the knowledge and judgement of the workforce. Moreover, difficulties in calculating returns on investment in skills and anxieties about competitors poaching trained workers may also curtail management action. In terms of *economic perform-ance*, joint regulation is superior to unilateral regulation. Joint regulation can make management train. Cooperation is compatible with conflict between unions and employers, 'indeed may require a conflictual capability of unions for its success' (ibid.: 264). Successful cooperation may entail high-wage policies and union involvement in standardized training curricula to bar employers from low-skill, low-cost policies. In many cases a productivist strategy requires unions to take on capital to educate it. Unions can develop this approach without sacrificing the integral part that conflict and militancy play in trade unionism and without sacrificing their egalitarian values (ibid.: 266–7).

We should never confuse strategic productivism with subaltern integration, which mistakenly insists on an end to adversarialism in this area and predi-cates that unions can influence a qualitative extension of training without joint regulation in the enterprise, and what is also indispensable, systemic regulation achieved through successful political action influencing the state. How far unions can get with strategic productivism is contingent on the context in which they operate and the balance of forces they confront. The power and orientations of the state and employers are inseparable from the situation of unions and their capacity to change things (Ashton and Green 1996). Streeck notes, although he does not address, the position of unions with declining organizational capacities – he refers to the situation in America. It is a charac-terization which certainly applied as a generalization to British unions in the 1980s and 1990s but which currently is more questionable – certainly for many organizations. Even here he notes that unions which develop the contribution they can make to skills formation may find it possible through bargaining to extract 'a political price for cooperation' (Streeck 1992a: 268).

Streeck's model is derived from Germany (Streeck 1992b). But his con-clusions are susceptible to generalization. They might appear particularly appropriate in Britain given the short-termism of British firms and their reluctance to invest in skills and training. His work was taken up by British scholars (Hyman 1994). Stuart (1996) insisted that the union role in imposing joint regulation was all the more salient in a liberal economy like Britain. The extent to which training as a bargaining issue offered integrative potential was open to doubt and any perceived mutual gains should be subjected to exacting scrutiny. Following Streeck, Stuart depicted skill formation as a distributive issue: 'To suggest that unions should relinquish any import over adversarial issues and engage in negotiations of a more cooperative kind seriously underestimates the likely gains for labour' (ibid.: 263).

The TUC itself emphasized that training was a bargaining issue (TUC 1992), although this was set within its turn to partnership[4] (see McIlroy, chapter 1, this volume). By the mid-1990s limited progress had been made (Claydon and Green 1994) and, on one estimate, only 17 per cent of shop stewards agreed training arrangements (cited in Keep and Rainbird 1995: 535). Nonetheless, these issues remained of intense relevance to trade unions with the election of New Labour. If realization of a strategic approach to skills and transcendence of subaltern integration depends on power and prevailing circumstances, as well as how these circumstances can be exploited by trade unionists, it is important to keep it in sight. It provides a useful measure of the trajectory and outcomes of TUC policy since 1997 to which we now turn.

The election of Tony Blair's government in 1997 rendered possible a renewal of union political action to achieve the re-regulation of skills formation. It encouraged a wide range of training which trade unionists, in accordance with the new tongues of the times, began to refer to as workplace learning. The demand for restoration of legislative scaffolding stood at the heart of TUC policy. Successive Congresses had urged the need for a training levy and rights to paid time off for employees for learning. A statutory framework, trade unionists believed, would underpin the development of social partnership, inspire a new tripartism and spark social dialogue with employers' organizations over skills. The unions took encouragement from their renewed access to government and particularly from the Green Paper *The Learning Age* which projected a 'new and modern role for unions' in training, pump-primed by the state-financed ULF. Workplace learning was pronounced 'a natural issue for partnership' and the statement promised to encourage 'workplace partnerships between employers, employees and trade unions to promote learning' (DfEE 1998a: 43).

But the doors were already closing. It was clear from the key statement, *Learn As You Earn*, that there would be no legal structure. The TUC appeared reluctant to accept this and was reticent in its criticism of government inaction. Although, by 1997, it had recast itself as a pressure group, pressure was limited to discussions with ministers as it sought to expand its new 'insider' role rather than develop public protest or campaigning. The view appeared to be that public dissension would be counterproductive in eliciting concessions from New Labour, a conception which continued to mark the TUC's stance (McIlroy 2000b). The general council's comments on *Learn As You Earn* encapsulated this approach. As far as the TUC was concerned, New Labour *was* proposing a statutory framework: this was presently based on the ILAs, Investors in People and the University of Industry, rather than 'specific obligations on employers to train the workforce'. But 'further statutory provisions' – presumably the unions' core requirements of a levy, responsibilities and rights – would be 'reconsidered' (TUC 1997: 32). Lobbying of Ministers to influence such 'reconsideration' was sustained. The TUC put their case to both the Department for Education and Employment (DfEE) and the Department of Trade and Industry (DTI) without success. Speakers on the floor of Congress were more forthright about New Labour's fudges and failures (McIlroy 2000a).

The TUC maintained a critical but cooperative stance, diluting the language of regulation where it felt it politically appropriate: 'The absence of a strong statutory framework for training was criticised by the General Council

... the General Council called for a modern system of rewards and incentives to employers and individual entitlements to learning' (TUC 1998: 109; and see TUC 1999: 96). Moreover, they believed that 'at long last there is a real political will to create a learning society' (TUC 1998: 108). Therefore, there was little point in quarrelling with a government which was delivering on other fronts, one which was prepared to acknowledge 'that trade unions have an indispensable role as advocates, negotiators and providers of education and training' (TUC 1998: 108). And which was prepared to generously finance that role. From the start the TUC worked closely with the DfEE and later the DTI to develop the ULF. There can be little doubt that the fund and the system of ULRs it helped create were intended by the government to act as compensatory substitutes for legal regulation, inducements which could entice the unions down the informal path of subordinate cooperation with management.

The ULF came on stream in 1998–9 with £8 million allocated for the first four years. Unions supported by the TUC made bids which were assessed by a DfEE panel with TUC representation. Projects ranged from IT development to equality and language training and covered workers from the railways to 'the home shopping sector'. The training of ULRs was central and 'a high proportion of activities are integrated with / focussed on basic skills' (TUC 2002: 118). Over £9 million was allocated to the fund by the government for 2002–3 and £11 million for 2003–4. By 2003, the TUC was reporting that the ULF had financed the training of 6,500 ULRs and fostered the establishment of 180 Learning Centres, while 36,000 people had been involved in learning (TUC 2003: 96). By 2005, the ULF's budget had increased to £14 million with an additional £3 million allocated for IT development and sectoral training and the TUC was reporting that in the last 12 months 67,000 people had been brought into learning and around 4,000 ULRs trained. In an important development it was announced that the Fund would be transferred to the new Union Academy (subsequently re-titled Unionlearn) which would merge TUC Education with TUC Learning Services (TUC 2005: 97–9, 105).

The ULR initiative developed from 1998. ULRs were involved in the workplace and the enterprise in arranging for members' attendance at courses, opening ILA accounts and helping to fund access to learning, although they were soon facing difficulties with paid time off and facilities from employers (TUC 2001: 80). By 2005, there were 12,000 ULRs and a year later, 14,000 such representatives. ULRs were essentially advisers on learning and organizers of provision; they were not learning shop stewards bargaining with management to regulate training and enforce union standards.

These positive developments did not distract the TUC from the necessity for legal intervention and a regulated system, objectives reiterated at annual Congresses. It saw the major aim of the ULF as developing unions' 'capacity to act as partners on workplace learning' (TUC 1998: 108). It was becoming apparent by this time that New Labour's conception of partnership was vague, voluntary and evasive. But for the TUC partnership remained specific and contingent on joint regulation. Joint regulation of training in workplaces was rare (Cully *et al.* 1999: 104–5). Thus legal support for partnership was necessary to extend it (see McIlroy, chapter 2; McIlroy and Daniels, chapter 3, this volume). The unions conceived ULRs as negotiators, rather than simply training advisers. They believed that if New Labour took partnership seriously it should place a duty on employers to negotiate over training (TUC 1998: 108; TUC 2001: 80). In the discussions with ministers over the Employment Relations Act (ERA) 1999 they lobbied for rights for unions to bargain over skills. The government was not prepared to go very far. The ERA introduced a restricted obligation on employers to *consult*, not *negotiate*, over training. Moreover, the obligation to consult was limited to a very small number of situations. It only covered enterprises where unions had invoked the ERA's provisions on union recognition and the Central Arbitration Committee (CAC) had, in consequence, issued an order requiring the employer to recognize a union but the parties had been unable to agree a procedure – leading the CAC to impose one. What the 1999 Act delivered was far from joint regulation and its coverage was extremely limited (ERA s. 5 introducing ss. 70B and C into the Trade Union and Labour Relations (Consolidation) Act (TULR(C)A) 1992).

Despite sustained efforts in ensuing years the unions were frustrated in achieving statutory support for joint regulation of training through the imposition of general duties on employers (McIlroy 2008: 293). Underpinning New Labour's neoliberal abstention was the fact that employers' organizations strenuously opposed obligations to bargain over skills (CBI 2001). This became transparent when the unions pursued another avenue to joint regulation. On the grounds that they should be not only advocates and providers but negotiators, that providing sometimes entailed bargaining and that some, although far too few, did bargain, the TUC argued for negotiating rights for ULRs (TUC 2001: 80). Again, union leaders insisted that legislative backing was imperative if there was to be any real progress towards joint regulation and the skills revolution. Again, the government refused to act (TUC 2000: 79; TUC 2001: 85). Again, the difficulty lay with the state's prohibition of further significant incursion into management prerogative in the aftermath of the ERA 1999. Employers did not wish to negotiate over training and they were not prepared to countenance extending ULR rights to that end (CBI 2001).

A typical New Labour compromise split the difference. The government conceded the key aspects of the CBI case: they denied the unions what they wanted most, but gave them something to be going along with. What unions got were rights to paid time off for ULRs, not rights to bargain for ULRs. The Minister of Skills, John Healey, observed: 'Legal recognition will go a long way towards raising the profile of these representatives and reinforce the job they do' (TUC 2002: 118). Negotiating rights would have strengthened ULRs far more. The Employment Act (EA) 2002 provided them with rights to reasonable paid time off for executing their functions. These were enumerated as analysis of the training needs of members they represented; provision of information and advice to their members; arranging and promoting training; and consulting with employers about these activities (s. 43 EA, s. 168 A TULR(C)A 1992). The new rights applied only to the minority of workplaces where unions were recognized. There was no right for union representatives to negotiate outside the exceptional situation of CAC involvement under the ERA procedure and there was no obligation on employers to even consult over training policy. During the DTI's review of the EA 2002, the debate about the ambit of the EU-inspired Information and Consultation Regulations and at the time of the Warwick Agreement with the government before the 2005 election, the TUC pressed the argument. They got no further (McIlroy 2008: 294).

From the point of view of any halfway effective productivist strategy the situation cried out for statutory support. The government's 1998 Workplace Employee Relations Survey (WERS) reported that in 43 per cent of workplaces union representatives received no information whatsoever about training. Negotiations over training took place in a derisory 3 per cent of workplaces (Cully *et al.* 1999: 104–5). The 2004 WERS found that union representatives received no information from management in 28 per cent of cases, received only information in 26 per cent of cases, were consulted by management in 38 per cent of cases and were involved in negotiations over training in a mere 8 per cent of cases (Kersley *et al.* 2006: 152–5). For trade unionists, even the small-scale improvements reported for 2004 compared with 1998 were welcome. After six years of New Labour the position remained unprepossessing. The slight coverage of collective bargaining placed the growth of ULRs and the ULF in a more critical perspective and put in question the viability of any productivist strategy.

Research has linked union presence with superior training performance in the enterprise (Green *et al.* 1995; Heyes and Stuart 1998) although union recognition rather than the presence of ULRs has been teased out as the crucial factor (Hoque and Bacon 2006). But the question of joint regulation remains central to union agendas and we still know little about how bargaining over workplace learning emerges and operates. The work of Munro and Rainbird (2000a; 2000b; 2004a; 2004b) on the Return to Learn courses, introduced by NUPE and developed by Unison in the 1990s, is sometimes referred to as exemplary (see, for example, Wallis, Stuart and Greenwood 2005). These valuable courses do not tell us a great deal that is new about bargaining over skills. First, they are distinctive in relation to the majority of skills provision resourced by unions through the ULF and work-based training. Second, although styled 'learning partnerships', they represent, in many aspects, a refurbishment of the conventional union day release courses pioneered by the NUM and other unions from the 1950s and continued, notably by the TGWU in the 1990s, in collaboration with universities, as well as the Second Chance to Learn courses, provided by universities and the Workers

Educational Association from the 1970s. Established unions, particularly those in relatively protected environments, were able to develop such provision through the post-war years. Third, such 'partnerships' are discrete expressions of goodwill by management which exceptionally spill over in any measurable fashion into similar generosity in bargaining over pay, conditions, work organization or job security. These learning agreements typically involve little more than the exercise of management prerogative to permit specified paid time-off and unions organizing courses with educational bodies. In terms of meaningful partnership between unions and employers they are relatively trivial and represent old wine in new bottles (McIlroy 2008: 300–1).[5]

The TUC reported on the basis of their own survey that in 2003, 51.3 per cent and, in 2005, 60.6 per cent of ULRs claimed that they had negotiated learning agreements covering paid time off for both ULRs and members and the establishment of workplace learning centres (Unionlearn 2006: 12). There is no suggestion that these agreements regulate the substance of enterprise training and they seem to be limited to the codification of rights of representatives and members to time off. There seems to be some disjuncture between these sorts of returns from ULRs and WERS' findings and we need to know more about the content, provenance and operation of these agreements and their relationship to collective bargaining arrangements.[6]

A study of three organizations in the public and private sector, selected by the TUC as examples of successful union involvement in learning, disclosed ULR involvement in a mix of basic learning from job-specific NVQs through provision for literacy and numeracy to language training and driving lessons. There was no focus on strategic productivism or bargaining over vocational training (Warhurst *et al.* 2007). Further research commissioned by the TUC found five learning agreements in the six organizations studied, although these were broad framework agreements which typically did not regulate vocational training. Rather, workplace learning was consciously separated from collective bargaining; and much of what was reported on was training for employability. It was conventionally viewed as a matter of partnership and mutual gains: the authors consider that unions adopting 'adversarial modes of engagement' are a barrier to effective learning partnerships, which are facilitated by the presence of ULRs, the availability of ULF funding and a roughly equivalent power balance between management and unions (Wallis and Stuart 2007). Overall, the research covers nine enterprises, all of which sought ULF funding. It contains little detailed analysis of the nature, distribution and regulation of employer-provided vocational training and how it relates to the workplace learning which is addressed. However, we are told in one of the reports that 'additionality' is not an issue: union-resourced workplace learning does not substitute for employer training (Warhurst *et al.* 2007: 12).

The tentative conclusion one can draw from this limited work is that workplace learning delivered by unions overlaps with, but is distinct from, employers' vocational training. The former seems to be developing as a state-funded service to managers and trade unionists. In some ways it provides a useful fringe-benefit sanctioned by management. On this restricted evidence there seems to have been a shift in union interest, away from encouraging bargaining over vocational training to brokering an alternative supply of learning for life, leisure and wider employability, with a workplace-related element. Rather than bargaining about training and workplace learning *in toto* as a distributive issue, including a focus on rewards in terms of remuneration, promotion and job enrichment, unions have constructed workplace learning as a consensual annexe to joint regulation. They have not extended collective bargaining over training.

There appear to be clear limits to progress in bargaining over skills. Equally there has been little advance on the creation of the social partnership espoused by the TUC (see McIlroy and Daniels, chapter 3, this volume). The goal of social partnership (TUC 1998: 108) has proved elusive. The TUC was granted three seats on the Skills Task Force and participated with the CBI in a working party on the Treasury initiative on productivity (TUC 2000: 74; CBI/TUC 2001). Nonetheless, the CBI remained hostile to any extension of social partnership: it was adamant that there would be no replication of the European model in Britain (Clough 2007: 15). The unions termed the Skills Alliance a social partnership body: it was a shadow of past tripartism or EU-style social dialogue. It operated fundamentally as a forum for discussion of pre-determined policy in which government and employer interests were predominant: it possessed little power and reflected social partnership in its weakest form (Keep 2006: 51). The unions indulged in wishful thinking when they claimed that the government was 'committed to a more systematic framework including social partnership arrangements at sector level' (TUC 2000: 74). Their representation on the SSCs, like their representation on the LLSCs and other skills bodies, tended to be the product of energetic lobbying and colonization. It remained restricted and these bodies were more a conveyor belt for New Labour initiatives than instruments of policy creation (McIlroy 2008: 291–2).

Even in the aftermath of Leitch, the TUC was urging 'strengthening the social partnership approach on skills' (TUC 2007b: 1). The approach needed introducing in meaningful fashion before it could be strengthened. In more sober moods the point was taken. In 2003, the TUC emphasized to the government the importance of 'the establishment of new social partnership arrangements at the national, regional and sectoral levels to drive forward the skills strategy' (TUC 2003: 92). In 2006, it argued: 'We need to build stronger social partnership arrangements on skills' (TUC 2006b: 16). Nonetheless, Congress House regularly claimed that its limited presence on the skills institutions was strategically fruitful. In 2003 it asserted: 'The General Council have continued to influence national policy through TUC representation on the Learning Skills Council and the boards of the Basic Skills Agency, Investors in People UK, UFI / Learn Direct, the Sector Skills Development Agency' (TUC 2003: 91). Similar sentiments were expressed in 2004 and 2005 (TUC 2004: 102; TUC 2005: 99). In reality only small successes were registered. For example, on the National Skills Task Force the TUC had championed entitlements to paid time off for less skilled workers to attain Level 2 qualifications, a policy which bore some fruit in the ETPs and the Leitch recommendations (Clough 2007: 16). On any balanced assessment and taking account of the big issues, the statutory framework and social partnership, its influence on the evolution of state strategy was marginal.

Explicit differences over policy have been rare. On the whole the TUC has been an enthusiastic advocate of the substance of state skills policy rather than a critic of it. The unions endorsed almost every initiative from the ILAs and the University of Industry to the LSC and the SSCs: their main objection was the need for more union involvement. The TUC's non-critical estimations of Investors for Industry or the ETPs may be contrasted with more searching evaluations from independent researchers (Hoque 2003; Abramovsky *et al.* 2005). The TUC substantially accepted New Labour's conception of globalization as the driver of the skills revolution, the economistic basis of government policy, its emphasis on human capital and the supply side and its eschewal of adversarialism (McIlroy 2000a; 2008: 288–9). Social inclusion, increased participation in education and the extension of opportunity were stressed. Facilitating competitivity was primary: 'There is recognition at the highest level that in today's global economy ignorance costs more than education in terms of lost competition and social exclusion' (TUC 1998: 214). TUC pronouncements were substantially aimed at augmenting union participation in a strategy which was predominantly taken as given. In a context where rigorous critique may have been perceived as 'unhelpful', even failing to facilitate the flow of funds, the emphasis was on more of the same.

The ever-flowing spate of TUC pamphlets devoted to workplace learning disclosed no extended statement on policy which critically engaged with neoliberal theory or prescription. There were occasional, typically terse, exceptions. In its response to the Porter report on productivity in 2003, Congress House referred to the problem of fragile employer demand for skills, the danger of mismatches between quality training and low-skill jobs and the need to stimulate demand by attacking low pay (Clough 2007: 20). The TUC submission to Leitch not only highlighted low levels of investment in skills training but argued that 'skills strategy needs to be linked to an active industrial strategy that addresses the opportunities of globalization while protecting potential casualties' (TUC 2006b: 3).

Over the New Labour years its expressed concerns were more procedural than substantive. Yet the TUC pursued the right to negotiate over training with admirable tenacity and attempted to outflank the government's refusal to grant ULRs rights to negotiate by pressing for statutory backing for learning agreements and learning committees as well as developing a new initiative, Collective Learning Funds (McIlroy 2008: 295). Its preoccupation with legal entitlements and extending the union role meant that it supported the ETPs and Train to Gain, yet challenged Leitch's insistence on a demand-led approach, which it saw as giving too great a role to employers (TUC 2007b). But again, protest subsided and criticism softened in the face of the offer of three seats for trade unionists on the CES and the government's acceptance of a review of legislation in 2010.

If we return to Streeck's analysis, which prefaced this review of TUC policy since 1997, we can conclude, on the limited evidence we have, that British unions have failed to develop a productivist strategy on the lines he adumbrated and that other academics applied to the British case. The unions have been unsuccessful in regulating management rule over skills and training in the workplace. They have been similarly unsuccessful in influencing state policy through collective political action to secure a significant share of responsibility for policies on skills formation, still less productive performance; they have not developed an independent industrial strategy. In the workplace they have acted to insulate learning from union bargaining agendas. They have generally characterized it as a non-adversarial issue, rather than a matter for conflictual cooperation and the imposition of joint regulation. In resourcing learning, unions, facilitated by extensive public funding, have delivered a service that has encouraged the confidence and enhanced the horizons and employability of their members. In terms of joint regulation and its outcomes, success has proved elusive and the approach developed questionable.

For example, a position of relative power parity between employers and unions suggests the opportunity for Streeck's strategic productivism, conflictual cooperation and mobilization to impose benign constraints on vocational training; rather than the occasion for insulation of learning issues and non-adversarial, integrative orientations. There is little evidence in the commissioned case studies for the assertions of TUC officials that an even balance of power and joint-interest approaches produces a wage premium for enhanced skills (Wallis and Stuart 2007: 2). Lack of success in relation to Streeck's strategic productivism has to be related to the wider context and to sustained union weakness. But it is arguable that unions have failed to maximize benign aspects of the current environment or mobilize adequately on the lines of Streeck's suggestions for unions with weak organisational capacities. The emphasis on learning as an integrative issue to be consciously separated from distributive bargaining constitutes an important fault line. It is tempting to conclude that this approach is influenced by government policy, particularly by the generous flow of revenue from the ULF and the consequent need to collaborate closely with the state and with employers in utilizing funds to resource provision and benefit members. The ULF may be achieving its purpose of encouraging desiccated 'partnership', New Labour style, in the workplace.

## The limits of neoliberalism

Social neoliberalism seeks to further social inclusion and productivist versions of welfare and redistribution by redefining citizenship in terms of the right and responsibility to participate in the market (Jayasuriya 2006). This approach may be applied not only to individuals, but to collective actors, such as trade unions. Constructive neoliberalism of the New Labour variety attempts to settle more satisfactorily the problem of trade unionism as an illegitimate constraint on the market and management, a problem that pioneering neoliberalism confronted but failed to resolve. In 1997, unions, despite the Conservatives' best efforts, represented millions of citizens and remained an integral component of the Labour Party. Instead of abolishing the welfare state, New Labour worked to reorganize it. Instead of sustaining their predecessors' exclusion of unions, they have sought to re-include them in economy and society, reconfigured as active, productive elements in the labour market. This is perceived as desirable generally, in terms of economic and social cohesion, and specifically, in terms of the effective management of the 'contentious alliance' of unions and the Labour Party.

If successful, this strategy turns market impediments into market facilitators. It removes constraints on the optimal operation of New Labour as a rational-efficient party playing the electoral market (see McIlroy, chapter 5, this volume). It centres on utilizing unions to deliver skills and training via contracts with the state. The British state's new social contract with the unions conditionally rehabilitates them as economic actors. It diverts opposition to neoliberalism. It promotes market inclusion and a new market agent which lubricates productivity, through the supply of skills, where it once stifled it through the pursuit of collective bargaining. The preamble to the new contract ordains that unions must mend their ways. The state's hazard is that unions can be pushed into doing something useful. They can be diverted from the negative work of interfering with management prerogative towards making it more effective. If not, little in terms of advantage or public expenditure is lost while the state still denies the unions key instruments necessary to any return to adversarialism and obstructive behaviour.[7] Moreover, emphasis on the extension of market opportunity may be perceived by neoliberal technocrats as a vote-winner. Neoliberal governments may take this path 'as much to guarantee themselves a successful niche in the political world of electoral markets as to guarantee their firms a successful niche in the economic world of commodity markets' (Coates 2000: 121).

Lucrative state contracts for skills compensate unions for the state's refusal to foster social partnership or impose a statutory framework for skills formation. They spread joint-interest ideology and they implicate unions in New Labour's conception that labour, not capital, not the restructuring of capitalist industry, is the answer to problems of production; redistribution of training opportunities, not redistribution of wealth and income, is the answer to problems of equality. At the micro-level, union representatives are 'in a unique position of trust and confidence in the workplace . . . best placed to encourage those with basic skills needs to come forward' (DfES 2002: 2–23). At the macro-level, unions constitute already-established national networks of experienced well-connected human resources for the organization and delivery of services. In a situation of relative resource-stringency, union activity is likely to follow funding opportunities as it has in the past (McIlroy 1996b: 102–4). Delivery of skills may help union recovery by providing services to members and demonstrating unions' utility to employers. The state's objectives of turning unions away from joint regulation towards subordinate collaboration with the state (Collins 2001; Ewing 2005) may bear fruit.

Hence the developing system through which trade unions have received over £100 million in modernization money, largely from central government. The learning money has been channelled through the ULF but also via the LSC, complemented by grants from the European Social Fund. The union role has been praised and pronounced a major success by government ministers, union leaders and academics. Its context, wider purposes, relationship to state policies and potential costs in relation to union revitalization, and the form it may take, should be kept in sight. Trade unionists are not, at least not in any conventional commonsense use of the term, partners in this endeavour or architects of the policy context in which delivery of training takes place. They are contractors and clients of the government. They are, to repeat the words of David Blunkett, 'foot soldiers' in an enterprise designed and directed by New Labour's neoliberal generals. They are carrying out a policy they have had no positive influence in determining, a policy consciously based on calculated rejection of TUC policy. The ULF prospectus states explicitly that its purpose is to maximize the union contribution to the government's skill strategy (Unionlearn 2008: 3).

Trade unionists have persuasively argued the need for a regulated system. Yet they are operating on behalf of the state and employers in an unregulated system. Moreover, it is difficult to see how union involvement will progress union policy. The more successful they are, the less compelling the case for change. And the vast majority of union literature describing and assessing the project is single-mindedly enthusiastic, although union objectives remain unrealized. There are obvious difficulties for unions in criticizing a system from which they benefit and more difficulties in expounding radical alternatives to it. The TUC seem more inclined to adopt the old adage 'Don't bite the hand that feeds you' than embrace Elvis Costello's updated version: 'I want to bite the hand that feeds me' (McIlroy 2008).

This new thriving union function may effect other functions such as organizing and bargaining, although its defenders emphasize that it is based on additional resources and complements rather than compromises existing activity. Nonetheless, the influx of new staff and the emergence of new activity require managing by existing staff and supportive resources. Financing learning through the ULF may lessen the urgency of bargaining for it with employers. In the workplace, unions are faced with a decline in activism (Charlwood *et al.* 2006) while the majority of ULRs have had previous involvement as shop stewards and health and safety representatives and may have added the ULR brief to their existing functions (Wood and Moore 2005: 10–11, 24). It is possible, against the background of pressure on bargaining and moves to consultation, that a drift towards emphasis on training within these representatives' functions, as well as the trend towards fewer bargaining stewards and more advisory ULRs, may presage further change in workplace organization, particularly when the literature contains references to members welcoming the less adversarial approach of ULRs (Munro and Rainbird 2004b: 155–6; and see Warhurst *et al.* 2007: 17).

Sustainability is certainly a problem. In 2006–7, 63 per cent of Unionlearn's funding came from the DfES and LSC, 22 per cent from the European Social Fund and 8 per cent from the TUC. Of the estimated £22 million income for 2007–8, only £1 million came from the TUC (Unionlearn 2007). Had the Conservatives been returned in the 2001 general election, TUC general secretary John Monks remarked, 'the future funding of the union learning services would have been put at risk' (TUC 2001: 4). New Labour may not be in office for ever (McIlroy 2008: 298).

If we situate all this in the wider landscapes of government policy, the TUC is making the best of an unsatisfactory job. On the one hand it is arguing that you will only crack Britain's skill productivity problem through robust regulation. On the other it is straining every sinew to make an unregulated system work and proclaiming that it is doing so successfully. On the one hand, it asserts that to do the job properly it needs adequate tools. On the other, it reports it is getting on very well without those tools. It would be unfair to say that the state is opposed to collective bargaining. It just refuses to do anything to extend it beyond the weak provisions in the ERA and the EA. It is denying the unions the weapons they need and in doing so can point to the progress the unions are, on their own account, making without them. Astute commentators take a more realistic view of the potential of unions as agents of change:

> Trade unions now have almost no formal input into national policy deliberations . . . Nor are they able to exert much influence on firms' competitive strategies by extracting wages that block off low-cost, low-quality routes to competitive advantage . . . the language of partnership has been a crucial device deployed by the state as a means of masking the deep, systematic asymmetry of power relationships within the system.
>
> (Keep 2006: 56, citing Streeck 1989: 58)

Green (1998: 137–9) puts his finger on the other side of the coin: we are dealing with what is first and foremost a problem of capital and the state. If they are inadequately committed, not only to the objective but to the means needed to attain it, then the unions are embarking on a labour of Sisyphus, albeit a well-paid one. Success is likely to prove chimerical because of the size of the task the unions are undertaking and the way they are tackling it. The TUC has repeatedly stressed the immensity of the challenge in terms of the numbers of employees who require training and the numbers of employers who do not train and who have little interest in training (TUC 2006b: 5). It is true that significant resources are involved: £22 million annually for Union-learn, 145 staff, scores of officials and activists across the unions, 18,000 ULRs and the enrolment of 100,000 learners a year. In its first nine years the ULF involved 50 unions in 700 workplaces. Situated against the size of the economy, the embedded nature of the problem, and the attitude of employers who are not committed to resolving it, this is a fleabite (Green 1998).

Moreover, the relationship between what the TUC is doing and how this impacts on skills formation requires further analysis. In the 1990s a lot of publicity was accorded to the Ford Motor Company's Employee Development and Assistance Programme (EDAP), an initiative emulated by other employers. EDAP offered workers a wide range of educational opportunities for self-fulfilment and employability. It was financed by the company and managed jointly with the unions. Although few spoke of 'partnership', it was intuitively and plausibly a valuable fringe benefit for employees and, perhaps, attracted goodwill to the company as well as expanding their employees' horizons. It was quite distinct from the company's vocational training provision, a different route to learning which did not encroach on management prerogative in that area (Beattie 1997).

The TUC set out in the 1990s to make vocational training a bargaining issue and stimulate employers to invest in skill formation. Today Unionlearn includes in its indicators of success 'an increase in the incidence of collective bargaining over training' (Unionlearn 2007). Judging by the recent research reports commissioned by the TUC from academics, that objective seems to have got lost somewhere. What seems to be emerging in these accounts is roughly the replication and extension of EDAP schemes, this time paid for by the state and resourced by ULRs. Through the ULF the state is moulding workplace learning. The guidelines for bids explain: 'It is not intended that ULF should be used to replace employer-funded train-ing, for instance, by funding purely job-specific courses for employees which should be the responsibility of employers' (Unionlearn 2008: 7). There may be issues of interpretation in this formulation and some overlap between workplace learning and employers' provision of vocational training. Overall, it seems that the ULF and ULRs are building-on additional learning enclaves separate from the collective bargaining agenda and from whatever enterprise training may or may not exist. Like the EDAP, the product of ULF is integrative and non-adversarial. It is an appreciable distance from strategic productivism.

The consequent increases in workplace learning meet state objectives: they increase the overall amount of learning for employability. Although doubts have been expressed about its lack of emphasis on broader education (Warhurst *et al.* 2007: 6), the new provision may fulfil individuals' aspirations for training for wider employability rather than training for the job they are in. Nonetheless, driven by individual choice, this kind of workplace learning may produce a mismatch between qualifications and jobs: supply does not always create demand. Much of the ULF provision focused on basic skills is questionably workplace learning in the sense that skill is significantly formed in the work process. And it remains unclear whether a path exists from collaboration with employers EDAP/ULF-style to bargaining with employers over vocational training. It is far from transparent how unions move from non-adversarial workplace learning and union learning centres to distributive bargaining; if they do at all. The former may become a substitute for the latter, even an obstacle to it. Unions remain weak. Generally they remain far from well placed to impose productivist strategies on employers. This does not go for all situations. Surely unions should be considering, particularly where 'labour parity' with employers exists, how to move towards strategic productivism as part of strengthening workplace organization and contributing to union revitalization?

The input that workplace learning can currently make to revitalization is debatable and depends on the cogency of the service model of union growth. In that model, potential members and members cast as individual consumers credit unions with provision of services and consequently join or remain in membership (Bassett and Cave 1993). By the end of the 1990s, research suggested that this approach was unlikely to impact qualitatively on union growth. Workers did not join unions for services – including learning. They joined for traditional collective reasons, centrally the desire for protection at work (Waddington and Whitston 1997; Waddington and Kerr 2000; Charlwood 2002). If providing learning did not provide growth – the central issue of British trade unionism – questions might be raised about why so many union staff were resourcing learning instead of organizing. Advocates of learning argued that, unlike other individual services such as financial benefits or legal aid, learning was collective because it was provided in a collective context (Munro and Rainbird 2004b: 152). So of course is legal aid. While the education of activists in trade unionism provides a collective classroom experience, this dimension may be absent from much workplace learning where members are dispersed across different courses, modes of provision and institutions. Workplace learning is often learning for individual employability and individual mobility as prescribed by social neoliberalism and opposed to collective conceptions of emancipation.

An allied approach responded to the lack of pulling power that research ascribed to the service model by claiming that learning was pregnant with possibilities for growth because it was intimately connected to the more fecund organizing agenda. Provision of learning services could increase recruitment and retention rates and stimulate activism. This seemed an unnecessary exercise in linguistic appropriation. The organizing agenda was conventionally perceived as representing a break with the service/servicing model. It was about workers combining collectively to protect themselves against employers. It emphasized self-servicing, self-regulation by members and building relatively autonomous workplace organization. In contrast with resourcing workplace learning it had strong, collective and adversarial implications (see Daniels, chapter 8, this volume). True, learning, for example in the case of migrant workers, might ignite or facilitate organizing. In the organizing model most learning is learning to organize. Commonsensically and logically, workplace learning as it presently exists is best conceived as the provision of a service, and recruitment and retention related to its provision is most usefully apprehended as illustrating the efficacy or otherwise of the service model.

State funding builds its own constituency and from 2002 the TUC began to emphasize that learning was part of the organizing agenda. Under John Monks, learning mission statements were about learning and partnership with employers. In conjunction with wider changes (see McIlroy and Daniels, chapter 3, this volume) involving rebalancing partnership and organizing, the refrain under Monks' successor, Brendan Barber, was that, for trade unionists, 'Learning is firmly part of their organizing agenda' (Unionlearn 2005: 1). Part of Unionlearn's mission is 'promoting integrated learning and organizing strategies' and it has recently appointed an organizing officer (TUC 2006a: 121). Attempts to utilize workplace learning to mobilize members and facilitate organizing are welcome. But enthusiasm for the organizing potential inherent in Unionlearn and the ULF may be related to the goal of legitimating, extending and protecting funding and deflection of criticism about it. It lacks a compelling evidential base. Academic studies which pose a connection between learning and significant increases in membership and activism, and on that basis predicate that learning has and can play a significant role in meaningful trade union revitalization, extrapolate unconvincingly from small-scale studies and a small number of cases. They fail to critically engage with the earlier research which demonstrated that provision of learning – in some cases provision of the same courses – was not a major generator of recruitment or retention, still less organizing (McIlroy 2008: 300–3).

At best the jury is still out on the question of whether workplace learning can meaningfully contribute to union revitalization. It seems unlikely. We can be less tentative about greater regulation of skills formation and collective bargaining to increase skills. Trade unions have not been successful in challenging state strategy or in significantly extending joint regulation of training and imposing benign constraints on employers to invest and upskill. The ULF/ULR model of partnership is not so much subaltern integration as the cultivation of a specialized HRM enclave, pump-primed by the state and insulated from bargaining mechanisms and mainstream industrial relations, and, crucially, the roots of Britain's skills problem: management prerogative. Britain's unions have not taken significant steps towards strategic productivism. They have come up against the limits of neoliberalism.

## Notes

1 American socialists used to observe: 'Ice is what the poor get in winter and the rich get in summer.'
2 There are different systems in England, Northern Ireland, Scotland and Wales, although the unions' role is broadly similar.

3   Lord Leitch (2006: 11) quoted from Adam Smith's *The Wealth of Nations* (1776):
    'the greater part of what is taught in schools and universities . . . does not seem to
    be a proper preparation for that of business.'
4   For contemporary arguments for an integrative accommodative approach by
    unions to skills formation see Mathews (1993).
5   See, for example, Croucher and Halstead (1990); McIlroy (1990, 1996a). For the
    TGWU courses see McIlroy (1989); Fisher (2005). For the Second Chance to Learn
    courses see Yarnit (1980).
6   We are not told a great deal about the survey, only that 'initial processing of the
    data was undertaken by the Labour Research Department' and that it was limited
    to England. Of the 841 responses, only 66.5 per cent were active as ULRs; 14 per cent
    were not currently ULRs and 19.5 per cent did not confirm whether they were or
    not so were excluded (Unionlearn 2006: no pagination).
7   For the British state, despite its embrace of neoliberalism, £100 million is a baga-
    telle. For the unions, it is money in fair words.

## Bibliography

Abramovsky, L., Battistin, E., Fitzsimons, E., Goodman, A. and Simpson, H. (2005)
   *The Impact of the Employer Training Pilots on the Take-up of Training Among
   Employers*, Nottingham: DfES.
Ashton, D. (2004) 'The political economy of workplace learning', in H. Rainbird,
   A. Fuller and A. Munro (eds) *Workplace Learning in Context*, London: Routledge.
——— (2006) *Lessons from Abroad: Developing Sector-based Approaches to Skills*,
   London: Sector Skills Development Agency.
Ashton, D. and Green, F. (1996) *Education, Training and the Global Economy*,
   Aldershot: Edward Elgar.
Bassett, P. and Cave, A. (1993) *All for One: The Future of the Unions*, London: Fabian
   Society.
Beattie, A. (1997) *Working People and Lifelong Learning: A Study of the Impact of an
   Employee Development Scheme*, Leicester: National Institute of Adult Continuing
   Education.
Brown, G. (1994a) *Fair is Efficient: A Socialist Agenda for Fairness*, London: Fabian
   Society.
——— (1994b). 'The politics of potential' in D. Miliband (ed.) *Reinventing the Left*,
   Cambridge: Polity Press.
Campbell, M., Baldwin, S., Johnson, S., Chapman, R., Upton, A. and Walton, F.
   (2001) *The State of Skills in England 2001*, Sudbury: DfES.
Castells, M. (1996) *The Rise of the Network Society*, Oxford: Blackwell.
Charlwood, A. (2002) 'Why do non-union employees want to unionize? Evidence
   from Britain', *British Journal of Industrial Relations*, 40:3, 463–91.
Charlwood, A., Greenwood, I. and Wallis, E. (2006) 'The dynamics of trade union
   activism in Great Britain, 1991–2003', paper presented to the 24th Annual
   International Labour Process Conference, April 10–12, London.
Claydon, T. and Green, F. (1994) 'Can trade unions improve training in Britain?',
   *Personnel Review*, 23:2, 37–51.
Clough, B. (2004) *From Spearholders to Stakeholders: The Emerging Role of Unions in
   the UK Learning and Skills System*, London: TUC.
——— (2007) *From Voluntarism to Post-Voluntarism: The Emerging Role of Unions in
   the Vocational Education and Training System*, London: Unionlearn.

Coates, D. (2000) *Models of Capitalism: Growth and Stagnation in the Modern Era*, Cambridge: Polity Press.

Collins, H. (2001) 'Regulating the employment relation for competitiveness', *Industrial Law Journal*, 30:3, 17–46.

Confederation of British Industry (CBI) (2001) *The CBI Response to the Consultation Paper 'Providing Statutory Rights for Union Learning Representatives'*, London: CBI.

CBI / TUC (2001) *The UK Productivity Challenge. Submission to Treasury Productivity Initiative*, London: CBI.

Crouch, C., Finegold, D. and Sako, M. (1999) *Are Skills the Answer? The Political Economy of Skill Creation in Advanced Industrial Countries*, Oxford: Oxford University Press.

Croucher, R. and Halstead, J. (1990) 'The origin of "liberal" adult education for miners at Sheffield in the post war period: a study in adult education and the working class', *Trade Union Studies Journal*, 21, 3–14.

Cully, M., Woodland, S., O'Reilly, A. and Dix, G. (1999) *Britain at Work*, London: Routledge.

Cutler, T. (1992) 'Vocational training and British economic performance: a further instalment of the British labour problem', *Work, Employment and Society*, 6:2, 161–83.

Davies, P. and Freedland, M. (2007) *Towards a Flexible Labour Market: Labour Legislation and Regulation since the 1990s*, Oxford: Oxford University Press.

Department for Children, Schools and Families (DCSF) and Department for Innovation, Universities and Skills (DIUS) (2008) *Raising Expectation: Enabling the System to Deliver*, London: DCSF.

Department for Education and Employment (DfEE) (1998a) *The Learning Age: A Renaissance for a New Britain*, London: HMSO.

—— (1998b) *University for Industry: Pathfinder Prospectus*, London: DfEE.

—— (1999a) *Learning to Succeed: A New Framework for Post-16 Learning*, London: HMSO.

—— (1999b) *The Learning and Skills Council Prospectus: Learning to Succeed*, London: DfEE.

Department for Education and Skills (DfES) (2002) *The Union Learning Fund – United Kingdom*, London: HMSO.

Department for Education and Skills (DfES), HM Treasury, Department of Trade and Industry (DTI) and Department of Work and Pensions (DWP) (2003) *21st Century Skills – Realising our Potential – Individuals, Employers, Nation*, London: HMSO.

Department for Innovation, Universities and Skills (DIUS) (2007) *World-Class Skills: Implementing the Leitch Review of Skills in England*, London: HMSO.

Ewing, K. (2005) 'The function of trade unions', *Industrial Law Journal*, 34:1, 1–22.

Fisher, J. (2005) *Bread on the Waters: A History of TGWU Education 1922–2000*, London: Lawrence and Wishart.

Gamble, A. (2006) 'Two faces of neoliberalism', in R. Robison (ed.) *The Neoliberal Revolution: Forging the Market State*, Basingstoke: Palgrave.

Gennard, J. (1987) 'The NGA and the impact of new technology', *New Technology, Work and Employment*, 2:2, 126–41.

—— (1990) *The History of the National Graphical Association*, London: Unwin Hyman.

Giddens, A. (2000) *The Third Way and its Critics*, Cambridge: Polity Press.

Green, F. (1998) 'Securing commitment to skill formation policies', *New Political Economy*, 3:1, 134–8.

Green, F., Machin, S. and Wilkinson, D. (1995) *Trade Unions and Training: An Analysis of Training Practice in Unionised and Non-Unionised Workplaces*, Sheffield: Employment Department.

Grugulis, I. (2003) 'The contribution of NVQs to the growth of skills in the UK', *British Journal of Industrial Relations*, 41:3, 457–75.

Heyes, J. and Stuart, M. (1998) 'Bargaining for skills: trade unions and training at the workplace', *British Journal of Industrial Relations*, 36:3, 459–67.

Hoque, K. (2003) 'All in all, it's just another plaque on the wall: the incidence and impact of the Investors in People standard', *Journal of Management Studies*, 40:2, 543–71.

Hoque, K. and Bacon, N. (2006) 'Trade union recognition, union learning representatives and training incidence in Britain', Paper to *British Journal of Industrial Relations* conference, Cardiff, May.

Hyman, R. (1994) 'Changing trade union identities and strategies', in R. Hyman and A. Ferner (eds) *New Frontiers in European Industrial Relations*, Oxford: Blackwell.

Jayasuriya, K. (2006) 'Economic constitutionalism, liberalism and the new welfare governance', in R. Robison (ed.) *The Neoliberal Revolution: Forging the Market State*, Basingstoke: Palgrave.

Keep, E. (2002) 'The English vocational education and training policy debate – fragile "technologies" or opening the "black box": two competing versions of where we go next', *Journal of Education and Work*, 15:4, 457–79.

—— (2006) 'State control of the English education and training system – playing with the biggest train set in the world', *Journal of Vocational Education and Training*, 58:1, 47–64.

Keep, E. and Mayhew, K. (1999) 'The assessment: knowledge, skills and competitiveness', *Oxford Review of Economic Policy*, 15:1, 1–15.

Keep, E. and Rainbird, H. (1995) 'Training', in P. Edwards (ed.) *Industrial Relations: Theory and Practice in Britain*, Oxford: Blackwell.

—— (2003) 'Training', in P. Edwards (ed.) *Industrial Relations: Theory and Practice*, 2nd edition, Oxford: Blackwell.

Kersley, B., Alpin, C., Forth, J., Bryson, A., Bewley, H., Dix, G. and Oxenbridge, S. (2006). *Inside the Workplace: Findings from the 2004 Workplace Employment Relations Survey*, London: Routledge.

King, D. (1993) 'The Conservatives and training policy: from a tripartite to a neoliberal regime', *Political Studies*, 41:2, 214–35.

King, D. and Wickham-Jones, M. (1998) 'Training without the state? New Labour and labour markets', *Policy and Politics*, 26:4, 439–55.

Labour Party (1996) *Learn As You Earn: Labour's Plans for a Skills Revolution*, London: Labour Party.

—— (1997) *New Labour: Because Britain Deserves Better*, London: Labour Party.

Learning and Skills Council (LSC) (2006) *National Employers Skills Survey 2005*, Coventry: LSC.

Leitch, Lord (2006) *Prosperity for All in the Global Economy–World Class Skills. Final Report*, London: HMSO.

Lloyd, C. and Payne, J. (2002a) 'Developing a political economy of skill', *Journal of Education and Work*, 15:4, 365–90.

—— (2002b) '"On the political economy of skill": assessing the possibilities for a viable high skills project in the United Kingdom', *New Political Economy*, 7:3, 367–95.

McIlroy, J. (1989) 'Back to the future', *Adults Learning*, 1:3, 10–18.

—— (1990) 'The triumph of technical training', in B. Simon (ed.) *The Search for Enlightenment: The Working Class and Adult Education in the Twentieth Century*, London: Lawrence and Wishart.

—— (1996a) 'Independent working class education and trade union education and training', in R. Fieldhouse and Associates, *A History of Modern British Adult Education*, Leicester: National Institute of Adult and Continuing Education.

—— (1996b) 'From the great tradition to NVQs: universities and trade union education at *fin de siécle*', in J. Wallis (ed.) *Liberal Adult Education: The End of An Era?* Nottingham: Continuing Education Press, University of Nottingham.

—— (2000a). 'Lifelong learning: trade unions in search of a role', in J. Field and M. Leicester (eds) *Lifelong Learning: Education Across the Lifespan*, London: Routledge.

—— (2000b) 'The new politics of pressure – the Trades Union Congress and New Labour in government', *Industrial Relations Journal*, 31:1, 2–16.

—— (2008) 'Ten years of New Labour: workplace learning, social partnership and union revitalization in Britain', *British Journal of Industrial Relations*, 46:2, 283–313.

Mathews, J. (1993) 'The industrial relations of skill formation', *International Journal of Human Resource Management*, 4:3, 591–609.

Munro, A. and Rainbird, H. (2000a) 'The new unionism and the new bargaining agenda: Unison-employer partnerships on workplace learning in Britain', *British Journal of Industrial Relations*, 38: 223–40.

—— (2000b) 'Unison's approach to lifelong learning', in M. Terry (ed.), *Redefining Public Sector Unionism – Unison and the Future of Trade Unions*, London: Routledge.

—— (2004a) 'Opening doors as well as banging on tables: an assessment of Unison-employer partnerships on learning in the UK public sector', *Industrial Relations Journal*, 35: 419–33.

—— (2004b) 'The workplace learning agenda – new opportunities for trade unions', in G. Healy, E. Heery, P. Taylor and W. Brown (eds) *The Future of Worker Representation*, Basingstoke: Palgrave.

Nolan, P and Slater, G. (2003) 'The labour market: history, structure and prospects', in P. Edwards (ed.) *Industrial Relations: Theory and Practice in Britain*, 2nd edition, Oxford: Blackwell.

Robison, R. (2006) 'Neoliberalism and the market state: what is the ideal shell?', in R. Robison (ed.) *The Neoliberal Revolution: Forging the Market State*, Basingstoke: Palgrave.

Shackleton, J. (1995) *Training for Employment in Western Europe and the United States*, Aldershot: Edward Elgar.

Shaikh, A. (2003) 'Who pays for the "welfare" in the welfare state?', *Social Research*, 70:2, 531–50.

Shaikh, A. and Tonak, E. (2000) 'The rise and fall of the US welfare state', in R. Baiman, H. Boushey and D. Saunders (eds) *Political Economy and Contemporary Capitalism: Radical Perspectives on Economic Theory and Policy*, Armonk, NY: M.E. Sharpe.

Streeck, W. (1989) 'Skills and the limits of neo-liberalism: the enterprise of the future as a place of learning', *Work, Employment and Society*, 3:1, 89–104.

—— (1992a) 'Training and the new industrial relations: a strategic role for unions?', in M. Regini (ed.) *The Future of Labour Movements*. London: Sage.

—— (1992b) *Social Institutions and Economic Performance*, London: Sage.

Stuart, M. (1996) 'The industrial relations of training: a reconsideration of training arrangements', *Industrial Relations Journal*, 27:3, 253–65.

Stuart, M. and Wallis, E. (2007) 'Partnership approaches to learning: a seven-country study', *European Journal of Industrial Relations*, 13:3, 301–21.

TUC (1992) *Bargaining for Skills: A Call to Action*, London: TUC.

—— (1997) *Report to Congress*, London: TUC.

—— (1998) *Report to Congress*, London: TUC.

—— (1999) *Report to Congress*, London: TUC.

—— (2000) *Report to Congress*, London: TUC.

—— (2001) *Report to Congress*, London: TUC.

—— (2002) *Report to Congress*, London: TUC.

—— (2003) *Report to Congress*, London: TUC.

—— (2004) *Report to Congress*, London: TUC.

—— (2005) *Report to Congress*, London: TUC.

—— (2006a) *Report to Congress*, London: TUC.

—— (2006b) *2020 Vision for Skills: Priorities for the Leitch Review of Skills*, London: TUC.

—— (2007a) *Report to Congress*, London: TUC.

—— (2007b) *Response to Delivering World Class Skills in a Demand Led System*, London: TUC.

Unionlearn (2005) *Changing Lives Through Learning – A Guide to Unionlearn*, London: Unionlearn.

—— (2006) *Making a Real Difference: Union Learning Reps. A Survey*, London: Unionlearn.

—— (2007) *Unionlearn Annual Report*, London: Unionlearn.

—— (2008) *Union Learning Fund Prospectus, Round II*, London: Unionlearn.

Waddington, J. and Kerr, A. (2000) 'Towards an organizing model in Unison? A trade union membership strategy in transition', in M. Terry (ed.) *Redefining Public Sector Unionism: Unison and the Future of Trade Unions*, London: Routledge.

Waddington, J. and Whitston, C. (1997) 'Why do people join unions in a period of membership decline?' *British Journal of Industrial Relations* 35:4, 515–46.

Wallis, E., Stuart, M. and Greenwood, I. (2005) ' "Learners of the workplace unite!": an empirical examination of the UK trade union learning representative initiative', *Work, Employment and Society*, 19:2, 283–304.

Wallis, E. and Stuart, M. (2007) *A Collective Learning Culture: A Qualitative Study of Workplace Learning Agreements*, London: Unionlearn.

Warhurst, C., Findlay, P., and Thompson, P. (2007) *Organizing to Learn and Learning to Organize*, London: Unionlearn.

White, S. (1997) 'What do egalitarians want?', in J. Franklin (ed.) *Equality*, London: Institute for Public Policy Research.

Wolf, A. (2007) 'Round and round the houses', *Adults Learning*, October, 23–5.

Wood, H. and Moore, S. (2005) *An Evaluation of the UK Union Learning Fund: Its Impact on Unions and Employers. Final Report*, London: Working Lives Institute.

Wood, S. (1998) 'Building a governance structure for vocational training? Employers, the state and the TEC experiment in Britain', in P. Culpepper and D. Finegold (eds) *The German Skills Machine in Comparative Perspective*, Oxford: Bergbahn Books.

Yarnit, M. (1980) 'Second Chance to Learn, Liverpool: class and adult education', in J. Thompson (ed.) *Adult Education for a Change*, Hutchinson.

# 10  Strikes

## Industrial conflict under New Labour

*Dave Lyddon*

The most explicit statement of New Labour's attitudes to strikes was in Prime Minister Tony Blair's foreword to the 1998 White Paper *Fairness at Work*: 'The days of strikes without ballots, mass picketing . . . and secondary action are over' (Blair 1998). Ten years of government have not changed New Labour's determination to maintain the Conservatives' legislative framework on industrial action. Yet, as with all governments, it has had to deal with strikes (particularly in the public sector) pragmatically, balancing the need to control public-sector labour costs with the state's preference for 'industrial peace', while avoiding fighting on more than one front at a time.

New Labour's antipathy to the exercise of the very limited right to strike has not differed significantly from that of its Conservative predecessors, as its language and actions testify. Even before he came to power, Blair observed that New Labour would 'not cave in to unrealistic pay demands' or 'be held to ransom' by the unions' (*Sun*, 4 April 1997). In a series of public-sector disputes, from the firefighters in 2002 – who were accused by some government ministers of playing into the hands of terrorists – to the prison officers in 2007, New Labour has excoriated strikers and threatened, or initiated, legal action (Seifert and Sibley 2005: 127; *Guardian*, 30 August 2007). To adapt Michael Frayn (1967: 160): New Labour 'concedes the right of men [and women] . . . to withdraw their labour. It just draws the line at strikes.'

New Labour's task has been made easier because it inherited a low level of strike activity. The annual number of strikes fell from around 2,000 in 1979 to about 200 through the 1990s. It decreased further in the 2000s, approaching 'close to a minimum level' (Edwards 2001). Working days 'lost' also declined in the early 1990s, in the almost total absence of large or long strikes, to the lowest levels since records began in 1893 (Lyddon 2007); in 2001 the official collection of strike statistics came under threat. The most strike-prone industries in the 1970s had been 'the large, strategically important industries most thoroughly entangled in . . . the pressures and tensions of the market' (Cronin 1979: 187). Several – manufacturing, transport and coal – were subject to market restructuring in the 1980s, involving major job losses and significant changes in working practices. Increasingly restrictive legislation facilitated tactical use of legal injunctions by employers to undermine some of the more important defensive strikes. The combination of economic and legal pressures resulted in some crushing defeats for unions and set up a powerful 'demonstration effect'. In this period of 'coercive pacification', 'each defeat discourages others from the risk of a strike' (Hyman 1984: 225). The miners' rout at the hands of the government in 1984–5 (and subsequent butchery of their industry) was a catastrophe, seared into the soul of the trade union movement, whose official response was first 'new realism' and then 'partnership'.

Edwards (1983: 233–4) once suggested that, as the 'character' of British post-war strikes was 'firmly embedded in traditions of workplace organisa-tion', it would take 'a major upheaval to destroy the practice of solving disputes at the point of production'. That is what happened in the private sector, with union density and collective bargaining coverage now signifi-cantly lower than their 1979 peak (see McIlroy and Daniels, chapter 3, this volume). Consequent on this, Elgar and Simpson (1993: 106) highlighted the 'increased awareness' of the 'complete vulnerability' of workers taking industrial action to disciplinary sanctions in an environment of employer and government aggression (and, at that time, high unemployment).

More recently, Edwards (2001) noted that while in some industries strike action had been 'a relatively normal extension of collective bargaining . . . it is now more considered and less organically part of industrial life'. Strikes remained important: 'as bargaining levers in pay negotiations'; and 'to signal discontent over new working arrangements', particularly in large organiza-tions or where there was a tradition of militancy. They still occurred in 'unexpected places'. But the low level of UK strike activity reflects a general 'tertiarisation of industrial conflict' in Europe and North America: there is a different pattern of action as it is 'the customers of these services and the citizens at large' who are (sometimes immediately) affected by tertiary (par-ticularly public-) sector strikes compared to the slower impact of stoppages in manufacturing and mining (Bordogna and Cella 2002: 605).

This chapter provides the first systematic account of strikes since 1997.[1] It analyses, in turn, the public services and transport, communication and dis-tribution – the sectors where most strikes now occur – followed by the media, entertainment and sports, and then the rest of the economy, including manu-facturing. The remainder of the chapter discusses employer and union tactics. It argues that the 'more considered' quality of strikes (to use Edwards's term), with protracted planning, balloting and action, along with the tactical use of ballots, ensures in some industries that disputes may go on longer than in the past. The low volume of strike activity does not necessarily indicate reduced conflict.

## The national picture

Table 10.1 gives annual averages (based on years experiencing a similar num-ber of strikes) for the main indicators. It demonstrates the remorseless decline

*Table 10.1*    Strike activity 1968–2006 (annual averages)

| Period | Number of strikes | Workers involved | Working days lost |
|--------|-------------------|------------------|-------------------|
| 1968–1974 | 2,846 | 1,684,000 | 11,703,000 |
| 1975–1979 | 2,310 | 1,658,000 | 11,663,000 |
| 1980–1984 | 1,351 | 1,298,000 | 10,486,000 |
| 1985–1990 | 838 | 702,000 | 3,600,000 |
| 1991–1996 | 244 | 226,000 | 656,000 |
| 1997–2001 | 192 | 145,000 | 357,000 |
| 2002–2006 | 134 | 438,000 | 728,000 |

*Sources: Employment and Productivity Gazette* 1969–70; *Department of Employment Gazette* 1971–9; *Employment Gazette* 1980–95; *Labour Market Trends* 1996–2006; *Economic & Labour Market Review* 2007.

*Note:*
The number of strikes refers to those 'beginning' in a year, which is lower than those 'in progress' during a year.

in strike numbers from the peak of 1968–74. Numbers of workers involved and days lost show that a similar fall in the average size and length of strikes only really operated from the mid-1980s and has been slightly reversed since the beginning of the 2000s.

These figures come from the official statistics:[2] 'Stoppages involving fewer than ten workers *or* lasting less than one day are . . . excluded unless the total number of days lost in the dispute is 100 or more' (Hale 2007: 35, added emphasis). There has been significant under-recording of the number of strikes meeting this threshold, though most of those excluded are likely to be close to it and do not greatly affect the days-lost figure, which is dominated by the largest strikes each year (Brown 1981).

Table 10.2 shows changes in strike numbers by broad employment sectors. The demise of coalmining in the 1990s ended strikes there. But manufacturing and construction remain large employers; the former has been most affected by globalization while construction has long been poorly unionized outside the engineering construction sector. Public services and transport and communication, while not always monopoly suppliers, deal with essential services, which makes most groups of workers difficult to replace.

Table 10.3 compares recent strike activity in the public and private sector. The fluctuation in total days lost is due to the presence or absence of large disputes in the public sector. Notwithstanding the decline in strike numbers in the early 2000s, there is evidence of increased activity in the public sector.

### Public services

Despite New Labour's initial tight spending limits, public-sector unions were 'largely quiescent' (Hyman 1999). But the 1999 local government pay negotiations for England and Wales were seen by the employers as 'a close run

*Table 10.2* Annual average number of strikes by sector for different periods 1968–2006

| Years | MESV | Other manufacturing | CTD | Construction | Coal | Public services | Other | Total |
|---|---|---|---|---|---|---|---|---|
| 1968–74 | 1,355 | 486 | 421 | 257 | 202 | 75 | 58 | 2,846 |
| 1975–9 | 966 | 457 | 263 | 211 | 277 | 98 | 67 | 2,310 |
| 1980–4 | 421 | 237 | 204 | 57 | 288 | 123 | 37 | 1,351 |
| 1985–90 | 203 | 98 | 157 | 24 | 199 | 164 | 13 | 851 |
| 1991–6 | 54 | 24 | 48 | 10 | 10 | 101 | 8 | 253 |
| 1997–2001 | 28 | 12 | 86 | 14 | 1 | 57 | 8 | 199 |
| 2002–6 | 16 | 14 | 45 | 3 | 1 | 55 | 8 | 137 |

*Source:* as in table 10.1.

*Note:*
Data before 1985 refers to stoppages beginning in calendar year. From 1985 it refers to stoppages ongoing in that year.
MESV = metals, engineering, shipbuilding and vehicles; CTD = communication, transport and distribution. Some disputes cover more than one sector; as a result the sum of the individual columns for each period is greater than the total.

*Table 10.3*  Public and private sector strike activity 1997–2006

| Year | Working days lost | | | Workers involved | | | Number of strikes | | |
|------|-------|-------|-------|-------|-------|-------|-------|-------|-------|
| | *Private* | *Public* | *Total* | *Private* | *Public* | *Total* | *Private* | *Public* | *Total* |
| 1997 | 163,000 | 71,000 | 235,000 | 127 | 89 | 130,000 | 127 | 89 | 216 |
| 1998 | 165,000 | 117,000 | 282,000 | 88 | 78 | 93,000 | 88 | 78 | 166 |
| 1999 | 172,000 | 70,000 | 242,000 | 102 | 103 | 141,000 | 102 | 103 | 205 |
| 2000 | 136,000 | 363,000 | 499,000 | 99 | 113 | 183,000 | 99 | 113 | 212 |
| 2001 | 128,000 | 397,000 | 525,000 | 83 | 111 | 180,000 | 83 | 111 | 194 |
| 2002 | 200,000 | 1,123,000 | 1,323,000 | 85 | 61 | 943,000 | 85 | 61 | 146 |
| 2003 | 130,000 | 369,000 | 499,000 | 87 | 46 | 151,000 | 87 | 46 | 133 |
| 2004 | 163,000 | 742,000 | 905,000 | 62 | 68 | 293,000 | 62 | 68 | 130 |
| 2005 | 59,000 | 99,000 | 157,000 | 56 | 60 | 93,000 | 56 | 60 | 116 |
| 2006 | 98,000 | 656,000 | 755,000 | 71 | 87 | 713,000 | 71 | 87 | 158 |

*Source:* Hale (2007)

*Note:*
Stoppages in progress during year.

thing' with agreement achieved only by assisted bargaining under ACAS auspices. There were one-day strikes over pay in the 32 local authorities in Scotland in August and September 2000. The GMB and TGWU then accepted an offer but Unison rejected it, undertaking indefinite selective action from November 2000 to January 2001; the dispute lost 273,000 days, involving 83,000 workers.

The largest national pay strike for many years, on 17 July 2002 (Nolda 2004: 380–4), was the first joint manual and white-collar national strike in local government (England and Wales), following the 1997 single-status agreement. It was probably the biggest-ever stoppage by women workers, whether the unions' estimate of 750,000 strikers or the employers' of less than 500,000 is accepted. John Edmonds, GMB general secretary, suggested 'some people in Downing Street have been telling Tony Blair he needs to have his own miners' strike and it would seem that ministers have picked local government' (*Guardian*, 13 July 2002).

But when the unions announced further strikes, with selective action in between, the employers feared alienating public opinion as the lowest hourly rates were still below £5. An immediate problem was that ministers and council executives could 'risk heavy criticism for being on holiday while parts of Britain grind to a halt' (*Guardian*, 20 July 2002). Even more significant was the expected confrontation with the FBU, 'a more formidable opponent', raising the prospect of two simultaneous disputes, which would be 'very difficult to manage'. ACAS brokered a settlement early in August. Charles Nolda, the local government employers' secretary, was relieved that the dispute had been 'nipped in the bud' (Nolda 2004: 382, 384)

For many, Labour's 'miners' strike' was its battle with the firefighters, whose demand for a £30,000 salary led to several strikes (one 24-hour, three 48-hour and one eight-day) in the winter of 2002–3. Just before the eight-day strike deadline, a settlement seemed to have been agreed: this amounted to 16 per cent over two years, linked to 'modernization'. It was dramatically snatched away in the small hours of 22 November 2002 when John Prescott, Deputy Prime Minister, intervened, despite possessing no constitutional role. Nolda, the employers' secretary, thought that 'the potential impact of this deal on public sector pay policy became more important than avoiding a strike' (Seifert and Sibley 2005: 144).

In January 2003 the government announced legislation granting it powers to impose settlements. This gave the FBU urgent reasons to reach agreement, especially in the build-up to the invasion of Iraq, with a claimed 19,000 members of the British armed forces engaged in providing emergency fire cover. A proposed 20 March strike was cancelled and the union agreed not to take further action while British troops were engaged in Iraq, though a settlement was not achieved until June 2003. It required a ballot, in August 2004, for another national strike, to force the employers to stick to the 2003 settlement (ibid.: 182, 222–4).

Overlapping with the firefighters' strikes was a 'festering series of disputes'

(*Financial Times*, 25 November 2002) through 2002 and 2003 to increase public-sector London weighting allowances. These received limited press coverage, with the (London) *Evening Standard* the only major newspaper to report some of the stoppages. Teachers struck twice: the NUT alone in March 2002, joined by the NAS/UWT in November. Education Secretary Estelle Morris was 'furious', fearing a return to 'the dark ages of dispute and conflict' (*Guardian*, 6 March 2002); another minister argued that giving evidence to the School Teachers Review Body was 'the way to negotiate – not through strikes' (*Guardian*, 27 November 2002).

There was a more sustained London weighting campaign in local government: Unison held a one-day strike in May and two days in June 2002, then another strike in October, this time involving the TGWU and GMB, followed by selective strikes in several boroughs in October and November 2002. Unison members also stopped work across London on the same day as the teachers in November. Further strikes, targeting individual boroughs, followed from March to December 2003, initially with the TGWU and GMB before these unions settled. Yet another all-London Unison strike in October 2003 coincided with the second of two postal workers' strikes on the issue. There were joint one-day strikes – in November 2002 and March 2003 – by the university unions, AUT, NATFHE, Amicus and Unison.

There was little coordination, although early stoppages coincided with the firefighters' strikes; the local government stoppages fed into the campaign for the 2002 national strike; and the postal workers' London weighting strikes spilled over into a major unofficial stoppage. A threatened large-scale one-day strike across several public services – over changes to pensions for civil servants and local government and associated workers – was averted in March 2005, with most of the so-called 'awkward squad' of new union leaders (see McIlroy and Daniels, chapter 4, this volume) reluctant to embarrass Labour. A 'fresh start' to negotiations meant that '[u]nion leaders and ministers have succeeded in putting off any chance of confrontation until after the expected election' (*Financial Times*, 22 March 2005). In October a deal was agreed protecting the pension rights of current employees, but not new entrants, in most public services apart from local government. As a result, there was a very large national one-day strike in March 2006 by unions with members in the local government pension scheme (including civilian police staff).

While the main local government bargaining units are still very large, 'pay delegation' in the civil service – one bargaining unit in 1994 had been replaced by 229 by 2004 (*PCS News*, 22 April 2004) – has fragmented its workforce. There have been some big PCS disputes, such as that over safety screens in job centres from September 2001 to April 2002 – with selective strikes and two national two-day strikes (in all, 251,000 days lost by 28,500 workers). The Department of Work and Pensions (DWP) pay dispute of 2004–5 involved three two-day national strikes, a 12-month ban on overtime (important given the reliance on overtime to meet targets) and non-cooperation with the 'Personal Development System' (which generated unofficial walkouts in Scotland, the north-west, Sheffield and London, when managers were suspended for refusing to carry out their duties under this system). An imposed pay deal in the DWP, including a virtual freeze for nearly half the workforce, also led to a 48-hour national strike in December 2007.

There have been civil service-wide disputes by PCS, over job losses, with one-day strikes in November 2004 and in January and May 2007. After many local actions over the years (Corby 2002: 288), the POA came close to a national strike in September 2006. It called the first-ever national strike in the Prison Service, in England and Wales, on 29 August 2007, without an official ballot, over the staging of a Pay Review Body award; strikebreakers were given a £500 bonus. In January 2008, Justice Secretary Jack Straw announced legislation to reintroduce the 1994–2005 ban on strikes by prison officers.

Many other civil servants have struck – particularly since 2001 – often for the first time, usually over low pay-offers or imposed or delayed pay-settlements, sometimes over job cuts or reorganization. This has periodically meant joint, but separately balloted, action by PCS (the main union) along with Prospect (organizing specialists and professionals). It typically involved one-day strikes, often accompanied by working to rule; sometimes a successful ballot in a previous year, sufficient to effect a settlement then, laid the groundwork for a later strike. Among those striking were the Crown Prosecution Service in 2001; the Parliamentary and Health Service Ombudsman, the British Museum and British Library in 2002; the Forensic Science Service, the Health and Safety Executive, the Driving Standards Agency and the Office for National Statistics in 2004; the Science Museum, English Heritage and magistrates courts' staff in 2005; and Ordnance Survey in 2006. Prospect's strikers included curators and conservators, forensic scientists, factory inspectors, driving examiners, statisticians and cartographers. Coordination was limited apart from a joint two-day pay strike in 2004 by PCS members in the Department of Constitutional Affairs, the Home Office, the Prison Service and the Treasury Solicitors.

Sustained selective action in the civil service was taken by the Northern Ireland Public Service Alliance (NIPSA) over eight months in 2004. Over 2,300 workers, from 14 departments and agencies, undertook selective stoppages involving from three to 167 members and lasting from three to 94 days; some workers came out two or three times and as many as 500 were on strike at a time. It was expensive, despite a voluntary levy on working members, too many members felt disconnected, and it did not deliver a 'killer punch' (NIPSA 2005).

In local authorities there are still selective strikes, usually of occupational groups, and occasional council-wide action. Some white-collar disputes are lengthy: for example, the 11-week strike by Unison members in Camden libraries in 1998; the rolling strikes by 300 Unison members in Glasgow libraries (1998–9); and the Saturday strikes at Hackney's libraries (2002). One Scottish pay dispute culminated in a rare indefinite strike: after 11 months of demonstrations and selective strikes, 5,000 nursery nurses struck for two months in March 2004; in six areas the strike continued for up to another six weeks (Mooney and McCafferty 2005). Another indefinite strike, by 270 Glasgow day centre workers, lasted eight weeks in 2007. More than 3,000 civilian staff in the police force across Scotland also struck, for the first time, over pay in 2005.

There has been little national action in the NHS since the early 1980s – apart from two 24-hour stoppages in 2006 by 1,000 Unison members against the privatization of NHS Logistics. Privatization has caused most recent NHS strikes, including those at University College London Hospital in the late 1990s that led to Unison being taken to court (McIlroy 1999: 530–1). The biggest dispute provoked a series of unsuccessful protracted strikes against privatization by 600 workers at the Dudley Group of Hospitals from August 2000 to May 2001, responsible for 92,000 days lost. Strikes have occurred at NHS contractors, such as that by 300 caterers, cleaners and porters (in Unison) employed by Sodexho at Glasgow Royal Infirmary in 2002, who won a £5 minimum hourly wage; Sodexho flew in strikebreakers but still lost.

This success inspired 900 workers for the same company at the Liverpool Royal Hospitals to strike later that year (Corporate Watch UK 2004). Other stoppages include those by 300 similar employees of Carillion at hospitals in Scunthorpe, Goole and Grimsby in 2003 and by 200 staff of Initial Hospital Services at Whipps Cross Hospital (London) in 2006. Successful strike ballots among contract staff at four hospitals in east London in 2003 led to increased offers of a £5 or more hourly minimum at three of them; the ISS Mediclean staff at Whipps Cross rejected their offer and took two days' strike action, achieving further improvement (Wills 2005). Strikes remain relatively rare among NHS clinical staff, though there were two one-day strikes by 250 community nurses, occupational therapists and team secretaries in January and February 2007 opposing cuts by the Manchester Mental Health and Social Care Trust; these were followed in the late summer and autumn by a prolonged series of strikes by 700 Unison members against the suspension of the community and mental health branch chair, Karen Reissman. After her dismissal in November, some 150 community-based workers struck for several weeks before returning to work when she lost her appeal.

There have been no large teachers' strikes (apart from over London weighting) but significant action short of a strike (see below); strikes at individual schools still occur. After the long dispute during 1993–6 over contracts, further education (FE) colleges remained a battleground (Williams 2004). The demand for pay parity with schoolteachers was one factor reviving national action. A national one-day strike by NATFHE members in 290 colleges in May 2001 was followed by a two-day strike in May 2002 and then an unprecedented joint one-day stoppage with ATL and Unison in November 2002 (over parity with teachers and school support staff). Lecturers at over 40 colleges struck, some more than once, in 2005 over their employers' failure to implement an existing national pay deal; this was followed by another national strike that year. In Northern Ireland about 2,000 FE lecturers took part in seven one-day strikes from May 2006 to March 2007 in all colleges in the province (they continue to implement a work-to-rule and withdrawal of goodwill), over failure to honour a commitment to pay parity with school-teachers. The UK government had set up a Public Sector Pay Committee early in 2006, which rejected this case despite support from the Northern Ireland Office (UCU press release, 29 March 2007). An 'independent adviser' was appointed in October 2007 to facilitate an agreement.

After one-day strikes in 1996 and 1999, lecturers in the 'old' universities organized a week of action, over pay, in February 2004: universities in England, Scotland, Wales and Northern Ireland each stopped on a different day, along with one UK-wide stoppage. After the one-day strike in old and 'new' (post-1992) universities in March 2006 there was sustained action short of a strike (see below). There have been individual university strikes, the longest being a week's stoppage at London Metropolitan in 2005 over attempts to impose a new contract.

### Communication, transport and distribution

This sector has been the other main locus of strike activity. The most significant national dispute of the 1990s was the postal workers' eight 24-hour strikes in 1996 (Gall 2003: 109–19). By then Royal Mail workers had the reputation of being 'the most unofficially strike-prone group' in Britain (ibid.: 63). This culminated in 330 instances of unofficial action and 25 of official action in the year to March 2001, including 'knock-on disputes' where CWU members refused to do work resulting from industrial action elsewhere (Sawyer 2001: 11–12). A moratorium on strikes, agreed in summer 2001, held for several months; there have since been periodic outbreaks of official and unofficial action (but a small majority voted in 2003 against a national pay strike).

An eventual showdown between Royal Mail and the CWU took place in 2007 over pay, 'modernization' of 92 alleged 'Spanish practices', and pensions. National 24-hour strikes were organized in June and July, then two weeks of continuous disruption around the country involving all members in two strike days each. Following five weeks of (unsuccessful) talks there were two 48-hour national strikes in early October, which Gordon Brown, the new Prime Minister, called 'unacceptable' (*Guardian*, 9 October 2007). A further week of selective action, with all staff striking for one day, was called off: the first two days as a result of an injunction and the other days suspended while the union executive discussed a new offer, brokered by the TUC. The issues at stake were so important that the executive tussled with them for several days before recommending the offer. Management action during the national dispute later led to a five-week official strike by 100 postal workers at Burslem (Stoke-on-Trent), over the suspension of 12 members, 'one of the bitterest strikes . . . for many years' (*CWU News*, 24 January 2008).

Fragmentation of the railways into separate companies, following privatization, has resulted in widely varying pay rates and cost pressures on employers. This has embedded conflict, with regular strike ballots, threats of injunctions (sometimes carried out) and last-minute agreements. One very long dispute at Arriva Trains Northern started in late 2001; the company responded to strikes over conductors' pay by cancelling rest-day working, which led to staff shortages. In one four-week period 37 per cent of trains were cancelled. The TSSA even broke its thirty-year strike-free record when ticket office and other staff at the same company participated, with RMT station and retail grades, in 48-hour strikes over several months in 2002.

In February 2003, after about 25 separate strikes by conductors, and despite members voting against the last offer, the RMT called off the action. The company claimed: 'Even on strike days, performance was good, and as the strikes went on customers got used to the strike timetable' (*Journal* (Newcastle), 7 March 2003). The union argued that the Strategic Rail Authority (SRA) had 'effectively bankrolled the company [see below] throughout this dispute', which 'removed the incentive to negotiate meaningfully' (*Rail Industry News*, 21 February 2003). The SRA also admitted that 'under franchise agreements . . . [it] could block wage rises above the increase in the average earnings index where a train licence had less than 12 months to run' (*Independent*, 28 June 2002). So the company was offering only 4 per cent (even though drivers had secured 18 per cent). ASLEF, the train-drivers' union, could settle most disputes once strike dates had been announced because of its members' strategic position; but it also fell foul of the SRA in the on-off series of 48-hour strikes at First North Western in 2002. At one point the SRA was 'taking control of wage negotiations in at least 16 of the 28 train companies' (*Independent*, 6 January 2003).

When simultaneous one-day strikes were held at nine companies over train guards' safety role in 2003, Richard Bowker, SRA chair, 'announced that as much as 10 million pounds was available for companies losing money during the current dispute' (*Rail Industry News*, 16 April 2003). The SRA indicated that train operators would receive compensation if they had taken 'all reasonable steps to avoid . . . industrial action and . . . to mitigate its effects' (*Financial Times*, 25 March 2003). More than £23 million was given to train operators for lost revenue due to strikes between March 2003 and November 2004 (*Rail Industry News*, 27 February 2006).

Industrial action threats by ASLEF and the RMT over the festive season are now common. Over 500 conductors at Central Trains were set to strike on bank holidays in December 2005 and January 2006 because there was no extra pay for working them; an agreement was reached. At Virgin Cross Country 12 consecutive Sunday strikes by more than 300 guards started on New Year's Day 2006 over Sunday payments. Some 350 RMT members on Midland Mainline voted to strike on Christmas Eve and New Year's Eve 2006 – both Sundays – and New Year's Day 2007 over shift payments. An agreement was reached but 550 senior conductors at Central Trains still struck over this issue and centralized rostering.

Network-wide action still occurs. A strike of 7,000 RMT signalling, maintenance and station staff at Network Rail in 2004 over pay, travel concessions and closure of the final-salary pension scheme was timed to coincide with a London Underground strike to increase its impact. It was averted by an offer that reopened the pension scheme to workers after five years' service. A 48-hour strike by Network Rail signallers shut the Scottish network in March 2007 and confirmed the vulnerability of the railway system.

Andrew Gilligan, the journalist, has argued that, on London Underground, the RMT's 'real weapon is not the strike, but the strike ballot' (*Evening Standard*, 27 February 2006): more strikes have been cancelled than have occurred. The RMT held 48-hour stoppages in June 1998 and February 1999, then, after an injunction, called one off in February 2001 (ASLEF went ahead with its strike). In May 2001, after talks at ACAS, the RMT was requested, in 'a strongly-worded letter' by TUC general secretary John Monks, to suspend another stoppage (*Financial Times*, 3 May 2001). Alternative strike dates were announced, including one on General Election day. This pressure point won the RMT an agreement that staff would be legally protected against changes in terms and conditions resulting from new ownership of sections of London Underground.

Two 48-hour strikes by ASLEF and the RMT in March 2002 were averted when Downing Street 'secretly ordered' London Underground to concede 'an inflation-busting pay rise' of the unions' full claim of 5.7 per cent 'in a desperate attempt to ease the pressure on beleaguered [Transport Secretary] Stephen Byers' (*Guardian*, 1 March 2002). Emboldened, the RMT struck for 24 hours in July over safety issues; in September and October it was joined by ASLEF for stoppages over pay. Blair condemned the second strike but a week later Ken Livingstone, London Mayor, offered the unions 'independent mediation' for when he took control of the network in the spring of 2003 (*Guardian*, 10 October 2002), which was accepted.

Airports are particularly vulnerable to strikes, and it takes time to resume normal operations when aircraft are in the wrong place. Various groups have taken action: pilots, cabin crew, check-in staff, in-flight caterers, baggage and cargo handlers, security staff, aircraft refuellers, maintenance workers and shuttle-bus drivers. Airlines have sometimes acted very aggressively: when British Airways (BA) cabin staff struck for three days in 1997, threats to dismiss them and sue them individually for damages meant that 2,000 took sick leave and only 300 openly struck.

Most airport strike threats occur during busy holiday periods, leading to settlements, though 500 check-in staff went on unofficial strike over clocking-in arrangements in 2003; a threatened strike by check-in staff in 2004 was preceded by a (highly disruptive) tripling of sickness absenteeism. BA had abandoned directly employing in-flight-catering staff when a work to rule in 1997 left aircraft short of food; then, in August 2005, 1,000 baggage handlers at London Heathrow took unofficial strike action to support Gate Gourmet airline catering workers, dismissed for staging a sit-in strike. Sir Rod Eddington, BA chief executive, admitted: 'Never before have we had to cancel the entire operation at our worldwide hub' (*The Times*, 18 August 2005). BA faced an even bigger challenge when thousands of cabin crew were on the brink of a series of three-day strikes in January 2007. The new chief executive, Willie Walsh, negotiated a deal with Tony Woodley, TGWU general secretary, but this was too late to stop hundreds of 'phantom flights' as passengers had made other travel arrangements (*Financial Times*, 30 January 2007).

The shortage of bus drivers has given them confidence to strike over relatively low pay levels. In big groups, such as First or Stagecoach, demands for pay parity have led to provincial strikes. A one-day strike by 2,500 Metroline drivers in 2006 was reputedly the first bus strike in London this century. Some 1,500 drivers for First South Yorkshire threatened action in 2003 and came out in 2004 in what was claimed as the longest bus strike in 30 years. Distribution workers are also beginning to exploit the vulnerability of supermarkets. Sainsbury warehouse workers on Merseyside held strikes in December 2003 and January 2004 while Tesco drivers, based at the Livingston distribution depot, struck in May 2007. Planned strikes in 2005 by TGWU and GMB drivers and warehouse workers for Morrisons secured national negotiating arrangements. ASDA averted a five-day strike by GMB drivers and warehouse workers in 2006 by conceding improved bargaining rights. The same year DHL Exel tried to break a strike of drivers and warehouse workers by using private security guards and agency labour. Finally, reminiscent of a more self-confident era, a two-week strike at the car delivery company Ansa Logistics in 2005 started with cars 'illegally locked' at Avonmouth and Liverpool docks: the keys had 'disappeared' (*Financial Times*, 3 August 2005).

### Media, entertainment and sport

After the collapse of their industry-wide agreement in the late 1980s, journalists on provincial newspapers eventually started taking action in 2002, particularly against low pay. A half-day strike at Newsquest Bradford, the first over pay in the provincial press for over ten years, was followed by a rash of disputes. An NUJ organizer later explained: 'The whole of the provincial press has been in revolt for the last two years. We have had a great wave of industrial action. Pay is so low that people will not take it any more' (*Independent*, 24 February 2004). Often companies settled after successful strike ballots; NUJ general secretary Jeremy Dear commented: 'For the first time in many years, members ... had a sense of their collective strength' (*Morning Star*, 22 May 2002). There were long strikes, as in Bradford in 2003 and Coventry in 2005, and very small ones, such as that by 13 journalists at the *Spalding Guardian* and the *Lincolnshire Free Press* in 2003.[3] A threatened strike in the national press, at the *Independent* on Budget Day in 2006, was not needed.

The NUJ has retained a strong base in broadcasting, where there have been regular short strikes over jobs cuts or pay. The most prominent was the one-day stoppage at the BBC by NUJ, BECTU and Amicus members in May 2005. There were also unofficial 'spontaneous protests' by BBC staff immediately after Director-General Greg Dyke's resignation in January 2004 (*BECTU News*, 29 January 2004). Thousands joined midday protests one week later. BECTU has been the most embattled union in television with action including a one-day strike across the BBC in June 1998 and a 24-hour strike at BBC TV News in November 2006. The biggest strike in commercial television was a 36-hour stoppage by BECTU and Amicus members at London Weekend Television (LWT), Granada, Yorkshire TV and a Manchester-based company, 3sixtymedia, in April 2005. The action disrupted filming of *Emmerdale, Heartbeat* and *Coronation Street*. During this action BECTU held simultaneous two-hour stoppages at Central TV, Anglia TV and ITV's southern control centre in London.

Strikes are not always practicable in entertainment but substitutes exist. Members of the actors' union, Equity, refused to sign new contracts in provincial theatres in 1997 in order to push up minimum rates; and on UK-produced films for four months from December 2001, for a reasonable share of the proceeds of television screenings and video and DVD sales of films. Some producers on high-profile projects (for example, the James Bond film *Die Another Day* and the second Harry Potter film) broke ranks to settle before a general agreement was reached (*Guardian*, 13 March 2002).

From May 1997 Equity members boycotted television commercials where there had been a reduction in fees. The action was relaxed to allow work on union-approved terms in January 1998 before ending in June. As commercials are produced months in advance of broadcast, it took time to bite. Stars such as Helen Mirren, Ian McShane, Tim Pigott-Smith and Robert Lindsay observed the boycott. Jeremy Clarkson (not an Equity member) and Cilla Black carried on working, though Chris Evans, the DJ (but not in Equity), refused work on Huggies nappies commercials. There are strikes and strike threats notwithstanding. The 60-strong chorus (of Equity members) at English National Opera voted for five one-day strikes in 2003 over job cuts. The only strike that took place forced the cancellation of Berlioz's *The Capture of Troy*, and the chorus gave a free performance of Verdi's *Requiem* in a nearby church on the night. When the Scottish Opera chorus faced disbandment in 2004, Equity instructed all members, including 3,000 singers, to boycott the company.

Entertainment workers can take advantage of immovable deadlines. Three television unions, BECTU, NUJ and AEEU, struck 'eleventh-hour deals' at Scottish TV and Grampian TV to avoid strikes over Christmas 1998 and New Year 1999. During a lengthy 1999 dispute by BECTU members at LWT, the union was not allowed to hold a meeting, on a revised offer, on site. A threatened two-hour stoppage to maximize attendance at an off-site meeting would have disrupted coverage of the opening ceremony of the Rugby World Cup, so a studio was found. BECTU members had won a £200 bonus payment for working over the Millennium New Year in most London and regional theatres. Strike action was balloted for in six West End theatres which had rejected this bonus: two others agreed to pay. Examples of BECTU strike votes (or even just balloting) leading to settlements include: Scottish Opera in the busy pre-Christmas period in 2002; the threat to a world premiere at Belfast's Lyric theatre in 2004; and a threatened Saturday strike at the RSC, Stratford, in 2001. Casino workers (in the TGWU) in London began a 24-hour strike at 7.00am on New Year's Eve 2006.

Industrial action, or its threat, is now more common in professional sport. PFA members had contemplated striking in 1992 and 1996. A strike vote, with a more than 99 per cent majority on a 92.7 per cent turnout, enabled the PFA to threaten a boycott of televised matches from December 2001 unless its share of the income (used for schemes to help present and former players) increased (*Financial Times*, 10 November 2001). A deal was eventually reached. After consistently late payment of wages, players at the Scottish football club, Hamilton Academical, voted to strike. When their wages were not paid on Friday 31 March, they did not play against Stenhousemuir the next day. A threat to continue the strike against Alloa on the following Tuesday was averted when pay cheques were cleared. Reporting the rearranged match with Stenhousemuir, one press headline joked: 'Accies play 11 strikers' (*Mirror*, 18 April 2000). Unfortunately for the players, the club was deducted 15 points, leading to its relegation, and seven strikers were released on free transfers.

'Player power' even infected the England rugby union squad, which refused, after a ballot, to play against Argentina in November 2000. The coach, Clive Woodward, gave the players a deadline of 11.00am the next day or he would drop them all. A settlement, giving improved pay, was thrashed out in time. *The Times* (23 November 2000) editorial accused the Rugby Football Union of behaving like 'a nineteenth-century mill-owner'. When the Jockey Club banned jockeys from using mobile phones at racecourses in September 2003, they 'reacted furiously, staging carefully choreographed [unofficial] walkouts from racecourses between races and ostentatiously using their mobiles' (*Financial Times*, 12 September 2003). The Jockeys Association, their trade body, boycotted a meeting on 14 September at Sandown Park (owned by a Jockey Club subsidiary) – the first ever UK race meeting cancelled through industrial action. In August 2005 jockeys also boycotted a meeting at Wolverhampton, over the decision to employ stalls handlers in-house. Earlier, TGWU stalls handlers started a series of strikes in June 2004. At Epsom, in the absence of stalls, the second favourite was facing the wrong way when one race started, to 'huge embarrassment' (*Guardian*, 5 June 2004). A settlement saved Royal Ascot.

*Construction, manufacturing and private services*

Most workers are more vulnerable than the above examples, but some can still exploit their market position. Workers in engineering construction took advantage of high-profile projects, particularly those connected to the Millennium celebrations. Electricians on the London Underground Jubilee Line extension engaged in a series of unofficial strikes and go-slows from 1996 to 1999 and negotiated a large termination bonus to meet the 31 December 1999 deadline; similarly, a small number of steel erectors won £3,000 bonus payments 'following threats to scupper the erection' of the London Eye Ferris wheel (*Construction News*, 30 September 1999).[4]

The reliance of supermarkets on UK suppliers for products such as poultry and meat has given food-processing workers leverage. Strikes at Grampian Food plants (in 2005, 2006 and 2007), supplying major supermarkets and Marks and Spencer, are one example. Even Bernard Matthews, the main supplier and processor of turkeys, backed down when faced with 'the UK's first family-friendly strike' and abandoned changing the working week from four shifts to five (*TGWU press release*, 15 July 2004).

With continuing contraction of employment and outsourcing of work abroad, manufacturing workers are particularly reluctant to strike. One stimulus has been the dismantling, or erosion, of final-salary pension schemes. At the Caparo steel group (owned by a Labour peer), ISTC members at Tredegar, Wrexham and Scunthorpe operated an overtime ban and work-to-rule before five one-day strikes, in August and September 2002, and planned several two-day strikes. Believed to be the first industrial action to defend a final-salary pension scheme, it was largely successful. This was followed by a one-day strike in October by TGWU members at Yuasa Automotive Batteries in Birmingham; a second strike was cancelled when the company postponed changes to allow talks. When GMB and Amicus members staged 24-hour stoppages at the French chemical company Rhodia's plants in Widnes and Oldbury in 2003, it agreed to keep the scheme open for existing workers until 2012. Rolls-Royce, the aerospace group, revised changes to its scheme under the threat of a strike ballot across the company in 2003.

There are still occasional indefinite strikes, such as that in 2005 by 96 engineering workers at Rolls-Royce, Bristol, for reinstatement of their dismissed Amicus convener, Jerry Hicks, abandoned when a ballot of the whole workforce was lost. In the once 'strike-prone' car industry, there are only sporadic stoppages (those at Peugeot, Ryton, in 2000 were the first for 20 years, followed by a one-day stoppage in 2003; those at Land Rover, Solihull, in 2004, the first since 1988). The solitary strike ballot at Nissan, Sunderland, in 2003 involved purchasing staff, who voted 17–5 to resist relocation south.

The jobs crisis at Rover, Longbridge (in Birmingham), saw up to 100,000 march on Saturday 1 April 2000 but no official industrial action. The news of closure (in September 2004) of Jaguar's Browns Lane factory and (in April 2006) of Peugeot's Ryton plant, both in Coventry, resulted in strike ballots;

unsurprisingly these were lost given the lapse of time after closure announcements. Amicus and the TGWU then spent £1 million on a 'boycott Peugeot campaign', launched in June 2006, which failed to capture the public imagination. The unions discovered that the Radio Advertising Standards code 'expressly prevents . . . [unions] from making statements about disputes or stating facts about employers' (*T&G News*, 10 July 2006).

Sit-ins are extremely rare. Since the successful two-month occupation at Glacier Metals in Glasgow in 1996–7, they have taken the form of demonstration protests. At a two-day unofficial occupation of Appledore Shipbuilders in north Devon, local residents and workers, who blocked the entrance with steel bollards, temporarily prevented a receiver from coming into the yard in September 2003. When two electronic component plants closed in Scotland in January 2007, the one at Kilwinning was briefly occupied.

Occasional strikes affecting the major banks occurred through the 1990s (Gall 1998: 126–30) but little has happened since. Among the more unusual strikes was one of several weeks in 1998 (eventually settled through ACAS) over the dismissal of the editor at the *Morning Star*, the Communist daily. Another was over breach of redundancy policy at Oakington Detention Centre, near Cambridge, in 2006 by workers at the Refugee Legal Centre. There were two one-day strikes by contract cleaners, in the TGWU, at the House of Commons in 2005, while the GMB organized strikes by National Car Parks attendants in Enfield in 2007. Even nuclear power workers have struck: at BNFL Sellafield in 2003 and at Hunterston in 2006. They fit Edwards's description of strikes 'in some very unexpected places'.

### *Action short of a strike*

'Action short of a strike' (ASOS) often complements strikes, but is sometimes used on its own, as with the 'Let Teachers Teach' campaign in 1998 when the NUT and NAS/UWT boycotted administrative tasks. Repeated in 2000 and labelled 'industrial action with a halo', it culminated in the 'cover-to-contract' action of 2001. This had a snowball effect as more and more areas implemented a refusal to cover for absent colleagues after three days. The local government employers' chair admitted that 'a strike would be easier to deal with' (*Guardian*, 15 March 2001).

The 2004 strikes in the old universities were followed by a four-week boycott of marking and exam-setting. The tactic was repeated in 2006 and continued into early June, by which time at least 19 employers were withholding, or threatening to withhold, pay. NATFHE's position (in the new universities) was to set, but not mark, exams while the AUT advised not setting exams. The action was sufficiently widespread to jeopardize the graduation process. A leading law firm's opinion was that 'the scripts . . . belong to the universities which they could retrieve with a court injunction'. Some universities contemplated this 'nuclear option', especially given the unofficial practice of 'marking and parking' where some lecturers marked scripts but held back the results (*Financial Times*, 27 May 2006). Academic boycotts are occasionally used to put pressure on a university by asking members in the rest of the sector to isolate it. Examples include those by the AUT against Nottingham in 2004 and Brunel in 2005–6. NATFHE boycotted London Metropolitan in 2004–5 over imposition of contracts and UCU agreed another boycott (over derecognition) there in 2007, which was not needed.

ASOS is especially potent in broadcasting, given tight production schedules. BECTU operated 'civil disobedience' in the BBC in February 2001, then won a ballot for a work-to-rule, over cuts in expenses, from 26 February, with further sanctions imposed on 28 March; this lasted six weeks until concessions were won. Another BECTU work-to-rule at the BBC in 2001 included refusing duties lasting more than 12 hours or any break between turns of duty of less than 11 hours. An appraisal boycott by NUJ and BECTU members at the BBC, starting in mid-2001, was still operating in March 2002. After a two-hour strike in February 1999, BECTU, NUJ and AEEU members at the four ITV stations in the Granada Media Group (Granada, Yorkshire, Tyne Tees and LWT) refused to work shifts with less than a 12-hour break between them. Two companies settled in June. With 'less than two weeks' material [for *Coronation Street*] in the can', Granada tabled a new offer in July (*BECTU News*, 29 June 1999). LWT staff carried on their action until November.

Similar measures were imposed by the NUJ at the *Birmingham Post and Mail* in 2004; two ten-minute 'screen breaks', a one-hour lunch break and no overtime operated at Sheffield Newspapers in 2005; at Newsquest Bolton in 2006 the NUJ chapel agreed that only one reporter and one photographer would work after 6 o'clock each evening. Other tactics are used for publicity. Science Museum staff held a 'Mad Hatter's Tea Party' outside the main entrance in February 2004. HSE staff either burned or shredded their payslips outside the main offices in London and Bootle in July 2004, when they also held a 'flexi-protest' (working only the core hours in a flexitime system), the latter tactic being used in the Inland Revenue in 2001.

The RMT called four 'no-revenue' days on South Central Trains in 2004, when members would 'refus[e] to handle money or to issue tickets' (*Rail Industry News*, 4 June 2004). The action was cancelled when the company intimated court action. When Central Trains conductors intended to stop issuing tickets in February 2007, they were threatened with losing half their pay. The RMT changed the action to a 24-hour strike, so the company stopped overtime and rest-day working, requiring cancellation or revision of services. The situation threatened to get out of hand and saw both parties go to ACAS. Finally, since ASLEF's adoption in 1995 of a drivers' charter, its executive has controlled rest-day working on the railways by giving or withholding permission (Weller 2006: 8). This has proved a powerful weapon.

## Employer and union tactics

### *Dismissals of strikers*

New Labour inherited several causes célèbres where strikers had been dismissed. The most famous was that of several hundred Liverpool dockers, sacked by the Mersey Docks and Harbour Company (MDHC) for not crossing a picket line in September 1995. Their unofficial action led to two major international days of solidarity in 1997: one in January saw action in 105 ports and cities in 27 countries; in September there were solidarity strikes in Australian and US West Coast ports. But in the UK, Bill Morris, TGWU general secretary, suggested there was 'no support for solidarity action whatsoever' within the union (cited in McIlroy 1999: 529). The union paid hardship pay of £12 per week (strike pay would have been about £30), totalling some £700,000. That the government owned shares in MDHC meant nothing to New Labour (Taplin 1998–9: 50). The employer's offer of compensation was accepted in January 1998, because 'the campaign had started to falter . . . [I]n order not to see good men and women lose everything or risk a collapse from within, we decided to conclude a collective agreement on the best possible terms achievable' (quoted in *Labour Research*, March 1998: 2).

At Magnet (Kitchens), Darlington, 350 TGWU, GMB, AEEU and UCATT members went on official strike in August 1996 when sections of the workforce were offered no pay rise after a three-year pay freeze. Fifty-two returned before a deadline; the rest were dismissed. Alan Milburn (Darlington) and Tony Blair (Sedgefield) were the MPs in whose constituencies most of the workers lived. Strikers and supporters leafleted Magnet's retail outlets on the strike's first anniversary and picketed them in the January sales of 1998. The campaign then shifted to demonstrating near the chief executive's Cambridgeshire estate, where redundant Derbyshire miners offered their assistance. Outside the company's AGM in January, three alternative comedians, Mark Thomas, Mark Steel and Jeremy Hardy, staged their own 'anti-fat-cat happening'; in February strikers occupied the Magnet store in London's Kensington High Street. The extra publicity produced a cash settlement in April 1998 – varying from £250, for strikers who had left immediately to find work, to £8,500 for the 82 who stayed the course.

When thirty-one CWU members at Critchley Labels, near Newport in South Wales, struck against derecognition in February 1997, they were dismissed. The CWU paid basic wages up to £150 per week; its conference voted to 'black' Critchley products but legal advice claimed that this would constitute (unlawful) secondary action and it was dropped (McIlroy 1999: 529–30). A 'cyberpicket', organized on the strike's second anniversary, flooded the company's UK plants with telephone and electronic calls, while international unions targeted its operations abroad. BT, the company's main customer, settled the dispute in June 1999.

The Hillingdon hospital cleaners' strike lasted even longer. Fifty-three workers, mainly British Asian women, had been dismissed in October 1995 after refusing to sign new contracts and going on unofficial strike against cuts in pay and conditions. Unison eventually supported the strikers financially – until January 1997, when it negotiated a pay-off. Thirty-one refused to end their strike and pursued tribunal claims, with Unison representation. Unison agreed again in 1998 to support the strikers and restore their union membership. Twenty-one won re-engagement and compensation at a tribunal in 1998 but it was not until October 2000 that some returned to work.

Without a change in the law, sackings of strikers continued under New Labour. For example, some 260 Unison and 45 GMB members at Tameside Care Group, a private residential-care provider,[5] were dismissed for striking against pay reductions in March 1998. A year later a limited settlement was made, though some continued to pursue tribunal claims. When the airline catering company LSG Lufthansa Skychefs imposed new working practices, 270 workers who took part in two one-day strikes in November 1998 were dismissed. According to the TGWU, Lufthansa 'was forced to negotiate . . . by "sustained and imaginative" action, involving maintaining a picket line outside Skychefs' premises near Heathrow . . . , organizing protests at the German embassy and undertaking an advertising campaign in the UK and Germany' (Hall 2000). A settlement came the day before the provisions of the Employment Relations Act 1999, making dismissal of employees engaged in lawful industrial action of less than eight weeks' duration automatically unfair.

The 86 TGWU members, who went on official strike on 30 April 2001 and were dismissed on 10 May by Friction Dynamics (in Caernarfon), discovered that this protection was full of loopholes before giving up their picket on 19 December 2003 (Pritchard and Edwards 2005). In another dismissal of strikers – at the foundries of William Cook (in the Sheffield constituency of Richard Caborn, a Trade and Industry minister) – the company insisted on changes that would cut earnings significantly, following previous cuts, which had to be agreed by 13 April 2001. One-day strikes were organized, with a work-to-rule on other working days. The employer then dismissed those who refused to agree, subject to notice related to individual length of service (UKEAT/0899/03/RN), which complicated the running of the dispute. The union's main advice was to apply to a tribunal (which, as with Friction Dynamics, has led to hearings spread over several years).

The Employment Relations Act 2004 extended 'protected industrial action' to twelve weeks. The dismissed, mainly British Asian, Gate Gourmet strikers in 2005 had taken unofficial action so they were not covered; of 813 sacked, 272 were eventually reinstated, 411 given the equivalent of their redundancy entitlement, and 130 received nothing (Hendy and Gall 2006: 249). Two of the stewards, sacked for organizing the solidarity strike, were eventually given a large payout by the TGWU (including £90,000 from BA for one). The union could have been sued if BA could prove 'involvement of its officials' in urging the strike, while the stewards had been advised that 'they could sue the

T&G for negligence for ordering them to take the illegal action' (*Guardian*, 18 September 2006).

### Ballots, discontinuous action, and the timing of strikes

Several factors facilitate settlements without strikes. From the decision to ballot, the process, dominated by legal constraints, plays out over a minimum of several weeks but sometimes months. Strikes are typically official and thus the union controls their organization. Where possible, unions will maximize a strike's impact while limiting loss of wages. Tables 10.4 and 10.5 show significantly more ballots than strikes, suggesting that unions use the former tactically as an extension of the bargaining process and that the strike

*Table 10.4*   Strike ballots 2002–6[a]

| Year | Number of strikes | Number of ballots | Ballots calling for strike action | Ballots voting in favour | Ballots voting against | Split result |
|------|-------------------|-------------------|-----------------------------------|--------------------------|------------------------|--------------|
| 2002 | 146 | 806 | 738 | 613 | 113 | 12 |
| 2003 | 133 | 899 | 825 | 684 | 125 | 16 |
| 2004 | 130 | 952 | 919 | 762 | 144 | 13 |
| 2005 | 116 | 815 | 775 | 663 | 109 | 9 |
| 2006 | 158 | 1,341 | 1,290 | 1,094 | 140 | 57 |

*Source:* Hale (2007)

*Note:*

a The higher number of strike (but not ASOS) ballots in 2006 probably reflects employers covered by the local government pension scheme strike. The discrepancy in figures for total strike ballots for 2005 and 2006 is in the original.

*Table 10.5*   Estimated percentage of workplaces experiencing industrial action 1998 and 2004

| | 1998 | | | 2004 | | |
|---|---|---|---|---|---|---|
| | Public sector | Private sector | All | Public sector | Private sector | All |
| Ballots | 20 | 3 | 6 | 22 | 2 | 5 |
| Any industrial action | 5 | 1 | 2 | 11 | 1 | 3 |
| *Of which:* | | | | | | |
| Strike | 4 | 0 | 1 | 8 | 0 | 2 |
| Non-strike action | 1 | 1 | 1 | 5 | 1 | 2 |
| Threatened action | 8 | 2 | 3 | 11 | 3 | 4 |
| Any industrial action, taken or threatened | 9 | 3 | 4 | 16 | 3 | 5 |
| Picketing | 2 | 0 | 1 | 5 | 0 | 1 |

*Source:* Kersley *et al.* (2006): 209, table 8.1.

*Note:*

Private-sector strikes (and picketing) are so infrequent as to be rounded down to zero per cent.

threat stemming from a successful ballot often acts as a proxy for a strike itself (Brown and Wadhwani 1990: 62).[6] The ballot result will carry legitimacy in the eyes of members and many employers and will often render the strike unnecessary (Elgar and Simpson 1993: 76).

Once strikes are called, employers may instigate court action. Some fifty-six injunctions were granted against unions from January 1997 to August 2005, usually stopping, sometimes only delaying, strikes. This is a lower annual average than for 1980 to 1996. It reflects decreased strike activity and unions' increased obedience of the law (confirmed by the absence of injunctions for secondary action and hardly any for picketing). The threat of injunctions (often for alleged balloting irregularities in increasingly complex procedures) was nearly as common as injunctions themselves and often led to suspended ballots or cancelled strikes (Gall 2006b: 330–2, 338).[7] While employers' resort, or threatened resort, to the courts can have serious effects for some workers, and sometimes the union, it functions more as a learning experience than a 'demonstration effect' for others.

When strikes proceed, 'discontinuous action' (such as a series of one-day strikes) is the dominant form. In the public services, where revenue collection is separate from service delivery, there have always been pressures to avoid indefinite strikes. Sustaining 'strike solidarity' (McCarthy 1964) is made difficult by the lack of 100 per cent union membership in most public services, thus the historic preference for strategic 'selective' strikes. When official action took place in manufacturing before the 1990s, plant-level strikes were often assumed to be 'indefinite' while infrequent industry-level strikes would be more tactical (Lyddon 1998). This situation has totally changed, particularly as a result of mass dismissals of strikers: discontinuous action is now the norm. Transport strikes have an immediate impact, encouraging discontinuous action, while their threat is more potent than in manufacturing ('stockpiling' is not possible in passenger transport and difficult – because of just-in-time deliveries – in goods transport). During an indefinite strike, 'an arbitrary deadline' has to be contrived but it cannot have 'the force of the one which marked the end of pre-strike negotiations' (Walton and McKersie 1965: 57). Since 1993, unions have to give seven days' notice of every separate instance of discontinuous action. This creates regular pre-strike deadlines, encouraging negotiations and cancellation of strikes to facilitate talks.

At any point, conciliation can be tried if both parties are willing. Despite declining industrial action, the annual number of requests for collective conciliation by ACAS remained remarkably stable (at about 1,200 to 1,300 per year) in the period 1987 to 2003 before falling. ACAS took the initiative itself in an increased proportion of cases from the mid-1990s (Goodman 2000; ACAS, *Annual Reports* 2000–7). Goodman (2000: 50) argues that union officials see conciliation as 'a possible means of making progress', though discontinuous action may make it more protracted 'in that it may take longer to cause sufficient damage to concentrate minds'.

The extremes can be illustrated from the fire service. In Suffolk there were no fewer than 22 stoppages of two, three, four or five hours, over an eight-week period in 2005. The opposite experience was a Merseyside strike in 2006, which used long strike periods but created a series of negotiating deadlines that would be missing in an indefinite stoppage. It consisted of a four-day strike, then two hours working, a second four-day strike, eight days back, then an effective continuous strike by regularly announcing new blocks of action to follow immediately after each other: eight days, two four-day blocks, then another two four-day blocks. In total, there were 28 days of action, with the last stoppage unnecessary.

Tactical timing has been a theme running through this chapter. Further examples show the creative timing and phasing of strike days. The civil service-wide strike on 31 January 2007 coincided with the last day for the return of self-assessment tax forms to the Inland Revenue and was followed by a two-week overtime ban (there had been a longer ban before the 2002 tax return deadline). The Science Museum strike occurred during schools' half-term holidays and that of English Heritage (whose sites include Stonehenge) was on the day of the summer solstice; one of the strikes by Ombudsman staff was on the day that the Ombudsman, Michael Buckley, was knighted. A strike by British Library assistants in 1999 was supported by Germaine Greer, who cancelled the launch party for her book *The Whole Woman* in order to avoid crossing their picket line.

In strikes at provincial newspapers, tactics are considered carefully. Thus twenty-nine journalists working on seven titles for the Greater Manchester Weekly Newspapers Group struck on crucial production days; a projected third strike would have stopped coverage of local elections in 2002. At Bradford in 2003 journalists varied the days of the week chosen for two- and three-day strikes. At Bolton and Bury in 2003, 'short strikes were not effective because they [management] were able to build up a stock of stories so after the second one we decided not to go back' (*Newsroom*, 2 May 2003).

## Conclusion

The evidence presented confirms the 'tertiarisation' of industrial conflict, with strikes mainly confined to transport and communication and public services. Blyton and Turnbull (2004: 340) characterized the strike record for 1997 to 2002 as 'Public Sector Discontent'. That was a premature judgement but undoubtedly would apply *from* 2002 as wage pressures, in particular, have built up.

Unions are now generally adept at utilizing ballots to achieve (limited) bargaining objectives. The balloting regime reinforces what Edwards (2001) calls the 'more considered' nature of strikes, brought about by long years of union and worker weakness. In this the law is, at best, an irritant, albeit an expensive one. At its worst, legislation ensures that unions cannot respond quickly to events, such as victimization, dismissals or closures. The unlawful nature of secondary action remains a major handicap in certain strikes. The long-standing official union preference for discontinuous strike action has become the dominant experience. This conserves funds, reduces the likelihood of dismissal (where there is now limited legal protection), and gives an aura of responsibility to what were once described as 'token' strikes.

One consequence of the legitimacy bestowed by secret ballots is the widening of the groups of employees who are prepared to take action (Edwards's (2001) 'unexpected places'). Another consequence is that unions can be on a 'conflict footing' for lengthy periods; some unions – especially those confronted by multiple employers – such as the RMT and, to a lesser extent, BECTU and the PCS, seem to be on a permanent war footing. Thus historically low strike activity masks, for much of unionized employment, a high level of antagonism in industrial relations.

The 'just-in-time' supply system of most manufacturers and retailers leaves them particularly vulnerable. While many manufacturing workers fear that action could lead to their jobs disappearing overseas, distribution workers are gradually appreciating their strategic position. Workers in passenger transport – railways, London Underground, buses, airports and airlines – control a perishable commodity and periodically exploit this. Public service workers still have relatively high job security but face work intensification, job degradation and tight pay controls (especially with the staging of Pay Review Body awards and the 'pre-budget report' announcement that annual public-sector pay rises will be held down to about 2 per cent for three years from October 2007). After 25 years of low inflation, who is to say that a significant rise in prices will not trigger a strike movement again? Prognostications of 'the death of the strike' will prove no more substantial than predictions of the dissolution of the working class or the demise of trade unionism.

## Notes

1 Where no source is given, it is a national newspaper or a union website.
2 Since 1996 the Office for National Statistics has collected the figures, using union websites and newspapers, including the *Morning Star* and *Socialist Worker* (ONS 2005).
3 See Gall 2006a for other NUJ ballots and strikes.
4 There have been walkouts in the construction of Wembley Stadium and Heathrow Airport Terminal 5.
5 Though Tameside Metropolitan Borough Council was part-owner (Centre for Public Services 1999).
6 The higher number of strike (but not ASOS) ballots in 2006 probably reflects employers covered by the local government pension scheme strike.
7 Other reasons for injunctions include strike notices and whether there was a lawful trade dispute. For current balloting provisions, see Simpson (2005).

## Bibliography

ACAS, *Annual Reports 1999–2000* to *2006–2007*, <http://www.acas.org.uk> (accessed 3 July 2008).

Blair, T. (1998) 'Foreword', *Fairness at Work*, London: DTI.

Blyton, P. and Turnbull, P. (2004) *The Dynamics of Employee Relations*, 3rd edition, Basingstoke: Palgrave Macmillan.

Bordogna, L. and Cella, G. (2002) 'Decline or transformation? change in industrial conflict and its challenges', *Transfer*, 8:4, 585–607.

Brown, W. (ed.) (1981) *The Changing Contours of British Industrial Relations*, Oxford: Blackwell.

Brown, W. and Wadhwani, S. (1990) 'The economic effects of industrial relations legislation since 1979', *National Institute Economic Review*, 131, 57–70.

Centre for Public Services (1999) *The Future of Tameside Care Group*, Manchester: Unison North West Region.

Corby, S. (2002) 'On parole: prison service industrial relations', *Industrial Relations Journal*, 33:4, 286–97.

Corporate Watch UK (2004) 'Sodexho: a corporate profile', <http://www.corporatewatch.org.uk/?lid=834> (accessed 1 July 2008).

Cronin, J. (1979) *Industrial Conflict in Modern Britain*, London: Croom Helm.

Edwards, P. (1983) 'The pattern of collective industrial action', in G.S. Bain (ed.), *Industrial Relations in Britain*, Oxford: Blackwell.

—— (2001) 'Strikes: scattered but not eliminated', *EIROnline* <http://www.eurofound.europa.eu/eiro/2001/10/feature/uk0110109f.htm> (accessed 16 July 2008).

Elgar, J. and Simpson, B. (1993) 'The impact of the law on industrial disputes in the 1980s', in D. Metcalf and S. Milner (eds), *New Perspectives on Industrial Disputes*, London: Routledge.

Frayn, M. (1967) 'A perfect strike', in R. Blackburn and A. Cockburn (eds), *The Incompatibles: Trade Union Militancy and the Consensus*, Harmondsworth: Penguin.

Gall, G. (1998) 'Union resilience in a cold climate: the case of the UK banking industry', in M. Upchurch (ed.), *The State and Globalization*, London: Mansell.

—— (2003) *The Meaning of Militancy? Postal Workers and Industrial Relations*, Aldershot: Ashgate.

—— (2006a) 'The National Union of Journalists and the provincial newspaper industry. From derecognition to recognition to fraught bargaining', in G. Gall (ed.), *Union Recognition: Organizing and Bargaining Outcomes*, London: Routledge.

—— (2006b) 'Injunctions as a legal weapon in industrial disputes in Britain, 1995–2005', *British Journal of Industrial Relations*, 44:2, 327–49.

Goodman, J. (2000) 'Building bridges and settling differences: collective conciliation and arbitration under ACAS', in B. Towers and W. Brown (eds), *Employment Relations in Britain: 25 years of the Advisory, Conciliation and Arbitration Service*, Oxford: Blackwell.

Hale, D. (2007) 'Labour disputes in 2006', *Economic and Labour Market Review*, June, 25–36.

Hall, M., (2000) 'Skychefs dispute settled', *EIROnline* <http://www.eurofound.europa.eu/eiro/2000/05/inbrief/uk0005172n.htm> (accessed 16 July 2008).

Hendy, J. and Gall, G. (2006) 'British trade union rights today and the Trade Union Freedom Bill', in K.D. Ewing (ed.) *The Right to Strike: from the Trade Disputes Act 1906 to a Trade Union Freedom Bill 2006*, Liverpool: Institute of Employment Rights.

Hyman, R. (1984) *Strikes*, 3rd edition, London: Fontana.

—— (1999) 'Strikes in the UK: withering away?', *EIROnline* <http://www.eurofound.europa.eu/eiro/1999/07/feature/uk9907215f.htm> (accessed 16 July 2008).

Kersley, B., Alpin, C., Forth, J., Bryson, A., Bewley, H., Dix, G. and Oxenbridge, S. (2006) *Inside the Workplace: Findings from the 2004 Workplace Employment Relations Survey*, London: Routledge.

Lyddon, D. (1998) 'Rediscovering the past: recent British strike tactics in historical perspective', *Historical Studies in Industrial Relations*, 5, 107–51.

—— (2007) 'From strike wave to strike drought: the United Kingdom, 1968–2005', in S. van der Velden, H. Dribbusch, D. Lyddon and K. Vandaele (eds), *Strikes Around the World, 1968–2005: Case-studies of 15 countries*, Amsterdam: Aksant.

McCarthy, W.E.J. (1964) *The Closed Shop in Britain*, Oxford: Blackwell.

McIlroy, J. (1999) 'Unfinished business – the reform of strike legislation in Britain', *Employee Relations*, 21:6, 521–39.

Mooney, G. and McCafferty, T. (2005) ' "Only looking after the weans"? The Scottish nursery nurses' strike, 2004', *Critical Social Policy*, 25:2, 223–39.

Nolda, C. (2004) 'Industrial conflict in local government since 1997', *Employee Relations*, 26:4, 377–91.

Northern Ireland Public Service Alliance (NIPSA) (2005) *Review of Civil Service Dispute*, Consultation Paper.

Office for National Statistics (2005) *Report of the Labour Disputes Inquiry: Mini Triennial Review June 2005*, London: Office for National Statistics.

Pritchard, T. and Edwards, I. (2005) *On the Line: The Story of the 'Friction Dynamics' Strikers*, Caernarfon: TGWU.

Sawyer (Lord), Borkett, I. and Underhill, N. (QC) (2001) *Independent Review of Industrial Relations Between Royal Mail and the Communication Workers Union*, London: Postcomm.

Seifert, R. and Sibley, T. (2005) *United They Stood: The Story of the UK Firefighters' Dispute 2002–4*, London: Lawrence and Wishart.

Simpson, B. (2005) 'Strike ballots and the law: round six', *Industrial Law Journal*, 34:4, 331–7.

Taplin, E. (1999) 'History in the making: the end of the Liverpool docks dispute, 1998', *North West Labour History*, 23, 49–54.

Walton, R.E. and McKersie, R.B. (1965) *A Behavioral Theory of Labor Negotiations: An Analysis of a Social Interaction System*, New York: McGraw-Hill.

Weller, S. (2006) 'We need to control rest day working', *ASLEF Journal*, August.

Williams, S. (2004) 'Accounting for change in public sector industrial relations: the erosion of national bargaining in further education in England and Wales', *Industrial Relations Journal*, 35:3, 233–48.

Wills, J. (2005) 'Organizing the low paid: East London's living wage campaign as a vehicle for change', in G. Healey, E. Heery, P. Taylor and W. Brown (eds) *The Future of Worker Representation*, Basingstoke: Palgrave Macmillan.

# 11 Europe

## The double-edged sword of justice? New Labour, trade unions and the politics of Social Europe

*Graham Taylor*

The relationship between Britain and the rest of Europe has provided an important fault line in the politics of British labour throughout the post-war period. The question as to whether Britain should be a member of the European Community proved an intractable source of division for most of the period and highlighted an important tension between social democratic internationalism and nationalistic labourism. In this context, the election of New Labour in 1997 marked an important transformation in the ideological and political orientation of the labour movement. Immediately following the 1997 election, the New Labour government agreed to the transposition of a raft of social and employment regulations into UK law that challenged the traditional industrial relations framework of 'voluntarism'. The New Labour project involved the reconstruction of the Labour Party into a 'modernized' European social democratic party which had adapted to neoliberalism, was unfettered by ideological commitments to the socialization of the economy and had distanced itself institutionally from the trade unions. The British unions embraced 'Social Europe' as the principal bulwark against neoliberal globalization and engaged enthusiastically with institutions and alliances at the European level. The 1997 election thus highlighted the extent to which British labour had undergone a process of Europeanization. 'Europe' had become an increasingly important 'frame' for trade union policy, identity and action.

The pro-European re-alignment generated optimism amongst both the UK's European partners and UK trade unions. Across Europe, there had been a growing frustration in respect of the obstructive attitude towards integration and harmonization of the Thatcher and Major administrations particularly the constant recourse to the opt-out on social issues. In the UK, the unions looked forward to a more progressive engagement with European Union (EU) social and employment policy under New Labour. One of the first acts of the New Labour Government led by Tony Blair was to reverse the UK opt-out of the Social Chapter negotiated by the previous Conservative administration. It is, therefore, somewhat ironic that in 2007, in his final act as leader of the New Labour Government Tony Blair, on the orders of future New Labour Prime Minister Gordon Brown, negotiated an opt-out for the

UK with regard to the incorporation of the Charter of Fundamental Rights into the 'Reform Treaty' (*Guardian*, 23 June 2007). A close inspection of the past decade, however, suggests that this is not quite the 'full circle' reversal that it seems.

Throughout ten years in office, New Labour has consistently attempted to articulate and legitimate a neoliberal policy agenda within a social democratic discursive framework. As this delicate balancing act became increasingly difficult to maintain, New Labour has reverted to a more explicit neoliberal discourse and practice. In terms of European social and employment policy, New Labour began the decade believing that neoliberal policy objectives could be delivered through social democratic forms of social partnership and social dialogue. Ten years on, New Labour invoked the power of inter-governmental veto to prevent further progress on the harmonization of European social and employment policy based on an explicit rejection of 'Social Europe'. This change of focus is reflected in an increasingly minimalist and obstructive approach to the transposition of European legislation into UK law. The approach of New Labour to European social and employment policy has deepened and intensified the tensions between New Labour and the unions. After a decade of New Labour, British union leaders increasingly view the struggle for 'Social Europe' as the only viable strategy to defend their members against the impact of neoliberal globalization.

In this chapter, I attempt to make sense of these contradictory developments. I begin by outlining the position of New Labour on the EU and European integration. This section will highlight the ways in which the New Labour project has involved a deepening commitment to European integration alongside a distinctive approach to social policy, social dialogue and social partnership based on the so-called 'Third Way'. The next section explores the Europeanization of British unions. This section highlights their increasing focus on 'Social Europe' as a major protection against globalization and increasing tensions between New Labour and the unions over EU legislation. The following section explores the development and transposition of a range of EU legislation, particularly recent initiatives on labour market regulation, industrial democracy and public services. I focus on the ways New Labour has approached these issues and the manner in which this has influenced the unfolding of European developments in the UK. The final section assesses how a decade of New Labour and European integration has influenced British unions and the prospects for progress in the deepening and extension of Social Europe. I argue that the politics of Social Europe, as developed over the past decade, has double-edged implications for unions. The EU has expanded the social and employment rights of UK workers in a way that threatens the long-term vitality of effective and autonomous trade unionism. I conclude with the argument that while this has recently been recognized by union leaders, there remain serious political and institutional barriers to the development of a more critical and incisive engagement with the politics of Social Europe by organized labour in Britain.

## New Labour, Europeanization and the 'Third Way': Neoliberalism in a social democratic shell?

The issue of the EU and EU membership formed the key foreign policy fault line running through the Labour Party in the post-war period. The party blew hot and cold according to the balance of power between a broadly pro-European right-wing leadership and a broadly anti-European left-wing membership (see Newman 1983; Featherstone 1988, 1989; Tindale 1992; George and Haythorne 1996; Callaghan 2007). It was only in 1988 that the Labour Party adopted an unambiguous pro-EU position. The main dynamics in this important policy shift were opportunistic, driven by the need to secure electoral advantage against a Conservative Party that was divided fatally on the European issue and to further marginalize the left within the Labour Party. The anti-EU stance of the left wing of the labour movement was based on the argument that the expansion of the Single Market, at least substantially, marked the 'export of Thatcherism' in the context of the undeveloped nature of 'Social Europe'. The adoption of a pro-EU position was thus part of an approach to move Labour onto the centre ground of British politics following the electoral disasters of 1983 and 1987. This involved the rejection of the Alternative Economic Strategy (AES) that had informed policy throughout the 1980s in favour of a strategy that recognized the increasing interdependence of the international economy. The influence of the trade unions was also instrumental in transforming the position of the party. In the context of the marginalization of the Thatcher years and the 'new realism' orientation of trade union leaders, Europe emerged as an important alternative means of advancing the agenda on employment rights and social policy. (McIlroy 1995: 313–48; Featherstone 1999: 6). The extent to which these developments, consolidated as New Labour emerged after 1994, mark the Europeanization of the Labour Party is a question that defies a simple or straightforward answer.

The process of 'Europeanization' can be defined as a 'process reorienting the direction and shape of politics to the degree that European political and economic dynamics become part of the organizational logic of national politics and policy making' (Ladrech 1994: 69). The development of a positive stance towards the EU by the Labour Party does indeed constitute one of the most significant developments in British party politics over the past two decades and has formed an important dynamic across a broad spectrum of policy changes (Holden 1999). There is evidence that the Labour Party underwent a process of at least partial Europeanization during the 1980s and 1990s. During the early 1990s, the party leadership adopted a positive approach to the single market, supply-side reforms and membership of the ERM. More importantly, the party declared support for the Social Chapter and in 1996 an important NEC statement argued that 'a new active partnership between government and business should be an essential feature of decision-making at the European level' (Labour Party 1996: 6). In the immediate aftermath of the 1997 election victory, Europeanization appeared complete. The New Labour government granted independence to the Bank of England in order to comply with the provisions of the Maastricht Treaty in preparation for Economic and Monetary Union (EMU) and reversed the opt-out of the Social Chapter.

These developments should not, however, be equated with total Europe-anization of the party. Following the election of New Labour, Tony Blair highlighted his opposition to both a marked extension of European legisla-tion under the Social Chapter or the introduction of European-style social security systems in the UK (Gowland and Turner 2000: 214–15). New Labour has pursued a minimalist approach to the transposition of European social and employment policy and delayed or blocked the implementation of European directives. Its principal objective has been to lead the reform of the EU according to the Third Way principles of 'employability' and 'flexibility'.[1] In the early days there was a clear attempt to present the British government as a key player in the future development and reform of the EU. The distinct-ive vision that New Labour offered was outlined by Tony Blair in his address to the Malmö Congress in 1997 where he outlined an innovative 'Third Way' allegedly distinct from the economic and social policies of both the old left and the new right (Hughes and Smith 1998: 95). At the 1999 Party of European Socialists (PES) Congress in Milan, Blair fleshed out this vision as based on the enabling not controlling state; welfare reform to tackle social exclusion and helping people back to work; the reciprocity of rights and obligations; and the promotion of international solidarity. Blair dis-tinguished his position from the Euro-Keynesian position that was becoming increasingly popular in France and Germany at that time (Featherstone 1999).

The most distinctive way in which New Labour has borrowed strategy and vision from its European partners is with regard to the adoption of their long-term policy models (ibid.: 12). This has involved the use of a 'social partnership' rhetoric to achieve what are essentially neoliberal policy object-ives. The UK remains distinctive in the European context owing to the degree to which the experience of Thatcherism resulted in the institutional and polit-ical decline of trade unionism or indeed the 'disorganized decentralization' or 'institutional collapse' of industrial relations (Crouch 1992). This decline has not been reversed under New Labour and the New Labour approach to social dialogue, social partnership and social policy needs to be viewed in this context. The New Labour project involved the ideological and programmatic repositioning of the Labour Party in terms of the renewal of the 'radical centre' and a 'symbolic rupture' with Old Labour (Moschonas 2002: 163–4). In policy terms, New Labour has positioned itself as the representative of 'Middle England' and sensitive to the demands of enterprise.

The style and appearance of New Labour has, however, changed from the overt hostility to unions displayed by the Thatcher and Major administrations. New Labour is consultative and consensual in areas such as social security policy (Hewitt 1999). The unions have in turn developed a more open and constructive attitude towards employers. Partnership has emerged as the dominant New Labour approach to industrial relations and was central to the *Fairness at Work* proposals that formed the basis of the 1999 Employment Relations Act. However, in the context of an enduring power deficit on the union side and the 'traumatic institutional memory' of the Thatcher era the construction of a new industrial partnership has proved difficult in the UK (Moschonas 2002: 184) and the reality is that New Labour has consistently excluded the unions from consultation on macro-economic policy (see McIlroy, chapter 2, this volume).

The substance of policy has been to combine a continuation of Conservative neoliberal macro-economic policy with social democratic-inspired social policies designed to reduce insecurity and maintain electoral support. These social policies include the introduction of a national minimum wage, the 'New Deal' programme of labour market activation, selective increases in public expenditure in the areas of health and education, a legal framework for union recognition and a selective reversal of opt-outs on EU social and employment directives. The 'Third Way' is not, however, equidistant from the Old Left and the New Right. New Labour downplays neoliberal rhetoric but accepts neoliberal practice, while at the same time rejecting in a fundamental way the established principles and practice of social democratic economic and social policy, including the rejection of a policy style that gave trade unions a central role in decision-making processes (Moschonas 2002: 196). Essentially, therefore, New Labour has pursued a delicate balancing act of simultaneously pursuing what were formerly seen as the opposing principles of the Old Left and the New Right (Hewitt 1999) in 'an enlightened and innovative administration of neoliberalism' where the big picture remains neoliberalism but the accompanying images are at least partially social democratic (Moschonas 2002: 196).

## The Europeanization of British Trade unions: The irresistible allure of 'Social Europe'

The TUC has pursued a strategy of positive engagement with the EU since the late 1980s (McIlroy 1995: 313–48). This period of stability stands in marked contrast to the period between the mid-1960s and the late 1980s when the official policy of the TUC on British membership of the European Community vacillated between support, opposition and indecision on five occasions (Teague 1989). There has been no serious challenge to the progressive TUC agenda on the EU since 1987. There is, however, a debate on the extent to which British trade unions have undergone a thorough process of Europeanization. It has been suggested that, under the TUC's enthusiasm, the dominant position of UK trade unions towards the EU following the 'Delors Conference' of 1988 remained one of scepticism, opportunism and pragmatism behind which was an enduring commitment to an essentially national form of trade unionism (Rosamond 1993). An alternative interpretation suggests that British unions have undergone a thorough process of Europeanization that involves a fundamental change in the economic perspective of the TUC and its main affiliates leading to a general acceptance of the efficacy of European integration (Strange 2002a).

According to Strange, the Europeanization of British unions has followed a rational assessment of the changing institutional and policy context generated by the ongoing process of European integration. Unions looked towards Europe as the efficacy and effectiveness of national demand management diminished and unemployment increased (Dorfman 1977; Teague 1989; McIlroy 1995: 313–48). We could add to this explanation the obstructive and generally negative approach of the post-1997 New Labour government on European social and employment reform as a further dynamic towards Europeanization. Such an interpretation, however, ignores divergent levels of Europeanization between unions organizing in 'transnational' and 'domestic' sectors (Bieler 2006, 2007) and enduring questions around the institutional compatibility between 'Anglo-Saxon' and Continental models of industrial relations.

In the UK unions have indeed devoted increasing amounts of resources to research and articulation of macro-economic policy in general and an engagement with these issues at the European level in particular. The TUC and GMB established permanent offices in Brussels in the early 1990s in order to promote and defend the 'social dimension' through the lobbying of the European Parliament and the European Commission (TUC 1992: 483–4; TUC 1993: 144). Unison has developed a 'memorandum of understanding' with Ver.di, the German public service union, on future cooperation and the coordination of strategy to defend European public services. The TUC and leading affiliates such as the GMB and AEEU, working both independently and through the ETUC, have been involved in the new institutional arrangements that have emerged as part of the EU social policy agenda. This includes engaging in negotiations with other social partners on a range of framework agreements and representation on the recently rejuvenated EU Standing Committee on Employment. The more active engagement with EU institutions has been facilitated by formalized legal machinery for social dialogue and potential collective bargaining, European Works Councils and a framework for union participation in decision-making on the issue of employment policy (Strange 2002b: 354).

There are, however, important differences between British unions and support for European integration and indeed full commitment to EMU has varied according to the sectors in which unions organize and the ideological and political orientation of individual organizations. In sectors open to the dynamics of global competition, unions such as AEEU supported EMU for both pragmatic/instrumental reasons and as a result of an ideological acceptance of neoliberalism. This position is, however, uncommon among unions organizing in competitive manufacturing sectors and the dominant approach has been the adoption of a 'Euro-Keynesian' orientation. The Euro-Keynesian paradigm was developed most forcibly by MSF, which combined support for EMU with a policy focused on support for deepening economic and political integration based on Euro-federalist macro-economic management (MSF 1993). The Euro-Keynesian position retains a commitment to full employment alongside a support for supply-side reforms to improve employability and social inclusion. The latter position was clearly dominant in Amicus, formed from the merger of the AEEU and MSF (Amicus 2005: 6). The GMB also supported EMU for sectoral reasons, particularly over the threat to manufacturing jobs posed by an unfavourable exchange rate between sterling and the euro (see TUC 2002), but has nonetheless been more critical of the neoliberal direction of European integration.

The position of public sector unions such as Unison was to view EMU as a threat to public services and public service employment and a threat to the political and economic sovereignty of the British nation state (Bieler 2006: 132–76). Despite its opposition to EMU, Unison has nevertheless developed an essentially positive approach to the benefits of European integration, based to some extent on the progressive Euro-Keynesian position of NALGO during the 1980s (Unison 1997). However, in the context of the increasing threat posed to public services by the liberalization agenda of the EU and following the re-election of a Labour government in 1997, Unison has focused on the national level and the attempt to influence the domestic trasnsposition of European directives (Bieler 2006: 168) alongside developing strategic partnerships with European public service unions such as Ver.di in Germany (Waddington 2005). The ambiguity of Unison's position was expressed in its support for the process underpinning the Employment Chapter of the Amsterdam Treaty. The EES provides an 'institutional framework formally in line with Unison's preferred intergovernmental approach to full employment policy despite the fact that its initial terms of reference . . . arguably reflected the drift towards neoliberalism of the post-Delors European Commission' (Strange 2002a: 349).

These divergent positions on EMU and European integration are indicative of a broader struggle to define the future trajectory of European development and in particular to set the determinants of a 'Social Europe' on the basis of a new 'historic compromise' in which market forces are embedded within a regulated social framework at the European level. An adherence to the 'Social Europe' project involves a challenge to the neoliberal dynamics underpinning European integration and an attempt to change or critically reinterpret the dominant categories underpinning the neoliberal paradigm. The notion of Social Europe has developed as a new utopian vision for trade unions in the context of the ideological and political exhaustion of the existing utopian vision of national, social democratic Keynesianism (Hyman 2001).

The GMB approach, and indeed the TUC leadership approach, has been to develop a radical orientation to the EU social partnership agenda which stresses 'negotiated involvement' or 'negotiated flexibility' based on an 'alternative compromise' of modernizing social democracy through the establishment of new collective bargaining mechanisms and new strategies of full employment.[2] The position of the TUC and the GMB, which organizes workers in the public and private sectors, reflects the benefits and dangers that further European integration poses for British unions (Bieler 2007: 115). The most recent and explicit commitment to Euro-Keynesianism is presented in the 2006 TUC Report on Europe:

> Europe needs to rediscover the benefits of macro-economic policies, taking action not just on the supply side . . . of the economy. The Stability and Growth Pact requires further reform – largely to give some meaning to the growth element of the pact . . . We need to protect the ethos of public service across Europe . . . The European Central Bank needs to have the objective of securing full employment, and needs in particular to abandon its obsession with countering inflation to the exclusion of jobs and growth.
>
> (TUC 2006c: 6–7)

Hence, pro-EU British trade unions have demanded expansion of the EU's macro-economic competence and increased attention to high levels of employment as part of a Euro-Keynesian project based on centralized fiscal and monetary policy in a federal union marked by EU-level social partnership industrial relations (Strange 1997: 21–3; Strange 2002b: 356–7). The position of Unison reflects a deeper ambiguity of British trade unions towards European integration. The shift towards 'new realism' and business unionism by many British trade unions during the 1980s predisposed unions to accept 'partnership' as a strategy of renewal during the 1990s and the possibility of a new historic compromise at the European level. The popularity of this position peaked in 1997 and has declined over the past decade, only to be reinvigorated as a decade of New Labour in power drew to a close. This does indeed seem to highlight a degree of pragmatic opportunism or indeed desperation with regard to the support of British unions for 'Social Europe'.

The issue of Europe also remains an important fault line between right and left in the unions, and 'left-wing' organizations such as the NUM and RMT have consistently proposed anti-European motions at the TUC Congress. This tension was highlighted in 2005 when a resolution critical of the proposed EU Constitutional Treaty was passed at Congress. This reversed the decision of the 2004 Congress that defeated a Eurosceptic motion. Both motions were put forward by the RMT. The motion rejected the 'increasingly neoliberal policies emanating from Brussels', including EU directives which liberalized passenger and freight rail services across Europe and the proposed directive on the liberalization of services. In essence, the motion rejected a European agenda that is 'elitist, militarist, corporate and anti-democratic' (EIRO 2005a). The RMT has spearheaded the 'Trade Unionists against the

EU Constitution Campaign'[3] which is focused on the issue of how the treaty exacerbates these tendencies. TUC general secretary Brendan Barber attempted to place the rejection of the resolution in the context of the positive approach of the TUC to the European Social Model and the importance of constructing a strong social dimension to the EU.

At the 2007 TUC conference, delegates backed unanimously a GMB motion calling for a referendum on the Reform Treaty. A more critical motion put forward by the RMT, which called for unions to campaign for a 'no' vote, was defeated despite the support of large and influential unions such as the PCS (*Guardian*, 12 September 2007). Clearly, therefore, British unions have undergone only a partial and to some extent pragmatic process of Europeanization. As I will demonstrate in the next section, this reflects more than enduring ideological and sectoral division between unions on the European issue. The directives and initiatives emanating from Brussels can be shown to have ambiguous and double-edged potential for the future prospects of UK trade unionism.

### European social policy and British industrial relations: Euro-corporatism or neo-voluntarism?

In this section I explore the main pieces of European legislation that have impacted on UK social and employment policy in order to highlight enduring tensions between New Labour and the unions over the form and trajectory of European integration. During the 1990s, the experience of mass unemployment across continental Europe provided the impetus for an increasing stress on employment policy, which resulted ultimately in the Employment Chapter of the Treaty of Amsterdam and the establishment of the European Employment Strategy (EES). The focus on 'employability' and 'flexibility' reflected the agenda of both New Labour and the European Commission. Consensus at Amsterdam was only attained through a restatement of the importance of subsidiarity and progress on the measure was achieved through the development of a multi-level form of negative regulation. The Treaty affirmed the enduring importance of national employment policy and the importance of avoiding costly job creation measures at the European level. In contrast to the Stability and Growth Pact established by the Dublin Intergovernmental Conference (IGC) in 1996, recommendations on employment issues are not binding on member states. The procedures adopted in respect of monitoring the EES are similar to the Stability and Growth Pact, but the non-binding nature of employment guidelines demonstrates the enduring imbalance between monetary and employment policy and the way in which employment and social policy remains subordinate to monetary restraint within the EU (Taylor 2006: 78–9).

This approach was reiterated and extended by the Lisbon Strategy. It set out a ten-year programme of reforms designed to make Europe the most competitive knowledge-based economy in the world, marked by sustainable economic growth, increasing levels of high-quality employment, social cohesion and respect for the environment. The Lisbon Strategy involved the invention of a new 'softer' model of EU policymaking: a shift from legislative action towards a so-called 'open method of coordination' (OMC) (de la Porte 2000). This amounts to an essentially neo-voluntarist approach to the development of 'Social Europe' (Streeck 1998) that involves invoking changes in policy at national level through the scrutiny of national policy outcomes at the EU level and through the exchange of information and best practice. The outcome of this process is a harmonization of policy objectives rather than a harmonization of policy outcomes or the development of a coherent European employment strategy. In this context, New Labour has adopted an essentially neoliberal interpretation of the EES in the domestic sphere and this is reflected in the way in which the British government has handled European directives on social and employment issues over the past decade.

New Labour has performed a delicate balancing act by simultaneously supporting the development of Social Europe whilst attempting to limit and obstruct those aspects of European legislation that threaten its neoliberal policy agenda. In essence, there is a tension between the 'Euro-corporatist' discourse associated with 'Social Europe' and the neo-voluntarist reality emerging from the dynamics of subsidiarity and the OMC. Consequently, those directives that build on the existing platform of individual rights that have developed as an integral part of the European 'common market' strategy of ensuring a level playing field for competition have been transposed in a relatively unproblematic way into UK law. In addition, New Labour has supported directives that result in further liberalization of European markets, such as the Bolkestein Directive on the liberalization of services. In contrast, New Labour has attempted to obstruct or minimize the directives that enhance the social or employment rights of workers or which threaten neoliberal policy priorities.

There is an established raft of individual rights at the European levels that recent directives have built on and which have been transposed in a relatively unproblematic way into UK law. The Treaty of Rome established the principle for equality of pay and treatment between men and women. The Equal Pay Directive (75/117/EEC) and the Equal Treatment Directive (76/207/EEC) established the principles of equal pay and equal treatment and the requirements of these directives form the basis of UK law including the 1970 Equal Pay Act and the 1975 Sex Discrimination Act. In the area of health and safety at work, EU directives establish minimum standards and the basic responsibilities of employers and employees. The Single European Act encouraged EU health and safety legislation and Article 129 of the Union Treaty confirmed the competence for the EU to act in that area. In 1989, a framework directive (89/391/EEC) and a directive setting out minimum requirements (89/654/EEC) established an EU-wide framework of minimum standards.

The development of an explicit EU competence in employment policy did not emerge until the 1990s. The attempt to coordinate European employment policy in the 1970s through the development of tripartite machinery was resisted by employers' organizations and national ministries of labour. Consequently, initial developments were the result of ad hoc and fragmented EC initiatives on collective redundancies (1975), transfer of enterprises (1977) and employee protection in the case of corporate insolvency (1980). The Acquired Rights Directive (77/187/EEC), as amended in 1998 and 2001, was transposed into UK law by The Transfer of Undertakings (Protection of Employment) [TUPE] regulations (SI 1981/1794) in 1982. The European Social Dialogue was re-launched by Jacques Delors in 1985 and following the Treaty on European Union (1992) enabled collective agreements between the social partners to be translated into European directives. These agreements have resulted in three directives on paternity leave, part-time work and fixed-term contracts.

The agreement on part-time work was implemented by Council Directive 97/81/EC under the 'Social Chapter'. This was extended to the UK when New Labour signed up to the Treaty of Amsterdam Social Policy Protocol in 1997 by Directive 98/23/EC. Following the provisions of the 1999 Employment Relations Act, this was extended into UK law by the Part-time Workers (Prevention of Less Favourable Treatment) Regulations (SI 2000/1551). The regulations make it unlawful for any business to treat a part-time worker less favourably than a full-time worker unless there are objective reasons for so doing. The regulations apply to rates of pay, overtime payments, training, maternity and paternity leave and pensions, perks and sick pay.

A framework agreement on fixed-term workers was reached in 1999 and adopted as part of the Social Chapter by Council Directive (99/70/EC). In the UK, the directive was implemented by the Fixed Term Employees (Prevention of Less Favourable Treatment) Regulations (SI 2002/2034) that took effect in October 2002. These regulations establish rights for temporary workers on fixed-term contracts not to be treated unfairly in comparison with workers on permanent contracts unless there are objective reasons for so doing. The regulations establish the right for fixed-term workers to consider their contract permanent if it is renewed without interruption for more than four years. The regulations also establish that fixed-term employers should have equal access to statutory redundancy pay, statutory sick pay and occupational pension schemes. Fixed-term employees have the right to be informed of permanent positions within their employer's organization and the right to a written response to a claim of unfair treatment under the regulations. The regulations exclude the armed forces, agency workers, apprentices and students on work experience placements.

The transposition of European directives into UK law has been less straightforward when the directive threatens aspects of pay and conditions that have traditionally been subject to voluntary regulation. This is evident in respect of working time. The Working Time Directive (93/104/EC) requires member states to limit working time to 48 hours per week within a four-month reference period, determines minimum rest periods and entitles workers to at least four weeks paid leave per year. The Conservative administration led by John Major attempted to block the directive by voting against it in the European Council; a position that was subsequently deemed unlawful by the European Court of Justice (ECJ). New Labour introduced the Working Time Regulations in 1998 (SI 1998/1833). These imposed a comprehensive statutory framework for the regulation of working time and the potential for heightened levels of litigation and juridification in areas of employment relations traditionally determined by voluntary agreement (EIRO 1998). The experience of the past decade suggests that this potential has been realized. The regulations stipulated that the right to paid leave applied only to workers with more than 13 weeks' continuous service. Subsequently, however, the Broadcasting, Entertainment Cinematograph and Theatre Union (BECTU) challenged this threshold in the ECJ and the New Labour Government was forced to remove the restriction in 2001 through the Working Time (Amendment) Regulations (SI 2001/3256).

The directive contained far-reaching derogations that allowed working time to be extended to an almost unlimited extent. First, the 'opt-out' clause enabled member states not to apply the 48-hour maximum based on voluntary agreements with individual workers (Article 18). Second, the four-month reference period can be extended to a maximum of 12 months by collective agreement (Article 17). In the UK, a number of collective agreements on the application of the directive were reached prior to the agreement coming into effect, including the agreement between the Heating and Ventilation Contractors' Association and MSF in 1996 which established an extended reference period of 12 months and between the Engineering Construction Industry Association and the AEEU, GMB, TGWU and MSF unions in 1997 to use the maximum collectively agreed reference period allowable under UK legislation. There are also examples of company-level agreements such as that between Group 4 and the GMB union (EIRO 1998). The Working Time Directive excluded most transport sectors. However, in 2000 a separate provision applied the directive to non-mobile workers in the sector while excluding mobile workers from the provisions on rest breaks and night work. The approach of the Commission has been to encourage social partner agreements in transportation sectors and agreements were achieved in the maritime and railway sectors in 1998, the civil aviation sector in 2000 and the road transport sectors in 2002.

A series of important rulings in the European Court of Justice (ECJ) in respect of the Jaeger and Pfeiffer cases ruled that 'on-call working time' should be defined as working time under the terms of the Directive and these judgments were used by several member states as a pretext for applying the opt-out. The opt-out was included in the 1993 Directive largely to satisfy the UK Government and it is widely recognized that the opt-out has subsequently been widely abused in the UK. Working hours are high in the UK owing to the lack of government regulation or sectoral agreement on working time and the comparatively low level of basic pay rates (EIRO 1997). Indeed, the UK was the only member state to have taken up the opt-out option under Article 18 of the Directive in a general way. The European Commission highlighted evidence from research it had commissioned (see Barnard *et al.* 2003) to argue that 'UK legislation and practice do not appear to offer all the guarantees laid down by the directive' and that 'the main characteristics of the system governing working time have remained unchanged despite the entry into the force of the directive, mainly as a result of using the "opt-out"' (EIRO 2004).

In May 2004, the European Commission published proposals for the revision of the Directive. TUC General Secretary Brendan Barber welcomed the 'much needed review' of the working time directive while reiterating his demand for the removal of the individual opt-out. At the 2003 Congress, the TUC launched the 'It's About Time' campaign with a key objective to end the individual opt-out of the 48-hour weekly limit and more generally 'to put long hours and work-life balance at the top of the workplace agenda'. This included the introduction of a telephone hotline and website to enable workers to report abuse (EIRO 2003). TUC research highlighted that UK workers put in the longest hours in the EU-15, two-thirds of UK workers were unaware of the 48-hour restriction and two-thirds of long-hours workers reported not signing the opt-out and one-third of those signing the opt-out said they were given no choice (ibid.). The research reported that the UK is tenth in the EU-15 with regard to productivity per hour and the long-hours culture tends to result in tired workers, mistakes and poor quality and creates a barrier to the expansion of education and training, perpetuating the comparatively unskilled and unproductive workforce in the UK.

In contrast, the CBI spokesperson Susan Anderson stated that 'The Commission is right to recognise the importance of choice over working hours and the value of the individual opt-out. This review must not lead to the removal of that vital freedom. UK employees have more choice about the hours they work than almost anywhere else in Europe . . . We do not believe that employers are routinely pressurizing workers into signing opt-outs' (EIRO 2004). The New Labour government remained committed to retaining the opt-out and therefore supported the position of the CBI.

The Commission proposed the maintenance of the individual opt-out, the definition of non-active parts of on-call duty as non-working time and the extension of the 48-hour reference period to 12 months with no safeguards. The ETUC found the revised directive unacceptable and questioned the legal validity of the proposals. The ETUC demanded the phasing out of the individual opt-out, the recognition of the binding nature of the ECJ rulings on on-call duty time and the maintenance of the four-month reference period except on the basis of collective bargaining or the provision of additional legal safeguards to information and consultation and health and safety (ETUC 2006). In May 2005, the European Parliament, backed by the ETUC, voted in favour of phasing out the opt-out within three years and the recognition of on-call time as working time in line with the ECJ rulings. The ETUC called on the European Council and the European Commission to accept the compromise agreed by the European Parliament. The June 2005 European Council, however, failed to develop proposals owing to the way in which a minority of member states, led by the UK, blocked progress on the initiative. The June 2006 Council also failed to develop a satisfactory and workable set of proposals for a new directive. This has resulted in a seemingly intractable stalemate on the issue of working time.

There is also deadlock with regard to the proposed Temporary Agency Work Directive. Temporary agency work is the most rapidly growing form of atypical work in the EU. Despite agreement on other forms of atypical work, framework discussions amongst the social partners have failed to reverse the position of UNICE (recently renamed BusinessEurope) that the pay and conditions of agency staff should not be on an equal footing with directly employed staff. In this context, the European Commission published its own proposals for a directive in 2002. However, a compromise on the directive has been difficult owing to the steadfast intergovernmental opposition of the UK, Ireland, Denmark and Germany in the European Council.

There is, however, regulation of transnational agency workers in the form of the Posting of Workers Directive (96/71/EC), which requires member states to remove restrictions based on nationality or residence that hinder employers posting workers to other member states to provide a service on a temporary basis. The directive states that employers have to guarantee equality of terms and conditions with workers in the member states to which they are posted. John Major's Conservative administration opposed the directive, as did the CBI, which argued that it could undermine competition and the free movement of labour and services and disadvantage the UK in comparison with more regulated economies. New Labour introduced legislation in 1999 in order to bring UK law in line with the regulations (EIRO 1999a). The comparison between the transposition of these two directives into UK law highlights the willingness of the Blair governments to acquiesce to measures that prevent distortions of the single market whilst resisting and evoking the principle of subsidiarity on measures that expand the substantive rights of UK workers.

There has also been tension between New Labour and the unions over the implementation of EU regulations on maternity and paternity leave. In 1995, a framework agreement on parental leave was reached and subsequently implemented by Council Directive (96/34/EC). The regulations provide that employers and employees can negotiate their own agreement on parental leave, which may take the form of collective agreements with trade unions, 'workforce agreements' with elected employee representatives or individual agreements, which may improve upon but not fall short of the statutory obligations. These obligations require that employees are able to take up to a maximum of four weeks' leave per annum in blocks or multiples of one week after giving their employer 21 days' notice. Employers may postpone the leave for up to six months where granting the leave would disrupt the operation of their business. The agreement holds that men and women have an individual right to at least three months leave for childcare purposes after the birth or adoption of a child until the child is eight years of age. The New Labour government agreed to implement the directive as part of its abandonment of the UK opt-out of the Social Chapter. An 'extension directive' (97/75/EC) extended the directive to the UK in December 1997 and the Maternity and Parental Leave Regulations (SI 1999/3312) transposed the directive into UK law.

These provisions were the subject of intense criticism by both the TUC and employer organizations. The British Chamber of Commerce expressed concern that small businesses would find it difficult to accommodate the absence of key members of staff and the CBI were instrumental in the establishment of the four-week annual limit. In 1998, the TUC and other pressure groups established the Parental Leave Campaign to lobby for parental leave to be paid. In March 1999, the TUC published an opinion poll that indicated that 34 per cent or 1.7 million parents would not be able to take advantage of parental leave if it remained unpaid. The TUC argued that the unpaid nature of the leave would particularly discourage take-up amongst lower-paid workers and would discourage male workers from taking an active role in childcare. The TUC calculated that providing a payment of approximately £60 per week (the current rate for statutory maternity pay) would cost the government approximately £250 million per annum. Then TUC general secretary John Monks stated that 'it is time to start a national debate about how best to ensure that every parent is able to take full advantage of parental leave – and it is clear that this is going to include moving from unpaid leave to paid leave' (EIRO 1999a). The TUC remains critical of the regulations owing to the unpaid nature of the leave and the lack of flexibility in the take-up of leave that has to be taken in blocks of at least one week. The TUC also questioned the extent to which limiting the provisions to children born after 15 December 1999 was inconsistent with the directive. In 2000 the TUC mounted a legal challenge to the Maternity and Paternity Regulations on the basis that the above restriction breached the EU Directive and the appeal was referred to the ECJ by the High Court.

The European directive on parental leave has provided an important catalyst for the review and reform of maternity, paternity and parental leave in the UK. In 2000, the government launched a review and published a green paper on the issue of how to increase the labour market participation of mothers without imposing onerous costs and administrative burdens on business. The most controversial proposal that was steadfastly opposed by employers' organizations was to establish the right for new parents to opt for part-time work. In 2001, the government announced that it was dropping the December 1999 restriction on parental leave, thus pre-empting the imminent decision of the ECJ. The TUC presented this move as a total climb-down and a victory for working parents, while the CBI stated that the move would stiffen the resolve of employers to fight the proposals to allow working mothers the right to work part-time (EIRO 2001).

Following a further period of consultation, the government published further proposals in 2005 (DTI 2005) that formed the basis of the 2006 Work and Families Act. The Act reflected the way the government was attempting to pursue its 'family-friendly' employment strategy in an employer-friendly way (EIRO 2005b). The act extends the period of statutory maternity pay, provides new entitlements for fathers to take paid paternity leave and enables carers to request flexible working hours. However, the Act also contains measures to help employers manage the administration of parental leave. While the TUC welcomed the Act, comments by Brendan Barber, TUC general secretary, on the publication of the proposal suggest that the unions remain concerned that the benefits of 'flexible' working are balanced in favour of employers (EIRO 2005b). Parental leave remains unpaid following the Act and the right to allow returning mothers to work part-time was not considered in the 2005 consultation.

There have been important innovations regarding the rights of workers to information and consultation. The European Works Council Directive (94/45/EC) established rights to information and consultation in large companies that have workforces spread across the EU and a more recent directive establishes an institutional framework for information and consultation in other large companies at the national level. The European Works Council Directive required companies with more than 1,000 employees and at least 150 employees in at least two or more member states to establish a European Works Council (EWC). The provisions were extended to the UK after New Labour signed the Social Chapter in 1997 by the Transnational Information and Consultation of Employees Regulations (SI 1999/3323) and came into force in January 2000. Prior to implementation, the New Labour government had come under intense pressure from UK companies and employers' organizations to develop a 'minimalist' approach to EWCs and to avoid unnecessary 'gold plating' of the directive and this was reflected in the final regulations, which did not go beyond the wording of the directive. There is no guaranteed role for unions in 'special negotiating bodies' (SNBs) or statutory EWCs and a minimalist and flexible approach to enforcement with minimal sanctions (EIRO 1999b). There is no obligation for companies to establish an EWC unless the company's management takes the initiative to establish one or employees or their representatives trigger the request procedure.

The directive provided the opportunity for companies to establish so-called 'Article 13' arrangements voluntarily before the statutory deadline and many UK companies decided to do this in the belief that a voluntary agreement would provide more flexibility for their organizational structure and industrial relations culture (Marginson *et al.* 1998). Following the statutory deadline companies have to conclude an 'Article 6' agreement that prescribes the negotiating arrangements that companies must follow. This involves establishment of an SNB, comprised of selected or elected employee representatives, that meets with management. The directive sets out the minimum substantive content of a transnational consultation and information procedure or EWC. In the UK, the regulations make no formal link between the EWC and other consultation bodies already established to cover the UK workforce. In contrast, in continental Europe local or national works councils and/or union recognition tend to determine employee representation to SNBs or EWCs.

Detailed case studies have highlighted the limited, management-controlled agenda of EWCs and the isolation of EWCs from established forms of workplace representation (Wills 2000). In the motor industry, EWCs have encouraged international competition for production capacity between plants (Hancké 2000; Whittall 2000). In non-unionized sectors, EWCs have developed as mechanisms of management communication rather than mechanisms for facilitating meaningful consultation between management and workforce (Royle 1999). In a recent study of EWCs in six British-based companies across a range of sectors, Redfern (2007: 302) highlighted the minimalistic and reluctant approach to EWCs by senior managers (see also Fitzgerald and Stirling 2004) and concluded that the forums remain remote from established bargaining and consultation mechanisms and have generally failed to improve the rights of British workers to information and consultation. The TUC has recognized these limitations alongside support for the directive and has called for the strengthening of the directive in order to increase the influence of workers in transnational corporations (TUC 2006c: 5). There remain a series of unanswered questions concerning the compatibility of Anglo-Saxon industrial relations systems with the 'continental' model of bargaining inherent to EWCs (Hall *et al.* 2003) or indeed the extent to which this 'dual system' threatens to undermine the representational role of UK unions within transnational corporations (Lecher and Rüb 1999).

The general framework for informing and consulting employees at the national level is the Information and Consultation Directive (2002/14/EC), which requires sizeable employers to inform and consult workforce representatives on the development of the organization, prospects for employment and substantial changes to work organization or contractual relations. In the first phase of implementation, the DTI published *High Performance Workplaces: The Role of Employee Involvement in a Modern Economy*. The consultation paper argued that the directive would provide a basis for both fair treatment at work and contribute towards 'high performance' workplaces, partnership and employee involvement (EIRO 2002). It argued for a flexible, essentially minimalist framework that did not cut across existing good practice or impose rigid arrangements across businesses (DTI 2002: 5) and a statutory minimum requirement that would only be invoked in the absence of a voluntary arrangement (ibid.: 11). Hence the paper stressed the limited suitability of the works council model, particularly in relation to small and medium-sized companies: it urged a diversity that combined 'representative and direct forms of participation' (ibid.: 28). The CBI expressed support for the proposals, arguing that 'the Government has recognized that employers need the freedom to inform and consult staff in a variety of ways. Now that this directive is to become law, it is vital employers get as much flexibility as possible' (EIRO 2002). The TUC were more circumspect, welcoming the initiative as part of a long-term process of increasing rights at work and a staging post in the long-term campaign to achieve minimum decent standards for UK workers.

The directive was implemented in the UK by the Information and Consultation of Employees Regulations (SI 2004/3426). This measure requires compliance by employers with more than 150 workers by April 2005, more than 100 workers by April 2006 and more than 50 workers by April 2008. What is important about these regulations is that for the first time the UK government strategy for implementing an EU employment law directive was achieved through tripartite discussions between the government, CBI and TUC. The TUC, in particular, perceived an important political advance owing to the way in which a national 'social partner' style framework agreement was used as the basis for the transposition of EU legislation into UK law. The importance of this directive for the unions is that it gives them a chance to gain a foothold in non-unionized, private sector workplaces. However, as Metcalf (2005) has noted, the long-term existence of works council arrangements in France and Germany has not reversed low and declining levels of union density and raises a nightmare scenario for UK unions whereby the indirect voice institution crowds out the union voice. The new information and consultation framework is therefore unlikely to reverse declining union density in the private sector without the restatement of a distinctive 'sword of justice' trade union orientation which itself is likely to rest on effective workplace organization and representation.

There is evidence that in certain sectors the shift to an organizing culture has resulted in a significant growth in union membership. Prominent examples include USDAW, where membership has increased by 17 per cent over the past decade, and the NUJ, which increased membership by 25 per cent between 2000 and 2005 (EIRO 2005c). The directive is thus unlikely to reverse the decline in the influence and effectiveness of UK unions in the absence of a parallel strategy to revitalize and renew workplace organization. Indeed, in common with the European Works Council Directive, the 'dualist' logic of the directive could pose a serious threat to the long-term representational role of unions in unionized workplaces that makes the revitalization of workplace trade unionism even more imperative.

Perhaps the most contentious directive developed by the European Commission in the past decade focused on liberalization of services. The Commission published a proposal for a directive on services in the internal market in January 2004. The proposal became known as the Bolkestein Directive after the Dutch Internal Market Commissioner who launched the proposal. Its objective was to open up a range of services to cross-border competition by the elimination of barriers between nation states that render it more difficult, costly or less profitable for a service supplier from one member state to operate in another. The definition of 'service' was broadly defined and included commercial services such as retailing, car rental, advertising, estate agents and hotels and tourism as well as the advice provided by professionals such as architects, lawyers, engineers and consultants. The directive was controversial owing to the way that it failed to specify adequately which services would be opened up to competition and, in particular, the extent to which the directive would apply to 'essential' services such as health care and social services.

The draft proposal was opposed by the French Government for its Anglo-Saxon, free-market bias and by the ETUC, TUC and individual UK unions. The two main concerns of unions were the 'country of origin principle' (CoOP), by which service providers would be subject only to the laws and conditions that applied in the country where they were based, and the failure of the draft to differentiate between commercial services and 'services of general interest' (SGIs). In the UK, the New Labour Government supported the 'market opening' objectives of the directive provided the proposed directive did not impinge on taxation, publicly funded health services, occupational pensions, social security policy or the criminal law. New Labour did not express opposition to the CoOP, much to the concern of UK trade unions.

In the context of these concerns, the ETUC and national trade unions campaigned against the draft directive on the basis that it would be against the interests of European workers and consumers. In March 2005, the ETUC organized a demonstration in Brussels against the draft directive which mobilized 75,000 protestors. In February 2006, the European Parliament voted in favour of a compromise that addressed many trade union concerns and the Commission subsequently put forward a new proposal that adhered to the principles of the European Parliament compromise. The compromise excluded labour law and sensitive sectors such as temporary work agencies and private security services. In addition, fundamental rights to collective bargaining and collective action were respected and services of general interest and some services of general economic interest such as health care were excluded. Most importantly, the country of origin principle was abolished, which enabled member states to exercise supervision and regulation in the 'public interest'. In May 2006, the Council reached agreement on an amended directive and this was approved by the European Parliament in November. The resulting improvements were hailed as a success for the trade union movement. However, the enduring concern of the ETUC was that the revised directive fails to include clear exclusions for labour law and social services of general interest and stronger support for fundamental rights. Amendments to take account of these concerns were rejected by the European Parliament Internal Market and Consumer Protection Committee in October 2006.

## Conclusion: Substantive reforms, utopian visions and the politics of Social Europe

Since the election of New Labour in 1997, the impact of EU social and employment policy on British industrial relations has increased. European legislation and directives have established a set of EU-wide minimum standards on a range of social and employment policy issues. It would be a mistake, however, to equate these developments with the end of voluntarism (cf. Sisson 1999) or to suggest that the UK is now part of a European industrial relations system (cf. Jensen *et al.* 1999). The strategy pursued by New Labour has been to support social and employment reforms that facilitate the smooth running of the European single market whilst attempting to maximize the competitiveness of the British economy. The focus has thus been on the transposition of European directives by voluntary agreement while simultaneously and strenuously opposing aspects of European legislation that provide additional substantive rights for UK workers. Indeed, one of the 'red lines' outlined by Prime Minister Gordon Brown in the context of the 2007 European Reform Treaty was that the Fundamental Charter of Rights should not impact on UK social and employment legislation (*Guardian*, 19 October 2007).

Notwithstanding its pro-EU rhetoric, New Labour has consistently pursued what is now an ingrained minimalist approach to social and employment rights, business regulation and trade union involvement. It has consistently aligned itself with the CBI to resist EU directives in areas such as information and consultation and on issues such as working time and agency workers. The example of the Consultation and Information Directive, which was transposed into UK law through a social partner 'framework agreement', highlights the ways in which the process of European integration is transforming the style of national industrial relations. The TUC hailed this development as a political advance on the road towards the strengthening of Social Europe. However, as I demonstrated in the previous section, the substantive benefits achieved by UK unions from the development of 'Social Europe' have been minimal. The irony is that 'Social Europe' has become the overarching ideological vision of British unions, perceived as key to union revitalization and to the protection and expansion of workers' rights. This was recently articulated by Brendan Barber:

> [S]ome of the most popular and worthwhile changes in the workplace have come direct from Europe. This is not just because the social European model balances the needs of employees, consumers and the environment in a way alien in unfettered US capitalism, but because it makes sense to introduce such changes throughout the world's biggest market.
>
> (TUC 2006a)

The 2006 TUC General Council statement declared that in light of the successful campaign against the Bolkestein Directive, it was time to relaunch the campaign for a social Europe. A strong social dimension was held to be vital if the security of EU citizens was to be protected against the vicissitudes of globalization. The statement suggested that the rejection of the proposed EU constitution by the French people was a sign that the necessary balance between drive for profit and the delivery of security had yet to be delivered. In order to achieve further progress on Social Europe the TUC highlighted the need to rebuild union membership and organization across the continent. It initiated a debate through a conference in 2005 on 'Organizing Across Europe'. It emphasized the need for a campaign bringing together unions, politicians and social movements in order to enhance the social model. Mustering 70,000 demonstrators in Strasbourg against the Bolkestein Directive demonstrated the potential of popular mobilization. These views were voiced by the TUC spokesperson on Europe, CWU leader Billy Hayes, in November 2006:

> In Britain, we remember that the anti-social excesses of the Thatcher and Major governments were tempered by the existence of a real European social dimension ... The European social dimension has delivered important rights for working people. However, despite some very real accomplishments – such as enlargement – Europe seems to have run out of steam in recent years. Indeed, after the French and Dutch 'noes' on the Constitution, the EU has stagnated ... Is there in fact an alternative? I'm afraid not. Looking around the World, Europe and the European Social Model remains our best bet.
>
> (TUC 2006b)

The prospects for further progress, however, remained dependent on the unwillingness of the New Labour government to play a more positive role in the Social Europe agenda. Hayes continued:

> [T]he biggest obstacle to progress with this agenda is the British government. On working time, it seems that the government opposes the end of the opt-out because it would prevent employers from acting flexibly ... The refusal of the government to give agency workers ... equal rights to other workers means that for some employers they are a cheap option.
>
> (ibid.)

The TUC still views Europe as the principal means to remove the obstacles to progress posed by New Labour. Moving on and moving forward requires a strengthening of the European Parliament and the mobilization of European unions as a social movement in European civil society. What are the prospects for the trade unions in Europe under a Gordon Brown premiership? Writing in the *Wall Street Journal*, Brown spelt out the New Labour agenda for the EU: it included an explicit rejection of 'Social Europe':

Economic reform should be embraced with even greater speed. The right response to global competitive pressure is to liberalize, deregulate and remove the old state aid subsidies, agree an open competition policy, and remove barriers that hamper companies crossing borders ... Europe must embrace labour market flexibility.

(quoted in Wainwright 2005)

In this context, the prospects for further expansion of social and employment rights through European legislation seem bleak. However, the development of EU social and employment policy over the past decade also provides the basis for a guarded optimism with regard to the potential for Social Europe to protect the interests of British workers. There have been undoubted benefits derived from the 'common market' measures associated with equal opportunities, health and safety and non-standard employment. Despite the opposition of the UK and other governments to the expansion of substantive social and employment rights at the EU level, these have nonetheless expanded on the basis of 'Russian Doll' incremental harmonization resulting from the decisions and rulings of the ECJ, the substantive concessions of neoliberal governments that have been necessary in order to achieve unanimity on market liberalization and the ways in which the 'variable geometry of the EU opens up new spaces of regulatory innovation' (Taylor 2006: 74–5).

In this context, it is clear why UK unions, faced with limited room for manoeuvre at the domestic level, should have constructed a utopian vision of Social Europe as the key to union revitalization and the maintenance and expansion of workplace rights. As I have demonstrated in this chapter, however, Social Europe, as it is currently constituted, has developed through powerful intergovernmental dynamics and the principle of subsidiarity is built into the institutional form of European governance. While the juridification of European social and employment policy has limited the scope and effectiveness of these dynamics, both subsidiarity and juridification tend to marginalize and exclude the interests of organized labour. The long-term survival and vitality of UK trade unions suggests that unions engage in a more critical and realistic assessment of how the 'double-edged' nature of the European 'sword of justice' produces both possibilities and dangers for the future of organized labour.

There is growing recognition among union leaders that the dangers of marginalization and exclusion can be countered by re-brandishing the original 'sword of justice' through the rebuilding of radical, campaigning trade unionism at workplace level, linked to a radical vision of Social Europe. This requires abandonment of the 'elite embrace' of EU institutions and the linking of workplace politics to a contentious and autonomous politics of Social Europe in European civil society (Hyman 2005; Taylor and Mathers 2004). This chapter has highlighted the limited progress of this project and the institutional and political obstacles to its development. The dominant approach of UK unions to Europe has been 'industrial legality' and 'partnership' and the New Labour government remains steadfastly opposed to the expansion of social and employment rights at the EU level. UK unions have started to recognize the double-edged nature of the European 'sword of justice' but the hard work of building an alternative is only just beginning.

## Notes

1 See Giddens (2007) for a 'Third Way' elaboration of the European Social Model.
2 See Lipietz (1988) for an exploration of the underlying theoretical rationale of the Euro-Keynesian position from a regulationist perspective and Habermas (2001) for a discussion of Euro-Keynesianism as a potential form of transnational 'cosmopolitan democracy'.
3 See <http://www.tuaeuc.org> (accessed 2 July 2008).

## Bibliography

Amicus (2005) *A Guide to AMICUS International Work* London: Amicus.
Barnard, C., Deakin, S. and Hobbs, R. (2003) 'Opting out of the 48 hour week: employer necessity or individual choice? An empirical study of the operation of article 18(1)(b) of the working time directive in the UK', *Industrial Law Journal*, 32:4, 223–52.
Bieler, A. (2006) *The Struggle for a Social Europe: Trade Unions and EMU in Times of Global Restructuring*, Manchester: Manchester University Press.
—— (2007) 'Co-option or resistance? Trade unions and neoliberal restructuring in Europe', *Capital and Class*, 93, 111–24.
Callaghan, J. (2007) 'Pivotal powers: The British Labour Party and European unity since 1945', *Capital and Class*, 93, 199–215.
Crouch, C. (1992) 'The fate of articulated industrial relations systems: A stock-taking after the "neo-liberal" decade', in M. Regini (ed.) *The Future of Labour Movements*, London: Sage.
De la Porte, C. (2000) 'Is there an emerging European consensus on social protection?', in E. Gabaglio and R. Hoffman (eds) *European Trade Union Yearbook 1999*, Brussels: European Trade Union Institute.
Department of Trade and Industry (DTI) (2002) *High Performance Workplaces: The Role of Employee Involvement in the Modern Economy*, London: HMSO.
Dorfman, G. (1977) 'From the inside looking out: the Trades Union Congress and the EEC' *Journal of Common Market Studies*, 15:4, 248–71.
EIRO (1997) *Working Time Moves to Top of the Agenda* <http://www.eurofound.europa.eu/eiro/1997/02/feature/uk9702103f.htm> (accessed 2 July 2008).
—— (1998) *New Working Time Regulations Take Effect* <http://www.eurofound.europa.eu/eiro/1998/10/feature/uk9810154f.htm> (accessed 2 July 2008).
—— (1999a) *TUC Poll Highlights Case for Parental Leave to be Paid* <http://www.eurofound.europa.eu/eiro/1999/03/inbrief/uk9903192n.htm> (accessed 2 July 2008).

—— (1999b) *UK Government Publishes Proposals for Implementing EWC Directive* <http://www.eurofound.europa.eu/eiro/1999/07/feature/uk9907220f.htm> (accessed 2 July 2008).

—— (1999c) *Postal Workers and the Implementation of the Directive* <http://www.eurofound.europa.eu/eiro/1999/09/study/tn9909201s.htm> (accessed 2 July 2008).

—— (2001) *Unions Hail Government Climb-down on Parental Leave* <http://www.eurofound.europa.eu/eiro/2001/05/inbrief/uk0105128n.htm> (accessed 2 July 2008).

—— (2002) *Government Issues Discussion Paper on Employee Involvement* <http://www.eurofound.europa.eu/eiro/2002/08/inbrief/uk0208101n.htm> (accessed 2 July 2008).

—— (2003) *Unions Launch New Campaign Against Long Working Hours,* <http://www.eurofound.europa.eu/eiro/2003/10/feature/uk0310104f.htm> (accessed 2 July 2008).

—— (2004) *UK Reaction to EU Working Time Report* <http://www.eurofound.europa.eu/eiro/2004/01/feature/uk0401104f.htm> (accessed 2 July 2008).

—— (2005a) *TUC Rejects EU Constitution* <http://eurofound.europa.eu/eiro/2005/10/inbrief/uk0510101n.htm> (accessed 2 July 2008).

—— (2005b) *Government unveils new family-friendly employment legislation* <http://www.eurofound.europa.eu/eiro/2005/11/feature/uk0511102f.htm> (accessed 2 July 2008).

—— (2005c) *Bleak Future Predicted for Trade Unions* <http://www.eurofound.europa.eu/eiro/2005/04/feature/uk0504109f.htm> (accessed 2 July 2008).

ETUC (2006) *Working Time Directive* <http://www.etuc.org/a/504> (accessed 2 July 2008).

Featherstone, K. (1988) *Socialist Parties and European Integration: A Comparative History*, Manchester: Manchester University Press.

—— (1999) *The British Labour Party from Kinnock to Blair: Europeanism and Europeanization*, Paper presented to the European Community Studies Association Sixth Biennial International Conference, Pittsburgh, PA, June.

Fitzgerald, I. and Stirling, J. (eds) (2004) *European Works Councils: Pessimism of the Intellect, Optimism of the Will?* London: Routledge.

George, S. and Haythorne, D. (1996) 'The British Labour Party', in J. Gaffney (ed.) *Political Parties and European Union*, London: Routledge.

Giddens, A. (2007) *Europe in the Global Age*, Cambridge: Polity Press.

Gowland, D. and Turner, A. (eds) (2000) *Britain and European Integration 1945–1998: A Documentary History*, London: Routledge.

Habermas, J. (2001) *The Postnational Constellation*, Cambridge: Polity Press.

Hall, M., Hoffmann, A., Marginson, P. and Müller, T. (2003) 'National influences on European Works Councils in UK and US-based companies', *Human Resource Management Journal*, 13:4, 75–92.

Hancké, B. (2000) 'European Works Councils and industrial restructuring in the European motor industry', *European Journal of Industrial Relations*, 6:1, 35–59.

Hewitt, M. (1999) 'New Labour and social security', in M. Powell (ed.) *New Labour, New Welfare State*, Bristol: The Policy Press.

Holden, R. (1999) 'Labour's transformation: searching for the point of origin – the European dynamic', *Politics*, 19:2, 103–8.

Hughes, K. and Smith, E. (1998) 'New Labour – New Europe?', *International Affairs* 74:1, 93–104.

Hyman, R. (2001) *Understanding European Trade Unionism: Between Market, Class and Society*, London: Sage.

—— (2005) 'Trade unions and the politics of the European Social Model', *Economic and Industrial Democracy*, 26:9, 9–40.

Jensen, C.S., Madsen, J.S. and Due, J. (1999) 'Phases and dynamics in the development of EU industrial relations regulation', *Industrial Relations Journal*, 30:2, 118–34.

Labour Party (1996) *A Business Agenda for Europe*, London: Labour Party.

Ladrech, R. (1994) 'Europeanization of domestic politics and institutions: the case of France', *Journal of Common Market Studies*, 32:1, 69–98.

Lecher, W. and Rüb, S. (1999) 'The constitution of European Works Councils: from institutional forum to social actor', *European Journal of Industrial Relations*, 5:1, 7–25.

Lipietz, A. (1988) *Mirages and Miracles*, London: Verso.

McIlroy, J. (1995) *Trade Unions in Britain Today*, 2nd edition, Manchester: Manchester University Press.

Marginson, P., Gilman, M., Jacobi, O. and Krieger, H. (1998) *Negotiating European Works Councils: An analysis of Agreements under Article 13*, Luxembourg: The European Union.

Metcalf, D. (2005) *British Unions: Resurgence or Perdition?* Provocations Series, 1(1), London: The Work Foundation.

Moschonas, G. (2002) *In the Name of Social Democracy, The Great Transformation: 1945 to the Present*, London: Verso.

MSF (1993) *Action on Europe*, London: MSF.

Newman, M. (1983) *Socialism and European Unity: The Dilemma of the Left in Britain and France*, London: Junction Books.

Redfern, D. (2007) 'An analysis of the role of European Works Councils in British workplaces', *Employee Relations*, 29:3, 292–305.

Rosamond, B. (1993) 'National labour organization and European integration: British trade unions and "1992"', *Political Studies*, 41, 420–1.

Royle, T. (1999) 'Where's the beef? McDonalds and its European Works Council', *European Journal of Industrial Relations*, 5:3, 327–47.

Sisson, K. (1999) 'The "new" European social model: the end of the search for orthodoxy or another false dawn?', *Employee Relations*, 21:5, 445–62.

Strange, G. (1997) 'The British labour movement and economic and monetary union in Europe', *Capital and Class*, 63, 13–24.

—— (2002a) 'British trade unions and European Union integration in the 1900s: politics versus political economy', *Political Studies* 50:2, 332–53.

—— (2002b) 'Globalization, regionalism and labour interests in the new international political economy', *New Political Economy*, 7:3, 343–65.

Streeck, W. (1998) 'The internationalization of industrial relations in Europe: prospects and problems', *Politics and Society*, 26:4, 429–59.

Taylor, G. (2006) 'European employment policy: governance as regulation', in G. Walzenbach (ed.) *European Governance: Policy Making Between Politicization and Control*, Aldershot: Ashgate.

Taylor, G. and Mathers, A. (2004) 'The European Trade Union Confederation at the crossroads of change? Traversing the variable geometry of European trade unionism', *European Journal of Industrial Relations*, 10:3, 267–85.

Teague, P. (1989) 'The British TUC and the European Community', *Millennium: Journal of International Studies*, 18:1, 29–45.

Teague, P. and Grahl, J. (1992) *Industrial Relations and European Integration*, London: Lawrence and Wishart.

Tindale, S. (1992) 'Learning to love the market: Labour and the European Community', *Political Quarterly*, 63:3, 276–300.

Traxler, F. (1996) 'European trade union policy and collective bargaining', *Transfer*, 2:2, 287–97.

TUC (1992) *Report to Congress*, London: TUC.

—— (1993) *Report to Congress*, London: TUC.

—— (2002) *Report to Congress*, London: TUC.

—— (2006a) UK *Workers Owe Much to Europe, and it's the Best Defence Against the Downsides of Globalisation* <http://www.tuc.org.uk/international/tuc-11995-f0.cfm> (accessed 2 July 2008).

—— (2006b) *Making the Case for Social Europe* <http://www.tuc.org.uk/international/tuc-12704-f0.cfm> (accessed 2 July 2008).

—— (2006c) *Europe: TUC General Council Statement*, London: TUC.

Unison (1997) *Unison European Report: Notes on the Inter-Governmental Conference on Economic and Monetary Union*, London: Unison.

Waddington, J. (2005) 'Trade unions and the defence of the European Social Model', *Industrial Relations Journal*, 36:6, 518–40.

Wainwright, H. (2005) 'The UK/US Presidency of the EU' *Red Pepper* <http://www.redpepper.org.uk/The-UK-US-Presidency-of-the-EU> (accessed on 2 July 2008).

Whittall, M. (2000) 'The BMW European Works Council: a case for European industrial relations optimism?', *European Journal of Industrial Relations*, 6:1, 61–83.

Wills, J. (2000) 'Great expectations: three years in the life of a European Works Council', *European Journal of Industrial Relations*, 6:1, 85–107.

# Index